D1521288

The American Critical Archives is a series of reference books that provide representative selections of contemporary reviews of the main works of major American authors. Specifically, each volume contains both full reviews and excerpts from reviews that appeared in newspapers and weekly and monthly periodicals, generally within a few months of the publication of the work concerned. There is an introductory historical overview by a volume editor, as well as checklists of additional reviews located but not quoted.

This book represents the first comprehensive collection of contemporary published reactions to the writings of William Faulkner from 1925 to 1962. These articles document the response of reviewers to specific works and chronicle the development of Faulkner's reputation among the nation's book reviewers. It has often been assumed that a poor reception in the popular review publications contributed to Faulkner's lack of commercial success. The material presented here tends to refute that assumption, clarifies the development of Faulkner's literary career, and provides a fuller understanding of the part played by book reviewing in the sales, promotion, and success of American literature.

AMERICAN CRITICAL ARCHIVES 5
William Faulkner: The Contemporary Reviews

The American Critical Archives

GENERAL EDITOR: M. Thomas Inge, Randolph-Macon College

William Faulkner

The Contemporary Reviews

Edited by
M. Thomas Inge

Randolph-Macon College

CAMBRIDGE
UNIVERSITY PRESS

Published by the Press Syndicate of the University of Cambridge
The Pitt Building, Trumpington Street, Cambridge CB2 1RP
40 West 20th Street, New York, NY 10011-4211, USA
10 Stamford Road, Oakleigh, Melbourne 3166, Australia

First published 1995
Reprinted 1996

Printed in the United States of America

Library of Congess Cataloging-in-Publication Data is available

A catalog record for this book is available from the British Library

ISBN 0-521-38377-3 hardback

Dedicated to
the memory of
Cleanth Brooks,
Faulkner's
best reader

Contents

Series Editor's Preface

The American Critical Archives series documents a part of a writer's career that is usually difficult to examine, that is, the immediate response to each work as it was made public on the part of reviewers in contemporary newspapers and journals. Although it would not be feasible to reprint every review, each volume in the series reprints a selection of reviews designed to provide the reader with a proportionate sense of the critical response, whether it was positive, negative, or mixed. Checklists of other known reviews are also included to complete the documentary record and allow access for those who wish to do further reading and research.

The editor of each volume has provided an introduction that surveys the career of the author in the context of the contemporary critical response. Ideally, the introduction will inform the reader in brief of what is to be learned by a reading of the full volume. The reader then can go as deeply as necessary in terms of the kind of information desired—be it about a single work, a period in the author's life, or the author's entire career. The intent is to provide quick and easy access to the material for students, scholars, librarians, and general readers.

When completed, the American Critical Archives should constitute a comprehensive history of critical practice in America, and in some cases England, as the writer's careers were in progress. The volumes open a window on the patterns and forces that have shaped the history of American writing and the reputations of the writers. These are primary documents in the literary and cultural life of the nation.

M. THOMAS INGE

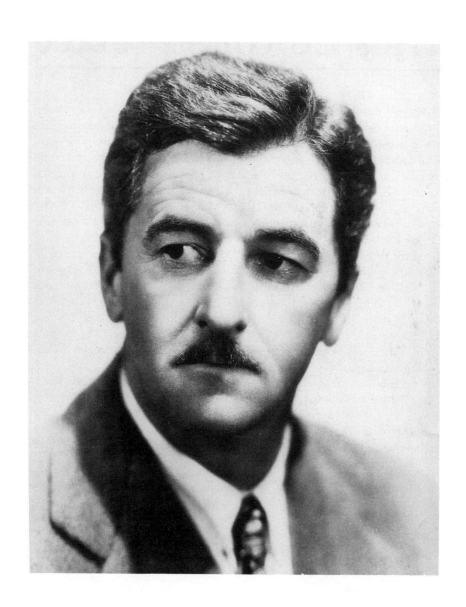

Introduction

Faulkner's first book, *The Marble Faun*, issued on December 15, 1924, was a subsidized publication from what we have come to call a vanity press. Of course, he was not the first major American writer to begin his career in print that way, since Walt Whitman not only self-published but even helped set the type himself for the first edition of *Leaves of Grass* in 1855. Unlike Whitman, however, Faulkner did not have to write his own first review. Indeed, as far as we know, there were at least three—a brief mixed notice in the *Saturday Review of Literature* and two lengthier appreciations. Monte Cooper in the Memphis *Commercial Appeal* found the book-length poem derivative from the British Romantics and certainly no better than his mentors' works, but fellow writer John McClure in the New Orleans *Times-Picayune*, probably out of friendship more than critical objectivity, offered high praise for a beginning performance and called Faulkner a "born poet, with remarkable ability." This was a writer, McClure correctly prophesied, "from whom we shall hear a great deal in [the] future," so we can praise McClure's ability to recognize a major talent in embryo, despite the unspectacular first step.

The next book, *Soldiers' Pay* (published February 25, 1926), was a novel issued by a respectable New York firm, Boni and Liveright. Writing under the inspiration, if not the tutelage, of Sherwood Anderson, with the encouragement of the community of writers in which Faulkner was living in New Orleans, gathered around the little magazine the *Double Dealer*, Faulkner had his eye on the contemporary literary marketplace then dominated by the satiric authors of the jazz age. F. Scott Fitzgerald's *Great Gatsby* had appeared the year before, and in England Aldous Huxley had begun his popular series of cynical society novels. The more than a dozen reviewers who took up the book tended to see it as an ineffective synthesis of the fictional styles of the time. John McClure at the *Times-Picayune* once again weighed in with warm praise and called it the "most noteworthy first novel of the year," but he was not alone in his admiration. Louis Kronenberger in the *Literary Digest* found touches of James Joyce in its wit and humor, and writing for his famed book page in the Nashville *Tennessean*, Fugitive poet Donald Davidson found it a "powerful book, done with careful artistry and with great warmth of feeling," superior in fact to another much praised novel of World War I, *Three Soldiers* by John Dos Passos of 1921.

If the first novel was perceived as too much of its own time, this was especially true of *Mosquitoes* (published April 30, 1927), a smugly satiric roman à clef based on the characters and adventures of the New Orleans artistic community of which Faulkner was a part. John McClure, usually the first with praise, seemed to have grown disenchanted with the sarcasm, cruelty, and eroticism he saw in the book, or perhaps he was simply being defensive because many of Faulkner's friends show up there, and there is even a self-portrait of the novelist himself. Lillian Hellman, writing for the New York *Herald Tribune*, despite spotting evident influences of Joyce and Huxley, thought the novel clever, versatile, brilliant, and "full of the fine kind of swift and lusty writing that comes from a healthy, fresh pen." Davidson maintained his support in the Nashville *Tennessean*, noting that "Faulkner sits in the seat of the scornful with a manner somewhat reminiscent of James Joyce, but... with such gracious ease that you almost overlook the savagery." The other reviewers, fewer than a dozen this time, were mixed in their responses, but nearly all found something to admire in Faulkner's emerging competence as a novelist.

With the third novel, *Sartoris* (published January 31, 1929), it became evident to most of the reviewers, the old faithful as well as the skeptical, that Faulkner had reached a maturity of style and had come upon the proper subject matter for his writing—his "own little postage stamp of native soil," the life and times of the people he knew best in Mississippi. Drawing on the history of his own family and that of his community, Faulkner created the people and county of Yoknapatawpha, a fictional universe he would spend most of the rest of his career developing, although the seeds in terms of themes and many of the characters were there in *Sartoris* already. The discerning critic Henry Nash Smith greeted the novel with the opinion that Faulkner was undoubtedly "one of the most promising talents for fiction in contemporary America" in the Dallas *Morning News*. Davidson in the *Tennessean* stated that "as a stylist and as an acute observer of human behavior, I think that Mr. Faulkner is the equal of any except three or four American novelists who stand at the very top." Anticipating the mythological and allegorical theories of George Marion O'Donnell a decade later, Davidson noted, "I cannot help suspecting some allegorical meaning is in *Sartoris*."

Before the year was out, Faulkner would prove that both Davidson and Smith were right in their prognostications and would completely vindicate their support by the publication of his masterpiece *The Sound and the Fury* (published October 7, 1929). Predictably, some reviewers did not know what to make of the novel's experimental structure and innovative style, despite an appreciative pamphlet by Evelyn Scott that came with the review copy. The perceptive critics, and there were many, praised the work for raising the provincial to the level of the universal, for expanding the boundaries of the American novel, and for restoring their faith in the art form and its emerging practitioners. Whatever the nature or tenor of the reviewers' responses, from sarcasm to adulation, it was clear that a major talent had arrived on the American literary scene.

Close on the heels of *The Sound and the Fury*, Faulkner published a second innovative and strikingly original novel, *As I Lay Dying* (published October 6, 1930). He switched his focus from a decadent Southern aristocracy to an eccentric family of poor-white sharecroppers, and he expanded his experiments in points of view, this time to let a large number of narrators tell the story in a style that borders on surrealism. Many reviewers were unsettled by the nitty-gritty details of the Bundrens' shabby way of life and some of the repulsive details of the novel (such as a rotting corpse), but most of them recognized the technical brilliance of the work and agreed with Ted Robinson in his review for the Cleveland *Plain Dealer* that Faulkner was "one of the two or three original geniuses of our generation."

All this praise and recognition must have gratified the precocious novelist, but Faulkner still lacked the kind of national respect and financial success that should have come his way by this point in his career. So according to his own testimony, which is not always trustworthy, Faulkner began a deliberate plan to write a novel so shocking and controversial that both fortune and fame (or notoriety at least) would surely follow. He did the trick exactly with *Sanctuary* (published February 9, 1931), a novel in which he maintained the development of the experimental techniques of the previous two efforts but with the use of such perverse and criminal characters performing such sordid acts that no reader could fail to take notice. Not only did readers take notice, but *Sanctuary* received twice as many reviews as any of the previous books. Even some of Faulkner's most ardent supporters couldn't take the novel's brutality—Ted Robinson in the Cleveland *Plain Dealer,* for example, called it "obscenely diabolical"—but one result of the notoriety in the press was that Faulkner came to the attention of many critics who previously had felt it safe to ignore him as a "promising" writer not yet in full stride. It was with *Sanctuary* that Faulkner became identified with the school of Naturalism— through the comments of such critics as Henry Seidel Canby and Alan Reynolds Thompson—a mistaken notion that it would take another decade of writing and finally some overt statements of the author, especially the Nobel Prize Address, to eradicate.

From the beginning of his career, Faulkner had fancied himself a short-story writer, and a steady stream of rejection slips did little to dissuade him. Beginning with the appearance of "A Rose for Emily" in the April 1930 issue of *Forum* magazine, and as his reputation as a novelist grew, Faulkner was able to place a striking series of distinctive stories in America's major periodicals, such as the *Saturday Evening Post, Harper's, Scribner's, Atlantic Monthly,* and *Story.* Thus, when he assembled a collection of stories for *These 13* (published September 21, 1931), he had an excellent body of material on which to draw and could include such masterworks as "A Rose for Emily," "Dry September," "That Evening Sun," and "Red Leaves." Except for two or three unfavorable reviews—most notably, one in the *Nation* by Lionel Trilling, who believed Faulkner's work was "too frequently minor"—this volume was warmly received, and the reviewers repeated a litany of praise for the writer as a major American talent, possessed perhaps by a moody spirit of gothic despair but brilliantly versatile in style and technique. Two publications in the summer of the following year received little notice—*Salmagundi* (published May 1932), a collection of three articles and five poems contributed by Faulkner to the New Orleans *Double Dealer* and the *New Republic* between 1919 and 1925, and *Miss Zilphia Gant* (published June 27, 1932), a limited edition of a short story originally accepted by the *Southwest Review*.

Given Faulkner's high reputation and the major accomplishments now behind him, one might expect the reviewers and critics to have been better prepared for what many consider another masterpiece, *Light in August* (published October 6, 1932). Several of them, however, were unsettled by what appeared to be a disjointed plot structure that failed to combine the separate stories of Lena Grove and Joe Christmas, by the frank treatment of social attitudes in the South on the subject of miscegenation, by the sensational depiction of prostitution and sexual perversion in sordid detail, and by the portrayal of the violence of decapitation and castration. Yet most of the reviews tended to be favorable, and their authors realized that this was not merely another chapter in Faulkner's history of the decline and fall of the South but a novel that touched on philosophic and social issues of broad relevance. In his treatment of the irrational reactions of man to the categories of race and color, Faulkner was ahead of his time. No other writer had dared explode the stereotype of the tragic mulatto in such a fashion. More important, however, he used racial identity as a metaphor to represent self-understanding in an increasingly disoriented world and thereby posited a situation of universal application.

Given Faulkner's standing by now as an author of undeniably powerful fiction, it is little wonder that the critics were taken aback by the ordinary quality of the poetry collected in *A Green Bough* (published April 20, 1933). It was clear in the reviews that the only reason the volume received the attention it did was that Faulkner the novelist had written it. Everyone felt obliged to call the poetry derivative, and among the names mentioned were Tennyson, Housman, Heine, Eliot, H.D., and Aiken. As the reviewer for the Cincinnati *Times-Star* put it, through the book "one may sketchily trace the history of English poetry from E. E. Cummings back to Marlowe or Jonson." Perhaps publishing the book served as a purgative for Faulkner, who never again nurtured the notion of being a poet.

The next book appeared a year later, *Doctor Martino and Other Stories* (published April 16, 1934), a collection of fourteen stories most of which had originally been published in popular magazines. The response was mixed, Faulkner's admirers seeking to find some few words of praise for an uneven selection of fiction, and his detractors taking delight in citing the inadequacies of the worst of the lot. Nearly everyone recognized the narrative power and gripping style of "The Hound," and the kind of respectful care exercised in discussing Faulkner, no matter the critical disposition, was itself an indication of the reputation he had achieved. From this point on, however, the press would never praise Faulkner's work again with anything like unanimity or ungrudging admiration.

If the two preceding books failed by and large to please the reviewers, the next novel, *Pylon* (published March 25, 1935), pleased them even less. The hostility that discreetly lurked behind the demeanor of Faulkner's sharpest critics burst into outright defamation. For instance, Sterling North wrote of *Pylon* in the Chicago *Daily News*: "Faulkner's new book is a sloppy, disgusting, nauseating performance by a half-articulate southerner who never entirely learned his job as a novelist and, aside from a few short stories and parts of *Light in August*, is a second-rater." In that the plot moved entirely out of the Yoknapatawpha cycle of fiction, which had earned him prominence, the book created problems even for his staunchest admirers. The disillusioned barnstormers who wandered through the story told by a cynical reporter were closer to the inhabitants of T. S. Eliot's *Waste Land* than to the decadent Southern aristocrats and stoic peasants of Faulkner's best work. Even John Crowe Ransom, who had applauded his earlier efforts, now noted in the Nashville *Banner* that "it is such a bad book that it seems to mark the end of William Faulkner." Ironically, *Pylon* came just as Faulkner was receiving wider press than for any of his previous books. A few reviewers did look beyond the novel's weaknesses to detect the hand of a better than average novelist at work, and Faulkner had the satisfaction of seeing *Pylon* reach the best-seller list in spite of the critical hostility.

The next novel seemed partly to make up for Faulkner's past lapses and would resubstantiate his claim as a major writer. As experimental in form as *The Sound and the Fury* and *As I Lay Dying*, and as closely focused on the psyche of the South as any of his Yoknapatawpha fiction, *Absalom, Absalom!* (published October 26, 1936) garnered more unreservedly enthusiastic reviews than any of his previous works. Of course, a few naysayers persisted, a minor chorus led most prominently by the arbiter of the book club set, Clifton Fadiman, who confessed in the *New Yorker* that Faulkner was beyond his grasp and concluded that *Absalom, Absalom!* marked the "final blowup of what was once a remarkable, if minor, talent." Fadiman and his followers were effectively drowned out by the unabashed adulation of scores of reviewers from all corners of the book world. Long analytic reviews became the order of the day, assessments that took into account Faulkner's past achievements and grappled for comparisons, analogues, and a critical vocabulary equal to the task of evaluating the novel. While some critics tried to ride the fence, most made up their minds decisively, and the favorable reviews outnumbered the unfavorable two to one.

In his next book, published more than a year later (February 15, 1938), *The Unvanquished*, Faulkner gathered together several of his best related short stories, such as "Ambuscade" and "An Odor of Verbena," and with minor revisions presented the whole as a novel. How well he succeeded may be gauged by the extent to which critics remained undecided about whether to treat the book as a novel or as a collection of short stories. Those who disliked the "blood and thunder" Faulkner of *Absalom, Absalom!* or *Light in August*, however, applauded the book for its lack of shock, sex, and perversity, while his admirers appreciated the fine writing but with considerably less enthusiasm than previous works had generated. In one odd, unexpected review, V. F. Calverton, writing for *Modern Monthly*, called Mississippi the "most backward state in the nation" and noted: "That fact is very significant in understanding Faulkner's fiction. He is dealing with a people who are inferior to all other Americans, who are living in a state of intellectual barbarism which is infra-medieval. . . . They are nothing more than the sick, stinking backwash of a dead but still rotting civilization." Faulkner usually irritated most of the conservative critics, but seldom had he received such a lashing from the press, although the bias was directed more at Mississippi than at the author.

Continuing his experimentation with structure, in *The Wild Palms* (published January 19, 1939) Faulkner juxtaposed two separate stories with alternating chapters and made no apparent effort to connect them, except for a thin reliance on the related themes of flight and refuge. While a few reviewers made a case for the success of the experiment, including Edwin Berry Burgum in *New Masses*, who found the two plots effectively integrated and called the book Faulkner's "most thoroughly satisfying" to date, most found it a failure.

Less innovative in form and style but more sensational in its bawdy humor and violent subject matter than the earlier major works was *The Hamlet* (published April 1, 1940), the first of a trilogy to be devoted to the history of the Snopes family. While the book seemed to test the patience of many of Faulkner's old supporters and slowly but surely to earn a few new friends, even some of his usually puzzled and wary readers began to show a grudging respect for his obvious talents in comic writing. His longtime booster Ted Robinson found himself flinging the book aside when he reached the passages about the idiot Ike's love affair with a cow, or so he reported in the Cleveland *Plain Dealer*, but Sterling North of the Chicago *Daily News*, who had earlier excoriated *Pylon*, took into account the magnificent sweep of *The Hamlet* in its depiction of Southern class and type, its vivid creation of characters from the sultry Eula Varner to the indomitable Flem Snopes, and its incredible range of style, to find the book one of the "outstanding novels of his [Faulkner's] brilliant career." Hardheaded Clifton Fadiman, of course, had to proclaim once more "I make no claims whatever to any ability to comprehend what Mr. Faulkner is about" in the *New Yorker*, and Don Stanford in the *Southern Review* thought the book phony, insensitive, and stupid in its delineation of character. The majority of reviewers, in any case, looked forward to the further adventures of the Snopeses as they took over Yoknapatawpha County economically and socially.

The Hamlet had been partly constructed of previously published short stories revised for their appearance within a new work. The next book was also a compilation of such stories, and Faulkner himself was uncertain whether to present the volume as a unified work or as an anthology; hence the first printing was entitled *Go Down, Moses and Other Stories* (published May 11, 1942), while subsequent printings were simply called *Go Down, Moses*. Perhaps there was intentional wisdom in calling the book a collection of stories at first, since this prevented the nitpickers from accusing him, as they had done earlier, of attempting to pass off a set of loosely related pieces as a unified work. If so, the strategy had the opposite effect. Many reviewers were quick to assert that despite its use of seven stories related primarily by their treatment of the adventures of the McCaslin-Edmonds family, the volume had a unified effect and dealt significantly with a period of rapid social and economic change in the South. By and large, the book garnered more consistent praise than many of his earlier works. Reviewers noted that Faulkner's style was impressive; his range of characterization and setting, realistic; and his themes, relevant to the times. Friend and foe alike were taken with "The Bear," a work that elicited comparison with *Moby-Dick* and other classic works of American fiction and that many rightly predicted would become a classic itself.

At this stage, it was perfectly clear that with or without large sales, Faulkner had arrived as one of the two or three top American writers in the estimation of the reviewing establishment. For this reason, it is doubtful that the main cause of the growing appreciation of Faulkner at this point in his career was the appearance of Malcolm Cowley's edition of *The Portable Faulkner* (published April 29, 1946), as has often been claimed. The appreciation and the reputation were already there, slowly building over the years, even though perhaps a bit out of the public mind with the lapse of four years since the appearance of the preceding book. What Cowley's compilation did accomplish, however, was its orderly establishment of a sense of the chronology and interconnected historical nature of the Yoknapatawpha cycle Faulkner had woven through Cowley's arrangement of short stories and excerpts from the novels. Faulkner's epic intent became clear for the general reader. Although it received few reviews, *The Portable Faulkner* did occasion an essay by fellow novelist Robert Penn Warren in the *New Republic* that proved a turning point in Faulkner criticism and an influential source of basic ideas to be developed in the following years. Warren's review has been frequently anthologized as one of the classic pieces of American literary criticism (and for that reason does not appear in this volume).

As Faulkner's career progressed, the number of journals and newspapers that reviewed his work gradually increased, especially on the heels of the notoriety of *Sanctuary* in 1931, with the most attention being paid to *Pylon* in 1935 and *Absalom, Absalom!* in 1936. *Intruder in the Dust* (published October 18, 1948), however, elicited twice as many reviews as any other book to that date. This polemical novel, in the form of a detective story, attracted such attention because of the political stance Faulkner adopted on the race question. Basically, he asserted that the racial conflict in the South could be resolved only by Southerners; that although the blacks deserved equality, it would never be accomplished through legislation; and that Northerners, liberals, and reformers were doing more to damage the cause of civil rights by interfering than to help in the achievement of justice. Needless to say, such an attitude antagonized both liberals and conservatives, both supporters of a strong federal authority and states-righters. Thus the reviews were full of political polemics for and against Faulkner, depending on the disposition of the journalist or periodical. Neither his friends nor his foes found it possible to deny the power and appeal of the novel as a work of fiction, and most called the book a literary event of the first order. After examining a cross section of sixty reviews, the New York *Times* on November 14, 1948, reported the score sheet:

> *Verdict*: Yes, by about 10 to 1. On the whole, amazingly well received, in view of the high style and the indirect defense of the South in the matter of South vs. Negro. Attacks generally from the North, and on political rather than literary grounds. Most of the attackers never got around to discussing the novel as a novel.

There appeared to be little doubt in the minds of *all* the commentators about Faulkner's status as a major figure on the literary scene.

Whereas *Intruder in the Dust* may have been a piece of social protest fiction disguised as a detective novel, *Knight's Gambit* (published November 27, 1949) was a collection of detective stories (all but one previously published) disguised as a novel. The presence of Gavin Stevens as a country-store Sherlock Holmes was the only thing the pieces had in common, and the delineation of his character was the main item of interest. Despite the book's weaknesses, the respect accorded *Intruder in the Dust* was sustained by the majority of the reviewers, with Warren Beck in the Chicago *Sunday Tribune* nominating Faulkner as the "Shakespeare of American fiction" and Malcolm Cowley rightly predicting in the New York *Herald Tribune* that he would win the Nobel Prize. Even though this ultimate literary prize was exactly one year away, Orville Prescott in the New York *Times* still found it possible to announce:

William Faulkner is considered by many Frenchmen and a few Americans as the most important living American writer. That he might have been, since his natural talents are so undeniably great, seems to me a defensible proposition. That he is not seems to me obvious. Undisciplined gifts, intermittent flashes of blazing power, a morbid preoccupation with violence and degeneracy and a monstrously turgid and obscure style are not convincing qualifications for literary pre-eminence.

The appearance of Faulkner's *Collected Stories* (published August 21, 1950) provided an opportunity to address the question of his considerable talents as a writer of short fiction, which he had steadily published since 1930 in popular magazines and collected or revised into several earlier books. His admirers came forward with many comparisons with other world masters of the short story, many apt and others mere exaggeration, including Poe, Chekhov, James, Kafka, Lawrence, and Joyce, but nearly everyone agreed that the collection itself was uneven, especially for the first-rate writer who just a few months after the release of *Collected Stories,* on November 10, 1950, would be announced as the winner of the Nobel Prize for Literature, as several critics had predicted.

The Nobel Prize would act as a lightning rod, attracting to Faulkner both the highest praise and retrospective I-told-you-so pieces from his supporters and the vehemence of his incredulous detractors, finally to be focused on the unlikeliest book to withstand such commentary, *Requiem for a Nun* (published September 27, 1951). It was presented as a novel in the form of a play, and the hybrid form and the experimental style again confounded the purists who had resisted the lack of traditional elements in the earlier works. As usual, people like Sterling North in the New York *World-Telegram and the Sun* waxed sarcastic about the "ungrammatical, clumsy prose"; Clifton Fadiman intentionally misspelled Faulkner's name throughout his review in *Holiday* magazine and recommended that he write for the comedian Jimmy Durante, since both had a genius for violating the English language; Maxwell Geismar in the New York *Post* thought the book "cold, empty, slick . . . trite, and sophomoric in its values"; and Carl Victor Little's review for the San Francisco *News* was a single sentence of 550 words parodying the famous sentence in *Requiem* of 49 pages. Several critics, usually discerning and fair, found it difficult to praise much in the book, but some of the most influential—such as Louis D. Rubin, Jr., Harrison Smith, Irving Howe, Robert Penn Warren, Malcolm Cowley, Granville Hicks, and Ray B. West, Jr.—saw no reason to hedge their enthusiasm despite the controversial nature of the work. *Requiem for a Nun* garnered even more reviews than had *Intruder in the Dust,* and given Faulkner's international prominence now, no one found it possible *not* to review each new volume as it appeared. When *Requiem* was actually staged on Broadway in 1959 as a play, the critical response was lukewarm, although it had been successfully staged abroad in a dozen countries. Some found the prose powerful but the dramatic values weak, so it had only a short run.

Each new book would, of course, receive from this point more careful scrutiny and considered attention than ever before. The reviews of *The Faulkner Reader* (published April 1, 1954) were largely positive and became occasions for reflecting on his entire career. Irving Howe, in a balanced overview for the New York *Times*, placed Faulkner in the company of such greats as Melville, James, and Twain, and saw him the equal of Hemingway or Fitzgerald, noting: "For once we have not begrudged an American artist the praise due him." Yet, a few insisted that Faulkner was receiving undue praise, including Charles H. Nichols, who wrote in *Phylon*:

> One has the feeling that all the grandeur of Faulkner's style—his Mississippi baroque—all his grotesqueries and posturing, all his high-flown bombast are attempts to wrest from his material a profound meaning which has persistently eluded him. It is high time that someone pointed out that the emperor has no clothes.

Faulkner had been working on the manuscript of his next novel for ten years; therefore it was much discussed and anticipated before publication as *A Fable* on August 2, 1954. Everyone rushed into the fray, eager to have his or her say on this most reviewed of all Faulkner's novels—more than two hundred reviews seeing print. Given the unusual theme and structure of *A Fable*— a retelling of the Christ story set during World War I and patterned after the Passion Week—extreme reactions were guaranteed. Orville Prescott (New York *Times*) found it "stiff and lifeless," Leslie Fiedler (*New Republic*) believed that the passion of Faulkner's rhetoric had "turned to stone," Nathan A. Scott, Jr. (*The Intercollegian*) regretfully called it "a great failure by our greatest novelist today," and James Aswell (Houston *Chronicle*) bluntly announced that Faulkner "ought to be hanged." Maxwell Geismar (*Saturday Review*), at the other end of the spectrum, noted, "It is by far the best novel Faulkner has published in the last decade," Granville Hicks (New York *Post*) described it as "a great novel and an act of Faulknerian heroism," Warren Beck (Milwaukee *Journal*) thought that more than ever it demonstrated Faulkner was "our greatest novelist," and Delmore Schwartz (*Perspectives U.S.A.*) declared it a "masterpiece." A good many reviews fell somewhere in between, their authors aware of being in the presence of powerful prose but unable to define or describe the nature of its grandeur. *A Fable* has remained a novel that rests uncomfortably in the canon and in the minds of critics, its importance in American fiction still an open question.

In 1955, Faulkner decided to draw together four of his hunting stories, including his famous tale "The Bear," and connect them with a surrounding narrative about the natural history and legendry of the South. The result was

Big Woods, which met with almost unalloyed praise. Perhaps reviewers were happy to see him return to the fictional territory of which he was undisputed master, or they were pleased to have a book more in the American grain, the pastoral tradition of Cooper, Thoreau, and Twain. In any case, most agreed with Lewis Gannett in the New York *Herald Tribune* that *Big Woods* represented "Faulkner at his finest."

The Town (published May 1, 1957), Faulkner's first major piece of writing since *A Fable,* occasioned a similar number of reviews (in fact, both remain the most frequently reviewed of all the novels, with *The Reivers* coming in a close third five years later). Because *Big Woods* returned to familiar territory and characters in its content and displayed the most popular brand of Faulknerian folk humor, the press was mainly positive, and many critics engaged in lengthy and often accurate assessments of his place in modern letters. A few claimed to remain confused by Faulknerian rhetoric and complexity, despite the relative clarity of the new work. As John L. Longley, Jr., put it in the *Virginia Quarterly Review*, "Those reviewers who in 1936 and 1942 decided never to forgive Faulkner have not done so." But more and more of the critical quarterlies—such as *Sewanee Review*, *Hudson Review*, *Epoch*, *Kenyon Review*, and *Western Review*—began to pay attention with review essays by leading literary critics that began to establish to a large extent the critical guidelines by which Faulkner was to be judged. Because *The Town* was the middle work in the trilogy about the Snopes family, it also allowed for further discussion of Faulkner's moral vision and view of modern society.

Two years after *The Town* came the final volume of the Snopes saga, *The Mansion* (published November 13, 1959). Largely relieved to see it completed, Faulkner's supporters found things to admire, although hardly anybody was satisfied with its disjointed structure and the distinctly political turn it took in introducing socialism and communism into Yoknapatawpha County. Paul H. Stacey in the Washington *Post* mentioned Melville and Hawthorne as points of comparison in his review, and he defended the structure as a "large cubistic painting put together in enormous chunks," but more frequently reviewers described the novel as repetitive, didactic, or, as Orville Prescott noted in the New York *Times*, "an intolerable bore." Prescott best summed up the status of Faulkner's reputation at this juncture when he wrote:

By this time every literate American citizen who reads contemporary fiction at all has made up his mind about William Faulkner and reached one of two possible verdicts: He thinks that the demon-ridden chronicler of a score of fantastic novels about a nightmare South is a master novelist who eminently deserved the Nobel Prize. Or he thinks that Mr. Faulkner is one of the most naturally gifted, but most disastrously undisciplined and sadly self-indulgent of American writers.

Many critics took note in their reviews of *The Mansion* of Faulkner's statement that "this book is the final chapter of, and the summation of, a work conceived and begun in 1925," and several misunderstood it to mean that Faulkner was through with writing and had completed his life's work. But there was to be one more novel, which indeed would complete the sizable bookshelf of fiction from his pen—*The Reivers* (published June 4, 1962). The publication date came just one month before Faulkner's sudden and untimely death on July 6, 1962. His writing career could not have been concluded in a more celebratory and fitting way, in that *The Reivers* was a return to the kind of rambunctious and rollicking humor that most of his readers, friend and foe alike, found enjoyable in his fiction. He resorted, as well, to a straightforward narrative and engaged in few of the stylistic pyrotechnics that both dazzled and irritated the critics.

The reviews were largely favorable. The critics appreciated the moral vision implicit in the events, the comic elements drawing on the frontier tradition of tall-tale humor, the folk idiom of the dialogue, and the easy flow of the story. They enjoyed, too, the simple pleasure of reading the entertaining adventures of a motorized Huckleberry Finn who takes an automobile ride to Memphis rather than a raft down the Mississippi and in the course of the trip is initiated into the pains and responsibilities of adulthood. The works of Augustus Baldwin Longstreet, the humorists of the old Southwest, Mark Twain, and James Thurber were the most frequently cited analogues for what Faulkner had done.

Some reviewers expressed doubts about certain coincidental plot elements and the credibility of an oral narrative told in one setting without pause for three hundred pages. Stanley Edgar Hyman in the *New Leader* found the novel a mere lightweight boy's book and "not even a superior specimen of the genre," and a semihysterical commentator for the *Catholic Register* was deeply offended by the "trashy" language and the stupidity of the Nobel Prize committee in recognizing Faulkner's wasted talent. She concluded, "Why waste good God-given moments on literature of this type?" Faulkner's old nemesis Clifton Fadiman, forced to deliver the selection committee's report in the *Book-of-the-Month Club News*, complimented the novel as a "highly sophisticated folk comedy" and admitted that although he was not "a Faulkner devotee... *The Reivers* caught, held, and delighted me, despite the impediments of the famous style, the crisscross structure, the acrobatic play with time sequence." The naysayers were a decided minority, and Winfield Townley Scott felt inspired to write in the *New Mexican*: "Take the book altogether, I can only, however awkwardly, record my curious sensation that I was reading a book which had long been a classic in American literature. I daresay that's what is going to happen to it." Willingly or unwillingly, most critics became reconciled to the idea that Faulkner was a major force in American letters. In what turned out to be a highly appropriate review, called "Prospero in

Yoknapatawpha," *Time* magazine compared the novel to Shakespeare's *Tempest*. Little did the anonymous reviewer suspect that as was true for the Bard, this was the work after which Faulkner would break his golden pencil and retire into immortality.

In making the selections for this volume, I examined every known review of a book by Faulkner. These were gathered through existing bibliographies, an examination of the Random House files, a study of all other files of reviews held by institutions or individuals, and other sources. Although I have aimed to be exhaustive, I am sure additional reviews will surface as research continues.

The texts of the reviews have been reprinted as they originally appeared, except that obvious typographical errors have been silently corrected and the names of books and characters are consistently spelled correctly. Omissions are indicated by ellipses. In some instances, full bibliographic data were not available for items reprinted or listed. All such items, however, may be found in the Random House or other files now housed at the University of Virginia, where they may be consulted.

Acknowledgments

The research for this volume was greatly facilitated by grants from the American Philosophical Society, Michigan State University, Virginia Commonwealth University, and the Southern Regional Education Board. The final stages of the manuscript were completed under the auspices of a resident fellowship at the Center for the Humanities of the Virginia Foundation for the Humanities and Public Policy in Charlottesville. I am grateful to all of these agencies for their essential support.

In gathering material, I was assisted by the efficient and cooperative reference staffs of the libraries at Virginia Commonwealth University in the 1970s, Clemson University in the early 1980s, and Randolph-Macon College since 1984. Faulkner's editor Albert Erskine kindly made it possible for me to examine the Random House files of reviews of Faulkner's books and promotional material, and additional files were made available in Special Collections of the Clifton Waller Barrett Library of the University of Virginia.

I have also benefited from the secretarial assistance provided by Virginia Commonwealth University, especially by Maria Borroni, and Clemson University, especially by Judy Payne, as well as Randolph-Macon College, including help from Geneva N. Bohannon and my student assistants John Baldwin, Michael G. Bond, Hope S. Thompson, Holly P. Preuss, and Jennifer L. Weisman.

My colleague and fellow Faulkner bibliographer John E. Bassett has generously shared his enthusiasm and information over the years from the time we first met in the Random House archives and pleasantly discovered we were on complementary rather than competing missions. His friendship is appreciated, as is that of William E. Boozer, editor of *The Faulkner Newsletter* and collector extraordinaire. The reproductions of the first edition title pages used in this book are from his collection. I am also grateful for the support of Andrew Brown and Julie Greenblatt of Cambridge University Press for making the series of which this volume is a part a reality. Finally, I want to thank at Randolph-Macon College President Ladell Payne and Provost Jerome H. Garris, who have encouraged the kind of scholarly climate that makes all things possible.

Acknowledgment is made to all of the newspapers, magazines, and individuals who kindly granted me permission to reprint reviews, including the following:

"From a Bookman's Notebook" and "Tiresome Faulkner" by Victor P. Hass.

Phylon for "Achievement of Faulkner" by Charles H. Nichols.

V. S. Pritchett for "Time Frozen" first published in *Partisan Review*, 21 (1954), 557–561. Copyright (c) by V. S. Pritchett.

Providence *Journal* for "The Waning South" and "Faulkner, His Critics" by W. T. Scott, "William Faulkner's New Novel" by B. K. H., "*Knight's Gambit* Annoys, Impresses" by J. Saunders Redding, and "Faulkner Tells a Fable" by Randall Stewart.

Raleigh *News and Observer* for "William Faulkner in the Air" by Emily Bridgers and "Faulkner Story" by Richard Walser.

Richmond *News-Leader* for "Novel, Modern Drama" by Louis D. Rubin, Jr., and "Faulkner Continues" by M. J. Bruccoli.

Rocky Mountain News (Denver, Colorado) for "Promise of Genius is Seen" by Pontoon J. Daakes.

Russell & Volkening as agents of the author for "Department of Amplification" by Eudora Welty from *The New Yorker*, January 1, 1949. Copyright (c) 1949 by Eudora Welty, renewed 1977 by Eudora Welty.

Sacramento *Bee* for "Plantation of Southland Is School of New Faulkner Tales," May 16, 1942.

San Diego *Union* for "Abraham, Abraham!" and "Faulkner Opus Fails" by Max Miller.

San Franciso *Chronicle* for "Faulkner's South" by Joseph H. Jackson. Copyright (c) San Francisco *Chronicle*.

Santa Barbara *News-Press* for "An Eye on the New" by Maurice Swan.

Southern Review and Don Stanford for excerpt from "*The Beloved Returns* and the Recent Fiction" by Don Stanford, *Southern Review*, 6 (1941), 610–628.

Southwest Review for excerpt from "Three Southern Novels" and for "A Troubled Vision" by Henry Nash Smith.

Time for "Haunted Landscapes," "Saga's End," and "Prospero in Yoknapatawpha." Copyright (c) 1950, 1959, and 1962 by Time Inc.

Trenton *Times* for "Book Fog: William Faulkner" by Harry A. Weissblatt.

Virginia Quarterly Review for "Galahad Gavin" by John L. Longley and "Told with Gusto" by Warren Beck.

Wallace Literary Agency as agents of the author for "Requiem for a Dramatist" by Anthony West, from *The New Yorker*, September 22, 1951. Copyright (c) 1951 by Anthony West.

Wheeling *News-Register* for "Faulkner's Newest Book—Intrigues" by Anne Chamberlain.

Every effort has been made to request permission from copyright holders for use of reprinted material in this book. Please forward any corrections to the editor.

THE MARBLE FAUN

THE
MARBLE FAUN

BY

WILLIAM FAULKNER

BOSTON
THE FOUR SEAS COMPANY
PUBLISHERS

John McClure. "Literature and Less." New Orleans *Times-Picayune*, January 25, 1925, Magazine Section, p. 6.

It is doubtful if there are a dozen thoroughly successful long poems in English. When a young poet attempts sustained production he is under Lloyd's or anybody's averages, predestined to failure. The most he can hope for, even if his name is Keats, is to fail with honor. Mr. William Faulkner, a Southern poet from whom we shall hear a great deal in future, has failed, it seems to this reviewer, but with real honor.

The Marble Faun, by William Faulkner, with a preface by Phil Stone, although not a completely successful work, is a book of verse rich in promise, and successful in part.

The candled flames of roses here
Gutter gold in this still air

is a couplet of fine poetry if this reviewer ever saw one. And *The Marble Faun* contains scores of excellent passages. The book, with all its immaturity, proves that Mr. Faulkner is a born poet, with remarkable ability.

This poem was written when its author was barely of voting age. It is the forerunner of a more mature volume of shorter poems which will be brought out this year. That volume of later work should contain some genuinely excellent sustained productions. The excellencies of *The Marble Faun* are sporadic: charming couplets or passages sandwiched between stretches of creditable but not remarkable verse. The general effect of the poem is vague. It is a prophetic book, rather than a chronicle of past performance. Mr. Faulkner possesses to an exceptional degree imagination, emotion, a creative impulse in diction and a keen sense of rhythm and form—all attributes demanded of a fine poet. The deficiencies of *The Marble Faun* are deficiencies of youth—diffuseness and over-exuberance, impatient simile and metaphor which sometimes miss the mark, and a general galloping technique which runs away with the author every now and then. Immaturity is almost the only indictment which can be brought against the work.

To say that *The Marble Faun* is a long poem is in a way incorrect. It is a series of fairly short poems, natural episodes, but it is bound into a whole by prologue, epilogue and thread of argument, and is apparently intended to achieve unity of effect. Mr. Stone in his preface refers to the book as a book of "poems." This is correct, literally, but the work is stronger when viewed as a whole, as one imagines Mr. Faulkner conceived it, when he wrote it in April, May and June of 1919.

Mr. Stone says of *The Marble Faun*:

> These are primarily the poems of youth and a simple heart. They are the poems of a mind that reacts directly to sunlight and trees and skies and blue hills, reacts without evasion or self-consciousness. They are drenched in sunlight and color as is the land in which they were written, the land which gave birth and sustenance to their author. He has roots in this soil as surely and inevitably as has a tree......
> The author of these poems is a man steeped in the soil of his native land, a Southerner by every instinct, and more than that, a Mississippian. George Moore said that all universal art became great by first being

provincial, and the sunlight and mockingbirds and blue hills of North Mississippi are a part of this young man's very being.

Nobody but the poet himself ever understands all the overtones and implications in a piece of imaginative verse. *The Marble Faun*, it seems—if it must be interpreted—is an excursion into direct experience. The marble faun, with its

> carven eyes
> Bent to the unchanging skies,

this creature of cold stone which "cannot break its marble bonds," yearns to know the warm and infinitely varied life of nature. Through the necromancy of the imagination, it tours the forbidden worlds of life and motion, becoming not merely a spectator but a pulsing part of the natural scene. When we recall the not too remote similarity of flesh and marble—even though few of us are statues in a palace of art, we are all automatons in a droll waxworks—it becomes evident that Mr. Faulkner's poem is full of food for meditation. . . .

This reviewer believes that Mr. Faulkner promises fine things. He is soon off for Europe. His new book of poems will appear shortly. Those who wish to keep in touch with the development of Southern poetry will do well to acquire *The Marble Faun* and the new book when it appears. One day they may be glad to have recognized a fine poet at his first appearance.

Mr. Faulkner, who served with the British Royal Air Forces, has taken a flier at nearly everything in his time (he is only 27 now). He has been in turn an undergraduate, house painter, tramp, day laborer, dishwasher in various New England cities, clerk in a New York book shop, bank clerk and postal clerk.

Saturday Review of Literature, 1 (March 7, 1925), 587.

An attractively-made book by a young poet who has led a varied and venturesome life. He is a Southerner, having been born in Mississippi. His verse is fluent and meditative, with an occasional phrase of beauty and an occasional flaw in the rhyming. Not much more can be said. He does not strain for effects, but, on the other hand, his sensitiveness to the poetic possibilities of the language is not sufficiently developed.

Monte Cooper. "The Book of Verses." Memphis *Commercial Appeal*, April 5, 1925, Section III, p. 10.

"From the time of Nathaniel Hawthorne," writes the charming Mr. Max Beerbohm, "to the outbreak of the war, current literature did not suffer from any lack of fauns."

It is some years since hostilities on the grand scale ceased, and current literature is again spared pain in this direction: for Mr. William Faulkner of Mississippi, has written a 50-page poem about a faun. Mr. Faulkner is splendidly atavistic, and does not in the least care how old fashioned he may be said to be; nevertheless it must have taken a fair amount of complacency to have had faith in the present significance of 48 pages of rhymed couplets—(two pages are given over to quatrains)—mostly in a plaintive minor key, where outworn phrases, such as "leafy glade" and its like, frequently occur.

Let us consider directly this little book so pleasantly bound in green paper boards. What has Mr. Faulkner attempted to convey in his poem? In what directions has he succeeded and what directions has he failed?

His present poetic credo is specifically expressed in an essay dated October, 1924, and entitled, "Verse, Old and Nascent: A Pilgrimage." In this essay the author traces his poetic lineage back to its Swinburnian beginnings; admits us to a view of his precipitate alliance with contemporary free verse writers; describes his haughty withdrawal, his ultimate divorcement from their encircling arms; makes pretty bows to Shelley, to Keats, to A. E. Housman and his "Shropshire Lad," and asks: "Is there nowhere among us a Keats in embryo—someone who will tune his lute to the beauty of the world . . . Is not there among us someone who can write something beautiful and passionate and sad instead of saddening?" The essay ends with this rhetorical question. The signature, William Faulkner, follows with magnificent simplicity.

The author would not pretend to claim, however, that his *The Marble Faun* is even embryonically Keatsian. The early allegiance to Swinburne coupled with two statements in the preface to the poem: "This is a first book . . . These are the poems of youth—"—enables us to avoid all speculation as to Mr. Faulkner's ability to carry on the sacred torch of universal beauty, unlighted, in his opinion, during these sordid times. It is with Swinburne, his master at the time of writing *The Marble Faun*, with whom we must compare him. The path for the critic is clearly marked.

Laying aside all question as to the uselessness of a return to the manner of a nineteenth century poet—(Swinburne has his admirers and his readers today)—we then ask: "What has William Faulkner to offer that his master has not said better?"

First, he has many pages of delicate rhyming couplets, that ring in their best lines with a silvery daintiness; that evoke the image of a kitten stepping fastidiously through wet leaves. There is none of the sweep and the swing of the best of Swinburne's verse—none of the stirring vigor of The Atalanta Chorus—but there is this delicacy voicing, for the most part, a sweet and rather plaintive resignation.

"Upon a wood's dim shaded edge
Stands a dusty hawthorn hedge
Beside a road from which I pass
To cool my feet in deep rich grass.
I pause to listen to the song
Of a brook spilling along.
Behind a patchy willow screen
Whose lazy evening shadows lean
Their scattered gold upon a glade
Through which the staring daisies wade.
And the resilient poplar trees,
Slowly turning in the breeze,
Flash their facets in the sun,
Swaying in slow unison."

This is Mr. Faulkner at his best. But what, then? Fifty pages of monotonous, if silvery, intoning, must prove to be soporific to the most alert mind, to the most favorably interested reader. All of the verse, however, is by no means of this degree of excellence. Besides an annoying return to the stupid inversions of the Victorians—besides an even more annoying use of accented last syllables. In past participles: "golden wi-red;" "thin-bran-ched shade;" "Lea-fed walls;" "dark etched bars;" there are glaring defects that occur, each more than once, in this poem of a faun of marble, planted in a garden and watching the seasons pass. These defects are: choice of metaphors not only mixed but only too often far from happy, indeed several times verging on the ridiculous, as

5

when, after the line, "Philomel dreams naked here—" a plucked, livid, reptilian nightingale is scarcely the image that any poet who uses the word Philomel intends to summon before his reader's eyes; second, a disregard for meaning, that, however, like his Swinburne, has yet been acknowledged by some of the long haired poet's admirers to be a real fault; and third, sudden descents into commonplace, even stumbling lines, devoid of distinction and of grace. These are quite inexcusable. We can overlook changes in cadence that are unsuccessful—(although Mr. Faulkner might learn much of the subtleties of irregular cadences from his contemporaries from whose contamination he has so definitely withdrawn). These are faults that might be outgrown with practice and the cultivation of what might be called a sense of rhythmical irregularity; but no poet, however young, should be commonplace; no poet of great promise would have been acquiescent in printing such ugly lines as these:

"And the moon that sits there in the
    skies—"
"To comb the wave-ponies manes
    back—"
"Why cannot we always be—"

These are clumsy descents from grace and beauty.

Mr. Faulkner evidently thinks that the same phrases, perhaps unusually felicitous in his opinion, can bear repetition. For whatever reason, he has repeated himself several times. "Inky trees," he has used twice and "velvet night." Again, his faun, remaining passive when surrounded by nymphs, and thereby proving his unlikeness to the more inflammable animal drawn by Mallarmé, describes these creatures who have come to bathe in the stream, where—

"......   .... they meet
Inverted selves stretched at their feet."

Only two pages farther on the "Swan's inverted graces" proves either that Mr. Faulkner was very careless or very devil-may-care. The result is equally repetitious and tedious.

There remains one more fault for which it is difficult to forgive him. Mr. Faulkner glories in his localism. We cannot but wonder, however, if his rhyming of "rim" with "them" and again "dim" with "them" was voluntary. He was educated in Oxford—Mississippi. If these were involuntary slips, due to a provincial accent, we can but respectfully point out a slip. If they were deliberate then it is high time that Mr. Faulkner should have learned that affected localisms are as unbearable in a writer as affected cosmopolitanism.

Taken in conjunction with the two essays, one of which has been already outlined, and another called "On Criticism" in which Mr. Faulkner tells the critics just what he thinks of them, the disarming simplicity of *The Marble Faun* is dimmed in part. The essays are dogmatic; there is in them a sneering quality, especially in regard to women, that is half baked and raw, and in one or two places rather evil smelling. Such words as entrails, masculinity, prostitution, are employed in a straining after the arresting phrase, a straining that was absent in the poem. It seems that Mr. Faulkner, in his splendid isolation from his American fellows is somewhat embittered—almost angry.

One turns away from the two essays, preferring the early poem, where an undeniably sensitive nature, so evidently now abrased, expanded before the contemplation of Mississippi mocking birds, Abyssinian nightingales, Italian formal gardens, hot noons, brooks, fields, Pan and his inevitable pipes, the whirl of the tired old earth, and the softness of falling snow.

"The soundless quiet flakes slide past
Like teardrops on a sheet of glass,"

Pretty sounds, but who has seen tears falling on a sheet of glass? Tears went into tearbottles could once be seen any day in Greece, we are told. We must let it go at that.

But we will not end on an unsympathetic note. There is real delicacy and a pensive charm about some of the verses in this first book, for which after all, not great pretensions have been made. Mr. Faulkner, in his essay "On Criticism," has said that: "With the American, the last word carries weight, is culminative." The critic, according to Mr. Faulkner, too often abuses his privilege of having the last word. In this case, the only gracious gesture is to reverse the usual order. Therefore, at the end, these quatrains from *The Marble Faun*.

"Let your finger, languorous,
Slightly curl, palm upward rest.
The silent noon waits over us,
The feathers stir not on his breast.

"There is no sound nor shrill of pipe,
Your feet are noiseless on the ground;
The earth is full and stillily ripe,
In all the land there is no sound.

"There is a great God who sees all
And in my throat bestows this boon;
To ripple the silence with my call
When the world sleeps and it is noon."

SOLDIERS' PAY

SOLDIERS' PAY

BY

WILLIAM FAULKNER

BONI & LIVERIGHT

NEW YORK   MCMXXVI

E. Hartley Grattan.
"A Book of Hatred."
New York *Sun*, April 3, 1926, p. 8.

This novel revolves about the almost silent and very sinister figure of Donald Mahon. He has been shattered physically and mentally in the world war. On his face is a horrible scar. On his spirit is a slaying apathy. About him are clustered a group of major figures and several minor. The major figures are his father, a rather extraordinary Episcopal minister; Joe Gilligan, an ex-private; Mrs. Powers, wife of a soldier killed in France; and Cecily Saunders, Mahon's fiancée (an alliance contracted before the war). The scene of the action is a small Southern town, but it is the peculiar quality of this novel that the characters and their interactions dominate the book almost exclusively. Scene is reduced to minimal importance.

These characters are thrown together in a fashion rather reminiscent of, say, Dostoievsky. That is to say, haphazard. And in consequence one feels that their being together is so fortuitous as to be almost inexplicable. Joe Gilligan is introduced drunk on a train bound West from Buffalo. Donald Mahon suddenly swims into his consciousness, and he enlists in Mahon's service to the extent of taking Mahon home and spending several months in close attendance upon him. Mrs. Powers comes upon Gilligan, Mahon and a third character only fleetingly and occasionally in the action, while walking through the train, and attaches herself to the party, becomes Mahon's other attendant and eventually marries him.

Januarius Jones ambles casually into the book shortly before the party arrives at Mahon's home. He has but little direct connection with Mahon and his satellites. His function will be indicated later. Cecily's relation to Mahon is obvious. But one is amazed that a man in Mahon's condition should be on a train unattended anyway, and that Gilligan and Mrs. Powers were so unattached that they could associate themselves with a quite casual acquaintance.

Once arrived in the Southern town the drama unrolls. Mahon sunk into apathy, terribly scarred, slowly goes blind. His fiancée is repelled, horrified by his appearance, and runs away from him. He cares for nothing that is going on around him. He is dying. His death closes the book. But whirled around him is a picture of postwar social life. And the burden of this life is sex released from the prewar restraints. Cecily is a flapper, so-called, and has her boy friends. To one of them she gives herself, to use a polite euphemism, and eventually marries him. Januarius Jones, pictured as fat and lazy, pursues women in his capacity as "magnificent hedonist" (Cf. the blurb).

Mahon is, of course, unaware of the saturnalia. But Gilligan and Mrs. Powers are actually aware of it, particularly Gilligan. So is William Faulkner, the author of the book. And into his novel he has pumped the most bitter, envenomed hatred of sex that one can well imagine. The whole passionate strength of his book is derived from his hatred. He hates it with his whole being. And I strongly suspect that he felt a relief when he finished the book and knew that to some extent he had freed himself from the burden it was upon him.

Fortunately, Mr. Faulkner is sufficiently the artist not to make his book a tract. Don't get that impression. His emotions are carefully directed into aesthetic channels. And fleetingly he writes passages of genuine beauty, showing the quality of his mind in another direction. But I do feel that the central, driving passion behind this book is hatred. Certainly it is not a comedy. It is not a humorous book. Nor is it an ironic book. Aside from the rather excessively casual manner in which the characters are thrown together, it is a good book, but not being Sherwood Anderson, I cannot go into rhapsodies about it.

Donald Davidson. "William Faulkner." Nashville *Tennessean*, April 11, 1926, Magazine Section, p. 6.

William Faulkner is a Southerner, and lives at Oxford, Mississippi. That is all I know of him, biographically speaking, except that he has contributed to *The Double Dealer*, that New Orleans magazine which has succeeded in disclosing to the world many young writers of talent lying hidden in this part of the United States.

However, it is unnecessary to know anything about William Faulkner. He reveals himself quite clearly in his novel, *Soldiers' Pay*, as a sensitive, observant person with a fine power of objectifying his own and other people's emotions, and of clarifying characters so that they possess the "real life" within themselves which it is one of the functions of art to present. Furthermore, he is an artist in language, a sort of poet tuned into prose; he does not write prose as Dreiser does, as if he were washing dishes; nor like Sinclair Lewis, who goes at words with a hammer and saw. Take this bit of description:

Solemnly the clock on the court-house, staring its four bland faces across the town, like a kind and sleepless god, dropped eleven measured bells of golden sound. Silence carried them away, silence and dark that passing along the street like a watchman, snatched scraps of light from windows, palming them as a pickpocket palms snatched handkerchiefs. A belated car passed swiftly.

Soldiers' Pay, then, is such a book as John Dos Passos might have written if he had not visualized life as such a mixture of harsh planes, intersecting in viciously haphazard ways. And *Soldiers' Pay*, which deals with post-war people in a Southern town, is superior to Dos Passos' *Soldiers Three*, that much-talked-about war book, because it digs deeper into human nature.

Mr. Faulkner's title indicates the irony which he discovers in the post-war situation, that irony familiar to returned soldiers, who came back, sometimes much broken and changed, to discover life moving as casually as ever in its old grooves, and people as much untouched by the war as by a polar exploration. Such a discovery makes a man turn a little grim and bitter, but life goes on, with formidable fructifying and budding. People must still live, love, eat, dance, go to the movies, and therefore it is better not to remain grim and bitter. It is better to crack a joke, light a cigarette, and go about one's business That is about what William Faulkner puts into his book.

The world of *Soldiers' Pay* is the post-war world, with a little Southern town given, let us say, as a typical specimen. Donald Mahon, a young aviator, returns to his place at a time somewhat indefinitely after the armistice. Although discharged from the hospital, he is a physical wreck, eyesight almost gone, feeble, useless limbs, a disfiguring scar across his face, just a hollow figure of a man with a mind hardly working. In effect, he comes back home to die. Around this central, inert figure, stopped midway in its experience of life, move all the persons of the book. Two people come with Mahon to see him safely home—Joe Gilligan, a typical soldier, bluff, good-natured, careless, kind-hearted; Mrs. Powers, an intellectual, far-seeing young woman whose husband was killed in the trenches. There are also the town people: Cecily Saunders, the pert flapper to whom he was engaged; Rector Mahon, the dying man's father; Joe Jones, a sort of Latin scholar intensely resembling a Greek satyr in his insistent pursuit of fleshly pleasures; Emmy, the servant-girl, and various other minor persons. The story consists in the unfolding of the situation created by bringing all these people together. For example, Cecily Saunders is at first romantically intrigued by the idea of marrying a wounded hero. But when she sees Mahon's horrible scar, it turns her delicate stomach. No, she couldn't marry a man with such a disfigurement. Besides, she is really in love with young George Farr, who has been assiduously wooing her while the heroes were absent. Cecily agonizes and debates tremendously, with her shallow nature torn by contrary impulses. Finally, the generous Mrs. Powers relieves the situation by marrying Mahon. And at last Mahon dies anyway. There is also the tragic situation of the old rector, who thought his son was dead, and who, when he gets his son back, naively hopes for a recovery. There is the tragedy of Emily the independent-minded servant girl who loved Mahon secretly. There is Jones, who goes after what he wants with deliberate hedonism. There is all the life of a Southern town, its secret as well as its obvious life, all the mingling of disillusionment and pagan recklessness that have characterized the postwar period.

It is, all in all, a powerful book, done with careful artistry and with great warmth of feeling. Mr. Faulkner is, as might be suspected, distinctly a "modern," and has used rather judiciously the special devices which Joyce and others have contributed to the technique of the novel. He has certain faults, such as a too insistent repetition of efforts which have an air of smartness rather than of fine art; he is too fond of phrases such as "faint lust"; he has too much of the current mania for depicting people "en deshabille"; he over-emphasizes sensuousness, as many moderns do. But he also has a sense of humor, is fairly equable, and avoids the nervous distortion which gives to so many modern novels an effect very much like that of the modern paintings and statues regularly reproduced in the *Dial*. His book will baffle and perplex some people who read it. Or at least they will say they are baffled and perplexed, largely because they are disturbed at the very core of their being. Nevertheless, it is an interesting and even an exciting book for persons who read with discrimination. Mr. Faulkner will perhaps do better books later, but meanwhile he is to be congratulated on a fine initial performance, for *Soldiers' Pay* is, so far as I know, his first novel. And I realize even as I write, that I have not halfway conveyed the flavor of it.

John McClure. "Literature and Less." New Orleans *Times-Picayune*, April 11, 1926, Magazine Section, p. 4.

William Faulkner in *Soldiers' Pay* has written a corking first novel on this theme of the return of the hero. Mr. Faulkner is already well known to readers of the *Times-Picayune* through his tales and sketches. He was known to observant crit-ics as a poet of great promise, but nobody expected him to produce a novel. He has fooled us all, and most pleasurably. *Soldiers' Pay* was written in New Orleans last spring, and a few Orleanians have read it in manuscript. It is a striking piece of work and should, if Mr. Faulkner con-tinues to write fiction, be the precursor of even finer things. Both in promise and in accomplishment it is probably the most noteworthy first novel of the year.

Donald Mahon, a young Georgian who fought with the Royal Air Force, returns as if from the grave, horribly scarred, go-ing blind and dying. He had been reported dead. With him on his return to the vil-lage where his father, a huge, gaunt man, is rector of the Episcopal church, come a strange pair whom he has encountered on the train, Joe Gilligan, a soldier just mus-tered out, and Mrs. Powers, a war widow. They come to help him because he is dy-ing. The village has changed. Mahon's fiancee, a flapper, now engaged in an ado-lescent intrigue with a jellybean, is terri-bly upset. In fact, she screams and faints at the sight of Mahon's face, so horribly scarred. Mahon, whose memory has left him, is like a dying child. The drama which is worked out as Mrs. Powers and Joe Gilligan battle to make his passing easy does not touch him though it revolves around him. He is the heart of it, the dying kernel, and it is strange to him. There is haunting poignancy in the situa-tion. Mrs. Powers, the strange Samaritan woman, is heroic. So is Joe. The back-ground is a village upon which jazz and prohibition have descended like a plague of locusts. In and out of the action moves Januarius Jones, a perfectly fabulous char-acter, who represents the world, the devil and the flesh. *Soldiers' Pay* leaves the reader with the haunting sense of life and death emotionally realized.

Viewed as a whole, the novel has the great merit of unity in design. It is formal in conception as tragedy ought to be. Its deficiencies—they are not serious—arise from a somewhat incoherent development of the theme, rather random motivation, and the author's tendency to get it over with in a series of spurts rather than in steady progression. The dialogue, often delightful, is not always convincing, and the action sometimes less so. As might be expected of a lyrical poet, there is more emotion and symbolic truth than objec-tive accuracy in the novel. In many in-stances in which a character says or does something that one believes he would not actually say or do, one feels that there is nevertheless a symbolic truth in the by-play—that something of this sort is what the character would like to do and, if he lacked inhibitions, would do. In point of style, *Soldiers' Pay* is admirable. This re-viewer can think of none of the younger novelists, and few of the older, who write as well as Mr. Faulkner.

Louis Kronenberger. "*Soldiers' Pay.*" *Literary Digest International Book Review*, 4 (July 1926), 522.

Soldiers' Pay might have been called *What Price Victory?* It deals, vitally and pun-gently, with the aftermath of the Great War; not with the social and economic adjustments the war necessitated and the soldier faced, but with the human and personal adjustments, or, as too often they turned out, maladjustments; with that, and with the passing away of an old scheme of things.

Whoever thinks Mr. Faulkner's story-people too fantastic to be human must remember that the world they moved in was an overturned world of bitter inverted fantasy, which, as it receded from their eye, advanced with increasing vividness upon their imagination. The war, annihilating conventions, moralities and ideals, not only left them primitives; it left them abnormal primitives. When, all three strangers to one another, a war-widow and an ex-private encountered a hopelessly doomed lieutenant on a Pullman, and forthwith forgot their destinations to accompany the dying man to his home in Georgia, their wild overthrow of earlier plans was not so absurd as it seemed. They probably had no real plans: a conventional world had crumbled, in mind and body and soul they were drifting, and to seize this tangible undertaking was probably the nearest approach to adjustment they could have found.

The story of *Soldiers' Pay* is the coming of these three to the town where scarred and dying Donald Mahon had left a father and a fiancee; the ironic, nervous, fantastic, sexually obsessed relationships that arose among them, complicated further by a fat satyr named Januarius Jones and a town youth named George Farr. Mr. Faulkner's method of presentation is as uncontrolled, unconforming, haphazard and desultory as his substance; but it very often achieves a vividness, a fervor, an immediacy which ordered procedure would not project. As primitives, these people are dominated by sex; as abnormals, they are stricken with continual consciousness of their obsession; it fills not only their bodies, but their minds. Mr. Faulkner employs a kind of Joycian pattern to describe them, reveals a kind of Joycian wit and humor, and has something of Joyce's precise recapturing of dialog. Yet he is much more than a disciple of Joyce. His book is not one for facile categories. It is a long way off from the typical war book; it has too much ironic pity and sense of futility to be an indictment; it is a study of the returned soldier, but not of his usual problems. Mr. Faulkner ignores the causes of the abnormalities in his people, to picture only the effects. His book seems to be a rich compound of imagination, observation and experience. In an isolated world of Faulkner's own making, shadows having the reality of men grope through a maze complex enough to be at once pitiful and comic, passionate, tormenting and strange.

Checklist of Additional Reviews

"Doughboy Who Returns Unexpectedly, Gravely Disfigured." Springfield (Mass.) *Sunday Union and Republican*, April 4, 1926, p. 7-A.

"War's Aftermath." *New York Times Book Review*, April 11, 1926, p. 8.

"Soldiers' Pay." Boston *Independent*, April 17, 1926, p. 463.

"The Bookman's Guide to Fiction." *Bookman*, 63 (June 1926), 472.

"Other Books Worth Reading." *McNaught's Monthly*, 5 (June 1926), 186.

Anderson, David Merrill. "Aftermath of War in the Person of One Broken Veteran." Baltimore *Evening Sun*, June 5, 1926, p. 6.

Barretto, Larry. "Men without Faces." *New York Herald Tribune Books*, June 6, 1926, p. 6.

Beckwith, E. C. "Soldiers' Return Theme of New Novel Called One of Biting Power." *New York Evening Post Literary Review*, April 3, 1926, p. 2.

Boyd, Thomas. "Honest but Slap-Dash." *Saturday Review of Literature*, April 24, 1926, p. 736. Also appeared as "Hysteric Moments." Minneapolis

Journal, April 25, 1926, City Life
Section, p. 11.

Morris, Lawrence S. "Flame and Ash."
New Republic, June 23, 1926, p. 148.

Sanford, John. *"Soldiers' Pay."* Detroit
News, April 11, 1926, Metropolitan
Section, p. 11.

MOSQUITOES

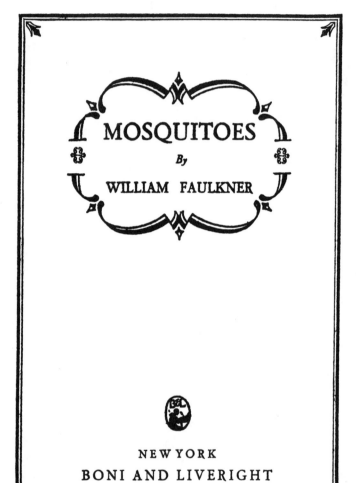

MOSQUITOES

By

WILLIAM FAULKNER

NEW YORK

BONI AND LIVERIGHT

1 9 2 7

Lillian Hellman. "Futile Souls Adrift on a Yacht."
New York Herald Tribune Books, June 19, 1927, p. 9.

Last year Mr. Faulkner wrote a novel called *Soldiers' Pay*. Many judicious readers thought it one of the few good books that came out of the war. Its tone was serious if its intent was ironic and its treatment imaginative. This year Mr. Faulkner has taken a quick turn, focusing his attention on an entirely different world. If his first novel showed more than the usual promise then this one, *Mosquitoes*, comes in time to fulfill it. But it must stand alone; a proof of the man's versatility.

It is perhaps unfair to any book, or at least unfair to an author's originality, should he have any, to compare his offering with another that has gone before. However, it remains one way to show excellence or demonstrate worthlessness. In 1923 Aldous Huxley wrote *Antic Hay*, which I think must still stand as the most brilliant book of the last few years. Since then there have been a host of people who have followed, or attempted to follow, in his footsteps. In most cases their literary worth has been as ephemeral as it was temporarily interesting. If any of these books have approached *Antic Hay* any more closely than *Mosquitoes* it must by now be forgotten. Not that the plot or the people in *Mosquitoes* are similar to those in the Huxley book. As a matter of fact the novel more closely resembles *Those Barren Leaves* in structure, but in the brilliant result it stands closer to the better book.

Mosquitoes takes place on a yacht. Mrs. Maurier, a collector of famous people in her own home town of New Orleans, has arranged a boating party for the more artistic of her friends. They come, some of them, because they have nothing better to do, some of them because they are assured of food, some because they cannot help themselves. She has gathered Gordon, a sculptor; Mr. Talliafero, a gentleman who knows much about ladies' lingerie; a young niece and the niece's mechanically inclined brother; a Jew and his sister; Mark Frost, a poet. The niece has found somewhere in New Orleans a young man and a young lady who on that particular day have nothing much to do with themselves. The niece invites them along. They are as cheap, as human, as vulgar as any two she could have found, and yet they furnish the wine for the party. It is a mad trip, this boat ride; the niece running off with the steward, an intellectual lady pursuing the vulgar young man and most of the other gentlemen of the party keeping to their rooms for fear of the grapefruit that is served for every meal. Together these people are a fine combination of wit and sophistication and naivete, but whatever their singularity, their problems, their frustration, are as important to you as if they were people who were more common. They are as tragic as other breeds are tragic, as authentic as your next door neighbor.

It is impossible to capture in a review the humor, the delight of Mr. Faulkner's writing. It approaches in the first half and reaches in the second half a brilliance that you can rightfully expect only in the writings of a few men. It is full of the fine kind of swift and lusty writing that comes from a healthy, fresh pen.

Undoubtedly certain portions of it are overwritten, certain Joycean passages that have no direct place or bearing, parts that are heavy and dull with overloaded description. But it is not spoilt. If it contained only the fine last scene it would still be able to stand up.

If you have waited with some feeling akin to longing to read about a modern heroine who is plausible and sympathetic in her sommersaults, or to watch a foolish and pathetic woman who has wealth and wants art, or perchance a decaying man who desires his youth; if you want a treat of really amusing conversation that depends upon its wit and not upon its flourishes; if you have waited to see these important matters done really well, then this is your book.

Donald Davidson. "The Grotesque." Nashville *Tennessean*, July 3, 1927, Magazine Section, p. 7.

William Faulkner's new novel, *Mosquitoes*, is like his first [one,] *Soldiers' Pay*, clearly an example of the principle of the grotesque in full operation. Faulkner sits in the seat of the scornful with a manner somewhat reminiscent of James Joyce, but with an easy languorousness befitting a Mississippian. And as he sits, he does dispatch mayhem, assault and battery upon the bodies of numerous persons with such gracious ease that you almost overlook his savagery. His device is simple in conception, but complicated in practice. The widow Maurier, a shallow lady who yearns after culture and patronizes genius, invites certain diverse people on a yachting party out of New Orleans; among the lot are a sculptor, a fool English man, a too-utterly-utter lingerie clerk with Don Juan ambitions, a flapperish niece and Penrodish nephew, a novelist, and, by the casual invitation of the quite casual niece,

a tough young bootlegger and his girlish sweetheart get mixed with the crowd and supply sufficient vulgar contrast

When the scientific-minded young nephew removes a part of the yacht's machinery, this medley of persons is stranded in mid-lake for some days. The ensuing period of boredom is punctuated, quite naturally, with some slapping and scratching as mosquitoes advance to the feast. There is also some of what the papers call "mixed bathing," a tragical-romantic escapade when the niece runs off to the mainland swamps with the steward, and an assortment of queer couplings and mixups. But we are chiefly aware that Mr. Faulkner is making all these people the butt of his irony. Most of them are, alas, a peckish, bloodsucking lot, like the mosquitoes. Only those who are physically and mentally spontaneous and natural escape the bite of Mr. Faulkner's wit, and even these nobler individuals are reduced somewhat to attitudes partaking of the grotesque. The novel runs on to its inconsequential end, and in spite of a really wonderful dexterity in the technical management of words to convey certain "slices of life," Mr. Faulkner makes us most aware, not of the people whom he is busy slaying, but of his own remorseless mind, most painfully ill at ease in Zion, wrenching his mortal world into a beautifully distorted cast, leaving us full of admiration for the skill of the performance, but conscious of some discomfort before the performer. Yet what he does, he does with buoyant zest.

20

John McClure.
"Literature and Less."
New Orleans *Times-Picayune*, July 3, 1927, Magazine Section, p. 4.

William Faulkner, who aroused hopes of fine things to come with his extraordinary first novel, *Soldiers' Pay*, still has that promise to fulfill. *Mosquitoes*, his second novel, is a clever interlude. It is made up of satirical character sketches. Each character is composite. There is much cruelty in the book. And, it may be remarked in passing, a good deal to affront the Puritan imagination.

The scene is a yacht. The novel is a picture of a yachting party. The title is derived from the irritating effect upon one another of people cooped up in small compass with nothing to do. They become as irritating to one another as the mosquitoes, always buzzing around. The best characterization in the volume is that of lowbrow Jenny, who, with her tough sweetheart Pets, somehow got invited to the party contrary to Hoyle. You sense the creative touch here. Elsewhere you detect the notebook or the retentive memory, and the critical sense. The work is fundamentally satirical.

That William Faulkner at his best writes with verve and gusto this book proves. There is capital stuff in it. Yet the conception, and to a certain extent the rendering, give the impression that it is a tour de force. The novel lacks the integrity of *Soldiers' Pay*. It is brilliant, but not profound. There is profundity in *Soldiers' Pay* and in some of William Faulkner's poetry. He was skylarking in *Mosquitoes*. The book, though cruel, is playful. It represents a day off.

Granted Mr. Faulkner's theme, it was inevitable that the fabric of his novel should be small-talk of one sort or another. The conversation is often extremely deft. It is often extremely unconventional, and Puritan readers are warned again that *Mosquitoes* is a most disconcerting book.

Here is a sample of Mr. Faulkner's prose. He is describing an interior in the old French Quarter:

> This unevenly boarded floor, these rough stained walls broken by high, small, practically useless windows beautifully set, these crouching lintels cutting the immaculate ruined pitch of walls with the age which had housed slaves long ago, slaves long dead and dust with the age that produced them and which they had served with a kind and gracious dignity—shades of servants and masters now in a more gracious region, lending dignity to eternity. After all, only a few chosen can accept service with dignity; it is man's impulse to do for himself. It rests with the servant to lend dignity to an unnatural proceeding.

That is Mr. Faulkner at his best. He allows himself throughout this book to indulge in horseplay, both in dialogue and description. "Twilight," he says at one point, "ran in like a quiet violet dog." That is Bill's little joke.

Checklist of Additional Reviews

"Other Books Worth Reading." *McNaught's Monthly*, 7 (June 1927), 188.
"Faulkner Discourses of Subject of Bores." Milwaukee *Journal*, June 4, 1927, p. 3.

"*Mosquitoes*." *Saturday Review of Literature*, June 25, 1927, p. 933.

"*Mosquitoes*." Boston *Evening Transcript*, July 2, 1927, Section VI, p. 8.

"Tedious Talk in *Mosquitoes*." Springfield (Mass.) *Sunday Union and Republican*, July 17, 1927, p. 7-F.

Aiken, Conrad. "William Faulkner, Who Wrote *Soldiers' Pay*, Again Manifests Brilliance, Promise and Foibles." New York *Evening Post*, June 11, 1927, Section III, p. 7. Reprinted in *A Reviewer's ABC*. New York: Meridian, 1958, pp. 197–200.

Eaton, G. D. "Not Generally Known." *Mc Naught's Monthly*, 8 (July 1927), 27.

McGinnis, John H. "The Southern Novelists Also Produce Literature of Revolt." Dallas *Morning News*, May 15, 1927, Section III, p. 3.

Suckow, Ruth. "South Wind Blows but Fitfully." New York *World*, June 12, 1927, p. 7-M.

Wylie, Elinor Hoyt. *Mosquitoes*. *New Republic*, July 20, 1927, p. 236.

SARTORIS

SARTORIS

---•---

WILLIAM FAULKNER

New York

HARCOURT, BRACE
AND COMPANY

Henry Nash Smith. "In His New Novel William Faulkner Broadens His Art." Dallas *Morning News*, February 17, 1929, Amusement Section, p. 3.

Most people have noticed casually that the hard-boiled school of younger novelists has been getting distinguished recruits from the South. But possibly the full importance of several recent Southern novels is even yet not recognized. As a matter of fact, if Sherwood Anderson's pronounced Southern associations are remembered and *The Time of Man* and *Mosquitoes*, it is possible to believe that the best novels of the last two or three years have borne a Southern imprint. This is especially true of William Faulkner's work. *Soldiers' Pay* and *Mosquitoes* undoubtedly represent one of the most promising talents for fiction in contemporary America.

Of course, there is a temptation to cry a local prophet's merits beyond their worth. But the chance of such an error is discounted in this instance by the wholly unexpected turn of Mr. Faulkner's talent. His books are simply not the thing that could have been expected from postwar Mississippi. He is, to be sure, one of the disillusioned young men who like to play with obscenity just to distress the censors, but there is disillusion and disillusion. When you get to the heart of almost any of the men called great in literature you find something a little chill and disturbing; they leave you with a sobering suspicion that perhaps life is like that. Mr.

Faulkner's disillusion is of this sort. I do not mean that he is a Southern Shakespeare or a Mississippi Cervantes; for he is not. What he may become lies inscrutably with the future. He learns his trade and broadens his thought almost visibly from chapter to chapter; and he is young. But he is able to confront and assimilate post war pessimism without falling into the sophomoric pose of his New York compeers, or the epicene dreaming indolence of Sherwood Anderson. In other words, like the hero of his newest novel, he carries his liquor steadily. From such a man one might well expect the definitive utterance of the generation who went to the war and came back when it was over.

But if he is to this extent representative of his time, he is in at least two ways unrepresentative of present styles in fiction. In the first place, he has revived and refreshed a literary manner which had almost wholly disappeared; he is for better or worse, eloquent. He likes processions of carefully accurate epithets; he likes jeweled, sensuous words shedding color and sound, words marshaled in swelling rhythms suggestive of blank verse. This is naturally heresy to the age of Dreiser; but the peculiar thing is he gets away with it. With the exception of a sentence here and there which grows too long for modern ears, his eloquence is moving, passionate, darkly remorseful. He speaks of the "baffled and mellow expostulations" of hounds; or he says, "About the doorstep the geese surged ecstatically with discordant cries, their necks undulant and suave as formal gestures in a pantomime"—but there is no use quoting snatches, I can merely suggest the full-chorded modulation of Mr. Faulkner's descriptions. The very fact that he makes words suggest music is quite unmodern. But sometimes he even expands into a sort of counterpoint, playing contrasting themes against one another; or again he flings upward in a crescendo to nothingness, only to return abruptly to a measured thin melody, light and graceful.

The other unrepresentative trait of Mr. Faulkner's writing is its poetry. His perceptions are Keats-like in their delicacy and richness; and his narrative moves among a constant series of pictures vivid beyond expectation. He is not ashamed to notice the moon; many of his figures thrown carelessly into a paragraph of conversation put the best efforts of the imagists to insipid shame, and his range includes smells and sounds even more keenly sensed and regarded than his pictures. His is a Southern countryside with the smell of boiling cane juice, of salt pork fried over a fireplace, of the reek of a negro cabin, of the banker's cigar smoke floating over a bed of saliva in the dusk.

> "The negroes gathered the puppies up one by one and tumbled them into a smaller box behind the stove, where they continued to move about with sundry scratchings and bumpings and an occasional smothered protest. From time to time during the meal a head would appear, staring above the rim of the box with blinking and solemn curiosity, then vanish with an abrupt scuffling thump and more protests, and the moiling, infant-like noises rose again."

I have not said enough about *Sartoris*, Mr. Faulkner's newest book. Sartoris is the name of an old Southern family which has for generations sent its men into reckless, lunging careers through aristocratic lives destined to violence and death at the end. In the hero, Bayard Sartoris, Mr. Faulkner takes up again the theme of *Soldiers' Pay*—the dazed inability of men recently come from France to fit into the peace they had left so short a time before. Again he remembers the war from the cockpit of a fighting airplane, this time as a searing image of John Sartoris thumbing his nose affectionately at his brother close behind him and then jumping without out a parachute from his burning plane.

But here more than usually the plot is unimportant. In *Mosquitoes* perhaps the intellectual attitude was most arresting. In *Sartoris* it is something else. Perhaps I can explain it by saying that Mr. Faulkner has got to be more of an artist and a little less of a social philosopher. He turns from scrutiny of the ideas of a certain New Orleans clique to the eternal task of the novelist—people themselves. *Sartoris* is not better than *Mosquitoes*, perhaps it is not quite so good. But with its publication Mr. Faulkner demonstrates that he is getting about novel-writing in earnest. *Mosquitoes* made the appearance of his next novel an event to be awaited with impatience and a little concern. *Sartoris* resolves a natural doubt about Mr. Faulkner's future and in no way decreases the impatience of waiting for his next.

Donald Davidson. "Two Mississippi Novels." Nashville *Tennessean*, April 14, 1929, Magazine Section, p. 7.

Even at the risk of being called an Old Confederate, I am obliged to say, after much reading of American novels, that the Southern novelists are doing about as well as anybody. Indeed, I think it would be a little hard to match the exhibit provided in the works of James Branch Cabell, Ellen Glasgow, T. S. Stribling, the late

Frances Newman, Elizabeth Madox Roberts, Julia Peterkin, DuBose Heyward, Isa Glenn, Roark Bradford, Maristan Chapman and others. The works of Lewis, Anderson, and Dreiser, which a few years ago dominated the field, now seem to belong to a phase that is passing. It is not impossible that the Southern writers, especially the younger ones, are partly responsible for the change. With one or two exceptions, they are romantic rather than realistic; they are bringing back a sense of style that almost vanished in the experimentalism of the post-war period; and they are perhaps more American than their predecessors in being nearer to an old native tradition that the Middle Westerners, in their desperate suspicion of commercial America, entirely forgot.

The immediate evidence may be found in two novels recently published, both of them by Mississippians, both sited in Mississippi: *Sartoris* by William Faulkner, and *The Devil Beats His Wife*, by Ben Wasson. They are two very different books, and really ought not to be discussed together. But they illustrate the point I have made, for both approach their material with vigor and freshness and do not fall readily into any of the categories which we have been used to establish for the endless series of contemporary novels that have virtually been repeating one another. Likewise, though they are so distinctly Southern in flavor as to tempt one to apply the term "regional," they do not betray the weakness of the "regional" or "local color" school, which is, as I see it, to write of negroes, poor whites and "colonels" in the terms best appreciated by Northern audiences.

Mr. Faulkner has already made his place as a novelist, though his work, for some strange reason, is not as well known as it should be. His two earlier novels, *Soldiers' Pay* and *Mosquitoes*, were clearly the product of a bold and original spirit;

but they somehow escaped attention while we were all engaged with *An American Tragedy* and *Dark Laughter*. Perhaps, too, they were more experimental and less well-conceived than *Sartoris*. Let me at once have done with nice distinctions and say that as a stylist and as an acute observer of human behavior, I think that Mr. Faulkner is the equal of any except three or four American novelists who stand at the very top. His sole difficulty so far seems to be that he has not found a theme or a character that really comes up to the possibilities of his style and his perception. For his style is a major style, not a trifling one; and his perception ought not to be lavished on weak or inconsequent persons.

In *Sartoris* as in the two previous books we discover a hero who is a bit cracked, and, as in *Soldiers' Pay*, it is the nervous strain of war that causes the sickness of mind and the feverish thirst for activity that is finally destructive. But in this novel the mad hero, "doomed" or "fey" person if there ever was one, is surrounded by a group of rather normal persons—the persons, major and minor, of a good Southern family in a good Southern community.

Bayard, the last of the Sartorises, comes of a "doomed" line. The Sartorises, like the men of the Irish song, always went forth to battle and always fell—fell unluckily, unnecessarily, and foolishly, but always with the utmost abandon and gallantry. The Sartoris women, when the men threw their lives away, were left with the braver and harder tasks of continuing the establishment and coddling the bruised warriors. The latest scion of the Sartoris line, that gloomy and inexpressive Bayard, was an aviator in the World War and came home to find himself dislocated from all reasonable relation with human affairs.

He had been lucky enough to get through the war alive, but his melancholy is not bettered by the loss of his brother,

27

also an aviator, whose death he has possibly caused. With no battles left to fight, Bayard dulls his misery with a series of meaningless anodynes: he speeds insanely along the country roads in a racing car, scaring negroes and keeping his family on edge; he rides wild stallions; he drinks fiery liquor. Literally he drives himself to death, for after he has tried all manner of machines which only wound and do not kill, he at last gets a full answer to his suicidal frenzy. He rides to his fate in a newly invented, untried aeroplane. And again the women are left to carry on the traditions; the indomitable Miss Jenny, scolding and realistic, says to Narcissa, the wife of Bayard who has named the new born child "Benbow" in order to escape or avert the fatality of family names:

> "Do you think that because his name is Benbow, he'll be any less a Sartoris and a scoundrel and fool?"

In this novel, though there are occasional touches of humor and though a diverse gallery of characters gives the narrative complexity, there is really nothing but tragedy. Tragedy is inherent in every syllable of Mr. Faulkner's careful sentences. There is fatality, there is inescapable despair, on every page. I cannot help suspecting some allegorical meaning is in *Sartoris*. The gloomy, unspeaking Bayard is a type of the man of this age whose only mortal satisfaction is in doing himself to death with machines. There is no end to his masculine foolishness; he is incurably romantic and childish. But the women are different; they are true realists. It is with more than a hint of a feminine world that the strong-minded Miss Jenny says: "It always does me good to see all those fool pompous men lying there with their marble mottoes and things . . . I reckon the Lord knows his business, but I declare, sometimes . . ."

Mary Ellen Chase. "Some Intimations of Immortality." *Commonweal,* 10 (June 5, 1929), 134–35.

Mr. William Faulkner's *Sartoris* brings to the mind of at least one reader the saying of Mrs. Robert Louis Stevenson about R.L.S.: "His faults are so much more lovable than other people's virtues." *Sartoris* has faults, but they are the faults of a style and a method crammed with virtues. There is such a wealth of figures, mostly good, that sentences too often seem mannered. Favorite words become intrusive, "sibilant," "myriad." Incidents are so well told that they seem detached, unable through their very individuality and power to take their place in the story. Characters live so completely and fully in themselves that they mingle with difficulty. In short, Mr. Faulkner's ingredients are so dear to him that he hates the stirring of them into a smooth whole.

Nevertheless, perhaps even because of these things, *Sartoris* is a memorable book. It is the name and story of a southern family whose troubled, overwhelming personality was so prodigal that even the dead Sartorises could not stay in heaven, must come back to linger on in their pipes, in the odor of the honeysuckle, in the rooms where they had once lived, and above all in the perturbed and desperate desires of their grandchildren. Thus they obtain their own immortality and ensure, sadly enough, the torturing mortality of succeeding generations of their name.

One wishes for space to recount the things in *Sartoris* which will be long remembered: the moon-swept Mississippi fields and hills on spring nights; the piping of young frogs "like endless, silver, small bubbles rising"; that inimitable Thanksgiving dinner; those charming interludes of conversation among the Negro servants. Innumerable details enrich the pages like beads of manifold colors. But above all else one will remember the suffering mind and imagination of young Bayard Sartoris, whose story this is. The prodigal creation of his forefathers, his is the body in which they survive, his the nature which they sustain and nourish and at last consume.

Checklist of Additional Reviews

Book of the Month Club News, March 1929.

"A Southern Family." *New York Times Book Review*, March 3, 1929, p. 8.

"*Sartoris.*" *Wisconsin Library Bulletin*, 25 (June 1929), 195.

Chattanooga *Times*, October 13, 1935.

"*Sartoris.*" Atlanta *Constitution*, December 1, 1929, pp. 7–8.

Brickell, Herschel. "Romance Has Its Gall." *New York Herald Tribune Books*, February 24, 1929, p. 5; also reviewed as "A Wild Southern Family,"*North American Review*, April 1929, advertising pages.

Morris, Lawrence S. "*Sartoris.*" *Bookman*, 69 (May 1929), 310.

Smith, Bernard. "More Talent than Theme." New York *Sun*, February 5, 1929, p. 10.

Tasker, J. Dana. "*Sartoris.*" *Outlook and Independent*, February 20, 1929, p. 311.

THE SOUND AND THE FURY

THE
SOUND AND THE FURY

BY WILLIAM FAULKNER

NEW YORK
JONATHAN CAPE AND HARRISON SMITH

Henry Nash Smith. "Three Southern Novels." *Southwest Review*, 15 (Autumn 1929), iii–iv.

... William Faulkner's novel calls for a re-examination of our premises. It raises at least two perplexing questions: first, does an unmistakably provincial locale make a book a provincial piece of writing? and secondly, what evidences of provincialism might one expect in the style of a novel written by a man who has, in the trite phrase, sunk his roots into the soil?

The first question suggests some consideration of a new Southwestern book, *Dobe Walls*. Stanley Vestal's novel, for all its wealth of frontier incident and description, is perfectly conventional in its plot, its technique, and its heroine; only in one of the men (Bob Thatcher for instance) does the influence of the Frontier on character become evident. *Dobe Walls* escapes from the here and now of life; it is a historical tale with unusually authentic information about the period and the region it treats. In this respect it is vastly different from *The Sound and the Fury*, which is concerned with a regional tradition only as it appears in the present, and from Mr. Faulkner's earlier novels, which often lean toward satire. Yet both novels have a regional setting, and both authors are residents of the provinces. Are both books to be related to the "new provincialism"?

The question of a provincial style is even more involved. One may always be suspicious when talk grows as theoretical as discussions of the "rhythm of a landscape" or "the spacious gesture of the frontier" tend to become. It seems entirely possible that some of us have been misled by an analogy, and have wandered a little into realms of speculation. Upholders of the idea of universal standards not dependent upon a genius of the age or a genius of the place have always been uneasy in the presence of such theories; and perhaps they are nearer right than we. Or maybe we are both right, but have not yet found the reconciling "nevertheless."

Let me, therefore, deliver myself from both points of view on the subject of *The Sound and the Fury*. No matter how universal the standard, there are certain pages in this novel which are very near great literature. I refer, for instance, to the character of Jason Compson, Senior, in which the typical cynicism of a decadent aristocracy is merged with—perhaps grows out of—an intensely individual delineation. They praise Chaucer for taking a stock character like Criselda and, without losing typical traits, making her a person; for writing that half-allegory, half-comedy, the *Nonne Preestes Tale,* in which a remarkable verisimilitude alternates with the complete fantasy of the beast fable as colors play back and forth with the shifting light on changeable silk. In both of these respects. *The Sound and the Fury* will easily bear comparison with the verses of the fat customs officer himself.

From another "universal" standpoint— the traditional definition of tragedy— Faulkner's achievement is also remarkable. Pity and fear are not often more poignantly aroused than they are in the scene where Candace Compson stands cursing her brother for the devil he is. The subject, too, is of an imposing magnitude; for as the story spreads its fragments before the reader there emerges the spectacle of a civilization uprooted and left to die. Scope such as this is not usual in American novels.

Faulkner's handling of the tradition of the Old South, nevertheless, is distinctly related to provincialism. He has realized minutely and understandingly a given milieu and a given tradition—to all intents and purposes, the milieu of Oxford, Mississippi, where the author has lived most of his life, and the tradition of the antebellum aristocracy. He has avoided the mere sophistication which sometimes is evident in his earlier novels, and is certainly at the farthest remove from a metropolitan smartness. That he has borrowed the stream-of-consciousness technique from Europe seems to me of minor importance; to say the least, he has modified it to his own use and has refused to be tyrannized by conventions, even the conventions of revolt.

In short, by the only definition that means very much, Mr. Faulkner is a provincial writer. He belongs to the South, if not to the Southwest. Though he is not a folklorist, though he is more concerned with life than with regionalism, his book has shown unguessed possibilities in the treatment of provincial life without loss of universality.

Harold W. Recht. "Southern Family Sinks into Dark Mental Decadence." Philadelphia *Record*, September 29, 1929.

This first [*sic*] novel, *The Sound and the Fury*, by a young Southerner, is an arresting portrayal of the decadence of an American family, done in a manner which owes much to James Joyce and Virginia Woolf and yet is far from being a blind imitation.

In these days in which so many books are hailed as the authentic masterpieces of the decade, one hesitates to inflict on it superlatives that are tiresome and ephemeral. Its admirers, and I hope that they

will be many, are going to find it unique and profound; those who refuse to follow the moderns in their devious pilgrimages through the human soul are going to be repelled on the first page, if only by the difficulties of Mr. Faulkner's method. They will thereby be spared annoyance at certain defects of which *The Sound and the Fury* is guilty, but they will also miss a great deal that is eminently worthwhile.

The book is divided into four parts which are four days in the life of the Compson family, provincial aristocrats of the South. The first day is presented through the eyes of Benjy, the idiot son, and here, unless I am misled by the novelty of the idea, Mr. Faulkner has done a brilliant piece of writing. No tale heretofore told by an idiot was nearly so sad or so beautiful.

Next we are transported back some years, to the day preceding the suicide of Quentin, another son, whose mind is harried by a love of his sister for which psychologists have, doubtless, a perfect explanation. It is this passage which is most reminiscent of *Ulysses*, and Stephen's mother-love motive rather shines by comparison. The third part has to do with Jason, the remaining son, and his attempt to subdue his fair and wayward niece, and in the final portion the author himself speaks in the third person.

Miss Evelyn Scott, whose sympathetic and intelligent estimate accompanies *The Sound and the Fury*, is too prone, I think, to find in it the elements of great tragedy. I see nothing of ultimate symbolism in the book; Mr. Faulkner is at the ancient game of telling a story, and our Twentieth century life is stripped for him of many of the old coatings that made it sweet. The devotees of the cult of unintelligibility are so sure of their advance that one is diffident about intruding the difficulties of the less gifted, but, since art must still be an exercise in communication, I wonder what principle they follow in knowing what to communicate. In the work at hand, for example, I should trade my knowledge that it was the eighth of April for a patronizing footnote that there were two Quentins. However, these are minor matters which need not detract from the merit of a novel much above the average, and if they inspire a second reading, so much the better.

Walter Yust. "Of Making Many Books." Philadelphia *Public Ledger*, October 4, 1929.

About 300 years ago there lived in Spain a poet whose name was Gongora. He came trailing along in the wake of the Golden Age of letters and lived during a transition period when the creative spirit had simmered down to fitful, meager burning; and because he himself had little enough to say, he took to inventing new ways to say old truths. His obsession became form, and he amused, and no doubt kidded himself, by experimenting with form. I don't know how deeply the old boy believed in himself and in the poems he wrote. I do know he wrote verses strangely similar to the unintelligible typographical contortions of today. He suggests Cummings, William Carlos Williams in his earlier manifestation, James Joyce when he is patently thumbing his nose at himself and readers, Gertrude Stein, hypnotized by repetitive sound.

Gongora, you see, endeavored to hide the weakness of his imagination by overdoing the tricks his fancy could handle. He was a decadent; a writer who wrote in handsprings because that was the best he could do.

Far be it from me to suggest that modern experimenters are without significance; far be it from me to insist that all they write is incomprehensible and somehow useless. They are merely tiresome; their rhetorical and printer's gymnastics require too much effort to be comprehended in this day of many books. There just isn't time to worry over them and their literary convictions.

And yet I must confess that whenever a new book comes to me in which some young man has been experimenting again, the book tempts me. And I'll spend hours over it, trying to decide whether I am mad or the author.

Harrison Smith, of Cape & Smith sends me William Faulkner's new novel, *The Sound and the Fury*. Mr. Faulkner is a young Southerner who's written two or three novels, all of them rich in promise and achievement. His present novel is a sport. Any page of it, except the closing ones (which are intelligible and conventional, sufficiently modern in spirit, of course, as the prose in *Main Street*) proclaims its difference from the traditional novel.

Mr. Faulkner adapts James Joyce, eschewing punctuation marks and ordered grammatical sentences, but not throughout the story. He tries, like Gertrude Stein, to dispense with the time element, or at least to break chronological sequence—until the closing pages of his novel. And he descends to the rather unforgiveable trick, or so it seems to me, of delaying the identification of personalities. (It's a toss-up, for the greater part, which of two Quentins you are reading about, or which Jason, and whether Quentin is a girl or a boy.)

Mr. Faulkner has the privilege of writing his novels as he chooses. It's none of my business. It is my business, however, to decide for myself when I wish to submit to a novelist's willfulness and his laborious attempt to play a game with me—to keep me puzzled by leaving out names of personalities and by scrambling incidents so that I am unable to follow any recognizable sequence. (A novelist at his peril plays hob with time; an idiot apparently can't help himself.)

And therein lies my chief objection to this novel. Mr. Faulkner plays these tricks on his readers for too obvious a purpose. Too obvious and arty. *The Sound and the Fury* comes from "Life's . . . a tale told by an idiot, full of sound and fury, signifying nothing." With that for a very literal text, Mr. Faulkner allows an idiot, for the first section of his story, to tell what he sees of the decline and fall of the Compson family of the South, a family decaying. The impress on the idiot's mind starts the confusion. I can't say that Mr. Faulkner has actually given us an idiot's mind; the matter's sort of hit and miss; who knows, anyway, what a deaf mute idiot sees? This one somehow hears, too, for he reports conversation. Unrelated conversation; and his time is utterly out of joint.

My feeling is that Mr. Faulkner's stunt—it's a convention you accept only out of kindness to the novelist—is too like an orchestrated farm yard poem, in which one hears the moo of the cow, the bark of the dog and the cluck-cluck of the chicken. Here one meets an idiot, who can't speak, telling his own story. It's as uninspired a device as the orchestra cow's moo is. Well——

As the book progresses, other characters tell the same idiot's tale, dropping here and there (as Mr. Faulkner willfully directs) bits of information which clear up slowly but surely the original mental mess Benjy the idiot gets the reader into. Before the novel closes, Mr. Faulkner's Japanese puzzle is pretty well solved, and one knows, for certain, that the Compsons are in a bad way, with the daughter and granddaughter déclassées, a drunken father dead, two sons at the end of their rope, a mother querulous and self-pitying who watches her kin desert her.

The novel carries, in Brother Jason, one of the most poisonous men, I know, in modern letters, whose character stands out bold and true. And there are situations in the novel when Mr. Faulkner rises above his distortions, which are unforgettable. I can't, for the life of me, understand, however, why so able a story teller will waste so much ingenuity and time trying to make a fine story a puzzle and a burden.

Ted Robinson. "Full of Sound and Fury, Horror Tale Sinks Spurs into Snorting Nightmares." Cleveland *Plain Dealer,* October 18, 1929, Amusement Section, p. 6.

I'm having nightmares in consequence of reading a strange book, and this psychic disturbance is responsible for my putting this book in the leading position this week. I expect what the analysts call a catharsis from talking about it in public—or, in the ordinary phrase, getting it off my chest.

The name of the book is *The Sound and the Fury*, the author is William Faulkner, and the publishers are Jonathan Cape and Harrison Smith. The characters are members of a degenerating southern family; the theme is the crisis of their decay; the method is unique; the technique is strikingly original and hauntingly effective.

36

I was sadly confused during my reading of the first part of this horrid story. That first part takes place on April 7, 1928. The second part goes back to June 2, 1910. The third part hops to April 6, 1928. The fourth and concluding section takes us through April 8, 1928. If I had had time I should have gone back and read the first part again, after I finished the book, just to get the chronological order straightened out.

That first part all takes place in the mind of Benjy, a dumb idiot, 33 years old. One understands the title of the book from this circumstance—

"It is a tale
Told by an idiot, full of sound and fury,
Signifying nothing."

However, from the standpoint of plot and atmosphere, this idiot's tale signifies a good deal. The confusion referred to results from the fact that in the idiot's consciousness there is no sense of time, and any chance smell, sound, or other physical stimulus will take him back to some past event that impressed him. His narrative is therefore an inextricable mixture of past and present; characters appear in their childhood and in their maturity; incidents that happened ten years ago are sandwiched in between the events of the present.

The second part is another Joycean narrative—the stream of consciousness of a neurotic brother who has been sent to Harvard. The horror of an unnatural sin he has committed drives him to suicide. After that, we go forward again to the events of the day begun by the idiot's tale. The daughter of an incestuous union is the sorry heroine of this story; she is a reckless nymphomaniac, like her mother, and refuses to stay in school in spite of the watchfulness of her uncle—himself a futile crook with a twisted mentality, a perverted moral sense and a diseased body.

The complete debacle of this pathetic family comes when the uncle, who for years robbed not only his invalid mother but his promiscuous niece also, is himself robbed by the latter when she runs away with a circus man.

It is a sordid and revolting story; and yet its sordidness has a certain tragic dignity, and so reminds the reader of *The Brothers Karamazoff*—to choose a Russian novel almost at random. Perhaps the method of *Ulysses* has been well employed here, if only for the reason that its confusion helps to veil much of what would be too painful if directly stated.

There may be much discussion about this book, if in spite of its manner it gains a large number of readers. I shall take no part in such discussion; but I shall credit its author with a large share of that proper proportion that constitutes what we call genius.

Winfield Townley Scott. "The Waning South." Providence *Journal*, October 20, 1929, Magazine Section, p. 27.

The Sound and the Fury, is a novel about a Southern family of descending social position. There is a father with considerable polish, a mother of far less education, a son who is a business man and another who is a Harvard student, two daughters who go wrong and a son who is a deaf and dumb idiot. There is little attempted on the part of the author beyond expression of these characters; the plot element is slight. It is the method in which the story is told that chiefly concerns us.

The narrative is divided into four sections. Three of these four are done in the manner of James Joyce, *Blue Voyage*, and Gertrude Stein. That is as near as one might approximate it. The story, in short, is told through the thoughts—jumbled, confused and wandering—of three different characters, with the exception of the last section which is written in quite conservative prose. Rambling, often capitalless or periodless or punctuation-less, the prose streams on for 330 pages in no very definite manner, although the manner is what concerns the author. And when one ascertains that the first section is through the mind of the idiot, one begins to appreciate the complications.

Max Eastman recently wrote an essay on the modernistic school of writers—Joyce, Cummings, Stein, et al.—in which he contended that the purpose of literature, primarily, is to communicate. Of course. And the chief indictment against the modernists is their utmost complete lack of communication. Under this indictment young Mr. Faulkner must fall. His novel tells us nothing. In one or two cases only does his method justify itself by a certain dramatic vividness. On the whole, his novel, over which Evelyn Scott has waxed so enthusiastic, is downright tiresome. It is so much sound and fury—signifying nothing.

Clifton Fadiman. "Hardly Worth While." *Nation*, January 15, 1930, pp. 74–75.

Probably someone has already remarked that the perfect enjoyment of great literature involves two factors. The reader should make an analysis of the methods employed by the artist to produce a given effect; and at the same time he should experience a synthetic appreciation of that effect in its emotional totality. The analysis must be almost instantaneous, almost unconscious. Otherwise the reader may become enmeshed in a tangle of aesthetic judgments, and experience difficulty in feeling the work of art as a whole.

Here, perhaps, lies the problem of comprehending the present-day revolutionary novelist. Frequently the intelligent reader can grasp the newer literary anarchies only by an effort of analytical attention so strained that it fatigues and dulls his emotional perception. He is so occupied in being a detective that by the time he has to his own satisfaction clarified the artist's intentions and technique he is too worn out to feel anything further. This is why the Joycean method of discontinuity has been entirely successful only when applied to materials of Joycean proportions. For it is obvious that if the theme is sufficiently profound, the characters sufficiently extraordinary, the plot sufficiently powerful, the reader is bound to absorb some of all this despite the strain on his attention. But if after an interval of puzzle-solving, it dawns upon him that the action and characters are minuscular, he is likely to throw the book away in irritation. The analysis has taken too long for the synthesis to be worth the trouble.

This seems to me to be the case with *The Sound and the Fury*, a novel by an extremely talented young writer dealing with the mental and physical disintegration of a Southern family. Mr. Faulkner's work has been magnificently praised by Evelyn Scott and other critics for whose opinions one must have respect. It is in all humility, therefore, that I record the feeling that the theme and the characters are trivial, unworthy of the enormous and complex craftsmanship expended on them. I do not see, for example, that Dilsey is more than a faithful old Negress; she is not, for me at least, "stoic as some immemorial carving of heroism," nor does she "recover for us the spirit of tragedy which the patter of cynicism has often made seem lost." I admit that the idiocy of the thirty-three-year old Benjy is admirably grasped by Mr. Faulkner, but one hundred pages of an imbecile's simplified sense perceptions and monosyllabic gibberings, no matter how accurately recorded, are too much of a good thing. Similarly, Quentin and Jason are not sufficiently interesting, not large enough, in a symbolic sense, to make it worth while to follow painfully the ramifications of their minds and memories.

Julia K.W. Baker. "Literature and Less." New Orleans *Times-Picayune,* June 29, 1930, p. 23.

William Faulkner in *The Sound and the Fury* has more than fulfilled the promise of his first novel, *Soldiers' Pay*, which contained the germ of greatness in its not quite realized tragedy. *The Sound and the Fury* is one of the finest works in the tragic mood yet to appear in America. With it Mr. Faulkner is definitely established as one of the most gifted of contemporary novelists. He is the only American who seems capable of rivaling James Joyce; in parts of this book he seems to have beaten Joyce, hands down, with a simplification of his own method. Not that the work is imitative. It is highly original. You have not read anything like it. But the style and method of approach—fluid and fragmentary and inconsequent as dream—represent something new in the world of letters that James Joyce more than any other one person brought into

it. Yet Faulkner's method is simpler, more direct than Joyce's. *The Sound and the Fury* is a work less bulky than *Ulysses*. It is, in this reviewer's opinion, in some respects a finer work of art. There is more force in it. Indeed, terrific force. There is more economy. There is a truer note of tragedy, not marred by a cynical tone of self-pity. It is a rare book, disturbing as all true tragedy is disturbing, heart-rending, terrible, yet gratifying. It is a difficult book too, for it requires of its reader an alert intelligence and keen sympathy. It is so rich in substance, so curiously handled, that it will repay many readings. No doubt two careful readings are necessary merely to clarify the simple outline of the history.

The confusion is designed, however. Mr. Faulkner sets the tragic note of his story of the disintegration and collapse of a proud family in the opening section, in which Benjy, the idiot son, 33 years old, babbles fragments of the sorry tale in a mad medley of past and present. Gradually, through his idiot brain, which has perceived everything in hard lines and bright colors but without understanding, you become acquainted with the figures of the tragedy and sense the march of the action. There is old Mr. Compson, proud and aristocratic, his wife, who resents the fact that he comes of a finer family than she, the daughter, Candace ("Caddy"), the sons Quentin and Jason, Uncle Maury, the grandmother, and the inimitable negroes (Mr. Faulkner's negroes are the most skillfully rendered in American fiction). Dilsey, the cook, T.P., Versh, Frony, Luster. In the second part Quentin, who is sent to Harvard with the proceeds of the sale of "Benjy's pasture," soliloquizes in a fragmentary way on Caddy's dishonor and his own nebulous sense of guilt that drives him to suicide. In the third part Jason, mother's pet, soliloquizes on the downfall of the family, and the cross he has to bear with Benjy slobbering and moaning in the house when he should have been sent to the asylum at Jackson long ago, his mother coddling herself with camphor and hot-water bottles, pretending to be ill, and Quentin, Caddy's scapegrace daughter, meeting lovers under the bushes. Jason, who is painted much too savagely, much too black, is the only unconvincing character in the novel. All the others live intensely and vividly. In the last short section of the book, Mr. Faulkner takes up the pen and sketches the final touches of the tragic scene. Mr. Compson, heartbroken by his daughter's dishonor, is in a drunkard's grave; Quentin, broken by the same fatality, is a suicide; Caddy is an exile, no doubt a prostitute, at best a kept woman; her madcap daughter Quentin who was taken into the family fold has, after many escapades, run away with a showman; Benjy is an idiot and gelded; the last male of the proud Compson line is not a Compson at all— Jason is an outcropping in every particular of his mother's inferior stock . . .

Caddy is a beautiful character. There is something uncanny in Faulkner's penetration of the feminine heart. Ask women how true his rendering is. They know it, men can merely sense it.

The benevolent tyranny of negroes over any Southern household is charmingly reflected in *The Sound and the Fury*. Faulkner knows and loves the negro. There is the fine inflection of sympathy and truth in his portrayal of Dilsey and her brood. The bossiness of a true Southern negro who lords it over the incompetent white folks in the big house is something that self-conscious Harlem negroes, or their white satellites, can never understand. The Southern negro, on the ante-bellum plantation or in later years, is part of the family. Dilsey tells her grandson, Luster, who looks after Benjy as T.P. did before him: "You got jes es much Compson devilment

in you es any of 'em." The Compson negroes are Compsons, too.

The Sound and the Fury is an excellent novel. It is one of the most remarkable novels that has ever come out of America.

This praise of a noteworthy achievement is not intended as a blanket endorsement of Mr. Faulkner's method in *The Sound and the Fury*. It is possible that the novel succeeds in spite of its more Joycean passages rather than because of them. The strongest portion of the tale is told by the idiot and here, though the author uses shifting sense and scene with more lightning-like rapidity than elsewhere in the book, the method of interpretation is extremely simplified. The muddled language of the "stream of consciousness" appears in more intricate variation in Quentin's soliloquy. It is at times remarkably successful, attaining a high degree of poignancy. At other times it is a difficult if not incomprehensible reading. The method, when carried to an extreme, is not a complete success. Conservative readers will no doubt consider the more involved passages in *The Sound and the Fury* grievous faults. But when the mass effect of a work of art is as powerful as that of this novel it is idle to pick flaws. Out of such experimentation as *Ulysses* and *The Sound and the Fury* will grow fine, new impulses in English prose.

Checklist of Additional Reviews

Charleston (W.Va.) *Mail*, October 2, 1929.
"Decayed Gentility." *New York Times Book Review*, November 10, 1929, p. 28.
Dallas *News*, December 1, 1929.
Indianapolis *News*, December 7, 1929.
Detroit *News*, January 5, 1930.

Charleston *Post*, February 15, 1930.

Montgomery *Advertiser*, February 16, 1930.

Davenport, Basil. "Tragic Frustration." *Saturday Review of Literature*, December 28, 1929, pp. 601–2.

F., R.B. Pittsburgh *Press*, January 12, 1930.

Fitts, Dudley. "Two Aspects of Telemachus." *Hound and Horn*, 3 (April–June 1930), 445–50.

Hansen, Harry. "The First Reader." New York *World*, October 9, 1929, p. 16.

L., R.N. "Told by an Idiot." *Scribner's Magazine*, December 1929, pp. 42, 46.

Martin, Abbott. "Faulkner's Difficult Novel Has Sin and Decay as Theme." Nashville *Tennessean*, November 17, 1929, p. 6; also reviewed as

"Signifying Nothing," *Sewanee Review*, 38 (January 1930), 115–16.

Myers, Walter L. "Make-Beliefs." *Virginia Quarterly Review*, 6 (January 1930), 139–48.

Robbins, Frances L. "Novels of the Week." *Outlook and Independent*, October 16, 1929, p. 268.

Rockey, Howard. "Fiction, Largely European and Very Good in the Average." Philadelphia *Inquirer*, November 30, 1929, p. 18.

S., M.L. "The Tumult in a Southern Family." Boston *Evening Transcript*, October 23, 1929, Section III, p. 2.

Saxon, Lyle. "A Family Breaks Up." New York *Herald Tribune Books*, October 13, 1929, p. 3.

Trilling, Lionel. "Tragedy and Three Novels." *Symposium*, 1 (January 1930), 106–14.

AS I LAY DYING

AS I LAY DYING

WILLIAM FAULKNER

NEW YORK

JONATHAN CAPE: HARRISON SMITH

Margaret Cheney Dawson.
"Beside Addie's Coffin."
New York Herald Tribune Books, October 5, 1930, p. 6.

Given the names: Darl, Jewel, Vardaman, Cash, Dewey Dell and Anse, you might think you were confronted with a comedy of the Herman-Sherman-and-Vermin type. On the contrary, these are the four sons, daughter and husband of a dying woman, Addie Bundren. Outside her window, Cash fashions her coffin. The neighbors come to see her, they sit like buzzards about her and talk. Presently Addie dies. Cash works all night in the pouring rain to finish her coffin. Then they load her onto the wagon and start for Jefferson to bury her with her folks. The rains have washed away the bridges, so they must try the ford. The wagon overturns, the mules are drowned, Cash breaks a leg. But Jewel rescues the coffin. They stop off a night and buy another team. All this takes time. Addie begins to smell. Buzzards sit on the coffin, when they can get at it, but most of the time they cannot because Cash—his leg set in cement—is lying on it. Little Vardaman is half crazy, Darl also. Darl, in fact, sets fire to a barn where the coffin is left one night. Jewel drags it out. Whenever possible Dewey Dell sneaks off to drug stores asking for something to cure her "woman's trouble," by which she means that she is going to have a child and is not married. But at last they reach Jefferson, bury the rotting corpse, send Darl off to an asylum.

This meaty tale comes to us through the consciousness of first one and then another of the characters. The method Mr. Faulkner used in his last novel, *The Sound and the Fury*, is here greatly modified, so that though something of that extraordinary madness hangs like a red mist over it, the lines of demarcation are mercifully clear. This is a great concession and a boon to people who are ready to weep with exhaustion from the effort to interpret and absorb what might be called a sort of photographic mysticism. But even so it cannot be said that for such readers *As I Lay Dying* will prove much of a picnic. Parts of it are written with that tense, defiant obscureness, the self-sufficient dislocation of thought which withdraws itself from facile understanding; and other passages, clear in themselves, are absolutely unhinged from the point of view of the character whose mind they expose and whose impressionistic portrait they seem to contradict. For instance, what are we to think of a small boy, farm-bred, whose reflections come to light as follows: "It is as though the dark were resolving him [the horse] out of his integrity into an unrelated scattering of components— snuffings and stampings; smells of cooling flesh and ammoniac hair; an illusion of a co-ordinated whole of splotched hide and strong bones within which, detached and secret and familiar, an *is* different from my *is*."

By perfecting and giving literary beauty to the half-formed images that floated through young Vardaman's brain, the author alters a whole contour. How shall we fasten this onto the child whose mind in the next chapter runs on bananas and toy trains and city boys? In such instances the method seems to miscarry and the reader's main reaction is likely to be exasperation. But in other cases, such as the chapter wherein the dead woman speaks, it builds the terrifying, mysterious and intimate picture of a soul as nothing else could. And the same hot, subterranean power carries over into his objective descriptions of Jewel catching the horse "enclosed by a glittering maze of hooves as by an illusion of wings," of the wagon overturning in midstream and the drowned mules whose "round bodies float and rub quietly together in the black water within the bend," of the Bundren family squatting in a wayside barn around the foul-smelling coffin, of Anse, "hangdog and proud too" with his new false teeth. The fecundity of an imagination like this is amazing, and the ingenuity, too, with which it skips from one sphere of action to another. One wonders what would happen if it were compressed into an even sterner form if Mr. Faulkner were to experiment with tradition? Something in the way his strength mounts when he externalizes his subject matter suggests that it would be very exciting. But surely, whatever the next move is, he will not lack for audience any one who had followed his work thus far.

Ted Robinson.
"Faulkner's New Book Engrossing."
Cleveland *Plain Dealer*, October 12, 1930, Amusement Section, p. 17.

It is unbelievable that I should have two more masterpieces to present this week, but so it is. First comes William Faulkner's new novel, *As I Lay Dying*, just published by Jonathan Cape and Harrison Smith. I wish I could describe this strange performance adequately. But you might refer in your memory to the enthusiastic words I spoke about Faulkner's former novel, *The Sound and the Fury*. In that remarkable book, events were described as they passed through the minds of the various characters; and one of those characters was an idiot whose clouded brain confused the time element. He mixed events of a year ago, ten years ago, his infancy, with the happenings of today and yesterday; and the reader had to disentangle this skein. This made the book difficult, but none the less fascinating. I was so impressed by the book that I could not get it off my mind— the method had been tremendously effective.

This new book is more orderly, though the method is the same. A woman, mother of a poor southern family, lies dying in her miserable mountain cabin, isolated from civilization. Outside her window, one of her sons is making her coffin, by her own orders. And the shiftless father; the adored illegitimate son; the son who is "queer"; the daughter who has been betrayed; the baby of the family; the doctor; the neighbors—these allow their thoughts to be read as the events unfold themselves.

Each chapter is headed by the name of one of these characters and each is told from the viewpoint of that character. And the tragic events proceed to a point of grotesque horror, unbearably inevitable. I defy anybody to read this book without becoming engrossed in its atmosphere to a painful and haunting degree.

I don't know much about this man Faulkner; but now that I know that *The Sound and the Fury* was not a mere tour de force, I am certain that he is one of the two or three original geniuses of our generation.

Julia K. W. Baker. "Literature and Less." New Orleans *Times-Picayune*, October 26, 1930, p. 33.

Most of the men and women of promise who have contributed to the brilliance of recent American literature have shown an unfortunate tendency, after a splendid beginning, to go backwards or to stand still. Their promissory notes have not matured. Ernest Hemingway has not advanced from the powerful sketches of *In Our Time*, though *A Farewell to Arms* was an admirable novel. What is true of Mr. Hemingway is true of most of his contemporary and of their immediate elders in American literature. Few of them have shown any true development. William Faulkner is a noteworthy exception. He has developed steadily and impressively and has become in a very few years an important figure in contemporary fiction. On the face of the papers, he may become the most important.

William Faulkner, a native of Mississippi who has done not a little of his writing in New Orleans, began as a poet. His first book, *The Marble Faun*, was a long poem. From that he turned to fiction, writing his first novel, *Soldiers' Pay* in New Orleans. In that book was apparent a remarkably keen and fine sense of tragedy, a very intense zest for life. It was in every sense a promising first novel. The promise was not fulfilled in his two succeeding books, *Mosquitoes* and *Sartoris*. It was amply fulfilled, however, in *The Sound and the Fury*, reviewed on this page a few months ago. That novel, too difficult in technique to become popular, is one of the finest pieces of tragic writing yet done in America. It has its faults, but they are minor. Its merit is major, for it is a novel of terrific intensity.

Mr. Faulkner's new novel, *As I Lay Dying*, is a worthy companion piece to *The Sound and the Fury*. It lacks the intensity and driving power that make the latter one of the most remarkable of American novels, but it has an integrity of conception and firmness of handling that make it a distinctive and noteworthy work. It fulfills the promise of *Soldiers' Pay*. It represents, in construction and technique, an advance beyond *The Sound and the Fury*. Mr. Faulkner continues to develop toward simplicity and power.

The Sound and the Fury dealt with the tragedy of the disintegration of an aristocratic family. *As I Lay Dying* deals with the tragedy of death among white trash. The tragedy of character is deeper than the tragedy of death, for death is a commonplace, whether among white trash or cavaliers. It stands to reason that *The Sound and the Fury* with its strange reverberations of madness should be a more striking novel than *As I Lay Dying* in which the action is sordidly matter-of-fact.

As I Lay Dying is a horrible book. It will scandalize the squeamish. But it is an admirable book, one to delight those who respect life well interpreted in fine fiction without attempting to dictate what subjects an author shall choose.

Addie Bundren lies dying. Outside the window her son Cash, an excellent carpenter, is making her coffin. She passes on every board with an appraising eye. Addie Bundren does not care to be buried with the Bundrens. She has made Anse, her husband, promise to bury her among her own folks in Jefferson community 40 miles away. When she is dead, they must wait three days for the wagon, which two of the sons have driven to town and wrecked. It begins raining. When finally they can start the trip to Jefferson the roads are quagmires, but they go, a bedraggled funeral cart on a dismal errand: Addie in the box, and accompanying her behind the two doomed mules, Anse and the children, Cash, the eldest; Darl, who cracks under the strain; Jewel, the highstrung son gotten in adultery, riding his blooded horse; Dewey Dell, the daughter who has been seduced and is in a desperate way, and Vardaman, the smallest boy in whose mind death has become a confused material symbol. The story is unrolled through the eyes of these actors and a few observers. The narrative, always in the first person, switches back and forth from one to another. It unrolls with sordid horror. The rivers are up and the bridges out. Again and again they retrace their course. The mules are drowned, Cash's leg broken and the coffin barely saved in a disaster in midstream. Jewel trades his fine saddle horse for a new team. Cash's leg is mended with a dime's worth of cement. Buzzards circle over the wagon. Passersby shield their noses, for the body was not embalmed. After eight days of this gruesome pilgrimage (which is never gruesome to the Bundrens, who are merely doing what Anse promised to do) they arrive at Jefferson, and Addie Bundren is buried. There is a surprise at the end, just enough to relieve the burden of horror as you close the book. The burden, however, is never insupportable for throughout you perceive the situation through the eyes of the Bundrens. These primitive souls are not sensitive enough to perceive the indecency, the enormity of their conduct. It is matter-of-fact to them. And the fact of death is offset throughout by a fine zest for life which Mr. Faulkner shares with the primitive types he so successfully interprets.

The hard, toilsome trip to Jefferson is a sore trial to Anse Bundren, but over and over he says "I don't begrudge her it." And the children, except for Darl who goes mad, are doggedly loyal.

The style, save in the passages of conversation, which are excellent, is not strictly in dialect. Mr. Faulkner repeatedly uses rhetorical devices of his own, and a vocabulary such as a Bundren never dreamed of, to render the thought in the mind. He does this particularly when the thought is so vague that a Bundren would be inarticulate, merely sensible of his feelings.

The Bundrens are touchy, with the fierce pride of white trash. They wish "to be beholden to no man." . . .

Mr. Faulkner has in a few instances exaggerated to attain the horror he desired, but the story as a whole is convincing. *As I Lay Dying* is a distinguished novel. With *The Sound and the Fury* it entitles William Faulkner to rank with any living writer of fiction in America. All but a scant half dozen—Dreiser, Anderson, Hemingway among them—he far surpasses.

Henry Nash Smith. "A Troubled Vision." *Southwest Review*, 16 (Winter 1931), xvi–xvii.

Someone has remarked before, I think, William Faulkner's kinship to the Elizabethans. In *As I Lay Dying*, it is still evident. There is for instance his preoccupation with unusual mental states—if not with actual imbecility, as in *The Sound and the Fury*, then with the insanity of Darl Bundren, with the morbid compulsion of Addie Bundren's family to bury her in the burying-ground back in Jefferson where she was reared, and with the boy Vardaman's conviction that his mother's soul has somehow got into the catfish he caught the afternoon she died. And even when it is seen through the eyes of the ostensibly normal characters, it is a morbid world, this rural Mississippi of William Faulkner's book: a Gothic world, productive only of hatred, passion, and frustration.

Faulkner is also like the Elizabethans in his touching of this violent matter with flashes of the poetry of rhetoric, a poetry which dwells lovingly on vivid colors and brave words, and seems almost to yearn for the blank verse which the modern democratic literary tradition has made impossible. When the men carry the homemade coffin into the room where Addie lies dead, "it is light, yet they move slowly; empty, yet they carry it carefully; lifeless, yet they move with hushed precautionary words to one another, speaking of it as though, complete, it now slumbered lightly alive, waiting to come awake." A woman's "wet dress shapes for the dead eyes of three blind men those mammalian ludicrosities which are the horizons and the valleys of the earth."

The theme of *As I Lay Dying* is the death and burial of Addie Bundren, the mother. Because they have promised her to do it, the family set out in an open wagon to take the body forty miles to Jefferson. A bridge is washed out, but they cannot wait; they try to ford the river, and the coffin must be rescued from the water. Cash, one of the sons, breaks his leg in the scramble. But they splint it crudely with cement and drive on. By the third or fourth day buzzards circle overhead. The family refuse to sleep, for they must watch with the body until it is buried. At the end Darl has been sent to the insane asylum, Cash's leg is gangrenous, and Dewey Dell has failed of procuring the abortion which she desires. But when the coffin is in the earth, Anse Bundren takes a hardly-saved ten dollars away from his daughter and at nightfall turns up with a set of false teeth, a gramophone, and a new wife.

Readers are now inured to unpleasant incident; but Faulkner is unusual in the lurid intensity of his outlook. His work is the sort that you either detest or like passionately. I like it. However atrocious and distorted his outlook may seem when it is judged according to conventional standards of sweetness and light, he has one of the most genuinely artistic imaginations in America. He also has eloquence and courage. It may be that he is lacking cheerfulness and restraint: but I began by saying that he was like the Elizabethans.

Checklist of Additional Reviews

"A Witch's Brew." *New York Times Book Review*, October 19, 1930, p. 6.
"Funereal Fiction." Detroit *News*, November 23, 1930, p. 6.
Chicago *News*, January 14, 1931.
"Twenty-four Novels of the Season." *Literary Digest*, January 24, 1931, p. 18.
Davenport, Basil. "In the Mire." *Saturday Review of Literature*, November 22, 1930, p. 362.
Fadiman, Clifton P. "Morbidity in Fiction." *Nation*, November 5, 1930, pp. 500–1.
L., R. N. "Faulkner—Pity and Terror." *Scribner's Magazine*, December 1930, pp. 158, 160.
Leek, John. "*As I Lay Dying*." *Daily Oklahoman* (Oklahoma City), February 22, 1931, p. 11–C.
Morgan, Morgen. "*As I Lay Dying*: A New Masterpiece." Wilmington (N.C.) *Star*, March 8, 1931, Magazine Section, p. 12.
S., E. C. "Faulkner Book Must Be Read." Winston-Salem *Journal and Sentinel*, November 30, 1930, p. 7–D.
Wade, John Donald. "The South in Its

Fiction." *Virginia Quarterly Review*, 7 (January 1931), 124–26.

Walton, Edith H. "An Eccentric Novel." New York *Sun*, November 7, 1930, p. 31.

White, Kenneth. "*As I Lay Dying*." *New Republic*, November 19, 1930, p. 27.

SANCTUARY

SANCTUARY

WILLIAM
FAULKNER

NEW YORK
JONATHAN CAPE & HARRISON SMITH

Paul H. Bixler. "In *Sanctuary* Wm. Faulkner Plumbs the Depths of Horrors." Cleveland *Plain Dealer,* February 7, 1931, Amusement Section, p. 16.

"He writes like an angel," said Arnold Bennett of William Faulkner. Presumably when the late lamented author of *Clayhanger* penned that compliment, he was thinking of style. Certain it is that when one considers content, the stuff of which Faulkner's stories are made, the young American is better described as writing like a devil.

Faulkner is interested in evil unadulterated. In *Sanctuary*, his last published novel but the first that has been at all widely read, out of a dozen or more carefully delineated characters only one approaches the normal; with each of the others there is something psychically wrong. The result is error heaped on error, perversion on perversion. The book is one long tattoo of horror. Were it not continued incessantly for 380 pages, the author's performance would be completely effective. As it is, some time before the end occurs, the reader is stunned and insensible from too many blows on his spinal column. The story is too much of an evil thing.

Sanctuary, though published the most recently, is not its author's last novel, incidentally. Its appearance in print was held up by the publishers until *As I Lay Dying*, Faulkner's own favorite among his longer works, was written and published.

These remarks, I hope, will not prevent anyone from reading the book. For six years now Faulkner has been the most gifted novelist writing in the United States. Too few people interested in good writing and in American literature have known this fact. The little group of intellectuals who had faithfully followed him since the publication of *Soldier's Pay* in 1926 came to believe that he was their own possession; that they would never have to share him. It has perhaps shattered their self-esteem, always in need of bolstering, that *Sanctuary* has been, and is continuing to be, a popular success. Its popularity, they explain somewhat regretfully, has occurred because the book is easier to read than any of its five brother novels; and because in the natural order of events the time had at last arrived for Faulkner to overcome the inertia of that public which is generally called discriminating and which buys books in sufficient quantities to make writers of literature famous.

A number of general remarks might be made critically of Faulkner's work. For one thing, he is an experimenter. If you read his earlier novels, you will find him playing all sorts of highly complicated narrative tricks, for the most part with a form of the stream-of-consciousness method. This made him interesting after a fashion, but it also made him a novelist's novelist; reading him was something like working a cross-word puzzle. In *Sanctuary* he happily settled upon an indirect manner that is not obscure.

Faulkner is a mental sadist, of course. He loves to stick pins in his characters and watch them wriggle; this is chiefly for the edification of the reader, who wriggles still more. His work goes back to an old tradition popular a hundred years ago, the tale of terror school. But he has introduced a variation and one far more fearful. Instead of concocting his novels out of ghosts, sliding panels and unexplainable shrieks at midnight, he has introduced

53

(along with a style far finer than "Monk" Lewis' or Mrs. Shelley's) all the terrifying possibilities of modern abnormal psychology. As I have already suggested, it seems to me that in this respect *Sanctuary* has overshot its mark.

Faulkner's liking for narrative tricks and for horrible detail would link him naturally in American literature with Poe and with Ambrose Bierce. But he follows yet another American tradition, that of local color. Though this last is clear throughout *Sanctuary*, it may be seen most clearly perhaps in a short story, "A Rose for Emily," in *These Thirteen* (recently published), in which the credibility for the horror comes directly from the setting. One could well imagine Poe writing such a tale of terror as this except for the one pertinent fact, localization. The story is not a five-finger exercise in creating vicarious fear, nor is it set, like "The Fall of the House of Usher," in a vacuum. It grows out of the background; only in the South could a woman kill a man in her home and keep clear from prosecution until she died.

Certain critics have begun recently to blow cold on William Faulkner. It appears, they say, that he has no philosophy. This, if true, is a defect. It may be noted also that the subjects of his fiction are calculated to narrow his appeal. And yet the number of his readers is likely to go on increasing. The truth is that the young man from Mississippi is simply too good a teller of tales to be ignored.

Ted Robinson. "Critic Finds Faulkner's *Sanctuary* Too Violent." Cleveland *Plain Dealer*, February 8, 1931, Amusement Section, p. 15.

Of course the books that stand out in one's mind are the ones one liked very much and the ones that one hated excessively. Perhaps you will be able to judge my likes and dislikes from my weekly selections. Unfortunately, however, the book I liked best this week is not yet released for review, and I can't tell you about it until it is published. And the book I hated excessively yet wins a tribute of reluctant admiration.

When I read, a couple of years ago, William Faulkner's remarkable novel, *The Sound and the Fury*, I was excited and astounded, and I warned my readers to look out for a new genius.

His second book, *As I Lay Dying*, justified my enthusiasm and prophecy. Now comes a third—*Sanctuary*. I seized it eagerly; I devoured it in large gulps. And I had indigestion; if I could spew forth its memory for good, I would do so.

Sanctuary is more simply and directly written than either of the others. Its construction is masterly, its style memorable. But it is the most brutal book I have ever read. I have a pretty strong stomach and I am fairly hard-boiled, but *Sanctuary* nauseated me. And I hereby warn readers against it if any squeamishness remains in their make-up.

It is so unutterably violent, so obscenely diabolical, that I find difficulty in talking about it at all. Its central point is an unthinkable act of degenerate outrage; its final catastrophe is an orgiastic lynching.

It is the uninhibited demonstration of hell on earth. And such is its perusal by persons of neurotic tendency. Jonathan Cape and Harrison Smith risk much in publishing this frenetic thing.

B.K.H.
"William Faulkner's New Novel *Sanctuary* Is Recommended for Its Vivid and Startling Story and Sheer Brilliance of Writing."
Providence *Journal*, February 17, 1931, p. 6.

We aren't going to be able to pass by William Faulkner's new novel, *Sanctuary,* with a proud and indifferent disdain. However much you dislike it (and it's about 10 to two you'll despise it) the thing has a tremendous power—some of the surge and thunder of the *Odyssey*, some of the terrific march of the great wind which once roared across Russia, sweeping giants in its path.

The fact is that William Faulkner is a tremendous probability, and very nearly an enormous fact. . . . One of the few troubling and provocative liabilities of a nation otherwise pretty comfortably asleep. . . . I don't mean in books only, but in every way. Not much is burgeoning and blossoming in these too-thoroughly United States just now—not much in art, not much in music, not much in engineering, not much in the obliquities of the spirit. . . . Depression is more than a matter of active money in the market: It touches the soul. And ours, for whatever reason you choose to give, is hibernating. . . . And so when a novel occurs that is huge and terrific and upsetting it behooves us to take note of the event—even if the novel is horrible. [All ellipsis dots in this review are in the original.]

And heaven knows *Sanctuary* is horrible enough—horrible with the wicked fascination of the completely damned. I can't think of anything which, in its incident and spirit, is more harrowing, more instinctively revolting. . . . Yet you can't let it alone, can't throw it across the room, into the fireplace as you'd like to, because under its sordid, creeping, haunting, terrifying context something sings. . . . You may think of Gorky, but you'll be falling short. Gorky couldn't, can't, write like this. You'll be nearer if you say Dostoievsky. But that won't quite do it, because Mr. Faulkner had in mind none of the great spiritual generalizations which excused Dostoievski's desperate pictures. . . . As far as I can see, indeed, he has no large message to shoot into the world, but only a bit more of perplexity for its consumption.

Here, he seems to say, is a foul and dirty fragment of American life in a certain weedy corner—yours to interpret, yours to regret: my job (and I think he is right) is only to report it to you so that you'll never, never forget it. . . . My eye! you never will! . . . Gowan Stevens, half-drunken and libidinous undergraduate of a neighboring university, drives out into the moonshine country to buy some more liquor, taking his wisp of a sweetheart with him into this evil backwoods. The consequences are unspeakably horrible. But they are reported with such restrained intensity, such power of delineation, such sheer brilliance of writing, that—well, we can't pass *Sanctuary* by. . . . That much and nothing more.

We said three years ago, somewhere in

these pages, that Faulkner would bear watching. . . . His last book, *As I Lay Dying*, backed us up immensely. . . . But we suspected nothing like this. . . . If he keeps his eye on his target he is going to hit something the like of which we haven't seen in a round century of blue moons. . . . Don't in the name of mercy, put this thing on the table where anyone can pick it up. Some will have the chills, some the creeps, some nightmares. And some just won't be able to stand it. . . . And from that very fact you'll see why we can't ignore it.

Henry Seidel Canby. "The School of Cruelty." *Saturday Review of Literature*, March 21, 1931, pp. 673–74.

In the powerful and distressing *Sanctuary* of William Faulkner, anti-romance reaches its limit. The plodding naturalism of Dreiser was merely evidence that the world was dingy, which the imaginative could disregard, the harsh staccato of Hemingway had sentiment as an undertone, Lewis's satire was at least based upon idealism. But this Mississippi writer (land of white columns draped in roses!) gives no quarter and leaves no field of the emotions unblighted. Others have written of the underworld and made it sinister, but in this story the underworld is less despicable than the frivolous creatures who descend into it. Others have done, and overdone, the trivial gin-drinking generation and the thin, hysterical debauchery of college youth, but with scorn, pity, or a secret admiration. Mr. Faulkner has come out at the further end of both Puritanism and anti-Puritanism, and in the dry light of complete objectivity weighs his sub-

jects for their pound or ounce of life with no predilection for "ought," no interest in "why," and no concern for significance. He is cruel with a cool and interested cruelty, he hates his Mississippi and his Memphis and all their works, with a hatred that is neither passionate nor the result of thwarting, but calm, reasoned, and complete.

Unlike his fellow workers in the sadistic school, Mr. Faulkner can make character. His Popeye, the gunman, an impotent defective, without emotions and unaware of morality, is the most convincing of all his lengthening line in fiction. And better than any of them, better, I should say than Hemingway, Mr. Faulkner can write a still and deadly narrative that carries with it an unrolling series of events as vivid as modern caricature and as accurate as Dutch painting. I say *can,* for in the attempt to tell a story by its points of emphasis; omitting explanation and connectives, he is frequently elliptical and sometimes so incoherent that the reader loses his way and must go back after later enlightenment to see who was who in an earlier scene. Mr. Faulkner seems then to be trying to write a "talky," where the dialogue gives the situation while the continuity is left to the pictures, which, verbally presented, are not enough to clarify the reader's imagination. Yet narrative skill of a high order he undoubtedly possesses.

But the story!—It lies in two planes; an upper and lower, like a Russian ikon. On the upper plane are three important figures, of whom a girl and a boy will be most detested. She is a predatory female, still too young to be fully conscious of the meaning of her desires, technically a virgin, technically a student in the local university, but absorbed in a series of "dates" where sexual escapes from the flesh-hunting town boys who wait with their cars in the darks of the campus are her preoccupation. On her own plane she is nothing but a shallow, pretty flirt, playing with lasciviousness. The boy has been to "Virginia," and speaks in the stale romantics of the "Southern gentleman," about hard drinking, hard loving, and chivalry. On his own plane he is an empty-headed fool who lives by words. On their own plane the two are engaged in a mildly romantic escapade,— she is to race with him ahead of the football train in his waiting car, drinking on the way. He is short of "corn," gets some, is told that he can't hold his liquor, gets drunk, misses the train, catches it further along the line and finds his girl, gets drunk again, and smashes the car on a side road near a bootlegger's headquarters.

Thus they slide into the lower plane, the underworld. In a rickety house, with a gunman, a rum runner, a helper at the still, and a bootlegger and his woman, the girl loses her nerve and becomes a whimpering child, fascinated but afraid of the evil around her. The boy gets drunk again, and leaves her to save his own reputation if he can. She is raped under circumstances of fiendish perversion, which she invites by her own depravity, which even in her climaxes of terror keeps her hovering like a soiled moth near the danger. Her gunman seducer, himself impotent, shoots the nit-wit helper who tries to protect her, and puts her in a house of prostitutes in Memphis where she takes to gin and drugs with convincing rapidity. The bootlegger is tried for the murder he did not commit, and she kills him by false testimony, having first out of sheer restless amorousness drawn a new and real lover to the spot where he is neatly and inevitably murdered by the jealous gunman, who had used him in their sexual relations, for purposes better left undescribed. Thus the Judge's daughter and the youth from "Virginia," when drawn down into the unmoral underworld are shown as trash, a hundred times less valuable even than the drunken mistress of the Memphis

house, the brutal rum runners, or the defective, soulless Popeye himself. These have a code. They are nothing.

And around this sordid tragedy hangs a kindhearted, liberal man, fascinated by the injustice of human misery. Moved by instinctive generosity he determines to save the bootlegger from an unjust indictment, because that sturdy criminal's faithful woman with her pathetic child has touched his sympathies, because he cannot stand injustice, because he has fallen in love with his stepdaughter and feels obscurely that her dangerous course in the flippant, sordid world of the upper plane will be safer if by his legal skill he can rescue the college flirt and avert injustice. With what results? The bootlegger has rape added to his charge of murder and is burned alive by the mob. Popeye goes off unscathed, and when hung, is hung for a crime he never committed. The girl is rescued by father and brothers, and is last seen in Paris, restless, vacuous, a menace to society now that she is awake.

Mr. Faulkner's Mississippi is, we trust, a partial portrait, but his vivid narrative style makes it convincing; nor can anyone doubt the force and truth of his characterizations—Popeye, the filthy politician, the bootlegger's woman, the nit-wit. Nor can any sane reader doubt that somewhere along the path he is following lies the end of all sanity in fiction. Here in this sadistic story is decadence in every sense that criticism has given the word, except dilettanteism—there is none of that. The emotions are sharpened to a febrile obsession with cruelty, lust, and pain which exaggerates a potentiality of human nature at the expense of human truth. These debased flappers and hideous mobs in a community which seems incapable of virtue in either the Christian or the Roman sense, are bad dreams of reality which no matter how truly set down are false to everything but accident and the exacerbated sensibilities of the author. To this disease Americans seem peculiarly liable, and there is a direct relationship between the drugged terrors, the unreal sadisms, and the morbid complexes of Poe's stories, and this new realistic decadence of which *Sanctuary* is an outstanding example.

Art is curious. Although it does not have to be representational of human life, when it does become more than design and gives form to human happenings it cannot and never has been able to go far into the abnormal, the unbalanced, the excessive without danger. Poe's more lurid stories are read now as drug phantasies, more interesting to the psychologist than to the man of letters, and so it will be with this new sadism, the novel cruelty by which the American scene with all its infinite shadings is made into something gross, sordid, or, as here, depraved with an ironic depravity in which the trivial by a kind of perversion becomes more horrible than professional evil, while what virtue exists in individuals only throws gasoline upon the lyncher's fire.

I have chosen Mr. Faulkner as a prime example of American sadism because he is so clearly a writer of power, and no mere experimenter with nervous emotion. He is distinguished above others in the cruel school by a firm grasp upon personality and his ability to enrich the flow of time with pertinent incident. No one who reads his description of the harlot's sob party and the drunken little boy will doubt his skill in prosaic horror. In *Sanctuary* I believe that sadism, if not anti-romance, has reached its American peak.

I say "has reached," for this is not Mr. Faulkner's last book. It was written before his imaginative and poetic *As I Lay Dying,* a book in which the intolerable strain of cruelty breaks down into one of those poetic escapes into beauty by which the real artist has always saved himself

from too much logic. In *As I Lay Dying* there is again a cruel mob, but it is withdrawn, watching the spectacle of a half-mad family who tell their stories by monologue in which one finds how far less intolerable is misery and violence if one sees into the hearts of the characters. It is almost as if Mr. Faulkner had said: I am not God. I am not responsible for these people. If I look at the outward aspects of life in the Mississippi I know, they are so terrible that I respond by impulses of cruelty which lead me to describe coldly events which when read can only arouse wrath or disgust. Let me start again with simpler people, naïfs and crazy folk, uncorrupted if also unmoralized, and tell my story as they must have seen it, thus forgetting my own scorns and cruelties, and so get closer to ultimate truth.

Perhaps *As I Lay Dying* is only a reaction from *Sanctuary* into a different morbidity. I do not think so. The creative artist is usually the first to turn from excess just when the weak and the imitative are racing ahead to their own destruction. He feels a call to a more important job.

The hard-boiled era is headed toward the dust heap where the soft-boiled era of the early 1900s has long preceded it. The post-war bitterness of wounded psyches has already subsided in England. Here it seems to be like an induced electricity where the pressure is higher but the substance less. The war-hurt generation is already too old for poetry, but just ripening for fiction. The candor behind their cruelties when they escape from the hard-boiled convention and grow wiser in life will give their work a substance and an edge which American fiction has too often lacked. They are not drugged, like Poe, nor have they his abnormal sensitivity which only the rightest of all possible worlds could have kept in bounds and only the most ethereal beauty could lift into the escape of real literature. They are—and I speak particularly of Faulkner and Hemingway—men of unusual ability who are working at their craft with a conscientiousness almost unknown to the easy going journalists who constitute so many of their contemporaries, and they have developed styles and methods, not better than, but different from, the practice of their established elders, such as Willa Cather or Sinclair Lewis, and perhaps better adapted to the new decades as they and theirs will see them. Yet, hurt themselves, they have so far vented their irritation upon, and transferred, as the psychologists say, their inferiorities to, a country and a personnel which can be hated, as they hate it, only when the imagination is still fevered. That fever, as it subsides, leaves the problem of rediscovering America, for America has to be rediscovered by every generation, the problem of discovering not just the drunkards, gunmen, politicians, near virgins, and futile, will-less youths which have so deeply engaged them, but the American scene in all its complexity. They will never do it while one ounce of sadism, one trace of hysteria remains.

Alan Reynolds Thompson. *Bookman*, 73 (April 1931), 188–89.

Those who relish the raw meat of fiction will find a whole butcher shop in this ostensibly realistic picture of Tennessee folkways. A considerable acquaintance with the ghastly details of human depravity and misery as painstakingly accumulated by modern naturalists may harden one against ordinary shocks; but Mr. Faulkner may well be granted the dubious honor of being extraordinarily shocking. Mere horror for its own sake usually misses its effect upon a sophisticated reader by reason of the obviousness of the attempt; and a more skillful treatment—even one as imaginatively powerful as that of Robinson Jeffers—may by its very extravagance provoke some to incredulous laughter. One would be happy to dismiss this book in some such fashion. But aside from an occasional obvious straining for the vivid epithet the author is at all times master of his medium; and his characterization and plotting compel our reluctant belief. Such things, we know, do happen; and they probably happen in just such ways.

The old argument about the themes of naturalistic horror need not be repeated. Most readers prefer not to mole through the sewers of life; and some who do are undoubtedly moved by abnormal tastes. An author is free to choose his subject; but readers are free not to read him if he chooses the depths of degeneracy and evil, and presents them not only without the softening effect of idealization but with an obvious desire to exploit the last nervous thrill to be got from a complete concrete visualization of every detail. Among other similar things, for example, the exact mechanical method and physical as well as emotional effects of a rape upon a young girl by an impotent degenerate are gradually but relentlessly exposed in this novel, skillfully held back to be revealed at the moment when they will shock the most. Those who play the game of exploiting the *frisson nouveau* find that its stakes are continually rising; each must raise his predecessor's ante. Mr. Faulkner has evidently determined not to be a piker. But unless a reader has a relish for sadistic cruelty, or a sort of medical interest in it, he will prefer milder pursuits.

A fair reader will none the less admit Mr. Faulkner's ability. The technique of *Sanctuary* is an example of the very promising method, gradually being perfected through many experiments, which fuses the cinematic scene-shifting of expressionism, the almost obscure brevity and vivid sensationalism of the imagists, and the intense exploration of momentary experience characteristic of writers like Conrad, with the classic formal beauty of an intricate plot skillfully implicated, rigorously unified, and implacable in its advance to a fore-designed end. The blurb on the jacket says that *Sanctuary* is "hideously and terrifically—and therefore beautifully—great." It would take a blurbist to identify the hideous with beauty; but we may assume that what he would say if he stopped for distinctions is that in spite of material ugliness the novel has the formal beauty of a complicated puzzle masterfully solved.

There are esthetes who are so fascinated by such virtuosity that they can ignore ordinary prejudices; some even take pride in doing so. But the normal reader, unskilled in suppressing his impulses toward kindliness and sympathy merely to appreciate the skill with which those feelings are outraged, is likely to judge otherwise. If any theory of esthetics leads to justification of such a book as this, he is tempted to say, better send theory to the devil and join the naïve majority who feel that the novelist should practise somewhat the same restraint in his imagination as is expected of him in his conduct. If modern naturalism provokes such immoderate reactions it has only its own immoderateness to blame.

Philip E. Wheelwright. *The Symposium*, 2 (April 1931), 276–81.

It may be that the novel, or something like what we now call the novel, is the white hope of American literature. At least, there is little positive evidence to confute the suggestion, what with drama selling out to the talkies and poetry borrowing more and more of its rhythms from prose. But if the American novel is to become something of literary as opposed to merely sociological or zeitgeistian importance, it must be something more than a collection of realistic snapshots and Freudian casebook gossip. It must create form. I say 'create' rather than 'have' because it is not enough that Americans should ape the forms invented by Hudson or Gide or Joyce. For the establishment of what can seriously be called an American novel it is required: (1) that there should be writers capable of giving form to American material—meaning American with respect principally to the tone and order of the emotions involved; (2) that the form should be moulded out of the material itself rather than imposed by European plaster-casts; (3) that the form should be principally justified by its ability to convey aspects of the material that could not be conveyed without it. I am not sure that the second and third requirements are quite distinct, though the third is intended to at once qualify and interpret the perhaps nationalistic connotations of (2). For naturally I do not mean that a serious novelist in this country can ignore, for example, Joyce. I mean that what of Joyce or any other writer comes through the prism of our own culture should be treated simply as one part of the, to a contemporary American, available material; and should if necessary be plagiarized, broken up, and adapted ruthlessly—as ruthlessly as Shakespeare dealt with Montaigne and the chronicles of Holinshed. Applying the general principle there seem to be very few writers who are properly speaking both novelists and Americans. There can be however, I think, little doubt that William Faulkner is one of them. With *Sanctuary*, his sixth novel, he has at length become established; and in considering it I wish also to consider

David Burnham's *This Our Exile,* which possessing the faults and ambiguous promises of a first novel and having a different tone from anything in Faulkner, does nevertheless share the one cardinal trait of striving towards a form that objectifies.

In *Sanctuary* Faulkner has used a variation of the technique that made *The Sound and the Fury* and *As I Lay Dying* such brilliant monstrosities. The principal devices are those already established in the earlier novels: a gradual clarification, chiefly through symbols, of the main events of the narrative; a type of conversation suggesting frustrated attempts at communication; a repetition of trivial statements for heightened emotional effect; a feeling for the automaton-character of bodily processes; an objectification of persons through the assignment of symbols special to each one; and an absorption of the person-symbols into the symbol arrangements that clarify the narrative and into those other symbol arrangements that sustain and intensify the emotional tone. At times these devices are used for effects almost melodramatic, as in the case of the means invoked towards the central revelation, which is accomplished by a group of partial disclosures ("I didn't know it was going to be just the other way," "You're not even a man!" "There wasn't no signs," etc.) and associations built around the roaring of shucks, the plopping sound, Popeye's whinneying, and the seeping blood.

The characters in *Sanctuary* have fullness, but a fullness as if in some other and rarely encountered dimension. This comes about from the unusual atmosphere which the symbol arrangements sustain and into which the characters are fixed. The in this respect most consciously and thoroughly developed charactcr is Popeye, a deformed creature who seems to cast a hypnotic evil spell all about him. His primary symbol is the eye. "From beyond the screen of bushes ... Popeye watched ..." the novel begins; and out of that beginning there arise not less than thirty separate similes describing human eyes, concentrated in sections of the novel where Popeye's presence is dominant. There are Popeye's eyes "like yellow knobs," a blind man's eyes "like dirty yellowish clay marbles" and "like two clots of phlegm," there is Temple Drake, Popeye's victim, with "eyes like holes burned with a cigar" and who saw something "with the tail of her eye." Imbued with another kind of quality is Miss Reba the brothel keeper, all breasts and lushness and hot glints and thick wheezy sounds. She "drank beer, breathing thickly into the tankard, the other hand, ringed with yellow diamonds as large as gravel, lost among the lush billows of her breast." Her dogs and even the inanimate trappings of her brothel partake something of her quality. The dogs, "woolly, white, worm-like ... moved about with an air of sluggish and obscene paradox ... or, rushing thickly in when the negro maid opened the door, climbing and sprawling onto the bed and into Miss Reba's lap with wheezy, flatulent sounds, billowing into the rich pneumasis of her breast and tonguing along the metal tankard which she waved in one ringed hand as she talked." In her brothel "the china figures which supported the clock gleamed in hushed smooth flexions: knee, elbow, flank, arm and breast in additudes [*sic*] of voluptuous lassitude." And then from a more dissonant arrangement of images comes malignant travesty:

> ... Her open mouth, studded with gold-fillings gaped upon the harsh labor of her breathing.
> "Oh God oh God," she said. ...
> She drew her breath whistling, clutching her breast ... "We was happy as two doves," she wailed,

61

choking, her rings smoldering in hot glints within her billowing breast. "Then he had to go and die on me." She drew her breath whistling, her mouth gaped, shaping the hidden agony of her thwarted lungs, her eyes pale and round with stricken bafflement, protuberant. "As two doves," she roared in a harsh choking voice.

Of particular interest is the quality of Faulkner's irony. The short sentence used as understatement is familiar from Hemingway and Lardner, but in Faulkner its use is specialized as a foil for an already constructed and violent complex of emotions. "Durn them fellers," repeated and repeated, and "Them fellers ought to quit pesterin her" are the only ways the half-wit Tommy can express his uneasy sympathy. And "But that girl, she was all right.... You know she was all right," repeated five times against the wall of the hill woman's silence produces a vague vast sense of something unnameably wrong. His most characteristic irony, however, is displayed in the frustration of attempts to communicate. There is the imaginative but incoherent discourse of Horace Benbow drunk, given a verbal form of heightened obscurity and mock-poetry to suggest the effect of its filtration into the consciousness of Ruby the moonshiner's woman. Again, there is the conversation between Ruby and Temple, where each led by her peculiar emotion builds her half of the conversation into a structure of its own, punctuating but not responding to the conversation of the other. The result is a kind of ironical epistemic, which is supplemented by irony of situation: Benbow's attempt to save Goodwin's neck bringing on a still more horrible death; the manner of Popeye's arrest and accidental retribution; above all, the final description of Temple—no reference to the moral enormities for which her weakness has been largely responsible—in the gray gloom of Luxembourg Gardens. . . .

That two such independently objective novels as *Sanctuary* and *This Our Exile* should be so unlike in material, in methods of objectifying material, and in tone is encouraging. Diversity is needful, and if diversity sometimes begets confusion, it is from a tradition of honest alive formalism that remedy must come. Formalism of this sort—the honest alive sort, growing naturally from the material—is what seems most to characterize the two novels I have been considering; and by this possession they are not only important as specimens of the nascent American novel but worthy also of enlightened, disciplined attention.

Julia K. W. Baker. "Literature and Less." New Orleans *Times-Picayune*, April 26, 1931, p. 26.

Max Eastman or somebody has said that "a poet in history is divine; a poet in the next room is a joke." Many who read the Greeks and the Elizabethans with fervent appreciation throw up their hands in horror when a contemporary touches upon those dark and malevolent impulses in human nature which so deeply concerned those magnificent dramatists. One feels sure that William Faulkner, probably the best living novelist in America, is rapidly becoming a scandal in Mississippi. Indeed a Memphis book-reviewer recently described Mr. Faulkner's new novel *Sanctuary* as "the most putrid novel that ever came out of the South," or verbiage to that effect.

It is indeed strange that the South of John Esten Cooke, Augusta J. Evans and James Lane Allen, should have produced William Faulkner. This son of Oxford, Mississippi, is a Greek. Tragedy concerns him. The terrific irony of life has impressed him more than the Bonnie Blue Flag. With his intense preoccupation with the agonies of the sentient individual soul, he might have lived in the Greece of Euripides, the London of John Webster. He is no more a son of a Confederate veteran than he is a Rotarian. He is Prometheus, gnawed by vultures. The cruelty and inconsequence of the human tragi-comedy obsesses him. He has as fine a tragic sense as any writer of fiction of his time, James Joyce not excepted. His two finest novels, *The Sound and the Fury* and *As I Lay Dying*, put to shame nearly every living American and English novelist. The only person that can pretend to match those books with two as good is Theodore Dreiser, with *Sister Carrie* and *Jennie Gerhardt*. Mr. Dreiser's work, by and large, the whole shelf of it, is today more impressive than William Faulkner's. It is bulkier and more mature. But Faulkner is hardly past 30 and Dreiser is past 60. Unless Faulkner is struck by a thunderbolt for his sins against propriety, unless Dreiser in a supernatural second youth produces masterpieces unforeseen, William Faulkner will surpass him in the end.

Sanctuary is not as good as *The Sound and the Fury* or *As I Lay Dying*. Apparently it was written between the two, or before either. Critics who call it Mr. Faulkner's masterpiece label themselves thereby as opportunists who failed to detect the greatness in *The Sound and the Fury* and *As I Lay Dying*, and are taking this occasion to clamber aboard the bandwagon. *Sanctuary* lacks the precision, the intensity and the finality of those fine novels. It is in many ways unconvincing. It is better certainly than *Mosquitoes* and

Sartoris, but not intrinsically better than its author's first haunting and evocative novel, *Soldiers' Pay*.

The story (which by the way could not have been conceived or executed except under prohibition) is the tragedy of Temple Drake, a slim and beautiful university co-ed.

Sanctuary is written in William Faulkner's nervous, vigorous style, a remarkably sensitive and intense medium of expression, delicate but virile. It is at once emotional and pictorial. Here, chosen at random, are two examples of its visual quality:

> The spring welled up at the root of a beech tree and flowed away upon a bottom of whorled and waved sand. It was surrounded by a thick growth of cane and brier, of cypress and gum in which broken sunlight lay sourceless.

> The cigarette weaved its faint plume against Popeye's face, one side of his face squinted against the smoke like a mask carved in two simultaneous expressions.

It would be possible to quote from *Sanctuary*, if space permitted, some of the most effective interpretation of emotion in American fiction.

Checklist of Additional Reviews

Tulsa *Tribune*, February 15, 1931. "Comments on New Books." Buffalo *Times*, February 22, 1931, p. 6–C. Toledo *Times,* March 31, 1931. "*Sanctuary*." *Forum*, April 1931, p. xviii. "*Sanctuary*." Bristol (Va.) *Herald-Courier*.

"Sanctuary." Charleston (W.Va.) *Gazette*, May 17, 1931, Magazine Section, p. 2.

"Sanctuary." *American Mercury*, June 1931, p. xviii.

Huntington (W.Va.) *Adventurer*, June 28, 1931.

"Sanctuary." Wilmington (N.C.) *Star*.

Benét, William Rose. "The Phoenix Nest." *Saturday Review of Literature*, 7 (April 18, 1931), 766.

Britt, George. "Behind the Backs of Books and Authors." New York *World Telegram*, February 17, 1931.

C., I. M. "*Sanctuary* Is Class by Itself." Raleigh *Times*, May 2, 1931, p. 12.

Canby, Henry Seidel. "The School of Cruelty." *Saturday Review of Literature*, 7 (February 21, 1931), 609.

Chamberlain, John. "Dostoyefsky's Shadow in the Deep South." *New York Times Book Review*, February 15, 1931, p. 9.

Coates, Robert M. "Books, Books, Books: About Murder, Criticism, and the South Pole." *New Yorker*, 6 (March 7, 1931), 84.

Cuthbert, Clifton. "The Morbidity of William Faulkner." *Contempo*, August 21, 1931, pp. 1–2.

Daniel, Frank. "*Sanctuary*." Atlanta *Journal*, March 1, 1931, Magazine Section, p. 22.

Dawson, Margaret Cheney. "Power and Horror." *New York Herald Tribune Books*, February 15, 1931, p. 3.

Emmart, A. D. "A Novelist of the First Magnitude Appearing Out of Mississippi." Baltimore *Evening Sun*, February 21, 1931, p. 6.

Fadiman, Clifton. "The World of William Faulkner." *Nation*, April 15, 1931, pp. 422–23.

Fleming, Roscoe. "Sees William Faulkner as America's Dark Genius." Pittsburgh *Press*, February 15, 1931, Entertainment Section, p. 5.

Hansen, Harry. "The First Reader." New York *World*, February 10, 1931, p. 13.

Heflin, Martin. "Faulkner's Book Full of Horror and Realism." *Daily Oklahoman* (Oklahoma City), April 5, 1931, p. 9–C.

Houser, Lionel. "A Black and Fetid Story Uncoils Its Hideous Length." San Francisco *News*.

Johnson, Oakley. "*Sanctuary*." *Modern Quarterly*, 6 (Winter 1931–32), 122–23.

McDonald, Edward D. "Out of Horror, Beauty Unfolds in *Sanctuary*." Philadelphia *Record*, February 14, 1931, p. 9–A.

Martin, Harry L. "Horrifying Tale Set in Memphis." Memphis *Evening Appeal*, March 26, 1931, p. 3.

Rascoe, Burton. "Among the New Books." *Arts and Decoration*, April 1931, pp. 50, 74.

Robbins, Frances L. "*Sanctuary*." *Outlook and Independent*, March 11, 1931, p. 375.

Seaver, Edwin. "A Chamber of Horrors." New York *Sun*, February 13, 1931, p. 31.

Sherwood, Robert E. "*Sanctuary*." *Scribner's Magazine*, April 1931, p. adv.–13.

Shipman, Evan. "Violent People." *New Republic*, March 4, 1931, p. 78.

Soskin, William. "Books on Our Table: William Faulkner Writes a Brutal and Tragic Novel in *Sanctuary*." New York *Evening Post*, February 10, 1932, p. 10.

THESE THIRTEEN

These

13

Stories by WILLIAM FAULKNER

· NEW YORK ·
JONATHAN CAPE & HARRISON SMITH

Edward McDonald. "Violent World of Faulkner in *These Thirteen*." Philadelphia *Record*, October 4, 1931, p. 14-B.

What, another book by William Faulkner! Yes, just that—his fifth since 1929, the year in which Mr. Hoover became President of these States.

Howsoever things have recently stood with the rest of us, all has been well with Mr. Faulkner. He has in the last three years just about walked off with the literary show. In an amazingly short time he has with breathless speed risen to fame—or, if you will, to notoriety at least. And *These Thirteen*, a first collection of short stories, will in nowise do discredit to the eminent position Mr. Faulkner has so rapidly attained.

Six of the stories in the present volume are already known to Faulkner readers; seven are here published for the first time.

But whatever their background, all of these stories are alike in this: all are composed out of their author's apparently inexhaustible literary resources, namely, his haunting knowledge of the frustrations, the perversions, the imbecilities, in a word, the compulsions of all sorts which drive his men and women into behavior which swings distractedly from the uttermost in heroism to the uttermost in degradation. The world of these stories is, then, like the world of Faulkner's novels: violent, disordered, cataclysmic. If any reader objects to the presentation, however brilliant, of such a world he had better give free rein to his inner check and leave *These Thirteen* alone. Certainly this is no book for humorists.

Since *These Thirteen* is the first opportunity to appraise Faulkner's short stories as a whole, we may expect to hear endless conjecture about the Hemingway influence upon Faulkner. There has been much of this already; there will be more.

It is important, therefore, to try to keep the record straight. Hemingway's first considerable book, *The Sun Also Rises*, appeared in 1926. In this same year, Faulkner published *Soldiers' Pay*, a work which subsequently made his English reputation. True, these books are novels, not short stories. But decidedly implicit in the episodic recitals of each of these books are the narrative methods for which both Hemingway and Faulkner are known. Consequently it must be clear that Hemingway could have had little influence upon Faulkner's early work. It is inconceivable that his influence could have been more than slightly indirect upon what Faulkner has done either in the novel or the shorter tale since *Soldiers' Pay*.

William Faulkner does not limp on Ernest Hemingway's crutch. He goes his own gait. One may not like that gait, nor the direction in which it is taking him. But there it is.

Robert Cantwell. "Faulkner's Thirteen Stories." *New Republic*, October 21, 1931, p. 271.

These Thirteen should be read after a reading of William Faulkner's novels; as brilliantly written as several of the stories are, they are mainly interesting as further examples of their author's work. Four of them are war stories, six are laid in the South, and the final three—which seem largely literary experiments—are set in France and Italy. The characters in the stories are like the characters in the novels; they act as people act while under some intense nervous strain, the source of which lies in some past condition, outside the story, not clearly stated. Sometimes the nervousness, the tension, is the story, as in "That Evening Sun" in the present volume, in which a Negro woman's fear that her husband has returned to kill her infects the members of the white family for which she works: the children are aware of it, and quarrel among themselves; the husband and wife quarrel because the husband walks home with the frightened servant. "Is her safety more precious to you than mine?" the wife asks, as almost her first response, and we suddenly see that the real story is not the written one of Nancy's foreboding, but the unexplained, unanalyzed condition of strain within the white family, the inner dissension, the battle for prestige that hampers the husband's attempt to help when he first feels that help is needed.

In "Dry September"—the story of a lynching—the attempt to save the Negro is halting in comparison with the savagery of the determination to destroy him; the barber can only remonstrate weakly, while McLendon, who leads the lynching party, is active and powerful. The emphasis is not on the conflict between the two men, or between two impulses, but on the lack of conflict, for the barber's effort dies in an attack of nausea. Yet at the end of the story there is a brief scene between McLendon and his wife, and McLendon is no longer powerful, but pathetic and nearly insane, so ravaged with his egotism that an imaginative flight is required to think of him as ever inflamed with purpose. Similarly, in *Sanctuary*, Popeye's strength was never adequately explained; indeed, the explanation—even the strange last chapter given over to Popeye's biography—was of his weakness, physical and mental; and although his power was felt all through the book, it was somehow mysterious; its source was not shown in the text.

In the present stories, as in Faulkner's novels, the conflict is not between two forces of equal strength, but between purposeful violence on the one hand, and half-hearted, ineffectual protest on the other. We can speculate as to whether or not this picture is complete, and whether or not this conflict is dramatically as cogent as one in which the characters possess equal determination and equal ability to act, but in the meantime William Faulkner insists on his version of the present more effectively, with greater imaginative resourcefulness, than any other American author.

The stories of the War, in which the tension he evokes so well would seem most fitting, are disappointing: "Victory" is a long, formless account of a boy who became a captain and ends by selling matches in the street; "All the Dead Pilots" is little more than an anecdote; "Ad Astra" and "Crevasse" seem allegories with their significance obscured by too precise detail. The best stories are those of the South, those that add to the picture presented by *The Sound and the Fury* and *Sanctuary*. It is the picture of a society in an advanced state of disintegration, but it is too generally applicable to be set aside with vague references to Southern decay. The society is in itself antisocial, intensely individualistic; the family is not a unit, but a battleground for its members; the community acts most efficiently to destroy any communal impulse. William Faulkner evokes this situation clearly, and if he does not suggest a remedy he does not, at least, contemplate the scene with detachment.

Lionel Trilling. "Mr. Faulkner's World." *Nation*, November 4, 1931, pp. 491–92.

Mr. Faulkner has the tone and emotional impact of a major writer. But despite the dramatic stress and portentousness of his work its implications are too frequently minor. It has so often been pointed out that Mr. Faulkner "creates his own world" that one at first assumes that his work tends to be minor simply because it is idiosyncratic. Yet one has only to take the example of Baudelaire to understand how even as esoteric symbolism may be consistent with that largeness of implication which we feel to be one of the primary requirements of major writing. In the work of Mr. Faulkner the absence of this largeness of reference seems to be the result of his particular social point of view rather than of the symbols that express it.

But for the present reviewer Mr. Faulkner is most interesting when he avoids social implications entirely. When he can exploit emotion in some strange and hitherto unexplored setting of mind or place he seems most at ease. Such settings are the minds of the children as they come into contact with primitive fear in the story "That Evening Sun" or the lost and fantastic colony of Negro-owning Indians in "Red Leaves" and "A Justice," or again the fear-hazed mind of the platoon and the caving chalk-field over which it wanders in "Crevasse." These scenes and moods, isolated from common reality, self-defined, not a little fantastic, offer Mr. Faulkner the possibility of complete success.

Such stories, depending as they do on mood, scene, and melodrama, are perhaps as unimportant as those of a writer like A. E. Coppard, but this question becomes irrelevant before their technical perfection. However, when Mr. Faulkner's material is not isolated, but is the material of the daily world, perfection dissipates. Pure event, pure emotion, acceptable enough in a special world, are given the lie by a common world which cries out for understanding as well as for rendition. "A Rose for Emily," the story of a woman who has killed her lover and lain for years beside his decaying corpse, is essentially trivial in its horror because it has no implications, because it is pure event without implication; and for the same reason the hero of "Hair" is, with his endless self-abnegation, little more than quaint— a "character," an "original." Moreover, when Mr. Faulkner does wish to hint implications, when he deals with philosophical emotions, the world in which he sets them has no vital contact with the world of common experience. In "Ad Astra" and "All the Dead Pilots" he uses an isolated society of inarticulate young men who in civilian life were separated from many of the realities of existence by their aristocracy, and who in the war are yet more isolated by the aristocracy of the flying corps and their love of death. Here, because the philosophical importance of emotions depends on their articulateness and their universality, Mr. Faulkner's emotions fail of final meaning and become high-flown and sentimental.

The social point of view which impairs the importance as well as the perfection of Mr. Faulkner's work may perhaps be traced to the ideology which animates two of his early novels, *Soldiers' Pay* and *Sartoris*. To the world of these books, with its sentimental nostalgia for past glory, Toledo rapiers, and lace ruffles, Mr. Faulkner gives fullest assent. In consequence, *Soldiers' Pay*, intended for a tragic post-war novel, is merely womanish and idyllic, and *Sartoris*, the story of a line of Southern gentlemen who do swagger bitter deeds and court death with a gallant despair, is shockingly close to a Michael Arlen confection of mad Marches, "despair," and "gallantry." As in every aristocratic society, there is to be found here a will to forget the physical basis of life; and tragedy robbed of its physical core and allowed to retain only its sad glow degenerates into slack softness and sentimentality. Like every aristocracy, this one is hostile to the generalization of experience, to ideas; hence the unilluminating inarticulateness of so many of Mr. Faulkner's people; hence, too, their quaintness, their mere melodrama and lack of significance, for what we mean by a "character" is a person whose qualities cannot be related to principles. A will to secede, to cherish its apartness and live out of the present is characteristic of Mr. Faulkner's particular aristocracy and to this one may trace the specialness and apartness of his artistic worlds.

It is when Mr. Faulkner breaks from this ideology that he is at his best. When he awoke from the aristocratic obliviousness to the physical which marred his two early books and, in his three later novels, used physical symbols, he left sentimentality behind and achieved both reality and generality of implication. Yet the other qualities of the ideology which we have noted still operate, even in the best of Mr. Faulkner's work, such as *The Sound and the Fury* and *As I Lay Dying*, to make it essentially parochial.

In the present volume perhaps the two best stories are "Dry September" and "Victory." The first is the story of a lynching, the second of a Scotch shipwright whom the war makes a gentleman and who remains one in waxed mustache and pressed suit even when reduced to selling matches. These stories seem best because they are aerated by contact with the common world, by the writer's acceptance of the common, an acceptance which by no means limits the originality, even idiosyncrasy, of their vision and style. Beside them the rest of the stories, for all their success in their own terms, have a subtle kind of stuffiness, shut off as they are in their interesting but hermetically sealed universes.

Pontoon J. Doakes. "Promise of Genius Is Seen." *Rocky Mountain News* (Denver), December 20, 1931, p. 4.

A book of short stories is difficult to review. In the light of my reputation for consistent conservatism, when that book is written by William Faulkner the difficulty appears insurmountable. Since my introduction to Faulkner's work, I have given it a good deal of thought. Unfortunately the conclusion of that thought goes against mental habits of many years standing. Those habits have not allowed me the experience of proclaiming in public print that any contemporary American writer had genius.

But now I throw away the key. William Faulkner has IT—literarily speaking, of course. It happens to be an element of a critical theory, evolved while attempting a book on esthetics, that the above adverbial qualification supplies all that is necessary to differentiate the definition of genius from that of it. Vague as the word is, when we see the attribute in the flesh we find not only a person (that is a power for synthesizing experiences) but a further ability to order relevant past experiences so as to intensify the present one. It is this that distinguishes what goes by the name of "personality" from the lackadaisical bundle of almost automatic experiences that is the average man. Genius needs only

70

the mastery of a technique subtle and precise enough to be able to communicate a concrescence of experiences as a single intensified experience.

Fauconnier writing of the Malays affords me a fortuitous example, and a theological one. He says that what they fear in the dead is "their thought, their passions, their deeds, freed at last and self-existent." To give to dead thoughts, passions and deeds the clarity of an immediate experience, a self-existence, they did not have in their temporal isolation, is the whole job of the literary gent so far as I can see. He's the only medicine-man we've got. To make big medicine he has to strike a very precarious balance between the two basic methods of thought, the inductive and the deductive. On the one hand he is not an experimental scientist communicating the data of knowledge, nor is he on the other a philosopher sweeping thru generalizations to find one universal enough to be a function of all the experimentalist's data. If he fails in the inductive side, his experience is so little referable to fact that it conveys nothing and he is merely talking to himself in public like Yvor Winters, etc., etc., etc. But if he has grasped no idea general enough to comprehend fully the particulars of the experience he is trying to convey, then the result resembles a mail-order catalog, of the sort to which Mr. Dreiser has too often treated us.

William Faulkner retains this balance better in his novels and in these short stories than any writer America has produced in a good many years. Moreover, he is young, and with an unusually fertile mind shows every potentiality for improving in technique and maturing in genius.

As the stories in *These Thirteen* are dissimilar in many respects, it were better within these limits not to take them up separately. They are there to be read by any with an interest in American letters. I will add that one of them, "A Rose for Emily," will knock your hat off.

Well, that's my story and I'm going to stick to it.

I doubt not that I am ill advised. Where literature has become on one hand a harmless cult of the slightly touched, and on the other, largely a commercial racket, criticism is subject to dictatorship. Under which happy auspices, as is the case in at least one nation I know of, it is better for the critical health to No Spika Zarathustra.

"The Literary Lantern." Durham *Herald*, December 27, 1931.

Our Mississippi novelist, William Faulkner, had been writing novels for several years before his work attracted any attention, even among critics. Now Faulkner first editions are coming into great demand among collectors, so much so that the *Publishers' Weekly* recently carried nineteen separate inquiries for "firsts" of his early war novel, *Soldiers' Pay*. A new story, presumably a short one, which Faulkner wrote while in New York City on business, is being published in a special edition of four hundred copies, each signed by the author. The title of this collectors' item is *Idyll in the Desert*, and it is issued by a publisher specializing in fine format and rare editions.

For those who have no acquaintance yet with Mr. Faulkner's novels there is a new volume of short stories which they may sample, *These 13*, containing most of his short pieces written during the last two years. In this time he has published three novels, yet so prolific is he that all his recent short stories could not be included in one volume. Among others, we miss the raucous "Spotted Horses," which appeared in *Scribner's Magazine* last summer, but the volume as it is, gives a fair idea of his work in all its varied moods. There are four war stories with their stark realism and macabre humor. There are three Italian sketches. And there are six pieces out of Mississippi in which the locale so strengthens the action that one cannot conceive of them as translated to another background. This thorough and organic rooting in a familiar life probably accounts for the fact that the Southern stories appear to be generally the most effective. "Red Leaves," introducing an unusual and very dramatic clash between the Indian and Negro races, is a picture of terror worthy to be ranged with the great horror stories. "That Evening Sun Go Down" is another superb impression of fear, gained in an entirely different way, through the puzzled yet realistic observation of children. "A Rose for Emily" is the ironic title of a macabre study in which the details are worked out with precise and telling effect, progressing from gossip-whispers of eccentricity to a terrible climax of perversion and ghastliness.

It is almost certain that Mr. Faulkner's audience will continue to be a small one. His subject-matter is not chosen for popularity, and his passion for experimentation leads him into a technique often stylized to the point of obscurity. But he is one writer, among the younger ones in America today, who is clearly possessed of genius. It is a dark, mysterious possession, like some outlandish spell, to be sure. But because he is in a way possessed, his books are individual and are full of the power which comes when a writer has the courage to select material peculiarly his own and the mastery to use it effectively.

Checklist of Additional Reviews

Youngstown (Ohio) *Vindicator*, September 26, 1931.

"Mr. Faulkner's Stories and Other New Works of Fiction." *New York Times Book Review*, September 27, 1931, p. 7.

"Short Stories by Faulkner." Detroit *News*, October 11, 1931, Part 10, p. 4.

"*These Thirteen*." Hartford *Daily Courant*, October 25, 1931, p. 6-E.

"*These 13*: Short Stories Are Tabloid Novels by William Faulkner Depicting the Sordid and Abnormal." Lewiston (Me.) *Evening Journal*, October 31, 1931, Magazine Section, p. 7.

"*These Thirteen*." Nyack (N.Y.) *Journal*, November 28, 1931.

"*These Thirteen*." *Forum*, December 1931, pp. x, xii.

"*These Thirteen*." *American Mercury*, January 1932, p. xxiv.

"*These Thirteen*." *Booklist*, 28 (January 1932), 201.

"*These Thirteen*." New Haven *Journal Courier*, January 1, 1932, p. 6.

"*These Thirteen*." Greenwich (Conn.) Press.

Ajax. "Themes and Variations." *Contempo*, February 1, 1932, p. 3.

Cushing, Edward. "A Collection of Studies." *Saturday Review of Literature*, October 17, 1931, p. 201.

Fraser, Hugh Russell. "Short Tales Penned by Faulkner." Albany *Knickerbocker Press*, October 25, 1931, Section IV, p. 5.

Grandy, Edwin T. "Courier Reviews of New Books." Berkeley *Courier*, March 26, 1932, p. 10.

Hansen, Harry. "The First Reader." Pittsburgh *Press*, October 25, 1931, Society Section, p. 14.

Hicks, Granville. "Faulkner and the

Short Story." *New York Herald Tribune Books*, September 27, 1931, p. 8.

Lutz, Mark. "Faulkner's Short Stories." Richmond *News Leader*, October 21, 1931, p. 8.

Milburn, George. "*These Thirteen.*" *Daily Oklahoma* (Oklahoma City), August 7, 1932, p. 5-C.

P[almer], C. B. "William Faulkner Writes Short Stories." Boston *Evening Transcript*, October 14, 1931, Section III, p. 2.

Phal, Armad. "Thirteen Stars in Faulkner's Sky." Richmond *Times-Dispatch*, September 27, 1931, Section III, p. 10.

Ralph, John H., Jr. "*These Thirteen* by William Faulkner." *Wisconsin State Journal* (Madison), November 15, 1931, p. 3.

Robinson, Ted. "Brilliant Story Telling." Cleveland *Plain Dealer*, September 27, 1931, Amusement Section, p. 16.

Shelton, Wilson E. "*These Thirteen.*" Beverly Hills *Bulletin*, February 25, 1932.

Sherwood, Robert E. "*These Thirteen.*" *Scribner's Magazine*, November 1931, pp. 14, 16.

Smith, Henry (Nash). "New Book Proves Southern Novelist Master of Technic." Dallas *Morning News*, October 11, 1931, Section VI, p. 8; also reviewed in *Southwest Review*, 17 (Autumn 1931), xxiv–xxv.

Stallings, Laurence. "Examples of Faulkner's Extraordinary Quality in His Volume of *These Thirteen.*" New York *Sun*, September 23, 1931, p. 29.

Vernon, Greenville. "Fallen Angel?" *Commenweal*, January 20, 1932, pp. 332–33.

Warren, Robert Penn. "Not Local Color." *Virginia Quarterly Review*, 8 (January 1932), 160.

Weeks, Edward. *These Thirteen. Atlantic Monthly*, January 1932, p. adv.-16.

SALMAGUNDI and MISS ZILPHIA GANT

SALMAGUNDI

By

WILLIAM FAULKNER

and a Poem by

ERNEST M. HEMINGWAY

MILWAUKEE:

The CASANOVA PRESS

MCMXXXII

Harry Hansen.
"The First Reader."
Greensboro *Daily News*,
May 15, 1932, Section II,
p. 4.

William Faulkner and Ernest Hemingway appear together in *Salmagundi*, a thin book of early writings just prepared by Paul Romaine and published by Casanova Press, of Milwaukee, Wis. True, the Hemingway is but four lines long, but it gets him on the title page. The articles and poems, with one exception, appeared in the *Double Dealer*, of New Orleans, and are being reissued with "the amusing permission" of Faulkner.

Upon reading these early writings of William Faulkner we find impressionistic sketches, irrelevant comment on American criticism, an autobiographical fragment discussing the influence of Swinburne on himself as a lad of 16 and a group of poems, including "L'Apres-Midi d'un Faune," said to be Faulkner's first published work. It appeared in the *New Republic*, August 6, 1919.

In 1925 we discover Faulkner writing:— "Is there nowhere among us a Keats embryo, some one who will turn his lute to the beauty of the world? Life is not different from what it was when Shelley drove like a swallow southward from the unbearable English winter; living may be different, but not life. Time changes us, but time's self does not change. Here is the same air, the same sunlight in which Shelley dreamed of golden men and women immortal in a silver world and in which young John Keats wrote 'Endymion' trying to gain enough silver to marry Fannie Brawne and set up an apothecary's shop. Is not there among us some one who can write something beautiful and passionate and sad instead of saddening?"

It is difficult to reconcile Faulkner's wish with his performance of later years, but in 1925 he was writing poems about dryads and fauns and youth and shepherd lads, invoking the dying gladiator and writing measured meters, and in this:—

"You are so young. And frankly you
   believe
This world, this darkened street, this
   shadowed wall
Are dim with beauty you passionately
   know
Cannot fade nor cool nor die at all.
"Raise your hand, then, to your scarce
   seen face
And draw the opaque curtains on your
   eyes.
Profoundly speaking of life, of simple
   truths,
The while your voice is clear with
   frank surprise."

In writing on criticism the youthful Faulkner complains that the American critic has become "a reincarnation of the sideshow spellbinders of happy memory, holding the yokelry enravished not with what he says but how he says it." He also adds that "when you ask him the author's name or the book's or what it is about he cannot tell you."

Apparently the Faulkner of 1925 fell in with a sad lot of critics. He declares that "the English review criticises the book, the American the author." By now, no doubt [of] it, Mr. Faulkner has found as much divergence among American as English critics and has also discovered among them men who can appreciate and sympathize with his unusual abilities and rich gifts.

"Faulkner Verses Show Wistfulness." Philadelphia *Public Ledger*, May 28, 1932, p. 11.

Paul Romaine in his rather facetious preface remarks, "This book was written by Youth, designed by Youth and published by Youth. The criticism can therefore be as harsh as it may—the bones are soft and do not break easily." May I add that the book is also being reviewed by Youth?

The volume is thin, containing three articles and five poems by Faulkner and a quatrain by Ernest Hemingway, the inclusion of which is apologetically justified in that all appeared anonymously in Walter Yust's distinguished, but now defunct *Double Dealer*. The entire content is early Faulkner, embracing the period 1919–1925.

The present work surprisingly enough shows a contented, harmonious, well-disciplined Faulkner. Few of his later acquired mannerisms are utilized, there is less of the exhausting penetration and trenchant figures of speech. Outside of a vitriolic denunciation of critics in general, there is little that characterizes the later Faulkner work.

Yet the volume is graced by some extraordinary material. Wistfulness, a quality seldom found in any of the man's work, is commendably expressed in a poem called "The Lilacs." In fact, the poetry in general is well rounded and palatable. William Faulkner is undoubtedly one of the motivating forces behind the shifting of the American literary scene from the Middle West to the South.

"A 'Prentice Faulkner." *New York Times Book Review,* May 29, 1932, p. 20.

This collection of William Faulkner's early sketches, articles and poems, culled with one exception from *The Double Dealer* of New Orleans, have a pronounced curiosity value. The section on New Orleans types—ranging from the longshoreman to the magdalen—wallows in color; the same color, restrained, chastened and made incidental to story demands, may be found in S*anctuary*. In these sketches Mr. Faulkner is trying his hand, and discovering an opulence in word-mongering that at least betokens gifts to master. The section on criticism makes a distinction between American and English critics. In London, Mr. Faulkner insists, the critic deals with the book; in New York he deals with the author of the book. Just where the dividing line comes here it is difficult to determine; obviously the book is part of the author, and the author is all of the book—unless he has hired a ghost. Possibly Mr. Faulkner means to chastise the columnists who deal largely in gossip. A section on poetry pays lavish tribute to Swinburne, whose influence may be noted in the poems that follow. One of these poems—"Portrait"—is quite beautiful in a fragile way. Another, "The Lilacs," is a weak echo of T. S. Eliot's "Portrait of a Lady," whose rhythm may be found in more than one modern poem. On the back cover of the book is a four-line poem, "Ultimately," by Ernest Hemingway, also taken from *The Double Dealer*. Paul Romaine, designer and publisher of the volume, offers the Faulkner salmagundi because it is "certain to reveal unsuspected qualities of a simple man."

"A Faulkner Item in a Limited Edition."
New York Times Book Review, July 17, 1932, p. 9.

This Faulkner story is here published for the first time, with an introduction by Professor Henry Smith of Southern Methodist University in Dallas. Dr. Smith, who casts a beam of light on the terrible mechanisms that move most of the people in the Faulkner novels by contrasting the author's methods with those of Meredith and Henry James, does well by this particular story when he says: "***Faulkner felt the remnants of Europe in America as unreal." Certainly the father, mother and daughter in the slight *Miss Zilphia Gant* are cut off from any sustaining tradition. Mrs. Gant, who kills her husband when he is unfaithful, has never been further from home than the county seat and has never seen a moving picture or read a magazine. She simply acts in a primitive fashion; then proceeds to ruin her daughter's life by a pathological insistence that the girl must be protected from all men. The story has a sort of bare horror, achieved by Faulkner's unerring use of the right words.

"A Southwest Book Club."
Contempo, November 21, 1932, p. 7.

The Book Club of Texas (Dallas), organized with the purpose of fostering the production of fine books, issues three or four original publications a year, available to members only. An annual payment of $2.50 in dues entitles one to membership, which is limited to three hundred.

The latest selection for publication is a Faulkner story—*Zilphia Gant*. The Club has Mr. Faulkner's word for it that this story is the basis of a future novel. Warped minds are again the protagonists of this story, but this time tempered by something less uncanny and more serene than other Faulkner pathological studies.

LIGHT IN AUGUST

LIGHT IN AUGUST

WILLIAM FAULKNER

HARRISON SMITH & ROBERT HAAS

James T. Farrell. "The Faulkner Mixture." New York *Sun*, October 7, 1932, p. 29.

William Faulkner's most apparent literary virtues are an impressive stylistic competence and a considerable virtuosity in construction and organization. It is his sheer ability to write powerfully that carries many readers through the consistently melodramatic and sensational parts that occur regularly in his writings.

For instance, when one strives to reconstruct or to tell a Faulkner plot in retrospect one sees this melodrama clearly, but when one is reading, one is swept along by the man's driving pen. Technically, he is the master of almost all American writers who fit under such a loose and general category as "realists." He has probably forgotten more about literary tricks than such writers as Ernest Hemingway or Sherwood Anderson will ever learn.

I have recently suggested, in these pages, a comparison between Faulkner and Julian Green. Another comparison, and perhaps a more apt one, is with the Irish novelist Liam O'Flaherty. In both cases, one finds an efflorescence of literary talents that is primarily employed in themes of violence. Of the two Faulkner is the more inclined toward out and out pathological cases, and also, his conceptions of character are the more unflinching. Both use melodrama literally. O'Flaherty is the more verbally excessive, and very often his melodrama consists in more metaphorical exaggerations. Thus, one of his hunted characters will skulk about nighttime Dublin, looking into store windows to see his face as the reflection of a ghoulish blob of flesh. With Faulkner, melodrama runs more to incident, to his sensational rapes, lynchings, and descriptions of the human being in sadistic and brutal moments. Faulkner, likewise, seems to have the more consistent viewpoint, and to grasp the social implications of his tales with greater clarity. Again and again, he has stated the problem of the intelligent individual, with some standards of justice, when he is forced to face mob fury: and with this statement, has gone a delineation of the impotency of the intelligent individual in the surge of that mob fury. A quotation, garnered from this new Faulkner novel, which might almost apply to the characters of an O'Flaherty book like *The House of Gold*, if one make a few slight alterations regarding religion, offers an explanation why Faulkner indulges in so many insanities and violences.

"Yet even then the music has still a quality stern and implacable, deliberate and without passion so much as immolation, pleading, asking for not love, not life, forbidding it to others, demanding in sonorous tones death, as though death were the boon, like all Protestant music. It was as though they who accepted it and raised voices to praise it within praise, having been made what they were by that which the music praised and symbolized, they took revenge upon that which made them so by means of the praise itself. Listening, he seems to hear within it the apotheosis of his own history, his own land, his own environed blood: that the people from which he sprang and among whom he lives can never take either pleasure or catastrophe from either without brawling over it. Pleasure, ecstasy, they cannot seem to bear: their escape from it is in violence, in drinking and fighting and praying; catastrophe too, the violence identical and apparently identical and inescapable. *And so why should not their religion drive them to crucifixion of themselves and one another.*" (Italics of author.)

83

Faulkner and O'Flaherty both afford the reader relief from a situation in these terms, by lyrical passages, or by strong and steady writing. In the Irish writer, the confessional strain runs strong, and the personal element is more direct and immediate. O'Flaherty seems to be more involved in his stories. Withal, the comparison is not nullified. They are both miniature editions of, say, Robinson Jeffers.

In *Light in August*, Faulkner adopts many of the tricks and mannerisms that have been termed "modernistic," and this without any great profit. Particularly, in some of the early pages, he is very free with metaphors, and they grow monotonous. He adopts the habit of using two verbs where one would often do. Thus, "The door opened, *inyamed.*" (Italics mine.) He runs words together, the same as Dos Passos does, although these words might just as easily [have] been separated. How "aweinspiring," or "womansmell" or "manvoice" or many other words are more effective by being combined is something I do not understand. Also he draws out distinctions between the sexes by such neologisms, which, for this reviewer at least, grow boresome. Finally, he even indulges in a bit of Gertrude Stein, again, to my incomprehension:

"Memory believes before knowing remembers. Believes longer than recollects, longer than knowing even wonders. Knows remembers believes a corridor in a big long gabled corridor . . ."

This novel has all the Faulkner ingredients. Also, despite the comments of adopted mannerisms, there is powerful writing, particularly some of the passages that describe the life of Joe Christmas, a life heaped with injustice. As a writer, I believe that Faulkner has been overpraised. Also, I believe that his preoccupations with violence and insanity will, with the accumulation of more Faulkner novels, wear

out. In other words, he is limiting himself. Because of these facts, there is no necessity of gravitating to the other pole and underpraising him. He writes with force and drive. He is worth reading, although consigning his work to posterity wholesale is another matter.

Fanny Butcher. "New Faulkner Writing Fits His Material." Chicago *Tribune*, October 8, 1932, p. 12.

Now and again there are seismic disturbances in the surface of our literary world, which goes on usually in its calm, fruitful way, bearing the seed planted in it by the past, accepted as a final fact by the present.

The most spectacular "trembler" of the last few years has been a young man named William Faulkner. His first writing was characterized by a violence of material, an absence of any of the old-fashioned forms in technique, and mannerisms of style which were so marked that they cried to be, and were, caricatured.

One of the most intricate of intellectual literary games is the pinning on of the donkey's tail, as it were. Give the guessers extracts of the works of classic or contemporaneous authors and let them figure out who wrote them. Incidentally there is exactly such a contest in this month's *Book Dial*, with prizes for the most accurate guesses and a short essay on *The Store*, by T. S. Stribling. One of the most amazing things, even to someone who reads continuously, as a literary editor must, is that almost all writing sounds alike. You might have a hard time telling from the style whether Thomas Babington Macaulay, Gen. Pershing, or Georges Clemenceau had written a piece about an historic occasion. In the *Book Dial* contest there is only one excerpt which—if you hadn't read the books and didn't know what they were about—you could label accurately just from the style, Ernest Hemingway's.

William Faulkner has had the distinction of writing always so much like himself and like no one else that anyone could spot his work—the description of an eye "like the upturned underbody of a dead fish" or words to that effect, and the running together of two or three words to express an idea, like "in the soft light downfalling upon the soft ungirdled presence of a woman prepared for sleep" for instance.

Such mannerisms are the most easily caricatured imaginable, and Mr. Faulkner was simply a lush hunting ground for the wits. On the other hand, Arnold Bennett's criticism of him will overbalance the caricatures, for about no one else living, so far as I know, did Arnold Bennett declare that "he writes like an angel."

It is too bad that Mr. Bennett did not live to see *Light in August* for Mr. Faulkner's most glaring idiosyncrasies in writing have been shuffled off his pen and there remains a style which, while just as peculiarly the author's own, has a solidness and a rightness that his previous writing had only part of the time. He has achieved something, not different for the sake of difference in *Light in August*, but a style which exactly interprets the mood and the matter of the book.

The mood is that of reality vibrant with brooding menace—not so much that of horror as in his earlier books were [*sic*]. The matter is the crisscrossed lives of people far from the norm, a white man with enough of the black in him to drive him to maladjustments as an orphan child, aimless wandering, casual loves and finally to murder, a ne'er-do-well who has run away as the book opens from the girl who loves

him and as the book closes has made his escape from her again, a white woman who loves the whole black race and dies for her love, a preacher who has stubbornly lived in the town a lifetime after being driven from his church and blood whipped by the K.K.K.

Even the characters who flit in and out of the action are all a little mad one way or another. Even the calm, fruitful Lena, who opens the book as she has tramped a month in search of her lover that their child may be born in wedlock, and who closes it, still tramping, with her three weeks old baby, in search of its father. And the simple Byron Bunch, who was an honest, God fearing and God serving man.

The book is without form in the conventional sense. It hops about on its toes, but the point is that it is on its toes all the time, never slumped into inactivity.

I should say that *Light in August* would make William Faulkner's popularity with the cognoscenti more understandable to the ordinary reader while in no sense disappointing his admirers.

Floyd Van Vuren. "William Faulkner Attains New Maturity in *Light in August*." Milwaukee *Journal*, October 8, 1932, p. 4.

A compelling power urges the reader through the 400 closely printed pages of this new novel by William Faulkner, the much acclaimed author of *Sanctuary*, *The Sound and the Fury* and *These Thirteen*. It is a power which transcends that of his earlier books, as if the power apparent in them was only a promise of the vital force that pervades *Light in August*.

The new book introduces a sounder and a more mature William Faulkner, a William Faulkner, it is true, who has not yet entirely conquered the art of the novelist, but who has now mastered the style and literary mannerisms to which in the past he was willing sometimes to sacrifice clarity and vitality. If Mr. Faulkner finds, after *Light in August* attains, as it will inevitably, to best sellerhood, that he is less a cult than he has been heretofore it will be because he has removed the taint of obscurity from his writing and has put more of his inherent strength and force as a novelist into his story than he has into its writing.

Which is not to say, however, that Mr. Fauklner is not still indebted, in *Light in August*, to James Joyce and the earlier followers of Joyce. His Joycean heritage is still apparent, but now it does not get in the way of the story Faulkner has to tell and his style and mannerisms seem more an integral part of his novel. The tendency toward style for style's sake has disappeared and his mannerisms have attained purpose.

The story in *Light in August* has its setting against the same Mississippi backgrounds that lent their atmosphere and color to his other novels and deals with characters of the same caliber as that of those who people his previous books. There is mention, even, of Col. Sartoris, a prominent character in earlier volumes.

Thus, *Light in August* opens with a picture of Lena Grove, young, courageous, on a month's trek that takes her from her father's tumble down shack in Alabama to Jefferson, Miss., in search of Lucas Burch, the itinerant young man who has betrayed her. There is Joe Christmas, product of an orphanage, bootlegger, scavenger, murderer, violator of women, whose doubt about his possession of negro blood leaves him no peace of mind and maddens him into unmentionable crimes.

There is Byron Bunch, of a meekness that verges on stupidity and that does not inherit the earth.

Then there is Hightower, preacher, philosopher, the soul of earnestness, and gentleness, figuratively crucified by his flock after the miserable, tawdry murder of a wife whom he cannot hold as his own. And there is Miss Burden, a descendant of northerners by birth, of northern carpetbaggers of the post Civil War period and who carries on their work in the name of abolitionists by befriending any and all of the negroes in the neighborhood. At 40, after a life of barrenness, she finds satisfaction for insatiable and unsuspected lusts in her relationship with Joe Christmas.

The characters in *Light in August* are too numerous completely to catalog. Their stories, perhaps, are too loosely woven together in Mr. Faulkner's novel (that, it seems to this reviewer, is the book's one major fault), but they are stories that hold the reader inevitably, relentlessly. Certain scenes in the book stand out as memorable after the final page has been turned: Joe Christmas' trek, maddened by starvation, in his efforts to escape punishment for the murder of Miss Burden; his death and mutilation at the hands of a mob; the killing of his guardian in his fiery, freedom curbed youth.

But Joe Christmas is not the only character of primary importance in the book and there are other scenes: Hightower, impervious to the tumult about him, as he preaches to a congregation that has walked out of his church after they learn of his wife's sinning; Hightower, a man of reclaimed youth, as he walks the two miles to his home after delivering Lena Grove of her baby. Finally, like an idyll after the horror and terror and lust described in the story proper, but an idyll which is filled with pathos and which is ever so slightly and amusingly Rabelaisian, is the chapter in which the consummation of

Byron Bunch's love for Lena Grove is re-counted.

It is not without contemplation that one discovers that the actual events in the story all take place within the limits of a few days. In reading *Light in August* it is as though the reader has lived through many lifetimes, so completely has he felt and realized to the full the significance or the futility of the lives of Mr. Faulkner's characters.

J. Donald Adams. "Mr. Faulkner's Astonishing Novel." *New York Times Book Review*, October 9, 1932, pp. 6, 24.

With this new novel, Mr. Faulkner has taken a tremendous stride forward. To say that *Light in August* is an astonishing performance is not to use the word lightly. That somewhat crude and altogether brutal power which thrust itself through his previous work is in this book disciplined to a greater effectiveness than one would have believed possible in so short a time. There are still moments when Mr. Faulkner seems to write of what is horrible purely from a desire to shock his readers or else because it holds for him a fascination from which he cannot altogether escape. There are still moments when his furious contempt for the human species seems a little callow.

But no reader who has followed his work can fail to be enormously impressed by the transformation which has been worked upon it. Not only does Faulkner emerge from this book a stylist of striking strength and beauty; he permits some of his people, if not his chief protagonist, to act sometimes out of motives which are human in their decency; indeed, he permits the Rev. Gail Hightower to live his life by them. In a word, Faulkner has admitted justice and compassion to his scheme of things. There was a hint of this to come in the treatment of Benbow in *Sanctuary*. The gifts which he had to begin with are strengthened—the gifts for vivid narrative and the fresh-minted phrase. His eye for the ignoble in human nature is more keen than ever, but his vision is also less restricted. He has learned justice and compassion.

Unlike *Sanctuary*, horror is not the predominant note of *Light in August*. There are two or three scenes in this book more searing than anything Faulkner has heretofore written, but they are also better integrated.

And although the pattern of *Light in August* is streaked with red, there is a blending here with colors both more subdued and more luminous than were customary to his palette. The locale is again the "deep South"; and the characters include the white trash of which he has drawn such relentless portraits, plain folk of a better strain, whites of a higher order, Negroes, and for the subject of his most detailed attention a poor white with a probable mixture of Negro blood.

The story opens with the flight from her home of Lena Grove, who takes to the road in search of the man whose child she is soon to bear, unquestioning in her faith that he will marry her when she finds him. Out of Alabama she trudges wearily into Mississippi, asking as she goes for the whereabouts of Lucas Burch. At the town of Jefferson she learns that a man named Bunch has been working at a local lumber mill, and thinks that her quest is ended. As, indeed, it is, for Lucas Burch is living in the neighborhood, under the name of Brown. Burch is a no-account, white-livered rascal who, in his flight from Lena, fell into company more evil than his own. He is carrying on a cheap bootlegging racket with Joe Christmas, the poor white whose fortunes provide the frame for most of Mr. Faulkner's story. Lena is given shelter by Byron Bunch, whom she seeks out at the mill in the belief that he is her missing lover. In its bald summary all this sounds much less convincing than Faulkner makes it. Byron is an insignificant but decent fellow, a humble Good Samaritan.

At this point the course of the narrative, after the Rev. Gail Hightower has been introduced, swerves to flash back over the background out of which Joe Christmas has come. The clergyman plays an important part in Mr. Faulkner's story. It is he against whose life, in the quiet of its closing years, the drama of evil engendered by the sinister figure of Joe Christmas plays itself out. There is a striking parallel in method here with that used by Ellen Glasgow in her new novel *The Sheltered Life*, in which the figure of old General Archbald serves much the same purpose as the Rev. Hightower in *Light in August*.

Faulkner's evocation of Christmas's childhood and youth is a masterly piece of work; the boy was inherently evil, no doubt, but environment and chance helped to mold him into what he is when we meet him, a creature soured and foul. With the story of Christmas's past unfolded, we are plunged forthwith into a maelstrom of terror and tragedy. He kills a middle-aged spinster, a repressed nymphomaniac with whom he has been living in a strange intimacy. Because of the puzzling circumstances of the murder, Lucas Burch also is held under suspicion. The murder itself, the mobbing of Christmas on his way to jail, his escape and horrible death— these are told with an intensity, a rush of force, which no one of Faulkner's contemporaries can equal. In remarkable contrast to these scenes are the episodes which

deal with the dumb love of Byron for Lena, the musing quiet of the chapter toward the end, in which the Rev. Hightower goes back in memory over his life, much as does General Archbald in Ellen Glasgow's novel. And there is a magnificent scene in which Lucas Burch is brought from jail to the cabin where Lena lies with her newborn child in her arms, a scene in which the man's character is shredded before our eyes.

There are phrases which are memorable: "Against his bare legs the wet grassblades were like strokes of limber icicles"; "Her eyes were like the button-eyes of a toy animal: a quality beyond even hardness, without being hard." "The faces of old men lined by that sheer accumulation of frustration and doubt which is so often the other side of the picture of hale and respected full years." And there are passages of considerable length which have a sustained beauty and burden of meaning to a degree which made this reader pause and exclaim.

Light in August is a powerful novel, a book which secures Mr. Faulkner's place in the very front rank of American writers of fiction. He definitely has removed the objection made against him that he cannot lift his eyes above the dunghill. There are times when Mr. Faulkner is not unaware of the stars. One hesitates to make conjectures as to the inner lives of those who write about the lives of others, but Mr. Faulkner's work has seemed to be that of a man who has, at some time, been desperately hurt; a man whom life has at some point badly cheated. There are indications in the book that he has regained his balance.

George Grimes. "A Rival to Popeye in Faulkner's New Novel of the Southland." Omaha *World-Herald*, October 9, 1932, Magazine Section, p. 7.

William Faulkner has abandoned, one may say, the cruel brutality of *Sanctuary* for brutal cruelty in writing his new novel, *Light in August*.

It is grim stuff, and if you don't care for grim stuff, you'd better avoid it. But if you do admit that there is a reason for realism in the writing of novels, grab this; it is extremely powerful.

It is again, as *Sanctuary*, a book about the south. A small town in Mississippi provides the scene. Drawn together there, as by inscrutable fate, are a girl, Lena Grove, calm and patient as she awaits her baby and goes in search of the child's father; the father, Burch, who has become involved with the man, Lee [sic] Christmas, who is partly of Negro blood. And Christmas is the character whose stolid acceptance of fate, whose relentless moving of his entire life toward murder and then his own lynching, stands out from the pages with terrible clarity.

Christmas is not such a malignant person as Popeye of *Sanctuary*, but he has in his character all the hardness of Popeye. Faulkner is at his brilliant best, it seems to me, in showing how society can compress the human heart and soul until all the milk of human kindness is squeezed out; all softness, all pity, all tenderness; leaving only the cold, flinty-hard will to live and do that which the moment suggests, no matter how deep the evil.

This sinister mulatto, Christmas, has for the reader (if he does not object to grimness) a fascination something approaching that which a deadly snake is supposed to exert. I could not set aside the book as it told about him, working in the saw mill, then turning bootlegger, then engaging in a horrible illicit passion with "Miz Burden." That passion brought to rottenness all the good that had been in her, until, in the end, he knew he had to kill her, and she, too, was aware of the fate that impended.

In his writing tricks, Faulkner again superbly achieves the feat of enabling his reader to see people and events through the eyes of the character who happens, at the moment, to be the center of the story.

George Marion O'Donnell. "A Mellower Light." Memphis *Commercial Appeal*, October 9, 1932, Section IV, p. 4.

The scene of William Faulkner's latest novel is Jefferson, Mississippi, the locale of four of the six novels that have made him a major writer. And the story is as characteristically Faulknerian as its setting. It will be probably well to warn those to whom *Sanctuary* was distasteful that Faulkner steadfastly holds the view that an artist must not be limited as to subject-matter, must not be restrained by outside pressure from exploring any fields of life toward which he is drawn and which seem to need exploration. For though *Light in August* is more human and less mordant than *Sanctuary*, it is decidedly tragic and decidedly unconventional in tone.

Mr. Faulkner utilizes almost 500 pages in the telling of his story. The plot is luxuriant, teeming with a thousand suggestions and implications and complications, but clearcut and lucid at last. As in his other books, Faulkner sheds light gradually upon the events that make up his narrative. There are long flash-backs in which one learns the life history of each of his major characters in turn; and these flash-backs, with their abrupt transitions from the present to the past, from one set of characters to another, give to the narrative a slight looseness that stands in the way of perfection, though it does not impair the cumulative effect of the whole.

The method which Mr. Faulkner has utilized in *Light in August* is interesting. It is simpler than any other he has used in his writing, yet it is a synthesis of all these methods. The author has employed third person, past tense, and present tense narration, the stream of consciousness, first person narration and conversation, blending the various methods that he has used separately in previous books into a whole that is admirably effective if not always smooth. This synchronization gives the impression that Faulkner is striving for a novel-form in which all modes will be blended into a perfect narrative. This perfection is not attained in *Light in August*, but it is approached.

In every respect *Light in August* is quieter than the author's earlier works. It is more restrained, less brutal, more leisurely and dignified in its movement. The author still possesses his power for dramatic, gripping writing about tragic events, and his descriptive epithets are usually so apt as to be startling; but the prose is less staccato than that of *Sanctuary*, being more like the prose of *Sartoris* and of portions of *The Sound and the Fury*. Even the characters are more human and less pathological than one expects Faulkner's characters to be.

On the whole *Light in August* is a greater work than any other book William Faulkner has written. It is more mature, broader in outlook, nearer to the final, truthful revelation of human potentialities for which the author is striving. It is a novel that no one who is interested in the growth of American literature can afford to neglect. And that William Faulkner is one of the major writers of our generation is proved here anew.

Ted Robinson. "Squeamish Critics Cramp Style of Faulkner's New Novel *Light in August*." Cleveland *Plain Dealer*, October 9, 1932, Amusement Section, p. 11.

There is not much fiction this week but what there is happens to be of great interest. William Faulkner's long expected new novel, *Light in August*, was published on Wednesday by Harrison Smith & Robert K. Haas, and since that is true there is no excuse for beginning with any other novel.

I might say at the outset that I am ever so slightly disappointed in *Light in August*. Perhaps it is the natural reaction against the squeamish critics of *Sanctuary*, but it seems to me that he has allowed them to cramp his style. This novel is not conventional, but it is nearer to the conventional in construction than are any of his earlier books. Faulkner's most striking talent lies in being able to describe a situation from the viewpoint of one of the characters concerned. In this novel he has refrained from that method and in so doing has sustained a distinct loss, both in style and in psychological significance. Perhaps he is tired of the "stream of consciousness" technique; I do not think that this should force him to the opposite or "omniscient author" viewpoint.

The book loses something in rapidity and inevitableness from just that shift in method. It moves more slowly than do the other books. Nevertheless, we have here a strong plot, some memorable characters, and a logical denouement. I refrain from giving any description of the narrative itself, and I do not wish to be understood as thinking this book unworthy of Faulkner, or as advising his many admirers not to read it. On the contrary, I believe that all will want to read it and that all will be interested in it. I am merely recording my impression that the author's earlier method is more powerful and that it would be an immeasurable loss if he should desert it.

Henry George Hoch. "Gray Realms of Faulkner: His Latest Novel, though Still Morbid, Reveals His Power and Versatility." Detroit *News*, October 16, 1932, Arts Section, p. 18.

Mr. Faulkner has never hesitated to reveal his most unlovely characters to the utmost, so it must be said of *Light in August* that it will shock the sensitive reader.

It must be added, also, that few serious readers who begin the book will be able to put it down until the last page has been read.

In his successive novels about the lowly,

ignorant and criminal peoples of the South, Faulkner gradually has risen above utter horror and morbidity by bringing in more and more characters who can command respect and affection.

The book has one major fault. For the most part there is a limning of character as good as Faulkner has done, a creation which makes the minor character of Percy Grimm in the manhunt an outstanding thing.

Yet the character of the Rev. Mr. Hightower, one of the major figures of the book, though given much attention and detail, is incomprehensible. Possibly it was intended to be so. But it irritates constantly, like a sore thumb.

The novel is the longest Faulkner has attempted, and has more plot and action than usual. It is unquestionably his best novel. It is much more palatable for the average reader than *Sanctuary*, but still a bad choice for those who dislike pictures of life in the raw.

Evan Shipman. *New Republic*, 72 (October 26, 1932), 300–1.

At the present time, most of the interesting writers are cautiously feeling their way with a realism that reduces the scope of their work in an effort toward absolute honesty. William Faulkner is in strong contrast to this tendency; his risk is considerable. He fills the realistic scene with drama; his characters are moved by exceptional and perverse impulses; their lives proceed toward violent ends. His powerfully individual books are written in a prose that at its best is poetic, at its worst confused and tedious. He has been highly praised; the strange, fervent quality of his work compared to the great Russians. But one feels that what is with them an evangelical force is with Faulkner a savage weariness with the puppets he means to destroy.

Light in August, his sixth or seventh novel, combines all the faults and some of the interesting qualities of his previous books. For instance the lack of unity in the handling of diverse themes is so marked as to seem a willful misleading of the reader. The extravagant style becomes ridiculous when, as often in four hundred pages, it is applied to the commonplace. It is hardly a supple medium. Much of the violence appears to be as formal a matter as in an Elizabethan "tragedy of blood." On the other hand, when describing a situation which justifies his elaborate prose, Faulkner controls the rhetoric so that it becomes an ideal expression of his nervous intensity. And he has a rare feeling for the poetry of rural speech; he indicates, contrasts, the difference in tempo of neighboring ways of life in the South with a perception that identifies him seriously with his country.

The story opens and ends with the migrations of a young country girl in search of her seducer. Neither she nor the man, however, is a principal character of the book. The central situation is the effort of Joe Christmas—believing himself, probably rightly, to have a taint of Negro blood—to escape that influence. His wandering, uncertain, sullen life culminates in an affair with a middle-aged Northern woman. She is an eccentric spinster living in the South, the last of a family of Abolitionists, alien and hated in that environment. Of course the affair ends tragically for them both. But there are other stories, not contributing to this, or contributing in the vaguest way, told in detail, with minute explanations going back to events that occurred perhaps generations before. These threads, or rather patches, constantly interrupt the pattern.

This is a long book; to me it reduces itself in importance to those chapters dealing with the strange, inevitably shifting relation of the thwarted, masculine woman with a suspicious outcast, essentially as starved and ingrown as herself. In Faulkner it is life that is inevitable; death is a clumsy stage property, a conventional dismissal of accumulated tension. It is because he can leave his action suspended in the short story that I think him more successful with that form; the contrast between the real implications of growth and change and the bravura of his imposed finality disappears. I find in all his work this importance of the fragment, this artificiality of the whole. *Light in August* is an ambitious attempt at an imposing form. For me, its ambition is the measure of its failure.

Barry Bingham. "Faulkner Flies by Night." Louisville *Courier Journal*, November 20, 1932, Section III, p. 6.

In all adverse criticism of William Faulkner's work there is one pitfall. It is that the critic is supposed to object to such writing because of the unpleasant subjects with which Faulkner invariably deals. This reviewer sees no objection to the subject matter per se of *Light in August*. Other writers have handled material far more sordid than this, and have shaped it into the substance of art. Faulkner has managed only to produce a rambling, inchoate, and slipshod novel that cannot be redeemed by occasional patches of good writing. It is his poorest published work.

Light in August gets off to a promising start with the tale of how Lena Grove comes up from Alabama all the way to Mississippi on foot to find the man whose child she is about to bear, and whom she believes to be waiting to marry her, if she can only discover the town where he has managed to find work. Her progress along the dusty roads through the somnolent countryside, has some of the epic simplicity of good folk writing, but all too soon she reaches Jefferson, the place where her lover has come to live. As she enters the town, she sees the sky reddened by the blaze of an old mansion that has been set afire to cover up a crime. Here had lived a middle-aged white woman, whose Negro lover hacked off her head before burning up her home.

From this point the story explodes feebly in a shower of sparks. Hundreds of pages are devoted to the story of one Joe Christmas (mysteriously dubbed Lee Christmas by the writer of the jacket blurb and nearly all the reviewers). Like all Faulkner characters, he is hag-ridden by a hideous obsession, in this case the belief that he has Negro blood. The tale of his downward career forms a sort of picaresque narrative that suggests a familiar Eighteenth Century form, a comparison surely capable of making some of the masters of that period writhe in their tombs. Through a succession of episodes that possess about as much reality as Mme. Tussaud's waxwork Chamber of Horrors, Christmas blazes his way to the rape, murder and arson previously mentioned, and at long last to a violent death.

It would be entirely possible for a writer to forge a fine novel out of these materials, and Faulkner has written with occasional spurts of vividness. The capital fault of the book, however, is one which showed its head in his earlier novels; his characters are too uniformly and monotonously abnormal. A novelist cannot hope to arouse more than a casual shudder from a reader if he writes of a mad house and makes all his characters equally insane. The effect must be obtained by placing one sane character, to represent the reader, in the midst of all the maniacs. The horror of Faulkner's *Sanctuary* would have been almost unbearable if his girl, Temple, had been a person of normal sensibilities and intelligence instead of a lowgrade moron. In *Light in August* there is again the crying need for one ordinary human being to provide contrast to the nightmare creatures who flit through the pages. Only Lena Grove has a touch of normality, and is made thereby the best character that Faulkner has created, but she is rudely pushed aside from the main current of the story.

It is obvious to anyone who has read this man's work that he has a real talent for writing, but small sense of form. His prose is like the poetry of a poet who has never attempted anything but free verse. He has been criticised, and lauded, too for producing such passages as this:

> In the less than half light he appeared to be watching his body seeming to watch it turn slow and lascivious in a whispering of gutter filth like a drowned corpse in a thick still black pool of more than water.

Such writing, however one regards it, is not the weakness of his style. The fault lies rather in the sadistic torturing of the English language in which he indulges himself when he sets down such phrases as "it seemed to him that that by which and because of which he had had ancestors long enough to come himself to be, had allied itself with crime." These faults have crept up on him since he began to reap the adulation of certain sections of the public. He is often stubbornly, unbearably repetitious. He plays with inversions of narrative style that were objectionable in Conrad and intolerable in Faulkner.

He uses the device of delayed suspense so endlessly that the classic example of that stylistic trick, de Quincey's "English Mail Coach," seems like a forthright nursery jingle by comparison.

To conclude, William Faulkner writes well enough not to write so badly, if such a phrase may be excused. He is frittering away a genuine talent. It was his boast that *Sanctuary* was dashed off in three weeks, and *Light in August* bears marks of the same injudicious haste. It should have been completely revised, cut down by at least a hundred pages, and subjected to a rigid control. The writer and the novel both stand sadly in need of one prime quality: artistic discipline.

Checklist of Additional Reviews

"Frivolous Mr. Faulkner." Baltimore *Evening Sun*, October 15, 1932, p. 6.

San Francisco *News*, October 15, 1932; October 28, 1932.

"*Light in August*." *Forum*, December 1932, p. vi.

"*Light in August* Is Psychological, Physiological Book." *Lasso* (Women's State College, Denton, Texas), May 10, 1934.

Adams, John R. "Faulkner Novel, *Light in August*, Full of Thrills." San Diego *Union*, October 30, 1932, p. 7.

Ball, George. "*Light in August*, Another Faulkner tour de force." Savannah *News*, December 11, 1932, p. 5-C.

Bernd, A. B. "Thwarted Souls." Macon *Telegraph*, October 16, 1932, p. 9.

Bessie, Alvah C. "*Light in August*." *Scribner's Magazine*, December 1932, p. 6.

Brickell, Herschel. "Mr. Faulkner Advances." *North American Review*, 234 (December 1932), 571; also

reviewed as "The Fruits of Diversity," *Virginia Quarterly Review*, 9 (January 1933), 114–19.

Canby, Henry S. "The Grain of Life." *Saturday Review of Literature*, October 8, 1932, pp. 153, 156.

Cantwell, Robert. "Fiction." *New Outlook*, November 1932, p. 60.

Davis, Elrick B. "And Faulkner 'Does It Again' with *Light in August*." Cleveland *Press*, October 8, 1932, p. 5.

Dawson, Margaret Cheney. "A Rich, Sinister and Furious Novel." *New York Herald Tribune Books*, October 9, 1932, p. 3.

Dromgoole, Will Allen. "Song and Story." Nashville *Banner*, January 15, 1933, p. 6-X; and "New Books," February 5, 1933, p. 6-X.

Field, Louise M. "The Modest Novelists." *North American Review*, 235 (January 1933), 63–69.

Grimes, Nancy. "Turning New Pages." Portsmouth (Ohio) *Times*, November 6, 1932, p. 6.

Hansen, Harry. "William Faulkner's Forlorn People." New York *World-Telegram*, October 8, 1932, p. 17.

Hickerson, Donna Davis. "Madmen Stalk in Novel." Minneapolis *Journal*, November 6, 1932, Editorial Section, p. 5.

Jackson, Joseph Henry. "A Book a Day." San Francisco *Chronicle*, October 19, 1932, p. 9.

Kaiser, Flora. "Faulkner's Latest Novel Morbid, but Has Brighter Side." St. Louis *Globe-Democrat*, November 6, 1932, p. 10-B.

Meade, Everard. "A Terrific Story Marching with Violence to a Bloody End." Richmond *Times-Dispatch*, October 9, 1932, Section III, p. 5.

Nash, Alan. "Faulkner's Inhumanity to Man Softened by Touch of Sympathy." Buffalo *Times*, October 9, 1932, p. 6-C.

North, Sterling. "Magnolias, Madness and Mississippi Mud." Chicago *News*, October 5, 1932, p. 16.

Polsky, T. E. "Faulkner Hits a New Note in Latest Volume." Akron *Times-Press*, October 23, 1932, p. 3-D.

Ratliff, Walter. "*Light in August.*" Atlanta *Journal*, October 23, 1932, Magazine Section, p. 18.

Schriftgiesser, Karl. "Bright Spots Are Many among the Season's Newest Books." Boston *Evening Transcript*, November 30, 1932, Section II, p. 1.

Shelton, Wilson E. "The Bookshelf." Beverly Hills *Call-Bulletin*, December 15, 1932.

Stone, Geoffrey. "*Light in August.*" *Bookman*, 75 (November 1932), 736–38.

Swan, Addie May. "Mr. Faulkner's New Novel Shows Surer Technique." Davenport (Iowa) *Daily Times*, October 22, 1932, p. 3.

Thompson, Frederic. "American Decadence." *Commonweal*, November 30, 1932, p. 139.

Tyler, Parker. "Book Reviews." *The New Act*, No. 1 (January 1933), 36–39.

Van Doren, Dorothy. "More Light Needed." *Nation*, October 26, 1932, p. 405.

Walsh, Wilbur. "*Light in August* Is a Story of Violence." Charlotte *News*, December 11, 1932, p. 8-B.

Weeks, Edward. "*Light in August.*" *Atlantic Monthly*, January 1933, p. adv.-10.

Williams, Sidney. "Wm. Faulkner Laboring in the Deep, Dark South." Philadelphia *Inquirer*, October 8, 1932, p. 12.

Wilson, Robert H. "*Light in August.*" Chicago *Herald and Examiner*, October 8, 1932, p. 7.

A GREEN BOUGH

A GREEN BOUGH

BY WILLIAM FAULKNER

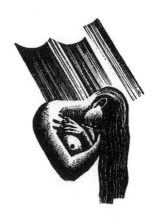

NEW YORK · NINETEEN THIRTY-THREE

HARRISON SMITH AND ROBERT HAAS

William Gorman. "William Faulkner, Poet." New York *Sun*, April 21, 1933, p. 25.

William Faulkner's new volume of poems is immediately notable for the number of experiments in imitation which it contains. Mr. Faulkner once confessed to an inquiring reporter: "Ah write when the spirit moves me, and the spirit moves me every day." It is now evident that he also reads a good deal, that he enjoys trying other people's forms.

In the first of his forty-four poems, Mr. Faulkner treats of a drawing room full of "All the Dead Pilots" in a strict "Prufrock" and "Portrait of a Lady" idiom. In the third poem he yields to the thrill of hallucination and he gets it with Hart Crane's means—a dazzling eruption of metaphors on a blank verse norm. In poem IV he writes a complete E. E. Cummings poem and throughout the volume he works in a few patented tricks (even Mr. Cummings's favorite prefix Un-). Almost any given student given the anonymous poems XI, XII, XIII, XIV, XV, would spot them as the work of A. E. Housman. This list of immediately apparent resemblances could be extended a little further.

One is not disparaging the particular poems in pointing out Mr. Faulkner's eclecticism. The poems are consistently able. But the author's eclecticism will come as a surprise to those who have been thinking of him as the powerful "original" from Mississippi. Evidently Mr. Faulkner is far less the slave to his corrosive vision of Southern Evil than the comparative consistency of his novels would indicate. In his own a little fatuously hard-boiled way, Mr. Faulkner admitted in the Modern Library Preface to his *Sanctuary* that he was something of a litterateur. This was a shock, for the country had given excited acclaim to the quick succession of novels based on a bare minimum of powerful obsessions. The present volume shows that, as Faulkner suggested, his talents are more diversified. It indicates that quite probably he can perhaps sustain himself in a long and varied "literary career"—a rare thing in America. From the evidence of this volume, that career will not be dull on the poetic side.

Generally, the material of the volume is not very directly related to the qualities of the novels. He does address some sonnets—at least one very good one, and certainly one very maudlin one—to Lilith, to "all Eves since the snake" and he writes one very amusing piece on the irony of courtship. But for the most part, Mr. Faulkner rings the changes on the tested fund of lyric themes: on the play of the elements in seasonal change, on sleep granting amnesty, on mortality, love. He proves his right to these conventions with a host of new metaphors that do them justice and with a general ease in managing quatrain and couplet forms. His only real trouble is in the sonnet form, which he uses ten times. He has not quite sensed the weight of this form; most of his sonnets, as the unsupple syntax and the difficulty of resolution reveal, are top-heavy. These are several fine short lyrics, one of them a new "watery dirge."

There is one connection between parts of the volume which it seems plausible to take as an assertion. The last lines of the first poem (dealing with the war pilots in the drawing room) read: "But I– I am not dead." The others lament: "Not dead, he's not dead, poor man; he didn't die—." The first line of the last poem (which probably yields the volume its title) reads: "If there be grief, then let it be but rain." And throughout the volume, Mr. Faulkner has praised pastoral peace:

"He finds but simple scents and sounds;
And this is all, and this is best."

He admits ecstasy before:

"the earth: his own,
Still with enormous promises of bread
And the clean smell of strength upon
    him blown."

With all this evidence any one who
wants to can make Mr. Faulkner the singer
of the Southern agrarian movement which
some two years ago issued a manifesto,
claiming the secret of salvation.

But whatever its significance for the
man, his land and its people, *A Green
Bough* with the possible exception of
Horace Gregory's second book, is the most
exciting volume of American poetry to
appear this season.

D. J.
"A Novelist's Poems."
Cincinnati *Times-Star*,
April 25, 1933, p. 16.

Not only is there a great difference between maturity of character and that of
the art production of that character but
this first published volume of poems of
William Faulkner enforces the conclusion
that maturity in one art does not automa-
tically enhance one's practice in another.
Faulkner, as a novelist, is a full-grown
artist, and although he may develop and
enlarge upon the stem he is already ripe.
These poems, published in full for the first
time in this volume, are callow.

That Faulkner is well read in English
literature is manifest from the congeries
of influences to be found throughout these
poems. There are, though rarely, specific

lines that recall almost identical ones of
other poets, but in the main it is the si-
militude in the tenor of both Faulkner's
lines and the characteristic lines of ante-
rior poets that is striking. There are, for
example, these lines from the second poem
that might have come from Tennyson:

"While music softly played
Softly flows through lily-scented gloom,
She is a flower lightly cast
Upon a river flowing, dimly going
Between two silent shores where
    willows lean,"

And again the Elizabethan line in the seventh poem:

"That, lastly, breath is to a man
But to want and fret a span."

There are others, so that one may
sketchily trace the history of English poetry from E. E. Cummings back to
Marlowe or Jonson. This is a characteristic of first poems and is significant only in
the poetic value of the poets followed.
Here there can be no complaint against
Faulkner; he chose the best of the tradition.

It would be a misapprehension of this
reviewer's intent were it to be taken that
these poems of Faulkner are worth only
adverse criticism. There is much more to
be said in praise of them than against
them. It is only to be suggested that going
to them the reader must not anticipate a
work as valid as that of his novels.

Faulkner's greatest talent, as revealed
in these poems, and one of the most fertile gifts a poet may possess, is for the
evocative and often profound metaphor
and simile: the new perception of old relations. A few of these are:

"Their voices come to us like tangled
    rooks."

"And silence like a priest on his gray
    feet
Tells his beads of minutes on beside."
"And polarised was all breath when
A girl let down her hair."

He also has a nice feeling for rhythm
and in some of the poems achieves an
almost perfect harmony between the suggestion of the content and the music of
the line, wherein the awareness, on the
part of the reader, of the technique disappears entirely.

There are minor faults to be recorded:
his touch in rhyming shows need of development as, for example, when he matches
"that'll" and "battle," and his use of the
dramatic line often tends to obscure, and
always prevents thorough unity in the
poem. But of the forty-four poems in the
volume there are a few that provoke the
exaltation of genuine poetry, and that puts
him, even in this beginning, way beyond
the common masses of poets.

Several of these poems, as evidenced by
their style and subject, were written during the World War. He was then apparently addicted to free verse, a habit which
he has fortunately abandoned.

Both in subject matter and attitude the
poems differ from Faulkner's prose, leaving the tradition of Poe which he has entered in the novels for the romantic attitude toward nature and the traditional
subjects of Life, Desire, Beauty and Death.

William Rose Benét. "Round about Parnassus: Faulkner or Poet." *Saturday Review of Literature*, 9 (April 29, 1933), 565.

A friend of mine, the other day, ventured
to say that those modern poets who ape
the more Frazerian portions of "The Waste
Land" may be said to have gone to the
Golden Bough-wows. There is, indeed, a
tendency among the more effete of our
modern metrists to cull passages from Sir
James George for the sweet uses of
adversification. But it is of another redo-
lence that I find our bleak and sinister
prosateur, Mr. William Faulkner, guilty
in his first large volume of verse, *A Green
Bough*.

The Raven bleak and Philomel
Amid the bleeding trees were fixed.
His hoarse cry and hers were mixed
And through the dark their droppings
    fell

Upon the red erupted rose,
Upon the broken branch of peach
Blurred with scented mouths, that each
To another sing, and close.

The commencement of that strain is a
whit rudely forced from Mr. Eliot. It is
certainly a far cry from "The Phoenix and
the Turtle."

Again, I turn a few pages back and
come upon

And bonny earth and bonny sky
And bonny'll be the rain
And sun among the apple trees
When I've long slept again.

Is this some Border Ballad abominably going Housman? The eminent English poet would presumably rather be murdered in his bed than commit all those "bonnys." It is over an ocean far away indeed from his Shropshire that they lie!

There are other signs on other pages that, as is perhaps natural in a young and sensitive poet, the nostalgic accent of the English Heine has stolen upon Mr. Faulkner unaware.

Again, the e-e-cummings typographical arrangement takes his fancy:

for a moment an œ on i pause plunging
above the narrow precipice of thy breast

and so on. There is an even worse apostrophe to lower-case cynthia, speaking of lower-case abelard and paris also lower-case that worms may, in the poet's own term, eviscerate for all of me.

"Lilith she is dead and safely tombed," he says in another place. Would she were! The trouble is that Philomel and Atthis and Cynthia and Paris and Lilith, and others, are all here again. Greetings, boys and girls! There is also the sonnet of the weary mouth and "pallid sly Still riddle of thy secret face" which really belongs back in the P.R.B. play-box of Rossetti and Swinburne.

Such things are strange in a writer whose impress upon prose is so individual. I had read in a newspaper review a callow affirmation that Faulkner's is the most important book of poetry of the season. But how is that possible?

The tendency among young reviewers is to become uncritical of any writer who has saliently achieved, and to gobble him whole. But that is assuredly to do him a disservice. Mr. Faulkner is an apt pupil in his poetry, choosing the most approved modern influences, but he can scarcely be said to have absorbed them.

The beginning of this book is the best, the broken conversation of the war-flier whose mind has been fatally injured and who lives in death—best of all, the chaos of his mind in the firelight, regarding a lady. The latter passage is vivid, strong, has something of the identity of Faulkner's prose, as he usually in his prose deals most convincingly with borderland cases.

Section III is good also, till IV goes e-e-cummings and V becomes wooden, and VI clumsily epigrammatic, and the Housman influence begins to assume proportions. It is too bad. Faulkner has something to say of Man the ploughman and youth first tasting love, but the voice is only intermittently his own. XVI—though now we are wary—seems better; but then follows the "o atthis" already referred to. XVIII, a youth's reverie on a hill, ends with a sudden and unexpected "chose vue." We almost exclaim at

And say the fleeing canyons of the sky
Tilt to banshee wire and slanted aileron,
And his own shape on scudding walls
Where harp the caseless thunders of the
    sun.

The first three lines of that are excellent, the last merely empty rhetoric of an old make. XIX gives us hauntingly the music of water. XX has a fine simplicity. Four poems later on comes a poignant fragment, as from the Greek. But the good and the bad are so mixed! There is no certain selection at work. Even in the last line of XXXV, "An old sorrow sharp as woodsmoke on the air," though one acknowledges a palpable hit, one cannot admit that a poem on the death of a courtesan, in such mood and cadence, is anything at all unusual. The dislocations of XXXVI, with the comparison of the wind to a leaping stallion, bring vaguely to mind Hart Crane. The poem is quite a tour de force. And in XL reappears a certain strange troubadour incarnation of

102

Faulkner's. His publishers quote from the next, about the lady whose breast is green by reason of the sun through leaves of apple trees. It is a pretty, pagan picture of old time, phrased with rather more precision than usual. But that is all. The lively eroticism of XLIII is more original. And yet it is pretty cheap.

A most mixed exhibit! I have tried not to be hypercritical. It is taken for granted that Mr. Faulkner is no mere gifted amateur as a writer of prose—and yet that is just what he seems when it comes to poetry. He does not truly know his way about. His hand is still prentice. He almost seems to be precocious, peculiarly enough, rather than accomplished. There are gleams. There should be. But where is the impressively original and strikingly integrated personality? Not in this book.

Checklist of Additional Reviews

"Famous Novelist Turns to Verse." Washington *Daily News*, April 22, 1933, p. 11.

"Faulkner as Poet." Macon *Telegraph*, April 30, 1933, p. 9.

"*A Green Bough.*" *Nation*, May 17, 1933, p. 565.

"*A Green Bough.*" Dayton *Daily News*, May 19, 1933, p. 26.

"Poems by William Faulkner." Boston *Evening Transcript*, July 15, 1933, p. 3.

Deutsch, Babette. "Poetry Out of Chaos." *Virginia Quarterly Review*, 9 (October 1933), 620–25.

Jack, Peter Monro. "Nature and Love Are Faulkner's Poetic Themes." *New York Times Book Review*, May 14, 1933, p. 2.

M., C. "'The Sun Lies upon the Hills. . . .'" *Sunday Florida Times-Union* (Jacksonville), May 7, 1933, p. 17.

Robinson, Ted. "Poems for That Spring Mood." Cleveland *Plain Dealer*, April 23, 1933, Amusement Section, p. 12.

Schappes, Morris U. "Faulkner as Poet." *Poetry: A Magazine of Verse*, 43 (October 1933), 48–52.

Walton, Eda Lou. "Faulkner's First Book of Verse." *New York Herald Tribune Books*, April 30, 1933, p. 2.

DOCTOR MARTINO AND OTHER STORIES

DOCTOR MARTINO

and other stories

by William Faulkner

NEW YORK · MCMXXXIV

HARRISON SMITH AND ROBERT HAAS

Peter Monro Jack. "William Faulkner Presents a Mixed Sheaf of Short Stories." New York *Sun*, April 16, 1934, p. 22.

William Faulkner's new collection *Doctor Martino and Other Stories*, representing about half of the stories he has written since *These Thirteen* was published two and a half years ago, is a familiar compound. The bulk and the best, that is to say, is familiar; the new direction that his story telling talent seems at the moment to be taking is not promising.

There is a good story of the end of the Civil War, a better story of the Great War, a brief addition to the Sartoris saga, two post-war airplane stories, four stories of Carolina or Mississippi mental or physical cruelty involving violence, rape and killing, an exciting detective yarn, and three fantasies of the kind Mr. Faulkner is becoming increasingly and some of us are becoming decreasingly fond of. These last include "Black Music" and "Leg," appearing here for the first time and persumably newly written.

The merit of his novels and stories, I think, has been to plunge from some sort of recognizable outward reality into the fatal mystery of the motives of human conduct. Sometimes the mystery is impenetrable, as in *The Sound and the Fury*, or complicated, as in *As I Lay Dying* or exhaustive, as in *Light in August*; occasionally no more than effective melodrama, as in *Sanctuary*, or in the story "A Rose for Emily."

To reverse the process, and try to make a fact out of a mystery, produces more common place work than I had thought Mr. Faulkner capable of. "Beyond"—in this collection—is Mr. Faulkner's characters in Robert Nathan's "There Is Another Heaven" and not so credible. "Black Music" reminds me of Saki's "Music on the Hill," and though I have never liked Saki's story, I like it better than Mr. Faulkner's evocation of a faun. The mere fact that he reminds you of other writers in these stories is unlike Mr. Faulkner, and to his disadvantage.

"Turn About" is a grand story of the war which was made into a movie, the story of an English "sissy," as the Americans suppose, being taken up for the first time in an airplane, and then inviting the American captain out in the English torpedo boat and scaring the life almost out of him. I have not seen the movie, but I must, if only to see where the Englishman gets his other hand in this episode when he was very drunk:

> "The English boy made an effort then. He pulled himself together, focusing his eyes. He swayed, throwing his arms about the policeman's neck, and with the other hand he saluted . . .!"

The Carolina stories are as good as ever, splitting up into a nice dialogue (from "Fox Hunt").

> "So now the old dame digs up about this boy, this Allen boy that the gal . . ."
> "I thought you said his name was Yale," the chauffeur said.
> "No. Allen. Yale is where he went to this college."
> "You mean Columbia."
> "No. Yale. It's another college."
> "I thought the other one was named Cornell or something," the chauffeur said.
> "No. It's another one. Where these

college boys all come from when these hotchachacha deadfalls get raided, and they give them all a ride downtown in the wagon. Don't you read no papers?"

"Not often," the chauffeur said. "I don't care nothing about politics."

This bright conversation is set against the slow garrulousness of the Negro stable boys: the one is done as well as the other.

The Southern stories and the airplane stories are as good as Faulkner can make them, which is better than most, and "Death Drag" and "Mountain Victory" and perhaps "Smoke" will have to be read by everyone who reads Faulkner. "Doctor Martino," the title story, may be skipped. It is a mildly interesting exercise in the occult, suggesting the manner of Scott Fitzgerald—but whenever I find Faulkner behaving like another writer I have lost interest in him. I prefer him to stick to his last.

William Rose Benét. "Fourteen Faulkner Stories." *Saturday Review of Literature*, 10 (April 21, 1934), 645.

It hardly needs to be said that William Faulkner is a "natural-born" writer. His stories are never according to any formula, they evolve out of his own unusual temperament. Some are better than others, but none is a prostitution of his natural gifts. In this book he appears to have enlarged his range. His command of the eerie and sinister is well known, but it develops that he can also be sardonically humorous in a high degree. Perhaps this might have been foreseen in an early novel of his, and probably his worst, *Mosquitoes* in which he created a certain dumbbell feminine character that I still remember. Of course, he can write with strong impact in his climaxes. You have only to read the last paragraph of "Leg," one of his very latest stories, in this volume.

"I told him to find it and kill it. The dawn was cold, on these mornings the butt of the leg felt as though it were made of ice. I told him to. I told him."

That is writing, I am sure, that the late Stephen Crane would greatly have admired; and it is absolutely and meticulously right for this particular story.

There are fourteen short tales. *Harper's*, *Scribner's* and *Story* have published the greater part of the collection. "Turnabout," which appeared in the *Saturday Evening Post*, was made into a talking picture. Two stories appear for the first time in this volume. In general the merit of the stories seems to me unusual. "Elly" I had been impressed with before. "Mountain Victory" is my favorite of them all. "There Was a Queen" almost comes next except for its not quite carrying conviction to me in regard to the daughter-in-law's final and crucial action concerning the letters. This action "makes" the whole story; and still, I don't quite believe it. But the character of the old lady is superbly drawn. "Fox Hunt" and "The Hound" are both good stories, which I have read before in magazines. "Doctor Martino" was new to me, subtle and interesting, but somehow minor for Faulkner. In "Death Drag" he deals in grim humor that is most effective. "Honor" is another story that involves flying. So far as I can tell, his fliers are the real thing, they sound authentic. This flying is of peace-time, but

"Turnabout," of course, was a story of the late war. It seemed to me, though an excellent yarn of its kind, to be, strangely enough, influenced somewhat by Kipling's method, even by Kipling's peculiar humor. "Wash" is fundamentally pure melodrama; "Beyond" an only half-successful treatment of the persistence—brief as it may be—of individuality after death; "Black Music" and "Leg" a couple of startling fantasies, the former possessing no inconsiderable humor. Altogether I found the collection much above the average run of books and short stories, as it should be. There is plenty of variety.

It is a peculiar circumstance that what seem to me the best two stories in the book, "Mountain Victory" and "Elly," involve men suspected of being negroes. We do not know the truth about Paul de Montigny of Louisiana, save that white or colored, he became involved with a girl whose environment impelled her into a passionate and murderous neurosis. On the other hand, Saucier Weddel is a noble, not an ignoble character, descendant of a French emigre and a Choctaw woman. Which brings me back to "Mountain Victory," a story in which all the characters, including the negro servant, are extraordinarily well drawn. The infatuation of the young girl, the pathetic quixotism of the young brother; the hatred of the elder brother and the woodenness of the father; the loyalty and childishness and inebriety of the negro; and the impressive fineness of Weddel, the Southern officer; all these qualities emerge in the most natural and absorbing of narratives through an intensely sinister atmosphere, the creation of which is the prime gift of William Faulkner. He is unsparing in presenting the tragedies of life. One might say that the darker they are, the more he is drawn to them. But in this particular story, blind fury is confronted by several kinds of heroism; which does not prevent the brave characters from being blotted out, but is not that exclusive parade of various types of ignobility to which a good deal of Faulkner's former work has accustomed us. In the character of Wash Jones, in the story "Wash," we also have dumb fealty assuming proportions of the heroic in the role of avenger; though as I have said before, this story seems to me rather a melodramatic "set-up."

I do not wish to wax sentimental in regard to so engrossing a story as "Mountain Victory." For it is the sort of Civil War tale that the late Ambrose Bierce, surely saturnine enough, would have respected. In closing, I see that I have neglected to comment on "Smoke," Faulkner's nearest approach to a detective story; on the whole well handled though somewhat amorphous.

Possibly the best of these narratives does not quite touch the best of the stories in *These Thirteen*, Faulkner's former book of short flights. But that must remain a matter of opinion. What I am sure of is that this writer is genuinely credentialled, in the short story as in the novel. In the more compact medium he is doing some of the most powerful and original work that America can claim in our time.

Monte Cooper. "Faulkner's New Book." Memphis *Commercial Appeal*, April 22, 1934, Magazine Section, p. 14.

These fourteen sharp, often staccato and sometimes brittle stories deal with many characters, a large percentage of them old or ageing persons, that are shown to the reader by action and conversation and only rarely by analysis, and that usually from the lips of another character in the story.

The scene of most of the stories is northern Mississippi that the author has used often before, and that he knows so well. "Turn About," however, is a tale of British and American men in a French seaport during the World War; and "Beyond" is an interesting excursion into life immediately after death, with an erstwhile judge searching for his little boy who had died at the age of 10, and giving up his quest because bereavement has made him what he is, and to find the child again would nullify the experience that has made him his own. Two of the stories are about barnstorming aviators, and "Death Drag" presents a remarkable and objective picture of a merchant named Ginsfarb, turned stunter, and displaying undaunted and unconscious courage because of greed for money.

"Doctor Martino," the title story, is, to this writer, one of the least successful of the book. Whether the fat physician, sitting all day, each year during the season, on a bench at the Mississippi spa, and dominating the life of a young girl, is a good or an evil influence, a I could not decide. And whether her mother, who, through trickery, breaks the spell and delivers the girl to marriage with her rich Yale suitor, is her savior or an old devil, I do not know. The story doesn't quite come off.

Very different is "The Hound," a story of a murder by a poor white of a man he has always known and against whom he has a grievance. This is a very powerful study of crime, and the atmosphere is especially authentic.

In "There Was Once a Queen" three women are portrayed: an old aristocrat, her negro servant, and her grand niece-in-law. The old lady is the heroine of the piece. Like Dr. Martino she just sits—in a wheel chair by a window; but there is no doubt of her essential quality. Nor is the character of the niece-in-law ambiguous.

Mr. Faulkner seems in these short stories to have considered with more care than he has in some of his novels the use of words. There are fewer distorted and intrusive images. At his best, his descriptive passages are very effective. Like Stribling he has observed how legal proceedings dominate the life of a small southern town; and in some of these stories lawyers and judges and sheriffs and grand juries play a relevant though not obtrusive part.

Louis Kronenberger. "Mr. Faulkner's Short Stories and Other Recent Fiction." *New York Times Book Review*, April 22, 1934, p. 9.

Mr. Faulkner's second book of short stories is by no means as good as his first was, nor good enough to add anything at all to his reputation. It will, if anything, detract from it. For the Faulkner who showed great promise in *Soldiers' Pay* and gave so good a performance in *As I Lay Dying* has abdicated here in favor of a rather hurried virtuoso with a bag of tricks. The virtuoso has had many bows before, and the tricks are by no means new ones. But in the past there has always been some touch of quality to go with them; there has always been something, no matter how disappointing the occasion, to inspire the reader with the feeling that at bottom Faulkner had a very special talent. To judge by the present book, it would seem that it may have been only a very special talent for highfalutin theatricality.

It is perhaps a little unfair to Mr. Faulkner that he should publish a book so undistinguished as this one just at the moment when many readers have already asked themselves why his work has gained so little in depth and toughness and meaning. It was easy to see that his earlier work needed discipline and direction; but it was impossible not to see how much imagination it revealed, how much personality and vividness. One excused Mr. Faulkner for overwriting and for writing unintelligibly because on occasion he wrote with such true power. One granted him his own special and singular world because it was anything but a dead world, and could be expected to produce lifesize and memorable creation. One did not grudge him his oddness because in it one saw a reflection of his independence. Many people, indeed, praised Mr. Faulkner chiefly for his differences.

But, granting that he has done some remarkable things in the past, certainly none of them is remarkable enough to live beyond its own generation, and certainly since *As I Lay Dying* there has been nothing so good as that book. *Dr. Martino*, made up as it is of magazine stories, should doubtless not be taken too seriously in itself. But it cannot be dismissed either; there is too much of Faulkner's method and manner. And the reader finds himself uneasy among them.

The effect aimed at in the bulk of these tales is something that, for want of a more inclusive name, must be called horror. It may be physical, it may be mental, it may be mystic. Sometimes it derives from fear, sometimes from uncanniness; at any rate it seldom has much humanity in it, and it plays upon our nerves and senses rather than our emotions. We feel no pity for Mr. Faulkner's characters, we distinctly do not identify ourselves with them, and we are not native to their world. We are not asked in many cases even to believe in them beyond their ability to achieve an effect for us. Such stories, obviously, must be judged by special standards; they are works of incantation, not of expression. In "Dr. Martino," however, no spell is worked and the result seems like flap doodle. In "Fox Hunt" a spell is partly worked, we are momentarily impressed, a little baffled, and ultimately indifferent. In "Beyond" incantation is somewhat shoved aside in favor of a sister-form fantasy; but fantasy fails to bear good fruit. In "Leg" (which the publishers say was "recently completed" but which is an old story by Mr. Faulkner) there are touches of macabre power, but the story is not intense enough to be horrible. The sardonic irony of "Death Drag" does produce an effect, even a moral effect, and it is in consequence one of the few stories in the book worth any serious attention. Quite the best of all the stories is "The Hound," a perfectly straightforward narrative of fear with a haunting atmosphere. In that story Mr. Faulkner uses a situation cleanly, with powerful effect.

For the most part Mr. Faulkner dresses up his stories in fancy and theatrical costumes. They go gliding about on the verge of the incommunicable; they end on high shrill notes of death and disaster; they pant through swamps of verbiage. At their worst they yield to a kind of bathos: a mere magazine story like "Smoke," for example, would never be more than crude entertainment, but at least in the hands of a straight magazine writer it would be slickly and swiftly told; Mr. Faulkner has puffed it up and made it pompous.

Here, where the Faulkner method and manner are pretty much in a state of collapse, we see him at his worst; but we do get a sense of just how much that method and manner are worth in themselves, even when they are functioning perfectly. They can have, on occasion, a very great baroque power, and they can create a universe which has vividness if not dimensions. They can saturate us with shocks and put all our senses on edge. They can even give us a temporary way of looking at life. But the bizarre writer, in whom there is imagination without vision and life without reality, is a phenomenon of every age whose hold on posterity varies according to his gifts of style, and subject-matter, and story-telling. He may fade out like the writers of the Gothic romances, or like the Mary Shelleys and the Peacocks. He may linger on, like the Poes; he may occasionally survive as a great eccentric, like the Sir Thomas Brownes. But the writers who at times seem to resemble him but actually see far beyond him—the Baudelaires, the Emily Brontës, the Dostoievskys—are in a different world.

Philip Blair Rice. "The Art of William Faulkner." *Nation*, April 25, 1934, p. 479.

Although Mr. Faulkner is on a number of counts the most interesting contemporary American writer of fiction, there is good ground for doubting that he is on his way to becoming quite first-rate as a novelist. All his readers agree that he can tell a story and that his use of language is dazzling; the general public buy his novels also because he gives them shivers and satiates their prurience; while the aestheticians are fascinated by his experiments in form. He is perhaps the only American whose achievement in this latter respect is at all comparable with that of Joyce, Mann, or Mrs. Woolf. After their several fashions, these writers have brought the novel closer to poetry, which in turn has aspired to the condition of the even more formal arts of music and paint-

ing. It is likely that the novel can no longer be the amorphous and pedestrian affair that it has been too often in the past, but there is also reason to believe that its matter will continue to be no less important than the manner. Mann and Joyce are bulky at least partly because they have something of consequence to say, while Mrs. Woolf's work appears slighter and Faulkner's tangential because their virtues reside almost wholly in the saying.

If Faulkner as a novelist is something of an eccentric, he is nevertheless quite in the main tradition of the short story. One hesitates to mention a novel of his in the same breath with *Tom Jones*, *War and Peace*, *The Brothers Karamazov*, or *The Magic Mountain*, but he seems the legitimate heir of Poe, Maupassant, Bierce, and Gorki. It is not only that the short story is largely a feat of craftsmanship: Faulkner's violent and morbid subject matter is better suited to the briefer type of fiction. In the short story a kick is obligatory; a few cocktails in the hour before dinner are in order, though one soon becomes groggy in the attempt to make an evening of them.

Faulkner's principal structural device, likewise, is more adequate to the short story than to the novel. It has been remarked that for all the abundance of action in his writings most of Faulkner's characters are static. The interest lies in the gradual revelation of character and of situation rather than in their development. When, toward the end of *Sanctuary*, the reader at last finds out what happened in the barn and is the matter with Popeye, he may very easily conclude that it was not worth all the mystification and the bother. This method, however, with the jolt of realization on the last page is an admirable device of economy in the short story, and it supplies the structure of many of the best tales in the present volume. "Turn About," a war story, builds up to discovery by an American aviator that a childish appearing English midshipman who goes about playing beaver with his captain is really engaged in operating a particularly dangerous kind of torpedo boat. In "Dr. Martino" a college man slowly comes to understand the Svengali-like spell that an elderly physician with heart trouble has over his fiancee. (The story, however, does not end here, but is forced on to a conventional melodramatic conclusion.) "Death Drag" reveals the preternatural stinginess of a Jew who risks his life daily by a leap from an airplane.

The device is, in fact, closely akin to the stock in trade of the detective author; and in "Smoke," Mr. Faulkner has written a perfectly orthodox, although superior, mystery story, with the classical list of suspects and the trick of the lawyer-detective to catch the murderer at the end. "The Hound," too, would not seem out of place in Miss Sayers's next *Omnibus of Crime.* Although Faulkner has gained renown almost exclusively for his blood and thunder, there are passages of humor here and there which are more than sardonic, which are almost cleansing. There is also not infrequently an authentic note of tenderness and wistfulness. It would be hard to surpass the deft portrayal, in "Fox Hunt," of the glamor which an utterly lost lady has for the poor white boy ("She's got her hair down. It looks like the sun on a spring branch"), and his inarticulate grief at the end upon learning that she can cry; or the glimpse of the great world that the Confederate major brings to the Tennessee mountain youth and his sister in Mountain Valley. Such touches, romantic and slightly sentimental as they are, testify to a side of Faulkner which is capable of development—into something less fragile.

His ventures into the realm of ideas, on the other hand, are rather distressing. There is the confused and pointless essay in eschatology entitled "Beyond," and the gratuitous conclusion of "Turn About,"

where one comes upon this thought which is placed in the mind of the aviator who hurls his plant with its two remaining bombs, at the chateau which serves as enemy headquarters: "God! God! If they were all there—all the generals, the admirals, the presidents, and the kings—theirs, ours—all of them." This morsel of social philosophy, crude and trite enough in itself, has not been in any way prepared for in the story, which is a plain tale of personal courage. Perhaps it is as well that Faulkner generally leaves ideas alone and sticks to the craft of story telling, in which he is unexcelled.

Frances Dawson.
"William Faulkner's New Short Stories in Different Vein."
St. Louis *Globe-Democrat*, May 12, 1934, p. 13-A.

Now that Mr. Faulkner has got a firm hold on his public, he is proceeding to give them what he likes and making them like it. For an audience which has been brought up on the sensual antics of morons, this sudden swinging over to more usual and less exciting fields may not be acceptable. He is setting out, however, to please himself and there is virtue in the decision.

He is the lone minstrel of the South who sings of forgotten grandeur. His tales of the fag ends of aristocracy are invested with unbelievable irony. The grimmer tales of poor white and caste, the puny race of mental and moral weaklings, all these find place in his pages. He works purely by suggestion, which often gives way to complete mysticism, and with touches of madness which by cumulative force become over-powering.

The outstanding story is "Mountain Victory," in which a Southern soldier and his negro servant returning from the war, fall among some mountain morons and are slain. This story has a stark outline of light and shade and a terrific climax. For a study in the psychology of a murderer there is "The Hound" which is a bit grisly in detail and turns on a strange sort of comedy relief. "Leg" is pathology, shell shock, or what you will. The title story is laid partially in St. Louis, but few natives will recognize the locale. Dr. Martino, its main character, is a mystic who dies when the power that he has over a young girl is broken. "Turnabout" and "Honor," which deal with post-war flying are lightly and nonchalantly written.

None of the characters is particularly outstanding. He handles his Negroes rather felicitously, but the men are grim, gaunt and hard bitten, and the women stolid or extraordinarily earthy.

Muriel Rukeyser. "The Virtuosity of William Faulkner." *New Masses*, May 22, 1934, p. 27.

William Faulkner has given us, in his second book of short stories, a collection of tense and single-minded people, living through events which are strange equations: passionless, accounted for in fact but not in meaning. The stories are remote and hard—the characters move against a hot and insidious Mississippi,

the Civil War, the World War, and remain half-people, touching no others, being touched by nothing. In the title-story, the main force is the influence of a doctor precariously near to death of heart disease, who pushes a young girl to rashness and bravery of a sort, feeding on her youth—but the girl, her lover, and the doctor are hardly connected in the relationship. In "Turn About" into which Miriam Hopkins was inserted to make the formula of a Hollywood movie, the men's reaction to waste and danger and war is violent and from the stomach alone. In "Elly" and "Death Drag," lust and danger are casual factors. Others range from fantasies of afterlife to a straight detective story.

These pieces are terse and ingenious; they might be vehicles for something of more account than unconcern. They are valuable for encounters and backgrounds; Southern society, now disintegrate, and yesterday sore with the defeat and pride and poverty engendered by the Civil War, is here. The share-cropper Wash—the decayed lady of "There Was a Queen"—the horror of "The Hound," while Cotton tried to remove the body from the treetrunk in one piece—the elements are here. Cause matches effect, everything is traced. But the sum lacks importance. There is a lack of emotional documentation. This work is apt and deft; it is not memorable, for the characters have no purpose nor passion, and the writer cares too little about his symbols to leave any mark of feeling in the reader's mind.

Much more could be done with this observation and the material that has gone into the stories. As they are, it is the deftness that is impressive; the maneuvering of situation rather than the internal motion coming out of the story itself. Because of his gift for manipulation and disinterest, Faulkner falls into the lists of precious writers. Less erudite than the academic authors concentrating on a society they would never remake, he nevertheless is in a position parallel to those writers of vignettes of the macabre who portray a civilization without explaining it. It is his merit that he is not didactic, that he has never pushed a point; but if a writer omits the earnestness of preaching, he must compensate with other values. The choice is left to him to drive his characters implacably by outside forces, or to dignify them, giving them enough consciousness to make meanings in their lives. Faulkner does neither.

The novels demonstrate his faults and strong points magnified. In works like *Light in August* and *Sanctuary*, observation is more important, the social backgrounds can be fully drawn, and the coldness piles up, setting horror upon horror, mathematically. But these are penny-dreadful virtues. If Faulkner is to assume the proportions his work still shadows, this dexterity—the skill of suspense, of deliberate characterization, and hinted interpretation—must be reinforced with the emotional sophistication which he now lacks, and which is the hallmark of literary maturity. Then his work will be what he is ambitious for it now to seem, having the living dimensions of the society he draws.

Checklist of Additional Reviews

"Tales Center around Title." Cincinnati *Enquirer*.
"*Doctor Martino*." *Newsweek*, April 21, 1934, p. 36.
"Another Batch of Faulkner Stories." Raleigh *News and Observer*, April 22, 1934, p. 5-M.

Dayton, *News*, April 27, 1934.
Danville (Ill., *Commercial News*, May 6, 1934.
"What's New in Fiction?" Pittsburgh *Press*, May 13, 1934, Society Section, p. 8.
"*Dr. Martino*." Boston *Evening Transcript*, June 30, 1934, p. 2.
"*Dr. Martino*." Birmingham *News*, June 24, 1934, Magazine Section, p. 3.
"*Dr. Martino*." Atlanta *Constitution*, September 9, 1934, p. 2-K.
Allan, W. "Faulkner Stories in New Volume Highly Praised." *Wisconsin State Journal* (Madison), July 22, 1934, p. 4.
Brickell, Herschel. "Others of Less Moment." *North American Review*, 237 (June 1934), 570.
Butcher, Fanny. "*Dr. Martino* Faulkner's Best in Short Story." Chicago *Daily Tribune*, April 21, 1934, p. 17.
Chamberlain, John. "Books of the Times." New York *Times*, April 16, 1934, p. 15.
E., D. K. "Some Clever Stories." Los Angeles *Times*, May 13, 1934, Section II, p. 7.
Fadiman, Clifton. "Fourteen Post-Gothic Tales." *New Yorker*, April 21, 1934, pp. 105–106.
Marsh, Fred T. "A Miscellany of Faulkner Stories." *New York Herald Tribune Books*, April 15, 1934, p. 7.
Matthews, T. S. "Rackety Jackets." *New Republic*, May 23, 1934, p. 51.
Patterson, Alicia. "Fourteen Horror Stories by Faulkner." New York *Sunday News*, April 22, 1934, p. 65.
Robinson, Ted. "Short Stories, Memoirs and an Unusual Travel Volume on Week's Reading List." Cleveland *Plain Dealer*, April 22, 1934, Amusement Section, p. 17.
S., D. "Vague Scenes in an Ominous World." Louisville *Courier Journal*,

May 6, 1934, Section III, p. 9.

Stevens, Marion Shutts. "A Crisis in Several Lives." Miami *Herald*, April 29, 1934, p. 31.

Walley, Harold R. "The Book Worm's Turn." *Ohio State Journal* (Columbus), July 25, 1934, p. 5.

PYLON

PYLON

By WILLIAM FAULKNER

1935 · HARRISON SMITH AND
ROBERT HAAS, INC · NEW YORK

A. B. Bernd. "Today's Book." Macon *Telegraph*, March 23, 1935.

More than ever, William Faulkner now writes like a man in a nightmare. To the tortured technique of story-telling which he developed to a high degree of obscurity in *Sanctuary*, he now adds the fantastic stylistic idiom of James Joyce. Into this idiom Mr. Faulkner has occasionally lapsed in the past; but never for such sustained passages as in this newest novel of his, nor quite so forthrightly.

Warning you in advance that this passage is descriptive of New Orleans streets in early morning hours during the Mardi Gras celebration, I give you a single sample culled from numerous opportunities, and ask if it [is] capable of evoking pictures in your mind:

"The scabby hoppoles which elevated the ragged palmcrests like the monstrous broomsage out of an old country thought, the spent stage of last night's clatterfalque Nilebarge supine now beneath today's white wings treading, the hyrdantgouts gutterplaited with the trodden tinseldung of stars."

This is impressionistic writing which gives a strange eerie quality to the narrative. Combined with the chronological distortions and evasive suggestions of incident that are part of the Faulkner method, it can make a commonplace tale seem other-worldly, unreal, some strange excursion of the subconscious or the alcohol-saturated mind.

Now, all this undoubtedly sounds derogatory,—and therefore is far from my intention. William Faulkner has written a magnificent book, a story that achieves much of its excellence from the very artificialities (literally legitimate or not) which I have tried to describe. The tale, throbbing, exciting, is there; the persons who make it, though all suffused with the very nightmare-quality which pervades the entire book, are living, sentient, predictable human beings. The obscurities of style and technique are not so frequent as to make unintelligible this chronicle of a handful of men and women in the midst of one of the saturnalias characteristic of our own time and place.

Mr. Faulkner has chosen to disguise New Orleans under the name of New Valois, Franciana. To the dedication of its new airport came, among others, Roger Shumann and Jack Holmes, pilot and parachute jumper, together with the woman they share and the child who is the son of one. A newspaper reporter, a gangling, moony fellow of nondescript origins, falls in with them and their mechanic Jiggs. At first the odd relationships of the group interest him; then the woman herself.

Involuntarily he plays King David to Shumann's Uriah. When the pilot's plane is damaged in a forced landing, the reporter urges the use of a borrowed machine, an unmanageable, admittedly dangerous contraption. Did the woman suspect the reporter's purpose in thus sending her husband to his death. The scrupulously objective Mr. Faulkner declines to answer. But the modern Bathsheba, a curse upon her lips, turns from him. This at least is plain: By the time the accident occurs the reader is sufficiently well acquainted with the reporter to know that he had acted innocently and in good faith.

The absorbing psychological perplexities of this tale Mr. Faulkner sets against the vivid background of the airport. The feel of the place, the impetuous speed-mad beings who are pioneers of our current frontier, the air—these make *Pylon* a breathless adventure in reading.

John Crowe Ransom. "Faulkner, South's Most Brilliant but Wayward Talent, Is Spent." Nashville *Banner*, March 24, 1935, p. 8.

It is painful to be disappointed by a young artist on whom you have counted.

Much the most brilliant of the creative talents in the South has been, by common consent, William Faulkner of Oxford, Miss. But we have known also that he was the most wayward. After *The Sound and the Fury* came *Sanctuary* and after *As I Lay Dying* there was a let-down in *Light in August*. His followers have had to admire him extravagantly for one book and take back their praises when the next appeared. But now comes *Pylon* and it is such a bad book that it seems to mark the end of William Faulkner. I do not refer to moral badness, either, for novels are not primarily moral or immoral; it is his artistic conscience that Faulkner has worn out.

Pylon is about a group of aviators— stunt fliers who make a poor living by performing at third-rate air meets. They are a hard lot but fearless. They neither talk nor think; they just fly; all through the book they are held at arm's length from us as if they were a mystery. The admiration which Faulkner feels for them is the same admiration that the boys in the poolroom have for public characters who are strong, silent, and vicious. Faulkner has never quite outgrown being one of those boys, but he likes to be a good deal more at the same time.

The scene is both mean and gaudy. A Southern city with a Latin quarter is celebrating the opening of its airport. There is a carnival atmosphere, with confetti, streamers, drunks, crowds, uproar; but the aviators pass through it all on their way between the air, where they really live, and the cheap hotels in which they barely exist.

The group consists in the pilot, the parachute jumper, the pilot's wife, the child (who is either the pilot's or the jumper's), and the mechanic. They compose a menage which is remarkable in many ways but not virtuous.

The action alternates between the flying business and the "domestic" life. In the end, the pilot crashes, trying to win a race with a condemned ship; the group moves along and the story is over. Newspaper men are talking about the accident. One says, "What do you suppose his wife was thinking about?" Another replies, "That's easy; she was thinking, 'Thank God I carry a spare.'"

These are the materials of Faulkner's new book; they are hopeless. He has found his tragedies in the dirt before now, but it has usually been country dirt, and the characters had some depth and human dignity; they were characters into whom a big novelist could enter and through whom he could express himself. In the present situation it is impossible for a sensitive novelist to stick to his subject and still be himself. Almost mandatory upon him, I should think, is the obligation to furnish his heroes with pretty much his own mentality, for there is no other way in which he can employ it.

Faulkner does make a half-hearted motion towards enthusiasm. He creates an eccentric newspaper reporter as his special narrator. The reporter is so taken with the fliers that he follows them like a dog, gives them of his scanty funds, takes them into his apartment, and cannot get enough of their company. But he is a limited fellow; Faulkner is not in him either.

In the end Faulkner is driven to fall back upon descriptive writing in order to express himself. It is frenzied and bad; the wildest prose he has ever written, with the possible exception of the monologue of the idiot boy in *The Sound and the Fury*, where there was some excuse for it. The excitement here is disproportionate to the occasion. The descriptions are not so much written as overwritten; they are a variety of poetry, not prose at all, and in fact they are a variety of the later writing of James Joyce, whose copyright few other novelists have thought it worth their while to infringe.

I quote from a passage describing a mere street scene:

"There was confetti here too, and broken serpentine, in neat narrow swept windows against wallangies and lightly vulcanised along the gutterrims by the flushing fireplugs of the past dawn, while upcaught and pinned by the cryptic significant shields to doorfront and lamppost, the purple-and-gold bunting looped unbroken as a trolley wire above his head as he walked. It turned at last at right angles to cross the street itself and meet the bunting on the opposite side marking its angle too, joining over the center of the street as though to form an airial and bottomless regalcolored cattlechute suspended at first floor level above the earth, and suspending beneath itself in turn the outward-facing cheese-clothlettered interdiction which Jiggs, passing, slowed looking back to read: 'Grandieu Street Closed to Traffic 8 p.m.– Midnight.'"

The most remarkable thing about this writing is that it is alien to the mind of any character in *Pylon*. This writing is Faulkner himself; a novelist designing so badly that, in order to have any part in his own story, he has to abandon his shabby characters and introduce a patch of very purple poetry. In this one act he violates so many canons of the novel that I think it is time to conclude: William Faulkner is spent.

Ted Robinson. "Faulkner Pens Mighty Tales of Flyers Who Are Gods in the Air, Pigs on Ground." Cleveland *Plain Dealer*, March 24, 1935, Magazine and Amusement Section, p. 15.

A new novel by William Faulkner must be regarded as the outstanding literary event of the week in which it is published. It would be so even were the novel a disappointment—and *Pylon*, published tomorrow by Harrison Smith & Robert Haas, Inc., is, let me hasten to remark, no disappointment to me. It is another inexplicably remarkable Faulkner masterpiece of characterization and atmosphere. It is bitter and sordid and somewhat true to the nature of things in the lives of the apparently futile people with whom it is concerned.

These people are an aviator who goes bad doing stunt flying at carnivals, a parachute jumper, a rather brutally stupid mechanic and a woman who is also a flyer and who lives impartially with the aviator and the parachute jumper and has consented to have the paternity of her six-year-old child decided by one flop of the dice. And besides these there is a drunken newspaper reporter. It is through his bleared eyes that we see the whole situation; he falls senselessly in love with the promiscuous aviatrix and during the carnival week at New Orleans he borrows money right and left to support the whole smutty and poverty-stricken crowd. At the end he is scorned and misunderstood by the woman whose putative husband has crashed to his death in a race.

121

Faulkner belongs with Mark Twain and Ring Lardner and he well completes and complements this trio of bitterly tragic comedians. He adds the power of loving the people whom he scorns and of sparing us no brutality or vulgarity concerning the people whom he loves. You are forced to sympathize with his characters to such an extent that you suppress your natural disgust for them. Faulkner loves these young men who live for aviation, who endure poverty for it, who are gods in the air and live like pigs on the ground. In the person of his reporter hero he loves this woman who is not true, lovable, but only dirty, stupid and somehow grotesque. It seems as if he had set himself an impossible task—the glorification of aviation accomplished by means of the most unpromising of people. Against these odds he succeeds brilliantly. If you are squeamish you may hate this book, but you will never forget it.

Harold Strauss.
"Mr. Faulkner's New Novel Strikes a Fresh Vein."
New York Times Book Review, March 24, 1935, p. 2.

Pylon marks an important turning point in William Faulkner's career. It brilliantly vindicates him from the current suspicion that his genius is limited to themes of violence, horror and the psychopathology of sex. In the novels preceding *Light in August* he revealed a bizarre style, a morbid though powerful imagination, and the ability to create terrific suspense by slowing down the passing of time at the moment of commission of an act of violence. These novels were isolated nightmares of the subconscious which tore themselves loose from the world of common reality, and therefore were limited in significance. And then, in *Light in August*, the range of his vision suddenly broadened.

Still uncompromising in probing vicious, terrified bestiality, he now proved able to tell the story of that pathetically impotent idealist, Gail Hightower, and to describe the dumb, persevering love of Byron Bunch for Lena. By admitting such themes to his scheme of things he gained perspective, and therefore a more just and compassionate view of life. He began to understand evil in its framework of social necessity—and wrote a great and memorable novel. *Light in August* must be regarded as definitely achieving the goal set in novels such as *Sanctuary*. Faulkner then seemed to have exhausted his potentialities. Furthermore, he began to write—very lucratively—for the popular magazines and for Hollywood. When *Dr. Martino and Other Stories* appeared in book form it seemed that there was nothing left of his art but the fantastic, baroque edifice of his style—hollow, unreal, deserted by life. He had mollified his themes, and in groping after what might be called decent horror, he seemed lost.

And now he has written *Pylon*. It has the explosive power and time-stopping intensity of the old Faulkner: and what is more, it reveals that at last he is able to handle a daylight theme. It is convincing proof that he can turn to any scene of human activity where there is tension and a wealth of nervous motion and treat it with persuasiveness, power and imagination. In itself it does not measure up to *Light in August*; it has not its substance, its perspective, its imponderable, living truth. Like *Sanctuary* or *As I Lay Dying*, it is an experimental book that contains a strong promise of leading to another major work.

The first result of Faulkner's emergence from the close confines of psychopathology is that he has no need to keep his motivation obscure. He no longer fears the taint of banality in handling the ordinary impulses which bridge our moments of intense or abnormal passion. *Pylon* is the story of a barnstorming air-race pilot who has come to a Southern city for the cash-prize races marking the opening of a new airport. In his troupe are Laverne (his wife), a child, a parachute jumper and Jiggs, the mechanic. These people live in a world of their own, a world of speed, iron nerve, small cash rewards for the greatest risks, chronic lack of money—a world which demands relentless precision of its inhabitants. From the outside world comes the reporter. This strange spider of a man—six feet tall, ninety-five pounds in weight, with a jangled nervous system—is drawn like a fascinated rabbit into the destiny of Pilot Roger Shumann and his four companions.

The reporter was first attracted to the group by the strange desires which Laverne awoke in him. She was a wild wench whom Shumann had picked up and trained as a parachute jumper. With Jiggs, the mechanic, they barnstormed around the country, eventually replacing Laverne with a professional jumper. Although Shumann was married to her, the jumper too possessed her, and neither she nor any one else knew which was the father of the child, Jackie. The reporter somehow acquired the hallucination that if she belonged to two men, she belonged to all men. He thought things would break for him. The troupe was broke. Although Shumann, flying a plane two years out of date, had won one of the early races by daring, diving turns at the pylons, he would not be paid off until the end of the

meet. The reporter, with some vague plan in mind, undertook to find food and lodging to keep Shumann in training.

This becomes the central link in a steel chain of cause and effect. If the reporter had not taken the troupe to his rooms in the Vieux Carré, if it had not been Mardi Gras and he had not stopped to buy a jug of absinthe on the way home—then the mechanic would not have been drunk the next morning, there would have been time to test the valves of the plane, and Shumann would not have cracked up. If the reporter had not still been thinking of Laverne, he wouldn't have helped Shumann get another plane for the big race—even Matt Ord's dangerous ship which had been powered with a motor too heavy for its light frame. And so on along the intricate but precise chain, until Shumann is dead and Laverne has escaped the reporter. By some suggestive magic—which upon analysis proves to be the fine forging of this chain—one senses the imminence of each event before it is recorded.

Do not suppose that this dulls the razor edge of suspense. On the contrary, it whets it. The fate of Shumann rests with beautiful inevitability upon the twin facts of his dangerous and tragically futile job, and the meddling of the reporter. That *Pylon* is in some ways an experimental work does not in the least distract from its breathtaking interest. It is a book that pounds on and batters the senses, that imparts the physical sensations of flying at 300 miles an hour and crashing plummet-like into the earth, that slings one through the gamut of emotions much as the winged bullets of cloth and steel dive in strut-straining swirls around the pylons that mark the bounds of the air-race courses. It is a book that must not be missed.

Mark Van Doren. "A Story Written with Ether, Not with Ink." *New York Herald Tribune Books*, March 24, 1935, p. 3.

Mr. Faulkner has never written a better story than this, or a more painful one. Like most of his stories, this one reaches the reader through a distressful medium which Mr. Faulkner has built up with bitter skill. The mere story, as always with its author, is less significant than the atmosphere it breathes. The important thing about its people is not what they do but the kind of thing they do, so that one is forced not so much to consider who they are as to reflect, not without horror, upon the species of creature they seem to represent, and upon the species of circumstance which has produced them.

The medium in the present case is, to use Mr. Faulkner's own diction, anesthetic. The atmosphere has been heavily charged with some kind of chemical which clouds the vision and numbs all those centers where human beings have been in the habit of feeling. It is not merely that we are oppressed by the lack of feeling in Mr. Faulkner's people. We finally are forced to recognize even ourselves as dead—and to be horrified, perhaps, by our lack of horror. Mr. Faulkner has written with ether, not with ink. He has anesthetized his readers as well as his characters. Whether this was a good thing to do is a special question the answer to which may be postponed until after the doing has been described.

The action lasts about four days and is confined to two localities—New Valois (presumably New Orleans) and a nearby airport where an aviation meet is in progress. The chief persons are four participants in the meet and a reporter from New Valois, who attaches himself to them until they become his obsession. The four participants are hard, treacherous, homeless and classless; they have drifted here to New Valois from anywhere and everywhere, in an old "crate" which one of them flies with an incredible, desperate skill and with an inarticulate passion that does not ask to be paid. A newspaper man says of him and his kind: "It ain't for money. It's because they have got to do it, like some women have got to be whores." This flyer and a parachute jumper are in common possession of a pale, metallic woman who has had a child by one of them—nobody knows which, though the flyer is legally her husband. (When the child had been born six years ago in California the men drew lots to see which one of them should marry Laverne.) In addition to these three there is Jiggs the mechanic, a foolish, unreliable little beast who spends most of his time dreaming about a pair of expensive boots into which he can stuff his hind legs.

And, indispensably, there is the reporter through whose strange mind and body we experience the quartet. He is one of Mr. Faulkner's strays, one of that impotent and disinherited class to which Popeye and Joe Christmas belong. He vaguely has a mother somewhere, so that his existence can be believed; but she has abandoned him to his states of mind, and here he floats, disembodied, cadaverous, mysteriously impelled, through the astonished lives of the four people he has taken unto his skinny bosom. Not that they are capable of much astonishment, since they too are anesthetized; but they can stare at him, and occasionally make speeches which are distinguished by the failure of any word in them to arrive at the loud, full truth.

Now, again, it is not what these people

do to one another that is the point of the book, though they do a plenty, and the action as such is most dreadful and exciting; it is the way they perceive and understand one another, the way they all look and listen, the way they surrender one by one to the idiot spell which the reporter, and behind him Mr. Faulkner, puts them under. The nature of this spell is only partially defined by the statement that alcohol has a great deal to do with it. There is drunkenness, to be sure; there are gallons of gin and paregoric, and there is much lurching around with pavements spinning deliriously. But there is also sleeplessness; the reporter, for instance, does not sleep through the four days of the meet, though he lives so hard each hour that the reader grows exhausted by the very spectacle. Neither the reporter nor the reader is allowed to relax from the weird strain which makes the world of the novel momently more fantastic and sickish. There is precious little food, too; and what food is taken into these bodies comes right up again. *Pylon* probably establishes a record among contemporary novels for the amount of vomiting it records, there being at least one major upheaval in each of the seven chapters, and many minor landslides. As much food and drink, indeed, remains outside of the characters, one way or another, as enters them. There is much spilling of liquor down shirt fronts, much drooling and slobbering generally. On one of the occasions when the reporter feasts his eyes upon Laverne she is "eating a sandwich, wolfing it and talking to the two men; he watched her drop the fragments back into the plate, wipe her hand across her mouth and lift the thick mug of coffee and drink, wolfing the coffee, too, the coffee, like the food, running down her chin from too fast swallowing."

"They ain't human," says the reporter to himself. But neither is he, for all the misty love he bestows upon them and for all the impotent longing he attempts in vain to let Laverne know about. They are all dogs—under dogs of this world—who in some cases snap wolfishly and in other cases merely chew their sandwiches with a sidewise tilt of the head or gaze dumbly out of whipped hound's eyes. The world has been too much for them. It is a world which cannot be experienced through clean and ventilated senses for the reason that it itself is vile and mad. Mr. Faulkner would seem to have grown utterly sick of what he sees. Newspapers, at least for his reporter, are "profoundly and irrevocably unimportant." Automobiles are "expensive, complex, delicate and intrinsically useless, created for some obscure psychic need of the species if not the race from the virgin resources of the continent to be the individual muscles, bone and flesh of a new and legless kind." Faith in mankind is for the parachute jumper a "dose," like consumption. Nobody ever smiles, though there is frequently a grimace that "looks like smiling"—more wanness and bewilderment than mirth. The aviators move mechanically about in a "bleak tense quiet" as the reporter speaks to them in a "tone of peaceful and bemused incomprehensibility." All is sub-human. All is weakness and pitiful mildness in Mr. Faulkner's New Valois.

The question whether Mr. Faulkner can afford to keep on publishing such novels is a question that had better be left after all to his audience. To repeat, he has never written a better one than this; but there is danger in that very fact, for he is so able at his job of outraging our emotions that we may end by having none for him. This of course would be a literary tragedy. For he has one of the greatest natural gifts to be found anywhere in America at the moment.

George Currie.
"Passed in Review."
Brooklyn *Daily Eagle*,
March 25, 1935, p. 16.

Mr. William Faulkner's *Pylon*, published today, concerns itself with the small occasions which determine the lot of man; his helplessness in resistance against what he has been pleased to call destiny; his pathetic endeavor to escape from self-knowledge and the inexorable passage of time, the brief duration of ecstasy, the lengthy intervals of frantic and bootless effort.

The bloody page, however, is absent from this novel. Though Shumann cracks up and dies in the end, his body is not recovered. But the butcher knife and the corncob, implements by which Mr. Faulkner forced his way into the appalled attention of the casual reader, are left at home. Instead we are given a combination of circumstances reeking with the hot smell of engine oil; with alcoholic nausea; with the dull devoted flirtation with death, which Shumann and the parachute jumper undertake daily for no apparent reason other than that it is what they are created for. Mr. Faulkner achieves an altitude record for passionate dalliance; it is an episode in which love literally soars to the clouds. And lest he might be accused of getting soft, he has included the ugly incident of the nympholeptic village cop and the bruised and almost naked Laverne, come to grief on her first exhibition jump.

There is also the reporter, a mad, drunken fellow, with a heart bursting with infinite compassion. He is fortunate in that he has an incredible city editor who will lend him considerable sums of money to pull Shumann and his wife, the parachute jumper and the putteringly irresponsible Jiggs through the four days of a Mardi Gras and an airport dedication. He is damned, for Laverne has cast upon him a spell. All that he does for the rest is for the love he has for the girl, but unlike most good news reporters, an articulate tongue is beyond his powers.

The girl Laverne symbolizes all the rest. She is a tuft of thistledown buffeted by the strong gusts of male passion. That which makes her unapproachable to the reporter is her obvious failure to come up to even the half-maudlin ideal into which he has molded her in a sick imagination. She is the wife of Shumann, but both he and the parachute jumper and herself couldn't have told you exactly which had been the child's father. The pair of them rolled dice to decide who should give the baby a name, while beside them mother and new born infant lay on an unrolled parachute.

The arrangement between this strange trio fully justified the reporter's explanation to his accommodating city editor that "they ain't human like us. . . . Burn them like this one tonight and they don't even holler in the fire; crash one and it ain't even blood when you haul him out; it's cylinder oil the same as in the crankcase."

The thin disguise of a name—New Valois—sets the scene away from New Orleans. As though to assure the reader that Shumann simply had to fly, come what may, Mr. Faulkner contrives to hold up the prize money, to get the aviators cheated into forking over the money to print new programs after one of their number is burned to death. They muttered, they grumbled, but they flew.

The climax is achieved in a mad-dog plane, but only after the four of them and the reporter have guzzled almost a whole gallon of alcohol flavored with paregoric. Laverne and the parachute jumper move on, the shadow of Shumann forever between them. The child is returned to

Shumann's father, the old country doctor who had mortgaged all he had to keep his son in the air, to keep him wedded to a woman the old folks despised. Utterly Faulkneresque is the scene in which the grandfather throws into a red and roaring stove the money the reporter had smuggled into the child's toy.

In this novel of speed Mr. Faulkner makes use of many a strange turn of phrase. He builds new words out of old ones. Thus: "The woman not voracious, not rapacious; just omnivorous like the locomotive's maw of his late symbology; he told himself with savage disillusion." Thus: "Jiggs tried to spell out the name, the letters inletted into the curbedge in tileblurred mosaic." Occasionally, in an uproar of rhetoric there spills out of his typewriter a word that must be gone over twice and even thrice, for in the violence of his sentences such a one as "dimlyseen" looks other than what it is.

He strikes cadences; speaks in howling crescendos and discontented diminuendos, and no imaginative picture in too incongruous. Thus: "Out of the last laggard reluctance of darkness—the garblement which was the city; the scabby hoppoles which elevated the ragged palmcrests like the monstrous broomsage out of an old country thought, the spent stage of last night's clatterfalque Nilebarge supine now beneath today's white wings treading, the hydrantgouts gutterplaited with the trodden tinseldung of stars."

He dopes his reader with generous dosages of such stuff, as if to say that like it or no, he will pound into each and all the enormity and outrage of the forces let loose by man upon the Earth for his own enslavement. If he can't do it legally, then perhaps he can succeed in completing the operation stealthily with the aid of the powerful anesthesia of his words. Mr. Faulkner's *Pylon* appears as the tempes-tuous March lion ordained to follow upon the trail of the lamb, which brought in the month. The author's anesthesia, it should be said, is harshly counter-irritant, rather than narcotic. This is not a book of which one would say, "I like it." Rather, it defies one to put it away unfinished; spits upon one; jeers and blows contempt. But it leaves one so hypnotized that the astonishing reporter appears credible; Laverne and her strange little court of the knights of monkey-wrench and cauter-pins appear as folks who really matter. Of such is the contrariness of an age in which a machine is more important than the hand which directs it. Mr. Faulkner rang it down our throats, so that all who read become aware they are a part of it.

William Soskin. "William Faulkner's *Pylon*." New York *American*, March 25, 1935, p. 17.

The strange case of William Faulkner:

In France and England certain critics will tell you that William Faulkner is the only important living Amercian writer. They will cite you his *As I Lay Dying* and his *The Sound and the Fury* as examples of his Dostoyevskian drama. In this country a large reading public took a less important Faulkner work to heart—*Sanctuary*, and was caught up in its study of perverted violence.

Today Mr. Faulkner publishes *Pylon*, a new novel about a troupe of stunt fliers in the South, and one that gives me, to coin a phrase, pause. When his earlier works appeared I shot off roman candles and indulged in a series of highly undignified celebrations in honor of the man and found myself one of a ridiculed minority in doing so. Even *Sanctuary*, a story that contained melodramatic elements not quite worthy of the talent Faulkner had already displayed, seemed to me an excellent book. Reading *Pylon* I experience that uncomfortable and sad sensation of disloyalty that comes with a repudiation of an old friendship or a creed of thought or belief.

By some chain of circumstance or other Faulkner has carried his pursuit of desperate action, his escape from an intolerable world, into a field that is no longer dramatically true. Here are his fliers, a bedraggled band of three men and a woman, a race apart "because they ain't human like us; they couldn't turn those pylons like they do if they had human blood and senses and they wouldn't want to dare to if they just had human brains. Burn them . . . and they don't even holler in the fire; crash one and it ain't even blood when you haul him out; it's cylinder oil the same as in the crankcase."

They are, in other words, insensible beings, just as the morons and idiots of Faulkner's other stories are insensible. And Faulkner flogs them, burns them, kills them, vents his sadistic fury upon them and tries to leave them, nevertheless, symbols of importance. In *Pylon* he carries the thing to meaningless lengths, however, and there is such a whirl of drinking, such an orgy of death-defiance and such large intimations of promiscuity among the men and the woman that the story remains blurred and pointless in my mind.

One may find many pages of brilliant narrative and description in *Pylon*. The air circuses, the atmosphere of the professional fliers' lives—a sort of mechanical gypsy trail, the newspaper office which is involved in the story through the intervention of a crazy derelict of a reporter; the drinking sessions and the individual

psychological trauma of these people whose pulses beat with alcohol and danger—all this Faulkner does beautifully.

Yet I found myself re-reading pages in order to discover what he means to say in the unnecessarily obscure writing of much of the narrative. I found myself wondering why the senseless circuit of futility these people traveled had to be prolonged. I had to look at words like "circuitriderlooking" and "cadaverface" a number of times before I felt their impact.

Often Faulkner makes us adjust our minds and muscles, to a fine conception of a machine—"expensive, complex, delicate and intrinsically useless, created for some obscure psychic need of the species if not the race, from the virgin resources of a continent, to be the individual bones and flesh of a new and legless kind." And then lets us down with chapter after chapter of relaxed, stupid action and flagrantly distorted stuff.

The story of *Pylon* is simpler than most of Faulkner's earlier tales, but it is simplicity of action rather than of meaning. He seems to me now to be an insecure writer, a fellow groping almost mechanically in a storm of furious, incessant action. I have the feeling he no longer cares very much about the meaning of all his words.

Sterling North. "Psychopathic Squirming of White Trash Marks New Faulkner, Caldwell and Wolfe." Chicago *Daily News*, March 27, 1935, p. 15.

Everyone to his own taste, but this reviewer is getting a trifle weary of the much-

128

heralded southern school of literature and particularly of its three most sacrosanct proponents.

If Faulkner, Caldwell and Wolfe wish to wallow in filth and subhuman bestiality for thousands of pages that is their privilege. And if several hundred thousand American readers wish to pay their good money to experience vicariously these subhuman emotions, excellent!

But if it were not for the fact that a critic's job is to read most of the new books that come along, we would forgo those pleasures from this date forth.

New York critics are busy raving about the new Faulkner novel. Raving about Faulkner is the thing to do. Just as repeating the latest insulting wisecrack of Alexander Woollcott is the thing to do, or slipping in a bit about Noel Coward or Lynn Fontanne or Alfred Lunt (preferably all three) is the thing to do.

Never mind the thing to do!

Faulkner's new book is a sloppy, disgusting, nauseating performance by a half-articulate southerner who never entirely learned his job as a novelist and, aside from a few short stories and parts of *Light in August*, is a second-rater.

Faulkner has admitted publicly that *Sanctuary*, with its perversion and melodramatic situations, was done purely for publicity purposes. Popeye and Joe Christmas, to take his two best-known and most thoroughly realized characters, are never for one moment human beings.

Both, however, are normal, healthy individuals compared to the disgusting characters in *Pylon*.

Briefly the story of *Pylon* is that of two flyers, a woman who is the wife of one and the mistress of both, and a small boy who is the son of the woman and one of the two men—not even the author apparently knows which—who come to New Valois (New Orleans) during the Mardi Gras to compete for pitiful prizes. They risk their lives daily, very nearly starve, sleep in a house of ill repute, get drunk, stay up all night and vomit on every second page.

They are joined by the most unbelievable reporter ever represented in fiction. Faulkner may know his flying, but he has obviously only the most hazy notions of newspaper work. His city editor is laughable.

This dirty scarecrow of a reporter who probably symbolizes death joins the family of flyers, who stalk like wooden Indians through the pages, dead, green, lifeless.

What is Faulkner trying to do?

Is he trying to do a more shocking book than his last one? He is saying that life disgusts him utterly. He is trying, apparently, to show that no human emotion is of the least importance. He is presenting speed-mad maniacs who in some way represent for him civilization. Men risking life daily for a few pennies, driving themselves toward inevitable destruction, even as the world is driving itself toward destruction.

But he has not bigness nor the genius to fulfill his self-assigned task. It would take a giant like Swift with honest hatred and searing satire to accomplish what Faulkner tries to accomplish with whimpering disgust. Where Swift used a broadsword, Faulkner uses a pail of mud and a broom. His prose is cheap, artificial and maudlin.

Caldwell's most recent book, *Journeyman*, is scarcely worth reviewing. It tells the story of an itinerant preacher who moves about the south in a broken-down Ford, raising the backwoods Georgians to sexual-religious heights, taking away their money with a pair of loaded dice, and sleeping with their wives.

Wolfe's *Of Time and the River* has a redeeming breadth. But he, too, is a southern whimperer.

There is a law of diminishing returns in this business both for the writer and the reader. Caldwell and Faulkner have reduced all human emotion to one particular type of bestiality. It is inconceivable that either can write another novel farther down the scale or more narrow in range. They have imposed upon themselves a southern boundary. As forces in American literature they are rapidly passing out of the picture.

For the reader, too, there is this law of diminishing returns. Even to the seeker after new sensations, Faulkner and Caldwell books prove that no new perversions exist.

The swing of the pendulum from "Moonlight and Roses" has transcribed its full arc.

Emily Bridgers. "William Faulkner in the Air." Raleigh *News and Observer*, March 31, 1935, p. 5-M.

To those of us who look on William Faulkner as one of that group of writers who lend to the South a particular distinction in contemporary fiction, *Pylon* must be a disappointment. As a full novel, it is without the rich imagination, the broad canvas, the human compassion of Mr. Faulkner's previous work, *Light in August*. As a study of people out of the ordinary experience of society, whom Mr. Faulkner presented so fiercely and understandingly in such books as *Sanctuary*, *The Sound and the Fury* and *As I Lay Dying* it fails to give the reader more than a surface picture, leaving him not even curious to know more about those in the book and untouched by what he does know. For although there is some engrossing writing in the book, Mr. Faulkner's expertly colored, suggestive, sometimes brutal, style, his half-revealing, half-concealing manner of telling his story, in the past so effective in ultimately bringing his characters to life, is used here to no satisfactory purpose. It is as though Mr. Faulkner had become so interested in how much information he could keep from his reader and still keep his pages exciting with the pyrotechnics of his writing, that he had inadvertently let his people disappear into death and the night without ever having brought them to life.

For his purposes, Mr. Faulkner has this time chosen a group of rootless people who make their living barnstorming the air circuses of the country. The group is composed of a racing pilot, a parachute jumper, a woman and her small son, and a mechanic named Jiggs. The pilot is the woman's husband, he and the parachute jumper having flipped a coin for that privilege after the birth of the boy, whose actual paternity is a question of considerable doubt. Marriage to the pilot has not, apparently, affected the woman's relations with the parachute jumper, and the three of them, with the child and the mechanic, travel fairly amicably together, barnstorming from one air meet to another, living no one knows exactly where or how between meets.

At the moment, Mardi Gras is being celebrated in New Valois, a Far South town, where as an added attraction a three-day circus is in progress at the dedication of the town's new airport. The pilot and the parachute jumper have entered the contests for the purses offered. On the first day of the meet, a reporter of the town, seeing the woman for the first time and hearing of her unconventional habits, becomes prey to a violent conviction that since the woman accepts two men she might as well make him the third. The woman is indifferent, contemptuous.

The mechanic and the pilot view his obsession with no particular interest. Only the parachute jumper shows resentment. Driven by his conviction and fascinated by the recklessness of the group, the reporter attaches himself to them. As usual they have no money until such time as they may collect some purses. The reporter makes himself responsible for their welfare in New Valois, and so becomes finally the instrument of the pilot's death.

Mr. Faulkner records faithfully and graphically what these people say and do and how they look. He gives one or two glimpses into the past life of the pilot and the woman. Rather comically he introduces the reporter's mother. But the light which she shed back over the springs of Popeye's actions in *Sanctuary* is never shed here for the reader's understanding of any one of the group. The rounded characterization to be found in *Light in August* is lacking. When, finally, the pilot lies dead in the lake where a rotten borrowed plane has landed him, and the reporter, futile and hazy, has let the woman escape him, and the book is done, the reader is both baffled and slightly irritated. The woman, with the parachute jumper still in her shadow, disappears into the darkness of a winter's night as enigmatic as when she was first spotted by her "blob of savage meal-colored hair" as she worked in dungarees around the pilot's out-dated racing plane. The reporter, flinging drunken defiance at his editor, is only more contemptuously futile, bitterer, madder than at the start.

Mr. Faulkner has written for effect at the expense of his characters, presenting them only in the half-light of his own making. From the first pages, the reader is conscious of a striving in carefully composed phrases and extravagant similes, in the use of almost too striking adjectives, in the piling up of odd incident and horrid detail—in the use of every means at Mr. Faulkner's command—for that bizarre atmosphere, that sinister tainted light in which Popeye and Benjy live with such reality in *Sanctuary* and *The Sound and the Fury*. But the careless recklessness of these people and their unconventional practices is not enough to taint the atmosphere as did Popeye's degeneracy and Benjy's idiocy, and the achievement of an atmosphere is not sufficient alone to explain them. *Pylon* for all its load of writing never comes through to life for the reader.

Malcolm Cowley. "Voodoo Dance." *New Republic*, 82 (April 10, 1935), 254–55.

The real plot of *Pylon*, if told straightforwardly, would run something like this:

Roger Shumann, the son of an Ohio country doctor, was supposed to study medicine, but his one lively interest was tinkering with engines, and his father bought him a second-hand airplane with the money saved to put him through medical school. He joined a flying circus. In Kansas, he met and carried off Laverne, a girl of fifteen who had been seduced by her brother-in-law. Laverne afterwards fell in love with a parachute jumper named Jack, but without separating from Roger. In California her baby was born, on a parachute unfolded in a hangar. She didn't know who the father was, but Roger and Jack rolled dice and Roger won, so Laverne became Mrs. Shumann. This family of air gypsies wandered over the country, risking their lives on aviation fields and starving in jerkwater hotels. After six years, Laverne was expecting another child. She knew it was Jack's, this time, and Roger also knew, but he was determined to raise money for her confinement at the cost of any danger to himself. At an aviation meet in New Orleans, during Mardi Gras, he flew an old plane in the first day's race and took second prize by cutting closer to the pylons than the other flyers. His plane crashed on the second day. A drunken reporter, who had fallen in love with Laverne, helped him to get another plane, fast and notoriously unsafe. The aviation authorities knew that Roger was likely to be killed, but they allowed him to enter the big race on the principle that the public was entitled to its thrills. When the plane went to pieces in the air, Roger managed to steer the wreckage away from the grandstand and into the lake before he fell. His body was never recovered. Laverne and Jack took the little boy to Shumann's father in Ohio, and then continued their hopeless and hungry wanderings. . . .

This is a plot that fifty novelists might have chosen to treat in fifty different fashions—as a chronicle of the Shumann family, as an American panorama, as a gallery of strange types, as romance, as adventure. Faulkner has found a fashion of his own, but at the cost of forcing the real plot into the background and revealing it only in scattered dialogues. The direct action of his novel is confined to five days during the New Orleans carnival. The principal character, instead of being Roger or Jack or Laverne, is the drunken and sentimental reporter. Many of the episodes are seen through his half-glazed eyes, and are thereby refracted and distorted; the story proceeds in what military historians call "the fog of war." For the rest, the general construction is that of a play rather than of the usual novel. The story moves in two directions as in a tragedy by Racine—that is, toward a future catastrophe and also toward a fuller understanding of the past. The characters are easy to recognize: every time they walk on the stage, the author identifies them by phrases that have the same function as the catch lines or gestures of actors doing character bits. Thus, the reporter is known by his flapping coat, Jiggs the mechanic by his bouncing walk, and Laverne by her "savage mealcolored hair." The action is quick, sharp, condensed; the mood is unified and is sustained by noises offstage—by a loudspeaker reporting the results of the air races, by the shouts and horn-blowing of the Mardi Gras crowds. There is even a Greek chorus of newspaper men to comment on Shumann's death.

And not only is the novel dramatic in structure; it is also a poetic drama, in the sense that Faulkner's style is often closer to verse than it is to prose. This fact is not apparent on a first reading. One is likely to be confused by the way he runs words together—sometimes forming unnatural and illegible combinations like "robin's-egg," "pavilionglitter," "electrodeitch"—and by his fashion of omitting commas even where they are needed. But one finds after reading a few paragraphs aloud that his style is extraordinarily resonant, that the accents fall naturally at the ends of phrases and that the pauses for breath recur at regular intervals. Many of his descriptions, even the more prosaic ones, can be broken into verses and printed as songs:

Above the shuffle and murmur
  of feet in the lobby
and above the clash and clatter
  of crockery in the restaurant
  the amplified voice still spoke,
  profound and effortless. . . .

I have not changed a word or a punctuation mark, but have merely divided part of a sentence into separate lines at places where the voice instinctively breaks. I might have continued in the same fashion. There are poems like this all through the novel, and their steady pulse-beat ends by having the effect of the tom-tom booming offstage in *Emperor Jones*; it is the stylistic device that Faulkner uses to orchestrate his voodoo dance of human passions.

There is one question that remains to be answered. Why did Faulkner choose this particular plot to dramatize with obvious care and to clothe in lovely rhythms? No matter how much he is interested in barn-storming aviators, they are still not his own people, not the sort of characters he can write about from the inside. Of course one can say that they lead picturesque lives and meet violent deaths, but I suspect that there is some other reason for their hold on him. I suspect that either consciously or unconsciously he reads a symbolic meaning into the lives of people like Roger and Laverne and the parachute jumper.

Consider again the nature of their adventures. They live among machines, and these machines become a symbol of sex transmuted into speed, of sex interfused with danger. The most sensational passage of the novel is a description of two people making love in an airplane high above the ground. Laverne in her daily life is conscienceless; she shares herself between two men, but "it ain't adultery," the reporter says; "you can't anymore imagine the two of them making love than you can two of them airplanes back in the corner of the hangar, coupled." This, however, is exactly what the reporter does imagine; it is one reason for his hopeless and bloodless and impotent devotion to a woman from another world.

And there is another symbol, this time hidden in the character of Roger Shumann. He comes nearer to being a hero than any other character in Faulkner's eight novels. He preserves his integrity in the midst of disorder; he is capable, strong, devoted, ready to sacrifice himself and to protect others even when his plane is crashing. He is also the technician, the type of modern demigod. And he is killed partly by the business men who control the Airport Commission and partly by the interference of a literary weakling. Thus, in two senses *Pylon* becomes a legend of contemporary life. The trouble is that the legend seems to have exerted more emotional power over the author than it exerts over his readers. Perhaps this fact explains the chief defect of what is otherwise an impressive novel—I mean the lack of proportion between stimulus and response, the air of unnecessary horror and violence. Reading some parts of *Pylon* is like looking through a window and seeing strangers making fierce silent gestures, without knowing the full cause of their anger or their sorrow.

Henry George Hoch. "Mr. Faulkner's Barnstormers." Detroit *News*, April 21, 1935, Arts Section, p. 17.

Mr. Faulkner's latest novel, as usual, is not pleasant reading. Its five characters are revolting people who do and say revolting things.

In other hands they would be just that—cheap, disgusting little people hardly worth hearing about. But Mr. Faulkner, who usually chooses such people for his novels, has the gift which lifts the book from the realm of smut and makes it compelling, powerful tragedy.

A writer of amazing versatility and power, he makes you see behind their words and actions the suffering and the grim irony in the lives of cheap little people tossed around by a world which is just too much for them.

Through his art it all becomes tragedy with a sting. Not many who pick this book up will put it down unfinished. And not many who finish it will escape a feeling that somehow they may be in part responsible for the suffering and the tragedy of such unlovely lives.

Pylon is not, to this reviewer, the best of Faulkner's books. Neither is it, as art, the equal of his short story, "Death Drag," which also deals with barnstorming aviators. But that does not mean that it is an inferior novel. Even though its characters and situations are unlovely, it has a power and depth of sympathetic understanding that make it a book of more than ordinary excellence.

"Under-Cover Works." New Haven *Journal-Courier*, April 29, 1935, p. 6.

With the exception of the mountainous and multitudinous Thomas Wolfe, there is no American writer of today with greater sheer natural talent than has William Faulkner. Certainly he has no equal for compressed power, for verbal virtuosity, for mind-wringing momentum. To read *Pylon*, as to read the previous books, is to submit to the fierce fascination of deliberately intensified tragedy and to emerge with mind limp, lagging, licked. To read [*Pylon* is to] become incredibly interested in persons who have the old familiar hungers but are never quite human, driven by terrific forces which must be given the old familiar labels but are not quite emotions. It is an experience which no one should miss, which will sink into the memory, but which few will enjoy.

Here again is displayed that unique Faulknerian technique of delayed action by which each vital instant is frozen for what seems an eternity and suspense heightened almost intolerably and of de-layed explanation by which the story is told only in lightning flashes, plot points withheld as in [a] puzzle which can be pieced together only bit by bit, motivations following rather than preceding actions. And that technique is used superbly to tell a tale which slips out of the mid-world of perversion [and] horror of most of the earlier books and into a new world, fully as part from the normal, but more natural, more understandable.

Three days only are compassed in the full novel; three days of the air races with which a southern city is celebrating its Mardi Gras and opening its airport. The story is of Roger Shumann, barnstorming pilot, his wife Laverne, a parachute jumper, Jiggs the mechanic, who also possesses the wife, Laverne's little boy whose parentage cannot be determined and a reporter. In particular a reporter, one of the most compelling portraits ever met in recent fiction, an intense young romanticist who is fascinated by the Shumann troupe as a rabbit by a snake and unconsciously starts the series of inevitable incidents which lead to the pilot's death. It is a story which rushes as the planes from pylon to pylon of the race-course, yet draws out suspense with a bitter, brutal grip until even tragedy is a relief.

G[eorge] Marion O'Donnell. "Faulkner and Insensitivity." *Direction: A Quarterly of New Literature*, 1 (June 1935), 152–53.

Pylon concerns a group of stunt flyers and an unnamed newspaper reporter, "something which had apparently crept from a doctor's cupboard and, in the snatched garments of an etherized patient in the charity ward, escaped into the living world." Against the background of an airport opening and Mardi Gras carnival in a Southern city, these people move somewhat like characters in an animated cartoon, or the people in James Joyce's *Work in Progress*, performing incredible antics and jerking galvanically with a semblance of life, but never being quite alive. Timeless and placeless, they stay drunk as much as possible, to aggravate their insensitiveness; the air is an obsession with them, and when they are not flying they do not live at all.

In this very choice of materials (characters and setting) lies, I think, the reason for the failure of *Pylon* as a novel. Heretofore, Faulkner has been dealing with characters who, however ignorant or however psychopathic, were at least sensitive. He has been able to enter his characters and to speak through them, and the result has been some of the most noteworthy books of our generation.

In *Pylon*, however, the characters are insensitive, and their lack of sensitivity has forced Faulkner to dispense with special narrators altogether and to intrude himself—writing as a poet with powers of omniscience—into the book. This intrusion produces the unfortunate, androgynous style in which the book is written, a style resembling in some respects the polyphonic prose of Amy Lowell or the prose-poetry of Paul Fort, but more closely resembling the style used by James Joyce in *Ulysses* and, much exaggerated, in *Work in Progress*.

Now this style is defensible in *Ulysses* on the ground that Joyce's special narrators are all sensitive people with unusual perceptive powers; but in Faulkner's case this defense is impossible, and his use of the method must be set down as a reversion to what we have come to call the

"purple passages" of Victorian novelists.

Faulkner has always lacked a sense of form. Only in *As I Lay Dying* and, to some extent, in *The Sound and the Fury*, has he ever approached formal perfection. In the last three of his novels, this lack of balance, of design, has been especially noticeable: *Light in August* was worse than *Sanctuary*, and *Pylon* is even worse than *Light in August*. This fault, in the case of *Pylon*, is caused directly by the style which Faulkner has adopted; and, as we have seen, the style is due to the nature of the materials which he selected.

The conclusion should be obvious: Faulkner has chosen unwisely in deserting the fury-ridden aristocrats and the naive but sensitive hillmen of Mississippi to write of rootless characters. His is essentially a provincial art, just as Joyce's art is provincial and as the art of Dostoievski and Tchekhov was provincial. His task, like theirs, has been to lift localism to universality. But *Pylon* lacks the regional accent; despite its Southern setting, the book is no more regional than it would be if it had been written by Ernest Hemingway or Waldo Frank. Faulkner has failed in *Pylon* because, turning away from his regionalism, he has seemingly lost his particularity as an author. And it will be a great loss to American letters if Faulkner does not choose to turn again to the red clay hills of Mississippi and to the people who live in those hills.

Checklist of Additional Reviews

Buffalo *Evening News*, March 23, 1935.
"Faulkner Genius." Camden (N.J.)
    Courier, March 30, 1935, p. 12.
"Air Circus: The Old Faulkner
    Characters in a New Setting."
    Newsweek, March 30, 1935, p. 40.

135

Newark *News*, March 30, 1935.

"*Pylon* Will Appeal to Faulkner Admirers." Sacramento *Bee*, April 6, 1935, p. 16.

Atlantic City (N.J.) *Press*, April 6, 1935.

"*Pylon* and Other Recent Books: Glamor of Flying in Vivid New Faulkner Tale." Richmond *Times-Dispatch*, April 7, 1935, Section V, p. 11.

"*Pylon* Tells of Barnstorming Fliers." Lexington (Ky.) *Herald*, April 14, 1935, Section III, p. 4.

"Faulkner Joins Obscurists' Cult in Newest Novel." Milwaukee *Journal*, April 21, 1935, Editorial Section, p. 3.

"Literature and Less." New Orleans *Times-Picayune*, April 21, 1935, Section II, p. 5.

"Faulkner Writes Gripping Tale of Air Barnstormers." Pasadena *Star-News*, May 4, 1935, p. 6.

"*Pylon*." Birmingham *News*, May 5, 1935, Magazine Section, p. 11.

"Vivid New Faulkner Opus." Salt Lake City *Tribune*, May 5, 1935, Magazine Section, p. 4.

"Machine and Men in Faulkner's Story." Springfield (Mass.) *Sunday Union and Republican*, May 19, 1935, p. 5-C; also reviewed in the Springfield *Weekly Republican*, May 25, 1935, p. 8.

"*Pylon*." *American Spectator*, August 1935, p. 13.

Adelberg, Julius. "In a Southern City at Mardi Gras." Boston *Evening Transcript*, March 20, 1935, p. 2.

Bell, Laurence. "Faulkner's Coming of Age." *Scribner's Magazine*, May 1935, p. 809.

B[enét], W[illiam] R[ose]. "Faulkner Fades." Nashville *Tennessean*, March 31, 1935, Magazine Section, p. 15.

Bowerman, Sarah G. "*Pylon*." Washington *Evening Star*, April 13, 1935, p. 6-A.

Brickell, Herschel. "Books on Our Table." New York *Post*, March 30, 1935, p. 7.

Cantwell, Robert. "Books." *New Outlook*, May 1935, p. 60.

Chamberlain, John. "Books of the Times." New York *Times*, March 25, 1935, p. 13; also reviewed in *Current History*, 42 (May 1935), xvi.

Clayton, Robert. "*Pylon*." Chattanooga *Times*, April 7, 1935, Magazine Section, p. 15.

Cooper, Monte. "*Pylon*." Memphis *Commercial Appeal*, March 24, 1935, Section V, p. 3.

Cooper, Sanford L. "William Faulkner Follows Usual Style in New Story." Pittsburgh *Press*, March 31, 1935, Section III, p. 11.

Corley, Pauline. "Inhuman Creatures of the Air." Miami *Herald*, March 31, 1935, p. 2-F.

Deutsch, Hermann B. "Faulkner Takes Wings." New Orleans *Item*, April 7, 1935, p. 8.

Fadiman, Clifton. "Books: Medley." *New Yorker*, March 30, 1935, p. 74.

Gannett, Lewis. "Books and Things." New York *Herald Tribune*, March 25, 1935, p. 13.

Grimes, George. "Faulkner's Tense, Bitter Novel of Flying Men, Seen through Haze of Drink." Omaha *Sunday World Herald*, March 31, 1935, p. 15-E.

Habich, William. "Faulkner Recaptures Power." Louisville *Courier Journal*, March 31, 1935, Section III, p. 4.

Hall, Theodore. "No End of Books: *Pylon*, William Faulkner's Powerful, Hypnotic Novel about Stunt and Racing Fliers." Washington *Post*, March 26, 1935, p. 9. Also see earlier mention in "Spring Fiction Proves of Varied Hue," March 24, 1935, Section III, p. 8.

Hansen, Harry. "Strange Tale, Strangely

Told." New York *World-Telegram*, March 25, 1935, p. 17.

Hanson, Grant D. "*Pylon*." Sioux City (Iowa) *Tribune*, June 1, 1935, p. 4.

Hayes. Stanford University *Daily*, May 28, 1935.

Hicks, Granville. "Melodrama." *New Masses*, May 14, 1935, p. 25.

Hippler, W. G. "A Line on Books." Buffalo *Evening News*, March 23, 1935, Section II, p. 3.

Hohlfeld, Adelin. "A Middlewest Lament." Madison (Wis.) *Capital Times*, April 7, 1935, p. 24.

Horan, Kenneth. "Faulkner Turns to Decent Horror." Chicago *Journal of Commerce and LaSalle Street Journal*, April 30, 1935, p. 16.

Hudson, Bill. "Reviewing the Book: *Pylon*." *Carolina Magazine*, June 1935, pp. 28–29.

Jane-Mansfield, C. "William Faulkner Has Produced a Novel of Social Significance." New York *Sun*, March 27, 1935, p. 24.

Jones, Howard Mumford. "Social Notes on the South." *Virginia Quarterly Review*, 11 (July 1935), 452–57.

Karant, Max. "Faulkner Cracks Up with *Pylon*, Reviewer Thinks." Evanston (Ill.) *News-Index*, April 25, 1935, p. 5.

Lattimore, Ralston. "*Pylon*: A Novel by William Faulkner." Savannah *Morning News*, April 7, 1935, p. 26.

McGill, Ralph. "Faulkner Writes On." Atlanta *Constitution*, April 7, 1935, p. 8-B.

Meyer, Luther. "Faulkner, Flying Scribe in New Opus." San Francisco *Call-Bulletin*, March 30, 1935, p. 8.

N., I. "Not Good Faulkner." Los Angeles *Times*, March 24, 1935, Part II, p. 6.

Patterson, Alicia. "The Book of the Week." New York *Sunday News*, March 24, 1935, p. 70.

Redman, Ben Ray. "Flights of Fancy." *Saturday Review of Literature*, March 30, 1935, pp. 577–81.

Riley, Edith. "*Pylon*." Houston *Post*, April 14, 1935, Society Section, p. 7.

R[oueché], B[erton]. "Faulkner's Furious Portrait of the Lost." Kansas City *Star*, April 13, 1935, p. 14.

Salpeter, Harry. "Memory and Experience." *Literary America*, 2 (June 1935), 418.

S[cott], W[infield] T[ownley]. "Some Americans of Our Time and a Couple of Faulkners." Providence *Sunday Journal*, March 31, 1935, Section VI, p. 4.

Stallings, Laurence. "Gentleman from Mississippi." *American Mercury*, 34 (April 1935), 499–501.

Troy, William. "And Tomorrow." *Nation*, April 3, 1935, p. 393.

Wagner, Charles A. "Books." New York *Mirror*, March 25, 1935, p. 25; and March 24, 1935, p. 29.

Warwick, Ray. "*Pylon*" Atlanta *Journal*, April 14, 1935, Magazine Section, p. 12.

Weeks, Edward. "Atlantic Bookshelf." *Atlantic Monthly*, June 1935, p. 16.

W[emer], W[illis]. "*Pylon*." San Diego *Union*, March 31, 1935, Feature Section, p. 7.

W[illiams], S[idney]. "Faulkner's *Pylon* and Bishop's *Act of Darkness*." Philadelphia *Inquirer*, March 30, 1935, p. 11.

ABSALOM, ABSALOM!

William Faulkner

Absalom, Absalom!

New York · Random House · 1936

A. B. Bernd.
"Today's Book."
Macon *Telegraph*,
October 25, 1936, p. 4.

When an author remains breathless for almost 400 pages, he should by rights expect his readers to reach that state of fatigue of which breathlessness is a symptom. Yet such is the magic of William Faulkner's style and method that the reader becomes only a fellow-panter, eagerly turning chaotic pages to learn the next terrifying tragedy that will overwhelm a group of forbidding and inhuman neurotics.

For Faulkner has imagination and power—qualities requisite to good literature. His fund of invention seems endless—though limited to such abnormal persons as we customarily prefer not to know intimately. He wastes in a single novel a dozen minor incidents that would make masterful short stories in themselves—and, as a matter of fact, he has used one of his own best short stories, "Wash," which appeared in *Harper's* two or three years ago, as a major incident in this book.

His driving force is tremendous. His words catapult from his pen with such impetuous violence that the wonder is, not that he is able to arrange them in order (for in this novel, at last, Mr. Faulkner boldly throws grammar overboard and follows his own private rules of syntax), but that he can communicate his meaning as clearly as he does. Naturally there are lapses. Occasional strings of words seem as relevant as the major output of Gertrude Stein. But for the most part, their meaning, in spite of some difficulty with pronominal reference, is perceivable, and their construction lamentable.

Reading Faulkner is an experience. Grant him his right to his own peculiar language (and he is a highly capable master of it). Grant him his circuitous method. Grant him his technique of creating suspense, not by something inherent in his story, but by a highly artificial means of arranging his revelations. Make these concessions, and sit down for an evening with *Absalom, Absalom!* You will find yourself absorbed, aroused, profoundly stirred, completely removed from your familiar world into the semi-lunatic asylum which is Mr. Faulkner's Mississippi.

For here again, the Mississippian writes of that world which is his by right of creation as surely as Poictesme belongs to Mr. Cabell. (May I insert a note for any aspirant to an M.A. in American Lit? A comparison of Faulkner and Cabell as products of the old South—and both of them assuredly are—should make as stimulating a dissertation as ever passed across a full professor's desk.) The town is the familiar Jefferson, with Benbows and Sartorises lurking hazily in the distance.

The chief actors this time are the families, right-handed and left-handed, which sprang from the loins of Thomas Sutpen "born in West Virginia mountains, 1807 . . . Major, then Colonel,—th Mississippi Infantry, C.S.A. Died, Sutpen's Hundred, 1869." Sutpen himself, seeking fortune in his youth, had wandered to Haiti and married a woman of alleged Spanish descent. Discovery of a flaw in her story caused him to desert her; and about 1833 he appeared in Jefferson, married a daughter of the town, and settled down to a turbulent and harried existence on a huge estate he had fraudulently wrested from the Indians.

Bizarre tragedy dogged his steps. Two children born of his American union, as well as the sole product of the West Indian affair, paid for the sins of their father. Everyone at all implicated in the unfolding of his life suffered—even the Confederate cause to which he devoted four years. An aura of hate surrounded him, a legacy of violence was all he could leave to a devastated world.

Essentially this is the familiar tale of the rise and fall of a Southern planter. Yet Mr. Faulkner has invested it with a freshness and new beauty by his heady style, his impatient flow of words and thoughts and figures, his unique narrative technique, no less than by his keen insight into human motives and his intense preoccupation with abnormal psychology. He writes like a man who is drunk, but he thinks like a coldly sober analyst. Racial and sexual relations dominate the world of his brain; and he penetrates them and exposes them as no other American writer does.

Incidentally, in this book, for the first time, he shows signs of going literary. He appends a chronology of the events in the tale, a genealogy of its characters, and a map of Jefferson and its surrounding territory (Area 2,400 sq. mi. Population, whites 6,298; Negroes, 9,313). On the map he shows the location of many incidents in *Absalom, Absalom!, Sanctuary, Light in August* and the other books: and he appends to it: "William Faulkner, Sole Owner and Proprietor." It is all a good deal like Mr. Cabell's Poictesme.

George Marion O'Donnell. "Mr. Faulkner Flirts with Failure."
Nashville *Banner*, October 25, 1936, Magazine Section, p. 8.

Seemingly coming out of nowhere, Thomas Sutpen appeared in Jefferson, Miss. in 1833, with a wagon full of wild Negroes and a frightened French architect. And, while the town wondered at him, Sutpen traded the Indians out of 100 square miles of land, built on his land the biggest house in the county, married the daughter of a respectable Jefferson merchant, fathered two children, and became the richest man in the community. All of this he accomplished with endless difficulty, but nevertheless accomplished, acting always in a kind of violent haste which made more than one person think of him as demoniac, mad in his desire to attain some goal which no one of them could define. Sutpen lived to see an impending incestuous marriage between his daughter and his son by the first wife whom he had married in Haiti and put aside upon discovering that she had Negro blood. He lived to see this marriage stopped when the bridegroom was killed by his own half-brother, the brother of the bride, who immediately fled from home. He lived to fight through the War of the confederacy, to hear of his wife's death, to return from war and start the rebuilding of his estate with the same violence which had characterized his original building of it. He lived to propose marriage to his wife's younger sister, to win her consent, then to insult her so that she hated him for the forty-four remaining years of her life. He descended at last to the keeping of a country store for a livelihood, still inspiring awe and some fear in his neighbors. And he died, at 62, violently as he had lived, killed by the grandfather of his sixteen-year-old paramour. This was Sutpen of Sutpen's Hundred. And he was all of this because, as a poor-white child in Virginia, he was turned away from the front door of one of the great mansions by a Negro servant, and because he had resolved to vindicate that child who was the demoniac Sutpen himself.

"He is bigger than all them Yankees that killed us and ourn, that killed his wife and widowed his daughter and druv his son from home, that stole his niggers and ruined his land," says Wash Jones, the man who later is to kill Sutpen, "bigger than this whole country that he fit for and in payment for which has brung him to keeping a little country store for his bread and meat; bigger than the scorn and denial which hit held to his lips like the bitter cup in the Book."

Returning for his setting to the Mississippi country of *Sartoris* and *As I Lay Dying* and *The Sound and the Fury*, Mr. Faulkner has built his new novel, *Absalom, Absalom!* around this man, who stands out as a new sort of figure in Southern fiction, in all his demoniac fierceness and strength. And with him in the book live also the people who lived around him and wondered at him during his lifetime. For in this novel, Mr. Faulkner has presented at once one man's life, the way of life in which he existed, a whole section of the country, and a whole passage of time.

But the story and the characters are not revealed in any conventional fashion. Mr. Faulkner is still experimenting with form; and this is probably a healthy sign, indicating that he is not yet finished as a novelist and is not likely to be finished for some time, despite the major artistic defects of his two previous books, *Light in August* (the formal structure of which does not stand the test of rereading), and *Pylon* (which is probably the worst of Mr. Faulkner's novels). For this new book, Mr. Faulkner has adopted a strange device: the story is revealed only as it takes form in the understanding of Quentin Compson (one of the Compson family who appeared in *The Sound and the Fury*) and becomes so much a part of him that "he was not a being, an entity, he was a commonwealth," so much a part of him that he can say of himself: "I am older at 20 than a lot of people who have died"—and say this without speaking falsely, without speaking with

the world-weariness of youth. This taking form of the story in Quentin's understanding occurs in the summer before he leaves for Harvard in 1910, and in the winter of his first year at Harvard, long after most of the events in the narrative have taken place.

Quentin functions as an actor, insofar as he is present at the startling denouement of the story. But primarily, Quentin might be called a Special Listener; his part is to hear people talk about Sutpen and about the doings surrounding him and his family. Those whom Quentin hears are his father, who tells what his own father knew and told him, and Miss Rosa Coldfield, Sutpen's sister-in-law whom he insulted.

Sometimes Mr. Faulkner reports their actual speech to Quentin. Sometimes he follows Quentin's mind as he thinks of the story. Sometimes he reports Quentin's speech as he tells the story to his roommate at Harvard. Sometimes the roommate, who has evidently heard parts of the story before this particular telling, interrupts Quentin to recount these parts of it. And in the last three sections of the book, all of these methods are combined, sometimes in such a manner that reading is difficult, the story is obscured, and it becomes necessary to refer to the beginning of a passage to determine just what character is acting as narrator. This is undoubtedly a stylistic fault. Difficulty is probably legitimate in fiction; but it has a very tenuous legitimacy, being always dangerous because it may perform the decidedly illegitimate function of standing between the reader and his final understanding of the characters and of the story, instead of helping him toward that understanding.

Moreover, when Quentin's roommate tells Quentin all over again parts of the story which Quentin himself must have told to the roommate, then the process seems a little ridiculous. It cannot fail to call to mind the device by which inexperienced dramatists make their exposition of antecedent action—those tense moments in which a husband reminds his wife that they have been married for five years and now have two children!

However, these are not major faults. Though the method of construction in this book is a dangerous one, it appears to succeed. The book seems narrowly to evade formlessness; yet it does manage the evasion, because of Mr. Faulkner's device of using Quentin as his Special Listener, even if it does not achieve perfect formal coherence.

One might question at times the realism of the narrator's speech, because they speak often in a kind of prose-poetry familiar to readers of *The Sound and the Fury*. But this is defensible in *Absalom, Absalom!* on the ground that Mr. Faulkner is dealing with characters who speak and think in the elaborate, Latinesque, sometimes oratorical style characteristic of the antebellum South. And it is defensible on the different ground that Mr. Faulkner is not writing just what can be said in narrative speech; he is writing all that cannot be said (trying thereby to project the very experience itself) along with what can be narrated. And experiences actually are projected in *Absalom, Absalom!* by means of this style. Here, too, Mr. Faulkner is daring; here, once more, he is flirting with failure. A novel can not be so complex and artistic a presentation of experience as a poem, since a novel necessarily excludes more of the minutiae of an experience, giving only the essentials where a poem may give much more of rich detail. And the ignoring of this limitation is a dangerous thing. Mr. Faulkner, however, is a conscientious and profound artist. And it is more likely that he deliberately accepts the danger than that he accidentally stumbles into it. That he does accept the danger, and still manages to defy it successfully, is one more evidence of Mr. Faulkner's artistry. For by this acceptance Mr. Faulkner manages to recreate the story of Sutpen whole, as it would be revealed in life, yet richer than life itself because of the strong, controlled power of his art.

With all of its minor stylistic and formal defects, *Absalom, Absalom!* is fiction of a high order of excellence, strong from its roots in the life of a people and in a land and in a time, rich from the experience of that people, and beautiful from its sincere telling by one of that very race, who has mastered his art as have few of his contemporaries.

Bernard De Voto. "Witchcraft in Mississippi." *Saturday Review of Literature*, 15 (October 31, 1936), 3–4, 14.

It is now possible to say confidently that the greatest suffering of which American fiction has any record occurred in the summer of 1909 and was inflicted on Quentin Compson. You will remember, if you succeeded in distinguishing Quentin from his niece in *The Sound and the Fury*, that late in that summer he made harrowing discoveries about his sister Candace. Not only was she pregnant outside the law but also, what seared Quentin's purity much worse, she had lost her virginity. In the agony of his betrayed reverence for her, he undertook to kill both himself and her but ended by merely telling their father that he had committed incest with her. This blend of wish-fulfillment and Southern chivalry did not impress Mr. Jason Richmond Compson, who advised his son to take a vacation, adding, in one of the best lines Mr. Faulkner ever wrote, "watching pennies has healed more scars than Jesus." Quentin went on to Harvard, where, however, the yeasts of guilt, expiation, and revenge that are Mr. Faulkner's usual themes so worked in him that he eventually killed himself, somewhere in the vicinity of the Brighton abattoir. But at the end of *The Sound and the Fury* not all the returns were in. It now appears that only a little while after he was pressing a knife to Candace's throat—I make it about a month—Quentin had to watch the last act of doom's pitiless engulfing of the Sutpens, another family handicapped by a curse.

Mr. Faulkner's new fantasia is familiar to us in everything but style. Although the story is told in approximations which display a magnificent technical dexterity—more expert than Mr. Dos Passos's, and therefore the most expert in contemporary American fiction—and although the various segments are shredded and displaced, it is not a difficult story to follow. It is not, for instance, so darkly refracted through distorting lenses as *The Sound and the Fury*. Though plenty of devices are employed to postpone the ultimate clarification, none are introduced for the sole purpose of misleading the reader, and in an access of helpfulness, Mr. Faulkner has included not only an appendix of short biographies which make clear all the relationships, but also a chronological chart which summarizes the story. If you study both of them before beginning the book, you will have no trouble.

Thomas Sutpen, the demon of this novel, has a childhood racked by the monstrous cruelties to which all Faulkner children are subjected. He has immeasurable will—like evil, will is always immeasurable in Faulkner. He forms a "design": to found a fortune and a family. In pursuit of it he marries the daughter of a Haitian planter, has a son by her, discovers that she has Negro blood, abandons her, and rouses in her a purpose of immeasurable revenge. He takes some Haitian slaves to Mississippi, clears a plantation, becomes rich, marries a gentlewoman, and begets Henry and Judith. At the University Henry meets his mulatto half-brother, Charles Bon, who has been sent there by his vengeful mother, who knows the secret of his parentage, and who is married to a New Orleans octoroon. Henry worships Charles at sight and helps to effect his engagement to Judith. Thomas Sutpen inconceivably does nothing to prevent the engagement till, just before the Civil War, he tells Henry the secret of Bon's birth, though not (and here again the motive is what Mr. Faulkner would call unmotive) that of his Negro blood. Through four years of war Henry remains jubilant about the contemplated incest, but when his father at last reveals the secret he cannot accept incestuous miscegenation, and so shoots Bon when he goes to claim his bride. Henry then disappears and Thomas Sutpen, still demonic, comes back to rehabilitate both his estate and his posterity. He informs the sister of his dead wife (who also was tortured in childhood and hates all men, though she contrives to desire two of them) that if he can succeed in begetting a male child on her, he will marry her. Being a Southern gentlewoman, she declines, and Sutpen begets a child on the fifteen-year-old granddaughter of a poor-white retainer. The child is a daughter and so Sutpen's design is ruined forever. The grandfather kills him with a scythe, kills the granddaughter and the child with a butcher's knife, and rushes happily into the arms of the lynchers. The relicts then send for Charles Bon's son and raise him, a mulatto, with further tortures. He rebels, marries a coal-black wench, and begets a semi-idiot, the last of the Sutpens who gives a tragic twist to the title of the novel.

The horror which Quentin Compson has to undergo occurs many years later, when Henry Sutpen has crept back to die in the ruined mansion, cared for by the shrivelled Clytie, another mulatto of Thomas's get. Henry and Clytie are burned up in the final holocaust, the ritualistic destruction of the house of hell and doom that is in part repeated from *Light in August*.

Mr. Faulkner, in fact, has done much of this before. This off-stage hammering on a coffin—Charles Bon's coffin this time—was used to make us liquefy with pity in *As I Lay Dying* where it was Addie Bundren's coffin. And when Addie's coffin, with the corpse inside, slid off the wagon into the flooded river, the effect then gained discounted the scene in *Absalom, Absalom!* where the mules bolt and throw Thomas Sutpen's corpse and coffin into the ditch. Much of Henry Sutpen's ambiguous feeling for his sister Judith was sketched in Quentin Compson's attitude toward Candace. When Charles Bon forces Henry Sutpen to shoot him, moved by some inscrutable inertia of pride and contempt and abnegation (or moved by unmotive)—he is repeating whatever immolation was in Popeye's mind when he refused to defend himself against the murder charge of which he was innocent, near the end of *Sanctuary*. These are incidental repetitions, but many fundamental parts of *Absalom, Absalom!* seem to come straight out of *Light in August*. It is not only that Etienne Bon undergoes in childhood cruelties as unceasing as those that made Joe Christmas the most persecuted child since Dickens, not only that he is moved by the same necessity to wreak both revenge and forgiveness on both black and white that moved Joe, not only that he commits some of the same defiances in the same terms, and not only that the same gigantic injustices are bludgeoned on the same immeasurable stubbornness and stupidity in the same inexplicable suc-cession. It is deeper than that and comes down to an identity of theme. That theme is hardly reducible to words, and certainly has not been reduced to words by Mr. Faulkner. It is beyond the boundary of explanation: some undimensional identity of fear and lust in which a man is both black and white, yet neither, loathing both, rushing to embrace both with some super-Tolstoian ecstasy of abasement, fulfillment, and expiation.

The drama of *Absalom, Absalom!* is clearly diabolism, a "miasmal distillant" of horror, with clouds of sulphur smoke billowing from the pit and flashes of hellish lightning flickering across the steady phosphorus-glow of the graveyard and the medium's cabinet. And it is embodied in the familiar hypochondria of Mr. Faulkner's prose, a supersaturated solution of pity and despair. In book after book now he has dropped tears like the famed Arabian tree, in a rapture of sensibility amounting to continuous orgasm. The medium in which his novels exist is lachrymal, and in *Absalom, Absalom!* that disconsolate fog reaches its greatest concentration to date. And its most tortured prose. Mr. Faulkner has always had many styles at his command, has been able to write expertly in many manners, but he has always been best at the phrase, and it is as a phrase-maker only that he writes well here. Many times he says the incidental thing perfectly, as "that quiet aptitude of a child for accepting the inexplicable." But, beyond the phrase, he now—deliberately—mires himself in such a quicksand of invertebrate sentences as has not been seen since *Euphues*. There have been contentions between Mr. Faulkner and Mr. Hemingway before this; it may be that he is matching himself against the Gertrude-Steinish explosions of syntax that spattered *Green Hills of Africa* with bad prose. If so, he comes home under wraps: the longest Hemingway sentence ran only forty-three

146

lines, whereas the longest Faulkner sentence runs eighty lines and there are more than anyone will bother to count which exceed the thirty-three line measure of his page. They have the steady purpose of expressing the inexpressible that accounts for so much of Mr. Faulkner, but they show a style in process of disintegration. When a narrative sentence has to have as many as three parentheses identifying the reference of pronouns, it signifies mere bad writing and can be justified by no psychological or esthetic principle whatever.

It is time, however, to inquire just what Mr. Faulkner means by this novel, and by the whole physiography of the countryside which he locates on the map of Mississippi in the vicinity of a town called Jefferson. This community is said to be in the geographical and historical South, and the Sutpens, together with the Compsons and the Sartorises and the Benbows and the Poor Whites and the Negroes, are presented to us as human beings. Yet even the brief summary I have made above shows that if we are forced to judge them as human beings we can accept them only as farce. Just why did not Thomas Sutpen, recognizing Charles Bon as his mulatto son, order him off the plantation, or bribe or kill him, or tell Judith either half of the truth, or tell Henry all of it? In a single sentence toward the end of the book, Mr. Faulkner gives us an explanation, but it is as inadequate to explain the tornadoes that depend on it as if he had tried to explain the Civil War by the annual rainfall at New Granada. Not even that effort at explanation is made for most of the behavior in the book. Eulalia Bon's monotone of revenge is quite inconceivable, and her demonic lawyer is just one more of those figures of pure bale that began with Januarius Jones in *Soldiers' Pay* and have drifted through all the novels since exhaling evil and imitating the facial mannerisms of the basilisk. Miss Rosa (another Emily, without rose) is comprehensible neither as a woman nor as a maniac. Why do the children suffer so? Why did Rosa's father treat her that way? Why did Sutpen treat Henry and Judith that way? Why did Judith and Clytie treat Etienne that way? Just what revenge or expiation was Etienne wreaking on whites and Negroes in that Joe Christmas series of attempts at self-immolation? Just what momentary and sacrificial nobility moved Wash Jones to kill three people? Just what emotion, compulsion, obsession, or immediate clairvoyant pattern of impotence plus regeneration plus pure evil may be invoked to explain the behaviour of Charles Bon, for which neither experience nor the psychology of the unconscious nor any logic of the heart or mind can supply an explanation?

Well, it might answer everything to say that they are all crazy. As mere symptomatology, their behaviour does vividly suggest schizophrenia, paranoia, and dementia precox. But that is too easy a verdict, it would have to be extended to all the population of Jefferson, the countryside, New Granada, and New Orleans, and besides the whole force of Mr. Faulkner's titanic effort is expended in assuring us that this is not insanity.

A scholarly examination might get us a little farther. This fiction of families destroyed by a mysterious curse (beginning with the Sartorises, there has been one in every novel except *As I Lay Dying* and *Pylon*), of ruined castles in romantic landscapes, of Giaours and dark "unwill," may be only a continuation of the literature of excessive heartbreak. The Poe of "Ligeia" and kindred tales, Charles Brockden Brown, Horace Walpole, and Mrs. Radcliffe suggest a clue to a state of mind which, after accepting the theorem that sensation is desirable for itself alone, has moved on to the further theorem that the more violent sensation is the more admirable, noble, and appropriate to fiction.

Surely this reek of hell and the passage to and fro of demons has intimate linkages with Eblis; surely Vathek saw this ceaseless agony, this intercellular doom, and this Caliph's heart transparent as crystal and enveloped in flames that can never be quenched. Surely; and yet that tells us very little.

Much more central is the thesis advanced in these columns a couple of years ago, that Mr. Faulkner is exploring the primitive violence of the unconscious mind. Nothing else can explain the continuity of rape, mutilation, castration, incest, patricide, lynching, and necrophilia in his novels, the blind drive of terror, the obsessional preoccupation with corpses and decay and generation and especially with the threat to generation. It is for the most part a deliberate exploration, Mr. Faulkner is at pains to give us Freudian clues, and he has mapped in detail the unconscious mind's domain of horrors, populated by anthropophagi, hermaphrodites, Hyppogypi, acephalites, and cynocephalites. It is the world of subliminal guilt and revenge, the land of prodigy which D. H. Lawrence thought was peopled exclusively by beautiful, testicular athletes, but which is inhabited instead by such races as Mandeville and Carpini saw. These are the dog-faced men, the men whose heads do grow beneath their shoulders, who feed on corpses, who hiss and bark instead of talking, whose custom it is to tear their own bowels. A far country, deep under the mind's frozen ocean. In Mr. Faulkner's words, a "shadowy miasmic region," "amoral evil's undeviating absolute," "quicksand of nightmare," "the seething and anonymous miasmal mass which in all the years of time has taught itself no boon of death."

Haunted by the fear of impotence and mutilation and dismemberment, hell-ridden by compulsions to destroy the mind's own self and to perpetrate a primal, revengeful murder on the old, cataleptic in the helplessness of the terrified young, bringing the world to an end in a final fantasy of ritual murder and the burning house—the inhabitants of the prodigy-land of the unconscious are also fascinated by those other primal lusts and dreads, incest and miscegenation. In Joe Christmas and Etienne Bon, neither white nor black, repudiating both races, inexplicably ecstatic with love of both, mysteriously dreading both, mysteriously wreaking revenge and expiation on both, we face a central preoccupation of Mr. Faulkner, a central theme of his fiction, and, I think, an obligation to go beyond the psycho-analytical study of his purposes. In spite of his enormous labor to elucidate these two mulattoes and their feelings and their symbolism in society, they are never elucidated. What is it that bubbles through those minds, what is it that drives them, what are they feeling, what are they trying to do, what do they mean? You cannot tell, for you do not know. A fair conclusion is that you do not know because Mr. Faulkner does not know. I suggest that on that fact hinges the explanation of his fiction.

It is a fact in religion. For the energy derived from primitive sources in the mind projects a structure of thought intended to be explanatory of the world, and this is religious, though religious in the familiar reversal that constitutes demonology and witchcraft. William James has told us how it comes about. The simple truth is that Mr. Faulkner is a mystic. He is trying to communicate to us an immediate experience of the ineffable. He cannot tell us because he does not know—because what he perceives cannot be known, cannot therefore be told, can never be put into words but can only be suggested in symbols, whose content and import must forever be in great part missed and in greater part misunderstood. This is a mysticism, furthermore, of what James called the lower path. There are, James said, two mystical paths, the one proceeding out of some beatitude of spiritual health which we may faintly glimpse in the visions of the saints. It is from the lower path, the decay of the vision, that witchcraft always proceeds. And witchcraft, like all magic is a spurious substitute for fundamental knowledge.

The crux of the process by which witchcraft came to substitute for the ordinary concerns of fiction in Mr. Faulkner's work may be observed in *Sartoris*. His first book, *Soldiers' Pay*, introduced the overwhelming despair finding expression in lachrymation and the creatures of unadulterated evil that have appeared in all his later books—curiously combined with the glibness and tight technique of magazine fiction. His second book, *Mosquitoes*, was his *Crome Yellow* effort, and had in common with his other work only a pair of lovers moving on some manic errand through a nightmare world. With *Sartoris* (which was published, if not written, before *The Sound and the Fury*), he became a serious novelist in the best sense of that adjective. He undertook to deal fairly with experience, to articulate his characters with a social organism, and to interpret the web of life in terms of human personality. Wherever he was factual and objective—in Loosh, Miss Jenny (who is his best creation to date), the unmystical Negroes, the crackers, the old men, Dr. Alford—he imposed a conformable and convincing world of his own on a recognizable American experience, in symbols communicative to us all. But he failed in the principal effort of the novel. What he tried to do, with the Sartorises themselves, was to deliver up to us the heart of a mystery—to explain the damnation, the curse, of a brilliant, decayed, and vainglorious family doomed to failure and death. And he did not do it. They were a void. We did not know them and he could not tell us

about them. They were without necessity, without causation. When he faced the simple but primary necessity of the novelist, to inform us about his characters, he backed away.

He has been backing away ever since. All the prestidigitation of his later technique rests on a tacit promise that this tortuous narrative method, this obsession with pathology, this parade of Grand Guignol tricks and sensations, will, if persevered with, bring us in the end to a deeper and a fuller truth about his people than we could get otherwise. And it never does. Those people remain wraiths blown at random through fog by winds of myth. The revelation remains just a series of horror stories that are essentially false— false because they happen to grotesques who have no psychology, no necessary motivation as what they have become out of what they were. They are also the targets of a fiercely rhetorical bombast diffused through the brilliant technique that promises us everything and gives us nothing, leaving them just wraiths. Meanwhile the talent for serious fiction shown in *Sartoris* and the rich comic intelligence grudgingly displayed from time to time, especially in *Sanctuary*, have been allowed to atrophy from disuse and have been covered deep by a tide of sensibility.

Mary-Carter Roberts. "Faulkner's Style Dwarfs Material in New Novel." Washington *Evening Star*, October 31, 1936, p. 2-B.

Fighting with his own prose like a man slashing his way through a forest of falling velvet curtains armed only with a dull knife, William Faulkner here writes

149

another novel of human disintegration in terms of the far South. It is on the whole a fine performance, though its excellence rests on Mr. Faulkner's formidable prowess as a consistent stylist rather than on any significance in his material.

For his story, just as a story, is purely conventional. It is the tale of a Mississippi plantation, from the time it was cleared out of virgin jungle by Thomas Sutpen in 1833 up to the destruction of the Sutpen family line in 1910. Such plots have been common to the point of weariness in the American novel in the past few years, though they have by no means always dealt with Southern scenes. They have told the tale of the sturdy New England skipper who built up a fortune with his clipper ships, erected a fine house in his pride and then saw his descendants degenerate into softness until nothing of his creative effort remained. Or they have told of the children of the New York patron, going through the same cycle, or the Pennsylvania German family, or have dealt with the descendants of sod-breaking prairie pioneers who went West with the light of conquest in their eyes.

The pattern has always been the same, however. It is the story of human resources dwindling to a vanishing point from a parent of original force and genius. Mr. Faulkner has not changed the outline in any remarkable degree. But he has contributed a luridly tragic coloring that lifts his book well above the ruck of the others.

Through the sheer pounding music of his prose he has invested his conventional stuff with conviction and significance. He writes here as he has in past novels—that is, as if he were the only writer in the world, and as if no one were expected to read his book except himself. To him, obviously, the story of the Sutpen plantation has been immensely tragic. Its conventionality simply has not occurred to him. He writes with newness about it,

with a profound personal sense of the horror of its decay and degeneration, not as if he were telling the tale to some other person, but as if, from that cycle of human regression he had drawn such a dark and dreadful beauty that for his own sake alone he must needs reproduce and preserve it. And so we have a novel that stands high among its contemporaries simply as a prose structure, a signal triumph of style over content and an example of artistic conviction as a force to give old tales new life and significance.

Beyond that there is not much to say about the work.

Cameron Shipp. "Confederacy's Hamlet: Faulkner's New Novel." Charlotte *News*, November 1, 1936, p. 8-B.

Through all of Mr. William Faulkner's novels, violence speaks dreadfully out of a muffled past, like the ghost of Hamlet's father mumbling under the boards, and his characters walk a dark stage, where kingly and terrible things are curtained and half-revealed in dark, rich rhetoric. And we see, when we have looked closely and studied the setting and the lines, that what Mr. Faulkner is showing, what he is striving to reveal—striving with the same burning repression of his stultified, noble and indecent characters— . . . is the South painfully groping between forgetfulness and a new way.

And to Mr. Faulkner, this groping is no easy thing to set down, no easy thing to see, or talk about. In him, somehow, there loom vast, atavistic impressions of evil; and in him burns a horrible shame and a hatred for the unclean, low people who rose on the cash crop when and after the South went to war, not, indeed, as an agrarian state, but as an industrial nation with something to produce and to sell, and niggers to make it.

I think, then, that Mr. Faulkner has fulfilled himself in *Absalom, Absalom!* and that this is his master work. It is, by its very genius, the hardest to read. I confess at the outset that many times I was lost and terrified in the shadows and thunders of his involved prose, lost and annoyed in his ramifications of chronology and ancestry.

The story is the starkest melodrama. It has to do with Thomas Sutpen, who came from nowhere with a tired horse and handsome pistols, with his crew of savage negroes from the swamps, and who built himself a fine mansion on acres in Mississippi thefted from an Indian. Sutpen, who was poor white trash of the meanest sort, bought his respectability by marrying the daughter of an upstanding Methodist. He had children, but his own past, his own son by a negress in Haiti, rose to commit murder, and his own life, in the end, came to despair. Mr. Faulkner shows, not clearly, but impressively, what happened when there came to power in the South the men who seized the stations and lands of the master classes, but were neither able nor willing to accept their responsibilities.

His method of telling this story is unique. The tale is revealed by Miss Rosa Coldfield, who was the aunt of Sutpen's wife, and once betrothed to him herself, in a narration to young Quentin Compson. It is the story a bitter old woman, haunted by the past, tells to a reluctant boy of this generation.

This book, like all of Mr. Faulkner's, is foreboding and powerful. In fulfilling his dark legend, it is his best. It may, though, be barred from the best seller lists by the hardships of its curious, symbolic and oftentimes beautiful prose.

"Disgusting."
Fort Wayne *News Sentinel*, November 7, 1936, p. 4.

Any pleasure to be had from this disgusting book must be described as little short of sadistic. Revolting as the whole volume is, perhaps Christian charity suggests the conclusion that Mr. Faulkner cannot be blamed altogether for insisting upon turning out such slime; for he apparently was just born to see things the way he does see them. But this fact does not alter the lacerating, bitter, repulsive result of his serious writing one bit.

This is the story of Sutpen's Hundred, a plantation of 100 square miles carved out of Mississippi by a poor white named Thomas Sutpen—a strange sort of feudal domain with the slaves, the crops, and the multifarious relationships and crosscurrents adding up to tragedy and idiocy rather than to moonlight and magnolias, lavender and old lace.

Gradually as the novel unfolds, Faulkner gives the reader a picture of the 103 years between the day when Sutpen was born of poor white stock in the West Virginia mountains and the day when a final catastrophe wipes the evidence of his life off the face of the earth—all the evidence but the illegitimate idiot great-grandson who goes howling off into the void.

The century is so full and so complicated that a synopsis is not possible, and so sordid that no such synopsis is desirable. A cloud of horror hangs over the whole story from the first to the last. The characters are so twisted and so tortured that there is almost no humor.

Max Miller.
"*Absalom, Absalom!*"
San Diego *Union*,
November 15, 1936,
Feature Section, p. 7.

In *Absalom, Absalom!* William Faulkner is still determined to be "different" at all costs, and this time the cost is a most elaborate inarticulateness.

Always he has wallowed in morbidity. That is no news. But this time he not only wallows in morbidity, but he adds to the confusion by making his sentences pages long, each sentence often interspersed with phrases in italics and with other phrases in parentheses.

And so if the secret of great writing is to write in a cross-word puzzle code that only the writer can decipher then Faulkner this time certainly should have the boys and girls buffaloed into the epitome of admiration.

I gathered somewhere that the novel was about the decaying south, beginning somewhere around 1807 with the birth of a poor white named Thomas Sutpen and ending in 1910 with the burning down of a house. But so many different persons are telling the story, and so many stories are being told within stories, that for the life of me I frequently thought that Faulkner in all this confusion of morbidity was trying to play a grand game of hide-and-go-seek with all of us.

Usually he has tried to shock us with sex, incest and all that sort of thing. He has a little of it here, too. But so many others by now have out-sexed him in this regard that he apparently has tried different tactics by being a little like James Joyce and a little like the Bible.

To give a plain sentence which can be understood apparently is obnoxious to him, now that for once he has stopped borrowing that tiresome mannerism of Hemingway's to follow each conversational remark with an "he said" or a "she said." It did attract attention once, but like all mechanical tricks in writing the trick soon wore out—but not soon enough.

If in the great show-down of years, *Absalom, Absalom!* does prove to be a great book then the joke is on me. But I have yet to know a great book which was built exclusively on tricky confusion.

Winfield Townley Scott.
"Faulkner, His Critics, and a Fresh Survey."
Providence *Sunday Journal*, November 22, 1936, Section VI, p. 8.

Let us be honest and admit that this review of William Faulkner's new novel has been delayed at least a month—a month put in in such matters as reading other reviews of *Absalom, Absalom!* The delay, as it happened was inevitable, but the reading of other reviews is unpardonable: a dangerous procedure, at best, for any reviewer-to-be. In the instance of *Absalom, Absalom!* nevertheless, I doubt very much if one's opinions could be guided by anything but the book. It is the kind of book which is so personally conceived and so individually executed that anyone, reading it, will have no time for other reactions; even though he may have noted that Carl Van Doren has called it Faulkner's best novel, and that nearly all other reviewers have joined the anti-Faulkner clan which grows apace—and which, by the way and for the sake of history, it must be admitted the present reveiwer anticipated: he being well-known and disliked in a small circle as the local scribe who shouted "nonsense" at *The Sound and the Fury* and thereby failed of a place among the discoverers of this writing angel of the decadent wastes of Mississippi.

Well, enough of that. Faulkner is long since discovered and, as I say, now well on his way to the abuse which grows out of any literary boom in this country. And as for *Absalom, Absalom!* I should venture—to be perverse—that Mr. Van Doren is nearer being correct in his judgment of it than its detractors are in theirs.

It is, like most of Faulkner's work, a violent tale of the South, plotted with the ingenuity of a dime novel, worked out in shuttle fashion so that understanding it is a labor, and written in a rushing prose of occasionally mystifying but always tongue-soothing richness. It will do little good to say that this is the tale of Thomas Sutpen, rugged individualist of the old South, who begot his own ruin in the begetting of a part-Negro child. It will do little further good to suggest in a few words that Sutpen and his ruin and result are symbolic of the crash of our pre–Civil War southern civilization. Of course, Sutpen is; but to translate all this from Mr. Faulkner's book would be like attempting a paraphrase of music—you may do it, but it's better to tell your listener to go listen to the music itself.

So here. I found *Absalom, Absalom!* deadening in certain parts of its back-tracking and forward-rushing (1807 to 1910, back and forth, several times). As a story, I found it bordering on the ridiculous—but many times with the sublime. Faulkner's sublimer passages are, simply, more frequent than those of most contemporary writers. Again and again in this novel there are those quick, raw glances into people or into time or into both (he has mixed them brilliantly here) which seem to leave one a more sensitive person than before. Few writers can do that.

W. E. Stegner. "New Technique in Novel Introduced." Salt Lake City *Tribune*, November 29, 1936, p. 13-D.

It is occasionally salutary for a reviewer to read other reviews of a book before he writes his own, if only for the caution it will give him about mistaking subjective judgements for truths. Where the book in question is difficult or involved or revolutionary in its approach, he will be astonished also to find how few critics are willing to let a writer do as he wishes, how few will judge a book on the standards it sets for itself instead of on standards the critic would impose upon it.

So, after reading half a dozen reviews of *Absalom, Absalom!* one is led to preface all his utterances with "I suspect." I suspect, for example, that Clifton Fadiman's review in *The New Yorker* is not only impercipient and lazy, but silly as well. I suspect that three other reviews in reputable papers are at least impercipient and probably lazy. I suspect that the only review that does Faulkner's last book anything like justice is that by Bernard De Voto in the *Saturday Review*.

I suspect further that one cannot dismiss *Absalom, Absalom!* as 400 pages of turgid and invertebrate sentences about psychopathic ghosts. It is true that with isolated lyrical exceptions the experimental sentences do not come off; they are frequently not only invertebrate but downright bad syntax. The characters are

153

admittedly ghostly and fleshless; the technique "cocks its snoot" at chronology and logic. Granted one reviewer's charge that Faulkner writes his guts out trying to tell a simple story in the most complex way possible, there is still reason to believe that he probably knew what he was doing, and why he was doing it.

If Faulkner had wanted to tell simply the simple story of demonic Thomas Sutpen's rise from poor white to opulent planter, his matrimonial experiments with whites and Negroes, his desire for a son and a perpetuated name, and the final dissolution of that dream in a flaming house haunted by the whimperings of a half-wit mulatto who is the only survival of the Sutpen blood, he could have told it as simply as that. The very fact that he didn't is proof enough that he didn't want to, that the manner is more important to him than the matter.

Instead of assuming the omniscience of motive and impulse and reaction that even the most realistic novelists in the past have felt obliged to assume, Faulkner presents his story through the mouths of seven different people, in what De Voto calls a "series of approximations." While there is plenty of character analysis here, it is frankly tentative, frankly the attempt of one character to understand another. The whole book, therefore, gives the impression of wavering uncertainty as Quentin Compson, Harvard freshman, tries to unravel the tangled threads of a tale which has reached him from a dozen incomplete sources, mutually contradictory in spots, filled with dark gaps where informants' knowledge gave out.

In other words, this novel, despite its shadowy, nightmarish quality, is in one respect the most realistic thing Faulkner has done. It reconstructs historical materials as any individual in reality has to reconstruct them—piecemeal, eked out with surmise and guess, the characters

ghostly shades except in brief isolated passages. As in life, we are confronted by a story whose answers even the narrator does not know, whose characters he (and we with him) guesses at and speculates upon, but does not attempt to explain fully.

What Faulkner is actually saying, as explicitly if not as simply as it has ever been said, is that no man, novelist or otherwise, can know another except in the trivial superficies of his life; that the mind and emotions of another are mysteries as deep as the hereafter; that we arrive at our knowledge—or rather, our surmises—of other people through these approximations, these driblets of information from six or 600 sources, each driblet colored by the prejudices and emotions of the observer.

That is how we know Demon Thomas Sutpen; how we arrive at a conception of Miss Rosa and her thwarted emotional life; how we know what little we do of the motives of Henry Sutpen and of Charles Bon, who was to marry Judith's sister and whom Henry killed. We know as much as Quentin does, as much as Faulkner does; and at the end of the book Quentin and his roommate are frankly guessing, extemporizing, trying to piece out sections of the plot which are wholly dark, creating plausible but wholly imaginary characters to fill in the gaps, endowing them with motive and action to fit the few surviving facts.

Perhaps that is what the critics are howling about, that they don't know any more about these "psychopathic ghosts" than they do about the people they associate with every day. Accustomed to having our fictional characters complete, fully rounded, we feel cheated if an author rejects the omniscient lie at the basis of most fiction. Perhaps, too, Faulkner doesn't entirely succeed; certainly the style is tortured beyond what most readers will stand. But I suspect, and strongly, that the mere technique of this novel may prove to be a significant contribution to the theory and art of fiction; and that *Absalom, Absalom!* will not be the last, or the best, to approach its materials in this way.

David Vern.
"*Absalom, Absalom!*"
Washington Square Review, December 1936, pp. 8, 23.

William Faulkner's *Absalom, Absalom!* continues his remarkable tradition of dividing the critics. Here is his thirteenth published volume, yet critical literature on Faulkner is as unsettled, or unformed as if he were just beginning to write.

One might expect by now that an attitude towards the man had begun to crystallize—like the general nod of approbation that soothes Sinclair Lewis no matter what he writes, the cerebral reception that Huxley gets, or even the jokes about length, etc., that a comparative upstart like Thomas Wolfe provokes. But every new Faulkner book is received like a first novel. All judgements are tentative pending . . . ah . . . surprise. The whole matter resolves itself, finally, very simply indeed. You are either for Faulkner, or against him. *Absalom, Absalom!* has come in for a good deal of extreme criticism. It has been called everything from masterful to muddled. It has been labeled a worthless bore, an idiot's exercise, and conversely a difficult and profound work. This reviewer found *Absalom, Absalom!* to be one of the best books to be found in many months, and probably Faulkner's best work.

The difficulties and obscurantism have been somewhat exaggerated. However, the one thing you must not demand from Faulkner is immediate understanding. You may finish a chapter without having discovered its relation to the book. Pay close attention, and keep on. Sooner or later it will fit in and make sense—beautiful sense usually. Faulkner is not writing chapters; he is writing a novel. And it is as a novel that you should judge its meaning. Often you will re-read a sentence or paragraph five or six times before it is clear. This is nothing to object to in itself, for we have all spent hours on a page of intricate economic theory, or an involved syllogism. The question actually is whether it is worth so much time to get the meaning. I would say yes.

But there are other questions. How necessary or valuable is this method? Could Faulkner use a more simple one? Both questions can be answered by saying that to change the method is to change the book. The essence of the book is its method—almost more than what it says. It must remind you in many ways of Gertrude Stein's laboratory novels, especially when you hit the new words that Faulkner has made for himself, actually more communicative than Stein's method of washing the old ones. Again, for some perverted reason, you may now and again think of Proust. Chiefly, this will be because of something as absurd as the fact that Faulkner's sentences run on and on—but occasionally you will get the wonderful whiff of reminiscence, not mellow, not sweet, but harsh, acrid.

Here the method has set the whole atmosphere of the book. There is the excellently conceived feeling of the dead appearing to live again—although not really—more in the way an embalmer paints the features of the corpse, and knows his ministrations will accent the fact of death.

The subject matter is again the South and the time is the Civil War period. The book is told as a story in jumps and jerks, with the memories which compose it given in studied disorder. But the author has provided a genealogy, a map and chronology. From the creator of Popeye, this is a serious gift. Indeed, Faulkner's whole bearing has changed noticeably. Not only has the vocabulary range been extended, but the style, that is, the actual wording in structure has gone on from what *Pylon* forecast, with at least one major deviation.

Faulkner's seeming, or actual, (depending which side you are on) emphasis on the abnormal is not very evident here. The crisp, short statements that Faulkner often used for higher explosive content is gone. He does not, anymore, state the bare facts. Rather, the story grows in layer after layer of fact, repeated, or rounded out, or given a new sidelight or different context. The resultant verisimilitude resembles that achieved by a social history. And if a character saves a bag of gouged eyeballs, it merely seems true. The method also has an unusual effect on the few characterizations in the book. They form slowly, as does everything else, but occasionally they flash into complete, luminescent figures. It is almost as if the author let gas escape for a while, and then lit a match.

The writing is rhythmic, cadenced, and reflective; the structure often is experimental. Unless thought and people excite you, it isn't terribly exciting. But much of it is first rate, and all of it worth reading.

Paula Snelling.
"Mr. Faulkner Adds a Cubit."
Pseudopodia, 1 (Winter 1937), 4, 16.

A parable recommends that tares be permitted to grow along with wheat until harvest lest an attempt to weed out the former result in uprooting the latter. Mr. Faulkner has adhered literally to the admonition. During the years he has developed a quality of wheat unsurpassed in many of its attributes. The tares have been cultivated almost as assiduously. When the critic in his temerity essays the role of reaper and would harvest first the tares to be burned then the wheat to be stored, he is confronted with a problem which Matthew 13:30 takes no cognizance of. For the two have become so entangled that a separation is well-nigh impossible.

No one can read William Faulkner's books without arriving at the conclusion that the man has truly remarkable powers. Nor can one read these books without recognizing that the stigmata of the third-rate recur in them with a frequency which cannot be dismissed. The writer demonstrates again and again an intuitive awareness of the hidden maelstrom of the unconscious, a mature knowledge of the sufferings an individual must endure when impulses are in too severe conflict with the demands of his civilization, a fierce hatred for the unnecessary suffering which man puts upon man, a deep pity for the victim of uncontrollable forces. And when he is writing of these things there is in his cadenced prose a surging power which few have achieved. These are qualifications of the very first order. But seldom can the reader turn a dozen pages without being confronted with some gratuitous horror; some spectacle which might have been lifted with no extenuations from the most shameless thriller. Or he encounters an appeal to race fears and prejudices having about the connection with the essential story that dinosaurs have with the superiority of a particular kind of motor oil. Or he is led to the brink of what seems a significant revelation only to have the scene shifted to a different time and place—often for the praiseworthy purpose of revealing a new facet which will make the delayed comprehension more complete; almost as often in what seems the spirit of moron Luster jerking the spoon from imbecile Benjy's opening mouth.

Several hypotheses, none wholly tenable, present themselves by which to account for the existence of such seeming incongruities in a mature and gifted artist. Perhaps he originally had (or early acquired) a "positive tropism" for all manifestations of the gruesome, as did Poe, and as he developed had the discrimination to bring his mature powers to bear primarily on those of deepest present significance; but has not rid himself of the vestigial inclination to display whatever hodgepodge of horror he can incidentally collect. Or, granted this fascination with the shocking, it may be that the emotional drive which carries much of his writing to so high a level, and which by its very potency testifies that it taps the writer's unconscious, short-circuits when its goal is too distant and requires frequent small stimuli to keep the current flowing. Or, again, it may be that he thinks as sorrily of mankind as the preface to *Sanctuary* indicates and believes that a reading public cannot be found for his books save through the lure of more and worse monstrosities; and is willing to barter his integrity. To shift the suppositions to a more philosophic level, it is possible that man is such that he cannot look directly at Truth. That when Jehovah would dole out a minimal decalog he can present it to even the great prophet only through the veil of a thick cloud and to the ludicrous and sorry fanfare of thunder and lightning, smoke and fire. Small wonder the prophet returns with not only a graven stone and a shining face, but with reverberations of thunder and after-images of lightning by which to bemuse himself and his people.

Mr. Faulkner's newest book reaches a higher level than do even *Light in August* and *Sound and the Fury*, in which the merely sensational and titillating had yielded the center of the stage to comprehension and portrayal. Though the primary object of his attention here as always is cruelty and decadence, he recognizes and throws more light upon the existence of these qualities in others than freaks. Yet here too he negates much of the major significance of his writings (that the "perversions" at which we shudder in the "abnormal" have their roots and often their more dire manifestations in the drab and circumspect "normal") by investing with a spurious and sinister halo of unusualness the very characters whom he otherwise draws so truly and understandingly. The tall tale element of which he so entertainingly showed himself the master in "Spotted Horses" and in the Indian stories of *These 13*, and which played a large part in *As I Lay Dying*, scarcely enters here. In his twelve books Yoknapatawpha county and the town of Jefferson, Mississippi, have become so thickly peopled with real and interesting characters whose lives overlap that the map and the genealogy appended to *Absalom, Absalom!* are useful as well as interesting. This last book centers around a man, Sutpen, whose silence concerning his past (and his present and future) and whose single-minded and at times ruthless pursuit of his uncommunicated ambition shroud him in unholy mystery in the eyes of the Jefferson people of the early and middle nineteenth century; so that now, in 1909, when most of the victims of the drama and destruction which came to those closely associated with Sutpen have died and the survivors are not willing or not able to unravel all the threads of mystery, the attempt to reconstruct the story resolves itself frequently into the speculations of first one and then another. The section in which Rosa Coldfield relives her part (tenuous, yet the core of her life and sufficient to make of her a poet and philosopher) is perhaps the richest section of the book. It would be unfair to summarize baldly a story whose value is derived largely from the significance and overtones which accrue as the reader learns first one incomplete part, then another tantalizing fragment and gradually arrives, as he does in life, at as full a comprehension as is permitted him. But it touches on several matters which have, at intervals, troubled man's sleep: ambition, conflicts of personalities, murder, poverty, war, gossip, courage, miscegenation, hate, love, marriage without love, sympathy, slavery, incest, friendship, blood ties, family pride, torture, reputation, loyalty, inadequacy, hope, imbecility, wealth, betrayal, suspense, loneliness . . . ; and is well worth anyone's reading. [Ellipsis dots are in the original review.]

Herman B. Deutsch. "Faulkner Provides a Design for Life." New Orleans *Item*, January 24, 1937, Metropolitan Section, p. 7.

Consciously or sub-consciously, any one who strives for understandable expression—writer, composer, painter, dramatist, or sculptor—has but a single goal in view, and this is the evocation of an emotional reaction in those by whom the finished work is seen or read or heard. Thus the old-time heavy of the melodramas, who twirled his mustachios, wore a silk topper, and—oh, ultimate depravity!—smoked cigarettes, the while he gritted: "I have you in my power, me proud beauty!"

felt definitely flattered when the audience hissed him, for he had roused in them the emotional response which was the final tribute to his artistry as a mime.

The appearance of Mr. Faulkner's latest book has been hailed, even in some quarters where one might least expect it, by such hisses, and the innocent bystander is entitled to the suspicion that certain scholarly critics have succumbed to a sort of Faulkner-phobia; that is, the fear that this one time Mississippi golf professional cannot possibly be as great a writer as he really appears to be, and that one had better take a sound swat at him for general results.

For, *Absalom, Absalom!* is a great book, a tremendous book, a novel of foremost importance. Essentially it is the expansion to book form of one of Faulkner's earlier short stories—"Wash" (see the volume: *Dr. Martino and Other Stories*). If its prose and its structure are both a bit more involved, possibly labyrinthine, than even the style to which Faulkner himself has accustomed us in the past it is likewise true that the novel is more searching, more profound and (in the progressive spell of inescapable doom which it lays upon the reader no less surely than upon the hapless characters that people its pages) more dramatic than anything Faulkner had hitherto given us.

When all is said and done, what are these indictments which have been lodged against *Absalom, Absalom!* by those whose views are entitled to serious consideration? (Obviously it is impossible to devote any regard to the "That nasty man!" school whose artless slogan is the question: "Can't he ever find anything pleasant to write about? There's enough trouble in the world as it is without borrowing more grief from a book"—these being the people who enshrined as best sellers *Green Light*, in this generation; *The Sheik* in the one before; and *The Winning of Barbara Worth* in the one before that.)

First: "The style is so involved that the story can be followed, if at all, only with great difficulty." It is quite true that Faulkner has cast aside and disregarded all limitations of time and space in this volume; that the narrative presentation is not sequent but shifts abruptly from place to place and/or backward and forward through the years; that a paragraph—even a sentence—which begins in a Mississippi hill county of the 1840's may well end in a Harvard dormitory on a winter's night of 1910 or on a Haitian sugar plantation in 1927. The only possible rejoinder to this criticism is: "What of it?—as long as the author brings it off," which Faulkner indubitably does. What matter how long or involved a sentence may be if it evokes an awareness of beauty in itself and brings the reader a fractional step closer to a realization of the implacable doom which is closing remorselessly down upon something that has been made real and warmly palpitant with life. One is almost tempted by way of reply to point out that the stately development of themes in Wagner's *Ring* series was once assailed as a meaningless lot of discords by those who saw in the melodic trivialities of "*Il Trovatore*" the ultimate goal of operatic achievement.

What else? "The book, the theme, the treatment, all are morbid." Morbid, of course, is a matter of definition. There are some to whom the cloying scent of tuberoses is morbid, because it calls to mind the mortuary atmosphere of funerals. To the surgeon and the medical student, there is nothing macabre about an autopsy of a corpse pickled in brine. It is true that, out-Faulknering himself, the author in this instance piles the Ossa of incest upon the Pelion of miscegenation. So what? So out of my own lifetime I yet recall the day when the word "legs" was shunned as the plague in polite discourse, when such things as underwear were re-ferred to—if at all—by speaking in hushed and bated tones of flannel unmentionables. So (likewise) is there more of the "morbid"—in this particular sense—in any of the salacious contes droles will hear at almost any cocktail party after the third (or if the gin was carelessly purchased) after the first round of what passes for a potable beverage, than can be found in the length and breadth of all Faulkneriana.

Absalom, Absalom! is the story of the frustration of a tortured soul's design for living. Thomas Sutpen is the son of poor white trash, born in a West Virginia hill cabin, and, at the age of 10 or there-abouts, is made aware for the first time of his place in the social scheme when, delivering a message at the nearby manor house, the Negro butler refuses to let him so much as state his errand unless he goes around to the back door. The plan and design for his life are thenceforth fixed. He must prosper and become the sort of figure who is admitted to any front door. Material wealth alone will not achieve this. He must found a family, a sort of Sutpen dynasty, with sons to carry on his name down the endless lighted corridors of time out of the darkness of his own squalid beginnings.

He runs away to Haiti, where he achieves success as manager for a sugar planter of French descent whose daughter, Eulalia Bon, he marries. A son, Charles, is born to the union. Within the year Sutpen learns that in Eulalia's veins—and consequently, in those of his son, Charles—there is an admixture of Negro blood. He divorces Eulalia, taking twenty of the wild plantation Negroes in settlement. With these he comes to Mississippi, purchases a hundred acres of land, virtually kidnaps a French architect from New Orleans and holds him prisoner while he and the slaves build the stateliest and most elaborate manor house in all the countryside.

He marries Ellen Coldfield, daughter of

159

a small storekeeper. Two children—Henry and Judith—are born. A slave girl, Clytemnestra, is also Sutpen's daughter.

Meanwhile Eulalia Bon has come to New Orleans with Charles, concealing from all the unnoticeable taint of Negro blood. In common with other gallants of the period, Charles adopts a quadroon mistress. Vengeful and unforgiving, Eulalia Bon has followed Sutpen's career. When he sends his son Henry to the University of Mississippi, at Oxford, she sends Charles there too. Henry invites Charles to come to Sutpen's Hundred for Christmas. Charles meets Judith and they fall in love. Sutpen forbids Charles the house, seeing in him once more the features of the woman he had banished from his life in Haiti 25 years ago. Henry feels—and so do we as readers—that it is because of Charles' involvement with the quadroon girl in New Orleans that Sutpen sends him forth.

There can be no climax yet, for the war of the states halts everything. Sutpen's Hundred is deserted. The colonel and Henry and Charles are all with the University Greys; the Negroes—the wild Haitian blacks and the others, have all left in the wake of the first blue-coated regiment to pass that way. Meanwhile Charles has learned that Sutpen is his father. If Sutpen will show his awareness of the fact by but one look or sign, he, Charles, will leave Judith, will drop out of their lives as though he had never entered them. But Sutpen refuses the sign. Henry, by now himself aware of the situation, kills him to save his sister from the incestuous and inter-racial union, and then flees.

Sutpen returns, an old man, a widower, and yet savagely determined to begin at this late day the grim task of building the plan and design of his life anew. He proposes to Rosa Coldfield, his very much younger sister-in-law, that they live together to see if it is possible for them to have a son; if the son is born he will marry her. Outraged, she leaves the place.

In a final despairing spring toward creation, Thomas Sutpen seduces the granddaughter of one of his retainers, a poor white named Washington Jones, and gets her with child. When the child is born—a daughter, not a son,—Wash kills Sutpen, his grand-daughter and the newborn infant, and is himself slain by the posse that comes to arrest him.

There is but one other remaining wellspring of the Sutpen blood. To dead Charles Bon and his quadroon mistress one son was born, Charles Etienne St. Valery Bon. In savage revolt against both the white race and the black, he finally marries the most apish black woman he can find and to them, one son is born—for Charles Etienne does not live long; he and Judith Sutpen both fall victims to a yellow fever epidemic. The son, a mulatto half-wit know as Jim Bond—a corruption of Bon—is finally all that is left of all the Sutpen blood.

Absalom, it will be recalled, murdered his brother for the rape of their sister, Tamar, and lost his life in revolt against his father. Just why the one tale should be morbid and the other not, is unclear to this reviewer. The tragedy of the father who is desolate in the knowledge that his blood must perish with him, is as keen in one year as it is in another—and across six thousand years the father's grief echoes in the poignant cry, from Mesopotamia to Mississippi: Absalom, Absalom, my son Absalom!

M. L.
"Cult of Infantilism."
American Spectator, February–March 1937, pp. 13–14.

Absalom, Absalom! makes pretensions of the first order. William Faulkner would be considered a giant of modern literature. His followers and satellites make grandiose claims for him. He deals in large themes; his prose is "revolutionary"; he is unbound by the technical traditions of the novel; he has been called one of the most "formidable" writers of our time. Thus Faulkner can not object if the severest tests are applied to his ability as a novelist.

This book concerns Tom Sutpen, who, with his twenty Negroes, strides into a little Mississippi town. He buys a hundred acres of land, builds himself a mansion in the grand style, engenders the fear and hatred of the townspeople. Tom Sutpen asks pity of no man and deals ruthlessly with all the world: he must accomplish the design which he evolved when, as a boy, he was turned away from the front door of a plantation mansion. He determines to build the Sutpen dynasty.

Sutpen marries, acquires two children Henry and Judith, as well as a miscellaneous collection of offspring by women of Negro blood. Sutpen is haunted throughout life by the black taint. His first wife had been tinged with Negro blood, though he had not known it, and borne him a son Charles. Charles and Henry meet in college, and Charles recognizes the younger man as his brother. He falls in love with Judith, and would commit incest with her. Throughout the years of the Civil War, even in the thick of battle, Henry and Charles are concerned with this problem.

Finally Henry grants his permission to Charles; his resistance to incest is worn down. But he learns of the tiny drop of Negro blood in his half-brother—and miscegenation he cannot permit. So he kills Charles and brings the body to his sister's feet.

Tom Sutpen is murdered by a poor white man whose grand-daughter he had seduced. The great mansion falls into decay, and finally is burned. And every person who strides through the book is dead—with the exception of a half-witted, half-caste son—the Sutpen dynasty.

Do not imagine it is easy to learn what the guiding motive of Sutpen's life is. Author Faulkner, macabre and sadistic, delights in rendering his plots so that the reader will not easily untangle them.

There are other plots interwoven with the major story: the story of Rosa Coldfield who tells part of the tale, poor old Rosa, the eternal old maid, who has "the rank smell of female old flesh embattled in virginity"; there is the story of Quentin, a Harvard Freshman, who set out to determine the facts of the Sutpen mystery, and whose brain weaves the story in such a manner that it is not always clear whether he is stating facts or imagining them.

Attempts undoubtedly will be made to read into *Absalom, Absalom!* a wider interpretation. Some will say that the book is an indication of the decay of the old South, and is symbolic of the eventual conquering of the old aristocratic civilization by the breed of Jim Bond, half-wit. Such would be a highly tortured interpretation upon a work which is itself already sufficiently tortured. Tom Sutpen, who wrestles with Negroes, is no southern aristocrat, is not typical of the southern ruling class. Jim Bond and Wash Jones, the poor white, hardly represent the spirit of revolt out of which a more equable southern civilization can grow. And those who know Faulkner will realize very well that he has no apology to make for southern aristocracy.

Any novel, to bear the stamp of quality, must be able to reveal motives and designs and emotions and events common to many individuals; it must evoke powerful sympathies by means of what psychologists call *Einfüblung*, or identification. Faulkner does not deal with people and with things in this manner. His individuals—the Sutpen family—are not to be frequently duplicated. Their violent course through life gives no meaning to other lives. The impact of social and economic forces upon the family is quite unlike the impact of these forces upon other families. In this sense, Faulkner's work is petty, unimportant. If one is held by the plot, by the sudden and inexplicable dropping of a strand here and the taking up of a new line of thought there, it is as one is held by a mystery movie—one wants to know what the outcome will be. The final impression will be of horror, of pervading sickliness. Faulkner's adherents may insist that he is uncovering elemental human motivations here: probably he is uncovering only Faulkner.

The line from Joyce through Gertrude Stein to Faulkner is clear. Joyce's clear chronology is lacking, but certainly the use of words is more intelligent than anything in *la belle Stein*. Still, in his attempt to achieve either a lyrical effect or some sort of mystic grandeur, Faulkner displays for words an almost surgical morbidity. He has a peculiar reverence for italics, and in some places page after page is filled with italics to indicate a stream of consciousness or a lack of certainty about the person who is engaged in discourse. And what logic is it that makes Faulkner revel in negatives of words—such as "not-husband," "notpeople," "notlanguage," "un-amaze." It recalls the acrobatic antics of the sleazy intellectuals who used to write for *transition*, that egomaniac's

dream, some years ago. But the literary world has since grown more mature. Such devices should draw only the contempt of an honest writer, for they give him a means whereby he can perpetrate bad writing and slovenly thinking under the guise of profundity, and at the same time gain the adulation of weakish ladies and gentlemen who adore anything they can't understand.

Such devices could not be summarily condemned, they would find ample justification, if they simplified the reading, if they rendered the story more lucid, if they clarified the text, or heightened the emotional content. But the reverse is true. They make reading difficult, they becloud the outlines of the story, they encase the details in a fog, and they add nothing to the understanding of thought processes.

The characterizations are disunified, only Sutpen excepted. Charles, who emerges as a suave, cultured, luxurious, sophisticated young man, changes completely and becomes almost naive when he first enters the Sutpen home—why? because Sutpen shows him no sign of recognition. It is doubtful whether so complex a personality as Charles would stake so much for a simple nod of recognition. Ellen, Sutpen's wife, is unclear throughout. She reminds one of a silhouette cut-out: one wonders what the features really are like. Rosa hates Sutpen with an implacable hatred, yet when he calmly announces he will take her to wife, she says nothing. Quentin Compson and Shrevlin McCannon, who tell the story to each other (sometimes they seem to be the characters themselves) are ghostlike figures, with little flesh and blood in them.

One thing a writer must remember: he writes not only for himself, but for readers. Insofar as he indulges in mumbo-jumbo or pseudo-mysticism, just so far does he forfeit his right to a permanent place in literature.

When literary historians essay our time, William Faulkner will figure as a curio. And he will be placed in a category which will bear some name like The Cult of Infantilism.

Checklist of Additional Reviews

"A Bog and a Clear Sky." Philadelphia *Evening Public Ledger*, October 26, 1936, p. 22.

"*Absalom, Absalom!*" Galveston *Tribune*, October 30, 1936, p. 5.

Council Bluffs (Iowa) *Nanpariel*, October 31, 1936.

"Faulkner Has Nightmare about the South in Civil War Days." *Newsweek*, October 31, 1936, p. 26.

Philadelphia *Record*, October 31, 1936.

"Southern Cypher." *Time*, November 2, 1936, p. 67.

Santa Monica (Calif.) *Outlook*, November 5, 1936.

Glendale (Calif.) *News-Press*, November 6, 1936.

"Best Sellers of the Season." Lewiston (Me.) *Evening Journal*, November 7, 1946, Magazine Section, p. 9.

Akron (Ohio) *Press*, November 8, 1936.

"The Deep South: William Faulkner's *Absalom, Absalom!*" Springfield (Mass.) *Sunday Union and Republican*, November 8, 1936, p. 7-E.

New York American (Rochester), November 22, 1936.

South Coast News (Laguna Beach, Calif.), November 27, 1936.

Greenwich (Conn.) *Graphic*, December 2, 1936.

"Brought to Book." New Haven *Journal-Courier*, December 3, 1936, p. 6.

Salisbury (N.C.) *Post*, December 6, 1936.

"*Absalom, Absalom!*" Sioux City (Iowa) *Tribune*, January 30, 1937, p. 4.

"*Absalom, Absalom!*" San Francisco *News*, February 20, 1937, Section II, p. 15.

B[eecroft], J[ohn]. "*Absalom, Absalom!*" *Wings*, December 1936, p. 12.

Becker, Charlotte. "*Absalom, Absalom!* Is Rated Faulkner's Most Important Contribution to American Letters." Buffalo *Sunday Times*, October 25, 1936, p. 2-C.

Bower, Helen C. "Tangled Threads." Detroit *Free Press*, November 1, 1936, Part III, p. 18.

Brickell, Herschel. "William Faulkner's New Novel Once More Sets Forth Theory that the South Is Doom-Ridden." New York *Post*, October 26, 1936, p. 13. Also see note in *Review of Reviews*, December 1936, p. 15.

Canfield, Dorothy, "*Absalom, Absalom!*" *Book-of-the-Month Club News*, October 1936.

Caperton, Mary. "William Faulkner's Macabre Imagination Puts Queer Zoocracy in Ante-Bellum South." Louisville *Courier-Journal*, November 1, 1936, Magazine Section, p. 4.

Chappell, John O., Jr. "Faulkner's Deep, Dark South." Cincinnati *Enquirer*, November 7, 1936, p. 5.

Childers, James S. "Novel Written by William Faulkner Is Strange Book." Birmingham *News*, November 22, 1936, Magazine Section, p. 7.

Colum, Mary M. "Faulkner's Struggle with Technique." *Forum and Century*, January 1937, pp. 35–36.

Corley, Pauline. "A Chronicle of the South from a Bitter Pen." Miami *Herald*, October 25, 1936, p. 11-C.

Cowley, Malcolm. "Poe in Mississippi." *New Republic*, November 4, 1936, p. 22.

Culver, Rae. "Mr. Faulkner at His Best." Unidentified newspaper, November 22, 1936.

Darrow, Mary B. "Southern Setting." Glendale (Calif.) *News-Press*, November 6, 1936, p. 8-B.

Dorais, Leon. "Three Novels Interpreting the South." San Francisco *Chronicle*, January 24, 1937, p. 4-D.

Fadiman, Clifton. "Faulkner, Extra-Special, Double-Distilled." *New Yorker*, October 31, 1936, pp. 62–64.

Gannett, Lewis. "Books and Things." New York *Herald Tribune*, October 31, 1936, p. 17.

Grainger, Paul. "*Absalom, Absalom!*" Minneapolis *Journal*, November 1, 1936, Editorial Section, p. 5.

Grimes, George. "Evil Blights Again in Another Faulkner Novel of the Deep South." Omaha *Sunday World Herald*, November 8, 1936, p. 11-E.

Hansen, Harry. "William Faulkner's New Book a Dark and Terrible Story. Its Prose a Triumph." New York *World-Telegram*, October 26, 1936, p. 19; Greensboro *Daily News*, October 28, 1936, Pittsburgh *Press*, November 11, 1936.

Hedger, Suzanne. "Dramatic and Powerful." *Pacific Weekly*, November 16, 1936, p. 333.

Hoch, Henry George. "Horrid Myth and Real Man: Curious Life Drama in Faulkner's Novel." Detroit *News*, November 15, 1936, Home and Society Section, p. 18.

Jack, Peter Monro. "Nightmares of Evil." New York *Sun*, October 30, 1936, p. 30.

Kilman, Ed. "Reviewer Finds Faulkner Book Task to Read." Houston *Post*, December 27, 1936, Section II, p. 7.

Lawton, Mary. "Different." Atlanta *Constitution*, November 23, 1936, p. 9-M.

Mann, Dorothea L. "William Faulkner as Self-Conscious Stylist." Boston *Evening Transcript*, October 31, 1936, p. 6.

Maslin, Marshall. Santa Rosa (Calif.) *Press Democrat*, November 28, 1936.

McClure, Robert E. "Strange Genius." Santa Monica *Evening Outlook*, November 5, 1936, p. 12.

M[ebane], J[ohn]. "*Absalom, Absalom!*" High Point (N.C.) *Enterprise*, November 22, 1936, p. 4.

Meyer, Luther. "Reading with the Bookworm." San Francisco *Call-Bulletin*, November 14, 1936, p. 6.

Murphy, Spencer. "Faulkner's New Novel Baffling but Effective." Unidentified newspaper, December 6, 1936.

N., D. A. "Dark Faulkner." Brooklyn *Daily Eagle*, October 25, 1936, p. 19-C.

Parks, D. W. "Can't Tell Story and Be Through." St. Louis *Post-Dispatch*, November 1, 1936, p. 4-J.

Parks, Edd Winfield. "Six Southern Novels." *Virginia Quarterly Review*, 13 (Winter 1937), 154–56.

Paschall, Walter. "*Absalom, Absalom!*" Atlanta *Journal*, November 8, 1936, Magazine Section, p. 12.

Paterson, Isabel. "An Unquiet Ghost out of the Old South." *New York Herald Tribune Books*, October 25, 1936, p. 3.

Patterson, Alicia. "Notes on Some of the Season's Better Books." New York *Sunday News*, November 22, 1936, p. 90.

Phillips, Russell. "The Literary Lantern." Charlotte *Observer*, November 29, 1936, Section III, p. 5.

Rahv, Philip. "Faulkner and Destruction." *New Masses*, November 24, 1936, pp. 20–21.

Ramsay, J. P. "The New Faulkner." Camden (N.J.) *Post*, October 31, 1936, p. 8.

Reynolds, Morgan. "*Absalom, Absalom!* Is Story of Strife, Not Easy to Read, but Entrancing." Richmond *News Leader*, October 27, 1936, pp. 9, 19.

Ritchie, Ward. "Some Tragic Ghosts Evoked in Faulkner Tale." Los Angeles *Times*, January 3, 1937, Part III, p. 6.

Roueché, Berton. "*Absalom, Absalom!*" *University Review*, 3 (Winter 1936), 137–38.

S., J. C. Birmingham (Ala.) *News*, November 22, 1936.

Selby, John. "Pleasure to Be Derived from New Faulkner Book Almost Sadistic." Gastonia (N.C.) *Gazette*, October 24, 1936.

Sloan, Sam B. "William Faulkner Writes His Most Ambitious Novel." Des Moines *Sunday Register*, November 1, 1936, Society Section, p. 6.

Smith, Henry (Nash). "William Faulkner Continues to Depict Decadence of South." Dallas *Morning News*, November 29, 1936, Section II, p. 9; also reviewed in *Southern Review*, 2 (No. 3, 1937), 583–85.

Smith, Russell. "Faulkner's Quality of Mercy." Washington *Post*, October 25, 1936, p. 8-B.

Sonnichsen, C. L. "Dusk in White Faces." El Paso *Herald-Post*, October 30, 1936, p. 5.

Strauss, Harold. "Mr. Faulkner Is Ambushed in Words." *New York Times Book Review*, November 1, 1936, p. 7.

Towne, Charles Hanson. "Pity Poor Reviewer on a Day like This." New York *American*, October 27, 1936, p. 36.

Troy, William. "The Poetry of Doom." *Nation*, October 31, 1936, pp. 524–25.

Van Gelder, Robert. "Books of the Times." New York *Times*, October 25, 1936, p. 15.

W., H. T. "Tragic but Gripping." Syracuse *Post-Standard*, November 8, 1936, Section I, p. 4.

Wagner, Charles A. "Books." New York *Mirror*, October 31, 1936, p. 12.

White, William Allen. "Books of the Fall." *Saturday Review of Literature*, October 10, 1936, pp. 16, 26.

Wile, Florence. "*Absalom, Absalom!*" Shreveport *Times*, November 8, 1936, p. 9.

Williams, Sidney. "Sinuosities of Faulkner, and Sterling North." Philadelphia *Inquirer*, November 7, 1936, p. 13.

THE UNVANQUISHED

WILLIAM FAULKNER

★

THE UNVANQUISHED

Drawings by
Edward Shenton

★

RANDOM HOUSE   NEW YORK

John Cournos.
"The Spirit of the South in the Civil War Lives in Faulkner's *The Unvanquished*."
New York *Sun*, February 16, 1938, p. 23.

William Faulkner knows his South, and it is possible that in the series of pictures he has penned of the Sartoris family in Mississippi during the latter days of the Civil War and the first days of the Reconstruction period he has not merely tried to perpetuate the spirit of a past age but also to indicate that the spirit is inherently alive to this day. The title of the book itself, *The Unvanquished*, is perhaps symbolic; the North has physically conquered the South, but there is something in the Southerner, especially in the woman of the South, essentially irrational and defying analysis; and this mysterious virtue, like John Brown's soul, goes marching on.

Some of the sketches in this book have already appeared in the magazines, but they have been skillfully rewritten and linked together to form one continuous narrative, which is episodic and atmospheric at the same time. It is for the most part the story of that very remarkable character, Rosa Millard, better known as Granny; and all of it is written reminiscently in the first person by Bayard Sartoris, son of the valiant Colonel, John Sartoris, and grandson of Rosa Millard. Bayard is only 14 at the beginning of the story, and the constant companion of his adventures, from the moment they hide under Granny's skirts to escape the just vengeance of the Yankees for having shot a horse, is Ringo, a shrewd, venturesome and depend-

able darky of his own age, who has a presence of mind and stout heart, neither of which forsakes him in an emergency; the emergencies are frequent and provide ample excitement, such as comes to civilians in war-time, passionately partisan. It is Ringo, young as he is, that is Granny's chief accomplice in the conspiracy to rob the Yankee army of mules by the simple device of forged orders signed by United States colonels; and the imperturbable old lady re-sells the same mules to the Yankee army at good prices, only to ply the patriotic and profitable trade elsewhere, a trade which seems to benefit the community of which she is a member more than it does her. This chapter is inevitably of an anecdotal nature, and amply entertaining, even if one is left to doubt that the Yankees could be consistently such fools as to allow a little old woman to get away with it for so long. The author at all times appears to be anxious to show that the Yankees, if they were fools, were always gentlemen, at least as far as women were concerned; and Granny, though faced with a whole sheaf of forged orders, gets off scot free.

There was no real war down where the Sartorises lived, not the first three years at any rate. Yet, atmospherically, and, in some curious degree physically, felt and experienced, particularly by the women and children, a war was in progress. "We knew a war existed; we had to believe that, just as we had to believe that the name for the sort of life we had led for the last three years was hardship and suffering. Yet we had no proof of it. In fact, we have even less than no proof; we had had thrust into our faces the very shabby and unavoidable obverse of proof, who had seen father (and the other men, too) return home, afoot like tramps or on a crowbait horse, in faded and patched (and at times obviously stolen) clothing, preceded by no flags nor drums and followed not even by two men to keep step with

169

one another. ..." It is this sort of reality that Mr. Faulkner has a superb knack of presenting, more often in terms of atmosphere, especially when Gen. Sherman's detachments find their way into Mississippi, and we have the extraordinary picture of freed Negroes on their nocturnal marches, and we are with Drusilla, who is yet to become the Amazon of Col. Sartoris's troop of cavalry, as she listens fascinated to the very breath of the, as it were, mystically moving, dark hordes, audible in the still night. Equally impressive is the persistent pursuit by Bayard and Ringo of Snopes and Grumby, one or the other of whom, or both, had done Granny in on her final venture. This happens when the war is over, but the war is by no means over for the South. Private feuds and vendettas, and resistance to Negro participation in government rule, replace the struggle with the North.

At times Mr. Faulkner writes with simple eloquence and power, and at times he is irritably obscure, both as to the identity of the characters and the nature of the action in which they take part; and now and then there is a piece of labored prose which means much or nothing, according to how much the reader is willing to read into it. An example of this is when Mr. Faulkner, with his fondness for perverse characters, has Drusilla, now married to Col. Sartoris, beg her stepson for a kiss, and he, kissing her, threatens to tell father. Then follows: "'Yes,' she said. 'You must tell him. Kiss me.' So again it was like it had been before. No. Twice, a thousand times and never like—the eternal and symbolic thirty to a young man, a youth, each time both cumulative and retroactive, immitigably unrepetitive, each wherein remembering excludes experience, each wherein experience antedates remembering; the skill without weariness, the knowledge virginal to surfeit, the cunning secret muscles to guide and control just as

within the wrists and elbows lay slumbering the mastery of horses: she stood back, already turning, not looking at me when she spoke, never having looked at me, already moving swiftly on in the dusk: 'Tell John. Tell him tonight.'" This is, indeed, "writing fiction as if it were a painful duty." But Henry James, of whom Wilde used these words, was superbly lucid compared to this, even at his worst. And it must be remembered that Mr. Faulkner writes of a milieu which is relatively primitive compared to the sophisticates who moved in James's drawing-rooms.

Charles C. Clayton. "Vivid Vignettes of War in the Deep South." St. Louis *Globe-Democrat*, February 19, 1938, p. 2-B.

William Faulkner's greatest gift is his ability to give contemporaneousness to the past. It has never been more impressive than in *The Unvanquished*, which although it is not his most powerful book, is in many respects the best book he has written.

The Unvanquished is a series of seven short stories set in that section of Mississippi Mr. Faulkner has adopted as his own, during and after the war between the states. All but one of them has appeared in magazines. They have been woven into a continuous narrative and the result is a series of sharply etched episodes of those years as they might stand out in retrospect in the memories of the people who experienced them.

They are not stories of the battlefield, but of the war as it was seen from the isolated plantation of the Sartoris family, where Bayard and Granny wait and watch. At first the war is something far off at Vicksburg or Corinth, but soon the first blue-clad soldier appears, and then there are federal troops everywhere, burning plantations, stealing silver, and bewildered Negroes hurrying northward at night.

There are many incidents which stand out: Granny sheltering Bayard and Ringo, his Negro companion, in the folds of her voluminous skirt after they had killed a Yankee horse; Granny cannily stealing confiscated Confederate mules and selling them to the invaders; and Brother Fortinbridge leaning on his shovel as he delivers his tribute at Granny's grave. And most impressive of all the final story, and the only one which has not been previously published, in which Bayard comes to know a higher courage than his father—the courage not to kill.

There is in these stories the warm feeling of having lived through those turbulent years with a gallant and courageous family. Granny and Bayard and Drusilla, who donned trousers and fought beside the men, must be ranked among the most real characters Mr. Faulkner has ever drawn.

This is not the hard-boiled Faulkner of old. This is a Southerner and sentimentalist, and, for all his pretense, he is a sentimentalist, writing sincerely and effectively about his own country.

Louis Kronenberger. "Faulkner's Dismal Swamp." *Nation*, February 19, 1938, pp. 212, 214.

The twisted heritage which the Confederate South bestowed upon its descendants is something few of them have renounced. It has got into their blood, and all that their weakened minds can do is resort to a rather vague, rueful, and inadequate irony. The truer irony is that they are its victims, forever driven on to commemorate their loss of Eden till one greater man (and where will he come from?) restore them and regain the blissful seat. The South languishes in race infantilism. The South is a fetish because of something that disrupted its childhood; it goes on fondling a faded gray uniform with epaulets, a sword put in its worn tired scabbard.

The South, to be sure, knows its moments of awareness and revulsion, as who would not, seeing impoverished brains and bodies in crazed retreat, seeing backward children lost in benighted folkways. But frequently these are moments of fascination also, for the process of decay can take on rich and gorgeous colors. We have evidence of this powerful revulsion and fascination in the works of Mr. Faulkner, who is a poet of disintegration, a necromancer of half-lights, but as yet no true visionary. Mr. Faulkner's saga of Jefferson, Mississippi, and its environs—spread out through half a dozen books—is, if not the only end, at least one end to a story that begins with drums and bugles, high-bred horses and gallant women. The decline and derationalization of the South can go no farther than Mr. Faulkner has taken them; it is now only possible for him to carry the story back to its source.

So here are tales of the Sartoris family during the War Between the States—a series of vivid exploits seen through the eyes of Bayard Sartoris as a boy, and set down by him long afterward. His father John, a reckless soldier and skirmisher, is away from home, where Bayard is living with his grandmother and the slaves. Always at his side is the Negro boy Ringo, presumably his half-brother. The status of Ringo in the family circle is one of the most interesting things in the book, as to my mind Ringo is by far the most interesting character. But for those who read *The Unvanquished* in the spirit that millions have read *Gone with the Wind*, it will be the grandmother who holds the stage—that indomitable ramrod, fierce as only sheltered and ladylike women can be. Lies, theft, murder itself count less with her than the twirling of a fan when it comes to saving the South, and her courage is quite equal to her criminality. I suppose that a great many women like Rosa Millard lived and behaved as she did during those desperate years. I am not so cynical as to refuse them homage. But they will never remind me of anything but the theater.

What Faulkner thinks of such women, and of such exploits as they achieved, and of all the disorder and valor and Marquis of Queensberry bloodshed that went on, is never altogether clear. The point of the book seems to be made when Bayard returns from law school after his father has been shot by an enemy, and defies the Southern code with a gesture that surpasses it. He will not kill his father's murderer; but neither will he ignore the insult. He goes unarmed to Redmond's office and lets Redmond shoot at him. This substitution of moral for physical bravura leaves the whole series of incidents uncomfortably question-marked. Certainly the tone and proportions of *The Unvanquished* are heroic rather than satiric. Certainly the merits of "the Cause" and the fortitude with which the Cause was defended—though I don't doubt that Mr. Faulkner has separated them in his own mind—are never clearly separated in the story. The very title of the book bespeaks an irony purely literary; it has the same double meaning as a pun. The book, at any rate, is pretty high-romantic stuff, cinema stuff, though where *Gone with the Wind* is purely Hollywood, *The Unvanquished* is coated with the expressionism of the foreign studio.

As writing, this is much the simplest book that Faulkner has written in a long time. To be sure, one keeps stumbling over nonsense like "Then he flung the door violently inward against the doorstop with one of those gestures with or by which an almost painfully unflagging preceptory of youth ultimately aberrates," but for the most part *The Unvanquished* gains from having been partly published in the *Saturday Evening Post*. As thinking, however, it seems to me as wilful, cluttered, sunless as ever. Faulkner is a master of sensation, the more lurid the sensation the better, and can throw marvelously strange lights over any scene he selects. But if he is fitted by neither temperament nor training to be a rational novelist, then, if he is to survive, he must move on from the company of the spellbinders to that of the seers; he must acquire and articulate a profounder moral sense, a capacity to enlarge life after the manner—to name the greatest—of a Dostoevski or an Emily Brontë. I do not see where, in this book, he has done more than brightly varnish rotten timber. I do not see where this book does more than repopulate a scene that Faulkner would do better to forget about. We are told, quite sensibly, that novelists should deal with the material they know best. But not forever, surely; and not if that material is a swamp, slowly, voraciously sucking the novelist in it.

Mary-Carter Roberts. "Faulkner Wit Covers Grim Action." Washington *Sunday Star*, February 20, 1938, p. 4-F.

Tastes seem to differ with a curious arbitrariness as regards William Faulkner. There are those readers who say that they like his short stories, but find his novels very hard going; and then there is that other school which says that he is the novelist of novelists in America, but that he only writes his short stories to sell magazines. For some reason few people seem able to think of him without thus mentally dividing his work. To the reviewer it would seem that he has worked with equal competence in both fields and given in each some performance of great goodness and no less obvious badness. The reviewer is aware, nonetheless, that that is not the way most people judge him.

His present volume, however, seems destined to please both schools of readers, for it can be called a collection of short stories or a novel with equal correctness. It is divided into seven chapters and each chapter is a complete story in itself. The same characters, however, are used throughout the book and the action is steady from one story to the next.

They are those tales of the Sartoris tribe, many of which have already been published in magazines, which trace the fortunes of a Mississippi plantation family through the Civil War and into the Reconstruction period. They are told through the experience of young Bayard, the son of the family. Bayard is no more than 14 when Vicksburg falls and the Yankee soldiers pour into the state, raiding and burning. Consequently the bloody and dramatic events of the stories are told as if seen by the eyes of a child, a manner of writing of which Mr. Faulkner seems fond, since he frequently makes use of it. They include—those events—the secret mass departure from the plantations of the Negroes, who have come to believe that the Yankee soldiers are going to lead them to "Jordan"; the burning of the plantation home, the pursuit of carpet-baggers and the desperate machinations resorted to by the Confederate women that they and their families might not starve. The mood of the book can be known from the title—*The Unvanquished.* Mr. Faulkner, who has sometimes written of his state in terms of the least prepossessing human types to be found within it, writes here of heroic behavior and heroic men and women, and does it appropriately, starkly and with surprising directness.

The reviewer likes best the chapters three and four, in which the grim action is high-lighted with humor. These stories tell how Bayard's grandmother followed the retiring Northern Army and made the commanding officer return to her mules and the trunk of silver which the soldiers had stolen, and of what fantastic use she later made of the written order for the restitution. They are richly funny tales, marked with a kind of humor which would have pleased the literary creator of the crafty Odysseus.

The collection has the sturdy, witty quality which is Mr. Faulkner's most familiar characteristic. It seems safe to recommend it both to readers who like his novels and those who declare preference for his shorter tales.

Ted Robinson.
"The Unvanquished."
Cleveland *Plain Dealer,*
February 20, 1938, All
Feature Section, p. 2.

What a toned-down and brushed-up Faulkner it is that appears in this new novel! No doubt this remarkable change is due to the fact that the chapters of *The Unvanquished* appeared as short stories in the *Saturday Evening Post* and *Scribner's Magazine,* which demand that the feelings of their wide circulation be spared too much violence.

The nearest we come to a truly Faulknerian scene is the incident where two fourteen-year-old boys kill the murderer of the grandmother of one of them and nail his hand to the headboard of her grave. And, of course, there is an occasional inordinately long sentence to remind the reader of the authorship of the book at hand.

This heavy facetiousness of mine is not fair to a fine tale, by the way. It is a dramatic and always fascinating story of Civil War days told from the viewpoint of a fifteen-year-old boy.

John Sartoris is a Confederate officer. His son Bayard stays at home on the plantation with his grandmother (a fine and notable character) and his inseparable friend Ringo, the Negro boy with whom he has grown up.

The war engulfs the plantation and the Yankees burn the homestead. A sympathetic Union officer gives Granny an order for some mules to replace the ones driven off by the soldiers. She practices a bit of forgery and duplicates the order many times, getting batches of mules from the federal army for all her neighbors. And there are other and less humorous adventures with tragedy and revenge and nobility of character involved.

It is picturesque and credible; it is indeed a very fine piece of sustained creation. And perhaps it will silence those critics who have proclaimed that Faulkner could not attract attention without scenes of unspeakable violence.

Granville Hicks. "Confederate Heroism." *New Masses*, February 22, 1938, p. 24.

Ever since Faulkner wrote the opening chapters of *Sartoris* in 1929, it has been clear that he would some day write this book. Of all the families with which he has people his Jefferson, Miss.—the Snopeses, Sutpens, Compsons, Benbows, and so on—only the Sartorises command his admiration. In general he is as complete a skeptic as our age has produced, but he retains an enthusiasm for Confederate heroes almost as unadulterated as that of Margaret Mitchell or Stark Young. And the Sartorises are the embodiment of Confederate heroism.

The Unvanquished is for the most part made up of stories that appeared in the *Saturday Evening Post*, and that too seems appropriate, because this is almost the only theme on which Faulkner could write in a way that would be satisfactory to *Post* readers. Not that these tales are free from gruesomeness, for "Vendée" is as brutal a piece as he has ever written, but they are cloaked with a glamour that he can summon up only when he is writing of the Old South. The dashing splendor of the narrator's father, the romantic (and incredible) audacity of his grandmother, and the general atmosphere of chivalry have their appeal to persons whose lives are unsplendid, unaudacious, and certainly unchivalrous.

The best of the stories—they have unity enough to be called a novel if the publishers insist—is "An Odor of Verbena," which has not been published before. In this study of conflicts, baffling emotions, and strange decisions there is some of the insight that made it worth our while to puzzle our way through *The Sound and the Fury* and *As I Lay Dying*. But for the most part the book is unpleasantly close to the general level of the Stars and Bars school.

In one respect, however, it is quite unlike any other Confederate novel. In *Soldiers' Pay*, his first novel, Faulkner hinted at a deep hatred of war. The hint recurs in *The Unvanquished*, rather surprisingly since the book is intended to glorify the Confederate dead. It is in no sense the book's theme, and it does not save Faulkner from the charge of triviality, but it is there, reminding us that there is more in the man than he has allowed to appear in his recent novels.

With every book he writes Faulkner become a more complex problem. But unfortunately with every book the incentive to try to solve the problem diminishes. Certainly *The Unvanquished* does not do much to encourage us, but it does make us conscious that this is one more tragedy of frustration, and a very real one.

V. F. Calverton.
"William Faulkner: Southerner at Large."
Modern Monthly, March 1938, pp. 11–12.

Philip Freneau, over a century and a half ago, declared that "a political and a literary independence . . . (are) two very different things; the first was accomplished in about seven years, the latter will not be completely effected, perhaps, in as many centuries." Like Jefferson, who expected a century to elapse before we populated the Louisiana territory, Freneau was in error concerning the time-element. Nevertheless, he was more correct than most of his contemporaries who believed that such independence would be attained with undoubted immediacy. If it did not take seven centuries, it definitely took one century before anything resembling cultural autonomy was achieved in America. More than that, it was not until the twentieth century that a *completely* liberated cultural pattern emerged.

It was in the teens and the twenties of this century, with the sudden appearance of Edgar Lee Masters, Carl Sandburg, Sherwood Anderson, Henry L. Mencken, Sinclair Lewis, Ernest Hemingway and others, that a literature which was indubitably American was born. In the nineteenth century the Americanizing impact and challenge of Walt Whitman and Mark Twain had failed to enter into the mainstream of our literature; it was this new group, scions of Twain and Whitman, who, in the teens and twenties, made it into a mainstream affair. Ever since, it has been impossible to confuse American literature with English literature. What is more, American literature, ever since it has become so distinctly and inimitably American has also become more vital, more colorful, and more significant than English literature. Today, for example, one finds in England, as I did last summer, that the most-read writers are American. The old school of Wells, Maugham, and Shaw, is considered effete and the younger school of Calder-Marshall, Greenwook, and others is regarded as promising, but still insignificant. Aldous Huxley, a betwixt-and-between man, belonging to a cultural third sex, is viewed as a literary pansy. It is not these people, but Ernest Hemingway, Thomas Wolfe, John Dos Passos, and *William Faulkner* who interest readers and critics in England today.

William Faulkner interests the English reading public for the same reason that Ernest Hemingway and Sinclair Lewis do—because he is so American and because his Americanness is not provincial but universal. The people he describes and the situations he depicts are national, or, what is even more limited, sectional, but the emotions he evokes are unconfined by geography or tradition. What makes American literature American or French literature French is something so subtly and inextricably involved with attitude, approach, emphasis that they can be easier recognized and felt than defined but the differences are there, however elusive and indefinable they may seem. Faulkner's approach to his people is as singularly American as Thomas Hardy's approach to his rustic mayors, school teachers, and commoners is unmistakably English. Faulkner is not concerned with the American agrarian in a general sense; he is concerned with the agrarian he has met, known, shaken hands with, lived with, in the deep south, in his native state of Mississippi, which is the most backward state in the nation. That fact is very significant in understanding Faulkner's fiction. He is dealing with a people who are inferior to all other Americans, who are living in a state of intellectual barbarism which is infra-medieval. In *Sanctuary*, one of his most revealing portraitures of Southern degeneracy, and in *Light in August*, his best novel to date, he introduces his reader to a collection of people who are totally incredible unless one lives in or has lived in Mississippi. What Caldwell and Kirkland did in *Tobacco Road* was gentle and generous compared with what Faulkner has done with the Mississippians he has described in so many of his novels.

To people who do not know the South, or Mississippi, Faulkner's characters seem fantastic, impossible creations, off-shoots of a morbidic imagination, but the fact of the matter is his characters are so absolutely and completely real, so forthrightly actual, that the very dregs of the country live in them, seep through them, distort and disfigure them. It is this fact which explains Faulkner's failure to create inspiring or admirable characters; to date, for instance, he has yet to create a single character of emulative quality. In his most recent novel, which is really a patch-work of short stories woven together to give the semblance of a novel, *The Unvanquished*, he comes closer in his depiction of the grandmother than anywhere else to providing us with a character whose experiences we can share with some slight degree of sympathy instead of with complete revulsion. No American writer since Poe has created such wild, macabre, forbidding characters. Poe, however, a child of the post-Waterloo romanticism of Europe, which found a fertile though remote rebirth in his work, invented his characters, contrived them out of the recesses of his weird imagination; Faulkner, on the other hand, gifted though he is with something of Poe's penchant for the macabre, didn't need to resort to *such invention and excogitation*. He had the characters before him, near him, with him.

Aside from his war experience, from which he emerged a lieutenant and a hero with wounds resulting from a plane crash (his novel *Pylon* is a produce of that aspect of his career), he has lived practically his entire life in the South and that, in itself, is an endurance test of a supreme variety. His work, therefore, has been inevitably soaked in Southern soil. His people are no more queer, relatively speaking, than Sherwood Anderson's characters in *Winesburg, Ohio*. Whatever difference exists results from the fact that the South is bankrupt and degenerate, living still upon forgotten frontiers of experience, whereas the Midwest, though stodgy, possesses something of promise and futurity. The Midwest characters in Sherwood Anderson, Sinclair Lewis, and Willa Cather are corrigible; the Southern characters in

Faulkner's fiction, however, are incorrigible. They are nothing more than the sick, stinking backwash of a dead but still rotting civilization.

The proliterati have complained that Faulkner does not deal with the class struggle and is not interested in the more progressive forces of American civilization. The truth of the matter is that the class struggle plays a relatively minor role in the semi-feudal life of Mississippi. There are abundant classes in the state but little struggle between them. Industry has made too little headway in Mississippi to have introduced the class conflict on a vast, active, belligerent scale. The majority of the Mississippians are an impoverished, exploited lot but they accept that lot without much protest or opposition.

In *The Unvanquished* Faulkner goes back to the Civil War for his types, and it must be said at once that as types these people are far superior to those in *Sanctuary* and *Light in August*. But these characters spring from a South which was old and defeated but not yet decadent, and there is a naturalness about their developments, their actions, their devotions, their deaths, and a simplicity which Faulkner has never attained in his previous novels. This is the least involved, the least obscure, and the least affected of his works. It is free of the literary tricks which made certain of his earlier novels sound "phoney" in places. It is free of all artifice, and it is to be fondly hoped that Mr. Faulkner's novels in the future will follow this novel as a model rather than go back to the distorted and contorted models of his earlier fiction.

Kay Boyle. "Tattered Banners." *New Republic*, 94 (March 9, 1938), 136–37.

There are two Faulkners—at least to me there are two: the one who stayed down South and the one who went to war in France and mixed with foreigners and aviators; that is, the Faulkner of the Sartoris saga (and the countless other savagely and tenderly chronicled documents of the South) and the Faulkner who wrote "Turn About," for instance, and "All the Dead Pilots" and *Pylon* with no perceptible cooling of that hot devotion to man's courage although the speech, the history, the conflict were no longer his strict heritage. I believe these two separate Faulkners (separated more by a native shyness of the foreigner than any variance in ideology or technique) possess between them the strength and the vulnerability which belong only to the greatest artists: the incalculable emotional wealth, the racy comic sense, the fury to reproduce exactly not the recognizable picture but the unmistakable experience, the thirst for articulation as well as the curiosity and the vocabulary—that rarity—to quench it. The weaknesses there are, the errors, the occasionally strained effects, are accomplished by the same fearless, gifted hand.

It is not difficult to reconcile the two Faulkners; perhaps as simple as recognizing that a man is a good host or a good guest, bur rarely both. On his own ground Faulkner is explicit, easy, sure; on someone else's he is a little awed, a little awkward, provincially aware of the chances he is taking. But I believe it is in the willingness to take these risks that Faulkner's whole future lies. That *The Unvanquished* happens to be one more chapter in the

Sartoris saga is no valid description of it, nor that it is a book about the Civil War—a Civil War in which the issue of black and white is lost in the wider issue not of justice and tyranny, subjection and freedom, or even sin and virtue, but merely of life and death. For one who loves Faulkner's work and has followed it closely and impatiently, the difficulty lies in isolating this book or any book from the others and trying to say this or that of it: his genius is not this book or perhaps any given book but resides in that entire determined collection of volumes which reveal him to be the most absorbing writer of our time.

On the face of it, this book is the story of an old lady whose home has been razed by Yankees and who sets out across the country, first driving two mules and then, when these are confiscated, two horses, wearing a borrowed hat on her head and holding over it a borrowed parasol. It is told in her grandson's words, at the outset a boy of twelve who goes with her on that imperiously reckless adventure which leads toward Jordan, toward her career of racketeering and, like any Chicago gangster's, toward atrocious death; a boy who in the twelve years covered by the story matures first in emotion, then in conviction, and finally in act. "Ringo and I had been born in the same month," he says of the Negro boy who is their sole companion on the drive toward retribution, "and had both been fed at the same breast and has slept together and eaten together for so long that Ringo called Granny 'Granny' just like I did until maybe he wasn't a nigger any more or maybe I wasn't a white boy any more, the two of us neither, not even people any longer. . . ." And toward the end of the book when they are both twenty-four, he says of Ringo in a man's language then: "He was sitting quietly in a chair beside the cold stove, spent-looking too who had ridden forty miles (at one

time, either in Jefferson or when he was alone at last on the road somewhere, he had cried; dust was now caked and dried in the tear-channels on his face) and would ride forty more yet would not eat, looking up at me a little red-eyed with weariness (or maybe it was more than just weariness and so I would never catch up with him). . . ." This process of development, subtly, heedfully, skillfully accomplished through the seemingly inevitable metamorphosis of speech makes the book a record not only of an individual's but a nation's, possibly a civilization's progression from violence to a passive and still undefinable bewilderment.

Elsewhere, the movement of that other group, the march of the liberated Negroes toward Jordan, starts like a whisper in the book, becomes "a kind of panting murmur" as they pass in the night, and swells to "women and children singing and chanting and trying to get to that unfinished bridge or even down into the water itself, and the cavalry beating them back with sword scabbards. . . . They just pass here without food or anything, exactly as they rose up from whatever they were doing when the spirit or the voice . . . told them to go. . . . Going to cross Jordan. . . ."

It is, then, the sentimental and glamorous story of one old lady who set out to find and ask a Yankee Colonel to return to her a chest of family silver tied with hemp rope, two darkies, Loosh and Philadelphy, and the two confiscated mules, "Old Hundred" and "Tinney"; and like a single and undaunted fife still playing, it is as well the essence of that war, a thing as intrinsically and nationally and gallantly the South's as the revolution is France's and the rebellion Ireland's: become now a legend, almost a fable of tattered banners, makeshift uniforms, incredible courage and inhuman ferocity. It has those weaknesses which can be found throughout Faulkner's work: the full-length portraits

178

which abruptly become caricatures not likenesses of the living, the "ladies" without face or substance, the repetitions, the maudlin lapses, the shameless voice of the evangelist declaiming in solemn, flowery passages. But it has that fabulous, that wondrous, fluxing power which nothing Faulkner touches is ever without. The word for it may be glamour or may be sentiment, but both these words are mutable and I have used them here without contempt, applying them in their best sense as attributes to fact. They can confuse, they can disguise, but they can as well bring to the familiar a heightened, an isolated and a therefore truer legibility. They were elements in that electric atmosphere and mystic climate in which Poe's men and women lived and have survived and they are a vital part of Faulkner's quicker, more comprehensive world. Faulkner and Poe, set far enough apart in time, are strangely kin: unique in our history in their immunity to literary fashion, alike in their fanatical obsession with the unutterable depths of mankind's vice and even more with his divinity.

If writing remain one of the Arts—with a capital A and be damned to the current mode of splitting it two ways in a poem or a fresco on a wall—if its sensitive execution still demand the heart and the endurance which have kept artists lying prone on scaffoldings painting year in, year out, and if its success depend on its acceptance as convincing tragedy or comedy, then it can quite simply be said of Faulkner that he is the rare, the curious, the almost ludicrously authentic thing. In this book, as in his others, he writes with that "fierce desire of perfection" which contemporaries said Michelangelo evidenced when "flinging himself on the material of marble," vehemently seeking expression for "the human elements of fervor and tenderness."

Richmond Croom Beatty. "Vitality of a Code." Nashville *Banner*, April 23, 1938, Magazine Section, p. 2.

Six of the seven stories which comprise this volume appeared originally either in the *Saturday Evening Post* or in *Scribner's*. The last one, and decidedly the best, "An Odor of Verbena," is new. A narrative that is fairly continuous runs throughout the collection. The book, I think, represents Faulkner in his most impressive manner— the manner of *Sartoris*. He deals with characters rich in a sensibility that has been conditioned by an unmistakably Southern environment. He writes from the inside, with an insight foreign, unfortunately, to the propagandists in fiction about the South.

Sartoris is the center around which these several narratives of the late Civil War and Reconstruction period revolve. Most of the plot is concerned with the activities of Granny, Mrs. Rosa Millard, who has got hold of some Federal Army stationery on which she forges orders demanding that horses and mules be turned over to her. These animals she promptly sells back to the Yankee chief-of-supplies in Memphis. Faulkner makes a great deal of this character. She dominates a small society which, though financially exhausted and overrun, is still able to live within the terms of a formal and clearly defined pattern. It is the projection of his characters against this well objectified way of life which, I believe, contributes largely to the sense of conviction with which one reads about them. Existence here has meaning, a purpose, and a code which no external calamity can destroy. The forces of disorder have not yet won out.

The result of this implicit attitude is a succession of figures which, if the term were not almost meaningless today, one might fairly call heroic. There is John Sartoris, Granny's son, commander of a small cavalry troop; there is Drusilla, who disguised herself as a man and went off to war to kill Yankees. There is the son of John Sartoris, from whose point of view the stories are written—a youth who resembles his father in everything except his appetite for blood. Each character, in his way, is noble and sensitively drawn.

As for the style of the book, the following example will serve both as a specimen of it and to focus the emphasis of Faulkner on the vitality of a code. He is describing the action of Drusilla—who married John Sartoris after the war—when John's son approaches the house, after his father has been slain by a political enemy:

"We rode on, toward the house where he would be lying in the parlor now, in his regimentals (sabre too) and where Drusilla would be waiting for me beneath all the festive glitter of the Chandeliers, in the yellow ball gown and the sprig of verbena in her hair, holding the two loaned pistols (I could see that too, who had had no presentiment; I could see her, in the formal brilliant room arranged formally for obsequy, not tall, not slender as a woman is but as a youth, a boy, is, motionless, in yellow, the face calm, almost bemused, the head simple and severe, the balancing sprig of verbena above each ear, the two arms bent at the elbows, the two hands shoulder high, the two identical duelling pistols lying upon, not clutched in, one to each: the Greek amphora priestess of a succinct and formal violence)."

It is a pleasure to read this sort of fiction. It is work whose authenticity grows out of a thorough understanding of the Southern temperament, an understanding which, alas, no text book can quite provide.

Earle Birney. "The Two William Faulkners." *Canadian Forum*, 18 (June 1938), 84–85.

Two writers have been struggling with each other for a long time inside the skin of William Faulkner. One of them is a stylized and morbid mystic attempting a sequence of novels on the scale of an epic. The other, the less publicized but more authentic author, is a sharp and brilliant narrator of short stories. The peculiar promise of Faulkner has always been that he was both of these; his failure is that he has never been able either to unite or to untangle his two powers within one book.

None of the nine novels which have given him a place in the immediate sun of American fiction can stand alone, nor do they make a satisfactory unit together. It is not merely that a major character in one work can be understood only by a knowledge of his sufferings in an earlier or a later book; or even one not yet written; it is not only that Faulkner eternally shies at his own plots, deliberately prancing and curvetting about a vital incident until a reader screams vainly to know what did happen and when and why. Deeper than this is his ability to do what he evidently most wants to do, that is, to make, out of the microcosm of "Yoknapatawpha County," Mississippi, a life-cycle of the essential American South from plantation days through the Civil War down to the World War and the present.

Such a theme demands an observation wide enough to scan the new industrial south and its problems as well as the decadent pastoral Confederacy and its anachronistic psychology, and the understanding which can unify the two. Instead Faulkner has given us a broken series of novel-fragments, each in turn disintegrated by separable passages of verbal experimentation. Octopus sentences emerge in fine undulating terror and then proceed to strangle themselves in their own straining tentacles; phrases soar into music and brilliant picture, and sink into discord and cubism. Motivation is equally incoherent; crime and sex abnormalities (constant in his fiction) are treated one moment as psychopathic, the next as products of Southern idealism, and finally as inexplicable, motiveless. By long reminiscences—all his characters are incurable brooders with prodigious and masochistic memories—the reader is led down the nightmare alleys of a character's mind, and then suddenly abandoned while the author leaps to a snorting horse of narrative and, like the schoolboy's cavalry officer, gallops away in all directions.

In other words Faulkner's handling of action is that of the short story, flashing, dexterous and brief, while his characterization and theme can be enclosed only in the epic cycle which he does not write. That is why the most steadily admired of his writings are not the once-fashionable *Sanctuary*, self-confessed pot-boiler, not even that amazing tour de force, *The Sound and the Fury*, but contes like "That Evening Sun Go Down" [*sic*] or "A Rose for Emily."

The Unvanquished, latest of his books, is a striking epitome of the two Faulkners. Its sections first appeared as separate stories in popular magazines; they have been insufficiently revised to appear as a novel and are now neither one thing or the other. "Ambuscade" was originally a fine simple story of two twelve-year-old boys, one black and one white, who played Civil War behind the Mississippi farmhouse while the white boy's father was playing it in earnest fewer miles away than they

thought. Lying "in ambush" with a real blunderbuss they shot the horse from under the advance scout of the first Yankee invaders, fled to shelter beneath their white granny's skirts and were saved by the shrewd courage of the old lady and the contemptuous chivalry of a northern officer. A Hollywood story-idea, perhaps, but made real by Faulkner's ability to step within the minds of both the adolescents and the aged, the rocket speed of his action at the moment of climax, and by that curious unsmiling humor-at-remote-control which pervades his best work. But, now that the story is fitted into a continuous book one is unable to forget that the white boy is Bayard Sartoris who, as an old man, had already brooded over this incident in an earlier novel, *Sartoris*, and that this Bayard's father, John, is now by the killing of two carpet baggers apparently setting in motion a family curse which was already being expiated in the earlier *Light in August* and which will probably pop up again in 1940.

Yet despite its curses, curse-words, and dozen odd murders, *The Unvanquished* represents, as De Voto has remarked, "a new high in purity and romance" for Faulkner. Even a rural Ontarian might risk a copy on the parlor settee. There is a blueblooded virgin who remains such despite a year's fighting in pants with Southern guerrilla corps. There's a treasure box buried, stolen, recovered, and reburied. There's Bayard's cocky grandmother who defrauds Sherman's men of mules, sells them back to them, and washes her sins away with prayer. Her spirit is conveyed in the title; she is eventually defeated but never licked. There is a sunny clarity about all this which is positively dazzling from Faulkner.

For the real Faulkner fan there are still a number of non-stop sentences, preposterous similes about whites of eyes, mystical smells (Bayard sniffs a "will to endure" on his pappa's uniform), a spot of corn-cob philosophizing, and the above mentioned entanglements with other Faulkneriana.

The reader looking for Faulkner's definitive treatment of the South must however continue to look. True, here is at last a book of his planted square in that Civil War which has been the great Trojan doom behind or before the melodramas of his other books; here he tackles the primum mobile; but at the best all that results are a few brilliant side-glances into the back-waters of the war. The movement of masses of men, the impact of great historic forces, of ideas and ideals, of economic motives and conflicts as reflected in the minds of representative men—all these are still over the horizon.

The one exception is a fine chapter, "Raid," which vivifies the mass hysteria of "freed" and bewildered slaves trooping like lemmings down the dusty roads to the rivers, chanting that Sherman is leading them to Jordan. But even this heart-compelling theme becomes a blurred Grand-Guignol, for Faulkner can see no real motive, no suffering negro race, behind the phenomenon. He looks at the black still through the dulled and provincial eyes of a slaveholder, ignorant of the humanity he surrounds himself with, ignorant of the essential anachronism of plantation feudalism, and ignorant of the real barbarousness of the equally outdated wage-slavery under which the contemporary black groans.

The Unvanquished, like Faulkner's other books, is a timepiece with a number of tiny jewels and delicate wheels, oiled and sparkling and ingeniously fitted; but there is no mainspring and the watch doesn't tick. Nevertheless, the wheels, regarded separately, are delights in themselves and the book is no worse, if no better, than Faulkner's others; as such it contains as good "action" fiction as any being written in the United States today.

Checklist of Additional Reviews

Brooklyn *Daily Eagle*, February 2, 1938.
"*The Unvanquished*." Youngstown (Ohio) *Vindicator*, February 13, 1938, p. 4-B.
Portland (Me.) *Press Herald*, February 19, 1938.
"War and Aftermath in Faulkner's Tale." Springfield (Mass.) *Sunday Union and Republican*, February 20, 1938, p. 7-E.
"Town-a-building." *Time*, February 21, 1938, p. 79.
Rutland (Vt.) *Herald*, February 22, 1938.
Chicago *Daily Tribune*, February 26, 1938.
"*The Unvanquished*." *Christian Century*, March 9, 1938, p. 306.
"*The Unvanquished*." Durham *Morning Herald*, March 13, 1938.
"Grim Note Threads Tale of Civil War." Oakland *Tribune*, March 13, 1938, p. 2-B.
"*The Unvanquished*." *Booklist*, March 15, 1938, p. 266.
"*The Unvanquished*." Sacramento *Bee*, March 19, 1938, p. 20.
"Faulkner Shows New Side to His Genius." Knoxville *Journal*, May 15, 1938, Section IV, p. 10.
"*The Unvanquished*." Birmingham *News*, June 5, 1938, Magazine Section, p. 7.
Anderson, Katherine M'Clure. "*The Unvanquished*." Macon *Telegraph*, March 2, 1938.
Barish, Mildred. "Civil War Setting for Faulkner's Novel." Los Angeles *Times*, February 27, 1938, Part III, p. 6.
Becker, Charlotte. "Civil War Days Theme of Book." Buffalo *Times*, February 27, 1938, p. 8–C.

Brickell, Herschel. "William Faulkner Returns to the Sartorises in *The Unvanquished*." New York *Post*, February 18, 1938, p. 19; Philadelphia *Record*, February 19, 1938.

Butcher, Fanny. "Faulkner Uses Softer Touch in His Writing." Chicago *Daily Tribune*, February 26, 1938, p. 8.

Chamberlain, John. "Books" *Scribner's Magazine*, May 1938, pp. 82–83.

Davis, Bennett. "Books of the Week in Review." Buffalo *Courier-Express*, February 20, 1938, Section V, p. 6.

De Voto, Bernard. "Faulkner's South." *Saturday Review of Literature*, February 19, 1938, p. 5.

F., A.M. "William Faulkner Writes His Own *Gone with Wind*." Milwaukee *Journal*, February 13, 1938, Editorial Section, p. 3.

Fadiman, Clifton. "An Old Hand and Two New Ones." *New Yorker*, February 19, 1938, pp. 60–61.

Fox, William. "A Mississippi Plantation during the Civil War." Boston *Evening Transcript*, February 19, 1938, p. 2.

Fuerbringer, Otto. "Fails to Excite One Reader." St. Louis *Post-Dispatch*, March 6, 1938, p. 4-B.

Gold, William J. "Books to Own." Roanoke *Times*, February 20, 1938, p. 24.

Govan, Gilbert E. "Wide Appeal." Chattanooga *Times*, March 13, 1938, Magazine Section, p. 11.

Grainger, Paul. "Faulkner Appears in Seven Shorts." Minneapolis *Journal*, February 27, 1938, Editorial Section, p. 7.

Hansen, Harry. "Southern Family's Tribulations under Yankees' Terrorism Related in *The Unvanquished*." New York *World-Telegram*, February 15, 1938, p. 19; also reviewed in *Harper's Magazine*, April 1938, advertising pages.

Hoch, Henry George. "More Tales by Faulkner." Detroit *News*, March 13, 1938, Home and Society Section, p. 16.

Hoole, William Stanley. "William Faulkner Forsakes Old Manner for New: Robust Portrayer of Southern Low-Life Has Go at Sweetness and Light." Dallas *Morning News*, February 27, 1938, Section III, p. 15.

Johnson, Robert. "Faulkner Retains Ability as Craftsman in New Book." Memphis *Press-Scimitar*, February 16, 1938, p. 7.

Kazin, Alfred. "In the Shadow of the South's Last Stand." *New York Herald Tribune Books*, February 20, 1938, p. 5.

Knowlton, Kent. "War and Reconstruction." Lowell *Courier Citizen*, February 18, 1938, p. 15.

Krank, Raymond C. "A Regenerate Faulkner." Brooklyn *Citizen*, March 7, 1938, p. 9.

Krey, Laura. "Southern Selections." *Sewanee Review*, 46 (July–September 1938), 365–74.

Lewis, Dewart. "Faulkner's Novel of the South in Rebellion." San Francisco *Chronicle*, February 20, 1938, This World Section, p. 27.

Lockhart, Jack. "Faulkner's New Book, *The Unvanquished*, Will Make Southern Hearts Beat Stronger." Memphis *Commercial Appeal*, February 27, 1938, Section IV, p. 9.

Murray, Marian. "Faulkner *Unvanquished* about Civil War South." Hartford *Times*, February 19, 1938, p. 7.

Neville, Helen. "The Sound and the Fury." *Partisan Review*, 5 (June 1938), 53–55.

Patterson, Alicia. "The Book of the Week." New York *Sunday News*, February 20, 1938, p. 56.

Rector, Beulah. "William Faulkner Has

a Vivid Story of the Post War South." Watertown (N.Y.) *Times*, February 17, 1938.

R[oueché], B[erton]. "Humor and a Heroine to Faulkner's Rescue." Kansas City *Star*, February 19, 1938, p. 14.

S., M. "Theatrical South." Milwaukee *Journal*, March 20, 1938.

S., M.W. "*The Unvanquished.*" *Christian Science Monitor*, February 16, 1938, p. 16.

S[elby], J[ohn]. "Among Faulkner's Best." Ansonia (Calif.) *Sentinel*, February 15, 1938; Bridgeport *Telegram*, February 15, 1938; Danbury (Conn.) *News*, February 15, 1938; Palo Alto (Calif.) *Times*, February 15, 1938; Nashville *Tennessean*, February 20, 1938, p. 6-D; Newport (R.I.) *Herald*, February 25, 1938; Huntington (W.Va.) *Advertiser*, February 27, 1938.

Shaw, Thomas J., Jr. "*The Unvanquished* Stands Out among Civil War Novels." Greensboro *Daily News*, April 10, 1938, p. 6-C.

Shipp, Cameron. "Mr. Faulkner Is Amusing." Charlotte *News*, February 20, 1938, p. 11.

Smith, Russell. "Mr. Faulkner Enters a New Phase." Washington *Post*, February 20, 1938, p. 9-B.

Smith, Theodore. "Dixie Becomes Grim in Book by Faulkner." San Francisco *News*, March 5, 1938, p. 7.

Stafford, Hazel Straight. "*The Unvanquished.*" Madison (Wis.) *Capital Times*, March 20, 1938, p. 16.

Strauss, Harold. "Mr. Faulkner's Civil War Novel." *New York Times Book Review*, February 20, 1938, p. 6.

Thompson, Ralph. "Books of the Times." New York *Times*, February 15, 1938, p. 23.

Van Doren, Carl. "Carl Van Doren Recommends." Boston *Herald*, February 19, 1938, p. 6.

W., C.E. "Faulkner's Latest." Syracuse *Post-Standard*, June 5, 1938, Section I, p. 4.

Waite, Paul. "Yankees Ride Rebel South." Boston *Herald*, February 19, 1938, p. 7.

Williams, Sidney. "Novels by the Lorimers, Faulkner, Anne Strawbridge." Philadelphia *Inquirer*, February 19, 1938, p. 26.

Wilson, Emma A. "*The Unvanquished.*" Chico (Calif.) *Record*, July 3, 1938, p. 4.

THE WILD PALMS

THE
WILD PALMS

~~~~~~

by William Faulkner

~~~~~~

RANDOM HOUSE · NEW YORK

Robert E. McClure. "Books Worth Reading." Santa Monica *Evening Outlook*, January 20, 1939, p. 10.

If the first mark of writing genius is power of creative imagination, William Faulkner of the Deep South is unquestionably such a genius and in the top flight of contemporary writers. Unfortunately for his popularity, his imagination is of a peculiarly morbid and tortured kind, and he delights in teasing and mystifying his readers before shocking them out of their senses and stunning them with nightmare horrors. So he is not for the tender-minded or for those who ask to be pleasantly entertained. Yet not to know Faulkner is to miss some of the most exciting writing of our time.

Moreover he is one of the most indigenous of our writers, who can tell us a great deal about certain parts of America and certain types of people and experience, without having to go to Loyalist Spain for inspiration. And he has matured. In his latest book, *The Wild Palms*, he no longer shocks for the sake of shocking, no longer reminds us of an over-imaginative youth too long exposed to the reptilian terrors and malarial fevers of a southern swamp, without benefit of sunshine and fresh air. He has taken, in this new book, two story themes that are as old as the Greek dramatists, and has adapted them to the American scene in a manner all his own, with brilliant artistry and a power of imagery not likely to be surpassed by any living writer.

The two stories are opposed to each other like contrapuntal themes in a musical composition. The first is that of a young medical interne in New Orleans who falls in love with a married woman, the mother of two children, and inspires an even greater passion in her. It happens to them not from any wantonness or desire for adventure in either one, but by spontaneous and overwhelming physical attraction. By a typical Faulkner device we are introduced to this couple at a time when their tragic passion has generated its own doom and theirs. We get baffling hints of this, of madness, despair, and horror, and then Faulkner breaks off to start their story from the beginning. He carries it to the first climax of their elopement and then launches his second theme, the story of an escaped and comparatively innocent convict who rescues a woman and then flees from her as from an intolerable incubus.

The convict is an ignorant young hillbilly doing time in a southern chain gang because he has tried to imitate his dime-novel hero, Jesse James. The Mississippi River goes on the rampage in one of its worst floods and the convicts are taken to the levees to help in the rescue work. By a perfectly natural chain of events, our hillbilly finds himself in a boat on the flood waters with a woman he has rescued, after an accident which has caused him to be reported as having drowned. The woman is about to have a child. The boat, already twice overturned, is in the raging main stream of the Mississippi and the hillbilly is still in prison stripes. That is what the movies call a "story situation"; if you can improve on it for suspense you may go to Hollywood right now.

Faulkner keeps switching from one story to the other, yet so skillfully that we are never annoyed but actually welcome the change from one kind of tension to another as a kind of relief. Both kinds are truly extraordinary; I think the description of the flood and what follows one of the greatest things of the kind I have ever read; and for the psychological drama between the man and the woman in the other story, for the way in which Faulkner makes their final doom seem inevitable and deeply tragic, I have the utmost admiration. Let me add that this love story takes the two people from New Orleans to Chicago, thence to a northern lake and thence to a northwestern mining camp in winter, with each different milieu beautifully created and the drama increasing in emotional pitch and intensity all the while. Such is the essential truth of these characters and the magic of Faulkner's narrative and descriptive power, that one is swept along to the final tragedy with a sensation of being hypnotized by a powerful drug.

Yet both stories are made too terrific—that is the chief fault of Faulkner, who must turn the convict's ordeal into a monstrous phantasmagoric nightmare, and bring his lovers across the borderline of madness. And while the writing is for the most part magnificent, it is sometimes mere sound and fury, if not just plain bad writing. Certainly the two opening pages are Faulkner at his worst and will discourage many possible readers. Altogether there is a good deal here to remind one of the horror writers of the Elizabethan Age, of Ford and Massinger and Webster, who also loved madness and violent melodrama expressed in torrential imagery.

Marian Murray.
"*The Wild Palms* Shows Faulkner at Low Ebb." Hartford *Times*, January 21, 1939, p. 7.

This latest novel of Faulkner's seems an unfortunate example of the way in which mannerisms may run away with an artist,

becoming so insistent that they obscure what he wants to say, and of the way a sense of power may betray that artist into giving less than his best.

Faulkner writes with the frankness which one associates with "realism." But he is no realist. One might perhaps best borrow a term from painting, and call him an expressionist. His desire and intention is to present the meaning behind action, the spirit behind thought itself. That makes for a shearing away of non-essentials, for the elimination of any sentimentality, for the direct and almost frantically sincere approach. But it means, also, often enough, a distortion of nature to enhance the emphasis. Carried to extreme it may so exaggerate the distortion that the ordinary spectator finds difficulty in seeing beyond it to the reality beneath.

There is no slightest doubt that William Faulkner is one of our greatest writers, or that he has something significant to say. One has to remember only, for instance, his unforgettable short story, "Dry September," or his Charteris series.

He wants violently to tell the world that sex is not indecent unless pruriency makes it so, that love is compounded of many elements, and deeper and more significant than the sum of those elements, that life has something more important to offer than money, that the soul can be destroyed by neither poverty nor prison so long as a human being keeps that integrity which will not permit him to be untrue to himself. In this instance, Mr. Faulkner wants to say also that the only immortality consists in memory, and that a lover may find reason for living on, even without hope, that the memory of certain aspects of the loved one may not die. What he has to say deserves a better handling than he has given it in *The Wild Palms*.

The story he evolves to carry his thought is so almost childishly naive that we couldn't believe a tenth of it. It's about a young interne, who has known nothing of women and suddenly falls in love with a married woman. They run away from it all, with the husband's consent, go through any amount of hell of various kinds, and eventually come to a horribly tragic end, while the wild palms of Mississippi still wave overhead. Mr. Faulkner seems to think they are very fine and noble, but he manages to make them almost inhumanly stupid. And along with his theme runs an obligato of a convict, released during the flood, who finds an unwanted woman on his hands and goes happily back to prison. The relation between the two stories is not too clear, and we couldn't believe in that convict either.

The author seems to think that all he has to do to create real characters is to have them talk gutter language every now and then.

The whole book impressed this reviewer as having been written with lazy effrontery. The author doesn't bother either to make a credible story. Some things, like the hero's making $5,000 a year writing confession stories (without the slightest preparation or indication of having either imagination or the ability to write), and his inability to cope with or understand matters that even a first year medical student should have grasped, are unforgiveable.

But even worse is the slack and careless writing, as such. One is used to long and loosely constructed sentences in Faulkner's writing but when they run over a page and a half apiece, and are so involved that the reader feels as if he were in a quagmire, that's too much. Even a great writer should edit his copy.

Mary-Carter Roberts. "Faulkner Expounds Realities." Washington *Sunday Star,* January 22, 1939, p. 4-F.

As far as the reviewer can make out, Mr. William Faulkner is a man who, if confronted by a brick wall, would prefer battering the obstacle down with his own head to climbing over it or walking around its end or to using any other method of passage. There is no question about it: he loves difficulty for its own sake.

Now the reviewer would not say that Mr. Faulkner is lacking in accomplishment. In battering over his various literary walls with his intrepid brow he has, unquestionably, a technique and a skill. The reviewer would even say that of all writers who habitually overcome their material by main strength and violence he is one of the most impressive. You get more violence, that is to say, in a page of Faulkner than you do in a couple of pages of anybody else. You can practically see him as you read, surrounded by malignant hosts of writhing parentheses, slippery adverbial clauses, dancing semi-colons, blocky synonyms and page-long sentences, struggling with them as with a nightmare, disdaining any victory which is too easy. It is an awesome vision, too. But nobody is likely to claim ever that it is a restful thing to read this literary gladiator. It is, instead, absolutely exhausting.

In his present book he has used his familiar turgidity to expand and expound the realities behind two such events as might be reported in any newspaper in about 50 words. The first would read something like this:

"Harry Wilbourne, former interne at

—— Hospital, New Orleans, was sentenced today to serve 50 years in the State Penitentiary for performing an illegal operation on Mrs. Francis Rittenmeyer. Mrs. Rittenmeyer died as a result of the operation. Wilbourne pleaded guilty to the charge."

And the second would read about as follows:

"—— ——, who is serving a 15-year term in the State Penitentiary for train robbery, had 10 years added to his sentence today for attempted escape. He was put to work on the levees during the flood seven weeks ago and broke away from the guards. Until his recapture he was thought to have been drowned."

Out of these two happenings, so routine in our civilized life that no one would pause for the reading of a report of them, and no one, having read the report, would remember it 10 seconds afterward, Mr. Faulkner has bludgeoned into being a powerful emotional book. It is actually two long short stories, completely separate as to characters and settings, told in alternate chapters. First one reads of the anguished doings of Dr. Wilbourne and his mistress, Charlotte Rittenmeyer. Then one reads of the despairing puzzlement of the train robber who never wanted to escape from his safe warm prison and who, having accidentally been swept away from his guards, had but one thought to his mind—to return and surrender.

The effect is as of a deafening counterpoint. In the Wilbourne story the theme deals with an effort to find liberty, ending in disaster. In the convict story we have the effort to escape from liberty, likewise ending in disaster. In both the atmosphere is one of pure nightmare, stiff, dreamlike, incredibly prolonged and devastating to the reader's instinctive resistance.

Of the two tales, the reviewer prefers the one dealing with the convict. In it there is some humor; hence it comes a

great deal nearer life than does the other one. The convict, with his fixed idea, is a sort of low-life Quixote. He is pitted against the awful force of the Mississippi River in flood; the stream carries him farther and farther from his desire—the warm penitentiary—and rolls and tumbles him about in a way which would utterly destroy the integrity and dignity of any human being except the one whose integrity and dignity lie in something beyond himself, that being, with the wretch in question, an unshakable determination to go back and surrender. He is a fantastic puppet tossed by the ruthless waters and by the no less ruthless hands of Mr. William Faulkner, but despite two such taskmasters he retains his gravity and his reader's respect. His story is an unforgettable bit of writing.

The other tale is less well grounded in essential truth. Its theme is a conventional one—that of the star-crossed lovers, no less, who flee the world only to find the world constantly at their door. The young doctor first abandons his career for his mistress and elopes with her on stolen money. She, in her turn, gives up her two children and a prosperous home for her love. Poverty besets the two, but they prove that it has no terrors for them. Then prosperity menaces their togetherness and they abandon their money success for the sake of their sacred passion. Finally the passion itself overthrows them; they are to have a child and they do not dare to. The doctor performs the illegal operation, his mistress dies and he is imprisoned for the rest of his life. He is given opportunity to escape and also to commit suicide, but he refuses it. A life punishment will be a life of memory of his beloved, and he would rather have that than any other possible existence. So he enters on his sentence.

The weakness of this story is in the characters themselves. The doctor is hopelessly vague; not once does he assume a believable shape; not once does he seem to be saying his own thoughts, but always those of Mr. William Faulkner. And the heroine is one of those awful monsters which male novelists from time to time create when they decide to forgo nature as a source of material and rummage about instead in the old grab-bag of desire, bringing up a half dozen or so isolated traits and arbitrarily shoving them together, making such a creature as has ahunted a good many dreams since the world began but which nobody has ever yet met in the flesh—or could endure. The poignancy of the adventure itself naturally suffers from the unnatural quality of the adventurers. The hero is pallid and the heroine is chromo.

The book on the whole is an impressive performance. It is, as said, deafening in effect. It produces that numb acquiescence which one notices sometimes after hearing too large a noise. As always, with Mr. Faulkner's work, the question of whether a reader can believe him or not is beside the point. He believes himself. And he has the force, for the moment at least, to ride down any kind of mental opposition.

Ted Robinson.
"Some of Faulkner's Best and Worst Found in *The Wild Palms.*"
Cleveland *Plain Dealer*, January 22, 1939, All Feature Section, p. 2.

Surface realism of the older school of William Dean Howells and the later school of Sinclair Lewis has always betrayed its less skillful practitioners into dullness. Psychological realism, following the canons of James Joyce, has the other handicap of re-

sulting more often than not in hard reading.

It is a little difficult to understand why this is so. It seems to me that William Faulkner, for instance, is by nature direct and simple, and that it is only by deliberate and frequently clumsy artifice that he forces his narrative into crooked paths and squirts clouds of sepia into the clarity of his exposition. Some of the best of Faulkner is to be found in his new book, *The Wild Palms* and a little of his worst. I think that this, the third sentence on his first page, is sheer impudence:

And the doctor wore a night shirt, too, not pajamas, for the same reason that he smoked the pipe which he had never learned and knew that he would never learn to like, between the occasional cigar which clients gave him in the intervals of Sundays on which he smoked the three cigars which he felt he could buy for himself even though he owned the beach cottage as well as the one next door to it and the one, the residence with electricity and plastered walls, in the village three miles away.

I ask you—"between the occasional cigar ... and the residence"—is that the syntax of it? One doesn't mind long sentences, or even sentences which contain too many different things to possess much unity; Faulkner has longer and more heterogeneous sentences than this, and they are quite effective. But the reader has a right to ask that the sentences come out somewhere and don't stay dangling forever. I say that is impudence: it is a cynical disregard of ordinary politeness.

For the rest, *The Wild Palms* is two novels, not one; and these two novels are printed in alternating chapters. Read every other chapter, beginning with the first, and you read the one properly entitled

191

The Wild Palms. Begin with Chapter Two and read alternate chapters, and you get another novel called *Old Man.* The two have no connection—though the jacket blurb calls his mixture "the orchestration of two major themes." You could get the same sort of orchestration by printing in one book alternate chapters from *Huckleberry Finn* and *Uncle Tom's Cabin.*

And now, having relieved myself of my impatience, I am in duty bound to say that these two stories are wonderfully imagined and consummately related. The first is the story of a tremendous passion: A young doctor gives up his career and a young woman abandons her husband and children, and the two live together in sordid poverty considering the world well lost. But they are ruined, body, mind and soul; and the story of their degeneration is as true and moving a tale as exists on a similar theme.

The other story is of a convict in Mississippi, who during a great flood is detached from his fellows in the chain gang and set to rescuing victims. He saves a woman, but the two of them are swept far down the river. He is free, but he does not want his freedom; he cannot get away from the woman. And this is the story of how he fights to get back to the blessed peace of prison again.

Oh, yes—perhaps the stories are complementary, being opposite in theme. And perhaps we are lucky to get two novels for the price of one. But I can't see the point in mixing them. Especially since both are extraordinarily fine pieces of fiction.

William McFee. "The Book of the Day: In Which a Writer with a Talent Outrages the Intelligence of His Readers." New York *Sun*, January 23, 1939, p. 10.

In this, the eleventh full-length novel by one of America's most distinguished and original writers, the reader who is not a Faulkner addict will find no surcease from his perplexities. He will find himself involved in all the same old bogs and swamps and miasmas as of yore. Nothing is changed except for the worse. Instead of broadening his appeal from the clever cognoscenti who first disseminated him to the general public, Mr. Faulkner seems to be following in the footsteps of his master, James Joyce, and restricting his clientele ever more narrowly to a cult who nourish their imaginations on the blood of werewolves, who regard literature as a sort of Voodoo devil worship and who relish the gory details of unnatural crimes.

The Wild Palms is a curious production likely to confuse the average reader because it presents, intertwined, two separate themes. *The Wild Palms,* which is about a woman named Charlotte Rittenmeyer and the man she is living with, Harry Wilbourne, has nothing to do with the convict in *The Old Man.* Harry Wilbourne is a doctor of sorts, and those conversant with the ways of Faulkner fauna will study Harry's early environment with attention if they wish to make sense of his later behavior. The entirely unrelated story of the convict is all the more confusing because of Mr. Faulkner's reluctance to illumine his prose with explanatory data. He has written two distinct pieces of fiction and then cut them and alternated their chapters in the same volume. Evidently an advance in the form of the novel. But *The Wild Palms* takes place in recent times whereas *The Old Man* deals with events that transpired during the great Mississippi floods of a decade ago, when Old Man River broke all bounds.

If Mr. Faulkner merely wants to make our flesh creep, like the Fat Boy in *Pickwick*, he is successful. If it is any satisfaction to him as a novelist he also makes one's gorge rise, one's blood freeze and one's desire to lay his book down become a passion.

The love story of Harry Wilbourne and Charlotte begins in New Orleans some months before the book opens. These two meet at a studio party in the Vieux Carré and plunge immediately into one of those frenzied affairs so dear to the modern school of novelists, affairs that seem to be modeled on the ferocious performances of Apache dancers some years ago, wherein the man tears the woman's hair out by the roots, flings her around the floor, smashes her jaw and gets his jaw smashed in return and finally kills her. Charlotte and Harry seem to be in an endless clutch of cold humorless sexual fury. She has walked out on her husband and two children and it is characteristic of the Faulkner technic that even her husband Rittenmeyer is refused the reader's sympathy. Mr. Faulkner does not believe in babying his customers. He reminds this reviewer at times, in his less unpleasant moods, of the badly brought-up child who responds to a caress by sinking his teeth in one's hand. When he really gets along with his banquet of horrors, one feels that it is time somebody took Mr. Faulkner's piece of chalk away from him.

This is said, not in sorrow, but in anger.

Mr. Faulkner was once quoted in these pages as having said that Arnold Bennett was the only man he had ever heard of "who set out to be a second-rate writer and succeeded." But what has Mr. Faulkner set out to be? And what are we to think of a man with a first-rate talent who outrages the intelligence of his readers and admirers with such preposterously distorted characters and incredibly sinister social forces? There are certain passages in *The Wild Palms* which are marvelous evocations of moods and scenes. There are others which are literally masterpieces of slothful perversity, beyond anything that Dreiser perpetrated at his worst.

To use a popular jargon, there is some maladjustment between Mr. Faulkner's genius and the medium in which he works. To use the vernacular, he resembles in his artistic capacity the tragic figure who lamented that "his clothes didn't fit and God hated him." Mr. Faulkner's thesis in *The Wild Palms*, that Charlotte (an incredible woman if there ever was one) and Harry were foredoomed to suffering, death and imprisonment because of their insensate and furious passion, won't hold water for a moment. There is no conceivable motive, that is, save that Mr. Faulkner had been in those parts, for Harry Wilbourne leaving Chicago and taking a job in a desolate mine in Utah and forcing Charlotte to share such a horrible existence. But Mr. Faulkner had been there and he can create some marvelous pictures of those dreadful regions. It is even less credible that a capable, healthy, mature woman, who has borne two children, who can earn money, should pester her lover, who is not a competent surgeon, to attempt an illegal operation on her. The whole thing collapses at the moment it is divested of the Faulkner art, or artifice.

The Old Man is even less comprehensible, through it is certainly in places an amazing technical performance. The birth of the child when the boat, in which she and the convict are being washed down the river, grounds on a lonely mud patch, is a tour de force of brilliant unpleasantness. Mr. Faulkner's idea of being a first rate writer, apparently, is to turn our stomachs. *The Wild Palms*, it is necessary to reiterate, contains passages of great beauty and is technically interesting. But the sumtotal is depressing and occasionally horrifying. Reading it is like a nightmare in a cesspool.

Malcolm Cowley. "Sanctuary." *New Republic*, 97 (January 25, 1939), 349.

In his latest novel, William Faulkner tries the experiment of telling two completely separate stories; let us call them A and B. He divides each of them into five chapters and prints the chapters alternately, like the black and white squares on a checkboard.

Story A has for its theme the flight from security into passion. When Harry Wilbourne meets Charlotte Rittenmeyer they fall in love, instantly and fatally, like two characters in a late-Elizabethan tragedy— say, Giovanni and Annabella in *'Tis Pity She's a Whore.* Harry is an interne in a New Orleans hospital, a poor boy who has starved himself to earn a diploma; in four months now he should be a practising physician. Charlotte has two little daughters and a prosperous and rather decent husband who doesn't believe in divorce. Yet they abandon all that, in order to nourish love as their one child and one career. A few months later in Chicago, Harry feels that he is getting respectable, that love is turning into habit, and so they flee once more, this time into the mountains of Utah. Charlotte is pregnant but refuses to bear the child because it might divide them. Their last desperate flight ends on the gulf coast of Mississippi, where she dies of an abortion. Harry, refusing to run away, is arrested for manslaughter.

Story B has for its theme the flight from passion and the search for security on an infinitely lower level than that from which Harry and Charlotte are escaping. At the Mississippi state prison farm, there is a tall young convict who is absolutely content to plow cotton for the rest of his days, so long as he is bossed and fed. But the cotton fields are flooded and the tall convict—we never learn his name—is set to work on the levee while the river rises hour by hour. Somebody gives him a boat and orders him to rescue a pregnant woman in a tree and a man on the roof of a cotton house. He finds the woman; then his boat is swept into the river. For the next six weeks, during the greatest natural disaster in the history of the South, his one aim is to get away from the woman (and her child, born in their wanderings), to get away from the need for making decisions and get back to his sanctuary in prison. The record of his journey is crazy and convincing: he is shot at by soldiers, crawled over snakes, rescued twice and abandoned, while he moves always southward with the crest of the flood. From New Orleans he makes his way northward again and lands on the levee from which he started. "Yonder's your boat," he says to the deputy sheriff, "and here's the woman. But I never did find the bastard on the cotton house."

Except that both of them end in the Mississippi state prison, there is no logical connection between the two stories. They don't even happen in the same year, since the great flood was in 1927 and Charlotte Rittenmeyer died in the era of the WPA. Their relation is almost purely allegorical. By putting the two stories into the same box, Faulkner is saying that some people fight and die to create their own precarious world, whereas others will perform deeds of physical courage, even heroism, in order to escape from the need for moral effort. The tall convict is the ideal soldier for a fascist army. Thus, the fable is effective, but it would have made a better novel if Faulkner had interwoven the two themes in counterpoint instead of merely setting them side by side.

Story A is so tense and somber with a sense of predestined doom that I found it very hard to read. Perhaps it will be equally hard to forget. My only complaint against Story B is that it half-uses a lot of outlandishly fine material and ends too soon. The book as a whole contains two or three of those authentic nightmares in which Faulkner is unequaled. One is the picture of the bankrupt mine in Utah where twenty Poles work furiously through the winter, under the delusion that they will someday be paid; another is the birth of the baby, with the tall convict as midwife, on an Indian mound where all the snakes of the Yazoo delta have taken refuge from the flood. On the other hand, the book seems negligently planned, as if Faulkner paid less attention to plot than to mood and tempo. What happened to the typewriter that Harry took to Utah, and what happened to the tall convict's alligator skins? Not many novelists would publish a book with these loose ends left hanging.

The style is clearer than in *Pylon* or *Absalom, Absalom!* There are only a few paragraphs of the high-flown gibberish, usually printed in italics, that Faulkner writes when he is trying to explain a complicated emotion. There are, however, a few apparently simple passages that are hard to decipher. One of these occurs at the very end of Story A, where Harry is wondering whether to commit suicide now

that Charlotte is dead and he must spend the rest of his life in prison. Finally he decides to live—

Because if memory exists outside of the flesh it won't be memory because it won't know what it remembers so when she became not then half of memory became not and if I become not then all of remembering will cease to be.—Yes, he thought, *between grief and nothing I will take grief.*

Only after reading the passage two or three times was I able to insert the imaginary punctuation marks that transform it into a straightforward soliloquy: "Because if memory exists outside of the flesh [comma] it won't be memory [comma] because it won't know what it remembers [period] So when she became not [comma] then half of memory became not [semicolon] and if I became not [comma] then all of remembering will cease to be." But the passage is better when printed as free verse, with each phrase on a separate line:

So when she became not
then half of memory became not
and if I became not
then all of remembering will cease to be.

Often when Faulkner writes bad prose he is really thinking in terms of poetry. What would he do, I wonder, with a five-act tragedy in blank verse? It might be that he could write his best work for the stage.

Michael March. "Page after Page." Brooklyn *Citizen*, January 27, 1939.

In reading *The Wild Palms* one lives again in the dank and turgid world of William Faulkner's morbid imagination. There is no fictional world quite like it, in which humans crawl upon the face of the earth like worms and serpents driven in their destinies to treacherous perversions. Illogical though this world may seem in relation to the normal world it is true within its own framework as are frenzied dreams within their own. And like dreams the Faulkner tales envelop the reader in their torturous convolutions. What happens in *The Wild Palms* seems, after one finishes the book, to have occurred under some powerful anaesthetic, something overwhelming and terrible which clings to consciousness like insidious cobwebs.

Objectively *The Wild Palms* seems impossible. Subjectively it is an experience. One experiences a good Faulkner novel, becomes involved in it as it grows like some heavy tropical growth. Two things happen in *The Wild Palms,* two themes run parallel. A young interne, deprived of the normal sexual life of youth, meets and falls terribly in love with a married woman with whom he flees to Chicago. Obsessed with their cataclysmic passion and the desire for uncompromising freedom they come to disaster. She dies in an illegal operation bunglingly performed by him, who is tried and found guilty of murder. The second tale, having no direct relation to the first, runs parallel with it, and describes the unwitting escape of a convict, who yearns for the security of the prison to which he returns contentedly in the end.

Here is the theme of what the publishers call "flight" and "refuge" played contrapuntally upon Faulkner's demoniac imagination. It is hardly important to draw conclusions from the novel's implications, which are many and obscure as is usually the case with this strange writer's work. It may be said that in the interne and his mistress Faulkner wishes to show the hopeless way of love in a world which seems always to betray lovers. Charlotte, the woman, declares that love never changes but lovers do; they become unworthy of love by compromises. This possessed couple through the time-span of the novel is frantically in flight from the compulsions of respectability. Actually they are in flight from their own fears, which bind them to the normality they so abhor. The convict, who has unwittingly escaped, wants nothing so much as his old safety and security within the prison walls. In one theme freedom is the goal, in the other security. The striving for freedom on the part of the impassioned couple is conditioned by intelligence, which in the end is overwhelmed by simple biological imperatives. The convict is the simple biological man not tormented by intellectual or emotional idealism.

Mainly, however, Faulkner creates the sense of life's terrible frustrations, the impersonality of the world we live in. In this case it is a crawling, slimy, ugly world, an evocation of an imagination that can conceive of no hope of any kind. There is not a person in the novel whom one would want to count as one's friend. There is no hope in these pages, only that hunted terror which lies behind the human mask. The events grow out of the moments when consciousness merges with sub-consciousness. The passions are not idealized by the author but brutalized, and the moments of these lovers in the full impact of their passions seem more related to death than to life. There is no ecstasy in them, no real fulfillment, only the frantic, terrorized awareness of their essential tragedy, which they cannot ultimately escape.

Although Faulkner may be said in this novel to be making a protest against respectability, the protest cannot be effective since the nightmare of his protagonists is so horribly dismal. His people are lost from the beginning, and a lost cause that has initially no high aspiration to commend it other than a driving physical passion is better lost.

As usual Faulkner's style is torrential in

its effect and as defective as a torrent. The words pour forth in entangled sentences, loaded with parenthetical phrases and grammatical flaws; they pour forth out of the depths of an imagination that is at times overwhelming. He expands the moment into grim analyses of motive; his descriptions emerge not objectively but as if one were inside a miasma.

The Wild Palms is, indeed, an experience. In it Faulkner casts an evil spell so unutterably fascinating that one cannot escape its black magical power.

Albert Guerard, Jr. "Faulkner's Two Jobs in One, His Best in Years." Boston *Evening Transcript*, January 28, 1939, Book Reviews, p. 1.

William Faulkner pays few respects to the accepted conventions of novel-writing. Last year's *The Unvanquished* consisted of seven short stories, strung together to make a "novel"; now we have two short and independent novels, *Wild Palms* and *Old Man*, broken up and intermingled to give a semblance of unity.

The two stories are not even concurrent. *Old Man* is the narrative of a convict caught in the Mississippi flood of 1927, whereas the all-for-love adventures of *Wild Palms*—timeless in themselves—are dated by a single casual reference to "the scant feminine underwear of 1937." The two themes, the lovers' flight from cloying respectability and the convict's struggle to regain the refuge from life's disorder which his penitentiary had become, achieve a very doubtful counterpoint. There are no placid moments to relieve the general intensity; the madness

of the characters is more or less intermittent. Perhaps the best excuse for Faulkner's arbitrary dislocation of form is that few readers could endure to read either "novel" at a sitting; that there is a certain relief in changing the embodiments of horror, in being whisked back and forth between frying pan and fire.

If *Old Man* takes on at times the unreality and inconsequence of allegory, *Wild Palms* is as real and immediate as *Manon Lescaut*. But Wilbourne, the young and inexperienced interne who gives up his medical career for the sole purpose of love-making, makes no effort to resist either Charlotte or his fate. They cut themselves off from normal life as completely as they can, whether in a lakeshore cabin near Chicago or in a western mining-camp. Their only fear is that they will not be "good enough" for love; that they will begin to look at things through respectability's jaundiced and corrupting eye.

Old Man is clearly intended to be an allegorical study of man's struggle against the incalculable and mysterious in nature: the pregnancy of the woman whom the convict rescues is a greater outrage than the monstrous river flood. But the allegorical or general significance of the story is surely hampered by the fact that the convict has (though not at every moment) a psychopathic adversion to women, and that he has, in many ways, the mind of a child.

There is much here, in brief, of the kind of incoherence that we have come to expect from Faulkner, an incoherence which limited Melville's greatness and which almost wholly vitiates the poetry of Robinson Jeffers. But it is, in Faulkner, the incoherence of a writer of genius. In his style particularly we find the glories and shames of literary intoxication: pages of uncontrolled rhetoric which rarely deviate into sense followed by pages of sharp and graphic intensity, pages revealing a gift of phrase shared by only two or three other writers in our time.

It is very doubtful whether any writer who ignores normal human character so deliberately and completely can write a great philosophical novel. Yet in spite of its pretentious and unrealized theme, *Wild Palms* is one of the most exciting and readable of Faulkner's novels. The story of Wilbourne and Charlotte has the terrible veracity of *Jude the Obscure*, and even the convict's heroic efforts have a kind of legendary and poetic truth. Faulkner has somehow resisted Hollywood's usual emasculation, and this present book seems to me a better one than any he has written in the last five years. It may come to be regarded as one of the great failures of our literature.

George Grimes. "Faulkner Tale Shocks; Shows Man in Flight." Omaha *Sunday World Herald*, February 12, 1939, p. 8-C.

Jeepers, creepers!

William Faulkner has done another novel guaranteed to give the reader the shudders and the creeps, to shock him bolt upright from his easy chair, to give him bad dreams at night.

Rather has he written two novels. The stories are told side by side, first one and then the other, with no apparent connection between the two, unless you probe for the philosophy of life's frustration that underlies both. And the connecting link between the two is not discovered until one reads the very last word in the book. I'll not tell you what that word is.

But here is a book containing two stories of flight. One of them, *The Wild Palms*, has to do with a young doctor who had worked and slaved and studied and was in his late 20's a virgin. Then he met a woman, a wife and mother of two daughters, a woman with the tawny yellow eyes of a cat and an overpowering urge to love. They went away together to make love, went from Mississippi to Chicago, went to a mine in Utah, found their way back down south and she died as the result of a criminal operation he bungled—because he loved her too much to do it efficiently.

The other flight, in the novel, *Old Man*, has to do with a tall convict, and a terrific flood of the Mississippi, with people clinging to trees and house tops. The convict was freed from his chains to go in a boat to try to rescue a woman perched on a roof top. He got her and they drifted with the flood, and she had a baby with him assisting, and finally he got back to prison and was given 10 more years by the warden for attempting to escape.

But how, in such brief outline, suggest the shocking realism of Mr. Faulkner's novel? How describe the desperate sexual urge of Charlotte, and the flight of Charlotte and Harry, their will to live for each other alone, disdaining all such enchaining comforts as home, and children, a job, pay checks, security? Or how describe the magnificent flood scenes with the tall convict caring for the woman he had rescued? How describe the pains of birth in a snake-infested swamp, the agony of despair, the futility of effort, the uselessness and folly of trying to flee from one's life, whatever that life is?

Anyone who has read Faulkner will know about his skill in such matters and will read this novel, in many ways, his best. He will read it despite its terribly long, involved, often meaningless sentences. He will read it despite scenes so barely suggested that one can only guess what takes place. He will read it wondering why he reads on in the tale of the woman with but one purpose, and the man with none, or the convict who had tried bank robbery and now could think of nothing in life but to get back to the prison from which a flood had once released him.

The Wild Palms will be anything to any reader. It may be brutal horror. It may be magnificent compassion. It may be supreme irony. It may be utter rot.

Bruce Catton. "*Wild Palms* Is Sinister but Dramatic." Huntington (W.Va.) *Advertiser*, February 5, 1939.

It is doubtful that the year will produce another book more somber, more sordid, yet so thoroughly dramatic as William Faulkner's newest novel, *The Wild Palms*. Very likely you may protest Mr. Faulkner's realism at every stretch of his incomparable book but if you start it at all you'll hang on to the grim and bitter end.

For that is just exactly what Mr. Faulkner guides you to in this novel, or rather two novels, within one cover. The first is *The Wild Palms* and the second, *Old Man*. You read a chapter of each alternately. Thus you are supposed to follow a sort of "orchestration of two major themes." The characters, incidentally, having nothing to do with each other at all.

But whether you perceive this "orchestration" or not you can follow each of the novels separately. *The Wild Palms* is first and is obviously Mr. Faulkner's leading story of the two. It is also the more horri-

fying for it traces the slow degeneration of a man and a woman.

In brief, this is the story of a young doctor who falls in love with a married woman, forsaking everything for her. In turn, she abandons her husband and children. So together the infatuate pair roam the face of the country, falling always to new depths. In the end death and an avenging nature climaxes their story.

Old Man is the story, on the other hand, of a convict who found a woman in a Mississippi flood he could not lose. Through disaster and every sort of misfortune she clung to him until at last this convict, already a free man, turned back to prison to get away from her.

Such is Mr. Faulkner's newest imagery. Take it or leave it, it is unforgettable fiction.

Edwin Berry Burgum. "Faulkner's New Novel." *New Masses*, February 7, 1939, pp. 23–24.

In his distinguished career Mr. Faulkner has not written a more thoroughly satisfying novel than *The Wild Palms*. He has been unusually sensitive to manner of expression and extraordinarily persistent in technical experimentation. Since he has at the same time insisted upon grappling with significant themes, his work has either presented the obvious flaws of construction of *Light in August* or achieved a form, like that of *The Sound and the Fury*, almost incomprehensible to the average reader. But in this latest novel he has come very near the successful expression he has been groping for. It not only reads easily; it grips the attention.

If such is really Faulkner's accomplishment in *The Wild Palms*, the comments the critics are making can scarcely be right.

Puzzled, apparently, by the fact that two unrelated stories unroll in alternate chapters, some of the critics have failed to find any organic connection between them, while others have discovered too simple a relationship. These latter believe the one story to be the mere opposite to the other. As the blurb puts it, the two themes are flight and refuge. On the one hand, a woman leaves the security of marriage for the hazards of life with an unstable young doctor. On the other, a prisoner, virtually given a chance to escape when he is sent to aid persons marooned by the overflowing Mississippi, prefers to return to his prison walls.

But the real relationship between the two stories must be more complex, for they both end within the "security" of prison walls. The pursuit of freedom, the escape from the conventional, has in neither instance been satisfactory. This is the basic ironic theme which both stories hold in common: in a demoralized age the prison affords the illiterate hillbilly and the educated neurotic doctor alike the only possible framework of social compulsions within which they can exist, if not with what Malraux would call man's natural hope and dignity, at least with the approximation of tranquillity. In this fundamental orientation of the novel, one can find a development of the paradox of Dostoevski. In Faulkner peace does not come after crime and suffering simply as a result of the compulsion imposed by society. The irony is more bitter, since these men who suffer and go to jail have become better men, better integrated men, than their sadistic jailers and the average respectable citizens outside. The "wretched of mankind" are in no mood to arise in Faulkner, but they have at all events escaped that pretense of freedom which our competitive world sets up as an ideal and translates, as these two stories hint, into the actuality of the undernourished body and the neurotic personality.

The dominant story, the story of Dr. Wilbourne, is in its general outline only the better retelling of Dreiser's *American Tragedy*. Wilbourne is the same sort of virtuous inexperienced weakling, whose suppressed sexual urges burst into control of him at the age of twenty-seven, and whose lack of that core of resolute selfishness which comes naturally to the boy on the street corner makes possible his eventual crime. But Faulkner is not content to leave Wilbourne the plaything of heredity and environment. He centers his attention on the intricate immediate conflict within the personality. He depicts the ineffectual rise of a deep masculine discontent with mere satisfaction in love, which leads Wilbourne, not to reject the "stability" (as the critics would say) of his being supported by his mistress, but to wipe out the offense to his pride in not being able to support her himself. And so they trek to the snowbound mine in Utah, where he fails as a doctor because he has fallen victim to a shady capitalistic enterprise.

One value of the subordinate story now begins to become apparent. It throws into contrast with the neurotic instability of this educated middle-class doctor the contrasting virtues of the proletarian. At the very time when the doctor is becoming hysterical because of his mistress' pregnancy, caught between her desire for an abortion and his fear and dislike of performing it, the criminal of the second story is rescuing from the swollen Mississippi a woman who is also pregnant. Actually the event, like the rest of the second story, occurred some ten year earlier. But the fact that Faulkner inserts this particular episode into his novel at this point can only mean that he intends the reader to learn something from the contrast of the two situations. If the doctor could hardly endure the cold of Utah winters, the hill-billy illiterate rises equal to this physical emergency. These scenes in which the man—who is never given a name, who is only described as tall and lean, as though the prototype of the underprivileged, not worth individualization in the eyes of dominant respectability—these scenes in which he keeps his boat afloat with the pregnant woman in it, in which he is shot at by officers on the bank he is seeking to hail, in which he delivers her baby on a mud bank to which he has dragged her no more weak with exhaustion than himself, may well be isolated in our textbooks as instances of Faulkner's mastery of the art of narration. But in the novel they furnish dramatic relief to the spasm of passion, the alternations of despair and futile ecstasy, the impotent hesitations, among which Wilbourne has been wallowing. They restore to the reader the pleasure and the confidence of certain elemental qualities which seem to have retreated from the higher social levels. But it has been nature and not society which has inspired this heroism in the tall lean man. And if after these weeks of heroism he returns to his prison, indifferent to the ten years which have been added to his sentence, "for escaping," it is because he knows he will enjoy there the friendship of his fellow prisoners and the comfort of tomorrow's hand upon the plough, which not merely his crime, his absurd, unsuccessful train robbery, but the very complexion of respectable society denies him outside.

It is not, however, on this note that Faulkner ends this novel. The heroism has been exceptional, something to be recounted with simple joy of recollection to his fellow prisoners, among whom someday, perhaps, Wilbourne, shorn by years of imprisonment of both his respectability and his neuroses, forgetful of length of love and the grief it has brought him, may be content to listen. For society has reduced these prisoners to the habitual level of Hardy's peasants who expect no more than toil and discipline. They get pleasure out of the day because they expect so little from it, and if they are deprived of love, remember with a laughter which has lost all bitterness that it does not submit to routine.

Henry Hart. "Books." *Direction*, 4 (March–April 1939), 21–22.

William Faulkner's *The Wild Palms* is so dismal a failure that one wonders whether his splendid talent is regressing.

Some collateral aspects of this question should be skipped: first, the obscurity and contrapuntual devices with which Faulkner tries to solve the problems of the novel form, in which he may not be interested, for his short stories are much more successful technically; second, the superficial aspects of his predilection for violence, the depiction of which makes few demands upon the artist because of the heightened emotions which inhere in it; third, his preoccupation with the female organs and his propensity for wreaking havoc upon them—(an unsuccessful abortion furnishes the action of one of the two main themes of *The Wild Palms* and a birth during the maelstrom of flood furnishes the other).

Let us deal only with this: Why does Faulkner expend his talent for original simile, and his mastery of the withering rhetoric of Ecclesiastes, upon inadequate exemplifications of the theme that fascinates him most—which, to my mind, is opposition to the corrosive effect of smug security upon all that is most precious in man and its tendency to frustrate man's growth? What prevents Faulkner from perceiving that his subject matter isn't adequate to the demands of his theme?

I think it is because he does not look in the right places for contemporary instances of bravery and hazarding the unknown. In Mississippi perhaps (though I doubt it) the immemorial courage of man, when bursting the bonds that distort or deaden the inextinguishable human spirit, may be manifested only in desperate little forays against petty private property, in trembling departures from monogamy, and in flouting the *mores* of a Baptist Fundamentalism. But such rebellions obscure rather than clarify Faulkner's theme. He will find adequate material in the actions of men who contend against the forces which cause the contented corruption that is Faulkner's bête noir.

Paula Snelling. "Out of the Gulf Stream." *North Georgia Review* (*South Today*), 4 (Spring 1939), 24–25.

In *Light in August* and in *Absalom, Absalom!* Mr. Faulkner seemed well on his way towards making of his vices the virtues they potentially are. About *Pylon* there was little good to be said. *The Wild Palms* lies somewhere between the two extremes. In it, the publishers say, he has "achieved a straightforward and smashing dramatic story in the best manner of his *Sanctuary* and *As I Lay Dying*." Their shelving is correct, and one quarrels only with the inclusion of the word "straightforward";—Mr. Faulkner's most cherished

trick in trade here and elsewhere being to march his readers through partially unintelligible, powerfully charged pages until they find themselves almost deciding what it is the author wishes to (or not to) tell them, then to jerk them into a new series of pages designed to the same end. For the rest of it, one looks again through the preface to the Modern Library edition of *Sanctuary*, glances through the subsequent corroborating pages, considers *The Wild Palms* and concludes that the author has not changed his spots. He even goes a step further here in that he tells two unrelated stories which have been placed in the same volume for little other discernible purpose than to afford him the pleasure, after engrossing you in one story to the point where you have forgotten what occurred in the other and have lost all interest in its characters, of transporting you to the other, there to remain until the same disinterest has arisen concerning the first set; then back again. Which bears more resemblance to the manner in which a fisherman disports himself with reel, rod and sucker than to the preoccupations of a serious and talented artist whose realm is the human soul. (The two stories, concerned with different characters, different locales, different times do of course permit the reader to make certain comparisons and contrasts, but the author does little in the choosing and the shaping of his stories to impress us with a relationship—unless it be the basic inevitability underlying the beguiling opulence of phrase in the "take-it-off, knock-it-off, or have-the-crow-to-pick-it-off" alternatives life frequently restricts us to.)

And yet Faulkner has gifts which, were his core of the same caliber, would place him in the foreranks of twentieth century novelists. For that reason only does one not accept his performances with equanimity. Those to whom ten talents have been given cannot escape the hard requirement that they produce therewith another ten. Whereas Mr. Faulkner seems to have selected as his goal the search for a corrosive with which to overlay each of his ten rarely duplicated talents. Yet it is perhaps useless, even stupid, to rail out at Mr. Faulkner for this. His books, more than those of any other American writer, seem to draw their power and their poison from their author's unconscious. They seem to be fashioned almost as dreams are fashioned: just as certain of our dreams are charged with an emotion far in excess of the requirements of their ostensible subject-matter, yet not too great for the deep elemental forces for which the dream symbols unrecognizedly stand, so Faulkner's novels have a surcharge of power and terror which though fully warranted by certain under-currents and conflicts of life, yet remain definitely excessive for the matters he chooses to write about. Or perhaps he no more chooses what to write about than we choose what to dream about—the subject-matter in both cases being that compromise material which simultaneously affords outlet for pent-up unconscious emotions and screen against conscious recognition of the basis of those emotions. One feels even that Faulkner's mad search for ever more and more bizarre material may be an attempt to find something spectacular enough, something awe-ful enough, to justify to his conscious mind (compelled to rationalize where it fears to reason) the emotion which he has and which he recognizes is out of proportion to what he sees in more conventional subject-matter—he not having attained that rare maturity of vision which sees that the most turbulent, the most distressing, the most exquisite emotions a human being can feel are not the outcroppings of lurid adventures, but have their roots in simple experiences which are the common lot of man; and that the bogey-men, the horror tales, the envisioned and the enacted perversions with which from time to time we confound ourselves are but feeble and inaccurate projections of simple and terrifying and hidden thoughts, conflicts, experiences that basically disturb us.

We are grateful to Mr. Faulkner for his certainty, and for his repeated powerful affirmations of this certainty, that life is not the stereotyped, mediocrity-encrusted affair which the conventional mind in and out of books contents itself that it is. That his fiction should impatiently and angrily state and overstate the inadequacy of customary assumptions concerning what is important in life is understandable and valuable. But it is not sufficient. There is great potential virtue, both artistic and psychological, in Mr. Faulkner's tendency to isolate one compelling factor, instinct, drive, perversion, character trait, in a person's life, taking a bulldog grip on it, following the person where this compulsive motive power leads him, refusing to be diverted from the scent by the false trails human beings lay to bemuse themselves and their fellow-travelers. But Mr. Faulkner does not give continuous evidence that he discards conventionalities discriminately or for the honest purpose of learning what lies beneath. More frequently he seems to be flaunting in our faces the cheapness in which he holds us—and himself; or to be following compulsions of his own which only coincidentally take him into the rich, inadequately explored bottom lands of civilization.

Checklist of Additional Reviews

Portland (Me.) *Express*, January 21, 1939.
San Francisco *Call*, January 21, 1939.
"Wm. Faulkner Displays Same Virtues, Same Faults in Unusual Novel."

Akron *Beacon Journal*, January 22, 1939, p. 9-D.

Buffalo (N.Y.) *Courier Express*, January 22, 1939.

Youngstown (Ohio) *Vindicator*, January 22, 1939.

Binghamton (N.Y.) *Press*, January 26, 1939.

"*The Wild Palms*." Boston *Herald*, January 28, 1939, p. 6.

Hollywood *News*, January 28, 1939.

"New Faulkner Novel Lacks Organization." Charlotte *Observer*, January 29, 1939, Section IV, p. 7.

"*Wild Palms* Written in Modern Way." Oakland *Tribune*, February 5, 1939, p. 2-B.

Milwaukee *Post*, February 11, 1939.

"William Faulkner at His Gloomiest." Knoxville *Journal*, February 26, 1939, Section IV, p. 8.

"*The Wild Palms*." *Christian Century*, March 22, 1939, p. 387.

Banning, Margaret C. "Changing Moral Standards in Fiction." *Saturday Review of Literature*, July 1, 1939, pp. 4–5, 14.

[Cantwell, Robert]. "When the Dam Breaks." *Time*, January 23, 1939, pp. 45–46, 48.

Chamberlain, John. "The New Books." *Harper's Magazine*, February 1939, advertising pages.

Childers, J[ames] S. "Mr. Faulkner Once Again Produces an Exciting Novel." Birmingham *News*, February 5, 1939, Magazine Section, p. 7.

Clayton, Charles C. "William Faulkner's New Novel Is Study in Passion." St. Louis *Globe-Democrat*, January 21, 1939, p. 1-B.

Conroy, Jack. "*The Wild Palms*." *People's Daily World* (San Francisco), February 4, 1939, Section II, p. 10.

DeJong, David Cornel. "William Faulkner Tries Two Themes." Providence *Sunday Journal*, February 19, 1939, Section VI, p. 6.

DeVoto, Bernard. "American Novels: 1939." *Atlantic Monthly*, January 1940, p. 73.

Doying, George. "Flight: It's Theme of New Novel by William Faulkner." Pittsburgh *Press*, February 5, 1939, Society Section, p. 11.

F., A.M. "Strong Meat in Faulkner's New Novel." Milwaukee *Journal*, January 22, 1939, Editorial Section, p. 3.

F., P.G. "A Book a Day." Spartanburg (S.C.) *Herald*, January 30, 1939; Bakersfield *Californian*, February 2, 1939; Erie *Times*, February 2, 1939; Greenville (S.C.) *Piedmont*, February 3, 1939; San Jose (Calif.) *News*, February 4, 1939; Macon *News*, February 8, 1939; Knoxville *News-Sentinel*, February 12, 1939; San Francisco *News*, February 25, 1939; Tucson *Star*, March 5, 1939.

Fadiman, Clifton. "Mississippi Frankenstein." *New Yorker*, January 21, 1939, pp. 60–62.

Fitzhugh, Eleanor. "Turns with Bookworms." Jackson (Miss.) *News*, February 6, 1939, p. 5.

Flournoy, Rose Boynton. "William Faulkner's Latest Novel, *The Wild Palms*, Is Brilliant Work by South's Foremost Writer." Columbus (Ga.) *Enquirer*, January 30, 1939, p. 2.

Gannett, Lewis. "Books and Things." Washington *Post*, January 20, 1939, p. 11.

Gardner, Jennie B. "Mr. Faulkner Scores Again with Novel Contrasting Two Contrapuntal Themes." Memphis *Commercial Appeal*, January 22, 1939, Section IV, p. 9.

Gewinner, Holt. "Today's book." Macon *Telegraph*, January 22, 1939, p. 4.

Hansen, Harry. "*The Wild Palms*, by William Faulkner, Is a Fantastically Absorbing Novel, Gripping as a Remembered Nightmare." New York

World-Telegram, January 19, 1939, p. 19; Norfolk *Pilot*, January 23, 1939.

Hogan, William. "The South of Faulkner's Mouth Leaves a Bad Taste." San Francisco *Chronicle*, January 29, 1939, This World Section, p. 16.

Hoole, William Stanley. "William Faulkner's New Novel Is Bible of Disintegration." Dallas *Morning News*, January 22, 1939, Section III, p. 15.

Jack, Peter Monro. "Mr. Faulkner's Clearest Novel." *New York Times Book Review*, January 22, 1939, p. 2.

K., M.S. "Faulkner's Pen Draws Monster with Two Heads." New Bedford (Mass.) *Standard*, February 26, 1939, Section III, p. 19.

Kazin, Alfred. "A Study in Conscience." *New York Herald Tribune Books*, January 22, 1939, p. 2.

K[ernodle], M[argaret] J. "Faulkner Has Strong Novel in New Effort." Greensboro *Daily News*, February 5, 1939, p. 6-D.

Knowlton, Kent. "Two Novels in One." Lowell *Courier-Citizen*, January 20, 1939, p. 15.

Lovett, Robert Morss. "Ferocious Faulkner." *Nation*, February 4, 1939, p. 153.

Maxwell, Allen. "*The Wild Palms*." *Southwest Review*, 24 (April 1939), 257–60.

Meyer, Luther. "Love Demands Strength." San Francisco *Call-Bulletin*, January 21, 1939, p. 14.

Myers, Bill. "*The Wild Palms*." Dayton *Daily News*, January 22, 1939, Society Section, p. 7.

N., R.W. "Contrasted Themes in *The Wild Palms*." Springfield (Mass.) *Sunday Union and Republican*, January 29, 1939, p. 7-E.

Needham, Wilbur. "New Faulkner Novel Teems with Brutal Frankness." Los Angeles *Times*, January 29, 1939, Part III, p. 7.

Nicholas, Louis. "Faulkner's *The Wild Palms*." Philadelphia *Record*, February 11, 1939, p. 7.

Patterson, Alicia. "The Book of the Week." New York *Sunday News*, January 22, 1939, p. 65.

Rector, Beulah. "*The Wild Palms*." Watertown (N.Y.) *Times*, January 21, 1939.

Redman, Ben Ray. "Faulkner's Double Novel." *Saturday Review of Literature*, January 21, 1939, p. 5.

Rollins, Steed. "Escape." Durham *Herald*, February 5, 1939.

R[oueché], B[erton]. "Faulkner's Desperate Love Story." Kansas City *Star*, January 21, 1939, p. 14.

Selby, John. "Books—." Johnson City (Tenn.) *Press*, January 20, 1939; New Haven *Register*, January 22, 1939; Bristol (Va.) *News Bulletin*, January 24, 1939; *Ohio State Journal* (Columbus), January 29, 1939; Lodi (Calif.) *Times*, January 31, 1939.

Shaw, Robert. "Life as Futility and Disaster." Oakland *Post-Enquirer*, February 11, 1939, p. 12.

Shipp, Cameron. "Mr. Faulkner's New Book." Charlotte *News*, January 29, 1939, p. 9-A.

Sonnichsen, C.L. "Two Battered Figures." El Paso *Herald-Post*, January 28, 1939, p. 5.

Stegner, Wallace. "Conductivity in Fiction." *Virginia Quarterly Review*, 15 (Summer 1939), 443–47.

Stevens, George. *Book-of-the-Month Club News*, February 1939.

Thompson, Ralph. "Books of the Times." New York *Times*, January 19, 1939, p. 15; also reviewed in *Yale Review*, 28 (Spring 1939), viii.

Van Doren, Carl. "Fiction." *Scribner's Magazine*, March 1939, pp. 55–56.

Van Liew, James. "*The Wild Palms.*" *Prairie Schooner*, 14 (Spring 1940), 68–69.

Wagner, Charles. New York *Mirror*, January 21, 1939.

Weigle, Edith. "There's Nothing Cheery in New Faulkner Novel." Chicago *Daily Tribune*, January 21, 1939, p. 10.

Williams, Sidney. "Faulkner Offers *The Wild Palms.*" Philadelphia *Inquirer*, February 11, 1939, p. 28.

THE HAMLET

by WILLIAM FAULKNER

RANDOM HOUSE · NEW YORK · 1940

Sally Harrison. "New Faulkner Novel." Brooklyn *Citizen*, March 29, 1940.

William Faulkner has gone back to his old writing-ground, Yoknapatawpha County, to come to grips with the common man. The glamorous in-love-with-death Sartorises, the beautiful and damned Sutpens of pre-war vintage, are gone from the earth, leaving the rock-bottom humanity of a sharecropper community. Even the negro-characters in *The Hamlet* are incidental. Here a southerner has ceased to blame the negro for the ills of the South (either blame or fear), just as in *The Wild Palms*, a man ceased from "blaming the woman." The hamlet is a group of common people who are in for it all right, but who cooperate raucously at their own undoing.

The story takes up at the turn of the generation, so to speak, when the shift of power out of the hands of the aristocrats had been consummated. A canny trader, old Will Varner, worked, financed and mulcted the hamlet. Most likely, everyone felt, he and his son after him would keep on gathering in the lands and the pennies of the citizenry in an iron process nothing could change. Or so it appeared, until Flem Snopes came to clerk in the Varner company-store, across the village street from the Varner gin scales.

The Hamlet is a cacophony of vicious, dirty laughs that punctuate his rise to power and explain how it could happen that a dehumanized underdog could gull a citizenry and spread his unseemly tribe like a stealthy fungus over an entire farming area. Only Ratliff, the enlightened sewing-machine salesman (and an occasional done-in wife or widow that didn't count) ever added anger or resolve to the general amusement. "Not frowning, but with a sort of fierce risibility," the village liberal watched it all, anticipating all but the last joke, which was on him.

I am not sure that the first guffaw wasn't the best. The Varner crown-prince saw a chance to do a stranger out of the fruits of his labor. That was old Ab Snopes, who came to the hamlet with the black gossip of a barn-burning trailing him close. Young Varner intended to scare him out of the country, come pay-off time. The natives laughed when it dawned on Varner that Ab and his son were actually capable of desperate revenge, perhaps even of mere unthinking violence. So, as a bribe, the son is offered a place in trade, and the saga of the terrible Snopeses begins. Soon Flem is weighing cotton and keeping accounts with the crown-prince running the errands.

The hamlet got another laugh when old man Varner deeded Flem the Frenchman place and heaven knew what else, to get a husband for his "ruined" daughter. Eula, lush personification of abundant femaleness, had driven her anchorite schoolmaster crazy when she was still 14. At 17, she was a fever on the whole male countryside, so that when the scandal broke, not one but three young men left town: One because he was responsible, and the other two because they could not bear not to be thought responsible. "A little lost village," mused Ratliff, "nameless, without grace, forsaken, yet which wombed once by chance and accident one blind seed of spendthrift, Olympian ejaculation and did not even know it." Snopes got her with a lot of Varner property thrown in.

If Ratliff was the repository of what conscience, pity, and intelligence was left in the hamlet, Ike Snopes, the full-grown idiot, was its innocence. In despair of the common citizen, the author lavishes his best poetry on the one person essentially without blame—in actuality the most horrible. The idiot commits sodomy, and becomes the village peep-show; but first Faulkner sets down a lyric love story of an idiot and a cow. Here is the Faulknerian tour de force, and it is an all-time high (or low). In passing, I might report that Faulkner is still writing like an angel when he isn't writing like a devil. The two fables, one about Snopes as Faust, another about the girl on the floor behind the store-counter, who "thought that was what the writin' in the ledger meant"; the climax in which Flem rides roughshod over the peasants, and particularly the way his wild horses drew the menfolks in from surrounding farms, over the fence, and in under their pounding hooves; the 33-line classic where you get the feel of sudden death from a gun-wound in the stomach: They are par. The imaginative faculty for sensory transference which D. H. Lawrence spent on bird-beast-and-flower life, Faulkner puts to the feel of deathly things—horrors, violences, aberrations.

But this is a "comic" novel, a long, mounting crescendo of practical jokes somewhat on the dirty side. They are just things that happen in a village. They are also the concrete symbols of the prize fight, the big business game, the "murder for profit" of war and punishment everywhere. They are indeed things that happen, but I am sure they didn't all happen in some corner-crossroads of Faulkner's precise memory. This is not realism, but tragedy—creative storymaking on a very high level of art and intention. The steps in the Snopes saga follow each other in a compulsive series of related explosions, each nicely calculated to give a lucky opening to the mean and greedy.

In spite of its wicked truth and the quick, exciting, objective narrative my final disappointment in this novel has been acute. I have felt through two of Faulkner's books now that he is on the very point of

finding a way out, a method of creative peace—between a man and a woman, between members of a society. His picture is honest; I think he has tried and has honestly been unable to find anyone working it out. But if his "hamlet" holds no such person, no such pair, let him imagine one! It is not Faulkner's job, as some would have it, to cease from his penning and go personally to some Yoknapatawpha County and start changing society. He is a writer. But it is a writer's job to imagine the truth he knows, and not merely to report the vast April Fool man-in-society is playing on himself today. This way, Faulkner's public is very likely to imitate his peasants and choose the shock, horror, and sensationalism of *The Hamlet* and let the lesson go: Reading *The Hamlet* for its cow as they read *The Sanctuary* [*sic*] for a corncob. Taken at probable net reader-value, *The Hamlet* is itself only commedia del arte, and Faulkner a defeated Ratliff playing into the hand of society's ubiquitous Snopes & co.

Frank Brookhouser. "Faulkner's Mississippian Lower Depths." Philadelphia *Inquirer*, April 3, 1940, p. 14.

That Mr. Faulkner has a way and a highly distinctive if sometimes chaotic way with words, that he is a writer of nightmarish imagination, that he combines the subtle with the slam-bang to produce the ultimate in weird effects, has been known for some years now. And once more it seems to be excuse enough for not having written a good novel, in the actual meaning of the word.

This, like all of his books, is thoughtful

and arresting and irritating. It is, at one and the same time, a wallowing in the mud, with the author's familiar subjects, and spasmodic flights in the sky, with his familiar flashes of strikingly brilliant writing.

In these four "long short stories"—they are only slightly inter-related and the book is not strictly a novel—of the fantastic Snopes family, which has wandered through some of his other books, you will find all the well-known Faulknerian traits.

The setting is Faulkner's Mississippi canebrake country, the time the late '90's, the characters the debased villagers and principally, the Snopes, who worm their way into the land, feed on it like leeches and gain complete control of it.

Flem Snopes, by canny trading, gains control of Frenchman's Bend, the hamlet, in the first story. The second story is concerned with Eula Varner, ready for love at an early age, drawing the men to her like molasses draws flies—and with the same romantic implications. This is just a warmup, however, for the idiot Ike Snopes' hopeless love for a cow in the third story. A band of wild Texas ponies gets loose in the village in the last story, creating another grotesque if more playful scene.

Thus Faulkner presents his people at their worst, at their nearest approach to the animal stage. His picture is probing, relentless, pitiless. And yet both the people and the picture seem to be getting tiresome. The point has been proved. Any Faulkner reader will know the defects of the book and yet shining through all of them is that amazing skill with words, that fertile mind, which has made the author one of the most original and ingenious talents in American letters. This book is both tiresome and tremendously interesting. That is no more a paradox than some of Faulkner's sentences.

Sterling North.
"Darker than the Moody Dane."
Chicago *Daily News*, April 3, 1940, p. 16.

Faulkner has always been writing *Hamlet*. He has been muttering to himself in midnight frenzy—staging his tragedies against the broken splendor of old Southern mansions, brooding over ancient injustice done to the human race.

But this time he has admitted to his brooding and has tried to define the nature of the injustice. In many ways this is the most articulate novel Faulkner has written, the most readable and the most carefully fashioned.

Often in the past he has substituted horror and mystery for those more difficult accomplishments—good character delineation and believable incident. His novels have been notoriously overwritten and undermotivated.

This is definitely not the case with Faulkner's *Hamlet*. The desire of Flem Snopes, son of Barn-burning Ab Snopes, to dominate Frenchman's Bend, and his long crooked climb to wealth and prominence have the essential solidity of *The Rise of Silas Lapham*—plus a satanic fury which seems less Hamlet than Lucifer.

As in all the Faulkner books, there are too many silences, too many completely inhuman characters, too many evasions of the novelist's responsibility to discover believable motivations. Eula, the supposedly attractive moronic Venus, is particularly underrealized.

But in Flem Snopes, the Varners (father and son) and Ratliff, Faulkner has achieved his best rounded characters since *Sartoris*. Faulkner's *The Hamlet* will certainly rank with *Light in August*—one of the two or three outstanding novels of his brilliant career.

Berton Roueché. "Faulkner Fills His Gallery." Kansas City (Mo.) *Star*, April 6, 1940, p. 14.

William Faulkner's twelfth novel tells the story of an incredible family named Snopes. In the course of his long and oblique Sartoris chronicles, Faulkner has provided an occasional glimpse of the upstart Snopese. *The Hamlet* describes their bizarre descent upon the village of Frenchman's Bend, a small Mississippi community, shortly after the turn of the century.

Faulkner followers will not be deceived by the apparent simplicity of such a summary. Between the appearance of the club-footed, barn-burning Ab Snopes and the departure some five years later of his shrewd, chilly son for a field of larger operations stretches a recital of horrific violence and tragic-comedy of the purest Faulknerian fury.

Yet, *The Hamlet* is one of Faulkner's more communicable narratives. There is less of his familiar tendency to withhold the vital clues to coherence. For the most part, he tells the story of the Snopeses with the conventional regard for orderly sequence of events. Because it is not unnecessarily difficult to follow, because it includes a gallery of memorable characters and because its up-piling of the gruesome and the revolting is relieved from time to time by wild flashes of humor, *The Hamlet* must take its place as one of Faulkner's most outstanding achievements.

Just what *The Hamlet* is designed to reveal, beyond the detailed recital of how Flem Snopes and his endless retinue of cousins take over the principal sources of wealth in Frenchman's Bend, is something for the individual reader to determine for himself. Perhaps most experienced Faulkner readers will be satisfied to accept *The Hamlet* as an exhausting emotional experience.

The Hamlet falls into four beautifully integrated parts, each discovering the life of the village and the impact of the Snopeses from a different point of view. The opening section relates the initial invasion, Ab Snopes's never proved but generally believed willingness to burn the barns of anyone who crosses him, and how his son Flem plays upon the fear of Jody Varner, operator of the village store and son of wealthy old Will Varner, to secure for himself the job of shop clerk. From his foothold in the store, Flem invites the influx of his fantastic kin, quickly and deviously begins the work of dethroning the long-established Varners.

Faulkner achieves one of his most remarkable portraits in Eula, Will Varner's great soft daughter who represents the embodiment of sex from the age of 8. This second section tells of the schoolmaster, the young men of the community and finally the older, well-to-do landowners who are reduced to an elemental lust by the young woman who exerts the power of her sex by the mere fact of her presence in the village. But it is Flem Snopes who marries Eula.

Most nightmarish is the third part which tells of the idiot, Ike Snopes, and the farmer Houston's sleek white cow, and of Mink Snopes, the murderer of Houston, and his insane 2-week vigil by the hollow tree in which he hid the shattered body.

The concluding section marks the triumph of Flem Snopes.

An outrageous novel, and a fantastic one. *The Hamlet* is placed by Faulkner's skill well within the bounds of plausibility. Few readers will know why they accept Faulkner's weird portraits, why they credit his scenes of improbable horror, why they find coherence in his sometimes inchoate rhetoric, his constant near-melodrama. But most readers will find themselves caught in his faculty to bring reason to delirium, to hypnotize not only during the process of his recital but also when the book has been read and put aside. Careful readers will find beneath the seeming abandon of his method, a rigid adherence to a form of his own fashioning, an exhaustive knowledge of the psychology with which he deals, a brilliance in dialogue, and a sense for the relations of time and place, of the present and the past.

Shields McIlwaine.
"Faulkner Begins a Trilogy about the Snopes Family."
Memphis *Commercial Appeal*, April 14, 1940, Section IV, p. 10.

This is the sixteenth volume of Faulkner. Sixteen years ago he published his first. Eleven novels, three books of short stories, and two of verse—these represent the industry, experimental courage, and studious craftsmanship of the proper man of letters. No American writer, except Eugene O'Neill, who, after all, belongs to an earlier group, has been such a daring eclectic in formal trial and error. No novelist of Faulkner's generation has a finer body of works to his credit than *The Sound and the Fury, As I Lay Dying, Absalom, Absalom!*, the *Old Man* part of *The Wild*

Palms, a half dozen short stories, and large sections of *The Hamlet*.

And yet Faulkner's position in current letters is unfortunate. In the minds of general readers he has been "typed" like a Hollywood actress; he is merely the author of *Sanctuary*, the movie of which gave most of America its first and only labeled acquaintance with the Mississippi writer. And it is true that in every novel appears material which shocks most readers, especially the older ones. Consequently they refuse to read and therefore miss some of the perfect writing of our time; thus Faulkner's audience is reduced largely to literary people, cultists, and connoisseurs of pornography. In his *Saturday Evening Post* stories he foregoes his physical gothic, but in his books he seems to write as he pleases. No intelligent reader, much less a critic, would wish Faulkner to enslave himself to the great American five-cent institution, or would demand that he write about anything except what is real to his imagination. But perhaps one's regret is mistaken, for Faulkner remains the cleverest American adapter of material and consequently the best literary merchant now writing.

The Hamlet perfectly illustrates the point. Its straight-away narrative, conventional sentence structure, and broad humor will appeal to anyone, but, as always, there is an episode (Book Three), based upon a barnlot joke familiar to men old enough to remember livery stables, which will prove too strong for all but the strongest stomachs. Yet it contains the most brilliant prose encountered by this reviewer since he read the opening section of *The Grapes of Wrath*.

But this novel is not merely another Faulkner novel of the expected elements. It has been announced as the first of a trilogy of novels about the Snopes family, trashy, cunning, and amoral, who under the leadership of their master crook, Flem, swarm into and largely take over French-man's Bend, a community 40 miles from Jefferson (Oxford), Mississippi. In the Snopeses, Faulkner adds a new social class to his world—one heretofore represented mainly by incidental characters—and a whole new settlement. Equally important and as enjoyable is the humor—a Faulkner quality not justly appreciated—of the book, strongly reinforced by two previously published short stories about horses, which are expertly worked into the novel. Witness, also, the drollery of the story about the poor white boy from a puncheon-floored hill cabin who became a somewhat bewildered football player at Ole Miss and sent five pairs of cleated shoes to his family of seven who thereafter clacked about in whichever pairs were handy. And the style, a compromise between the rhetoric of *Absalom, Absalom!* and the plainness of *The Unvanquished*, may be an approximation of Faulkner's final instrument.

In *Absalom, Absalom!* is a map of the Mississippian's fictional country, signed "William Faulkner, Sole Owner." When the Snopes series and perhaps other books about the same region are completed, Faulkner's little world of North Mississippi may well be mentioned with Hawthorne's New England and Thomas Hardy's Wessex—and not patronizingly either.

Ted Robinson.
"The Hamlet."
Cleveland *Plain Dealer*, April 14, 1940, Feature Section, p. 3.

This book was published nearly two weeks ago, and so it is already stale as news—and I don't care at all. I got provoked enough to throw the volume across the room when I was halfway through with it and it was 10 days before I could trust myself to pick it up again and now I shall say this: Ever since I read *The Sound and the Fury* all those years ago, I have been waiting patiently for Faulkner's masterpiece. Now I know that *The Sound and the Fury* was his masterpiece, and that his childish obsession with the unspeakable will forever keep him from doing as honest and unsmudged a piece of work.

Having said that, I am ready to acknowledge the many virtues of *The Hamlet*. It contains some of the keenest character drawing Faulkner has ever done. The Snopes family is unique in literature: Flem Snopes is such a sinister figure as would be worthy of Dostoievsky or Balzac. He sets himself patiently to work to acquire every business and every property in the community; and as each parcel comes into his power, he imports a relative to manage it, until finally he has exhausted all the possibilities of the place.

Eula Varner is another shudderful figure: a whole section of the book is given over to this fat, stupid, dangerous female animal. And then there is Ike Snopes, the village idiot. This is no mere halfwit, but a disgustful creature who cannot even speak intelligibly, and who is a prey to the most deplorable instincts. It was Ike who made me throw the book. I ask you: Is there anything for human amusement or instruction in the day-by-day activities of a completely mindless imbecile? Why, but for the gratification of the author's perverted judgment, should any reader endeavor to interest himself for 60 pages in a minute description of a gruesome creature who grovels habitually in filth?

Suit yourself about this book. I am tough-minded; no kind of vulgarity offends me if it serves any artistic purpose. But my impatience is aroused by an author who makes a point of inserting in each of his books as if he had made a wager that he could get away with it, some hitherto unprinted nastiness. It is not an idea worthy of an intelligent adult.

Malcolm Cowley. "Faulkner by Daylight." *New Republic*, 102 (April 15, 1940), 510.

The Hamlet is a new sort of novel for William Faulkner, less somber, more easygoing and discursive. Except for a few short stories, it makes better reading than anything else he has written since *Sanctuary*.

Until now, almost all his books have been war novels—Civil War novels, in a sense, although most of them have been laid in the twentieth century. They have been based on aspects of the same plantation legend that appears in *So Red the Rose* and *Gone with the Wind*. This seems a curious statement, considering that Faulkner is usually described as a realist and a rebel against the Southern tradition. In reality he accepts the tradition, but in an altered form, making it less material than moral. He does not insist in his books that ante-bellum life was glamorous, and he is not interested in white-pillared plantation houses except as symbols of decay. What he does tell us is that there used to be men in the South who were capable of good and evil, who observed or failed to observe a traditional code of ethics. These men, he says, were defeated in the Civil War, but not by the Northern armies. Surviving into a new era, they were weakened by a sense of guilt resulting from their relations with the Negroes; and they were finally destroyed by new men rising from among the Poor Whites. The point is made sym-

bolically in *Absalom, Absalom!*, where the plantation owner is killed after the war by a white squatter. His only surviving descendant is a halfwitted mulatto. Until now *Sanctuary* has been the one novel where, in spite of hasty writing, he has suggested the full range of his effects—including not only terror and pity but also homely realism, Freudian illogic and wild humor.

The Hamlet is different from any of the novels in the Sartoris cycle. Reading it one feels that Faulkner has suddenly emerged from his Gothic midnight into the light of day.

The scene is a community so humble and remote that it is outside the plantation system; it might exist almost anywhere in the American backwoods, from Florida to Oregon. There are no surviving heirs of the slaveholding caste in Frenchman's Bend, and there are comparatively few Negroes. Most of the natives are white and poor, but they are too self-respecting to be called Poor Whites. Only the Snopes family, which has come from richer land to the westward, has been corrupted by living among people with higher economic—and moral—standards.

The principal theme of the novel is the rise of Flem Snopes, by consistent meanness, from clerking in the village store to lording over the whole community. Very soon he has peopled Frenchman's Bend with a whole swarm of his relatives, little men gnawing at money like rats at cheese. One of them, Mink Snopes, commits murder for pure spite. Another, Ike Snopes, is an idiot boy who falls in love with a cow (and this passage is the least effective in the novel because it seems deliberately intended to be shocking). Flem Snopes himself cheats the shrewdest man in the county by making him dig for an imaginary treasure. The book is composed of separate episodes like these, tragic, sensational or hilarious. Some of them have little to do with the Snopes family; and they are bound together chiefly by dealing with a community where Faulkner seems to have known every single inhabitant from birth to deathbed.

The new quality I find in this book—new to Faulkner at least—is friendliness. Pity he has often shown in the past, but never before the amused liking that he extends to almost all the people of Frenchman's Bend. He likes their back-country humor, he likes the clean look of their patched and faded shirts, he likes the lies they tell when swapping horses. In a curious way, he even likes the invading tribe of Snopeses; at least he likes to write about them. And Flem Snopes himself—with his little bow tie, his mud-colored eyes, his jaws rolling a cud of tobacco till the suption is out of it—is made so unfailingly mean, so single-hearted, that he arouses a sort of admiration. When he exhausts the resources of Frenchman's Bend and moves on to the county seat, one feels sorry to see him go and relieved at the promise of meeting him again.

The Hamlet was written as the first volume of a Snopes trilogy. In the novels to follow, Flem will certainly become a leading banker—that much has been promised —and possibly a Senator as well. Anything, one believes, is possible to a man so tight-fisted and empty-minded. Twelve years ago we had a President Snopes, from Vermont.

Eda Lou Walton. "The Snopeses Move Up." *New Masses*, April 16, 1940, p. 27.

Two criticisms have been brought against William Faulkner as a novelist. He has been said to have not so much a style of his own as a great facility in adapting styles to his purposes. Gradually, however, it has become apparent that Faulkner uses various narrative methods as a poet would use different poetic forms for different moods, and usually successfully. His frequent use of the stream of consciousness method, moreover, is admirably suited to his purpose of portraying almost completely inarticulate and shrewdly instinctive mentalities.

Second, Faulkner has been said to rely too much on the perverse or abnormal in human action for horror and suspense. His last several books, however, have proved that his distortion can function when used to portray a distorted or disintegrating social scene. The distortion and violence of some of Faulkner's scenes are as functional, indeed, as was distortion, for example, in Picasso's *Guernica*. His oblique approach to his story clarifies the fact that it is not the crimes or perversions that produce horror. The horror lies rather in the casual submission of his characters to any violence. Faulkner's characters itch for anything that breaks the monotony of their impoverished lives.

Primarily, of course, Faulkner's studies of the South are studies of a decaying culture. And this new novel is no exception. It is concerned with the Snopeses—hill people who have become "soured" by mistreatment at the hands of the decadent aristocrats. These aristocrats were succeeded first by the traders; then, as the traders grow lazy and indifferent, the struggle begins all over again. It is the same struggle for power and for money. And *The Hamlet* is a study of the methods (totally amoral and petty and vicious) by which the shrewder of the once tenant or small farmers of the hills turned the tables against the older traders. What the Snopeses knew, they had learned by being cheated. Now they begin to prove that small dog can eat larger dog—if nothing, not even kinship (the greatest loyalty among earlier landowners), is sacred.

The various members of the Snopes family have appeared in Faulkner's earlier books. In short stories we have heard of barn-burnings and of a murder in which the murderer is tortured into acknowledging his crime by the hound of the man killed. Both these tales are incorporated in *The Hamlet*. In *Absalom, Absalom!* Faulkner published a map of Frenchman's Bend, the scene of this story, and this map indicated that the Snopeses would rise to a financial leadership even greater than they attain in this new novel. *The Hamlet* is a tale of only their first victories, which are all small but significant. The Snopes family gradually get into their own hands farms and farmers, and finally they outwit the interpreter of the story, Ratliff, a sewing machine agent who "gets around."

Certain chapters in this book are unforgettable. Faulkner's study of an idiot's (the weakest Snopes') passion for a cow is sheer primitive myth—apocalyptic poetry, too. And always Faulkner has handled, better than any modern writer, scenes of flight and frenzied escape. In *The Hamlet* the chapters describing the horse-trading for wild Texan mustangs and the mad race of these frenzied animals through barns, bridges, even houses, are intensely exciting and, I think, symbolic. Only wild animals or maddened people, in Faulkner's books, seek freedom. Most men are caught, caught in part by their own stupidity, in part by poverty. (Faulkner does not deal with the industrialized South or with organized labor.) The book closes with an appalling scene in which a man, driven mad by being cheated and by wanting to cheat back, hollows out his own grave, digging for money not there.

Led to believe in the existence of a treasure by deliberately planted bait, this man and Ratliff (the shrewdest character in the book) complete the Snopeses' victory by buying the old Frenchman's place itself, a worthless ruin. The Snopes family move on, then, to Jefferson to become bigger businessmen. One of them takes with him as his wife Eula, symbol of female fertility, damned now to give birth to a money-mad race.

Although Faulkner's sympathies cannot be said to be clearly with "the people," he has a (possibly aristocratic) horror of the middle class passion for money. But he has also a deep sense of identification with and understanding of frustration and can interpret inarticulate, angry little minds by seemingly swimming through their very inchoate images and by ironically and yet sympathetically recording their few words. The phase of the South with which he is obsessed rots, and he knows it. He recreates the very stink of Frenchman's Bend as it slowly decays, while group succeeds group of money-mad men.

John Selby.
"Faulkner Is Still Busy at His Old Tricks."
Charlotte *Observer*, April 21, 1940, Section III, p. 5.

According to the publisher of William Faulkner's *The Hamlet*, this is "a key column in the literary edifice he has been erecting these many years." Perhaps so, but after a couple of weeks' thought this reader cannot help but believe the edifice will fall if it leans too hard on the key column.

The Hamlet is a collection of stories strung together roughly to form an episode and rather terrifying novel. It is too much to call it a novel, perhaps, but it must have a name. The story, such as it is, concerns the people of Frenchman's Bend in Mississippi, and especially the Varner and Snopes families. The Varners have swallowed the village and the county as a whole and are digesting it more or less peaceably until Ab Snopes and Flem come in. Then the Snopes clan proceeds to eat the Varner clan, and with them the village and the land. The Snopeses are no better and no worse than the Varners—both groups are dreadful. The reader has no interest in whether one group or the other controls Frenchman's Bend. Therefore the process of change must be made interesting.

But this, for this reader, also fails because of Faulkner's almost fanatic devotion to the dull and the horrible. At best the people of *The Hamlet* are sluggish, dirty and worthless—excepting only one or two and they have typically Faulknerian faults. Most of the people in the story are definitely degenerate, many of them are vicious as well. It is possible that such communities exist, but since it is safe to say that no reader of *The Hamlet* has ever seen one, the author must therefore force him to believe in this one. Perhaps he will succeed with some, but it seems doubtful.

Thus, since the people and the incidents of the story are distasteful, Mr. Faulkner has only one resource left and that is to make his effect by the strength and beauty of his prose. But it is difficult for prose as involved as Faulkner's to be strong—a simple trick of grammar would straighten most of it out, but the author does not want it straight. He must, as a result, rely almost wholly on shock to carry the book. There are plenty of shocking, even terrifying things in *The Hamlet,* but Faulkner has been shocking right and left so long that the reader, like a little boy's dog, finally tires of running from his master's "Boo!"

Harlan Hatcher. "Faulkner's *The Hamlet* Is 'Exercise in Horror.'" Columbus (Ohio) *Citizen,* April 28, 1940, Magazine Section. p. 4.

Reading one of the last several novels by the wildly talented William Faulkner is like crossing the mountains from North Carolina into Tennessee on U.S. 64. You climb through timber and green shrubbery on a pleasing road, reach the crest of the hill and look down on one of the most desolate and unhuman regions on this earth—the eroded, scarred, copper-colored acres around Ducktown and Copperhill. No tree, no blade of grass, no green thing whatever survives the sulphurous poison spewed over it by the copper works. The houses hang over deep gullies on the naked ground, and the mute and sickly people move about like condemned souls in some undreamed of circle in Dante's *Inferno.*

Mr. Faulkner's novels are the Ducktown of contemporary American literature. He has just added a new and interesting panel to the exhibit called *The Hamlet.* It is subtitled "A Novel of the Snopes Family," that slimy crew of whom Faulkner has given us a few choice glimpses in previous novels. But I doubt if even these previews will quite prepare the reader for all the new twists and turns in this psychological exploration of shrewd, subhuman minds and the occasional enlargement upon horror that had, we thought, reached end point.

It would be hard to summarize the story in *The Hamlet.* There is not one, but several, and readers of *Scribner's, Harper's* and the *Saturday Evening Post* will recognize the short stories that appeared in their pages which serve as a narrative thread for the fourpart symphony of this novel. The most central strand tells how the Snopes gang, a migratory, sullen and vicious lot of share-croppers and barn-burners, drift into Frenchman's Bend, "a section of rich river-bottom country lying 20 miles southeast of Jefferson," and owned by lazy William Varner. Jefferson is Faulkner's Paris for his sub-human comedies.

By some mysterious but unexplained power and method, Flem Snopes gets his head in the master's tent, practically takes over the store, then the management of the estate, marries Varner's nubile, cybelean daughter Eula after she had upset the entire male population around Frenchman's Bend, goes to Texas, returns with wild horses to scare the countryside and finally moves on Jefferson as a wider field for his operations.

The side stories, tall tales and character sketches which accompany Flem's rise are scarcely subordinate to it and are connected with it only in the most tenuous fashion. Much of the first section is taken up with folk tales of sharp bargains and the malpractice of horse traders. Centering around a traveling sewing machine salesman who spreads the news, these tales have a rough, unsmiling humor about them which helps set the half-serious, half-ironic tone of the novel as a whole.

The second part is the story of Varner's Jittite goddess of a monstrosity, Eula, a woman at 8, passive, immobile, remote and molesting. She seems to me something of a failure, even within her own primitive symbolism; and despite all the mammalian adjectives heaped up around her massive curves, she remains unfeminine. She is the exact extreme in sex type from the slim co-ed in *Sanctuary*.

The most masterly exercise in horror is the story of idiot Ike and his infatuation with a neighbor's cow and of the attend-ant murder of Houston and the fight between Houston's hound and Mink Snopes, his murderer. It is a strange paradox that William Faulkner does some of his best writing, and that is good enough for any man, when he hits his stride in such animalistic episodes.

What all this adds up to I do not exactly know. The first several pages, with the superb character sketch of old Varner, "at once active and lazy," who could sit away a day "in a homemade chair on the jungle-choked lawn of the old Frenchman's homesite," prepare us for another *As I Lay Dying*, a *Sanctuary* or *The Sound and the Fury*. But that hope is quickly dispelled as the folk tales crowd in.

We are left with another close and disturbing study of the degeneracy of certain southern types and with a display of pyrotechnics in stylizing the English language unequalled in modern writing. Readers who have been following Faulkner's work will find in *The Hamlet* a little more than usual, but still not much, of the quality that held them captive in the earlier novels culminating in *Sanctuary*.

Luther Meyer. "The Bookworm Takes Pen in Hand." San Francisco *Call-Bulletin*, May 4, 1940, p. 14.

The Bookworm does not apologize for being a little late as usual in reviewing a William Faulkner novel. His unvarying procedure when a Faulkner novel emerges from the publishers is (i) to pick it up, heft it, decides that it's an awfully heavy book and then put it down for a few days. Next (2) he begins to read the thing in gingerly style with a rather sour look on his face and some bewilderment. Then (3) he decides that he doesn't like the book. Faulkner has such an oblique method of telling a tale. He goes round and round his subject like a coyote around a piece of rotten meat and frequently bewilders the unwary reader. Finally (4) the Bookworm becomes fascinated by the Faulkner opus and is unable to put it down until the last page. On two or three occasions he has even taken a Faulkner novel into the bath tub with him ... And that's the course the Bookworm has run with *The Hamlet*—William Faulkner's ugly novel about the Snopes family, the meanest, greediest, cruelest mess of sub-human beings he has ever encountered anywhere. [All ellipsis dots are in the original review.]

Flem Snopes is the son of a barn-burner, who comes to Frenchman's Bend, the site of an enormous pre–Civil War plantation dominated by Will Varner, and before the book ends he has devoured the whole village and countryside. Oddly enough, although Faulkner rounds out the characters of all the other individuals in the story, he does little more than sketch the outline of the unspeakable Flem.

And yet, he is all the more real because we know him only through the distrust and hatred of his neighbors. There are vivid, breath-taking scenes in the novel and more than once the Bookworm paused in admiration of the frantic, frenetic, ribald, skeltonic and even humorous dash of Faulkner's story telling ... And sometimes one hears in his pages the trumpet call of William Shakespeare's extravagance, as when he describes that instant of sunrise when the day, "melodious with the winged and jeweled throats, upward bursts and fills night's globed negation with jonquil thunder" ... And so far, in only one month, the sale has been greater than for any other Faulkner book and that tireless author is already working on a sequel in which Flem Snopes is to be "meaner, richer and more repellent still."

Maurice Swan.
"An Eye on the New."
Santa Barbara *News-Press*, May 6, 1940, p. 5.

A great many books are coming off the presses now that are a result of research work among the dusty volumes of minor incidents in American history. Faulkner's isn't a strained effort to catch the stars and stripes in hectic rhetoric. He has been immersed in his genre until it has ripened into a classic; the articulation may be strange but it has all the earmarks of an authentic master like the particular style wrought by Conrad or Cabell. It is not mere poetic form or obvious music that makes me say that he is a poet but the sheer genius to ignite images that cut open new worlds upon our sensibilities. *The Hamlet* is his greatest book for the parts that reach the ultimate of his writing powers but not for its unity and ambitious grasp of components to coagulate a vision. The tendencies are blunted by too many inchoate sections and cannot meet to evoke an integral unity.

The story takes place in the usual haunt of Faulkner near the Mississippi, unwinding from the delectable gossip in front of the general store in Frenchman's Bend. It centers around the peculiar but entrancing family of the Snopes. Flem Snopes gradually consumes the entire village until he is forced to leave it to his kinsmen to gain a foothold in Jefferson.

Like peanuts is an incomplete protein Faulkner is an incomplete poet. The chemistry hasn't been fully processed. The chemistry of his nerve to his vision is not completely metamorphosed to poetry.

There are too many orientated chunks to permit pure osmosis through the tissue, but in spite of the dismal outcome of many of his remarkable preludes, Faulkner is an indisputable genius. He has the uncanny sensibilities to wrought from the particular, mythic significances like John Cowper Powys has of the specific to personal esoteric cosmologies. If the spirit of Faulkner continues in Heaven I imagine he will sit with the great bards on Olympus telling bawdy stories with classic allusions.

Faulkner takes away the shibboleth and all its sophisticates from sex and bares its primitive flow, reeking and bubbling in the humid air. The bow-tie gives the neck decorum, the neck through which the cells in the cortex shape schemes to tangle people into harness by the immutable civil laws of man. This is Flem Snopes, this is dignity as banker squeezing with deeds and loan notes. The book is made up of certain sections that grow out complete from Faulkner's sub-consciousness. He bound them together with the same elemental vision that a poet coerces lines and images and reflection to a theme that startles the subconscious to turn up its pattern. The seminal flow drawing the drooling imbecile to hymenal dawns tinting the flecked flanks of a cow is the unbridled sex of the unconformed, untutored virgin and the mad ones in innocent war against the diplomatic, wise and sophisticate. The relative, Flem Snopes, of this drooling imbecile, Ike Snopes, is totemed with high hat and bow-tie; compromised with his sex (the basic proclivity of the animal) for money. The law is grappled in his palm of ducats, and the innocent and well-intentioned are beaten into obeyance of the distorted and the hypocrisies. Flem's wife is the innocent flesh calling males; shaped by Vulcan into the beatific flesh of Venus and rolled down the sunslopes of Paradise. She is unknowingly seduced by the intelligent will of the male, and her father sells her like a cow to Flem. Flem bought her, paying respectability to cover her shame. For the avarice of money Flem made a deal to buy the kind of flesh the imbecile, his relative, moans after chasing the cow. It's a distorted picture of our distorted society wrangled and mangled by money and sex.

The study of Eula, the future wife of Flem, is a masterpiece and so is the brilliant creation of the drooling imbecile watching the pearl-dewed cow, knee deep in water and mist. This is one novel I will certainly reread again and again for its beautiful passages and to fish up more clues. I agree with the publishers that this is a prominent pillar in our literature. The characters will haunt you, they are not cut out in pasteboard, they breathe and live.

Partee Fleming. "Faulkner's Twelfth." Nashville *Tennessean*, August 4, 1940, p. 4-B.

It is an at least interesting coincidence that two writers who would come off second best in comparison with no other living American novelists should this year publish books with the famous Hamlet in the title.

But while James Branch Cabell (author of *Hamlet Had an Uncle* published this spring), who is the all-time master of the American phrase, seems already to have put his best work behind him, Faulkner adds to his stature with each new novel.

And now, as he stands on this twelfth novel, he towers over the rest of the contemporary output. It is not fair to the number one master of modern writing technique to judge him, as a large public does, on his popular success, *Sanctuary*, which he calmly admits that he wrote

221

for the one purpose of making money.

If you have an adult mind and read *The Hamlet* it is a better than even-money bet that you will indulge yourself in more of Faulkner.

Don't worry about trying too hard to get the purpose and meaning of each sentence and paragraph and page. If you know the meaning of his words, and the gentleman from Oxford, Miss., does have quite a vocabulary, you will understand him just about as well as he himself understands what he is writing.

The importance of Faulkner is this. He believes in the primary psychic importance of evil in man's world. He is in direct contact, through very sensitive feeling, not intelligence, with the world which most people try to block out of their senses so that they can hew closely enough to the line of the "normal" that no one, most of all themselves, will suspect their sanity.

These "most people" succeed in denying this other world so well that only when their intelligence is asleep and primal instincts, their sub-conscious, is rampant, do they get an alarming touch of this buried life which has more to do with the way this world is run than they would ever admit. Then these "most people" jerk their intelligence back into control of the situation, block out the senses it is easier to deny than to live with, wipe the cold sweat off their brows and say, "But it was only a dream."

In *The Hamlet* Faulkner turns his dream-searchlight on a small Mississippi community, Frenchman's Bend, as he imagines it was in what seems to be the years 1885 to 1895. And the author shows an acute awareness of the personal history of the people of his state.

There are four parts to the book, bound together with their mutual concern with Frenchman's Bend and with the Snopes family and with little else.

The first part deals with Flem Snopes, one of the coldest characters in literature, and tells how he concerns the community's meager financial market through unbelievable, but rational, jugglings of very small amounts.

Part two is titled "Eula" and is concerned with the life which revolves around this sex-carrier who infects every male within eye or nose range. She is the ruination of a large group which includes her school teacher who is the subject of an anachronism. Faulkner has the school teacher, who hangs on to his poorly-paid teaching job at the Bend for three years after his graduation from the University of Mississippi because he can't stand the thought of some other man getting Eula, outfitting his family with stolen football shoes with cleats at a time when the game wasn't played in Mississippi.

The third part of the novel deals with Ike Snopes, Faulkner's almost inevitable idiot. The murder, marriage trial and the like here are only incidental to the pathos of Ike's romance with a cow. This is some of Faulkner's most serious comedy.

The last part of the novel is a farce dealing with buried treasure. Except that the plot is unimportant in relation to the whole this would not be worthy of Faulkner.

George Marion O'Donnell. "Not Pleasant, but Truthful." Nashville *Banner*, August 21, 1940, p. 4-x.

For years William Faulkner has been writing what amounts to a Southern "Human

Comedy," presenting the South as Balzac strove to present his France. Mr. Faulkner now turns his attention, in *The Hamlet,* to the landless, scheming, poor-white Snopes family. The Snopeses have appeared in earlier novels as minor characters; *The Hamlet* begins the detailed presentation of their story. The book adds another significant chapter to Mr. Faulkner's account of Southern life. As such, it is of more than timely interest; it is a permanent contribution to Southern Literature.

The Hamlet is laid in the neighborhood of Frenchman's Bend, twenty miles back in the hills from Jefferson, Miss. Flem Snopes, the protagonist of the novel, comes into the settlement during the period just following Reconstruction and takes a job clerking in the store of Will Varner, who is the leading property-holder of the community. Flem's special talent (a characteristic one in the Snopes family) is for clever, unscrupulous trading; and Flem knows how to use his talent. He schemes his way to the domination of the community, displacing Varner as the leading property-holder. He installs his numerous down-at-heel relatives in the best jobs in the village. He marries Varner's daughter, Eula. Finally, he moves off to Jefferson, to find new fields of activity.

The Hamlet is much more than the story of Flem Snopes; it is the prototype of the whole rise of the new, commercial, metropolitan South. But the important thing about the book, as literature, is that the characters and actions always remain particular and vivid in themselves although they have more general meaning. Mr. Faulkner's protagonists are people, and they live in a recognizable South.

He never theorizes or argues about it; he simply allows his readers to live in it and know its people, little by little, as one gets to know a new neighborhood.

Flem Snopes acts out his history within a fully peopled locality. The minor characters are presented in the round; and their stories are always lively. In fact, Mr. Faulkner can concoct more downright good stories, as such, than any other American novelist; and there are a great many examples of this skill in *The Hamlet.* Moreover, the book is enriched by the quality of grotesque, outrageous frontier humor which has appeared from time to time in Mr. Faulkner's earlier books and which is a significant, though frequently overlooked, aspect of his writing.

The form of the novel owes a great deal to the most characteristically American of literary traditions—the Tall Tale. Ratliff, an itinerant sewing machine salesman, is the principal narrator. Neither a Snopes nor an aristocrat, of humble breeding but having a decency that the Snopeses lack, Ratliff is a member of the middle class that is too often entirely omitted from Southern fiction. In another era, he would have been a yeoman, probably a pioneer yeoman; and it is significant and right that he should tell most of the Snopes story in a literary form descended from the oral tradition of his forebears. Most of the book has the tone of gossip around a country general store. It is just the tone that the book ought to have.

Mr. Faulkner violates this tone in several instances—notably in the section dealing with the idiot, Ike Snopes—and draws on the full resources of his wide-range vocabulary to produce brilliant pages of the "ore rotundo" prose to which his readers have become accustomed. Although these passages are often excellent in themselves, they contrast so violently in tone with the rest of the book that they make it seem disordered and formless. But they seldom fail really to convey an experience more thoroughly than it might have been conveyed in any other way.

These passages result from Mr. Faulkner's scrupulous literary honesty, which is one of his great assets as a serious artist but which is a detriment to the orderly form of his work. He is so honest that he is not afraid to dare failure, at times even to appear ridiculous, for the sake of rendering the whole content of an experience.

Mr. Faulkner is never willing to omit the elements of experience that are not easy to handle with technical smoothness. He attempts to render human life in its full complexity, even in its incomprehensibility. How to manage the presentation is the problem of every serious artist. Mr. Faulkner's solutions of the problem, although they are not uniformly successful, seem to be among the best and most honest solutions that any contemporary novelist has managed to produce. His work is not all pleasant reading, but it tells the truth.

Don Stanford.
From "*The Beloved Returns* and Other Recent Fiction."
Southern Review, 6 (Winter 1941), 610–28.

... *The Hamlet,* Faulkner's latest explosion in a cesspool, with a plethora of attempted rape, seduction, murder, and sodomy, is a series of loosely connected episodes depicting the rise through shrewdness and treachery of the Snopes family to a position of power in Frenchman's Bend, once the site of a large pre–Civil War plantation, now fallen into decay. The creatures of Faulkner's world are completely phony, but even if we believe in them, they are so insensitive and stupid that their actions have no meaning for us; they are not even capable of an interesting kind of evil, as for instance the evil of Hardy's *Barbara of the House of Grebe.*

One incident will illustrate Faulkner's method. Labove, a football player for a university on weekends and a school teacher in Frenchman's Bend on weekdays, acquires an overwhelming passion for Eula, one of his sexier pupils who had reached puberty at the early age of eight. Because of her youth he restrains himself for three years, and eventually obtains a job in the city in an effort to forget her, but one day, at a boarding house, someone sets a sweet potato in front of him. Now Eula always had a sweet potato for lunch which she was accustomed to eat on the school steps every noon. The association is too much for Labove. He returns to Frenchman's Bend and teaches school again, still keeping his distance from Eula, but every day, just after school is dismissed, he kisses the warm seat of the chair which Eula has vacated. One afternoon Eula catches him in the act; he makes a flying tackle for her and starts to rape her, but she lays him out cold with her elbow. Here we have the exact reverse of the sentimental commercial story. Instead of a haunting perfume which reminds the lover of his sweetheart, we have a sweet potato; instead of a treasured glove kissed in secret by the lover, we have a chair still warm from Eula's bottom. There is also murder, seduction in which one of the participants has a broken arm, and sodomy between an idiot and a cow during which the cow defecates on the idiot. This scene is the climax of Faulkner's literary career. ...

Checklist of Additional Reviews

"*The Hamlet.*" Oakland *Post-Enquirer,* March 30, 1940, p. 12.

"Rural Scum: Faulkner Pens Tale of an Ornery Tribe Given to Lust and Homicide." *Newsweek,* April 1, 1940, p. 32.

"Genius-à-la-King." *Time,* April 1, 1940, p. 73.

"William Faulkner's *The Hamlet* Is a Study of a Backward Community in the Hinterland of Mississippi." Newark *Evening News,* April 2, 1940, p. 8.

Chicago *News,* April 3, 1940.

"William Faulkner Etches Acid Vignettes of South." Milwaukee *Evening Post,* April 6, 1940, p. 5.

Catskill (N.Y.) *Mail,* April 13, 1940.

Canton (Ohio) *Repository,* April 21, 1940.

"William Faulkner's World Is Enlarged by New Novel." Dallas *Morning News,* April 21, 1940, Section IV, p. 10.

"The Hamlet." San Francisco *Argonaut,* May 31, 1940, p. 21.

Knoxville *Journal,* June 30, 1940.

Bender, Naomi. "The Book Rack." Akron (Ohio) *Journal,* April 21, 1940. Miami *Herald,* May 28, 1940, p. 4-G.

Benét, Stephen Vincent. "Flem Snopes and His Kin." *Saturday Review of Literature,* April 6, 1940, p. 7.

Bonnoitt, Murray. "Under the Covers." *The State* (Columbia, S.C.), August 18, 1940, p. 5-B.

Butcher, Fanny. "Another by Faulkner." Chicago *Daily Tribune,* April 3, 1940, p. 14.

Cameron, May. "William Faulkner's *The Hamlet* Casts a Spell." New York *Post,* April 1, 1940, p. 9.

Clayton, Charles C. "Faulkner Writes Novel of Decay in the Old South." St. Louis *Globe-Democrat,* April 13, 1940, p. l-B.

Davis, Bennett. "Books of the Week in Review." Buffalo *Courier-Express,* March 31, 1940, Section VI, p. 2.

DeJong, David Cornel. "The Newest Faulkner." Providence *Sunday Journal,* April 14, 1940, Section VI, p. 7.

Drewry, John E. "New Book News." Atlanta *Constitution,* July 21, 1940, P. 6.

Dupee, F. W. "William Faulkner's Anger at Humanity Puts Forth Another Bitter Flower." New York *Sun,* April 2, 1940, p. 40.

Fadiman, Clifton. "Horrors, Charm, Fun." *New Yorker,* April 6, 1940, p. 73.

Gibson, Edmond P. "Mississippi White Trash." Durham *Herald,* April 21, 1940.

Guerard, Albert. "Snopes Family Devour Village." Boston *Evening Transcript,* April 13, 1940, Section V, p. 1.

Hansen, Harry. *"The Hamlet,* by William Faulkner, and *The Crazy Hunter,* by Kay Boyle, Are Characteristic of Their Best Work." New York *World-Telegram,* April 3, 1940, p. 27.

Hoch, Henry George. "Slick Tricks with Horses." Detroit *News,* April 7, 1940, General News Section, p. 22.

Jackson, Joseph Henry. "Faulkner Again Writes Strongly about Extremely Nasty People." San Francisco *Chronicle,* April 8, 1940, p. 15.

Jackson, Katherine Gauss. "Fiction."*Harper's Magazine,* May, 1940, advertising pages.

Johnston, Esther. *"The Hamlet." Library Journal,* 65 (April 1940), 300.

Kronenberger, Louis. "The World of William Faulkner." *Nation,* April 13, 1940, pp. 481–82.

Lindauer, Sydney. "Book Chatter." Red Bluff (Calif.) *Daily News,* April 6, 1940, p. 6.

Littell, Robert. *"The Hamlet." Yale Review,* 29 (Summer 1940), viii.

Mann, E. L. "Turning the Pages." Cincinnati *Times-Star,* April 2, 1940, p. 7.

Maslin, Marshall. "The Browser." Lawrence (Mass.) *Eagle*, May 18, 1940.

M[cClure], R[obert] E. "A Faulkner as Really Is Faulkner." Buffalo *Evening News*, April 6, 1940, Section II, p. 7.

Merlin, Milton. "Earthy Humor Alleviates Tale of Nightmare Folk." Los Angeles *Times*, April 21, 1940, Part III, p. 7.

Nicholas, Louis. "The Book Shelf." Philadelphia *Record*, March 31, 1940, Metropolitan Section, p. 13.

Parsons, Eugene O. "Novel of Soil and Sky in Mississippi." Worcester (Mass.) *Telegram*, March 31, 1940, Section IV, p. 8.

Patterson, Alicia. "The Shocking Snopes." New York *Sunday News*, March 31, 1940, p. 72.

Porteus, Clark. "Faulkner's *Hamlet* Like Bridge Hand." Memphis *Press-Scimitar*, April 11, 1940, p. 11.

Rascoe, Burton. "Faulkner's New York Critics." *American Mercury*, 50 (June 1940), 243–47.

Rhodes, Arthur. "William Faulkner Tells of the Snopes Family." Brooklyn *Eagle*, April 1, 1940, p. 20.

Roberts, Mary-Carter. "Rise of a Sharecropper Family Told in Novel by William Faulkner." Washington *Sunday Star*, April 7, 1940.

Rugoff, Milton. "Out of Faulkner's Bog." *New York Herald Tribune Books*, March 31, 1940, p. 4.

Selby, John. Columbus (Ohio) *State Journal*, April 15, 1940; Raleigh (N.C.) *Observer*, April 21, 1940; New Haven *Register*, April 24, 1940.

Snell, George. "Fantastic and Evil Brood, Sucking Life of a Town, Truly Faulknerian Product." Salt Lake City *Tribune*, April 21, 1940, p. 6-D.

Snelling, Paula. "Three Native Sons." *North Georgia Review*, 5 (Spring 1940), 7–12.

Stegner, Wallace. "The New Novels." *Virginia Quarterly Review*, 16 (Summer 1940), 464.

Strauss, Harold. "Mr. Faulkner's Family of Poor Whites." *New York Times Book Review*, April 7, 1940, p. 2.

Thomas, Aubrey L. "Book of the Day." Philadelphia *Evening Public Ledger*, April 1, 1940, p. 23.

Thompson, Ralph. "Books of the Times." New York *Times*, April 1, 1940, p. 17.

Warren, Robert Penn. "The Snopes World." *Kenyon Review*, 3 (Spring 1941), 253–57.

GO DOWN, MOSES AND OTHER STORIES

Go Down, Moses
AND OTHER STORIES

by

WILLIAM FAULKNER

RANDOM HOUSE : NEW YORK

Ted Robinson.
"*Go Down, Moses.*"
Cleveland *Plain Dealer*,
April 12, 1942,
All Feature Section, p. 3.

This book of stories will be published Tuesday morning. If I should print this review next Sunday, I should be five days late. There are reviewers who violate the publication date by printing their notices a week before release, and thus they annoy bookseller and publisher alike, violate agreements, and disappoint the public. I mention this merely to disclaim any desire or intention to join that class.

Go Down, Moses is named for the last story in the book. There are only seven, all told, but one is what publishers nowadays call a "novella." It is called "The Fire and the Heart" and it runs to a hundred pages.

But that last story was certainly the one to choose for the christening of the book; it is a bright, bitter story, as clean as a cameo. Indeed, some of the best of Faulkner is in this volume; and when I say that, I am calling the book important. You can get up a quarrel in almost any company by mentioning Faulkner, and there are critics as well as readers who froth at the mouth when his name comes up. And this is all very silly.

I do not go forth on a missionary crusade to tout this writer as the Great American Genius; I do not even think he should be on the required reading list for the eighth grade. Indeed, I will go so far as to say that I find certain passages in his works unpalatable. But since similar things have been said about most of the world's important authors I cannot feel that they are particularly worth discussing any more.

The only intelligent criticism that can be applied to the works of William Faulkner is this: that he does not always succeed in what he sets out to do.

And for those who have been offended by some of his novels I might say that the stories contained in this book have been previously printed in the *Atlantic Monthly*, *Harper's Magazine*, *Collier's*, *The Saturday Evening Post* and *Story Magazine*. So there is little to fear.

All seven stories are good Faulkner and good literature. They are merciless; they are a searchlight turned upon the dark places of the south.

Harry Hansen.
"The First Reader: *Go Down, Moses and Other Stories*, by
William Faulkner,
Illuminate the Racial Situation in the South."
New York *World-Telegram*, April 14, 1942, p. 19.

As a novelist William Faulkner is often a highly sensitive social historian. When he stops plotting situations like *The Wild Palms* and lets people reveal themselves by the lives they lead—as do the tricky Snopses of *The Hamlet*, he may be said to humanize the statistical tables of the Department of Agriculture. Something of this sort happens in his new book, *Go Down, Moses and Other Stories*, which purports to be seven short stories assembled from seven magazines. But it adds up into the family chronicle of the McCaslin-Edmonds family, which is unlike any other family

229

Faulkner has portrayed and indirectly illuminates the racial situation in the South.

According to the census the state of Mississippi is half white and half black, but obviously its appearance is as if someone had shaken white and black beans together in a peck measure and added a supply of brown beans to account for the mixtures. The McCaslin-Edmonds clan exemplifies this creeping amalgamation, and, curiously enough, it is described with more sympathy than Faulkner usually gives his creatures. Perhaps the dedication gives an indication of Faulkner's feeling in the matter. It reads: "To Mammy Caroline Barr, 1840–1940, who was born in slavery and gave to my family a fidelity without stint or calculation of recompense and to my childhood an immeasurable devotion and love."

Here, once more, is Faulkner's favorite subject, the decaying Southern family, the landowners whose Negroes, for the most part, stayed on the land, but this is not the conventional family of aristocrats, living in white-pillared houses beloved of Hollywood. Here, too, are the aging men Faulkner portrays so well; they mull over the memories of family events, bicker about current crises and reveal, gradually, the relationships of the whites and Negroes in the tale.

Their motives are not always clear; their acts are often shrouded as if in the light of dusk and the whole community seems strangely unreal, yet Faulkner's indirect manner provides a feeling of saturation in a community. This is particularly true of the two longest stories, "The Fire and the Hearth" and "The Bear." The latter will offer some difficulties because Faulkner has complicated the story with symbolism and a running monologue in which the subject-matter shifts like the plot of a disjointed dream. While I am aware that some readers get much pleasure out of deciphering puzzles and tracking down hints,

my preference is not for old men who can't keep their minds on the subject.

"Was," the first story, offers an interesting sidelight on the Southerner's love of a wager; in "The Old People" McCaslin offers the conviction that life is best when thoroughly lived and the earth is here to be used, which recurs in other stories. "Delta Autumn," however, is Uncle Ike's rather mournful musing about the passing of the good hunting and the exhaustion of the land, and he resents the irresponsibility of human beings who have corrupted it. *Go Down, Moses* is not subtle, but it might be described as Faulkner's final, and perhaps cynical, comment on the strength of a family bond.

William Abrahams. "William Faulkner at His Best in Collection of Seven Stories." Boston *Globe*, May 6, 1942, p. 19.

Mr. Faulkner continues to occupy his own ambiguous position in contemporary American letters: our most distinguished unread talent. That such a position should be his reflects no discredit on Mr. Faulkner, but rather on ourselves.

It is time that someone pointed out that his so-called faults—an involved, convoluted style, and a certain narrowness of range—are paralleled in the works of an even greater writer, Henry James. It is time also, as in the case of James, to recognize that the faults, if such they be, are characteristic portions of a work that, when all is said against it, remains as valuable and imposing as anything produced in this country in recent years.

Go Down, Moses, Mr. Faulkner's lat-

230

est book, is a collection of seven vaguely unified stories, ranging in tone from light-hearted farce to almost Grecian tragedy. That they are difficult reading must be admitted, but they are sufficiently rewarding to justify the close attention required for any proper appreciation and understanding.

Mr. Faulkner's scene is once again the deep South. His characters are of two sorts. There is, first, the played-out aristocratic strain—exhausted ghosts who move through crumbling mansions like accusations against their own exalted past. And second, there are the Negroes, who have maintained through the years a kind of primitive health and integrity that baffles and annoys the whites at whose side they live.

The stories, taken singly, seem almost trivial; the attempt of a spinster to capture a husband; a Negro who goes berserk at the death of his wife. But their cumulative effect is movingly impressive. We feel that we have seen a society in action, that we have been given a picture artistically, perhaps even sociologically, right.

Here are seven stories that should be read by anyone who cares about the progress of American fiction. They represent William Faulkner at his best. Which is equivalent to saying the best we have.

Harry A. Weissblat. "Book Fog: William Faulkner." Trenton *Times*, May 9, 1942.

The name of William Faulkner does not flow with any great regularity in the public places where the people meet to discuss the questions of the day. If you have the fortitude and inordinate tolerance to attend a hundred parties where the artistic ladies and gentlemen gather to parade their shallow knowledge of human affairs, you will hear Hemingway discussed before the second round of drinks has been passed and, if you stay long enough, the conversation might even get around to Shakespeare. But the name of Faulkner remains unsaid, his literary effort and his extraordinary talent hidden away in the corner, like the bust of Beethoven in the niche, his presence aware of but only by silent allusion. There was something in this shying away that made me feel that all these people, the people who read the books and go to hear music and see shows, these people who hover perennially on the fringes of what we smugly and unknowingly call culture, had accepted Faulkner, had set him off as having adequately mastered a certain subject, and therefore, nothing could be said of him that would add or detract from his reputation. That's what I thought at first, but later with the passage of years and quiet little conversations here and there, I reached another conclusion. A great many people who read Faulkner don't even begin to comprehend what his prose so wonderfully relates. I came across people who seemed to think they had another Dos Passos or an Erskine Caldwell in the personality of William Faulkner, and that he stood for one thing in life, the grim side of the South, with overtones of sadism and mystery enveloping the product. You will hear these people talk about Faulkner as if he were a surgeon continually on the prowl to carve the secrets out of the old Southern families, to probe and examine with scalpel and knife those dreadful bits of super-gossip stored away in somebody's mind long before the Civil War.

William Faulkner is not so easily disposed of. For me, his writing has never ceased to be astonishing. Even that much-bruited book, *Sanctuary*, which caused the nice people to raise one eyebrow in shocked artistic surprise, and furnished for the dirt-diggers several long week-ends of undismayed hilarity coated with unfeigned and synthetic ribaldry, even this book was to me a sort of an oblique revelation, for it was apparent that while Faulkner pays strict attention to story, building carefully in concentric circles, there is a quality, a certain mysterious perception, not the mysteriousness of the spooks and goblins, nor that of the fifth dimension, but a certain indefinable quality which only a few writers seem to possess. Arnold Zweig had it and, before him, Joseph Conrad had it, the mystery of the human mind and of the soul. A writer must be very humble to feel and write about these things. It was of Conrad that I thought as I read Faulkner's latest collection of stories, *Go Down, Moses*, for while their geography was different, and their upbringing separated by the vast spaces, their minds were in unison in the quest for the secrets of the soul. You find it running like a clear line of silver in anything and all things written by Joseph Conrad, and you find it in the books of William Faulkner, in every story, no matter how small or seemingly insignificant. It is this quality which so many people have failed to grasp and understand and this is a curious thing, for it requires no great mind to perceive the goal toward which Faulkner is always walking. It stands out with dignity and nobleness in the longest story of the collection, entitled simply "The Bear." I can think of no story in recent years or in the years before which has worked so profoundly upon me. Here the race of mankind stands exposed in the brave humility, matching strength against Nature; hunters seeking a bear as they would seek the secret of life itself; returning again and again to the hunt, something impelling and driving them back to

the woods each year, a something which they could not quite understand or even begin to translate into the words of speech, but nevertheless driving with a compelling fury until the bear was run to earth and his noble life stilled forever. If you ask for plot, that's all there is to it, and you may wonder why Faulkner could take so much time and writing space to tell his story of the hunt. But this is no ordinary pursuit. No pursuit conducted in dignity ever is. Not only are men's lives at stake, but also their sacred things, their character, their honor and their truthfulness, for if they could not be honest with the bear they sought with such anxiety, how then could they find honesty in their own souls?

And while it is a bear upon which this story is centered, the bear, in turn, gives it back to them, so that the whole story of the South is brought to bay, the story of slavery and of the lush days before the Crusade, and the days of darkness and thought which followed. And it is in the telling of this story that the prose of Faulkner rushes into the world of consciousness, even as the hunters rushed to test their strength with a worthy foe. The dog, "Lion," which flew at the throat of the bear, knowing in his firmly desperate way that even accomplishment would bring death, did not hang on more tenaciously at the throat of Old Ben than does this story hang on to your own throat. Call it a symbol or what you will, and draw from it as many conclusions as you please, but if you are only remotely aware of what is going on about you, and particularly what is going on inside of you, you will not only understand these words of William Faulkner, but you will go back to them, over and over again, like the hunters returning to the woods for the quest, seeking in the words running across the page in even type, seeking in the phrases so wondrously woven from the common words of the English speech, some explanation of that business gnawing at the heart.

There are other stories in the book which hold your attention, uncommonly good stories, such as William Faulkner always writes, but it is "The Bear" that dominates everything in sight, making of the other stories something very satisfactory but somehow only in a supporting role. You will find sights and sounds in those other stories and there are some scenes you will not forget in a hurry, especially that one of the old tough man seeking buried money with a divining machine, but these, too, seem to be there for the purpose of making "The Bear" the thing that it is, an astonishing story that has its geography in the South and its impulses in all parts of the world where man awakens in the morning for new deeds. And all of this was contrived by a man who brought it out from some mysterious recesses of his soul, some secret place where it had been stored for years, perhaps for centuries. You won't find its equal in a hurry.

Gilbert E. Govan. "Genuine Faulkner." Chattanooga *Times*, May 10, 1942, p. 5-M.

It was, as I recall, Arnold Bennett who said that William Faulkner "writes like an Angel." To one accustomed, as was Mr. Bennett, to the orderly attitudes and practices of the British Isles, it must have seemed that the themes of Mr. Faulkner's writings must have been derived from the devil, himself. For they contain every form of violence known to man. These are no people willing to accept authority of law. They, themselves, are judge and jury. Incest, rape, miscegenation, murder, suicide, and minor crimes—all the modes of anti-social attitudes may be found somewhere in Mr. Faulkner's pages.

Yet, it is definitely true, as Mr. Bennett said, that only the top few among our writers are his peers. Abnormal as his characters are, intentionally obscure as his writing sometimes is, there is also a nostalgic appeal which throws about his every story a glamour for every southerner willing to admit that life in the south cannot be compressed into a single pattern. Familiar as many of these scenes are, the actors involved in them do not always follow the paths we are accustomed to. Partly, that is due to the natural differences between people; partly, it is attributable to these familiar circumstances having been given us through the unique perspective of one particular brain, that of William Faulkner. It was Somerset Maugham who pointed out that "the artist gives you his private view of the universe." Many of these scenes and circumstances have a familiar ring to all southerners—hunts and hunters, cotton plantations, their owners and the Negroes who work on them—but the particular form that they assume here is Faulkner's, and only his.

That, though, does not detract from the validity—or the reality—of his representations. The stories of this volume revolve about one family, the McCaslins, their plantation, and the Negroes who work it, first as slaves and then as free men. Some of the latter have in their veins McCaslin blood. They are neither more nor less loyal as a consequence. Probably the chief figure is that Isaac McCaslin who gave up his patrimony because he saw it as an "edifice intricate and complex and founded upon injustice and erected by ruthless rapacity and carried on even yet with at times downright savagery not only to the human beings, but the valuable animals too, yet solvent and efficient." "I am free," said this McCaslin, when it was done, and then goes on to say, "Yes. Sam Fathers set me free." And if you wish to know how, you can find out only by reading "The Bear" in this book. Nor is that all you'll find in the story. There is great excitement—no one has ever described better a hunt and a bear's fight with the dogs and men, and the remembrance of the camp and the stands, where Isaac waited on his daily vigil, will remain with you a long while. And then there is something of further value: the realization that came to Isaac after the fight: "Courage and honor and pride, and pity and love of justice and of liberty. They all touch the heart, and what the heart holds to becomes truth, as far as we know truth."

There are seven stories in this volume. All have the same merits—and demerits. They are all strangely realistic and immaginative, hard and sentimental, direct at times and then confused. But—as does the writing of fine writers always—they introduce you to a world which, while resembling the everyday world in which we live, is yet queerly different. It is a world though which repays the effort necessary to become acquainted with it.

James Robert Peery.
"Critic Outfaulkners
Faulkner in Praise of New
Stories."
Memphis *Commercial
Appeal,* May 10, 1942,
Section IV, p. 10.

An hour's hard writing of connective or explanatory matter, or perhaps only mortising, jointures, no matter whether he felt, or even feels compulsion to make explanatory mortisings, or any other kind of concession to intellectual laziness in a reader, when telling one of his wild, ribald, outrageous tall tales of his McCaslins and Beauchamps and Tulls and Compsons, an hour of setting down connectives to the diverse urgencies, roarings, lustings, petty evasions of the five generations of blacks and reds and whites of his Frenchman's Bend and Jefferson in his own dominated domain called something like Yakanatchatawbee County (these multicolored ones alive not only as descendants of the old people but somehow profoundly coeval and even shadowcasting into a future wombed in the present and the past as well, and permeate in his brain like patent furious unpoured lava and flowing like a dark mixture of all the bloods, the black, the white, the red, from the brittle scurrying nib of his pen which is itself a projection of the sharp styles of his impatience and preoccupation, as if he, this Faulkner, wanted not only to reveal his own immersed brain but, by use of deliberate trickery and befuddlement which finally betrays even himself, to grapple with and engage the last brain cell of his reader, not only to demand attention but to capture and rape the whole attention until at last, human curiosity surmounts bewilderment and wades through turgid, massed, floundering rhetoric—like this one-sentence review of his book of stories—in order to end amazement over what this fellow can be writing about, for he believes in the profundity of his subjects and so will not tolerate in his readers any less devotion than he himself has given to his half-breed Lucas Beauchamp who, of all the black and black-and-white descendants of old Carothers McCaslin, never made apology for failing to deliver every day the promise implied in just being a descendant nor felt the need of underscoring in any way the fact of his patrimony, and who beats Roth Edmonds at every turn of treasure-hunting or whisky-making or mule-stealing, not by a more dextrous chicanery than the white man can muster but by simply knowing that he himself is a man-made McCaslin and that Roth was woman-made; and to that Uncle Buck who, when he inadvertently after midnight and in the company of 9-year-old Ike McCaslin crawled under a mosquito-net and into the bed occupied by a spinster who had already tried every other method of ensnaring him as salvation from a more chronic form of spinsterhood, heard the brother of the spinster say, "You come into bear-country of your own free will and accord. All right; you were a grown man and you knew the way back out like you knew the way in, and you had the chance to take it. But no. You had to crawl into the den and lay down with the bear. And whether you did or didn't know the bear was in, it don't make no difference. So if you got back out of the den without even a crawl-mark I'd be a damn fool. . . . Yeas, sir. She got you 'Filius, and you know it. You run a hard race and you run a good one, but you skun the hen-house one time too many"; and to Ike McCaslin tutored by Sam Fathers to shoot fast and shoot slow when the buck arrows the glade, not only tall gargoylish tales embellished so realistically that unwary readers are trapped into belief that he, this Faulkner, instead of simply embellishing the monstrous tales told first in jungle and cave, and later in every horse-swapping camp in the new America, is trying to blanket the whole Southern scene with the last criticism, but tales of mysticism smelling of Choctaw voodooism like blood of a slain deer mopped on the boy's face—; and his devotion to the ravaged and retreating forest and its civilization which not even that last Indian chieftain was rightful owner would have made these stories (that extra hour of writing he did not accomplish), the five alone

and others joined in novella length, a novel to set beyond *The Hamlet* and *Absalom, Absalom!* yet, even without the hour because of gusto, sincerity, humor, and craftsmanship, still beside them on your shelf.

"Plantation of Southlands Scene of New Faulkner Tales."
Sacramento *Bee,* May 16, 1942, p. 17.

From the author of *Sanctuary, As I Lay Dying,* and *Absalom, Absalom!* has come this collection of seven stories ranging from the length of the novella to the less than twenty pages in the title story, "*Go Down, Moses.*"

As in his past books, Faulkner has drawn inspiration from his native southland and its people, the whites and the Negroes. In this series, the action revolves around the McCaslin plantation, its founders and inheritors, and although each story could be read divorced from the others, each has a bearing upon the whole, so much so that some of the episodes and the character motivation in one story are explained later in another.

The volume leads off with "Was," a story of the Uncles Buddy and Buck and tells of a gamble in which Buck won for himself, all unwillingly, a bride. It is in this story we first meet Tomey's Turl and Tenny who are the forebears of the Negroes whose blood later is mixed with that of the McCaslins. The second story, "The Fire And The Hearth," is the longest, and portrays a portion of the life of Lucas Beauchamp, a descendant of the original McCaslin and Tennie Beauchamp, a slave.

"Pantaloon in Black," the third, describes the torment of Rider, a young Negro whose wife had just died, and the agony which follows him till, seeking release in liquor, he winds up his life by killing a white man for cheating at dice, and is subsequently hanged. This tale is the only one in the collection which has no bearing upon the others, and paradoxically is the most readable from the standpoint of clarity of episode and chronological sequence.

The fourth story, "The Old People," relates the first hunting trip that young Isaac McCaslin takes, at the age of 10, with his cousin and a group of older hunters. "The Bear," the following story, is again bound up in the woods of the hunting trip of the previous tale and pictures of the taming of a doglike wild animal which will be brave enough and strong enough to catch the old bear who is regarded as master of the forest. Also included in this story is more material on the McCaslins and their history.

"Delta Autumn," the sixth in the series, tells of Isaac's last trip to the woods and of his kinsman, Roth, and his code of living. The concluding story relates with etched sharpness the return of the grandson of Mollie Beauchamp, the wife of Lucas, to whom we were introduced in "The Fire and the Hearth," after his execution for murder.

These, in briefest outlines, are the focal points about which the various stories turn, but it must not be imagined the sum total is contained therein. Any reader who is familiar with Faulkner's work will realize he incorporates much which seems irrelevant, and expands his material until plot is buried beneath an overload of crisscrossing patterns.

To a reader who may be encountering this author for the first time, there is much bewilderment in store. Faulkner has a style which is definitely his own. Although not using the stream of consciousness technique altogether he does make use of it when his characters soliloquize at any great length, which they frequently do. The reader will become inured to casting a wary eye at sentences running a page or more, taking a deep breath, and diving into them, only to flounder at times over the heaped up phrases, the thoughts within thoughts, and the time, which the author is prone to juggle from the present to the past with nary a nod to warn the reader. The author has an apparent fear of the obvious which leads him, oftentimes, far afield in the motivation of his characters.

With these handicaps and obstacles inherent in the mere technique of Faulkner's writing, it is difficult for the reader to weather these stream of consciousness portions, with a clear idea of just what the man is getting at.

In subject matter, Faulkner's predilection for the morbid, the psychologically misfit, the mysterious, is less obvious here than in many of his previous efforts, but the quality he instills is yet that of the decay, the decadence which followed the Civil War in the South.

In reading these stories one has the feeling the author's main idea is less what he says directly than what he implies through symbolism, yet often his symbolism is too obscure to be effective.

Yet with all the author's shortcomings one has the distinct feeling that here is a writer who has something fine to offer, which makes it worth the effort it takes to read his material. What this something is is not yet clear. It is more than his ability to bring the forest into your room, to make you feel the essence of decay, and to smell the side pork cooking in a Negro's shack. These things he does, and more, with infinite skill, but it is not this alone which forces the reader on, intriguing and bewildering him to the completion of the book.

236

Robert Molloy.
"The Book of the Day:
William Faulkner Writes
about Deep South
He Has Made Familiar."
New York *Sun*, May 19,
1942, p. 40.

If we are to accept as true the saying that easy reading comes from very hard writing, we may be tempted from time to time to say that the converse is true while we are reading William Faulkner's *Go Down, Moses*, a collection of related stories in the familiar Faulkner's setting and atmosphere.

For here, mingled with passages of somber poetry and sometimes of a power that makes you think of Dostoevsky, are the tortuous sentences, the elliptic phraseology and the almost unfathomable mumblings that must make even the Faulkner fans wince. The first page and a half, for instance, ends with this passage: "Not something he had participated in or even remembered except from the hearing, the listening, come to him through and from his cousin McCaslin born in 1850 and sixteen years his senior and hence, his own father being near 70 when Isaac, an only child, was born, rather his brother than cousin and rather his father than either, out of the old time, the old days" (no period). Start a reader off like that and he is very likely to exclaim, as Douglas Jerrold is said to have exclaimed after puzzling over a passage in Browning: "My God, I'm an idiot!" And the first story which contains their master stroke of concealed meaning is illuminatingly entitled "Was."

We don't believe there is any justification for writing of the sort, particularly in the case of an author of Faulkner's immense talents. Perhaps Herbert J. Muller was correct when he wrote, in 1937 in his *Modern Fiction* that "Even Faulkner's style is hardening into strained, grotesque mannerism."

The foundation of these stories is the relation between the white descendants of the McCaslin family and their part Negro children half-brothers and cousins. We see the McCaslins in several generations and during a period of about one hundred years. The dominant figure of the stories is Isaac McCaslin, Uncle Ike, who learned hunting and woodcraft from a part Indian, Sam Fathers, and who refused his inheritance out of his conviction that no one could really bull or sell the earth. We see him as a boy, witnessing a strange and comic poker game for human stakes in "Was"; killing his first deer under Fathers's tutelage and partaking of a mystical experience in "The Old People"; and we meet him again in "The Bear."

This short novel, some 140 pages in length, tells, in its first part, a thrilling story of the hunt and the woods. Young Ike McCaslin is one of a party that for years hunts down a giant bear, Old Ben, whose tough hide, cunning and terrible ferocity have for years defied the huntsmen and their dogs. For a little more than half its length this is a thrilling performance, full of drama, poetry, and atmosphere, and yet as clear in the writing as the most matter-of-fact passages of Hemingway. After that we skip to the years of Ike McCaslin's majority, with extracts from an old family account book and many pages of baffling discourse, and at last we come to a rather pointless conclusion.

Another novelette presents more clearly the strange relationships of the white McCaslins and their dusky kin. It is called "The Fire and the Hearth," and its central character is Lucas Quintus Carothers McCaslin Beauchamp, Negro descendant of the McCaslins. Lucas, now an old man, works a farm on the land of Carothers

Edmonds whose grandfather and Lucas grew up together and had a mortal dispute over Lucas's black wife. Lucas, descendant of the McCaslins on the male side, despises the Edmondses, who are descendants on the distaff side. Their peculiar relation comes to a crisis when Lucas becomes interested in a treasure-finding machine and spends his nights in trying to find the treasure that, tradition says, is buried on the land. The human values here are clearly brought out, and there are kindness and humor.

Completing this strange picture of the South are the title story, relating the execution for murder of Samuel Worsham Beauchamp, grandson of Lucas Beauchamp's wife, Mollie, and his stately funeral. "Delta Autumn," another episode in the life of old Ike McCaslin, and "Pantaloon in Black," the story of a giant Negro lumberman who runs amok after the death of his young wife. If you are a regular Faulkner reader you will want to have read this volume for the fine things in it, and for a further clew to the author's attitude toward the land of his birth. But we repeat the warning that it's often very hard going.

Jack Keller.
"Faulkner Southern Stories Gather under One Title."
Columbus (Ohio) *Citizen*, May 24, 1942, Magazine Section, p. 4.

William Faulkner never is easily digested. *Go Down, Moses*, latest of the Faulkner books, is a collection of stories about the South and seems to have been treated with bicarbonate prior to publication because fortunately the stories are interesting, understandable and of some other value than literary.

Faulkner has tried for years to bulldoze his reading public into thinking the South is something most of us think it isn't. He's been helped in this endeavor by Erskine Caldwell among others.

This new collection of Faulkner's Southern stories range from a novella, "The Fire and the Hearth," to the bright, slight, titlepiece "Go Down, Moses." All of the seven stories contain the family names of the Edmonds, the McCaslins and the Beauchamps. And, as usual, Faulkner stresses interbreeding and inter-marriage between whites and Negroes with the problems it produces.

Ike McCaslin carries through three of the stories. Ike at 12 is the chief character in "The Old People" as he kills his first buck and is initiated into manhood by an Indian ceremony. He again appears in "The Bear" as a 16-year-old who witnesses the death of Old Ben, an almost immortal bear, and also sees the death of his beloved wilderness. This is one of Faulkner's best.

Ike at 70 is introduced into civilization in the story "Delta Autumn." He says of the people who brought the ruin of his woods and civilization to the delta: "The people who have destroyed it will accomplish its revenge."

There's no questioning the sound authenticity of William Faulkner's South. It's solid. It's a South that few other authors dare attempt to put in printed word. He knows the details of the Southerner's farming, hunting and folkways. Gifted, brilliant William Faulkner has written many novels, poems and short stories. He's one of America's foremost writers—yet his misfortune has been to miss immortality in literature by never having done a book which has deserved permanent fame.

Lionel Trilling. "The McCaslins of Mississippi." *Nation,* May 30, 1942, pp. 632–33.

William Faulkner's latest volume is brought out as a collection of stories, but six of the seven stories deal with a single theme, the relation of the Mississippi McCaslins to the Negroes about them, and they have a coherence strong enough to constitute, if not exactly a novel, then at least a narrative which begins, develops, and concludes. The seventh and alien story, "Pantaloon in Black," is inferior both in conception and in execution; why it was placed in the midst of the others is hard to understand, for it diminishes their coherence. But conceivably Mr. Faulkner intended it to do just that, wishing to exempt the collection from being taken for a novel and judged as such. Yet it is only as an integrated work that the group of the McCaslin stories can be read.

Mr. Faulkner's literary mannerisms are somewhat less obtrusive than they have been, but they are still dominant in his writing, and to me they are faults. For one thing, I find tiresome Mr. Faulkner's reliance on the method of memory to tell his stories. No doubt we can accept what so many Southern novelists imply, that in the South a continuous acute awareness of regional, local, and family history is one of the conditions of thought. But the prose in which Mr. Faulkner renders this element of his stories is, to me, most irritating; it drones so lyrically on its way, so intentionally losing its syntax in its long sentences, so full of self-pity expressed through somniloquism or ventriloquism. Then, too, while I am sure that prose fic-

tion may make great demands on our attention, it ought not to make these demands arbitrarily, and there is no reason why Mr. Faulkner cannot settle to whom the pronoun "he" refers. Mr. Faulkner's new book is worth effort but not, I think, the kind of effort which I found necessary: I had to read it twice to get clear not only the finer shades of meaning but the simple primary intentions, and I had to construct an elaborate genealogical table to understand the family connections.

These considerations aside, Mr. Faulkner's book is in many ways admirable. The six McCaslin stories are temperate and passionate, and they suggest more convincingly than anything I have read the complex tragedy of the South's racial dilemma. The first of the stories is set in 1856; it is the humorous tale of the chase after the runaway Tomey's Turl—it takes a certain effort to make sure that this is a slave, not a dog—of how old Buck McCaslin is trapped into marriage by Miss Sophonisba Beauchamp and her brother Hubert (rightly the Earl of Warwick), and of the poker game that is played for Tomey's Turl; the humor is abated when we learn that Turl is half-brother to one of the poker players. The last story is set in 1940; its central figure is the Negro murderer Samuel Worsham Beauchamp, descendant of Tomey's Turl and related to the McCaslins through more lines than one.

The best of the book does not deal directly with the Negro fate but with the spiritual condition of the white men who have that fate at their disposal. The Edmonds branch of the McCaslin family—there are three generations of Edmonds, but Mr. Faulkner likes to telescope the generations and all the Edmondses are really the same person: this does not exactly make for clarity—represents the traditional South; Isaac McCaslin, who is by way of being the hero of the narrative, represents the way of regeneration. The Edmondses are shown as being far from bad; in their relation to their Negroes they are often generous, never brutal, scarcely even irresponsible; but they accept their tradition and act upon their superiority and their rights, and the result is tragedy and degeneration both for the Negroes and for themselves. The effects are not always immediate and obvious; one of the best passages in the book, and one of the most crucial, is that in which, as a boy, Carothers Edmonds asserts his superiority over his negro foster-brother and then, seeking later to repent, finds the tie irrevocably broken and his foster-family, though wonderfully cordial, stonily implacable; and this failure of love which Edmonds's tradition imposed upon him seems to affect his whole life.

As against the tradition which arrests the dignity of possession and the family, Isaac McCaslin sets the dignity of freedom and the unpossessable wilderness. The experience by which his moral sensibility is developed is a kind of compendium of the best American romantic and transcendental feeling. Cooper, Thoreau, and Melville are all comprised in what he learns from Sam Fathers, the Chicasaw Indian (but he was enough of a Negro to be glad to die), from the humility and discipline of hunting, from the quest after a great bear, a kind of forest cousin to Moby Dick, from the mysterious wilderness itself. So taught, he can no longer continue in the tradition to which he is born; at great and lasting cost to himself he surrenders his ancestral farm to the Edmonds branch.

It will of course be obvious that so personal and romantic a resolution as Ike McCaslin's is not being offered by Mr. Faulkner as a "solution" to the racial problem of the South; nor, in representing that problem through the sexual and blood relations of Negro and white, is he offering a comprehensive description of the problem in all its literalness. (Though here I should like to suggest that Mr. Faulkner may be hinting that the Southern problem, in so far as it is cultural, is to be found crystallized in its sexual attitudes: it is certainly worth remarking of this book that white women are singularly absent from it and are scarcely mentioned, that all the significant relations are between men, and that Isaac McCaslin is the only man who loves a woman.) But the romantic and transcendental resolution and the blood and sexual ties are useful fictional symbols to represent the urgency and the iniquity of the literal fact. They suggest that its depth and its complication go beyond what committees and commissions can conceive, beyond even the most liberal "understanding" and the most humanitarian "sympathy." Mr. Faulkner not only states this in the course of his book; he himself provides the proof: the story "Pantaloon in Black" is conceived in "understanding" and "sympathy," like every other lynching story we have ever read, and when it is set beside the McCaslin stories with their complicated insights it appears not only inadequate but merely formal, almost insincere.

Jeanette Greenspan. "Faulkner at His Best." Brooklyn *Citizen,* June 5, 1942.

With *Go Down, Moses*, a collection of seven stories of varying length, six of which are so interwoven as to be sequels to each other, William Faulkner rises Phoenix-like from the funeral pyre which the critical gentry have been building for him for the last few years. The warmth and depth of the writing, the newly revealed philosophy of man's relation to pure nature and pure truth, and his understanding of the deep southland's problems which are to be found in such stories as "The Old People" and "The Fire and the Hearth" are his answer to the doubters who have been wailing that he had become "a writer's writer" and that his preoccupation with sheer violence and horror had taken him too far off the path of reality ever to return. When Faulkner chooses to write "straight" as he does in the greater part of these seven tales about the relationship of white and negro in the Mississippi Delta country, there is little better in the literature of our time.

The stories in *Go Down, Moses,* although they possess different titles and were apparently at different times, ought to be considered as part of a whole. They are like a fugue with repetitions and variations on the central theme of the ethnic closeness of southern Negroes and whites—an affinity by blood, by proximity and by labor, which the white men have tried to conceal and to obliterate, and in so doing have persecuted and exploited their fellow creatures, while creating within themselves galling conflicts, passions and a totally false and artificial approach to life, itself.

When Faulkner dedicates this book to Mary Caroline Barr "who was born in slavery and who gave to my family a fidelity without stint or calculation of recompense and to my childhood an immeasurable devotion and love," he is not being sentimental, nor nostalgic. He is simply stating a fact which the white men of his stories are loath to acknowledge and which they have even endeavored to hide with cruelty and hatred.

The prototype of this kind of white man is Carothers Edmonds, owner by inheritance of the McCaslin plantation, whose "haughty ancestral pride" which he discovered at seven dissolves into an abject and infuriating sense of inferiority when he contemplates the effrontery of Lucas, the old Negro who had lived on McCaslin land half a lifetime before the young man was born, and whose blood was better than his because he was descended from the first McCaslin through the male line. To make it more difficult for the young man it was his white man's burden to pay the taxes, insurance and interest and "keep ditched, drained, fenced and fertilized" the land on which the old Negro seemed the host and the white man the intruder and guest.

In every story, except "Pantaloon in Black" which is a clever, ironical tale of a lynching told completely by indirection, there is the comparison, the conflict between white and black as well as their mutual interests, the accent on superior blood and pure ancestry against a constant background of a receding wilderness. This is the forest of the delta land inhabited by deer, bears, dogs and the reincarnated spirits of Indian warriors who were first on the land; and there is their revenge upon the plantation owners and farmers who keep gnawing at the wilderness and pushing it back until it was necessary to ride two hundred miles from Jefferson for good hunting. "The white man's hold on the land actually was as trivial and without reality as the now faded and archaic script in the chancery book in Jefferson which allocated it to them."

All that Faulkner has to say in the preceding half-dozen tales reaches its logical climax in the last and title story, "Go Down, Moses" in which the prominent citizens of Jefferson bring home the body of an executed Negro murderer for a traditional burial because of their respect for his venerable and ancient Negro grandmother. It is the shortest story in the book; but it is the one in which most is said in the fewest words. Samuel Worsham Beauchamp, a petty thief banished from the plantation by the choleric Carothers

241

Edmonds, goes wrong all the way. Samuel was the bad seed of a bad father, and they electrocuted him for murder in Chicago. But down in the bottomland of the delta country, white men solicited money from door to door to collect two hundred dollars so that Aunt Molly could bury her grandson in a gray and silver casket and ride through the town in a big black car behind the hearse. It is with such simple symbols and with consummate artistry that Faulkner has made the deep South a place of humanity and reality instead of a bit of lush regionalism.

George Snell.
"New Faulkner Tales Keep to Tradition."
Salt Lake City *Tribune*, June 7, 1942, p. 13-C.

William Faulkner has been slowly producing an impressive saga of southern life in a series of remarkable books, the most recent of which is *Go Down, Moses*. It is a collection of seven stories, macabre in quality, even gruesome at times, which carry on the Faulkner tradition with no diminution of intensity, power and eccentricity.

They are concerned always with the changing social mores of a decadent South, and in their nostalgia (implicit always, never stated) for a vanished serenity and elegance and integrity, they reveal Faulkner as the lamenting historian of a dead day rather than the ruthless nihilist he has sometimes been called.

The stories in *Go Down, Moses* are independent and may be read as such, but the whole book centers its attention on an old, decaying plantation owned by the McCaslin-Edmonds clan, and the narrative action is interrelated. Again it is the story of the infiltration of Negro blood into the once aristocratic McCaslin strain, and the concomitant degeneration of this proud family. The "white trash" clan of Edmonds gradually usurps the privileges, even the property, of the McCaslins, spreading upon the land like some loathsome fungi.

Like the termite Snopeses of *The Hamlet*, the Edmondses overrun everything; they represent a new and terrifying class of parvenus, without grace, mercy or anything but greed and chicanery, to entrench themselves as a social group.

Among the most convincing and memorable of the tales are "Pantaloon in Black," "The Bear," and the title story. The first shows an essentially "good" Negro gone berserk with grief at the death of his wife, and his eventual lynching. "The Bear" is a strangely tender story of a boy who learns how to hunt under the tutelage of an old man, half Indian, half Negro, who inspires him with a strength of spirit that the McCaslins have long since lost. "Go Down, Moses" is a nostalgic evocation of the days when there was respect and love between master and slave—a subject hard to treat convincingly, but Faulkner manages it.

The stories are "difficult" in the sense that their narrative pattern is intricate, the style involved, at times wildly luxuriant as foliage in the Delta bottoms, but they repay reading for their startling psychologic insights and earnest presentation of a tragic problem.

August Derleth. "The New Books: Excellent Short Stories." Madison (Wis.) *Capital Times*, July 19, 1942, p. 22.

In the long view, there are comparatively few contemporary American writers of short stories who will survive the test of time; but it is certain that both William Faulkner and Sally Benson will be among those few. That is not to say that everything these writers have written is top-flight work: not at all—every writer may be expected to write stories of varying worth, and that is especially true of a man who can write as much as Faulkner, for instance.

Faulkner's place in American literature of the first half of the present century seems to me secure. No one can say how he will weather, but such novels as *Light in August*, and such short stories as some of those seven in his new collection are as good as anything that has been written by Americans since 1900. Faulkner is perhaps one of the outstanding regionalists in America today; he has selected a corner of Mississippi about which to write with merciless sincerity, and in his mosaic of life in his home country there is everything ranging from high comedy to dark, brooding tragedy. As usual, these stories in *Go Down, Moses* add to his reputation; there is nothing here of the confusion of *The Wild Palms*, for instance, despite those points about that novel which made some critics tend to regard it as among his best, particularly its pattern; there are subtle, dramatic interplay of character relationships, comedy, and pathos in these stories, and above all, there is a credibility that brooks no doubt. *Go Down, Moses* must rank as one of the best collections of short stories to come out of the forties in America.

Checklist of Additional Reviews

Rochester *Democrat-Chronicle*, April 19, 1942.

Columbus (Ga.) *Inquirer-Sun*, April 26, 1942.

Savannah *Press*, May 9, 1942.

Norfolk *Pilot*, May 10, 1942.

"South Preoccupies Faulkner." Dallas *Morning News*, May 10, 1942, Section IV, p. 12.

Newsweek, May 11, 1942.

"*Go Down, Moses*." *Time*, May 11, 1942, p. 95.

New York *Journal*, May 16, 1942.

"*Go Down, Moses*." *New Yorker*, May 16, 1942, p. 74.

New York *News*, May 17, 1942.

Syracuse *Post-Standard*, May 24, 1942.

Cincinnati *Times-Star*, May 27, 1942.

"The Decadent South." San Francisco *Argonaut*, June 5, 1942, p. 24.

Amberg, George. "Paradoxical." El Paso *Herald Post*, June 6, 1942.

Andrew, G. C. "*Go Down, Moses*." *Canadian Forum*, 22 (August 1942), 155.

Boutell, C. B. "Series of Seven Faulkner Tales." Boston *Herald*, May 13, 1942, p. 17.

Brookhouser, Frank. "Black, White and Faulkner." Philadelphia *Inquirer*, May 20, 1942, p. 20.

Burke, Harry R. "A Mystery of Bloods." St. Louis *Globe-Democrat*, May 16, 1942, p. 4-A.

Cheney, Frances Neel. "Three Volumes of Short Stories." Nashville *Banner*, May 13, 1942, p. 4-X.

Cowley, Malcolm. "Go Down to

Faulkner's Land." *New Republic*, June 29, 1942, p. 900.

Danielson, Richard Ely. "Atlantic Bookshelf." *Atlantic Monthly*, September 1942, p. 136.

Graves, John Temple. "Faulkner. . . ." *Saturday Review of Literature*, May 2, 1942, p. 16.

Gregory, Horace. "New Tales by William Faulkner." *New York Times Book Review*, May 10, 1942, p. 4.

Helbert, James E. "Latest Books." Elmira *Advertiser*, May 5, 1942, p. 4; Bakersfield *Californian*, May 15, 1942; Beloit (Wis.) *News*, May 21, 1942.

Hoch, Henry George. "Short Stories by Faulkner: New Collection Reveals His Unusual Talent." Detroit *News*, May 17, 1942, Classified Section, p. 24.

K., H. "New Faulkner Tales Are Powerful Stuff." New Bedford *Standard*, May 10, 1942, Section IV, p. 26.

Littell, Robert. "*Go Down, Moses*." *Yale Review*, 31 (Summer 1942), viii.

Maslin, Marshall. "The Browser." San Bernardino *Sun*, May 24, 1942.

P., M. "Family Tree in Black and White." Worcester (Mass.) *Telegram*, May 10, 1942, Section IV, p. 8.

Patrick, Corbin. "*Go Down, Moses*." Indianapolis *Sunday Star*, May 10, 1942, p. 19.

Patterson, Alicia. "Stories of the Southland." New York *Sunday News*, May 17, 1942, p. 73.

Peeples, Edwin. "Master at His Best." Atlanta *Constitution*, July 12, 1942, p. 6.

Putnam, Samuel. "Quaint, Soft or Desperate." *People's World* (San Francisco), January 27, 1943, p. 5.

Rugoff, Milton. "The Magic of William Faulkner." *New York Herald Tribune Books*, May 17, 1942, p. 2.

Russell, Cara Green. "Faulkner Writes Well but Obscurely." Durham *Herald*, May 10, 1942; Greensboro (N.C.) *News*, May 10, 1942.

Sargent, Marvin. "Way Down South in the Land of Problems Still Unsolved." Oakland *Tribune*, April 12, 1942, p. 4.

Seaver, Edwin. "Books." *Direction*, 5 (Summer 1942), 31.

Selby, John. "The Literary Guidepost." Salisbury (N.C.) *Post*, April 12, 1942; Wilmington (N.C.) *Morning Star*, April 14, 1942, p. 4; Santa Monica *Outlook*, April 16, 1942; Charlotte *Observer*, April 19, 1942; New Haven *Register*, April 19, 1942; Toledo *Times*, April 19, 1942; Youngstown (Ohio) *Vindicator*, April 19, 1942; Culver City (Calif.) *Star-News*, May 1, 1942; Monrovia (Calif.) *News-Post*, May 1, 1942; Redondo Beach (Calif.) *Southern Day Breeze*, May 1, 1942.

Shattuck, Charles. "*Go Down, Moses*." *Accent*, 2 (Summer 1942), 236–37.

Voiles, Jane. "*Go Down, Moses*." San Francisco *Chronicle*, May 17, 1942, This World Section, p. 12.

Weigle, Edith. "Stories Cover Broad Range in Collections." Chicago *Daily Tribune*, May 13, 1942, p. 16.

Wellington, Gertrude. "A Book a Day." Honolulu *Star-Bulletin*, June 1, 1942, p. 4.

Weston, Sam. "Book Gives Tales of Southern Life." San Diego *Union*, May 24, 1942, p. 7-C.

Zwart, Elisabeth Clarkson. "Here Are Four of the Most Unusual Books of the Spring." Des Moines *Sunday Register*, May 31, 1942, Society Section, p. 9.

THE PORTABLE FAULKNER

The Portable

FAULKNER

Edited by Malcolm Cowley

THE VIKING PRESS • NEW YORK

1946

Caroline Gordon.
"Mr. Faulkner's Southern Saga: Revealing His Fictional World and the Unity of Its Patterns."
New York Times Book Review, May 5, 1946, pp. 1, 45.

William Faulkner, alone among contemporary novelists, it seems to me, has the distinguishing mark of the major novelist: the ability to create a variety of characters. He is also a poet, or, as the Germans would put it, a *dichter*. It is Malcolm Cowley's distinction to have presented in his preface to The Portable Faulkner the first comprehensive survey of Mr. Faulkner's work that takes into account his symbolism. In 1939 a young Southern writer, Marion O'Donnell, published in *The Kenyon Review* an essay in which he traced in great detail an allegorical scheme in Mr. Faulkner's work. In his view the Snopes, hillbillies who have moved in to town from the piney-woods section and have become horse traders, ginners, merchants and finally bankers, represent the forces of corruption at work within the South.

The Sartoris, Millard, Compson and other families stand for the old order. Their powerlessness to avert disaster, partly through the combination of circumstances and partly through their own weakness, is best symbolized by Colonel Sartoris, who, coming back from the Civil War with a citation for bravery at the hand of General Lee, turns politician and degenerates into such a forensic old windbag that his son Bayard finds himself unwilling to avenge his death. So far as I know, these two critics are the only ones who have read Mr. Faulkner's work in the way I think he wants to be read: seeing in it not a series of novels with sociological implications, but a saga, a legend that is still in the making.

"I call it a legend," Mr. Cowley says, "because it is obviously no more intended as an historical account of the country south of the Ohio than 'The Scarlet Letter' was intended as a history of Massachusetts or 'Paradise Lost' as a factual account of the Fall."

Mr. Cowley thinks of Mr. Faulkner as an epic poet or a bardic writer in prose, whose books form a number of interconnecting cycles. "Just as Balzac, who seems to have inspired the series, divides his 'Comedie Humaine' into Scenes of Parisian Life, Scenes of Provincial Life, Scenes of a Private Life, so Faulkner might divide his work into a number of cycles: one about the planters and their descendants, one about the townspeople of Jefferson, one about the poor whites, one about the Indians (consisting of stories already written but never brought together), and one about the Negroes." The whole, according to Mr. Cowley, forms a record of the adventures of people who live in a mythical kingdom which Mr. Faulkner himself calls "Yoknapatawpha County" ("William Faulkner, sole owner and proprietor") and all the books in the saga are parts of the same living pattern.

It is this pattern and not the printed volumes in which part of it is recorded, that is Faulkner's real achievement. Its existence helps to explain one feature of his work: that each novel, each long or short story, seems to reveal more than it states explicitly and to have a subject bigger than itself. All the separate works are like blocks of marble from the same quarry: they show the same veins and faults of the mother rock. Or else—to use a rather strained figure—they are like wooden planks that were cut, not from a log but from a still living tree. The planks are planed and chiseled into their final shapes, but the tree itself heals over the wound and continues to grow.

William Faulkner was born at New Albany, Miss., on Sept. 25, 1897. His family soon removed—as one of his own characters might put it—to the county seat, Oxford, where William, the oldest of four brothers, attended the public schools, but without graduating from high school. He served in the Royal Flying Corps during the first World War and returned to Oxford to become a student at the University of Mississippi, since veterans could then matriculate without a high school diploma. Mr. Cowley records that he "neglected his class work and left without taking a degree. He had less of a formal education than any other good writer of his time," Mr. Cowley adds, "except Hart Crane—less even than Hemingway, who never went to college, but who learned to speak three foreign languages and studied writing in Paris under the best masters. Faulkner taught himself, largely, he says, by 'undirected and uncorrelated reading.'"

Mr. Faulkner's first novel, *Soldiers' Pay*, which reflected to some extent his experience as a flier, was published in 1926. It was followed by *Mosquitoes*, a satire on artistic life in New Orleans, which shows little promise of what is to come. In 1929 he published *Sartoris*, a novel of uneven merit, in which members of the Sartoris family who will figure in later books appear. It was followed by fifteen other books in which the same characters appear, disappear and reappear in ever widening circles. Of them all, *Sanctuary* is the only one that received wide distribution. In 1945 Faulkner's seventeen books were out of print, some of them unobtainable in second-hand book stores.

One of the masters whom Faulkner evidently studied in his "undirected and uncorrelated reading" is Flaubert. He handles details with Flaubertian precision. It is perhaps no accident that the American writer achieved his first fame in the same way that the great French writer did, through the public's appetite for erotic detail—and, in Mr. Faulkner's case, through the Eastern critics' desire for examples of Southern degeneracy. Mr. Cowley thinks that the story of Temple Drake and Popeye has more meaning than appears on a hasty first reading—"the only reading that most critics have been willing to give it." "Popeye," he says, "is one of several characters in Faulkner's novels who represent the mechanical civilization that has invaded and conquered the South. *Sanctuary* is not a connected allegory, as one critic explained it, but neither is it an accumulation of pointless horrors. It is an example of the Freudian nightmare turned backwards, being full of sexual nightmares that are in reality social symbols."

Mr. Cowley has made his selection for *The Portable Faulkner* with a view to giving a general panorama of life in the mythical Yoknapatawpha County, "decade by decade, from the days when the early settlers first rode northward along the Natchez Trace." There are complete novels but there are two stories of almost novel length: "The Bear"—in my opinion as good a story as has been written by any American—and "Spotted Horses." Among the notable shorter pieces are: "Percy Grimm," the story of a man who asked only to live and die uniformed and regimented—"I created a Nazi before I ever heard of Hitler," Faulkner says of him; "Red Leaves," the story of a Negro slave of a Chickasaw chief who tried to escape being sacrificed on his master's grave, and "Was," which exhibits a brand of frontier humor reminiscent of Mark Twain.

The selections from the novels, the section from *The Wild Palms* called *Old Man*, and the chapter entitled "A Wedding in the Rain" from *Absalom, Absalom!* are complete in themselves yet they retain what Mr. Cowley calls "the unity of the Faulkner legend." But the reader who makes Mr. Faulkner's acquaintance only in *The Portable* will hardly be aware of the full scope of his talent, for he will not have had an opportunity to observe the brooding intensity with which, in the full-length novels, moving backward and forward in time, he hovers over a theme—presenting the experiences of the characters from every conceivable angle, as a man in a lifetime of recollection might suck the marrow out of some event of his youth.

He will also not have had a chance to discover Mr. Faulkner's worst faults: an obscurity that comes partly from over-ambition and partly from succumbing to his own rhetoric, and an occasional weakness of structure. *Absalom, Absalom!* the story of Thomas Sutpen, the mountain boy, who being sent to the back door of a Tidewater mansion by a Negro servant resolved to acquire a mansion as large as the one he had been denied entrance to, with its concomitant land and slaves, has perhaps the strongest, most coherent structure; but *As I Lay Dying* seems to me the most perfect in proportion, presenting in a many-faceted design the lives of all the members of the Bundren family.

Mr. Faulkner's stories, as Mr. Cowley says, have "the quality of being lived, absorbed, remembered, rather than observed." It is indeed, as if the author had squatted among the blue jeans that ring a Southern court house on Saturday afternoons and regarded natural objects long enough for them to take on other than their pristine shapes. One of Flem Snopes' wild calico ponies rushes past. The man leaping to catch it realizes, as if for the first time in his life, how long a horse's head is and, as the butt of his pistol hammers its nose, how hard the skull is.

The saw which Addie Bundren's son, Cash, uses to saw the planks of her coffin buzzes as insistently as the lathe which Binet kept turning in the courtyard when Emma Bovary, clutching Rodolphe's letter in her hand, looks down and sees the pavement rushing up to meet her. A little boy totes a monstrous catfish home and, cleaning it, finds it "as full of blood and guts as a hog." A log, rearing up suddenly out of a swollen current, confounds the men who are trying to carry a coffin across the river.

The solidity and immediacy of such details stand Mr. Faulkner in good stead when he will suddenly expand some image so that it seems to take in the whole of life. The saw, rasping on through scene after scene, of *As I Lay Dying* becomes a symbol of the discords of human life. The fish, "bleeding quietly in a pan," reveals to the boy what he could not have guessed from his elders' whispered comments: the fact that mortals must die. The log, rearing up, assumes in the eyes of the dazed and thwarted men such supernatural proportions that for an instant it stands "upon that surging and heaving desolation like Christ."

The Faulkner characters, like his incidents, stand for more than themselves. It is no accident that he continually uses words like "grave, absent, bemused" to describe them. They move rapt in the contemplation of their individual fates. At some time—early, like Thomas Sutpen, or late, like Joe Christmas—they leave everything else and go to meet it.

He has another characteristic which often marks the major novelist: compassion for all created beings. This compassion sometimes has subliminal objects. "The Long Summer" portrays the love of an idiot boy for a cow. The story, in spite of its Gothic language, is classical in feeling. The cow grazes, Io-like through windy leaves. He weaves a chaplet of flowers for her brow; and, when she is taken from him, squats, holding the crudely carved, wooden cow that has been given him for a toy, moaning. Mr. Faulkner is as tender toward man raising himself from all fours as when he walks upright.

The American author whom Mr. Faulkner most resembles is Hawthorne, in Mr. Cowley's view. "They stand to each other as July to December, as heat to cold, as swamp to mountain." And Hawthorne, he points out, had much the same attitude toward New England as Mr. Faulkner has for the South. ("New England is quite as large a lump of earth as my heart can really take in.")

As Mr. Cowley expresses it:

> Like Faulkner in the South, he applied himself to creating its moral fables and elaborating its legends, which existed as it were, in his solitary heart. Pacing the hillside behind his house in Concord, he listened for a voice; you might say he lay in wait for it, passively but expectantly, like a hunter behind a rock, then, when it had spoken he transcribed its words—more slowly and carefully than Faulkner, it is true, with more form and less fire, but with the same essential fidelity.

It is this fidelity to a voice, a voice which speaks of more than human endeavor, that makes the similarity between the two writers, I think. Mr. Faulkner's characters, like Hawthorne's, seem emanations from the land. It is fortunate for Mr. Faulkner's genius that he was born in northern Mississippi, a land he describes in *As I Lay Dying*, as a country "where everything hangs on too long. Like our rivers our land: opaque, slow, violent, shaping and creating the life of man in its implacable and brooding image."

No land less implacable and brooding

could have given him his spiritual geography. As Hawthorne's imagination was colored by the dark, narrow houses, the sombre streets of Salem, so is Mr. Faulkner's attuned to the savage, short springs, the even more savage droughts of the upper Delta. He writes like a man who so loves his land that he is fearful for the well-being of every creature that springs from it.

Sylvia B. Richmond. "In Spite of the Fact!" Chelsea (Mass.) *Record,* September 7, 1946, p. 3.

Recently a distinguished European journalist who was visiting the U.S. decided to make a trip to Oxford, Miss., to see an American whose writings he admired—William Faulkner. "There are too many people coming down here," Faulkner is reported to have complained. "Just last month there were two other journalists. This place is getting to be as bad as Hollywood." And, when the European arrived, Faulkner was nowhere to be found.

From time to time he has been persuaded to write for a movie film company. One day he told the studio he was going to work "at home." Later, when they tried to call him in Santa Monica, they found he had returned to Mississippi. That was what Faulkner had meant by "at home."

In spite of the fact he does none of the customary things to gain public attention, Faulkner's reputation as a writer grows steadily—nationally and internationally. Now we have *The Portable Faulkner* edited by Malcolm Cowley, a collection of some of his best stories about his Mississippi county. The selections are arranged chronologically and cover the history of the county from the days it was inhabited by the Chickasaws to the Second World War.

Checklist of Additional Reviews

"*The Portable Faulkner.*" *Kirkus,* February 1, 1946, p. 49.

"Bookwright." "Faulkner Consolidated." *New York Herald Tribune Book Review,* June 2, 1946, p. 20.

Davidson, Will. "A 'Portable' Reveals the Real Faulkner." Chicago *Sunday Tribune,* May 26, 1946, Part IV, p. 10.

Warren, Robert Penn. "Cowley's Faulkner." *New Republic,* August 12, 1946, pp. 234–37.

Wilson, Edmund. "*The Portable Faulkner.*" *New Yorker,* July 27, 1946, p. 65.

INTRUDER IN THE DUST

Intruder in the Dust

by

William Faulkner

Random House

New York

John Chapman. "New Faulkner Novel Expands Prior Ideas." Dallas *Morning News*, September 26, 1948, Section VI, p. 6.

William Faulkner in his first novel since 1940 seems to me to be expanding a series of problems which he first stated explicitly in the collection of short stories, *Go Down, Moses* (1942), but which had been implicit in almost all his previous writing. *Intruder in the Dust* may well be one of the larger fragments which originally was meant for *Go Down, Moses*, since the setting and the characters are all identical, and since it is not greatly longer than one of the stories in that collection.

The argument, briefly, is that Lucas Beauchamp, a mulatto with some of the best white blood of Jefferson in his veins, is in prison following the murder of one of the Gowrie clan who live in the nearby hills. A lynching bee is imminent, but for some reason the Gowries, ordinarily a dangerous group of men, remain strangely quiet. The town awaits them, but while they delay Gavin Stevens' nephew, named Chick, a colored youth about Chick's own age and an elderly spinster set out to discover the real killer of the Gowrie. Since in some measure the effect of the story depends upon the solution of the crime, one need not elaborate the plot further.

That plot, however, is incidental to the character of Lucas Beauchamp, as intractable and stiffnecked a Negro as ever irritated a Southerner. What Chick Stevens discovered to his amazement was that Lucas possessed the same feelings and followed the same code as did the best white men of the region. His double origin imposed upon Lucas not only the conduct proper to a white man of good blood, but also burdened him with certain characteristics of the colored, in such manner that he could not act consistently either as the one or as the other.

Faulkner's preoccupation with the Negro question both in *Go Down, Moses* and particularly in this current novel has led to the suggestion that the writer has undergone considerable change in recent years. Such a statement is in my opinion an entirely uncritical one. It is very doubtful indeed that any major writer of this country has been as little understood as William Faulkner.

The naturalists, the psychoanalysts, the surrealists have all claimed him as their own. In 1932 Henry Smith in a preface to *Miss Zilphia Gant* suggested that Faulkner was both a lyric poet and a naturalistic novelist. In Europe the tendency has been to regard him as belonging to a Gothic school that includes in America pre-eminently Edgar A. Poe. It is not unusual at all to hear the statement that Faulkner's sole interest is in brutality for the sake of brutality, that he is of the brotherhood of Baudelaire, and so on.

All of these comments have some degree of validity, perhaps, but not one of them perceives a rather fundamental characteristic of William Faulkner. His first novel, *Soldiers' Pay*, received very little notice at all, although it was a rather competent satiric job. In 1927 when Faulkner's second novel, *Mosquitoes*, appeared, John H. McGinnis on this page hailed the writer as one of the most efficient and caustic satirists of the young postwar group. McGinnis' perception was characteristically acute: one does not write good satire unless he feels deeply and thinks profoundly.

Shortly after this, however, Faulkner abandoned explicit satire and began to write in the manner which has come to be associated with his name. Because he dealt nearly always with instincts at the lowest human level, critics assumed that he was naturalistic. Because those brute instincts led to the most revolting forms of violence, critics again assumed that Faulkner created obscenity for the fun of it. Because about 1932 he ceased writing in dialect and undertook a peculiar and complicated style, the surrealists claimed him. And now when he writes something that is explicitly social no doubt the sociologists will take him over.

My argument is that Faulkner has been consistent throughout his entire work and that the good mind, the acute feeling and the sharp perception of the satirist have never deserted him. In no single piece of his writing can one find him indulging in horror as Poe, for example, concentrated on it as an end in itself. Rather, as in *Soldiers' Pay*, *Sartoris*, and *Mosquitoes*, Faulkner was concerned with the displaced persons of World War I; in the next set of novels, which come to be called characteristically Faulknerian—*The Sound and the Fury*, *As I Lay Dying*, and *Light in August*—his concern is generally with the same types of people whom Steinbeck and his counterpart Saroyan write of.

Faulkner's position seems to me to be merely that these people, prevented either by nature or by opportunity from the ability to reason, respond to impulses which can best be represented by the fragmentary, unpunctuated, half-conscious style he adopted for depicting them. The brutality that characterizes Joe Christmas, for example, arises less from the man himself than from that society that treats him as a brute.

Therefore it should not seem particularly strange that Faulkner, having dealt with the displacement of people from war and from poverty, should finally come to deal explicitly with the most dispossessed and displaced of all, the Negro. His concern with the relation of Negro to white in the South—not Dallas, but Mississippi where there is really a problem—dates even as far back as *Sartoris* and recurs with varying importance through most of his other works. It might also be said that no little of his writing represents the daytime equivalent of a nightmare in which the writer attempts various possible solutions of the racial question.

This argument by no means undertakes to establish Faulkner as a great humanitarian of the school of Victor Hugo but merely urges that he be considered as a serious and thoughtful writer who has very good reason for the use of such forms and styles and topics as he has chosen. *Intruder in the Dust*, though sections of it may be of use to certain literate Dixiecrats, is no more an answer to the question of the Negro than some of Faulkner's other productions. Perhaps Faulkner himself supplies by implication in the words of Gavin Stevens as intelligent a beginning as we possess: "Which proves again how no man can cause more grief than that one clinging blindly to the vices of his ancestors."

Paul Flowers. "Faulkner Offers Logic, Not Passion." Memphis *Commercial Appeal*, September 26, 1948, Section IV, p. 16.

To mention the name of William Faulkner in his home state, often is to precipitate controversy, for many of his fellow Mississippians resent the pictures he etches. Beyond the confines of Mississippi and the South, the name of Faulkner is spoken with something akin to reverence, and his admirers elsewhere are as vocal in their belief that he executes true portrayals of characters, as some of his neighbors are in the denial.

Intruder in the Dust is a novel which ought to bring these two conflicting elements closer together, for in this novel, William Faulkner has struck an admirable balance.

The story deals with a negro, Lucas Beauchamp, who has been accused of shooting a white man in the back. Through the medium of a young white boy, a negro of like age, and an aged spinster, there is an exhumation of the victim's corpse, another murder, an episode of body swapping and burying in quicksand, events which prove Lucas Beauchamp's innocence and which logically enough forestall the lynching of Lucas. There are fratricide and stealing of lumber within the ranks of shiftless whites, but the story seems chiefly to be a medium for Faulkner to point up circumstances which produce and encourage violence in backwoods communities such as Beat Four of Yoknapatawpha County. It presents a compelling argument on behalf of a man who insisted on living as a human being instead of a servile, cringing subhuman, and balanced against that, the book submits with telling eloquence the most pertinent arguments for state and local action against lynching.

If Southerners and reformers from afar would read Chapter 7 of *Intruder in the Dust*, there would be no excuse for the current wrangling and political trickery based on minority questions. Mr. Faulkner's character has spoken so eloquently and at the same time so logically, with so much common sense.

Intruder in the Dust has its ghastly aspects, but Mr. Faulkner has employed these elements effectively to get his idea across.

Here again the author has demonstrated his great skill in character portrayal, his photographic eye amazing in its capacity for small detail, his objective understanding of degenerate breeds and the forces that drive them. *Intruder in the Dust* should add hordes to the legion of Faulkner devotees.

In contrast to the majority of so called "problem novels," *Intruder in the Dust* is designed to make the reader think instead of feel. For that alone it should be ranked high among the year's books.

Horace Gregory. "Regional Novelist of Universal Meaning." *New York Herald Tribune Weekly Book Review,* September 26, 1948, p. 3.

It may be difficult to convince the majority of William Faulkner's contemporaries that among living writers he is America's major novelist, and it is perhaps more tactful, and certainly more prudent, to withhold a title of such magnitude that its weight is of dubious value until the writer who receives it is safely lowered into the grave and is, at last, deaf and blind to the gratuitous patronage of praise and blame. But William Faulkner's position today is an extraordinary one, as it has been since the publication of *Sanctuary* and *Light in August,* and it is now clear, on the publication of his seventeenth book, which in mere bulk is scarcely greater than a long short story that he has not yielded to, and is not concerned with, the pretensions and temptations of writing "The Great American Novel."

The kind of fiction (short stories as well as novels) that Faulkner has been writing since 1926 is cumulative in its depth and scope; he is one of the very few novelists of the twentieth century (of which James Joyce is one and Marcel Proust another) who have transformed the avowedly "regional" setting of their writings into one of universal meaning and application; he is one of the few—and there are not many writers of his kind in any age—who are most "universal" when most "at home." As his writings testify, William Faulkner's Mississippi has become as complete a world of his imagination as Herman Melville's and Joseph Conrad's metaphors of human existence in the humors, the melodramatic temper, the sunstruck calms, the stormy darknesses, the physical beauty and terrors of the sea. There is an affinity, quite aside from the question of the slight probability of "influence," between Melville's imagination and William Faulkner's and the likeness extends to the character of their prose; both writers, each in his singular way, possess a style which is both illuminated and darkened, one almost says, "by flashes of obscurity"—that is, the very texture of their prose is both dense and fluid, rich in its wealth of "poetic ambiguities," intertwined with meanings that may seem innocently descriptive, but, on second thought or reading, yield psychological, moral, religious and even social interpretations. Nor is it well to read both writers in a mood of consistently heavy seriousness, seeking out profundities that do not allow for the presence of comic relief from the stresses of imaginative insights, semi-tragic irony and melodramatic action.

Faulkner's present novel is written in a lighter vein than *The Sound and the Fury*, and *As I Lay Dying*, and is a sequel to one of the less successful long short stories, "The Fire and the Hearth," in his recently published volume of stories, *Go Down, Moses*. *Intruder in the Dust* is one of the rare examples in fiction in which a

sequel far exceeds the promise of its beginnings in an earlier story, and for the reader who does not care to "go behind the scenes" of action the present novel is an independent series of episodes, told from the point of view of a sixteen-year-old boy.

The novel, not unlike the earlier short story, is a melodramatic comedy, and has for its central character the same figure, Lucas Beauchamp, an elderly Negro, descendant of one of the great white land-owning families in the county, an inheritor of family pride and courage, and possessed of an intractable wit that is quite his own. Lucas Beauchamp is no mere "Uncle Tom," that Pantaloon of sentimental abolitionist literature, but one of the most convincing Negro characters in American fiction, a rare figure of unmarred dignity, and it is one of the marks of Faulkner's genius that he can write of the Negro without false pity, without the usual haze of shallow sentiment in which so many "men of good will" scatter patronage, and the sweet, slightly rotted fruits of "good intentions." The melodramatic action of *Intruder in the Dust* involves the threat of a "lynching party" and the digging up of a body from a grave at midnight, situations which have become "stock properties" in Southern melodrama and fiction; it is what Faulkner does with the action that makes it new, that gives it an air of perennial freshness and sense of motion. For behind the story emerges the conflict of racial and class pride, Negro as well as white, and there is also the opposition of the collective, huge, abstract "face" of the mob against the intelligence and humane wit of a few individuals whose insight is classless, raceless, and less concerned with "good intentions" than with doing good.

Perhaps no American novel of recent years has so many admirable characters in it as *Intruder in the Dust*, and, unlike most "good people" in fiction, they are neither stupid nor dull. This does not mean that Faulkner has lost his famous "sense of evil," for he permits the uncle of the boy, whose point of view reflects the action of the novel, to speak of the political, intellectual, and cultural evils of our time.

Not all white people can endure slavery and apparently no man can stand freedom (which incidentally—the premise that man really wants peace and freedom—is the trouble with our relations with Europe right now, whose people not only don't know what peace is but—except for Anglo-Saxons—actively fear and distrust personal liberty; we are hoping without really any hope that our atom bomb will be enough to defend an idea as obsolete as Noah's Ark); with one mutual instantaneous accord he forces his liberty into the hands of the first demagogue who rises into view: lacking that, he himself destroys and obliterates it from his sight and ken and even remembrance with the frantic unanimity of a neighborhood stamping out a grass fire.

There is the kind of truth in this statement that cuts against the grain of current prejudices and platitudes, that refreshes and does not hamper the action of human intelligence and understanding particularly in a year of Presidential campaign oratory. It is in these remarks that Faulkner again resembles Melville, who did not see reality in literal terms, but was always mindful of a "wind" that "spins against the way it drives."

It is all too easy to say: "The stories and novels of William Faulkner are, of course, reactionary—reactionary and nostalgic as the South itself with its long memories of a once fought Civil War." All of which is shortsighted generalization of his accomplishments. Rather than being merely "nostalgic," Faulkner is imaginatively aware of a past which exists and has its dual appearances of life and death within the present. He may find himself, from time to time, as in *Intruder in the Dust*, given to write editorials on the present state of the world and its misfortunes, but the larger truths of his insights are implicit in the stories he has to tell and the actions of his characters. In the mastery of his style which he constantly refreshes with technical variety and invention, Faulkner is the least "reactionary" of all living American novelists, and in his perception of enduring human situations he is well in advance of younger writers who have rested too long and too heavily upon the mere formulae of "scientific" psychology and the devices of topical "realism." Surely, the conflicts of pride in *Intruder in the Dust* are not likely to be "out-moded" tomorrow, and the "tyrannies" of "the one, the few and the many," as Faulkner touches upon them in the present novel, are as meaningful today as they were when Jonathan Swift perceived them as a young man, and William Butler Yeats rediscovered them in Dublin twenty years ago.

It is hardly necessary to add that the action of comedy and melodrama in Faulkner's new book involves the reader in thinking about seriously controversial matters including the question of "State Rights" in the South, but it is one of the essentials of Faulkner's gifts as a novelist seldom to fail in leading his readers, either intellectually, or in physical surroundings where they least desired or expected to go. This is one of the elements of "suspense" in a Faulkner novel, a quality which is by no means lacking in his new book. Although *Intruder in the Dust* is a book of less than 250 pages, it leaves the impression of being a novel of twice its number of words. The compression and fluid density of its prose may frighten away a few readers who have formed the habit of reading prose in telegraphic sentences. Yet even those few will find the rewards of reading it salutary. If the book is not the most sensational of William Faulkner's novels, it is one of the best of his shorter books, one in which the adventures of a sixteen-year-old boy, an elderly maiden lady of positive convictions, a middle-aged lawyer, and an intractable Negro are endowed with the qualities of life beyond even the faintest memories of nine-tenths of the fictional heroes and heroines who are more loudly spoken of today. And in their company, William Faulkner's so-called "isolation" in the South has been transformed into a position of great advantage.

Ben Wasson. "William Faulkner's New Novel." *Delta Democrat-Times* (Greenville, Miss.) September 26, 1948, p. 18.

It is not an easy thing to write a critical piece about a book written by a friend. One approaches the job with hesitation, timidity and a sense of inadequacy. A balance of detached critical judgment is almost desperately strived for.

For so long a time, I have felt that William Faulkner is the most important of living American novelists, and I do not believe that this conviction has anything whatsoever to do with my personal affection for him. Faulkner is, undeniably, in the big tradition of novelists. Even in the most minor of his themes he suggests the wide scope, the very broad canvas. The overtones of the big, the large, are ever present, in either the Faulkner short story, the Faulkner novella or the full length Faulkner novel.

Malcolm Cowley, in his distinguished essay on Faulkner, (which is an Introduction to *The Portable Faulkner*) states: Essentially he (Faulkner) is not a novelist, in the sense of not being a writer who sets out to observe actions and characters, then fits them into the architectural framework of a story. For all the weakness of his own poems, he is an epic or bardic poet in prose, a creator of myths that he weaves together into a legend of the South."

Intruder in the Dust might be labelled another legend of the South—not a soft, magnolia scented legend, but one in which violence and the hope for justice is passionately presented.

This is the briefest, in length, of any Faulkner novel. It follows the pattern of the mystery or detective story. In fact, it might well be reviewed by the critics of mystery yarns, who would, most of them, be pretty well mystified!

Briefly, the plot concerns the murder, several miles from the by-now fictionally familiar town of Jefferson, Mississippi, by a mulatto of a white man. The murder takes place in a particularly violent, hot-blooded section of the county, known as Beat Five. The Negro is arrested, and, though he is safely gotten into the town jailhouse, the threat of lynching overhangs him.

A sixteen year old white boy, who feels an obligation to the accused, is resolved to save the Negro, Lucas. He is joined in this effort by a more than seventy year old spinster, Miss Fabersham, and a Negro youth with whom he had grown up.

This trio of detectives is unique, and in the truest sense of the word, extremely humorous, outrageously ludicrous. The efforts of the three to extricate Lucas from the jail offer some of the most ghoulish and outlandish situations ever presented in a novel.

It is a simple enough framework for a story. It is likely that much will be written about the possible symbolism of the three sleuths: the old, aristocratic lady, the white Southern youth, and the young Negro. I will leave the fancy surmises to those critics who care for suchlike. I do know that again William Faulkner has written a legend and one which contains deep penetration and a controlled wild beauty. The author has, in the central section of the book in three pages, written a magnificent and superb thesis of what the South represents today. I do not know any author who has said so eloquently and so succinctly what he has to say in this particular passage.

A thing that interests me particularly, is the fact that Faulkner continues, even in his seventeenth published work, to experiment with his medium. It is a sign that he is not tired, that he knows that the author, who believes in his trade, must continue to find new uses for his tools, which are words.

Intruder in the Dust is not a major opus in the true sense of the phrase. But it is a major book compared to the products of the great mass of fiction which pour daily from the publishers.

To those readers who are interested in reading a novel in which the overtones are Olympian I say "Read this book." To those readers who are interested in sitting on the backstairs and peeping over the shoulder of the servant girl as she peruses the newest best seller, I say: "Stay away from this book."

Not only the South, but all the United States, should be proud that William Faulkner is one of our authors.

Henry Seidel Canby. *"Intruder in the Dust." Book-of-the-Month Club News*, October, 1948.

This may be the best, it is certainly the most readable, of Faulkner's longer stories. Regarded as a tract on lynching, it has historical importance, for the purpose of the novel is to show in action what Faulkner regards as the conscience of the South; and its argument does not differ materially from the slogan of the new Southern party. The Southern white is the Negro's best friend. He accepts his guilt from the past, and if allowed to handle affairs in his own way, will give the Negro his rights when his rights can be safely given to him. But the *Intruder in the Dust* is not really a tract, it is a powerfully written and very dramatic story. The Negro who was about to be lynched by the uncontrollable poor whites of an outlying district, was innocent of the crime. But that he was saved only by the efforts of an old woman and two small boys, one colored, seems to be not a very effective argument for the power of conscience. Nevertheless, in the novel they are truly symbolic of a moral force. And the vivid reality of the scenes, the sharp and intensely individual reality of all the chief characters, make this book a novel of high distinction. Whatever one may think of his thesis, Faulkner's drama could have been written only by a major novelist. His great achievement is, I think, in character and in the atmosphere of a Mississippi which seems scarcely a part of the modern United Slates. His plot is a great advantage in a novel written in a style as mannered as it is effective, and difficult to read until one gets the swing of the rhythm. For the plot as it develops becomes a story of mix-up in murder, of disinterment and discovery, which will make any detective story writer gasp in envy. *Intruder in the Dust* is one of the really outstanding books of the American fiction year.

Alex Murphree. "Faulkner's Novel Offers Parable on Southerners' Duty to Negroes." Denver *Post*, October 3, 1948, p. 4-C.

William Faulkner's new novel reaffirms the unique quality among writers which has earned Faulkner a pre-eminent place among modern novelists despite a predilection for Gothic horror, melodramatic violence, macabre humor and an almost complete absence of sweetness and light—except for a cold glimmer of eerie illumination as by foxfire.

The unique quality is one of seeming. While other writers seem to know their characters and the life they report from the probing of imagination, the factualness of analytical observation, Faulkner seems to have lived with his characters in Jefferson, Miss., as a brother waking up with them in the morning in the room over the kitchen. He seems to have met them in friendliness when the hound was baying the moon. He seems to have met them in hot anger and outrage on a dusty, rutted country road. With his characters he seems to have come in such close contact that any emotional reaction between character and author is justified.

Intruder in the Dust is neither Faulkner's greatest nor least great novel. He has, with sincerity, drama and a wry sort of comedy, treated a subject which other novel-ists have dealt with, but those others have stacked the cards, have pulled the strings, have loaded the dice.

Faulkner is writing about the Negro-white relationship as it exists in the south—writing neither in defense nor censure except that he lets one of his characters, who may be considered the author speaking, describe the southerner's point of view rather more exactly than has been customary lately.

Lucas Beauchamp is a Negro with enough white blood to make him related to one white family but not enough—because by the folk ways of the south there is never enough—to make him white. He is uppity; he doesn't "say mister" as though he means it. He is proud of paying his way, of never asking a favor—and of his gold toothpick.

A white man is shot in the back, a "po' white" from the hills of the country where lynch mobs come from, and Lucas is found standing over him with a smoking pistol. Lucas is doomed to die by rope and flaming gasoline.

It takes the belief, born of imagination and not of faith, of a 17-year-old white boy and a 70-year-old aristocratic white woman to save Lucas. Lucas insists that his pistol did not kill Vinson Gowrie and that Gowrie's body must be dug up to prove it. He knows better than to ask any white man to act as a ghoul in his behalf. He asks the boy.

For a strange reason, the boy is able to conquer his loathing for the task and his fear of the consequences. When the boy was 12 years old, Lucas had spurned his proffered payment for a meal and the youth owes it to his white man's integrity, his southern manhood, not to permit himself to lose face before Lucas, a Negro. Lucas has become his unwanted obligation by a process not known in the north.

The corpse is dug up and another murder revealed. Lucas is saved almost as the mob gathers. Mob hatred turns to mob shame.

Faulkner emphasizes that the tornadic force which results in down-south lynchings comes from the family solidarity of the hill men with a simple code of vengeance and of hatred of the Negro, the solidarity of families who are "integrated and interlocked and intermarried with other brawlers and fox hunters and whisky makers not even into a simple clan or tribe but a race, a species." And he notes they live "where peace officers from town didn't even go unless they were sent for and strange white men didn't wander far from the highway after dark and no Negro anytime."

What Faulkner is saying, beyond telling a story, is that the south, that large and important part of the south which doesn't ride with the Kluxers on Saturday night, is the only part of the land which has ever aided the Negro, the only section which stands ready to do so and that the interference of outlanders can only make the Negro's lot more unbearable.

"We are defending . . . simply our homogeneity from a federal government to which in simple desperation the rest of this country has had to surrender voluntarily more and more of its personal and private liberty in order to continue to afford the United States," Faulkner has his most enlightened and kindliest character say.

"Sambo is a human being living in a free country and hence must be free. That's what we are really defending: the privilege of setting him free ourselves; which we will have to do for the reason that nobody else can since going on a century ago now the north tried it and they have been admitting for seventy-five years now that they failed.

"But it won't be next Tuesday. Yet people in the north believe it can be compelled even into next Monday by the simple ratification by votes of a printed paragraph."

There is more to that argument and it is inherent in Faulkner's thinking and the thinking of most southerners.

It must be confessed that Faulkner has become steadily more difficult to read in recent years. He has freed himself of commas and burdened himself with parentheses within parentheses as a means of giving his sentences a tidal ebb and flow. But sufficient concentration will master the difficulties and Faulkner's prose burns with a steady fire and will compel concentration.

David Carpenter. "Faulkner's *Intruder in Dust* Apology for South's Jimcrow." New York *Daily Worker*, October 6, 1948, p. 13.

In *Intruder in the Dust*, William Faulkner finally penetrates to the core of the obsession which has haunted him in all his previous novels, but which he has evaded up till now.

In practically all his prior writing, Faulkner dealt primarily with effects. His South was degenerate. His people were psychopathic, insane or idiotic. The world they inhabited was an unreal, fantastic, corrupt and immoral nightmare.

Faulkner's style of writing, his own unique inchoate, almost inarticulate stream-of-consciousness technique fitted the content of his writing like a glove.

But the reader of his novels was always left without an understanding of why Faulkner's South was degenerate, why his people were always so "peculiar," why their lives was only a "bad dream."

In his new novel, Faulkner provides the answer. He seeks to justify his degenerate South by giving his exploration of the cause of that degeneracy. And he thereby uncovers his own obsession, which has forced him to see only evil in his South. Correctly enough, he recognizes that the problem which he—and all other Southern whites—face is their relation to the Negro people. But he distorts the problem and its solution to fit his obsession.

Faulkner realizes that he and his fellow middle-class whites must bear responsibility for the degradation and enslavement of the Negro people in the South. But he seeks to shift the basic guilt away from himself and his fellow white Southerners. They have sinned, of course, but their sin was forced upon them by outside forces. They had no choice but to sin against the Negro people. That is the theme, intent and net effect of *Intruder in the Dust*.

To prove his point, Faulkner has abandoned the degenerates, the idiots, who were the protagonists of his previous novels. The three main characters of his new novel are all healthy people—a clear-thinking upper-middle-class boy of 16; his uncle, who is a lawyer, and an old Negro, who respects himself and refuses to kowtow to white supremacy.

The story concerns itself with the prevention of the lynching of the Negro, who has been falsely accused of murdering a no-good white man.

The first 150 pages or so of the novel are a brilliant evocation of the development of the consciousness of the adolescent Southern youth to a realization of the injustice inflicted on the Negro people by Southern whites. Faulkner shows how contact of the youth with the old Negro farmers clears away the prejudices foisted upon him by a white supremacy tradition and propaganda. The stream-of-consciousness technique lends itself admirably to a portrayal of this type.

But Faulkner's style of writing is meant to do more than just that in this particular novel. The form has a deliberately shrewd and sly motive which becomes obvious on page 153 and the following pages. The style of the writing is blended with the content of the story to hypnotize the reader into a belief in the righteousness of the white heroes so that he will accept everything they do or say as righteous.

The white boy has come to realize the injustice done the Negro people. The white boy, with the aid of a Negro youth his own age, an ancient white spinster, his lawyer uncle, and the sheriff, has saved the life of the old Negro farmer by finding the real murderer.

Then suddenly, without prior warning, the lawyer uncle introduces a new note. He must justify the white lynchers.

"It's because we alone in the United States (I'm not speaking of Sambo right now; I'll get to him in a minute) are a homogeneous people. . . . The New Englander is too of course back inland from the coastal spew of Europe which this country quarantined unrootable into the rootless ephemeral cities. . . ."

So Faulkner finally comes out into the open. The reason for the degeneracy of his South is the influx of "foreigners," who are destroying his "Anglo-Saxon civilization."

Faulkner has the lawyer uncle expand his theme: "That's why we must resist the North: not just to preserve ourselves nor even the two of us as one to remain one nation because that will be the inescapable byproduct of what we will preserve: which is the very thing that three generations ago we lost a bloody war in our own back yards so that it remain intact: the postulate that Sambo is a human being living in a free country and hence must be free. That's what, we are really defending: the privilege of setting him free ourselves..."

Faulkner thus lies about history and his own motives. He blames the non-Anglo-Saxons for his plight. But it was the Anglo-Saxons—and the "foreigners"—in the North, in New England and the West, who fought to free the slaves. And the Southern white supremacists fought the Civil War not for the privilege of freeing the slaves but to maintain the slave power.

But Faulkner is frightened by his realization that the Negro people are not waiting for the Southern white supremacists to free them. That is the real meaning of the proud figure of the old Negro farmer in *Intruders in the Dust*.

Faulkner recognizes that the Negro cannot be beaten by force. And he sees the danger involved in the possibility of unity between the Negro people of the South, the poor whites of the South, and the people of the rest of the United States. So Faulkner would bribe the Negro people with honeyed promises to come over to his side in a civil war to conquer the United States for the white supremacists.

Thus does Faulkner finally reveal the stinking sore whose pus has infected all of his previous writing. Yes, there is this evil in the South. But it is not his fault, he cries out. It was forced upon his people. And now, he says, the time has come to root out this evil by fighting and conquering the North, the East and the West which imposed it on them.

But Faulkner does a service for the people of our nation of which he is unaware. He exposes once and for all the hypocrisy of those so-called southern liberals, who beg piously to be left alone to solve the problems of Negro-white relations. Their real objective is conquest of the United States for the white supremacists. Fascist dictatorship by the Southern Anglo-Saxon superman.

If you think this is an exaggeration, here is what Faulkner has the adolescent white youth declare near the end of the book: "We are in the position of the German after 1933 who had no other alternative between being either a Nazi or a Jew...."

Max Miller.
"Faulkner Opus Fails to Impress Reviewer." San Diego *Union,* October 17, 1948, p. 11-D.

For an author who has received so much national publicity as William Faulkner, and who is considered almost legendarily "great" by so many, I still wonder why he feels obliged to resort so much to the old hokum of mumbo-jumbo. But he does this old trick again in his new novel, *Intruder in the Dust*, his first novel since 1940.

And if you ask me to name exactly what the novel is about, or what the author himself is trying to say, I am afraid I cannot tell you.

And simply because the author himself wants it that way, I suppose. For if readers cannot often understand what an author is writing, the readers are likely to think: "Ah, this author must be deep. He must be very deep, ah me."

Yet the truth is more likely not to be that way at all. What such authors are doing really is throwing out their words, letting them stay where they fall, and leaving the work up to the reader to sort them out into any kind of sense, if there is any.

For instance, one sentence in *Intruder in the Dust* occupies more than five pages without a stop or a period or a paragraph.

And that, sir, is just plain theatricalism. Such is not good writing or necessarily "deep" writing. It is merely a stunt.

Of course if readers do want to wade through all such underbrush, and try to untangle it, and if the readers do happen to find a thought or two which makes sense, then the readers may flatter themselves with their own wisdom. "I'm the only one who can understand this author. He's too deep for others."

But that's merely kidding oneself. For the best writing is always the simplest writing, the writing in which the author has done his utmost not to have a superfluous word, not to be running all around in circles in hopes that sooner or later in the dangling paragraph he may say something.

William Faulkner proved in *Sanctuary* long ago that he does not have to put on a tricky sideshow every time he writes anything. But in *Intruder in the Dust* he sideshows himself all over the place. He screams for attention. So much so that one of these days they may have to develop a "code" for him, the same as with James Joyce or with Gertrude Stein. And this may be considered the ultimate of success.

But to me it's still just plain old baloney. The English language is sufficient enough, if used simply enough, to get any idea or story across—providing the author has one.

August Derleth.
"Three Novels."
Madison (Wis.) *Capital Times*, October 24, 1948, p. 40.

Not since the memorable *Light in August* (1932) has Mr. Faulkner done as good a novel as *Intruder in the Dust*. The entire action of this curious but impressive novel, which is impressive despite manifest flaws, concerns a projected lynching which does not, after all, occur. It does not take place because Lucas Beauchamp once befriended a white boy who, believing him innocent, undertakes to prove it, and does so. Lucas Beauchamp is one of Faulkner's most major characters; his concern is not with the attempt to lynch him, but stubbornly, with the conviction that he is as good as anybody else, white or black; he is thus a focus for community hatred, and at the same time the symbol of the entire conflict between whites and blacks in the South.

Beauchamp endures despite everything, and that, in a very real sense, is typical of the southern Negro, of the problem of racial discrimination, of the social forces at work within that problem. *Intruder in the Dust* is not a long novel, but it is singularly complete within its frame; it is in a sense a very skillfully constructed novel, and yet, in another it annoys because its rhetoric is involved, and needlessly so. It has in it some remarkably bad passages, but these are greatly offset by the greater number of singularly fine passages. Indeed, some of the prose in this novel is among the best Faulkner has done.

What *Intruder in the Dust* demonstrates above everything else, whatever its shortcomings, is that Faulkner is almost alone among the novelists of the 1930's who has developed consistently, making a slow but steady progress upward. This novel is unquestionably one of Faulkner's best; it is a novel that must be read by anyone who pretends to be seriously interested in American letters, for, both as one of Faulkner's best, and as one of the best among contemporary American novels, it demands an understanding audience.

What Faulkner has to say in this book has grown out of a long apprenticeship not only in writing of the South but in living in that important region of the United States. Its 247 pages mark a significant return to trends first discernible in *Light in August*.

Joseph Henry Jackson. "Faulkner's South." San Francisco *Chronicle*, November 10, 1948, p. 20.

It is possible to judge Mr. Faulkner's prose confusing indeed; most readers find themselves balked, time and again, by the wandering sentences, the double-packed parentheses, often the outright lack of grammar, in the style he employs.

Nevertheless, Faulkner has adopted his style for a purpose, and if the reader is willing to work at reading him, he accomplishes that purpose. He is difficult, but, as has been said before, what one gets from a work of art depends greatly upon what one is willing to bring to it.

Those who have (a) learned to accept Faulkner's manner, or (b) are willing to roll up mental sleeves and sweat over his prose, are likely to find *Intruder in the Dust*, rewarding as a work of art. Such readers, however, may also discover, hand-

in-hand with a certain brand of tolerance, some of the intransigence, not merely of the Old South but of other parts of the U.S. which "hate foreigners." It is easy to underline both these aspects of the book, as this review will do in a moment.

First the story and its immediate purpose:

The trouble with Lucas Beauchamp was that he had too much self-respect for a Negro in his part of the South. He had white blood in him, but that wasn't all of it. Lucas simply did not register the automatic humility required of any Negro in Mississippi. He was not aggressive. He was not arrogant. He was just himself. But that was too much for the white people there. For years they had been thinking: "We got to make him be a nigger first." No one said it, exactly, nor did Lucas do anything definite to which they could object. He simply acted like a man, not like a man of a particular pigmentation.

Then he was suspected of killing a white man. By an accident—it was Sunday—the lynching that would otherwise have followed immediately was put off. That afforded certain interested people—notably a white boy in whom a clarification of ideas and emotions had taken place after Lucas had pulled him out of the creek some time before—an opportunity to clear him of the crime. Lucas came closer to being lynched than any Negro had ever come and lived to see another day. He had not changed; he was the same Lucas. But the whole community had been through a spirit-shaking readjustment, a kind of moral purge.

As far as it may be boiled down so briefly, that is Mr. Faulkner's story here.

Some of what he intends to say by his story is clear enough. He feels, so it seems to me, that the South must be left to take care of the Negro problem itself, and that bit by bit, it eventually will realize that

"Too many of us . . . are willing to sell liberty short at any tawdry price for the sake of . . . a constitutional statutory license to pursue each his private postulate of happiness and contentment regardless of grief or cost, even to the crucifixion of someone whose . . . pigment we don't like."

This is plain, and suggests that Mr. Faulkner is carrying the torch of tolerance. But what becomes of his attitude when he makes special mention, apropos the homogeneity of the U.S., of New England's failure to recognize the menace of "the coastal spew of Europe which this country quarantined unrootable into the rootless ephemeral cities?" One can deduce only that Mr. Faulkner has made up his own definition of homogeneity, (and of tolerance), and that this definition will admit the Negro (though only after the South, in defiance of the North, exercises "the privilege of setting him free ourselves"), but does not admit "the coastal spew of Europe," whatever that may mean.

It is worth noting here, I think, that those who use such terms never define the parts of Europe they mean. Or perhaps, come to think of it, such writers would find it rather awkward to say in cold print—the U.S. still being what it is—"the coastal spew of Europe, excepting, of course, such immigrants as have been of Anglo-Saxon, Celtic, Teutonic or Scandinavian backgrounds."

To be sure, Mr. Faulkner may mean something else, though I don't know what. As I've noted, it isn't always easy to be sure exactly what he does mean, since he chooses to sacrifice clarity for strength of effect in his writing. In any event, *Intruder in the Dust* is a powerful novel if you are pleased to forget clarity for the sake of the cumulative effect of its style. Maybe, anyway, it is not fair to expect an artist whose chief interest lies in producing strong effects to be both clear and logical as well.

Granville Hicks. *"Intruder in the Dust." Tomorrow*, January 1949, pp. 57–58.

William Faulkner's new novel has not only reached a wider audience than any of its predecessors, with the possible exception of *Sanctuary;* it has interested and challenged the reviewers, calling forth an extensive and impressive body of critical analyses. I do not know how many critics would vote for Faulkner as the "best" or the "greatest" living American novelist, and I don't suppose that such a poll would mean much, but it is significant that there is no other contemporary writer about whom the critics can find so much to say.

As almost everyone must have gathered by now, *Intruder in the Dust* is among other things a beautiful example of Faulkner's narrative skill, readable, exciting, even melodramatic. In its fundamentals it has the lovely simplicity of a fable, the fable, say, of the lion and the mouse, with a stubborn old Negro in the role of the lion and a white boy figuring, very much to his credit, as the mouse. Needless to say, Faulkner is not content to deal with the situation in these simple terms, but he keeps the dramatic effectiveness of the fable, and righteousness triumphs in satisfying fashion.

It is also generally known that *Intruder in the Dust* is the most overtly political book that Faulkner has written. However, it is not true, as some reviewers seem to have assumed, that he has only recently become aware of the Negro problem. The ideas, as well as most of the characters and themes, of *Intruder in the Dust* are carried over from the short stories published in *Go Down, Moses* (1942), and essentially the same ideas will be found in *The Unvanquished* (1938). Faulkner has always had a passionate sympathy with the Negroes and a tragic sense of the problems involved in Negro-white relationships. He has always felt, furthermore, that southerners must solve these problems and that only southerners can.

What he has done in *Intruder in the Dust* is to create a highly articulate lawyer, the uncle of the boy who saves the old Negro, and let him set forth sundry arguments in defense of the position Faulkner has held for so long. That Faulkner bothers to put these arguments in the altogether suitable mouth of Gavin Stevens indicates, of course, that the issue now has for him a special urgency: the time has come when the south must act and the north must not. It is this sense of crisis that is new, and because of it Faulkner seems to have concocted some of his arguments rather hastily, but there is nothing new or hasty about the general position they are intended to defend. Nor does the novel stand or fall by the turgid dialectics of Uncle Gavin; even as a statement of faith, and certainly as a novel, it is validated by Faulkner's extraordinary insight into the complicated structure of human responsibility and human guilt.

Finally, something must be said, though much has already been written, about the style in which Faulkner has chosen to tell his story and communicate his insights. It is a difficult style, chiefly because of the long sentences, some of which run to six or eight pages. These sentences have their own clarity; they can, for instance, be read aloud with little or no trouble; but they do stagger the eye. The question anyone has to ask is why Faulkner, who can write a prose as crisp as Ernest Hemingway's whenever he wants, has chosen thus to impose upon the reader's patience.

Although his handling of syntax has always been reckless, the six-page sentence, hurtling along without much punctuation except parentheses and double parentheses, has been a recent development, introduced in *Go Down, Moses* and perfected in *Intruder in the Dust*. Its purpose in the latter book can sometimes be discerned, notably in the wonderful description—a sentence of merely three and a half pages—of the lynchers' flight from Jefferson. Here, while Chick is kept poised on the brink of hysteria, his fantastic vision unfolds, until he is just caught back from the edge of wild laughter and tears. Here the device does work, making us feel that the vision is instantaneous and complete. And perhaps that is what Faulkner is always driving at, trying to circumvent the damage that grammar, or any other kind of logic, does to all vital processes, to thought and speech and life itself. At any rate he has to be given the benefit of the doubt; he has won that right by the seriousness of his devotion to his art and by the magnitude of his indisputable achievement. Whatever effort *Intruder in the Dust* demands of the reader, it fully repays.

Eudora Welty. "Department of Amplification." *New Yorker,* January 1, 1949, pp. 50–51.

Jackson Mississippi
December 15, 1948

To the Editors, *The New Yorker,*
Gentlemen:

How well Illinois or South Dakota or Vermont has fared in *The New Yorker* book-review column lately, I haven't noticed, but Mississippi was pushed under three times in two weeks, and I am scared we are going to drown, if we know enough to.

It's that combination "intelligent . . . despite" that we're given as a verdict each time. The "intelligent" refers to the books or their characters and the "despite" refers to the authors' living in Mississippi. Now there's one who is not only intelligent despite, but, it appears, not quite intelligent enough because of. In fact, one of this country's most highly respected critics writes three or four pages in a recent *New Yorker* on one of the great writers and begrudges him his greatness, and I do feel like "noticing."

Edmund Wilson, reviewing *Intruder in the Dust*, by William Faulkner, reaches one of his chief points in the paragraph:

> To be thus out of date, as a Southerner, in feeling and in language and in human relations, is, for a novelist, a source of strength. But Faulkner's weakness has also its origin in the antiquated community he inhabits, for it consists in his not having mastered—I speak of the design of his books as wholes as well as of that of his sentences and paragraphs—the discipline of the Joyces, Prousts, and Conrads (though Proust had his solecisms and what the ancients called anacolutha). If you are going to do embroidery, you have to watch every stitch; if you are going to construct a complex machine, you have to have every part tested. The technique of the modern novel, with its ideal of technical efficiency, its specialization of means for ends, has grown up in the industrial age, and it has a good deal in common with the other manifestations of that age.

In practicing it so far from such cities as produced the Flauberts, Joyces, and Jameses, Faulkner's provinciality, stubbornly cherished and turned into an asset, inevitably tempts him to be slipshod and has apparently made it impossible for him to acquire complete expertness in an art that demands of the artist the closest attention and care.

That last sentence, born in New York, has the flaw of a grammatical mistake; I don't know what being out of date in feeling means; and I didn't mind looking up "anacolutha"—but to get through to the point, *Intruder in the Dust* itself having been forgotten earlier in the piece, I shy at this idea of novel writing as a competitive, up-to-the-minute technical industry, if only for the picture it gives me of Mr. Faulkner in a striped cloth cap, with badge and lunchbox, marching in to match efficiency with the rest only to have Boss Man Wilson dock him—as an example, too—for slipshod bolt-and-nut performance caused by unsatisfactory home address. Somehow, I feel nobody could go on from there, except S. J. Perelman, and he works in another department.

It's as though we were told to modify our opinion of Cézanne's painting because Cézanne lived not in Paris but by preference in Aix and painted Aix apples—"stubbornly" (what word could ever apply less to the quality of the imagination's working?).

Such critical irrelevance, favorable or unfavorable, the South has long been used to, but now Mr. Wilson fancies it up and it will resound a little louder. Mr. Faulkner all the while continues to be capable of passion, of love, of wisdom, perhaps of prophecy, toward his material. Isn't that enough?

Such qualities can identify themselves anywhere in the world and in any century without furnishing an address or references. Should this disconcert the critic who cannot or does not write without furnishing his? Well, maybe it should.

Mr. Wilson has to account for the superior work of Mr. Faulkner, of course he has to, and to show why the novelist writes his transcendent descriptions, he offers the explanation that the Southern man-made world is different looking, hence its impact is different, and those adjectives come out. (Different looking—to whom?) Could the simple, though superfluous, explanation not be that the recipient of the impact, Mr. Faulkner, is the different component here, possessing the brain as he does, and that the superiority of the work done lies in that brain?

Mr. Faulkner (if report of his custom is true) has probably not bothered to look at the reviews of his book; he certainly doesn't need a defender of any sort; but it's hard to listen to anyone being condescended to, and to a great man being condescended to pretentiously. Nearly all writers in the world live, or in their day lived, out of the U.S. North and the U.S. South alike, taking them by and large and over random centuries. (Only Mr. Wilson is counting for the city vs. the country, to my sketchy knowledge.) And it does seem that in criticizing a novel there could be more logic and purity of judgment than Mr. Wilson shows in pulling out a map. In final estimate he places Faulkner up with the great, as well he might, but with a corrective tap asks him—maybe twice—to stand on just a little lower step for the group picture, to bring out a point in the composition. I still don't think the picture turned out too clear, somebody was bound to move.

For of course there's such a thing as a literary frame of reference that isn't industrial New York City in 1948, just as there's a literary frame through which one can look and not find "pages" of Mr. Faulkner's "The Bear" "almost opaque." "Opaque"—to whom? To Mr. Wilson I would say that I believe they are clear to me (for one example—((queer eyesight and all))), remembering too that each of us is just one looker. The important thing is that Mr. Faulkner's pages are here to look at.

Yours sincerely,
EUDORA WELTY

Anne Chamberlain. "Faulkner's Newest Book Intrigues." Wheeling *News-Register*, March 6, 1949, Part III, p. 9.

Intruder in the Dust, by William Faulkner, combines a hairraising narrative with the brooding, subtle literary style that has made the writer famous. It's an expert blending. It makes this—Faulkner's first novel in 10 years—one of the best books of this time, and certainly one to be reckoned with for years to come.

The suspense story unwinds with all the chills and thrills of a master whodunit. If Lucas, that arrogant and quiet Negro, did not shoot the white man in the back, who did? Will Lucas be lynched before his innocence is proven? What will the frightened 16-year-old boy, the old lady, and the loyal servant find when they dig up a corpse in the middle of the night? Who lurks in the shadows beyond the graveyard and who stalks free and murderous as the mob gathers outside of Lucas' cell?

Gripping as it is, the plot is a minor consideration in the worth of the novel. It binds the story tightly; it makes the reader turn the pages too rapidly; it practically forces one re-reading. For the narrative is the vibrating cord on which Faulkner strings the rich and intricate history of this little southern town. Into it is woven his understanding and his horror, his love, his prejudice, his blind, basic devotion to his people. The race question has never been treated with more intense and brilliant objectivity, or with more feeling—for both sides. Few characters in modern fiction can surpass the proud and hateful Lucas. Or the confused white youth, so abruptly hurled into adulthood.

A word about Faulkner's prose style, which has sometimes seemed too involved for the average, impatient reader. Either we have just learned how to read him, or this book is a vast improvement on his other novels. The sentences are often nearly page-long; the leap from present to past and back is sometimes momentarily disconcerting, but the final effect is one of crystal clarity. There is, we think, a trick of adjustment to reading Faulkner. Conditioned as American readers are to short, staccatic sentences—or to long ones which wind up senselessly—we simply have to orientate ourselves to the relaxed and graceful flow of this writer's prose. Do not try to read him hurriedly; do not—mentally—hold your breath when you plunge into a sentence. Take it easy; let the sound and the rhythmical motion of the phrases roll deep into mind and memory. If the violent plot of this book sends you gasping and struggling through the pages, you can look forward to a wealthy second reading. He's worth it.

Mary Auld. "What Do You Like to Read?" McKeesport, (Pa.) *News,* March 23, 1949, Section II, p. 23.

If it's the new Faulkner book:—

Unlike many of the leading writers of his generation William Faulkner has not, in his latest book, *Intruder in the Dust,* been reduced to licking around the edges of contemporary American life and taking little snarling nips at its fringes. He, on the contrary, plunges into the heart of a dramatic situation—and one not uncommon in the South, the district of which he almost invariably writes—and produces a novel of depth and affirmation, philosophically speaking.

Mr. Faulkner's style of writing, although it has influenced many young hopefuls during the past two decades, has proved to be most difficult to imitate. His words pour onto the page, apparently direct from his subconscious rather than his conscious thinking; sometimes their juxtaposition is highly unconventional; punctuation, sparingly used, leans toward the semicolon; often the choice of vocabulary startles the reader, but always the thought flows surely and distinctly. It's the sort of thing that grates on the nerves a bit at first, —gradually, however, becoming natural and pleasant and preferable.

The story, although basically simple, is so cleverly contrived that it carries the reader along from one level of suspense to the next in a pyramidal build-up. Only a master of narration could achieve so stirring an effect without the aid of the least suspicion of melodrama. Scenes of gruesome horror become feasible through the author's matter of fact approach and his effective use of understatement.

But by all odds the most startling aspect of the novel to those familiar with Mr. Faulkner's work lies in its richly affirmative philosophy. The bestiality of men in the mob is here frustrated by the moral stature and basic integrity of a very young man, an old woman and a faithful servant.

That good triumphs over evil, thereby producing repercussions through the community for good, makes this novel strangely incompatible with the other products of the school of writing with which Mr. Faulkner has always been associated in the reader's mind. Perhaps maturity is responsible for this excellent book in which the characters, setting and action blend into what may well be considered the author's finest book to date.

Charles I. Glicksbery. "*Intruder in the Dust.*" *Arizona Quarterly*, 5 (Spring 1949), 85–88.

If a newcomer to fiction had submitted the manuscript of this novel for consideration by a publisher, it would most likely have been rejected as promptly and decisively as *Sanctuary* was before Faulkner achieved recognition. It has all the glaring faults that would disqualify a beginner: a pretentious vocabulary, a baroque style, a thesis which, though skillfully integrated within the context of the story, is ridden hard for all it is worth. Even so, the most memorable feature of this novel is not the story but the "moral," which stands out sharply and challengingly; the entire plot is so constructed as to elaborate and emphasize the author's central convictions about the Negro problem in the South.

The story itself does not amount to much, but, as is usual with Faulkner, his method of presentation is so subtle, so powerful, and so complex that he carries the reader along with him, in spite of the purple patches and the rather pretentious theorizing. Lucas Beauchamp, a Negro, is accused of having shot a white man in the back. The rest of the plot is taken up with the attempt to prove his innocence and to frustrate the milling mob, many of them kinsmen of the murdered man, from lynching the Negro. The grave of the murdered man is dug up in the thick of night by a white lad, helped by a Negro boy and an elderly lady. When the news finally gets around that Lucas Beauchamp did not commit the deed, the lynching mob quickly disperses. The Negroes come out of hiding; the town resumes its normal life.

A bare outline such as this is totally inadequate to suggest the nightmarish intensity with which each incident is developed, nor can it suggest the vibrant metaphysical overtones of the novel. *Intruder in the Dust* is of special importance in that it demonstrates unmistakably that Faulkner's rigorous naturalistic method in the past was but a mask worn for the occasion. Here the disguise is thrown off and his views on the vexed Negro problem are revealed in all their reactionary violence. Faulkner, like some other Southern writers, is still engaged in fighting the Civil War. In effect, he is telling Northerners and Westerners who suffer from the reformer's itch (and anyone who wishes to raise the condition of the Negro is, by definition, a "reformer"), to mind their own business, since they have no comprehension of the complexity of the problem and how it must be solved gradually, if it is to be solved at all. The South, we are given to understand, will clean house in its own scrupulous, fair-minded, traditional way. Though this will take time it will eventually be done—but not by the ineffectual methods of legal compulsion or force recommended so urgently by humanitarians and liberals up North.

Yet Faulkner is fundamentally too honest and too conscientious a novelist to gloss over the truth. Lucas Beauchamp is drawn as a singularly compelling character, self-composed, sure of himself, a man not to be contradicted. The South is pictured as hagridden by a guilty, paranoiac awareness of the Negro's presence. The youngster, Charles, the peg on which the story is made to hang, makes the exciting discovery that even Negroes can grieve for the dead, that Negroes have their integrity and incorruptible pride. But much, too much, is made of the penetrating odor of Negroes. Most Southerners, according to Faulkner, accept the smell as irrefutable proof of ingrained racial differences. They cannot imagine an existence in which that disturbing "racial" odor would be missing. In addition, Lucas is portrayed as being too independent in spirit, too indomitable, for the comfort of the whites in that region. He must be humbled, taught a lesson, made to act the part of a "nigger."

Faulkner is at best in describing the psychology of the mob waiting for the inciting word of command, the mob morbidly drawn to this scene of purgation by blood, this apotheosis by fire. Yet Faulkner, strangely enough, endeavors to exonerate these people of guilt. The code requires that all such violations by Negroes be punished by lynching the offender; then the slate is wiped clean, and it is possible to begin all over again. These are the rules according to which "the game" is played in the South. Indeed, that is what the Negroes themselves count on. The Negroes must behave like Negroes and the whites like white folk. When this happens—once the blood-fury is appeased—there is no hard feeling on either side.

Still the instinct for justice is not to be denied; Charles is determined that Lucas shall not die simply because his skin is black. He digs up a grave to save a reputed Negro murderer from the wild vengeance of the community. The uncle, another Faulknerian mouthpiece, philosophizes at some length on the capacity of the Negro to endure all sorts of suffering, and still survive. Now all this may be defended as the dramatic projection of a character in the story, representative of a certain point of view to be found in the South, but it is repeated too often and given too much space, to be accidental. What Faulkner is doing (if he is present all the time behind his creation) is to reject the postulate on which the concept of democracy rests; namely, the assumption that just as people, black or white, cannot endure slavery, so all men yearn to achieve genuine freedom, the recognition of their fundamental humanity. The amazing thing is that the youngster Charles, really the protagonist in the story (if it can be said to have any protagonist), the spokesman for the author's point of view, is made to agree with the uncle. He discovers a mystical identity between man and the soul of his forebears, an identity which the alien, forever cut off from this blood-communion, cannot hope to understand. The North is incapable of comprehending the condition of the South, the problem it must work out for itself, without aid or interference from the outside. The North is the plague to be resisted and defied. It is intolerable that the North, filled with alien, gullible masses, should pass outrageous, slanderous judgements on the South.

It is the uncle who articulates the thought of the presumably enlightened members of the South. The South, he feels is the only community which still has a homogeneous population, and this is sufficient reason for resisting the colossus of the North. Faulkner, speaking through the medium of the uncle, is willing to concede that the reforms the Northerners are clamoring for are desirable and indeed inevitable, but it cannot be done, he insists, by legislation or constitutional amendments or dint of force. It must be a slow evolutionary process, the outgrowth of folk-accommodation. The uncle is willing to accept even Lucas Beauchamp (or Sambo, as he calls him) as a homogeneous man. What he deplores is "Sambo's" efforts to imitate not the best but the second-best of the white race, its flashy vulgarity, its mediocrity, its political corruption, its passion for wealth. He believes in the "Sambo" who has rooted himself firmly and lovingly in the Southland, the "Sambo" who can endure because he is sustained by patience, even when he is without hope, because he is in love with simple elemental things; his mule, his land, his hearth, his children, his religion.

Yet the uncle is perceptive enough to recognize the tyrannical influence Lucas Beauchamp and his brethren exercise over the conscience of the white community. However vindictive in temper, the community knows that this is so. It is a feeling which cannot be beaten down, a feeling for justice, a sense of conscience, and even of pity. In fact, the uncle maintains that he is defending the cause of Lucas Beauchamp against the North and East and West, against those who seem to believe that man's injustice to man can be abolished overnight by the police. He admits the injustice frankly and the need for expiation, but this expiation must take place without help or advice. At the end, Charles, too, comes to the realization that he is one with his people, bearing their shame and need for expiation. He understands at last what his mission is: to defend not only the South but also the United States against the meddling North and East and West, for their aim is to divide the nation. All Southerners would band together with unanimous solidarity against the use of force or any interference on the part of outsiders, especially theorists and do-gooders who are miles removed from the scene and do not understand the situation in the South. After all, in the North are to be found irrational hatreds and discriminations and forms of vengeance against foreigners and racial minorities even more cruel than those operative in the South.

It is unfair, of course, to tear all this out of context, but if it is meant as Faulkner's intransigent message to the North and the West, his apologia for the condition of the Negro in the South, then it is deplorable and appaling. No amount of genius can disguise the propagandist character of these fulminations. The South, convinced of its own righteousness, determined to keep the Negro in caste-bondage until such time as it sees fit to release him from this state—the South is again threatening to secede from the Union.

Intruder in the Dust represents dangerous doctrine. It marks a regression from the fine objectivity and naturalistic insight of the author who had composed *Light in August* and *Absalom, Absalom!* An angry, embittered, tendentious novel, it is by no means Faulkner at his best. The psychological analyses are crude and amateurish; dog-eared dogmas are offered as profound revelations of the human soul; stale metaphysical reflections and inept anthropological lore are trotted out to vindicate the backward and oppressive tribal code of the South. If Faulkner is maintaining that the South harbors some noble and exalted spirits, men of tender conscience, high sense of honor, and profound humanity, who would deny it? If he is asking that the South, because of its rich past, racial homogeneity, and historic traditions, be granted a special dispensation, exempt from the laws of democracy that are supposed to apply to all men, black as well as white, then he is guilty of darkening counsel.

Checklist of Additional Reviews

"Intruder in the Dust." Kirkus, August 1, 1948, p. 374.

Retail Bookseller, September, 1948.

Syracuse (N.Y.) Post Standard, October 2, 1948.

"Intruder in the Dust." Newsweek, October 4, 1948, p. 91.

"A Way Out of the Swamp?" Time, October 4, 1948, pp. 108–12.

"Intruder in the Dust." Wichita Eagle, October 6, 1948, p. 6.

"Of This 'n' That." Wilmington (N.C.) Morning News, October 7, 1948, p. 9.

Santa Maria Times, October 8, 1948.

"Intruder in the Dust." San Francisco Call Bulletin, October 19, 1948, p. 12.

"Faulkner Novel." Knoxville News-Sentinel, October 24, 1948, p. 2-C.

"Intruder in the Dust." College English, 10 (December 1948), 178.

"Intruder in the Dust." Promenade, December 1948.

"Intruder in the Dust." Booklist, December 1, 1948, p. 120.

Saturday Review, December 4, 1948.

"Intruder in the Dust." South Bend (Ind.) Tribune, December 6, 1948, p. 6.

"Intruder in the Dust." Burlington (Vt.) Free Press, January 13, 1949, p. 6.

"Intruder in the Dust." Southside Journal (Los Angeles), July 21, 1949.

"Intruder in the Dust." Radio broadcast on KSAL (Salinas, Calif.) (copy in Random House files).

Arnold, Betty Lou. "Intruder in the Dust." Weymouth (Mass.) Gazette, January 20, 1949, p. 4.

Ashford, Gerald. San Antonio Express, November 22, 1948.

Avery, Emmett L., and L. E. Buchanan. "Faulkner Novel a 'Civil Rights' Mystery." Spokane Spokesman-Review, October 10, 1948, Magazine Section, p. 13.

B., B. "It's Still Faulkner." Rochester (N.Y.) Democrat and Chronicle, November 7, 1948, p. 10-D.

Barzun, Jacques. "The New Books." Harper's Magazine, December 1948, pp. 102–8.

Beauchamp, Elise. "Faulkner on Murder." New Orleans Times-Picayune, October 17, 1948, Section II, p. 17.

Bole, Allen. "Faulkner Novel Probes South's Racial Problem." Hartford Times, September 25, 1948, p. 19.

Brady, Charles A. "William Faulkner Continues His Soliloquy on the South." Buffalo Evening News, September 25, 1948, Magazine Section, p. 5.

Breit, Harvey. "Faulkner after Eight Years: A Novel of Murder and Morality." New York Times Book Review, September 26, 1948, p. 4.

Bruce, Bill. "Mass Mind in Lynching Is Topic of Faulkner's Latest." Daily Texan (University of Texas), October 17, 1948.

Bunker, Robert. New Mexico Quarterly Review, 19 (Spring 1949), 108–15.

Butcher, Fanny. "William Faulkner Novel Pleads Negro's Case." Chicago Sunday Tribune, September 26, 1948, Part IV, p. 6.

Cheney, Frances Neel. "Novel Treats Race Problem." Nashville Banner, October 1, 1948, p. 36.

Comee, Edgar A. "Holiday Season Roundup from the Editor's Bookshelf." Portland. Sunday Telegram and Sunday Express Herald,

December 19, 1948, p. 20-A.

Conroy, Jack. "William Faulkner's Dixieland Is Getting More Sedate." Chicago *Sun-Times,* September 26, 1948, p. 8-X.

Cournos, John. *"Intruder in the Dust."* New Yerk *Sun,* September 27, 1948, p. 18.

Cowley, Malcolm. "William Faulkner's Nation." *New Republic,* October 18, 1948, pp. 21–22.

Daniel, Frank. "Yoknapatawpha County Law." Atlanta *Journal,* October 13, 1948, p. 35.

Daniel, Thomas H. "A New Faulkner Book, and Strange Writing." Columbia (S.C.) *Record,* October 28, 1948, p. 1-D.

Dean, Mary Scott. *"Intruder in the Dust."* El Paso *Herald Post,* November 13, 1948, p. 4.

Demarest, Michael. "Man's Injustice to Man." San Francisco *Argonaut,* October 1, 1948, p. 18.

Douglas, Marjory Stoneman. "Faulkner Probes Racial Relations." Miami *Herald,* September 26, 1948, p. 4-F.

Dwight, Ogden G. "Conscience of the South Stirs in the Latest Faulkner Novel." Des Moines *Sunday Register,* November 21, 1948, p. 5-A.

Elconin, Victor. "Hope Rests in the South." *Daily Oklahoman* (Oklahoma City), October 31, 1948, p. 8-D.

Filler, Louis. *"Intruder in the Dust."* *Antioch Review* (8 December 1948), 512.

Fineman, Morton. "William Faulkner Probes Conscience of the South." Philadelphia *Inquirer,* September 26, 1948, Book Section, p. 1.

Fuermann, George. "Notes on the Artistry of William Faulkner's Parables and Legends." Houston *Post,* October 3, 1948, Section IV, p. 16.

Gannett, Lewis. *"Intruder in the Dust."* New York *Herald Tribune,* September 28, 1948, p. 21.

Gehman, Richard B. "Faulkner's First in Eight Years." *Kirkeby Hotels,* October 1948, p. 61.

Geismar, Maxwell. "Ex-Aristocrat's Emotional Education." *Saturday Review of Literature,* September 25, 1948, pp. 8–9.

Giles, Barbara. *"Intruder in the Dust."* *Masses and Mainstream,* November 1948, pp. 78–81.

Glick, Nathan. "The Novelist as Elder Statesman." *Commentary,* 7 (May 1949), 502–4.

Gloster, Hugh M. "Southern Justice." *Phylon,* 10 (First Quarter 1949), 93–95.

Goldman, Rosetta. "Faulkner's New Novel." Brooklyn *Eagle,* October 10, 1948, p. 12.

Govan, Gilbert E. "Faulkner's South." Chattanooga *Times,* October 17, 1948, p. 25.

Grauel, George E. *"Intruder in the Dust."* *Best Sellers,* November 1, 1948, p. 163.

Greene, A. C. "South Finds Defender at Last in Faulkner's Novel." Abilene *Reporter-News,* September 26, 1948, p. 4.

Hanlon, Frank. "More Light on Race Problems." Philadelphia *Sunday Bulletin,* September 26, 1948, Metropolitan Section, p. 13.

Hansen, Harry. "Faulkner's New Novel about Negro." New York *World-Telegram,* September 27, 1948, p. 17. Also reviewed in "Books." *Redbook,* November 1948, p. 34.

Hardwick, Elizabeth. "Faulkner and the South Today." *Partisan Review,* 15 (October 1948), 1130–34.

Hart, H. W. *"Intruder in the Dust."* *Library Journal,* 73 (August 1948), 1089.

Howe, Irving. "The South and Current Literature." *American Mercury,* 67

(October 1948), 494–503.

Ingalls, Jeremy. "Victory and Tragedy in Human Relations." *Common Cause,* February 1949, pp. 277–78.

Jones, Carter Brooke. "Faulkner Novel Shows Radical Change in Style." Washington *Sunday Star,* September 26, 1948, p. 3-C.

Kielty, Bernardine. "Undercover Stuff." *Ladies' Home Journal,* October 1948, pp. 14–21.

Kiessling, E. C. "A New William Faulkner Novel." Milwaukee *Journal,* September 26, 1948, Section V, p. 4.

Killalea, Ed. "Faulkner's Latest Novel of South Has Seed of Hope." *Rocky Mountain News* (Denver), October 31, 1948, p. 16-A.

Klein, Francis A. "Faulkner Waves Reformers Away from the South." St. Louis *Globe-Democrat,* September 26, 1948, p. 7.

Kuhl, Arthur. "Faulkner on a New Tack after Eight-Year Silence." St. Louis *Star-Times,* September 29, 1948, p. 25.

Logal, Nelson W. "Prophetic Drama of Race Tensions." *Books on Trial,* 7 (October–November 1948), 126.

Lord, Ruth K. "A Picture of Mississippi." Louisville *Courier Journal,* October 31, 1948, Section III, p. 10.

Lytle, Andrew. *Sewanee Review,* (Winter 1949), 120–27.

Martin, Gertrude. "Treatment of Negro South's Own Business." Chicago *Defender,* October 23, 1948, p. 7.

Martin, Robert. "Faulkner Preaches on Southern Problems." Dallas *Times Herald,* September 26, 1948, Section VI, p. 4.

McGarey, Mary. *"Intruder in the Dust."* Columbus *Dispatch,* October 31, 1948, p. 9-F.

McVicker, Daphne Alloway. "Faulkner Changes Pace in New Novel *Intruder in the Dust.*" Columbus *Citizen,* October 31, 1948, Magazine Section, p. 8.

Merlin, Milton. "New William Faulkner Novel One of His Best." Los Angeles *Times,* October 17, 1948, Part IV, p. 6.

Mikules, Leonard. "The Common Reader." *Crenshaw Mirror* (Los Angeles), October 8, 1948, p. 10.

Milano, Paolo. "Faulkner in Crisis." *Nation,* October 30, 1948, pp. 496–97.

Millstein, Gilbert. "Faulkner the Mystic Turns Polemicist." New York *Star,* September 26, 1948, Pleasure Section, p. 13.

Minot, George. Berton *Herald,* September 29, 1948.

Moose, Roy C. *"Intruder in the Dust." Carolina Quarterly,* 1 (Fall 1948), 65–67.

Morrill, Claire. "Freedom Is Faulkner Book Thesis." Taos (N. Mex.) *Star,* December 2, 1948.

North, Sterling. *"Intruder in the Dust."* New York *Post,* September 26, 1948, p. 15-M.

Norton, Dan S. "This Man's Art and That Man's Scope." *Virginia Quarterly Review,* 25 (Winter 1949), 132–33.

Parsons, Eugene O. "Oddity of Fiction." Worcester (Mass.) *Sunday Telegram,* September 26, 1948, p. 4-C.

Paulus, John D. "William Faulkner's Novel Fails Because of Writing." Pittsburgh *Press,* November 28, 1948, p. 60.

Peyton, Ernest. "The Southern Problem of Negroes and Mob Violence." Fort Worth *Star-Telegram,* October 3, 1948, Section II, p. 11.

Phipps, Robert. "Jacket Blurb Proves a Help." Omaha *World Herald,*

September 26, 1948, p. 29-C.

Prescott, Orville. "Books of the Times." New York *Times,* September 27, 1948, p. 21; also reviewed as "Outstanding Novels." *Yale Review,* 38 (Winter 1949), 382.

Price, Emerson. "Faulkner's New Novel Is Unusual Thriller of South's Social Pattern." Cleveland *Press,* September 28, 1948, p. 25.

Querol, M. N. "The Black and the White." *Philippine Education Company News Magazine,* April 2, 1949.

Reynolds, Horace. "The Interior Country of William Faulkner." *Christian Science Monitor,* October 7, 1948, p. 11.

Robinson, Maude. "He's Allergic to Periods." Salt Lake City *Tribune,* October 3, 1948, p. 5-M.

Rogers, Leona. "Southern Rift Fatally Slow in Being Mended." Fort Wayne *News-Sentinel,* November 13, 1948, p. 6.

Rogers, W. G. "Lynching Problem Examined Anew in Faulkner's Novel." Cleveland *Plain Dealer,* September 26, 1948, p. 6-E.

Rolo, Charles J. "Yoknapatawpha County." *Atlantic Monthly,* November 1948, pp. 108–10.

S., M. *"Intruder in the Dust."* Columbia *Missourian,* November 17, 1948, p. 4.

Schuyler, Josephine. "An Unusual Mississippi Novel." Pittsburgh *Courier,* January 8, 1949, p. 25.

S[cott], W[infield] T[ownley]. "William Faulkner's Novel." Providence *Sunday Journal,* September 26, 1948, Section VI, p. 8.

Sherman, John K. "Faulkner Takes Lynching for Non-Comma Spin." Minneapolis *Sunday Tribune,* September 26, 1948, p. 15-W.

S[izer], A[lvin] V. "Bold But Involved Probing of the South's Conscience." New Haven *Register,* October 24, 1948, Magazine Section, p. 6.

Smith, Harry L. "Advice to Northerners." Richmond *Times-Dispatch,* September 26, 1948, p. 11-D.

Spearman, Walter. "Faulkner and the South." Durham *Morning Herald,* October 31, 1948, Section IV, p. 7.

Thomas, George Pryor. "Arty-Artful Style." Hartford *Courant,* December 12, 1948, Magazine Section, p. 12.

Truax, Charles. "Harsh Story of the South." Dayton *Daily News,* September 26, 1948, Section 10, p. 7.

Turner, E. S. "Faulkner Considers South's Race Problem." Syracuse *Herald American,* October 3, 1948.

W., W. "Puppets to Anger." Greensboro *Daily News,* October 31, 1948, Section II, p. 7.

Walton, Clarence. "Book Markers." Norfolk *Ledger,* February 2, 1949, p. 6.

W[eissblatt], H[arry] A. "Faulkner and the South." Trenton *Sunday Times Advertiser,* February 27, 1949, Section IV, p. 8.

Welty, Eudora. "In Yoknapatawpha." *Hudson Review,* 1 (Winter 1949), 596–98.

White, Mary Ann. *"Intruder in the Dust."* Los Altos (Calif.) *News,* January 6, 1949.

Wiener, Max. "Faulkner Falters." Newark (N.Y.) *Sunday News,* October 17, 1948, Section III, p. 42.

Wilson, Edmund. "William Faulkner's Reply to the Civil Rights Program." *New Yorker,* October 23, 1948, pp. 120–28. Reprinted in *Classics and Commercials.* New York: Farrar, Straus, 1950, pp. 460–70.

W[ood], D[aniel]. *"Intruder in the*

Dust." Pasadena *Star-News,* November 7, 1948, p. 41.

Wright, John A. "Novel Retells Negro Plight." Los Angeles *Mirror,* October 23, 1948, p. 34.

Yeiser, Frederick. "Faulkner Rings Some Changes on One of Favorite Themes." Cincinnati *Enquirer,* September 25, 1948, p. 5.

KNIGHT'S GAMBIT

WILLIAM FAULKNER

Knight's Gambit

RANDOM HOUSE NEW YORK

Blanche Hixson Smith. *"King's Gambit [sic]."* Meriden (Conn.) *Record,* November 11, 1949, p. 6.

"A new book by America's foremost novelist," is the Random House statement on the jacket of William Faulkner's *Knight's Gambit* just released from that publishing house. William Faulkner is certainly famous. This is his eighteenth volume and most of its predecessors are available in many translations in as many foreign countries. We are not sure whether he should be called "America's foremost," but he certainly slings English with powerful force. Likewise he has no formidable rival in his own generation to dispute with him the championship as teller-of-tales. He can make a simple story both exciting and profound.

However the story, or rather stories in *Knight's Gambit* are not simple. The book is really five separate stories told by a single narrator and built upon the activities in pursuit of justice-with-mercy of Uncle Gavin Stevens, who has appeared in other Faulkner stories about this same Mississippi county. We finished the first section entitled "Smoke" with great excitement. "Here," we said, "is the GREAT AMERICAN WRITER." The story is a superb study of twin brothers in whom inherited traits of character develop with such vast difference. Moreover these brothers are actors in a tremendously exciting mystery,—a whodunit of the cleverest type. Uncle Gavin is more interested in justice than in truth. He proceeds to demonstrate that there are tricks in all trades, and when the trick of a county prosecutor brings the real criminal to light it is justified.

But then we turned to the next chapter about a pathetic character named Monk.

Smack in the eye we were hit by this sentence in the first paragraph: "Because it is only in literature that the paradoxical and even mutually negativing anecdotes in the history of a human heart can be juxtaposed and annealed by art into verisimilitude and credibility." Now there ought to be a law against a sentence like that one. It almost stopped us in our tracks which would have meant that we would miss the balance of one of the finest books of the year. We assure all our readers that Mr. Faulkner indulges in no more such laborious obscurities. That is actually such bad writing that one wonders if he didn't put it in on purpose to bait his readers, and more particularly his critics. It is AWFUL.

But the story of moronic Monk, and his pitiable gropings for a free life is at once heart-breaking and horrifying. "Hand Upon the Waters" is superficially an exposition on the fallacy of believing there can be a "perfect crime," that is without leaving evidence that will trip the smartest criminal. It is also a tale of fidelity and devotion. "Tomorrow" and "An Error in Chemistry" are both murder stories, but their main purpose is to show that appearance of crime may be deceiving. And all these tales, connected as they are because of Gavin Stevens and his eternally swinging Phi Beta Kappa key earned at Harvard, are studies of the manners, superstitions, loyalties and shortcomings of the South. Gavin says "I am always more interested in justice and human beings than in truth." It is the human beings and the impact upon them of circumstances and environment that make these Faulkner tales far more important than most murder mystery writings.

The five incidents of these separate titles are rounded off by a long-short story from which the volume obtains its title. In this last section written about the narrator of the other five stories and his Uncle

Gavin, this white-haired, kindly, wise and witty gentleman is shown in a romantic, rosy light. We are entranced at this picture of a lover so faithful and so philosophical. And we are excited over the author's background for the romantic chronicle.

We have to admit that the Faulkner pen grows heavy here at times. We discovered one paragraph about inherited libraries and inherited experience that contained a single sentence running to twenty-five lines in length. And in the story are such things as "protagonist of a young girl's ephemeris." Indubitably (another Faulkner word) there are people who will read Faulkner and not need a dictionary at hand, but that doesn't mean this kind of phraseology is excusable. Its erudition is awkward. Having written so much about morons, cretins and deafmutes, it is as if Mr. Faulkner for his own satisfaction must prove he can wind his way through involved sentences and place in their proper context a nice variety of sixty-four-dollar words.

Christopher Matthew. "William Faulkner's New *Gambit*." Milwaukee *Journal*, November 6, 1949, Section V, p. 3.

The people you meet most often in William Faulkner's stories are the strange, substandard folks who inhabit the backwoods and backwaters of Mississippi. These animalistic bayou billies, naive and ferocious by turns, are also in the majority in Faulkner's new work, *Knight's Gambit*. But the hero of the six stories that comprise the book is an altogether different type of person. Gavin Stevens is one of nature's noblemen, a practitioner of the law who stands out among lawyers as Sherlock Holmes stands out among detectives.

As district attorney of "Yoknapatawpha" county Stevens is in fact a kind of Sherlock Holmes himself, and his Dr. Watson is his bright young nephew and protégé, Charles Mallison. Charles is a mere boy in the first story. He has just turned 18 in the last. He is sometimes the narrator, and always the admirer who is properly awed by his uncle's unpredictable moves in his favorite game of chess or in the larger game of checkmating criminals.

Uncle Gavin is a bachelor and a scholar. For years he has devoted one hour every day to the colossal task of translating the Old Testament from the original Hebrew into Greek. No one knows that it is a kind of penance for a youthful mistake that ended his chances with a 16 year old plantation belle.

Years before, when Stevens was a carefree student at Heidelberg, he happened to be carrying on a correspondence with two girls. One was the aforementioned belle whom he intended to marry, the other a Russian émigré with whom he was flirting by letter in German. One day he got his letters into the wrong envelopes.

The sultry Russian obviously couldn't make much of the English letter, but the southern miss had her German one translated. She decided that Gavin was poking fun at her. Not long after, she married a man she never loved—a bootlegger—and bore him two children, a boy and a girl who turned out to be hellions.

Thus the destiny, or shall we say the destination, of crossed letters ruined Uncle Gavin's best chance for marriage. But the day finally came when the bootlegger died and the young wildcats stormed into his office seeking legal advice. Their family affairs and emotions were tied into knots. With masterful skill Uncle Gavin unraveled every knot, then tied another large one which ended his days as a translator and began his career as a husband.

Thus the knight had finally won the fair lady, and the 25 years of bachelorhood had been a gambit—a sacrifice play in chess to gain a later advantage. During those 25 years he had become a folk hero in his county. The stories Faulkner tells about Stevens in the courtroom rival those told about Abraham Lincoln or Judge Priest.

He once convicted a murderer with a wisp of smoke enclosed in a tiny cigaret box; he tripped another by detecting a mistake in his fish story and a third by watching him mix his toddy. This last fellow, a Yankee showman, put the sugar in his whisky instead of in his water, as every southerner does.

Though each of the six stories is complete in itself, together they form a unit held together by the chief character. The copyrights indicate that they were published at various times during the last 17 years. All of them are written in what for Faulkner is straightforward prose, which is likely to enhance the enjoyment readers will derive from them.

Edward Parone. "What, No Images of Curve?" Hartford *Courant,* November 6, 1949, Magazine Section, p. 14.

The Critic and the Book Reviewer meet to talk over the SIGNIFICANCE of Bill Faulkner . . . [All ellipsis dots are in the original text.]

CRITIC: What we should be concerned with is the Overall pattern of the works, not the perfection or imperfection of mere parts. The Achievement of Faulkner is the success with which he has created a world, even a universe, or a form co-equal with content, so that you cannot discuss one aspect without keeping the other in mind. The world of his creation is a true art world, a world he made, alone and unafraid . . .

REVIEWER: But, sir, what about this book? Should anyone read it? Should anyone BUY it? Isn't it a good book all by itself? Can anyone walk up to the clerk and say, "I'll take this one here, please," without taking the rest of Faulkner too?

CRITIC: (Tolerantly) You cannot pick up this book without taking the rest of Faulkner too. Everything he has been has created this book.

REVIEWER: But you talk about art worlds, and drive people away by telling them they have to know all about a dozen other books before they can read this one. Don't you want anyone to read this book?

CRITIC: Yes. But I don't think anyone should be allowed, without warning, to read *Knight's Gambit* at the expense of not reading Faulkner. That is too high a price to pay for any book. If you mean, however, can the reader just grab the book and have what is called, by *Time,* a "bang-up" good time reading it, yes, I suppose so, but what an ultimately unsatisfying time he will have. The Elizabethan had a bang-up good time watching a play by Shakespeare, but whose satisfaction is keener from the play, his or ours?

REVIEWER: There you go, bringing in Shakespeare!

CRITIC: (Who cannot bring himself to say what he should say, i.e. "Ah, shut up".) You mistake me. I am not comparing Faulkner with Shakespeare; but I am saying that when we have perspective thrust upon us we cannot look at a thing as though we had nothing but bare facts.

REVIEWER: (Anxiously) Anyway, let's just take this one book, just for the sake of argument and see if it's any good. I know we shouldn't and all that, but let's do it anyway.

CRITIC: Very well. Begin.

REVIEWER: The story "Smoke" is a kind of thwarted *King Lear* affair with the man who instinctively wouldn't divide up his land with his children and ended up . . .

CRITIC: Perhaps. Then again, these are kinds of detective stories, no? And this is a story about Gavin Stevens, isn't it, and only incidentally about Old Anse and his sons? The hero of this story and the book is Stevens; and the town of Jefferson, which makes up the world of Faulkner, is part of him and he part of it, and he is not on another side of the fence from his "enemies"; they are both on the same side, in the same world. The same world produced both of them.

REVIEWER: But what about the madman who comes down from the hills on the roads that civilization brought; and the House Beautiful monstrosity the bootlegger built out of a wonderful old house?

CRITIC: The madman and the monster house are, so to speak, both latent in the world, and no more of another world than the car Gavin Stevens uses to accomplish his missions.

REVIEWER: And that's another thing. Stevens is the God of Light descending on the scene to dispense justice, almost in his spare time.

CRITIC: Stevens's justice takes up all his time. He does not descend, any more than Faulkner does. He is not naive, though he may seem to be. He gives you people without cuteness. Unlike Sherwood Anderson, he opens all the doors he finds, and is not content with merely supplying facts but meanings too, and the morality of this book is a piercing scrutiny by people of the world in which they live, not by the consent of the author, but because they must.

REVIEWER: (Persistent to the end) The story "Tomorrow" is the embodiment of the sunless South. It leaves one with a feeling of cold.

CRITIC: You are getting warm, but you have leaped to an implication of one story without getting the point of the whole thing.

REVIEWER: Ah, but I have perceived an image of a curve, a linear discreteness between this story and the one on King Lear.

CRITIC: (Shuddering) Please drop dead.

REVIEWER: Just the same, that's all I found, and if that's not a valid conclusion, then there isn't any. Because you know as well as I do that you can't understand what he's talking about half the time. I think he's just obscure without complexity.

CRITIC: There is a surface obscurity; you have to work hard over him; sometimes he sounds like a breathless boy; and his writing seems to achieve its results, like a Saul Steinberg drawing or an O'Neill play, by sheer ineptitude, but with an overpowering perfection of its own because (and therefore) it carries his potent truth. Yes, "Knight's Gambit" is the worst story in this book, a slick magnolia romance cum Pearl Harbor.

REVIEWER: All in all, then the book is terrible.

CRITIC: All in all, it is far better than 98 per cent of most other books published this year. Spend your money, read it, and you'll get more than you bargained for. And man to man, kid, just between us, you have a hole in your head.

Warren Beck.
"Unique Style of Faulkner Still Is Tops."
Chicago *Sunday Tribune*, November 13, 1949, Part IV, p. 3.

All six stories in *Knight's Gambit* feature Gavin Stevens, the county attorney who dominated Faulkner's preceding novel, *Intruder in the Dust*. Again Stevens is a Faulknerian agent, like Benbow in *Sanctuary* or Ratliff in *The Hamlet*. These acute incorruptible spectators comment humanely, a veritable chorus in modern tragedy. Outraged moralists, they wryly locate sympathy and despair in irony. Stevens rises above frustration, however, being the instrument of legal justice, a helpful conciliator, and finally an accepted suitor.

Five of these stories concern murders, and in one an intended death-trap is barely avoided thru Stevens' alertness. All exhibit intricated plots and ingenious detection. But they go beyond melodrama. They abound in Faulkner's penetratingly grotesque characterizations and witty dialogues with somber overtones. They display his unique style, like a river in flood, its surface giving the hallucination of slow eddying, but its volume immensely urgent. Stevens' "bland immediate quick fantastic voice which lent not only a perspicacity but a solid reasonableness" is again Faulkner's familiar paradoxical voice, whimsical and incisive.

The title story, a substantial novelette, brilliantly orchestrates complex events and themes of hatred, love, accident, design, cultural contradictions and individual development. It resolves crises in five lives, including Stevens' own, and is filtered re-vealingly thru the maturing mind of Stevens' nephew, as interlocutor and philosophical understudy.

At one denouement a sheriff remarks, "The Book itself says somewhere, 'Know thyself.' Ain't there another book somewhere that says, 'Man, fear thyself, thine arrogance and vanity and pride'? . . . What book is that in?" Stevens answers: "It's in all of them. The good ones, I mean. It's said in a lot of different ways, but it's there." It's in *Knight's Gambit* too. This dispensation of pity and terror, this acknowledgement of right principle transcending human folly and validating moral fortitude, has permeated the protean dramatic variety of all Faulkner's work.

By these august standards of the tragic and tragi-comic most imaginatively rendered, Faulkner remains pre-eminent, the Shakespeare of American fiction.

Shelby Foote.
"Five Stories, One Novella and Crime Themes Comprise Faulkner's Newest Collection."
Delta Democrat-Times (Greenville, Miss.), November 13, 1949, p. 18.

Some people read stories of crime detection for relaxation. William Faulkner *writes* them, apparently for the same purpose.

His eighteenth book—containing five short stories, most of them written in the Thirties, and a new short novel, "Knight's Gambit," which lends its title to the

287

collection—has probably the lowest specific gravity of any book by this author since *The Unvanquished*, his thirteenth, or possibly even since *Mosquitoes*, his second.

This is not to infer that the book is one to be overlooked or set aside. No Faulkner book is ever that. Mr. Faulkner's ability to communicate sensation and invoke a mood, which he possesses to a degree that no writer anywhere has ever surpassed, is as much in evidence as ever. And in places, particularly in the title story, the dialog positively sparkles. The writer's wit—so conspicuously avoided or hidden before, or at best merely suggested—comes into its own.

Gavin Stevens, the lawyer from *Intruder in the Dust*, is the tie that binds them together; he is the central character in all six stories. Chick Mallison, his nephew, who also will be remembered from *Intruder*, is narrator of three of the stories and the title story is seen through his eyes, just as in the novel.

All six are "detective" stories—at least they are hung on a detective-story frame. Five concern murder and the sixth concerns the threat of murder. The first five came out in magazines between 1932 and 1946, one of them having been entered in a mystery-fiction contest. They are reprinted chronologically.

"Smoke" (1932) has already appeared in the *Doctor Martino* collection. Readers presumably are acquainted with it.

"Monk" (1937), the best short thing in the book—and indeed one of the best stories Mr. Faulkner has ever written—concerns a cretin who commits a suggested murder in order to link himself with "the world of living men." There is incidentally an acid portrait of an amoral governor-politician whose identity is hardly mistakable.

"Hand upon the Waters" (1939) is a revenge story. A deaf-mute revenges the murder of his benefactor, a feeble-minded fisherman.

"Tomorrow" (1940) runs "Monk" a close second for first place among the shorter things. It is also a revenge story, dedicated to the Southern belief "that only a life can pay for the life it takes; that the one death is only half complete."

"An Error in Chemistry" (1946), the story that was entered in the magazine contest (it won second place), is the most patently contrived and therefore least successful item in the collection.

So much for the short stories. "Knight's Gambit," the novelette, is written in Mr. Faulkner's latest manner. The mood and style are those of *Intruder in the Dust*, except that the seriousness of purpose and theme in the earlier novel (purpose, the justification of the South; theme, the coming of age of a Southerner) are lacking here, for this is a romantic comedy. It might have been called "The Courtship of Gavin Stevens."

As such it is a complete success. Nowhere has Mr. Faulkner's touch been surer, his style more applicable to content. At his worst he can be sentimental and melodramatic (here at times he is both) but the style saves all; its brilliance carries him through anything. The reader, with evidence on every page that he is in the hands of a master, will find nothing to regret.

Two features of this short novel make it especially welcome to Faulkner fans. 1) He writes of horses—which no one has ever done so well—and 2) he describes the establishment of a "barony." He has done both before, and now he does them again, as well or better than ever.

Some readers have shied away from Mr. Faulkner's books, believing them too "profound," too "complicated." This is regrettable, particularly here in Mississippi, for no readers have a better chance for enjoyment than we have. Speaking Mr.

Faulkner's idiom, we catch overtones and implications that no outlander would suspect. He writes for us.

So perhaps this collection will serve a noble purpose. It will give reluctant, self-deprecating readers an entering wedge, a chance to become acquainted with one of the greatest bodies of work in all the world's literature, an introduction to the world of William Faulkner.

J. Saunders Redding. "*Knight's Gambit* Annoys, Impresses." Providence *Sunday Journal,* November 13, 1949, Section VI, p. 8.

The first five stories in William Faulkner's new book are banal. They are banal in the same way that *Sanctuary* was, and they are as if, like *Sanctuary*, they were written merely out of an excess of technical skill and virtuosity.

One is annoyed and impressed by them in exactly the fashion one is by a woman who, profoundly and irrevocably in love with a man, idles her time in being coy with other men of one-tenth her true love's worth.

The first five are murder stories—just murder stories with a touch of mystery. And not true mystery; but rather as if William Faulkner and Erle Stanley Gardner had made a trade with one another and each was cheated, the one not giving the magic of his thunder-and-lightning emotionalism and the other withholding the tensive, awesome logic of his ingenious plot.

The result is Faulkner disemboweled and thunder without God.

All the Faulkner characters are in these stories: Gavin Stevens, for instance, that Mississippi cosmopolite (a contradiction both in terms and concept), who here serves as a sort of draw-string; the big-bellied, hard-eyed sheriffs; the driven men and women of "Jefferson" and its environs; the colored people, and the poor, faded blue-denim whites.

But they are here for nothing. The man, young Anse Holland, in the first story "Smoke," is wasted on a mystery-murder story ending.

The same is true of Tyler Ballenbaugh in "Hand Upon the Waters." Except that in this story, Faulkner himself got lost—not in the alleys of mystery, but in characterization and purpose. Tyler didn't murder the feeble-minded Lonnie Grinnup, but he should have, and when one finds he did not, then characterization is sacrificed to plot. "Hands Upon the Waters" is probably the worst story Faulkner ever wrote.

"Tomorrow" is the best of the first five. It is almost true Faulkner. The psychopathia is in its characters for a reason other than that Faulkner characters are supposed to be psychopathic.

Told in a series of flashbacks, the story gets very close to those elements and items of frustration, despair and tragic degeneracy that Faulkner sees as the invariables in the character of the South.

But here again, the author plays coy with mystery, and Stonewall Jackson Fentry in the end is sacrificed, not to credibility or even probability, but to the mere necessity of making the plot come out.

But there is "Knight's Gambit," the title story, and the first five seem but semi-digestible preliminaries the host has not bothered to freshen up, knowing that a solid, palate-teasing meal was to follow.

For "Knight's Gambit" is such a meal. Not a feast, mind you, and not a banquet (though with some of a banquet's trimmings), but a good warm plate of substantial fare. Faulkner is not fooling here.

In this novelette he goes back to his primary concern—the mystifying but totally unmysterious (as a genius handles it) relation of one human being to another and to life.

There is the old fullness of emotional communication in it, the old regard for truth and also the old regard for story. And this story has, one feels, a special significance for the author's future work, for in it Gavin Stevens, the romantic saviour and explicator of the South's terrible conscience, marries.

The next Faulkner book will be worth waiting for.

Donald Heritage.
"Faulkner Polishes Up Six Cameos of Crime."
Newark (N.J.) *Sunday Star-Ledger*, December 4, 1949, p. 56.

Six cameos of crime, polished, glinting with somber and cold light, sharply yet ever so carefully cut, make up this all too quickly read volume. These stories stand by themselves, still bear close relationship in their common Yoknapatawpha soil and in their peripatetic private-eye, the intellectual, philosophical and deucedly clever county attorney, Gavin Stevens. These are masterpieces of fictional fabric, cut from a bolt probably a bit less rich in texture than *Go Down, Moses*, yet still far superior to most cousins of its cloth.

If you are a Faulkner fanatic, you must feel much the same way about Gavin Stevens. He has been seeing justice done the human way for the past 15 years or so and in that span of time has become one of Faulkner's favorite characters; he also is one of ours and should be one of yours.

In these half-dozen whodunits he is the interpreter of Southern mores and chronicler of unthinking passion, a compassionate guide to psychically battered mentalities, an expert in human relations.

In "Smoke" he traps a murderer who forgot too many things about horses, wills and smoke. "Monk" measures the mentality of a sub-moron who kills to free his soul. In "Hand Upon the Waters" a deaf-mute settles conflict between brothers. "Tomorrow" wakes to superstition and love and violent death.

"An Error in Chemistry" turns the tables on a magician murderer whose cold toddy becomes too hot to handle. And "Knight's Gambit" deals at length with fiftyish fancy and nineteenish love, a foreign affair, and Gavin Stevens' own mercurial emotions.

If this is not Faulkner's best work, it still is Faulkner and even not-so-good Faulkner is so very much better than the best of many another.

Ruth Chapin.
"The World of Faulkner."
Christian Science Monitor, December 8, 1949, p. 20.

William Faulkner is reported to be the most widely read American novelist in Europe today. A certain die-hard European concept of American cultural inferiority, a view centered in Babbitt and bounded on the East by Wall Street, on the North by Chicago gangsters, and on the West by cowboys, may well have received fresh impetus and a whole new dimension in Faulkner's southland. For this reason, if for no other, he merits careful critical attention.

Out of the skeletons in the southern closet, Faulkner has constructed some seventeen casually related sagas of Yokna-patawpha County and Jefferson township: narratives of violence, degeneracy and soured integrity. Sometimes he invests his sordid relationships with a crude social symbolism; always he carefully documents them. He may trace through generations the warping effects of jealousy, and worn-out land, and a wayward daughter, on a dirt farmer of original good intentions. The pattern of his work is never formal but loose, disparate, an uncovering of the twisted roots and stem—in character and environment—which lie beneath each culminating violence.

The present book, *Knight's Gambit*, is both quieter in tone and better organized than most of its predecessors. It comprises six separate short stories, all centered in Jefferson and all concerned with the uncovering of a murderer, or of the motives of those who are contemplating murder. The stories are unified by a figure mentioned in previous books: Gavin Stevens, the county attorney, who here takes over, either officially or unofficially, the unravelling of each problem.

The word problem is used advisedly. These pieces resemble nothing so much as miniature detective stories. As before, Faulkner has delved into men's pasts, bringing up clues from their characters and from their lives.

But it is Gavin Stevens who holds the trump card, the special, circumstantial knowledge which tells him who is the sinner; and, further, whether the sinner deserves conviction. For Gavin believes that truth and justice are two very different things; and he is not beyond a bit of legal horseplay to aid a man who, though tech-nically guilty, is morally innocent.

For Gavin is not quite of Faulkner's world. Educated at Harvard (Phi Beta Kappa) and Heidelberg, urbane, cultivated, yet thoroughly at home with the men squatting against the store fronts on Sat-urday afternoon, he seems to have dropped straight from a ready-made, humanistic heaven. With the same finished ease with which he wins a game of chess, he solves the present crop of Jefferson's difficulties. He is a beguiling character, but he is dan-gerous in his implications.

For the benevolent paternalism which Gavin embodies in such a fresh and at-tractive form is, as surely Faulkner knows, a familiar serpent in the southern Eden, with a long history of luring men to sur-render individual responsibility for a par-tial good—which almost inevitably degen-erates into a consuming evil. Individual rededication and rebuilding alone can scotch this serpent.

Considered in a vacuum as a literary craftsman, Faulkner is uneven and undis-ciplined, but his occasional best is very good. He can sketch in a landscape with vivid economy, and transmit the slightest nuances of common speech (though much of the prose in the present book is per-versely prolix). But Faulkner is not writ-ing in a vacuum, nor is he being read in one. On the contrary, he is projecting a negative, twisted, highly personalized con-cept of the South with such apparent force that it is being widely taken, on its own terms, as of positive value. But sheer en-ergy, and technical facility, are as wind in the desert unless based on a premise some-how justifiable. In Faulkner's work such a premise is difficult to find.

291

Lawrance Thompson.
"With *Knight's Gambit*
Faulkner Takes a
Disturbingly
Quixotic Turn."
Louisville *Courier
Journal*, December 11,
1949, Section III, p. 19.

For the past 17 years, William Faulkner has been turning out highly readable novels and short stories in which a minor character named Gavin Stevens has become familiar. He is an honest lawyer, attorney, amateur detective, in Faulkner's mythical Yoknapatawpha County, Mississippi. In *Knight's Gambit*, five short stories involving Gavin Stevens have been collected and supplemented with a title novelette. Further unified, these six stories share a common theme: the ironically paradoxical ways in which justice and injustice are made to confront each other.

Nobody wants to be told details of a detective story, and even if these are not equal to Faulkner's best they are too good to be spoiled. Yet there is a larger relationship worth discussing. *Knights Gambit* offers greatest enjoyment to those who are so well acquainted with Faulkner's elaborately chronicled saga that they can recognize all the overtones and undertones and extension of Gavin Stevens' life-story. His family roots go deeper into the history of this unreal-real microcosm of the South than those of the more notorious or famous families such as the Snopeses, the Compsons, the Sartoris. Stevens appeared as far back as 1932, in *Light in August*; he figured prominently in Faulkner's latest novel, *Intruder in the Dust*; but he must not be confused with

his namesake who started all the trouble in *Sanctuary*.

Stevens has an additional significance, in this broader Faulknerian frame: his author and creator has set him apart from both the common and the uncommon people in the celebrated town of Jefferson. Having left the South, long enough to obtain a Harvard education, having traveled in Europe and having studied in Heidelberg, Stevens prides himself on his detached and penetrating vision of his fellow townsmen. Put it another way. Gavin Stevens shows himself to be something of an artist, whose raw materials (like Faulkner's) are people, whose main interest (like Faulkner's) is in the "clotting" of justice and injustice, of good and evil. In his latest novel, *Intruder in the Dust*, Faulkner seemed to feel such a close kinship with Stevens that Stevens was drafted to serve as Faulkner's own personal loudspeaker. Furthermore, in the climactic novelette of *Knight's Gambit*, this reviewer senses a different but equally ominous kinship between Stevens as puppet and Faulkner as puppeteer: each shows for the first time a certain disconcertingly mellow and mystical attitude toward the tenderizing power of love.

Has Faulkner just turned a corner, in his career as storyteller? His familiar bent, in the past, has been predominantly tragic and bitter. His case histories of murders, rapes, violence, have led many critics to say that none of Faulkner's characters has a soul, that even the author himself seems to lack one. Perhaps these critics might have been more accurate if they had pointed out that Faulkner's tragic itches and agonies still reflected his lost-generation disillusionment. He has always been a man of too much feeling, and mixed with his dark broodings over what man has done to man—what the South has done to the South (with the help of the

North)—there have always been some sentimental tears. As long as Faulkner was
horrified and fascinated by grim aspects
of past and present, he afforded his readers an engrossing literary experience, to
say the least. And that was the Faulknerian
bent which won him a following, at home
and abroad.

Is Faulkner leaving all that? Is the mel-
lowing Gavin Stevens the tip-off, with his
utopian sermonizings at the end of *Intruder in the Dust*, and with his symbolically hopeful surrender to love, in
"Knight's Gambit?" If so, those of us
who are his cautious admirers must brace
ourselves.

Always there has been a pleasantly quixotic aspect to Faulkner's chivalric
knightliness, nice so long as he kept it
under wraps. But the emergence of the
sentimental in the once hard-headed Gavin
Stevens—and the growing sense of identification between Stevens and Faulkner—
is disturbing. Faulkner's next literary gambit may even more quixotic.

Lawrence Olson.
"*Knight's Gambit.*"
Furioso, 5 (Winter 1950),
86–88.

None of these six stories equals Faulkner's
best. "The Bear," for instance, is worth
more than any combination of them. But
four of them are exciting to read, and one
stands out. All six are mysteries, five are
about murder, and the earliest was published in 1932. Together their greatest interest lies in Gavin Stevens, the Oxford,
Mississippi intellectual lawyer-detective
whom Faulkner invented in the early 30's,
used in *Light in August* and *Intruder in
the Dust,* and who solves all six myster-

ies, comments upon them, and makes
rhetoric about the south.

"Smoke" is least memorable, a murder
trial story with a trick ending, what the
magazines would buy. A man commits
murder because he is the beneficiary of
the man who is the murdered man's beneficiary. Stevens, as county attorney, solves
this, and we learn about him that "he was
a Harvard graduate: a loose-jointed man
with a mop of untidy iron-gray hair, who
could discuss Einstein with college professors and who spent whole afternoons
among the squatting men against the walls
of country stores, talking to them in their
idiom. He called these his vacations." He
talks a lot, and he is more interesting than
the story. But he is embarrassing, and he
seems merely eccentric; one is not sure
whether Faulkner's sympathies lie with the
Harvard man or with the men squatting
against the country stores.

The next story, "Monk," is much better. It is about a moron ("perhaps even a
cretin") who is framed into two murder
charges and finally hanged. Stevens alone
takes an interest in his case, and after
Monk is dead, proves his innocence. In this
story Stevens appears as an idealist in a
world of practical politicians—a "knight"
whose gambit is in defense of elementary
justice. Faulkner slams at politicians: "at
that time we had for Governor a man
without ancestry and with but little more
divulged background than Monk; a
shrewd man who (some of us feared, Uncle Gavin [Stevens] and others about the
State) would go far if he lived." The lawyer clearly is set over against this demagogue and the "identical puppet faces" of
his "battalions and battalions of factory-
made-colonels." One learns no new facts
about Stevens, but his notions, his values
are clearer. In a typical Faulknerian passage, he leaves the Governor's presence,
and starts back to Jefferson, "riding across
the broad, heat-miraged land, between the

cotton and the corn of God's long-fecund, remorseless acres, which would outlast any corruption and injustice. He was glad . . . to be sweating-out of himself the smell and the taste of where he had been."

In "Hand Upon the Waters" Stevens solves a murder through his intimate knowledge of folkways. He is more intricately bound into the action than in the earlier stories. He blends more smoothly with the "country store" people, and he is built up into an intellectual with folk-cunning and folk-courage. His relation to the people is more nicely stated: "they knew him, voting for him year after year and calling him by his given name even though they did not quite understand him, just as they did not understand the Harvard Phi Beta Kappa key on his watch-chain." But he understands them. He is no longer merely a courtroom orator, but a convincing man of action. This story is notable, moreover, for the clarity of its setting. In a few sentences which foreshadow the assurance of his maturest style Faulkner sets a scene:

"The two men followed the path where it ran between the river and the dense wall of cypress and cane and gum and brier. One of them carried a gunny sack which had been washed and looked as if it had been ironed too. The other was a youth, less than 20, by his face. The river was low, at mid-July level."

I pass over "An Error in Chemistry" to get to "Tomorrow," the most memorable of these stories. The plot of "Tomorrow" is as contrived as a silent film serial; but for the first time in this book, the dialogue and the dialect reach a pitch of fluidity and conviction and accuracy sufficient to carry the reader incredulously to a dead stop at the story's end. In this story one learns that Stevens went not only to Harvard but to Heidelberg; but the embarrassment one felt about him in "Smoke" has gone. Perhaps this is because he doesn't talk, he listens while the countrymen talk, and for the space of a story he is believable.

As he so frequently does in his later books, Faulkner squeezes the history of a family or of a whole region into a paragraph or two of the truest colloquial yet written down for that area. It is impossible to do more than suggest the flavor of that language. A country woman is telling about a country widower and his child:

"He didn't even have diaper cloths. He had some split flour sacks the midwife had showed him how to put on. So I made some cloths and I would go up there; he had kept the nigger on to help his pa in the field and he was doing the cooking and washing and nursing that baby, milking the goat to feed it; and I would say, 'Let me take it. At least until he can be weaned. You come and stay at my house, too, if you want,' and him looking at me—little, thin, already wore-out something that never in his whole life had ever set down to a table and et all he could hold—saying 'I thank you ma'am. I can make out.'"

The title story, though longer, more ambitious, and more recent, has nothing in it to match the uncanny rightness of that dialogue. In "Knight's Gambit" Stevens plays raisonneur; the story is presented from the point of view of his nephew, Charles Mallison. So it is roughly contemporary with *Intruder*. It is a long story, or short novel, which (in my opinion) fails because most of the people in it simply aren't there, and the story is (in my opinion) unbelievable. It is just a fantastic story about some rich adolescents and rich middle-aged Mississippians with an Argentine cavalry captain tossed in. Slabs of Faulkner's great lean humor bob up through the fat here and there, but after the achievement of "Tomorrow" the whole affair seems very pale indeed.

If I have succeeded in suggesting some of the qualities of these stories, I should like to make one final observation about them all. It seemed to me as I read them through once and twice and three times, that while the sentences grew longer and longer, the antecedents more obscure and the adjectives more rhetorical and profuse as I grew nearer to Faulkner's present style, still the first story, "Smoke," required fully as unremitting an effort as the last, the title story. But clearly the difficulty I experienced in following all six plots arose not from the progressive elaboration of the sentence structure—the letting loose of more snakes through more lace—but from a more mysterious cause, which in this book has to do with the character of Stevens and the half-legendary, half-real society in which he moves and to which most of Faulkner's books have contributed. I have not read the critical magazines on Faulkner for a good many years, but I have read his fiction and lived in Oxford, Mississippi and Gavin Stevens seems to me to be one of his most complicated characters. He is, as I have just indicated, partly real and quickly recognizable—the Harvard-Heidelberg-Rhodes Scholar prototype who comes home and settles down. But he is also partly unreal and unbelievable; part of him never came back home, and the archaic courtliness of his personality for 1950 isolates him in his harsh and violent climate. At any rate, it is the job of estimating his complexity which is Faulkner's own complexity, which makes the action of these stories so hard to follow.

Checklist of Additional Reviews

"*Knight's Gambit.*" *Kirkus*, September 1, 1949, p. 485.

"Faulkner Writes 18th Book." Miami *Herald,* November 13, 1949, p. 4-F.

"Faulkner's Detective." *Newsweek,* November 14, 1949, pp. 92–93.

"*Knight's Gambit.*" *Booklist,* November 15, 1949, p. 97.

"*Knight's Gambit.*" Jersey City *Justice,* November 15, 1949.

"Yoknapatawpha Sherlock." *Time,* November 21, 1949.

Waldorf-Astoria (N.Y.), December 1949.

"*Knight's Gambit.*" Daly City (Calif.) *Record,* December 1, 1949, p. 2.

Rocky Mount (N.C.) *Telegram,* December 4, 1949.

"*Knight's Gambit.*" Burlington (Vt.) *Free Press,* December 7, 1949, p. 14.

"*Knight's Gambit.*" San Francisco *Argonaut,* December 9, 1949, p. 20.

San Francisco *Call-Bulletin,* January 7, 1950.

U.S. Quarterly Book List, 6 (June 1950).

"*Knight's Gambit.*" South Bend *Tribune,* date unknown.

Algren, Nelson. "Faulkner's Thrillers." *New York Times Book Review,* November 6, 1949, p. 4.

Armour, Lloyd. "More Adventures in Faulkner Land." Nashville *Tennessean,* November 27, 1949, p. 8-E.

Ashford, Gerald. "Faulkner Again." San Antonio *Express,* November 6, 1949, p. 24.

Bedell, W. D. "A Changed William Faulkner." Houston *Post,* November 6, 1949, Section IV, p. 16.

Bernstein, Doris. "*Knight's Gambit.*" *Labor Herald,* February 24, 1950.

Bradley, Van Allen. "Faulkner at Best in *Gambit.*" Chicago *Daily News*, November 9, 1949, p. 44.

Brady, Charles A. "Faulkner Introduces New Southern Sleuth." Buffalo *Evening News*, November 5, 1949, Magazine Section, p. 6.

C., T. "*Knight's Gambit* Is Newest Novel by Faulkner." Fort Worth *Star-Telegram*, November 13, 1949, Section II, p. 13.

Champion, Hale. "New Faulkner Novel Is Impressive Writing by a Fine Talent in Search of the Truth." Sacramento *Bee*, November 19, 1949, p. 29.

Coughlin, William J. "No. 18 for Faulkner." Detroit *Free Press*, November 6, 1949, p. 7-B.

Cournos, John. "*Knight's Gambit.*" New York *Sun*, November 8, 1949, p. 10.

Cowley, Malcolm. "Faulkner Stories, in Amiable Mood." *New York Herald Tribune Book Review*, November 6, 1949, p. 7.

Crume, Paul. "Again Faulkner's Work Has Violence as Theme." Dallas *Morning News*, November 6, 1949, Section II, p. 10.

Dunkel, Wilbur. "A Faulkner Gambit." Rochester *Democrat and Chronicle*, October 30, 1949, p. 11-D.

Dyslin, George E. "*Knight's Gambit.*" Indianapolis *Star*, December 25, 1949, Section III, p. 14.

E., L.B. *Promenade*, date unknown.

Farber, James. "A New Collection of Vivid Stories by Faulkner." New York *Journal-American*, November 12, 1949, p. 8.

Fee, Marge. "Crime under Cover." Omaha *World Herald*, November 13, 1949, Magazine Section, p. 25.

Fineman, Morton. "Faulkner's Version of Private Eye." Philadelphia *Inquirer*, November 20, 1949, Magazine Section, p. 37.

Flowers, Paul. "Faulkner Offers *Knight's Gambit.*" Memphis *Commercial Appeal*, December 4, 1949, Section IV, p. 12.

Garcia, Rolando A. "*Knight's Gambit.*" Manila *Bulletin*, October 30, 1950, p. 16.

Gibeau, R. F. "Character Delineation, Aspects of Prayer Admirably Presented." Fort Wayne *News-Sentinel*, January 21, 1950, p. 6.

Goldsmith, Ida W. "The South Mirrored in William Faulkner's Mind." Tyler (Tex.) *Courier-Times-Morning Telegraph*, November 6, 1949, p. 3-A.

Greenberg, Martin. "Gambit Declined." *Commentary*, 9 (January 1950), pp. 103–4.

H., F. "*Knight's Gambit.*" Columbia *Missourian*, January 23, 1950; *Missouri Clipsheet* (University of Missouri), February 3, 1950.

Harris, Geraldine C. Columbus *Dispatch*, November 20, 1949.

Harrison, W. K. "*Knight's Gambit.*" *Library Journal*, September 15, 1949, p. 1321.

Hicks, Granville. "The Yoknapatawpha Saga." *New Leader*, December 31, 1949, p. 10.

Horan, Kenneth. Dallas *Times Herald*, date unknown.

Howe, Irving. "Minor Faulkner." *Nation*, November 12, 1949, pp. 473–74.

H[uling], E[lizabeth]. "*Knight's Gambit.*" *New Republic*, November 21, 1949, p. 19.

Hunter, Anna C. "Books in Review." Savannah *Morning News*, November 8, 1949, p. 9.

J., B. "Faulkner Turns to Mystery Stories in *Knight's Gambit.*" Jackson (Miss.) *Daily News*, November 20, 1949, p. 5.

Jarman, Frances. "*Knight's Gambit.*" Radio broadcast on WDNC (Durham) (copy in Random House files).

Jones, Carter Brooke. "New William Faulkner Volume Is One of His Most Engrossing." Washington *Sunday Star*, November 6, 1949, p. 3-C.

Jones, Howard Mumford. "Loyalty and Tiresias of Yoknapatawpha." *Saturday Review of Literature*, November 5, 1949, p. 17.

L., C.V. "*Knight's Gambit.*" Houston *Press*, November 11, 1949, Section I, p. 22.

Lind, S. E. "The World of Books." *Sunday Compass* (unidentified city), November 20, 1949.

M., N.B. "Mystery by Faulkner." Oakland *Tribune*, January 8, 1950, p. 2-C.

Manausos, Demetrius. "Tales of Mississippi by William Faulkner." *Books on Trial*, 8 (December 1949– January 1950), 159–60.

Marshall, Eloise M. "*Knight's Gambit* Is Typical Faulkner." Columbus *Dispatch*, November 20, 1949, p. 7-F.

McAdory, James. "Tense, with Suspense." Birmingham *News*, November 12, 1949, p. 4.

Miles, George. "*Knight's Gambit.*" *Commonweal*, December 9, 1949, pp. 275–76.

Minot, George. Boston *Herald*, November 20, 1949.

Murphree, Alex. "Faulkner Introduces Gentleman Attorney Who Knows Human Heart and Values Human Life." Denver *Post*, November 6, 1949, p. 4-C.

Overall, Tiny. "*Knight's Gambit* Welcomed by All Faulkner Fans." Jackson (Tenn.) *Sun*, February 5, 1950, Section III, p. 3.

P., J. "Old Faulkner in New Grouping." New Orleans *Times-Picayune*, December 11, 1949, Section II, p. 7.

Parsons, Eugene O. "Moves like Chess Knight." Worcester (Mass.) *Telegram*, November 6, 1949, p. 11-D.

Patrick, Peggy A. "*Knight's Gambit.*" Des Moines *Sunday Register*, January 8, 1950, p. 11-W.

Paulus, John D. "Faulkner Dissipates Gifts in Meaningless Prose." Pittsburgh *Press*, November 13, 1949, p. 70.

Pickrel, Paul. "Outstanding Novels." *Yale Review*, 39 (Winter 1950), 382.

Plumb, F. M. "Faulkner Poor Whites Ride Again in *Knight's Gambit.*" *Rocky Mountain News* (Denver), November 13, 1949, p. 16-A.

Prescott, Orville. "Books of the Times." New York *Times*, November 8, 1949, p. 29.

Price, Emerson. "Violence—By Faulkner." Cleveland *Press*, November 8, 1949, p. 26.

R., R. "Faulkner Disappoints." Greensboro *Daily News*, December 18, 1949, Feature Section, p. 3.

Rolo, Charles J. "Studies in Murder." *Atlantic Monthly*, January 1950, pp. 85–86.

Rovere, Richard. "Faulkner, Mrs. Roosevelt, and Social History." *Harper's Magazine*, December 1949, pp. 108–10.

Rubin, Louis D., Jr. "Five Southerners." *Hopkins Review*, 3 (Spring 1950), 42–45.

Sandrock, Mary. "*Knight's Gambit.*" *Catholic World*, 170 (January 1950), 314.

Sherman, Thomas B. "Faulkner's Latest a Set of Short Stories." St. Louis *Post-Dispatch*, November 20, 1949, p. 4-B.

Silberman, Lee. "*Knight's Gambit.*" Wichita *Eagle*, January 1, 1950, p. 6.

S[izer], A[lvin] V. "The Bookworm Turns." New Haven *Register*, November 6, 1949, Magazine Section, p. 6.

Spearman, Walter. "Three Southern Authors' New Books Disappointing."

Charlotte *Observer*, November 6, 1949, p. 18-C.

Steinberg, David. "Faulkner's Mysteries." Newark (N.J.) *News,* November 13, 1949, Section III, p. 52.

Strong, Russell. "The Failure of Faulkner." Kalamazoo *Gazette*, December 22, 1949, p. 9.

T., J.C. *Sunday Times Magazine*, February 19, 1950.

Tripp, Frederick. "Faulkner Scores in Whodunit." Amarillo *Sunday News Globe*, January 8, 1950, Section II, p. 21.

Truax, Charles. "Gavin Stevens—a Spokesman for Faulkner and the South." Dayton *Daily News*, December 18, 1949, Society Section, p. 14.

W., E. "Life in Mississippi Depicted in Series." San Diego *Union*, February 12, 1950.

Ward, Mary Jane. "Faulkner Tries His Hand at Sherlock Holmes Tale." Chicago *Sun-Times*, December 4, 1949, p. 134.

Wilson, Edmund. "Henley and Faulkner Not at Their Best." *New Yorker*, December 24, 1949, pp. 57–59.

Yeiser, Frederick. "*Knight's Gambit.*" Cincinnati *Enquirer*, November 5, 1949, p. 5.

COLLECTED STORIES

Horace Gregory.
"In the Haunted, Heroic
Land of Faulkner's
Imagination."
*New York Herald Tribune
Weekly Book Review,*
August 20, 1950,
pp. 1, 12.

In the early years of the present century when undergraduates in colleges made their first discovery of Chekhov, every one who dreamed of writing a book some day felt the sudden impulse to write, if nothing else, the perfect short story. It seemed so easy: if almost any one on a fortunate occasion could tell a story, then it followed naturally that any one could write it and with the slightest effort could become both rich and famous. And today when more short stories than ever are being written, the perfect story, or if less than that, the story worthy to be remembered, is just as rare as ever. In contemporary literature a number of the stories and short novels of William Faulkner seem to possess an immortality; some few of them have haunted the imagination of their readers, including other writers, for nearly twenty years. Are the stories perfect works of art? Not many, for William Faulkner is not that kind of artist: some of the stories, no matter how highly we may regard them, contain blurred passages of prose, or if read for themselves alone, seem willfully obscure. Why is it then that Faulkner's writing has the sign of genius and the promise of an enduring life?

One answer to this question is that Faulkner always has something to say, but beyond that answer there is the likeness that he bears (which does not mitigate in the least his individual qualities) to certain writers who have stirred and guided the sub-channels of fiction during the first half of the twentieth century—if one becomes literal, three of them are not of this century at all. I refer, of course, to Henry James, Herman Melville, Dostoevsky and Franz Kafka, James Joyce and D. H. Lawrence.

A generation ago most of these writers were considered too obscure in meaning, or too dark, too complex, too gloomy to read for pleasure, or to some readers, too dangerously modern. Today their names are the familiars of academic discourse and are among the clichés of reference in quarterly reviews. However in or out of fashion these writers are or may become, each carries within his prose the essentials of poetic insight and imagination; beyond the rules of art, of critical taste and controversy, each conveys an awareness of the mystery of being and of moral integrity. Within this company where the independent spirit is kept alive, in the company of the sometimes difficult and more obscure, the writings of William Faulkner find their natural environment.

The present volume of Faulkner's stories—there are forty-two of them—has the almost literal appearance of an omnibus; it is a collection made from earlier volumes, now unobtainable, and it includes seventeen stories that have been published separately in magazines, but not between the covers of any of his books. It contains all the varieties of Faulkner's writings, rearranged for this occasion in something that approximates a topographical order: The Country, The Village, The Wilderness, The Wasteland, The Middle Ground, Beyond.

The first impression that the book conveys is one of an Elizabethan richness: here is the variety of life itself, its humours, its ironies, its ancient tempers, its latest fashions, its masks of horror, its violence, its comedy, its pathos. It is gratuitous to say that the stories are uneven in depth, quality and interest. After a closer view, what emerges from the casting of this wide net, is Faulkner's extended chronicle of Mississippi, a country in which his novels, *Sanctuary, Light in August, Absalom, Absalom!, The Hamlet,* and *The Unvanquished* have their being. The stories that venture beyond that particular topography are less convincing; only one, "Mistral," with its scene in post–World War I Italy, is the exception to the rule. Faulkner's Mississippi is of the same authority as scenes in Joyce's Dublin and Kafka's Prague; and in Faulkner's stories, as in stories of Joyce's *Dubliners* and Kafka's *The Penal Colony*, the writer draws upon the sources of universal truth where he is most at home.

For the last fifteen years it has been obvious enough that Faulkner is a regional novelist; he is of Mississippi and of a country that fought the Yankees during the Civil War and many of the long, difficult years that followed it, but it is also clear that he is a regional novelist with a difference; whenever he raises the ghostly image of the Confederate flag, it is in memory of those who fought a losing cause with honor—honor and pride and a not unconscious sense of irony. The idea of honor, however thinly worn, however gray it may appear, floats behind the panorama of Faulkner's writings; his people, rich or poor, red-skinned, or black or white, carry that idea as though it were an unnamed element of blood within their veins.

D. H. Lawrence once remarked that America was haunted by the Indian; something very like that conviction and that feeling enters into Faulkner's tales of The Wilderness, particularly his "Red Leaves," one of the memorable stories reprinted in the present volume. Surely no one has written of a deeper South than Faulkner's wilderness where Chickasaw Indian, Negro and white American conquered the land and lost it to one another. In another story, "The Bear" (which is part of *Go Down, Moses,* and is not included in *The Collected Stories*), and in the speech of one of its characters, another aspect of "Red Leaves" is shown:

> Don't you see? This whole land, the whole South is cursed, and all of us who derive from it, whom it ever suckled, white and black both, lie under the curse?

It is by this kind of penetration into the psyche of the South and of America that Faulkner retains his kinship to Melville, for like the elder writer, Faulkner looks downward and inward to the causes of guilt (which is also the subjective, inward look of Dostoevsky) before the sense of sin can start its long journey toward expiation.

Of the South that is now America there are three stories of World War I in *The Collected Stories*: "The Tall Men," "Two Soldiers," and "Shall Not Perish," in which the gods of family honor and devotion are invoked; there the emotions aroused by the interweaving of pathos and irony are resolved in the ancient truth that patriotism has its deepest roots at home. The closing paragraph of "Shall Not Perish" ends in a statement that has an air of particular timeliness today:

> ... The men and the women who did the deeds, who lasted and endured and fought the battles and lost them and fought again because they didn't even know they had been whipped, and tamed the wilderness and overpassed the mountains and deserts and died and still went on as the shape of the United States grew and went on. I knew them, too: the men and women still pow-

erful seventy-five years and twice that and twice that again afterward, still powerful and still dangerous and still coming, North and South and East and West, until the name of what they did and what they died for became just one single word, louder than any thunder. It was America, and it covered all the western earth.

So much then for one aspect of what Faulkner has to say. What of the less known side of Faulkner in which serious, half grotesque farce and comedy are in the foreground of his scenes and in which the themes of honor, devotion and personal integrity are woven into the fabric of the story? It is important, I think, that at least two of these stories, "Uncle Willy" and "That Will Be Fine," are told in the person of an all-seeing, shrewd, half-innocent, adolescent boy, a boy who seems to be the direct descendant of Melville's Ishmael through Mark Twain's Huckleberry Finn and Sherwood Anderson's George Willard of *Winesburg, Ohio*.

This line of heritage is of no discredit to Faulkner, and it shows how well he adjusted the character of his own gifts to the example set before him by Anderson. Uncle Willy, who was all too fond of drugs and drink and who resisted reform through the commands of well meaning relatives and ladies of the church, is one of the memorable characters of American fiction, and another is Uncle Rodney in "That Will Be Fine." These figures are of the romantic but no less real American who will never be fenced in, whose independence is inviolate, whose ingenuity almost, but not quite, circumvents the laws of ethical behavior and social propriety.

Among the best of *The Collected Stories* is also "Hair," which is a comedy of the first order; nor is there a better story anywhere of the barber and the peculiar delicacy of his craft. The story teeters on the verges of the ridiculous, the absurd, the sentimental: the precisely mild, neat shabby figure of the barber reminds one of Venus's victims in Lucretius's treatise on the nature of love; it is the nature of his devotion to the images of beauty and honor held in his mind's eye which lends him dignity even in his devotion to an angular little girl of easy virtue and rescues him from oblivion in pathos.

Of the stories reprinted in the present collection, "A Rose for Emily" is the best known, and it is also among the best of its kind in a genre which includes Walter de la Mare's "Seaton's Aunt," Henry James's "Last of the Valerii" and Edgar Poe's "Fall of the House of Usher." It has, I fear, provided an inspiration for large bales of creeping moss, magnolia fiction from the South, and which has now, even as I write, grown into giant, mushroom-like proportions, has escaped the modest bindings of several books (not by William Faulkner) and is heard weeping behind adolescent smiles of drunken laughter upon the Broadway stage. This is, of course, dubious flattery to Faulkner's gifts and insights, and it is the price that every writer pays for writing supremely well.

The least fortunate side of Faulkner's gift in drawing upon the wells of memory are in his stories of airplane pilots—"all the dead pilots" of World War I; the stories have all the pathos of personal tributes paid to unworthy friends: but are they heroes? They were once young, and possessed of physical beauty in skill and action; they are cursed by the passage of time, but not by the deeper forces that are at work in Faulkner's tales of the South; nor do Faulkner's pilots hold so clearly and with almost religious fervor the codes of honor and loyalty possessed by his other characters, the codes by which they expiate their sins of violence, their taint of madness.

To the general reader perhaps the greatest difficulty in reading a Faulkner short story is the experience of coming upon one that seems meaningless or incomplete. Unfortunately the true answer to the reader's question must be sought for in *Go Down, Moses*, or in *Light in August*, or another one of Faulkner's books. For at least twenty years, Faulkner has kept in mind, as though they moved upon a turning wheel, the fabulae, part family legend and part history, of Mississippi; yet he is seldom provincial in the sense that many regional writers feel compelled to be. His South with its mingling of races, with its remains of Baroque horror and decay, with its bartering of lands and birthrights, with its interludes of the shrewd, half-innocent eye of half-grown children, with its Puritanical hold upon the rights of individual being, action and thought is, as Faulkner would say it, of the America that covers all the western earth.

If Faulkner's extraordinary rhetoric is at times obscure, and is at times as baroque as the plot and substance of some of his stories, he has also written more passages of unmistakable lucidity than any writer of his generation. He is more distinctly the master of a style than any writer of fiction living in America today. Surely few writers of the short story can withstand the test so well as he in having a story read aloud; more than half the art of Faulkner's prose is in the meaning and the pleasure it conveys to the reader's inner ear. To keep the rhythms of his prose within the range of the human voice is one of the reasons, I think, that Faulkner, in the writing of a story, so often employs the use of the monologue; it is the tone of voice in which the words are spoken that gives color to the meaning of the story.

Above, beyond all questions of Faulkner's style rises the evidence of his ability to haunt the imagination of those who read his stories. Even when his stories are not at their best, the conviction of encountering a moment of human action and reality remains. One finds it difficult to forget the little melodrama of Elly, the self-obsessed young woman, the all-too-obvious victim of self-pity. "The Brooch," the story of the son dominated by his mother, is another part of the same glimpse into reality, and the black-out of resolving self-love through violent injury and death. Faulkner's solution is, of course, too easy, but he has caught within a very few pages the moral horror of self-destruction and the too-often sentimental motives of suicide.

The secret of Faulkner's hold upon the imagination is that he moves always to the unseen, unliterary and essential springs of human action; and on occasion he destroys a few of his more profound revelations of evil by an impatient thrust of counter-violence. His great accomplishment is of one who is never blind to the conflicting forces of evil, of honor, of loyalty, of spiritual death and earthly love, and if, like some of the Elizabethan dramatists, he is regional and of the American South in the same sense that they were island Englishmen: if, like them, he leaves his dead sprawled across the footlights of the stage, like them he has succeeded in giving the public of his time a vision of the quickness, the romantic mutability of life which survives the subtle passion of decay.

304

William D. Patterson.
"Short Tales by Faulkner
Show Range."
New Orleans *Times-Picayune,* August 20,
1950, Section II, p. 7.

The somber periphery of passion and disintegration, "the tragic fable of Southern history," that William Faulkner has created in his writing is a world of people possessed, of cruelty and violence. His stories so reek of social decay that a critic once called him "a minor Balzac of the sub-human world." This world is revealed in all its enervating reality in *The Collected Short Stories of William Faulkner.*

Although it is questionable whether the short story is his strongest metier, these 42 tales cover so great an area of Faulkner's career and fictional milieu that they constitute a notable body of achievement.

The reader is immediately impressed with the mastery of style and the great range of subject, from the decaying grandeur of the plantation aristocracy or the day-to-day dramas of the townsfolk, to the Indians retreating reluctantly into the back country or the sophisticates leading their predatory lives in the concrete canyons of the East. The moods pass from the grave and the grim to the haunting and the humorous.

All of it adds up to a literary landscape that makes Oxford, Miss., and its surrounding country as much a part of American letters as Hawthorne's New England or Sherwood Anderson's Ohio.

(*Collected Stories* has been chosen as a release by one of the book clubs for September, said to be the first time for a Faulkner work.)

Faulkner's apparent disregard for style,

his "flouting of the rules of grammar and syntax without rhyme or reason, running on for page after page without pausing for breath," has drawn complaints from some.

It is also a frequent criticism that Faulkner ignores the sui generis nature of his expression. "If a story is in you," he has said, "it has got to come out the way it is." He never fits a story to a form, but puts it down the way it came to him.

Some of the World War I tales in this book, such as "Victory," "The Middle Ground," and "Beyond," are not only heavily mannered in their telling but also conventional in form. Compared with later products like "A Rose for Emily" and "Shingles for the Lord," they show how far Faulkner has come since he dropped formal rules to write his own way.

Faulkner's nightmare world reminds the reader of Dostoievsky, except that Faulkner is not so obsessed with the spiritual. His hell is here, and now.

Which is one way of describing this flame of a book.

William Peden.
"Sartoris, Snopes and
Everyman."
*Saturday Review of
Literature,* August 26,
1950, p. 12.

William Faulkner is beginning to emerge rather clearly as the most considerable twentieth-century American writer of short fiction; the present volume is a publishing event of real significance. Because of its importance, because of the complete lack of information concerning its inclusiveness or data about the prior publications of the selections, and because of Mr. Faulkner's reticence concerning his work, a few facts may be of some value.

William Faulkner has published four volumes of short stories, all but the last of which are out of print. At least two of his novels might just as accurately be described as series of integrated short stories. He has published numerous magazine stories, many of which have never been reprinted. The *Collected Stories of William Faulkner* includes seventeen magazine stories, all but two pieces from *Dr. Martino and Other Stories*, and all those from his first and best collection, *These 13*.

This volume, then, is hardly representative of Faulkner's total contribution to the literature of the short story. It does not include, for example, such excellent stories as "Spotted Horses" or "Raid" or "Smoke," all of which ultimately found their way into Faulkner's novels although originally published as short stories.

The best of Faulkner's stories are those connected directly or indirectly with the saga of Yoknapatawpha County. They include a wide variety of characters, aristocrats, poor whites, Negroes, and Indians; they embrace a time span of more than a century, the most important event of which was the defeat of the Confederacy. Yoknapatawpha's leading citizens, the Sartorises, Sutpens, and Compsons, fought gallantly in the War; their descendants were never able to forget it; some of its poor whites, like Abner Snopes, profited by it. The decay of a Sartoris-controlled world and the rise to importance of a Snopes is a basic theme with Faulkner, to be repeated again and again in stories like "A Rose for Emily" or "Wash." In the decay of this world, the War was a major precipitating agent, Faulkner suggests, rather than the ultimate cause. Faulkner's Yoknapatawpha is undermined as much or more by the ferretlike rapacity of the Snopeses and the failure of its Sartorises as by Yankee bullets or carpetbag occupation. The Sartorises, Faulkner comments, men who had galloped in the old days on fine horses across the fine plantations, were symbols of admiration and hope; they were instruments, too, of despair and grief.

Faulkner is first a Mississippian and second a Southerner; Yoknapatawpha has, of course, been frequently identified with Faulkner's own country and Oxford, its county seat. Yet Faulkner at his best is no more a sectionalist in any limited interpretation of the word than, say, Hawthorne. With Faulkner place and setting are basic structural elements, not a mere decorative device. Inescapable and all-pervading, place is a vital influence on the lives of his characters. Faulkner's heritage is as much a basic element in his art as was Hawthorne's. Yet his greatest achievements have been in his sure, penetrating, and frequently devastating comprehension of the universal, translated into fictional terms by means of the local and the specific: Sartoris and Snopes are two aspects of the emblem which is everyman.

Too much has been written concerning Faulkner's preoccupation with violence, decay, abnormality, and melodrama. It is true that many of Faulkner's best stories— "A Rose for Emily," "That Evening Sun," "Dry September," "Red Leaves," and "Barn Burning,"—are somber or tragic. Such works, however, do not indicate the author's variety of subject matter and mood. In stories like "Shingles for the Lord," "A Bear Hunt," or "Mule in the Yard" Faulkner displays a robust sense of humor, a combination of horseplay, shrewdness, and sheer trifling far removed from the world which one of his critics has called one of "manias of doom." Faulkner, too, has been criticized for his lack of compassion, his creation of a gallery of soulless individuals. Of the many glaring misconceptions of Faulkner's work, this is perhaps the most striking.

Concerning the hitherto unpublished

pieces included here, the less said the better. With the exception of "A Courtship," which is as good as anything Faulkner ever wrote, a noteworthy addition to his series of Indian stories, most of the others serve only to illustrate the melancholy fact that even a very great writer can be very bad at times.

Hodding Carter. "Faulkner Tells of All of Us." *Delta Democrat-Times*, August 27, 1950, p. 4.

The publication of any book by William Faulkner is an important event, not only to the reader and student of contemporary literature but to the observer of the American social scene. The inclusive adjective American is used advisedly; for although Faulkner generally restricts himself to the easily identified eroded hill regions of Mississippi, what he says is not bounded either by time or space, but rather is timeless and without geographical limitations.

This is one way of saying that William Faulkner is a genius, which is a description too loosely given to too many who are not deserving of it. But certainly, this remote fabulous Mississippian is a genius; a rare writer whose senses are attuned not only to sound and sight and smell and touch but to the soul of mankind, so that, writing, he spins the very thread of life itself.

So much in preface to some comments, not literary, on the publication of a book entitled *Collected Stories of William Faulkner*, containing forty-two short stories. These short stories go back in time

thirty years and more. What Faulkner writes about the eroded people and lands of the 1920's is tragically accurate. He does not revel in the degeneration and savagery and bitter pride and hopelessness he found, for he pities, even loves, the people whose doomed tales he tells. But these stories, written in and about the earlier years of this century, offer no hope for people or land.

This is not true of the later Faulkner. His recent novel *Intruder in the Dust*—which, of course, is not included in the short story collection—is concerned with the spirit of the lynch mob, just as in the dreadful short story "Dry September." In the short story, set in the early 20's, there is no hope. In the novel there is.

What this means—and the observation is more important, I suppose, to the historian and sociologist than to the literary critic—is that Faulkner's works, in the aggregate, reflect not an immutable but a changing South, almost imperceptibly and perhaps without conscious intent. And that is meaningful.

We Southerners fall into many subdivisions. There are still those who say that the evil and the sordid do not exist among us at all or that such matters should not be publicly aired. There are some few who would have us believe that violence and malice and prejudice and ignorance are the primary and unchanging characteristics of our region; there are others who seek the changing whole, recognizing that the South of today is not the South of Faulkner's twenties; and no one sees this any more clearly than does William Faulkner himself, whose portrayals of the recent past have shocked and goaded and shamed and at the last afforded hope.

But these are asides. I envy the thousands who in these collected stories will come across William Faulkner for the first time.

"Haunted Landscapes." *Time*, August 28, 1950, p. 79.

Mississippi novelist William Faulkner (*The Sound and the Fury, Light in August, Sanctuary*) has no time for literary circles. An iron-grey, taciturn man of 52, he much prefers hunting and fishing. Nonetheless, for 20 years, he has been one of the leading enthusiasms of U.S. literary-intellectual pundits. Next month, for the first time, a book by William Faulkner is a Book-of-the-Month Club alternate selection. A fat collection of 42 Faulkner tales written over the past quarter-century, *Collected Stories* will let a brand-new layer of U.S. readers judge for themselves what all the critical whooping is about. The stories are also pretty sure to bring a spate of re-estimates by the critics themselves.

As a writer, Faulkner shuttles between two worlds. One of them is easily recognizable because most people spend most of their time in it: the grey one of everyday life. Faulkner describes its persons and places: down & outers in Manhattan's Penn Station, war veterans living on pride, hungry poets mooching from a successful colleague. If this were all that Faulkner could do, he would be buried in an obscure corner of U.S. letters, as a minor realist in the tradition of Dos Passos, Hemingway and F. Scott Fitzgerald.

The other Faulkner world is the one he has made his own: mythical Yoknapatawpha County in northern Mississippi, a landscape haunted by an unsettled past and an unwanted future. The past survives in the memory of the old South, its code of courage and chivalry, its moral stain of slavery. The future is the creeping new world of Northern commerce and industry; in Faulkner's view, it promises to make life impersonal, mechanized and "depthless."

In his stories, the Sartoris family represents the past—former aristocrats who lose themselves in gentility, alcohol, rhetoric and madness. The Snopes family symbolizes the future; they are coldly, and crudely, on the make. The process of degeneration hits bottom when a third type appears: people who use the Sartoris pretensions to veil the Snopes greed.

Faulkner's instinctive sympathies are with the founders of the Sartoris clan, who tamed the country and fought in the Civil War. But he realizes that their way of life is dead forever, largely because they allowed it to be corrupted by slavery. Some of Faulkner's most viciously satirical passages are directed against the sickly remnants—the gentlemen who drink morning toddies while the floors beneath them are visibly rotting away. At the same time, he desperately hates the hard-souled, faceless Snopeses, whose only purpose in life is to accumulate money. In the present-day South, Faulkner admires only such stiff-back Negroes as Lucas Beauchamp of *Intruder in the Dust*, who endure humiliation with patience and dignity, and those poor whites who cling to their land, their families and their old morality.

This view of the South as an area trapped between Sartoris impotence and Snopes viciousness explains Faulkner's harshness and fury. He is a man possessed and tortured by his vision: too honest to deny it, too sensitive to tolerate it. The horrors of his books—the rapes and castrations, the incestuous romances and idiot flirtations with cows—fall into place, not as exhibits of sensationalism, but instead as images of the social and moral disease that he is constantly probing.

If taken as realistic reporting of Southern life, Faulkner's Yoknapatawpha saga makes little sense. It is based on his life-long devotion to the Mississippi scene, but it is no mere copy of that scene. Rather it is a grotesque, symbolic version, in which the dimensions of reality are wildly distorted to make them more vivid. Some-times, his writing seems almost like a pro-longed hallucination—a hallucination crowded with extraordinary characters and violent actions. Moreover, for any Northerner to believe that Faulkner's world is limited to the South would be complacent provincialism. When Faulkner describes his Yoknapatawpha County, he is writing not only about the South but also the North, not only about the North but all of modern life.

Often enough, in his furious haste to get things down on paper and his weak-ness for pyrotechnics, Faulkner trips over his own inventiveness. His tales of vio-lence then become preposterous and cheap; his livid rhetoric creates a verbal log jam, with prepositions flying wild, clauses drift-ing crazily and parentheses multiplying like rabbits. But when he is really in com-mand of his story (about half the time), Faulkner makes his rhetoric work for him, even when it is full of echoes of Ciceronian oratory and of overripe Elizabethan poetry.

And he can be direct and simple. When he wants to describe Flem Snopes's eyes, he calls them "two gobs of cup grease on a hunk of raw dough."

He is particularly gifted at recording Negro speech: "I can't hang around white man's kitchen . . . But white man can hang around mine. White man can come in my house, but I can't stop him. When white man want to come in my house, I ain't got no house."

In the *Collected Stories*, Faulkner's blaz-ing skill and lazy improvisations, his rich humor and corny folksiness, his deep sense of tragedy and tasteless gothic excesses

are all brought together. About half a dozen stories are as good bits of fiction as have ever been written in the U.S.: "Barn Burning," a poignant sketch of a boy's anguished love for his arsonist-father; "A Rose for Emily," that hair-raising classic of a lady's decline to necrophilia; "Wash," a magnificent portrait of a poor white who, after years of loyalty, rebels against his landlord; "Dry September," a lynch-ing story to end all lynching stories; "A Courtship," a richly comic tall tale about the love rivalry of a white man and an Indian in early 19th Century America; and "Death Drag," a harrowing story about three hungry, neurotic stunt flyers.

The final impression left by Faulkner's work is that he is a writer of incompara-ble talents who has used and misused those talents superbly and recklessly. But his book has the excitement that comes from never knowing when, amidst pages of fail-ure, there will come a masterpiece.

Edward Parone. "A Mane like Tangled Fire." Hartford *Courant*, September 3, 1950, Magazine Section, p. 14.

His syntax would give Harold Ross the creeps. (It is much tougher than Proust. He uses fifty words where five would do; he uses one long word where ten short ones would do. His punctuation is sparse.) His opening passages would make any newspaper editor or teacher of creative writing want to throw himself into a pit full of cottonmouth moccasins. (He intro-duces three characters on the first page about whose subsequent importance you are not sure. He mentions people and events and thoughts which he explains in his own sweet time. He almost takes it for granted that you know the genealogy of everyone in Yoknapatawpha County and vicinity. He forgets small details.)

We haven't got another writer in America who can compare with him in breadth and variety. (The best ones can match him in depth.) Beside him, Hemingway looks like a flash in the pan.

There is no such thing as a born writer, but he is the closest thing there is to it. He is not, of course, artless. Yet you get the feeling that his great compulsion to speak overcame or was unaware of any sense of incapability or self-doubt or the impossibility of the job—as though a flower has pushed itself painfully up out of the arid dust of a Mississippi dooryard, showing, as part of its character and beauty, all the blemishes and deformities acquired in merely being born. When he tells a story you get the feeling that this is the way you would hear it and repeat it if Herman Basket, the Choctaw, had told it to you. (James and Hemingway you admire, but they amaze you with their art and always a little you hold them at arm's length. He is like the old man full of stories who used to run the dirty watch repair shop around the corner or like the old uncle you have had around the house for years who is a talented gossip.) That takes great art.

When the world speaks it is as general and confusing as four winds blowing at once. When his world speaks it speaks with his voice, which, with all its human failings, is the voice of order. Without ever intruding upon the stage he has set as an embarrassed, all-hands actor, he has made himself an intrinsic part of the play. It is as though he had not only produced but was produced by the universe he created: Yoknapatawpha County, a mythical territory in Mississippi whose geography and people are more real than Fairfield County.

A Gertrude Stein or Ezra Pound would have ruined him. They would have imposed upon the art which a good writer develops in transit an added layer, a "tone" of art. In making him impeccable they would have made him untrue to his need and his purpose. What he wants to say depends on his "primitive" sincerity, his imperfections, his headlong dive into a bottomless vat. It is "we" who tell the stories which have been pieced together from bits heard and seen here and there. They are composites (which he blankly states about one story, "All the Dead Pilots") and because "we"—a city or village with a searching scrutiny—speak, there is confusion. For out of what chaos of the mind have things been thought? with what chaos of actions have deeds been done? from what chaos of impressions has order come and a story been made?

This is apparently what makes him "difficult" reading. (You do not have to like him, but if you take him you must be willing to take all of him.) Yet it is part of his genius, part of his originality, this illusion of order rising out of chaos right before your eyes. It gives him a bardic quality. And these things, together with his subjects, his conception and his accomplishment make him the first great American writer.

The only old time hero in those stories is "we," whether the country, city, village or wilderness. In the best sense of the word it is indifferent and it survives all the stories it relates—adding, because it is human after all, a bit here and there of guilt, wisdom and glory. (Lawyer Gavin Stevens comes close to being a hero—Harvard and Phi Beta Kappa but virile nonetheless and aware of those who are not any of the three and open to mistakes himself. But because of his qualities he is not suitable for the hero's part.) Most typically and significantly the "we" is a young boy, pouring out extravagantly, in breathless profusion, all that his innocence has let him hear, see and feel. He is perfect for the role. Indeed, he was created for it, since (there the art reveals itself) his own father and mother and family are often negligible characters. He is related to them only for convenience's sake. He is most like the town of Jefferson or the mind of a writer both of whom have a "naive" or ignorant way of being right or revealing truth.

It took this volume to reveal that there is more universality and virtuosity in the work of one man than in a recent anthology containing the work of 55 different writers. There are no extrinsic trappings, no introduction, only intelligent grouping which ends the book wisely with the voluptuous death dream "Carcassonne": "I want to perform something bold and tragic and austere . . . me on a buckskin pony with eyes like blue electricity and mane like tangled fire, galloping up the hill and right off into the high heaven of the world . . ." That is what has been done in this work.

It is silly to tell people that they "ought to" read certain books. Usually it is better to leave them to their own devices. Some people should not read anything at all. Some do not have to read. But if you must read, then there are certain books you ought to read and among these there are some that you ought to own. This is one of them. And the name is Faulkner. William Faulkner.

Paul Engle.
"Collected Stories of William Faulkner."
Chicago *Sunday Tribune*, September 17, 1950, Magazine of Books, p. 3.

This is the book which may at last bring William Faulkner the position and praise he has so long deserved. Many of his novels have been out of print. He has been extremely criticized by some because of the violence of his books. Others have objected to his refusal to accept popular slogans which blurred over the reality of experience as he saw it. From the beginning he has gone his own individual and original way.

What these stories suggest is that we have had in this country for some time a writer of imagination, of power, of literal recording of truth, of brilliance in prose and scope of conception. In brief, we have had a fiction writer of genius, one of the few, quietly working away in Mississippi while the latest writer of a best seller gracefully took from the hand of his grateful publisher the literary gin. Reading this collection, one can only feel that bourbon and branch water have here produced a finer thing.

At their best Faulkner's stories have the qualities of the supreme examples of modern literature—they are rigorously accurate in speech, in concrete detail, in weather and landscape and clothing, and at the same time are highly symbolic of large areas of moral meaning. Faulkner has, indeed, created many levels of social, economic, class, regional, racial, and intellectual significances, and all in terms of the most dramatic incidents.

His stories, like his novels, cover the

decline of a plantation life whose high principles he admires, although he admits the infection of slavery which destroyed the life. And they cover the rise of that political money-grabber, the family of Snopes, symbol of the petty group which had replaced the older and nobler Sartoris type. Faulkner likes neither, but admires the older men for their adherence to convictions, whereas the Snopes tribe had no conviction save that of money. But Faulkner never permits this larger view to interfere with the fictional texture of his tales.

As his medium for narrating, Faulkner has devised a rich and various prose, full of startling images and wry jokes and sharp psychological insights. He is one of the few recent American novelists to have a distinguished and at the same time realistic style. Sometimes it shatters into rhetoric, but when successful it is an instrument of amazing force.

The stories of the south in this volume have a quality of intense accuracy lacking in those dealing with Europe or New York. But there is not a story in this book which does not have elements of great fiction.

Robert Cantwell. "Faulkner's World." *The Freeman*, October 2, 1950, pp. 26–28.

There are forty-two stories in *The Collected Stories of William Faulkner*, and the book runs to 900 pages. It must be said at the outset that, considered as a whole, they seem his best work. They are plainly the product of one of the most powerful and original imaginations in American literature, and they justify including Faulkner among the world's masters of fiction.

The town of Jefferson that Faulkner has

been building for the past thirty years, the Negroes with their grave and oblique comments, the cunning and pettiness of the monstrous Snopes family, with their eyes like stagnant water, the romantic Sartoris descendants, the world of courthouse squares, barber shops, mountain cabins, bus stations, old houses, lawyers' offices, swamps, plantations, is no longer only potentially a Balzacian creation: it is, like the Paris of Balzac, a living environment, with a history, heroes, mythology, codes, and a life of its own.

These stories gain their strength from being part of the whole Faulkner environment. They can be read independently of the novels, but they take on their deepest meaning as exemplifications of one side or another of the people and the practices of Faulkner's own specific Mississippi civilization. There are six sections in the book. The first, "The Country," contains six stories, newer ones, and generally Faulkner's best: "Barn Burning," "Shingles for the Lord," "The Tall Men," "A Bear Hunt," "Two Soldiers," and "Shall Not Perish." The second section, "The Village," begins with the famous "A Rose for Emily," and includes ten stories, ending with the equally famous "That Evening Sun," the only one of the stories Faulkner wrote in the early thirties that can be compared with his newer work. The third section, "The Wilderness," is made up of four of those baffling Indian tales of Faulkner's that seem to have come from nowhere and to bear no relation to anything else in literature. The next, "The Wasteland," consists of five war stories. The fifth section, "The Middle Ground," is principally made up of the stories Faulkner published in the middle thirties—"Wash," "Dr. Martino," and "The Brooch"—along with a newer piece like "Golden Land," of corruption and publicity in Los Angeles. The final section, "Beyond," includes "Black Music," "The Leg," and such very early works as "Mistral" and "Divorce in Naples." They are so different from the later ones, and so much like the expatriate fiction of the time, that they seem almost the work of another writer.

As to what is in them: in "Barn Burning" we come upon Abner Snopes and his family thirty years after the Civil War. The Snopeses, for readers who are not familiar with the novels, are that extraordinary clan of amoral, cunning, and yet essentially comic opportunists who have been inundating the country. They wheedle their way into jobs, they graft, lie, cheat, steal, they set one Negro workman against another by telling each that the other is after his job, they trade their wives for minor political posts or junior partnerships, they stage accidents to collect insurance, and they climb, climb and climb, devoting to their tireless self-seeking their considerable brains, their cold hearts and their sacred honor. The name is synonymous with a kind of ludicrous shrewdness and stupid cunning—little snide deals worked out like diplomatic maneuvers. As a symbol the Snopeses are probably a good deal more representative and significant than the Babbitts ever were. We now learn of another side of them: old Ab Snopes, crippled and vicious, accompanied by his sons and bovine daughters, is burning the barns of any landowner who crosses him. His son, Colonel Sartoris Snopes, rebels against this destructive pilgrimage across the land (and apparently, it seems, against the Sodom-and-Gomorrah home life of the family), warns a landowner, and flees.

Heretofore the Snopeses have been maddening, or contemptible, or funny, but old Ab in his villainy, limping with a wound in his heel (dating from the days he was stealing Confederate and/or Union horses), longfaced, taciturn, dark and merciless, is a powerful figure, rightly feared; Faulkner's portrait of him is his clearest example of his mastery of backwoods dialect of this type of mentality. Heretofore, too, the rise of the Snopeses has been in worldly terms. They get political jobs. But the boy's revolt is not merely the awakening of a moral sense—it is an heroic act; not a glimmering awareness of right and wrong, but a sudden leap from a world of hatred and primitive cunning.

The Flem Snopes who steals the brass fitting from the city power plant (including the safety valve) is kin to the Snopes of Jefferson who buys mules and runs them on the railroad track so he can collect damages from the railroad. The Sartoris drunk on Armistice Day in France ("Ad Astra") is of the same family as the ninety-year-old Virginia Sartoris of "There Was A Queen," listening to the confession of her daughter-in-law. The Compsons of "That Evening Sun," trying ineffectually to prevent their negro maid from being murdered, is the Compson family of *The Sound and the Fury*, the character of the children foreshadowing their later tragedy. The Major Waddell of "Mountain Victory," killed after the Civil War as he is trying to get back to his plantation, is the son of the Indian and Frenchwoman, named Waddel or Vidal, who appeared in Washington, calling on the President, in Faulkner's cycle of Indian stories.

These interrelationships are not only a part of the story—often they *are* the story, what it is that adds significance, movement, emotion, a sense of mystery, what prevents it from being only a picturesque or dramatic incident. They link the individual stories to something, in the way that Hawthorne's stories, in Van Wyck Brooks's phrase, were links with the Middle Ages. They link them to the past, to history, to the world of quality in the crude family-tree sense of the word, of course, but a world of quality in which action and expression is in accord with the truest and deepest impulse, and free of calculation and guile. The vision of this quality lies over Faulkner's novels; it hovers over the town of Jefferson like a mirage; the Sartorises and a few others understand or glimpse it; the Snopeses have no conception of it whatsoever. The linkages to the whole are so important to Faulkner's work that it is doubtful if it would mean anything like what it does without them. Faulkner's war stories could have been written by others, and so could his stories of flying. The intricate interrelationships of Jefferson, ancestry, the delicate filaments of inheritance and recollection, are unique: there is never a question but that they are a positive force in the life of the people.

Faulkner is no antiquarian. When he does recount known history, it is often superficial. His people like to talk it, like a preacher quoting a text—not a text actually relevant, but one that is supposed to be. The interconnections in his stories are to the past, but he has had to create a past as well. I do not understand his Indians, but I marvel at them, at the imagination that conceived of these torpid redskins and their Negro slaves, and gave them speech, clothes, emotions; the chief who hauled the steamboat overland to his plantation; the mixture of tribal rites and Paris education; the flight of the Negro slave who is to be killed to keep the dead chief company in the other world. It is true that they provide Faulkner with much material for satire, but unlike the Snopeses they have so few points of contact with a recognizable world that it seems too labored and difficult for the effect, like raising a building in order to paint a caricature of a WPA mural on the wall.

This collection of his short stories is so much clearer than Faulkner's work in general that it is inappropriate to do more than mention the familiar exaggerations and repetitions. When he began to write, when he was half way through his second novel, "I discovered," he said, "that writing was a mighty fine thing. It enabled you to make men stand on their hind legs and cast a shadow." Sartoris made him feel that "I had all these people" and when he discovered them "I wanted to bring back all the others." To a considerable extent he has done so, and this recreation of an hitherto unimaginable past is what lay behind those first rather conventionally rebellious tales. It may also serve to explain, partially, why Faulkner stands in an oblique relationship to the life of his time, why his picture of Jefferson does not have the kind of relationship to the country that Balzac's Paris bears to France and the world.

The material for his art does not lie on the surface; it is not around everywhere in Jefferson's streets and houses and schools and stores; it has to be dug and scratched for, fabricated, added to, joined and connected. A past has to be created for it, and a political theory. Faulkner digs up his extraordinary incidents and characters, and by sheer will power and a powerful narrative gift and a command of common speech almost makes them seem part of ordinary experience. He almost convinces us that his Jefferson is the South, and his stories representative. They are very often not: they are fragments filling in one part or another of the pattern, compelling enough to make us accept an obvious weakness of motive, or to overlook some vague and affected writing ("time and despair rushed as slow and dark under him as under any garlanded boy or crownless and crestless girl . . .").

In "The Tall Men," for example, a draft investigator comes to arrest two farm boys for failing to register for the draft. Their father has been hurt in the mill that day, and the investigator is led into the old man's room, where he finds himself surrounded by silent and watchful men. They keep him there while the boys go to enlist.

The old man has been drinking so much that the doctor cannot give him an anesthetic and amputates his leg without it, while the sheriff talks to the investigator about war, government, the AAA—"Life has done got cheap, and life ain't cheap. Life's a pretty durn valuable thing. I don't mean just getting along from one WPA relief check to the next one, but honor and pride and discipline that makes a man worth preserving . . . " In "Shingles for the Lord" the volunteer workmen reshingling the church argue about the time each one is to give: "You don't seem to have kept up with these modern ideas about work that's been flooding and uplifting the country these past few years." There is a kind of conservative Democratic wish-fulfillment in this picture of the government and the people, and it is part of the same view of life that turns so much of the humor of Faulkner's novels into grotesque horseplay, that turns so many of their big scenes into static tableaux, and that turns so much of the narrative into impressions, sequences of words—outraged, violent, voiceless, indignant—"Then he left," or "Then we were alone"—in place of the clear development we have been led by his own graphic powers to expect.

Yet with this granted, his stories are marvelous. The old man and his son tearing off the shingles of the church in the darkness in order to put one over on another volunteer workman for the Lord, and then dropping a lantern and burning the church, are unbeatable: their story is a masterpiece. The Negro dialogue, especially in "Mule in the Yard," has never been surpassed by Faulkner, which probably means by anyone. And in "Two Soldiers" it seems to me that Faulkner has stated his case more clearly than in all the novels that preceded it. This story of a country boy running away to find his brother in the army—"You got to have water and wood to cook with. I can cut it and tote it for you-all"—has a wild and passionate simplicity; it really is the love of the country without reservations or restraint. This is what he has been driving at, the quality whose absence has been the source of his estrangement from Jefferson, the quality that the Snopeses cannot comprehend. In the past, in the Sartorises or the gallant Southerners in the Civil War, it has often been distorted, emerging as a momentary acceptance of impulse, bravado, show, a scornful rejection of compromise, but it is here perfectly fused with the setting—the bus station and the recruiting office—and the time—the days after Pearl Harbor—whose mood and character have never been better expressed. This is one of Faulkner's stories that was right on the street, all around him, requiring no past or explanations, and it is his best.

George Smart. "Good Variety in Faulkner." Boston *Post*, October 8, 1950, p. 2-A.

If the novels of William Faulkner fall into a pattern of horror, violence, poetic introspection and sensitively rendered natural beauty, his collected stories most emphatically do not. So if you are inclined to shy away from a Faulkner book on the theory that it's just too durned depressing to read in such overwrought times as these, let us recommend this collection to you on the ground that many of the stories are beautifully symbolic, a number of them are funny in the, believe it or not, Thurber manner, and quite a few are cheerful and optimistic. Furthermore, nearly all of them indicate beyond all doubt that William Faulkner is an unmistakably superior writer, one of the very finest literary craftsmen now working in America. His grasp of human psychology is at times truly amazing; his gift for finding the right turn of phrase to suggest deep spiritual and emotional meanings is as unmistakable as it is rare. Finally, no writer we know of is better at recreating the varied and limitless beauties of nature.

Any book of stories is hard to review and Mr. Faulkner's collection, running to some 900 pages, is especially complex and multifarious. The stories are grouped in patterns: The Country (these deal with the rural Mississippi people Faulkner has made both famous and infamous); The Village; The Wilderness; The Wasteland (mainly war stories); The Middle Ground; Beyond (stories built around a kind of psychological mysticism almost impossible to define). These classifications serve to suggest an over-all theme in Faulkner's work, one not very clear-cut but more or less implied. That theme is the corrosive and deepseated effects of defeat in war and defeat in competition on human nature.

Yet to say that this is the Faulkner theme and at the same time to suggest that many of these stories are poetically beautiful and even cheerful may seem a paradox. Well, so be it. Faulkner's limitless talent for seeing all sides of life in all sorts of places (very many of these stories deal with neither Mississippi nor the South) brings him inevitably to the position of realizing that no one theme, no matter how central, can ever categorize or pigeon-hole human experience, not even in the war-ridden 20th century. So much for the overall effect of this book. To be more specific, we can only say that here you will find such well-known Faulkner people as the Snopeses and the Sartorises, that some of the classic tales like "A Rose for Emily" are here,

and that there are also some of the Faulkner *Saturday Evening Post* stories. The stories are nearly all complete in themselves, have to be read pretty much at a one-at-a-time pace. Almost any one of them is likely to ring some sort of bell for any reader. In short, this is a rich collection of very superior fiction. Our guess is that, so far as creative writing of a high order goes, it's the year's best book buy.

Morris Freedman. "Collected Stories of William Faulkner." Chicago Jewish Forum, 9 (Summer 1951), 288–89.

William Faulkner's short stories serve well to pose his paradox. He is certainly an important American writer worthy of discussion on a high level. However, aside from Robert Penn Warren (his imitator and a more calculating craftsman), Faulkner is the only American writer who has regularly published both for the mass production audiences (*Saturday Evening Post*) and for those who read respectable literary journals (*Sewanee Review*). Nor is it merely a matter of doing hack work to support art. Possibly Faulkner separates the two worlds and knows what's for a twenty-five dollar market and what for a thousand dollar one. But his artistically tawdriest stories are distinguished by flashes of originality and style, certainly signs of skill, if not genius, in writing; and his best pieces are often marred by the lapse of taste, of the total absence of it, which characterizes American slick magazine fiction.

Faulkner is not an artist, then, in the sense of attempting—omnipotently, omnisciently—to control every element in his chosen medium with a high consciousness of art. He is not a Joyce or Mann—who examine and reexamine and are sure they know why every comma is in its place; he is in the tradition of Byron and Lawrence, and probably Hemingway—who, to use Byron's image, leap like tigers at their prey: if they don't kill with the first blow, they withdraw to the bush to lie in wait for another victim. (Lawrence never rewrote; if he didn't like a draft, he threw it away and started a new one.) Faulkner's reader must constantly struggle with the problem of whether a certain confusing detail in plot or characterization, a lapse in syntax, an ambiguity in language, is accidental, the result of this tigrish relationship to his work, or quite intentional. For Faulkner is no primitive. He surely knows Henry James; a chapter in an early book, *Pylon*, is titled "The Lovesong of J. A. Prufrock"; an early novel is slavishly imitative of Huxley.

But if he is not an artist in this sense, if he is not totally and perpetually conscious of every effect, then neither was Shakespeare. And as one comes to Shakespeare ready to accept and shrug off the meretricious in the total context, one should approach Faulkner with a somewhat similar tolerance. This book offers a good picture of the high and low in Faulkner. On the positive side, there is his luxurious love of language; his piling on of adjectives in search of the exact nuance; his repeated use of certain ones in unexpected contexts, jarring the reader into attentiveness ("furious" and "outrageous" are favorites); his absorption with plot and the technique of unfolding revelation; his creation of a gallery of fullbodied characterizations we can as little make out unequivocally as real people; and so on. On the negative, we have stories that start off brilliantly and then suddenly collapse (as though Faulkner lost interest and just wanted to get the thing over with); aimless, anecdo-

tal ones about foolish people involved in foolish messes; mawkish, sentimental ones that read like dehydrated synopses of slick magazine fiction; and so on.

A number of rarely anthologized Faulkner stories appear in this collection. We find here "Elly," a brooding, intense tale of familial and race relations, one of the finest things he has ever done; "Crevasse," one of his early stories about World War I, concentrating on the wasteland-like loneliness of war; "Lo!" a remarkable fantasy, frightening yet funny, about how a tribe of Chickasaw Indians besieged the White House; "Artist at Home," a wry comment on the artistic life; "Honor," a flying story, in which a struggle of wills is dramatically carried on without ever being articulated. The usual Faulkner pieces are here also: "A Rose for Emily," "That Evening Sun," "The Bear Hunt." Someday, perhaps, there will be a collection called "The Best of Faulkner," in which the good will not be tainted or made questionable by the bad. In the meanwhile, this collection offers a full picture of the kind of work done by a literary genius in our time who has not let his touch become inhibited by self-consciousness or a too great awareness of literary art, or his production limited by a compulsion toward perfection.

Checklist of Additional Reviews

"*Collected Stories of William Faulkner.*" *Kirkus*, June 15, 1950, p. 340.
Long Beach *Press Telegraph*, August 27, 1950.
Quick, August 29, 1950.
Houston *Press*, September 1, 1950.
"Faulkner Collection Offers 42 of His Stories." Syracuse *Herald*, September 3, 1950.

"Faulkner Volume." Rocky Mount (N.C.) *Sunday Telegram*, September 3, 1950, p. 5-A.

"*Collected Stories of William Faulkner.*" *Newsweek*, September 4, 1950, p. 79.

Pasadena *Star News*, September 17, 1950.

"*Collected Stories of William Faulkner.*" *Atlantic Monthly*, October 1950, p. 90.

"*Collected Stories of William Faulkner.*" *College English*, 12 (October 1950), 64.

"*Collected Stories.*" *Best Sellers*, October 15, 1950, pp. 118–19.

"*Collected Stories of William Faulkner.*" Radio broadcast on WSTC (Stamford, Conn.), October 15, 1950 (copy in Random House files).

"*Collected Stories of William Faulkner.*" *Wisconsin Library Bulletin*, November 1950, p. 18.

"*Collected Stories of William Faulkner.*" Roanoke *Times*, date unknown.

Kentucky School Journal, November 1950.

Negro Digest, April 1951.·

The Cresset, October 1952, p. 61.

Allison, Margaret. "William Faulkner Collection Arrives." Bay City (Mich.) *Times*, September 21, 1950, p. 22.

Ashford, Gerald. "Faulkner's Stories." San Antonio *Express*, August 27, 1950, p. 10-B.

Beck, Warren. "The Stature of Faulkner." Milwaukee *Journal*, September 10, 1950, Section V, p. 4.

Bradley, Van Allen. "Genius of Faulkner Brilliantly Displayed in His Short Stories." Chicago *Daily News*, August 30, 1950, p. 33.

Brady, Charles A. "*Collected Stories of William Faulkner.*" Buffalo *Evening News*, August 19, 1950, Magazine Section, p. 8.

Branigan, Alan. "The Great Mr. Faulkner." Newark (N.J.) *News*, September 17, 1950, Section III, p. 54.

Brennan, Dan. "Faulkner Due for Fame." Minneapolis *News*, August 25, 1950, p. 10.

Burt, Jesse. "A Passport for Adventure in Faulkner's Vivid World." Nashville *Tennessean*, September 3, 1950, p. 14-A.

C., C. "Collected Work of a Southerner." Augusta (Ga.) *Chronicle*, August 20, 1950, p. 8-B.

Cady, Ernest. "Something for Every Faulkner Admirer in His *Collected Stories.*" Columbus *Dispatch*, August 27, 1950, p. 7-F.

Cargill, Oscar. "*Collected Stories of William Faulkner.*" *Tomorrow*, December 1950, pp. 52–53.

Carroll, Calvert. "*Collected Stories of William Faulkner.*" Baltimore *News Post*.

Carter, Hodding. "William Faulkner's Collected Stories." Atlanta *Journal-Constitution*, August 27, 1950, p. 3-F.

Carver, Wayne. "Faulkner's Work at Last Overcomes Mrs. Grundy's Heroic Resistance." Salt Lake City *Tribune*, December 31, 1950, p. 5-M.

Chapman, Mary Chilton. "*Collected Stories of William Faulkner.*" Charleston (W.Va.) *Gazette*, August 20, 1950, p. 3.

Clough, Ben C. "Faulkner Stories." Providence *Sunday Journal*, August 27, 1950, Section VI, p. 8.

Derleth, August. "New Short Stories." Madison (Wis.) *Capital Times*, September 2, 1950, p. 3.

DuBois, William. "Books of the Times." New York *Times*, August 24, 1950, p. 25.

Elconin, Victor A. "Faulkner Brilliant and Inconsistent." *Daily Oklahoman* (Oklahoma City), November 19, 1950, Magazine Section, p. 15.

Fiedler, Leslie A. "William Faulkner: An American Dickens." *Commentary*, 10 (October 1950), 384–87. Also see "Style and Antistyle in the Short

Story." *Kenyon Review*, 13 (Winter 1951), 155–72.

Fratoni, Alba. "Collected Short Stories of William Faulkner." *Westporter Herald* (Westport, Conn.), January 18, 1951, Section II, p. 3.

Govan, Gilbert E. "Of Books and Writers." Chattanooga *Times*, September 10, 1950, p. 21.

Hart, H. W. *"Collected Stories." Library Journal*, 75 (July 1950), 1180.

Haswell, Richard E. "Faulkner's Virtuosity." St. Louis *Post-Dispatch*, October 8, 1950, p. 4-C.

Haxton, Josephine A. *"The Collected Stories of William Faulkner." Delta Democrat-Times* (Greenville, Miss.), August 20, 1950, p. 20.

Hedges, Edmund H., S.J. *"Collected Stories of William Faulkner."* Kansas City *Sun Herald*, February 15, 1951, p. 7. Reprinted Peoria (Ill.) *Register*, February 25, 1950.

Hicks, Granville. "Our First Novelist." *New Leader*, November 20, 1950, pp. 20–22.

Hunt, Douglas L. "William Faulkner's Stories—Sensitive, Tender, Shocking." Birmingham *News*, August 27, 1950, p. 6-E.

Hunt, John. *"Collected Stories." Wake*, 9 (1950), 122–24.

Hunter, Anna C. "Books in Review." Savannah *Morning News*, September 3, 1950, p. 39.

Hutsell, James K. "Here's Faulkner in Provocative Cross-Section." Pensacola (Fla.) *News-Journal*, September 10, 1950, Section III, p. 4.

J., D.W. *"Collected Stories of William Faulkner."* Lewiston (Me.) *Daily Sun*, November 3, 1950, p. 4.

Jackson, Margot. "Collection of Faulkner Stories is Best of Publishers' Offerings." Akron *Beacon Journal*, August 27, 1950, p. 4-B.

Jensen, Arthur E. "Human Sympathy and Craftsmanship." Boston *Sunday Herald*, August 20, 1950, p. 3-B.

Jones, Carter Brooke. "Short Stories of Faulkner Collected." Washington *Sunday Star*, August 27, 1950, p. 3-C.

Kelly, James E. "Faulkner Fans Given Rare Treat in New Collection of Stories." Denver *Post*, September 3, 1950, p. 4-D.

Kervin, Roy. "Touched by the South." Montreal *Gazette*, December 9, 1950, p. 31.

Kohler, Dayton. "Collected Stories Exhibit Faulkner's Full Range." Louisville *Courier Journal*, September 3, 1950, Section III, p. 6.

Krim, Seymour. "Short Stories by Six." *Hudson Review*, 3 (Winter, 1950–1951), 633–36.

Kuhl, Arthur. *"Collected Stories of William Faulkner."* St. Louis *Star-Times*, September 27, 1950, p. 17.

Lysenko, Vera. "Man—Mean, Magnificent." *Globe and Mail* (unidentified city), November 4, 1950.

Nicholson, Henry. *"Collected Stories of William Faulkner."* Radio broadcast on WSAY (Rochester, N.Y.), November 14, 1950 (copy in Random House files).

Olofson, Phil. *"Collected Stories of William Faulkner."* Fort Wayne *News-Sentinal*, September 30, 1950, p. 4.

Partridge, David. "Salute to Faulkner— Nobel Prizewinner." New York *Post*, December 10, 1950, p. 12-M.

Petrone, John F. *"Collected Stories of William Faulkner." The Militant*, December 4, 1950, p. 2.

R., S. *"Collected Stories of William Faulkner." Westchester Life*, May 1951.

Ready, W. B. *"Collected Stories of William Faulkner." The Sign*, October 1950, pp. 66–67.

Record, E. D. "Faulkner Stories Now Collected." Rochester *Democrat and*

Chronicle, October 8, 1950, p. 11-E.

Ritter, Ed. *"The Collected Stories of William Faulkner."* Cincinnati *Times-Star*, October 25, 1950, p. 25.

Rose, William. "Forty-two Stories by Faulkner." San Francisco *Chronicle*, August 20, 1950, This World Magazine, p. 18.

Rosenfeld, Isaac. "Faulkner and Contemporaries." *Partisan Review*, 18 (January–February 1951), 106–9.

Rovere, Richard. "New Books." *Harper's Magazine*, November 1950, pp. 100–9.

Sandrof, Ivan. *"Collected Stories of William Faulkner."* Worcester (Mass.) *Sunday Telegram*, August 20, 1950, p. 7-D.

Shaw, Mildred. Grand Junction (Colo.) *Daily Sentinel*, September 21, 1950.

Simak, Clifford D. "Faulkner Tales Belong to Permanent Library." Minneapolis *Sunday Tribune*, August 27, 1950, Feature-News Section, p. 10.

Sivia, Harry. "The Artistry of William Faulkner." Houston *Post*, September 3, 1950, Section IV, p. 11.

Sizer, Alvin V. "Faulkner Stories Superb." New Haven *Register*, August 27, 1950, Magazine Section, p. 8.

Skelton, Bill. "Faulkner Best, Worst and Inimitable." Jackson (Miss.) *Clarion-Ledger*, September 10, 1950, Section IV, p. 3.

Spearman, Walter. "New Faulkner Book." Greensboro *Daily News*, September 17, 1950, Feature Section, p. 7.

Sylvester, Harry. "The Dark, Bright World of William Faulkner." *New York Times Book Review*, August 20, 1950, p. 1.

T., W. "A Feast of Faulkner." Philadelphia *Inquirer*, September 3, 1950, Magazine Section, p. 34.

Truax, Charles V. "New Collection of Faulkner Stories." Dayton *Daily News*, September 10, 1950, Section II, p. 7.

Tunstall, Caroline Heath. "Faulkner's World." Norfolk *Virginian-Pilot*, August 20, 1950, Part IV, p. 10.

W., A.M. "Faulkner Anthology Good Book Shelf Item." Hartford *Times*, August 19, 1950, p. 16.

W., L.A. "Romantic Cynicism Rambles Through Faulkner's Sad Tales." Columbia *Missourian*, October 16, 1950, p. 4.

Washburn, Beatrice. "Man's Inner Nature Gets Attention." Miami *Herald*, August 20, 1950, p. 4-F.

Willingham, John R. "Some Rank with the Greatest." *Arkansas Gazette* (Little Rock), October 1, 1950, p. 2-F.

Wilson, Edmund. "Magazine Stories by Masters: Faulkner, Edith Wharton, and James." *New Yorker*, December 9, 1950, pp. 161–62.

Wilson, Gloria. "Faulkner School Strikes Bonanza." Houston *Chronicle*, September 3, 1950, p. 11-B.

Wolin, Don. Rochester *Democrat and Chronicle*, June 10, 1951.

Yeiser, Frederick. "Faulkner's Lode." Cincinnati *Enquirer*, August 26, 1950, p. 5.

NOTES ON A HORSETHIEF

WILLIAM FAULKNER

Notes on a Horsethief

DECORATIONS BY ELIZABETH CALVERT
THE LEVEE PRESS GREENVILLE MISSISSIPPI

1950

Richard Walser. "Faulkner Story of Good and Evil." Raleigh *News and Observer*, February 11, 1951, Section IV, p. 5.

This is the first book to come from the pen of America's leading writer of fiction since his elevation some months ago to the ranks of Nobel Prize winners. Whether it is a long short story or a brief novel, one must take his choice. Faulkner has a habit of denying the usual classifications. At any rate, it is a postscript to his 1948 novel, *Intruder in the Dust*—a story which put clearly upon the conscience of white Southerners the psychological requisites to the solution of their racial problem as well as one which defined the psychological posture of the Southern Negro regarding this problem. The conscience has not changed in Faulkner's story, though the fictional situation has somewhat altered.

It is April, 1914. A famous imported racehorse, with a leg irreparably injured in a train wreck, is stolen by his English groom, and with the aid of a Negro preacher-stableman is nursed and cared for sufficiently for him to win races in out-of-the-way county seats and country fairs, always eluding the pursuing detectives, police, insurance adjusters, and others interested in his apprehension. The chase ends in a small Missouri town, where the escape of the English groom is effectuated as a tribute from the community to the groom's efforts to have the horse serve his natural purpose—racing—instead of imprisoning him in a veterinarian's ward to provide procreation for future thoroughbreds. The community also saves the Negro from the law as a reward for his role in the escapades—thus reversing the basic situation in *Intruder in the Dust*.

Faulkner would be telling us here that the conscience of the Southern white, though he is the "captive" of the Negro, has built his law not only to punish "the evil but of protecting the weak." When the old Negro gives himself up, the turnkey, who is really the hero of the story, ponders the situation of the Negro and the money he is supposed to have made from the winning racehorse: "What a shame he has to defend it with only his black skin which itself is the first and deadliest enemy to his keeping it." The Negro's money is the concern of the outsiders, but not of the Missouri jailer and his townsmen. The Negro is allowed to go free, even though he did not seek freedom. When the issues are clear to him, Faulkner would say, the Southerner will exact justice in spite of the law and in spite of the color of the accused, just as he is frequently misled when the issues are clouded, as they were in *Intruder in the Dust*.

Notes on a Horsethief has been published in a limited edition of 975 copies from the press of Faulkner's famous fellow Mississippian, Hodding Carter. There are decorations by Elizabeth Calvert. And I especially am happy to add that it is not, as the *New York Times* reported last summer in announcing the book, a story in one sentence. The difficult Faulkner style, however, burnishes the entire piece, and I counted a single sentence seventeen pages long. The story is a necessary link in Faulkner's expanding concepts (there is a three-page treatise on war); it will hardly achieve popularity, nor does it seem likely that Faulkner intended it to.

Irving Howe.
"Genius as Windbag."
Nation, March 10, 1951, p. 233.

Though it comes from the one living American who can lay claim to greatness as a novelist, this privately printed and fabulously priced story is a bad piece of writing. Faulkner is cultivating a literary paunch: he has become impossibly garrulous and preposterously oracular. To anyone who admires *The Sound and the Fury*, *The Bear*, and *The Hamlet* for the superb things they are, it is extremely irritating to see not a decline in Faulkner's powers but something almost worse, a cavalier abuse of them.

In conception *Notes on a Horsethief* is marvelous. An English race horse is brought to America and wins every contest in sight. It is a proud animal, which responds, in "no mere rapport but affinity," only to the word of its groom, a grimy little Englishman. One day the horse is badly hurt in an accident, and the groom, fearful that some meddlesome authorities may have it shot, spirits it away with the help of some Negroes and then nurses it back to life. Though it now has only three legs, the horse can still run faster than any mere four-legged creature, and the groom, together with a stubborn old Negro preacher and his twelve-year-old grandson who doubles as jockey, tours the South and Midwest cleaning up on the races. The horse soon becomes a popular legend and, for the groom and the Negro, an object of passion. When its wealthy owner sends detectives to hunt it out, no one will inform on the horse thieves, and when the old Negro surrenders himself, a mob insists that he be freed. The American public insists on "man's

serene and inalienable right to his folly."

Until the full work of which *Notes* is part becomes available, it will be difficult to make out the deeper intentions behind this fable, but it obviously raises memories of Sherwood Anderson's horse stories and is certainly the sort of thing Anderson would have loved. Loved, that is, if Faulkner took the trouble to tell it. As it is, he throws up a thick screen of rhetoric which is forever getting in the way of the story: the "not only ... but" construction, extremely effective in previous stories, is here greatly overdone, and the writing is strained beyond any need of the fable itself. There are fine bits of observation about Negroes—toward whom, by the way, Faulkner is fundamentally shy—but there is no thematic need for the kind of anguished and magniloquent rhetoric that might be justified in *Intruder in the Dust*. Instead of the economy this humorous story obviously demands, Faulkner has allowed himself to ramble along about matters that have little relation to the horse, the groom, or the Negro.

One wonders whether this self-indulgence is partly due to the fact that Faulkner's critics have recently been rolling over and playing delightedly dead each time he publishes something. And one can only hope that when *Notes* appears in final form it will be ruthlessly pared of home-made rant. The talent is still there in all its fabulous luxuriance, and so is the capacity for inventing situations no one else would even dream of; but Faulkner badly needs some ordinary self-discipline. And if his critics, at whatever risk of seeming presumptuous, don't tell him so, who will?

Checklist of Additional Reviews

Collins, Carvel. "Faulkner Story from a Novel to Come." *New York Herald Tribune Book Review*, February 25, 1951, p. 8.

Morrissey, Ralph. "Important Faulkner Story." Nashville *Tennessean*, June 20, 1954, p. 19-C.

Poore, Charles. "Books of the Times." New York *Times*, February 8, 1951, p. 31.

Wilson, Edmund. "*Notes on a Horsethief*." *New Yorker*, April 14, 1951, pp. 136–37.

REQUIEM FOR A NUN

WILLIAM FAULKNER

REQUIEM
for a NUN

RANDOM HOUSE   NEW YORK

Anthony West. "Requiem for a Dramatist." *New Yorker,* September 22, 1951, pp. 109–12.

Mr. Faulkner's new offering, *Requiem for a Nun*, is in the main a sequel to *Sanctuary*, and is concerned with the further misadventures of Temple Drake, a tomboy whose qualities have always had an unsettling effect on her creator. Even for the heroine of a novel of violence in the heyday of the genre, she was experience-prone to an unusual degree: Between the time she slipped off the train at Taylor and the time she was to be seen yawning at the watery charms of the Luxembourg Gardens on a wet autumn day, a good deal had happened to her. She had been in an automobile wreck, she had been involved in two murders, she had been raped in a manner new to the novel, and raped old-style by proxy, she had been kidnapped and held prisoner in a Memphis brothel, and she had committed perjury that resulted in an innocent man's being burned to death by a mob. It may seem that fate, playing fair, could not have had more in store for a simple Southern girl. But it did.

We now learn that after a year in Europe, Temple went decked in virgin's white to the American Embassy in Paris and there married up with Gowan Stevens, the well-bred lush whose bout of drinking landed her in her mess of trouble. She added to that slightly incredible step the wholly incredible one of returning to Jefferson, her home town and the county seat, to settle down. For any but Faulkner characters, this ill-advised choice of part-ners and of a place to live would have meant a year—if that—of embarrassment, social slight, and domestic tension, followed by a move into the barely cognizant, unremembering vastness and anonymity that surround Yoknapatawpha County, with Temple headed for Nevada or the Virgin Islands. But being what they are, they stay right on there among the old, familiar faces, waiting for their doom. Mr. Faulkner picks them up eight years later, when it, or at least the first installment of it, has caught up with them. The reader is brought up to date on the Stevenses by means of a three-act play that tells of the blows that have hit the young couple. Wadded between its acts, for reasons of the higher symbolism (to do with law, the continuity of affairs human and divine through the effluxion of time, and so forth), there is an entertaining anecdotal history of Jefferson's jail and courthouse and the State Capitol from the earliest times to the present day, but the play is the thing—and a rather startling thing, too, when one analyzes it.

In Act I, Scene I, a brief courtroom scene, we see Nancy Mannigoe, a colored former prostitute who has been employed as a nursemaid by the Stevenses, being sentenced to death for the murder of Temple's second child, and we are shocked to learn, from a stage direction, that Gowan Stevens' Uncle Gavin, the County Attorney, has been defending the murderess. This piece of tactlessness, noteworthy even in Yoknapatawpha circles, is pushed to the point of unprofessional conduct in Scene 2, which follows on the death sentence by thirty minutes. Gavin pursues the Stevenses into their home to press them for details of the crime that he believes were suppressed during the trial. He badgers them but makes no progress. All he gets at is the invisible worm that is eating away at the heart of the young folks' marriage—Gowan's knowledge that Temple just loved the time she spent in the Memphis bordello. This excites him, and he immediately starts probing on the new line it opens up. "What else," he asks Gowan, "happened during that month, that time while that madman held her prisoner there in that Memphis house, that nobody but you and she know about, maybe not even you know about?" This ranks high in the category of what Bergson, in another connection, called "*les questions que ne se posent pas*," and its effect on Gowan is considerable. It deprives him of the power of coherent speech, and all he can do is mutter "So help me" and offer to hit Uncle Gavin with a whiskey bottle. Uncle takes the hint and leaves, and Scene 2 comes to an end.

The young marrieds go to California the following morning with their surviving infant and their memories, and it is hard to imagine what earthly power will be able to fetch them back to Jefferson and into a room with Gavin Stevens ever again. The answer is that preFreudian concept, the innocence of a little child, which used to reform burglars and reconcile the unhappiest of married couples:

"We were on the beach, Bucky and I. I was reading, and he was—oh, talking mostly, you know—'Is California far from Jefferson, mamma?' and I say 'Yes, darling,' you know: still reading or trying to, and he says, 'How long will we stay in California, mamma?' and I say 'Until we get tired of it' and he says 'Will we stay here until they hang Nancy, mamma?' . . . I say 'Yes, darling,' and then he drops it right in my lap . . . 'Where will we go then, mamma?'"

Convinced by this that there is no place to hide, the party return to Jefferson, and Scene 3—same room, same company, same badgering, but four months later—becomes possible. Gavin is harping on Temple's sense of guilt now, convincing her that she must go to the Governor and tell him the whole background of the murder, even as far back as Memphis, for the ostensible purpose of saving Nancy's neck. After turning every which way, she agrees and the curtain falls.

Act II takes place in the office of the Governor, a singularly patient and long-suffering public servant. Wakened at two in the morning, he listens unprotestingly by the hour while Gavin Stevens, spouting rhetorical nebulosities about the moral law, takes Temple apart with no discoverable motive and squeezes her little secrets from her. What had impelled the Stevenses to employ Nancy? Temple was drawn to her because her teeth had been kicked out on the steps of the bank one morning by the cashier, who resented her choice of the moment when he was opening the place for the day's business to present an apparently valid claim for a two-dollar fee that had been outstanding for a fortnight. This had convinced Temple that of all the people in Jefferson Nancy was the one who could speak her language, so she had hired her to have someone around she could talk to. What she wanted to talk about was how wonderful Red, the dance-hall bouncer Popeye had procured for her as a lover, had been. And later she had had her affair with Red's younger brother to talk about. While she was mewed up in Miss Reba's in Memphis, she had whiled away the duller hours by writing obscene letters to Red, and Junior had treasured these down the years. Then he had turned up to do some blackmailing. Blackmail and a happy physical resemblance to Red were, of course, foundation enough for a romance, and Temple just naturally fell in love with her new charmer. But sporadic adultery proving inadequate, Temple planned to run off with him, as she had once intended with Red.

Here she was faced with a scruple, humanitarian rather than moral, that she had little cause to suspect in Nancy. Gowan has, all along, had his doubts of the paternity of his first-born, and the second child is still too young to be left behind. You can't be meaning, says Nancy, to "leave one with a man that's willing to believe the child ain't got no father, willing to take the other one to a man that don't even want no children." Temple is, so Nancy, unable to frustrate the elopement by hiding the jewels and the loose cash that were to finance its initial stages, murders the younger child. All this comes out, as reluctantly and painfully as an impacted wisdom tooth, in Scene 1 and in Scene 2, a flashback to the night of the murder.

Scene 3 opens with a line for the producer: *Temple does not know that the Governor has gone and that her husband is now in the room.* This switch depends on some sort of conniving and tiptoeing in and out of the room that is more than hard to believe in, but we are already far, far beyond logic and credibility anyway. When Temple realizes that this has taken place, she rounds on Uncle Gavin, asking for an explanation of exactly what is going on, and learns that the Governor had finally rejected all appeals for clemency in Nancy's case the week before. The moment has clearly come for Temple to add justifiable homicide to her record, but she keeps on talking. You just fixed this to make me suffer, she says, it wasn't even to make me "confess to my husband, but to do it in the hearing of two strangers, something which I had spent eight years trying to expiate so that my husband wouldn't have to know about it." (She does not explain what manner of expiation her carnal traffic with Red's brother has been, but no matter.) No, says Uncle Gavin. "You came here to affirm the very thing which Nancy is going to die tomor-

row to postulate: that little children, as long as they are little children, shall be intact, unanguished, untorn, unterrified." The text does not seem to support this statement. The child has been butchered. Temple's affirmation has been, if anything, that girls who sleep around with members of the criminal classes and write them smutty letters will presently regret it; and Nancy is not going to postulate anything. Society, the law, or whatever you like to call it is going to break her neck in the hope of dissuading private persons from killing other private persons. At any rate, it is now after 3:30 A.M. onstage and there is nothing to do but bring down the curtain on Act II and get the characters off to bed.

They meet for Act III, seven hours later, in the Jefferson jail, where Mr. Faulkner's big surprise is waiting for us. Something— contact with Temple, perhaps; the satisfactions of murder, possibly—has transformed Nancy Mannigoe into a Saint. Serene and calm, at peace with God and man, and coached about such problems as the existence of evil in God's creation by Gavin Stevens, ever ready with a leading question, she offers her former employer the consolations of religion. But if Temple has succeeded in becoming the agent of Nancy's salvation, she has not got to the point of salvation herself. She leaves the jail murmuring that there must be something, "anyone to save it [her soul]. Anyone to want it. If there is none, I'm sunk. We all are. Doomed. Damned." It is a dim revelation, and it has cost the lives of Tommy, Red, Popeye, Goodwin, Temple's second child, and Nancy to bring it to her. Temple is still just twenty-seven, and one can only wonder what dread events, what fearful harvest of mortal flesh, will be required to fetch her the whole way back home to a knowledge of Mr. Faulkner's fierce and frightening God.

One's feelings about this concoction as

the work of the one unchallengeable and unquestionable genius at present functioning at the full tide of his creative powers on the American literary scene cannot be very happy. They may be softened by the joking thought that Henry James, too, wrote plays, and that Shaw wrote novels. Or they may be dodged by classification, by saying that this book belongs on the shelf alongside *Mosquitoes*, a long way from *Soldiers' Pay*, *Light in August*, *The Sound and the Fury*, and *The Hamlet*, and is a mere aberration at the outer fringe of the work of a major artist. But the puzzle remains: why the genius who has given Jefferson and the County such reality and substance should have populated it with such people, so brutishly and incredibly entangled.

Maxwell Geismar. "Faulkner's New Novel Will Win No Prizes." New York *Post*, September 23, 1951, p. 12-M.

"What do you want? What in God's name do you want?" cries the heroine of Faulkner's new play-novel. "I told you. Truth," says the hero. So let us accept Faulkner's thesis and admit at once that this new work by a serious and gifted artist is absolutely worthless.

It is cold, empty, slick. It is not only trite and sophomoric in its values, but it is pretentious and, I happen to think, badly written. I'm not sure whether it is worse to conclude that Faulkner wrote it as a potboiler for the Broadway and Hollywood stage, or that he honestly believes in it.

And I say this not as a detractor of Faulkner's work but as an admirer of whatever has been good in it—notably *The Sound and the Fury, Light in August*, and *Absalom, Absalom!*

This one is a sequel to *Sanctuary*, and you might ask why he picked the most sensational and least serious of his early works to make over into a cheap thriller and a puerile morality play.

Temple Drake is married to the southern boy whose drunken driving got her into the Memphis sporting house. She has two children and is a respectable member of the Mississippi country club set. All is forgiven apparently—only her colored nurse has murdered her youngest child and has been condemned to death, quite rightly, one would think.

However, Gavin Stephens (who is Faulkner's prototype of a true Southern gentleman, and has defended the Negro girl in court) is not satisfied. During the rest of the book he attempts to get the truth out of Temple, and while this takes some time since all the characters revert into the language of Greek tragedy at the crucial points, it all—ultimately, which is too late for my taste—comes out.

Temple Drake has been blackmailed by the brother of the man she fell in love with during her imprisonment in the sporting house. She has also fallen in love with her blackmailer. (It seems that all three of them, the two brothers and her husband, Gowan Stephens, look somewhat alike.)

The fact is that Nancy Mannigoe, the colored nurse, has committed the crime in order to prevent Temple from ruining her life again by deserting her husband and children for the sake of another impure love. And Temple must confess her sin publicly not indeed to save the Negress (who is also a former dope-fiend and prostitute) but to save her own soul.

Does it seem a little far-fetched? It is; and perhaps the ornate, mysterious and bombastic language that Faulkner uses here is designed to prevent us from ever understanding the real plot of his play.

Anyhow Temple has one child left, and at last atones for her sin, while the Negro girl is happy, presumably, to die for the sake of the white folks' salvation. The problem of the Negro has always bothered Faulkner (that is to say, the problem of denying the true Negro problem in the South today), and what a convenient solution this is!

But even in Heaven, as we are told, Nancy Mannigoe will be destined to play a menial role—and do work that has to be done—while "the harp, the raiment, the singing" are not for her, not now.

So *Requiem for a Nun* is still a requiem for a second-class nun, and *Sanctuary Revisited*, which might be a better title for the play, is a flop.

Faulkner has also surrounded the play proper with a longish prose narrative of Jefferson, Mississippi's early history, which is a better piece of writing, but which has very little to do with the main action. If it isn't presumptuous, I'd like to add that Faulkner doesn't seem to understand the South.

Carl Victor Little. "A Comment on Mr. Faulkner's Latest, *Requiem for a Nun*." San Francisco *News*, September 24, 1951, p. 14.

William Faulkner in this new novel—but is it a novel—writes one sentence that consumes 49 pages which seems to be almost a life sentence but who am I to criticize the Old Master of the vultures-in-the-magnolias school of Southern novelists;

and, as I sit here dreaming of life and death and incest and murder and other happy events in old Jefferson, Miss., and in the sordid expanse of ghost-haunted Yoknapatawpha County, Miss., a political subdivision also dreamed up by Mr. Faulkner, I wonder how it goes with the Compsons and the Snopeses and the Sartorises and the Sutpens and the Popeyes and the Temple Drakes and then my feeble mind drifts inevitably back to myself and I say if a Nobel Prize winner can write a 49-page sentence why should I worry whether I drive my readers nuts; and this brings me to Faulkner's new novel which is a novel if a play is a novel when shuffled with three long essays on the code of the Southland, how the poor white trash ever got that way and how Jefferson County got its name and the lock on its jail to begin with; but hell I might as well face it, review this latest Faulkner opus and get on with my work; even so, believe not that I am presumptuous enough to hoot at the Old Master because I am a Faulkner moderate which means that I can take him or leave him alone and this I take in large doses but thank the Lord there is only one Faulkner in the world for two Faulkners would drive me crazy but first let me discuss the play that is interrupted by the yards of Faulkner prose, a play which undoubtedly will lay the customers in the aisle when it opens in New York (and I'm waiting to see George Jean Nathan's review of same) because it is a dramatic triumph which in a way is an extension of the early Faulkner novel *Sanctuary* in which Temple Drake, an all-Mississippi coed, was kidnapped and held a willing captive in a Memphis bawdy house but I must remember that this is a family newspaper and now Faulkner projects the *Sanctuary* story into a play and you have Temple Drake married to Gavin Gowan, the young fellow who in *Sanctuary* didn't seem to give a damn whether the white slavers got his darling or not and the play opens with Nancy, Temple's colored maid who is a retired prostitute and drug addict, being sentenced to death for smothering Temple's baby and in flashbacks we have Nancy doing this dastardly deed because Temple is about to run away with the low brother of Red, this being the same Red who was killed in *Sanctuary* by Popeye the white slaver (not the sailor man) because Red and Temple were in what passes for love; and verily, Faulkner is saying something in this novel which isn't a novel at all unless a novel may be defined as one would define a bed—anything with covers—but why should I do all the work for you and if you don't like this attitude drop around and I'll give you your nickel back; so, see what I mean?

Sterling North. "Sequel to *Sanctuary*." New York *World-Telegram and the Sun*, September 24, 1951, p. 22.

The jacket of this book states categorically: "*Requiem for a Nun* reaffirms William Faulkner's almost undisputed position as the most renowned novelist in the world today."

Not to quibble over the meaning of the word "renowned," which at least suggests that the acclaim is justified, we would like to go on permanent record as saying that if the above statement is true world literature definitely requires a requiem.

It has been this reviewer's painful duty over more than two decades to wade through the gumbo of 19 books by William Faulkner.

In that time I have seen not the slightest improvement in his ungrammatical, clumsy prose, and I have long since ceased to hope for a book from Faulkner which does not wallow in the sensational and melodramatic.

Requiem for a Nun contains two elements, one of which might have made a fairly good guidebook article, the other a long short story or (if vigorously rewritten) a three-act play. The two elements, very poorly integrated, add up to the first draft of what might have been a powerful novel.

Element number one is a series of miasmic essays on the history of the mythical Yoknapatawpha County of Mississippi, with special symbolic emphasis on the county courthouse and the jail.

Element number two is a three-act play concerning the sordid life of Temple Drake, whom we first met in *Sanctuary*, whose hunger for evil finally brings a far more admirable woman—her Negro servant—to the gallows.

Both women are ex-prostitutes, and the Negress in addition is an ex-dope fiend. We are informed, if we are capable of wading through the exasperating obfuscation, that Temple Drake (now Mrs. Gowan Stevens) has had an abnormal appetite for sin ever since she was the feted all-state debutante who was kidnapped and held prisoner (but not against her will) in a house of prostitution.

We are also informed that the negress, Nancy Mannigoe, now sentenced to hang for killing Mrs. Stevens' second child, a baby of 6 months, is not only the victim of her environment and later Temple's viciousness but is almost Tolstoyan in her understanding and love for Temple, Temple's ex-alcoholic husband, Gowan, and their two children.

Faulkner, who writes in three shades, black, white, and mud-gray, makes neither of his extreme characters believable.

But they come nearer to living on the page than Temple's shadowy husband, Gowan (another drunk from the University of Virginia), and Gowan's noble uncle, Gavin, defense attorney for the negress.

With typical disregard for his readers, Faulkner calls Gavin "Stephens," which is of course, Gowan's last name. So we find "Stephens" being ordered from "Stephens' living room," which is, of course, Gowan's. All of the motivations and most of the action is highly unbelievable. Several times in the book Faulkner makes a three-year error in his own chronology of events. In fact, one wonders whether Random House employs even a proofreader to say nothing of an editor, when handling Faulkner's books.

Faulkner once admitted that his early shocker, *Sanctuary*, was written rapidly and for the express purpose of scandalizing the public. This sequel, though more serious in intent, still contains the revolting sex-pervert, Popeye, who enjoys Temple vicariously in some shadowy scenes as decadent as anything in modern literature.

The author's attempt to give this whole jumbled narrative a high moral meaning will deceive no one who is not already bamboozled by Faulkner's histrionics. And although there are moments in this book when the fortunate discipline of the drama form comes close to making the author write clearly, they are not frequent enough to save the novel.

Despite the rave reviews you will be reading elsewhere, don't waste your $3 on this one.

Louis D. Rubin, Jr. "Novel, Modern Drama, Morality Play Merge in Faulkner Book." Richmond *News Leader,* September 24, 1951, p. 11.

A girl, Temple Drake, is brutally raped by a gangster and pervert called Popeye. Because she was also a witness to Popeye's murder of a farm youth, she is taken by him and hidden in a house of ill fame. There, instead of trying to escape, she falls in love with a tough called Red, whom Popeye also kills later on.

Meanwhile, a moonshiner, Lee Goodwin, is falsely accused of killing the farm boy. At the trial, the intimidated Temple testifies that Goodwin both murdered the farm boy and raped her. Goodwin is lynched; Popeye is later executed for another murder, which ironically he did not commit; and Temple is taken to Europe by her father to recover.

This is the plot of William Faulkner's novel, *Sanctuary*, published in 1931. Faulkner wrote it, he declared, to make money. For a time it was considered as just that: a gory thriller, one of its author's less important works.

But after a while, people began to realize that *Sanctuary* was no mere sex novel. Critics, particularly George Marion O'Donnell, showed that *Sanctuary* was really an allegory: a sermon on morality. Temple Drake was not only a Southern girl; she was also the symbol of southern womanhood corrupted. Gowan Stevens, the sottish professional Virginian who had abandoned Temple, instead of trying to protect her from Popeye, stood for the

335

hollow tradition. Popeye was godless, root-less, impotent modernism, the symbol of evil incarnate, Faulkner has since called him. Red is natural lust.

In *Sanctuary*, the corrupted Southern woman succumbs to evil and lust. The result: the lynching of an innocent man—absolute chaos, the end of civilization and order.

So instead of having produced a mere potboiler, Faulkner had dealt with figures of tragic violence, and was delivering a devastating judgment on the world in general and Yoknapatawpha County, Miss., in particular.

As such, however, *Sanctuary* ended on a despairing, negative note, and William Faulkner is no man for that kind of thing. After all, as he said last year in his speech in acceptance of the Nobel Prize, "It is the poet's privilege to help man endure by lifting his heart, by reminding him of the courage and honor and hope and pride and compassion and pity and sacrifice which have been the glory of his past. The poet's voice need not merely be the record of man, it can be one of the props, the pillars to help him endure and prevail."

So in 1951, 20 years after *Sanctuary* appeared, Mr. Faulkner has produced a sequel, another novel about Temple Drake: *Requiem for a Nun*.

In form, *Requiem for a Nun* is experimental. Indeed, it is really no novel at all, but a play, with each of three acts preceded by long prologues, describing the building of the courthouse and jail of Faulkner's mythical Yoknapatawpha County, the founding of the capital city of Mississippi, Jackson, and the history of the Yoknapatawpha jail, in that order.

It is not until he finishes the novel and begins thinking about it that the reader begins to realize what the descriptions of the courthouse, capital, and especially the jail have to do with the story of Temple Drake. But of this, more later.

The action proper of *Requiem for a Nun* opens as Nancy Mannigoe, a Negro nurse and a former prostitute and dope fiend, is sentenced to be hanged for smothering to death the infant child of Temple Drake, now Mrs. Gowan Stevens. Gowan's uncle, Lawyer Gavin Stevens, tries to learn from Temple the true story of events on the night of the murder. Temple remains silent, however, and she and Gowan leave for the West Coast.

Gowan had married the then-disgraced Temple shortly after the action of *Sanctuary* had ended. He had done it to atone for his abandonment of her; he was facing up to his moral responsibilities. The marriage was thus built on guile and forgiveness, and both Temple and Gowan were busy forgiving each other, and being reminded of their guilt in order to be grateful for being forgiven. The tension is becoming unbearable.

Gowan shows his resentment by doubting their older child's paternity, and threatens to tell this to the child. Temple fights back against this for a time, but she is in even worse straits herself. The strain of being good is almost too much to bear; especially after the birth of the second child, she has felt hopelessly trapped.

At this point, along comes the brother of Red, Temple's lover in *Sanctuary*. He attempts to blackmail her with some obscene love letters she had written to Red while she resided in the house of ill repute. This is Temple's chance: she not only takes money to pay the blackmailer, but makes him her lover and prepares to take the younger child and run off with him.

But Nancy Mannigoe, the Negro nurse and confidante, moves in. After trying every other way she knows to stop Temple from going off with her new lover and thus ruining the lives of her children, she does the only other thing possible: she kills the infant. Only this, she realizes, will prevent Temple from running away, keep her with her family, and thus give the remaining child a chance to grow up in kindness and love: "that a little child shall not suffer in order to come unto Me," as Gavin Stevens put it. And though the younger child must die to permit this for its older brother, it at least is spared a childhood of hate and suffering because of its mother's sins.

Thus, the Negro nurse Nancy has chosen to die by hanging in order that "little children, as long as they are little children, shall be intact, unanguished, untorn, unterrified."

The final scene occurs in the jail. How, Temple asks the condemned Nancy, can she prove equal to the task of making good Nancy's sacrifice? There is tomorrow and tomorrow and tomorrow, Temple says; how can she know that, after she has endured and overcome a lifetime of penitence for her son's sake, there will be the forgiveness of God at the end, as Nancy postulates?

"Believe," Nancy replies. "Believe what, Nancy?" Temple asks. "Tell me."

"Believe," Nancy says again, and follows the jailer back to her death cell.

So at the end, Temple sees that the only answer to any of this, the only possible way to live, is in trust and belief. She will forgive Gowan, who has forgiven her, and will fight to keep her home together for the sake of the remaining child.

"Temple," her husband calls from off-stage.

"Coming," Temple says.

So there is Faulkner's morality play: it took the Negro nurse, Nancy Mannigoe, former prostitute and dope fiend, to hold together Temple's family, because Nancy had the faith to do it. The theme of *Requiem for a Nun* is: Believe. It is necessary, Faulkner says, for man to accept full responsibility for himself, to die if need be, so that life may go on—that little children may grow up with love and affection.

The role of the jail in *Requiem for a Nun* we realize, is to remind us that there must always be awareness of evil, wherever there is mankind. It can be hidden deep, but it must always be there, because it is emblematic of the recognition of sin as evil. It is the jail, the same one in which Nancy Mannigoe waits to die, that provides for the town of Jefferson and the county of Yoknapatawpha and the state of Mississippi, and the South, and the world, the symbol of man's moral purpose: "to help him endure and prevail."

So constituted, *Requiem for a Nun* is one of Faulkner's strongest novels, one of the high points in the work of this great moralist.

Irving Howe. "Faulkner: An Experiment in Drama." *Nation,* September 29, 1951, pp. 263–64.

Almost alone among the older American writers William Faulkner continues to show creative restlessness, experimenting with new forms and widening the bounds of his subject matter. Though his latest book is uneven, partly magnificent and partly an ambitious failure, it is an admirable example of his continued exertion, his refusal to rest on laurels, his undiminished curiosity about problems of craft. Since the praise of Faulkner is now so fulsome and indiscriminate, I had better say, however, that there is nothing here equal to his best work: nothing like the tragic lyricism of *The Sound and the Fury* or the scenic power of *Light in August*.

A three-act play with narrative intervals setting the background for each act *Requiem for a Nun* is a sequel to one of

337

Faulkner's weakest novels, *Sanctuary*. In *Sanctuary*, you will recall, the feather-brained bitch, Temple Drake, after an accident with her drunken escort, Gowan Stevens, found herself captive of a satanic mobster, Popeye. And liked it. In the Memphis brothel to which Popeye took her she developed a passion for Red, a young tough whom the impotent Popeye provided as his sexual substitute.

Now, in *Requiem*, Temple and Stevens are respectably married, parents of two children, but still tortured by a need to show each other gratitude and forgiveness. Wearied by this regimen of cautious goodness, Temple decides to run off with Red's younger brother, who has appeared in Yoknapatawpha to blackmail her with the lascivious letters she had written during her Memphis excursion.

To this plan there is only one obstacle: a Negro woman named Nancy, a reformed dope addict and ex-prostitute whom Temple employs as a nursemaid and confidante for an exchange of memories about youthful sin. Nancy, in the name of the children, begs Temple not to run off, and when she is rebuffed, strangles Temple's baby to forestall the greater tragedy of both children being left homeless. Condemned to die, Nancy shows no fear: she is in God's hands.

If this play is produced, it is likely to suffer from the same weaknesses it reveals in print: Faulkner hardly troubles to dramatize his story, the bulk of it is told by Temple—after many tedious hesitations—to auditors on the stage. This is the familiar Faulkner strategy of spiraling back from a troubled narrator to a troubling action, but in a play it won't do unless the action is *shown*.

The strength of the play rests in its characterization of the whites. In previous books Faulkner has expressed a striking distaste for the doings of young women, partly as an accommodation to foul humor

and partly from an obscure governing bias; but Temple, one of the foulest of his females, is treated with surprising sympathy and a fine sense of how even slight aging can modify character. Gowan, who had learned to drink like a gentleman in his southern college, is also well done: far more resonant a character than in *Sanctuary*. But Nancy is a problem.

All Faulkner's recent books reveal an intense concern with the Negroes, an inability to rest in whatever his latest opinion of them may be, a need to keep pressing at the limits of his mind. This, and not his much-quoted philosophical sermons, seems to me the sign of his strength as novelist and moralist. Unfortunately, in *Requiem* he is so obsessed with the Negro as a force or a presence that he does not establish a Negro as a person. Lacking the rich particularity of a Dilsey or a Lucas Beauchamp, Nancy never comes to life; featureless and bloodless, she is merely a moral wraith, a Voice. Her murder of the white child is hard to take in terms of ordinary human motivation, and therefore hard to take in terms of Faulkner's intended symbolism. More troublesome still is the weight Faulkner seems to be imposing, from the most admirable of motives, on the Negroes—nothing less than the salvation of the whites. In a way opposite to his advocacy of "states' rights" in *Intruder in the Dust*, he may here be a little unfair to the Negroes: isn't he asking too much of them? What they want and need is equality, not the job of saving the whites—*that* the whites will have to do for themselves.

Before her death Nancy engages in a religious dialogue with Temple and Uncle Gavin Stevens, the one Faulkner character who is consistently boring. Nancy proclaims, "Believe." Temple asks, "Believe what?" Replies the Negro woman, "Believe." No doubt, this will excite those critics who adore the simple faith (in others), but to me it seems mere sentimental piety. Temple's question is very much to the point, and Nancy's answer—well, it is no worse than most of the answers one gets these days. In general, it really does Faulkner no service to glide over his recent fondness for pontificating, or to treat all of his work as if it were gilded gospel, beyond evaluation and requiring only hushed exegesis.

The narrative interludes are another matter: here is the major Faulkner, the imaginative chronicler of a region and a people. One interlude, called "The Courthouse," is written in a winding breathless style which serves beautifully for a humorous recall of the Yoknapatawpha past. This section is partly a paean to the vanished American wilderness, for Faulkner the source and scene of mobility, freedom, and innocence; partly a witty anecdote of how the loss of a lock, the vanity of a mail rider, and the shrewdness of an early settler led to the building of Yoknapatawpha's first courthouse.

Still better is "The Jail," a loping forty-nine page sentence of rich but clear prose; rhetoric splendid and controlled. Both rhapsody and elegy of the Yoknapatawpha past, "The Jail" is also a review of Faulkner's own legend, touching on most of his past books and ending with a recognition that the South, now absorbed into "one nation," barely exists anymore as a separate region, the "old deathless Lost Cause" having become "a faded (though still select) social club." Faulkner will probably write more books about Yoknapatawpha, but "The Jail" seems likely to serve as a valedictory to his world; time has caught up with him or he with time; and for those who have immersed themselves in this world, even if with the consciousness that they are not of it, his impassioned farewell will seem a gesture infinitely sad.

Harrison Smith. "Purification by Sacrifice." *Saturday Review of Literature*, September 29, 1951, p. 12.

William Faulkner is the most complex of our writers but for those who have discovered the quality of his genius and have traveled backward and forward through the world in which his conscious and his subconscious mind has dwelled there is no modern author whose work is more fascinating and rewarding to explore. In short stories and novels he has written the saga of the deep South since 1825, and for his purposes has invented mythical Yoknapatawpha County and has created its people dwelling in cities and villages, old mansions and scattered shacks. It was the fashion among the reviewers of the late Thirties to deny his talent, to accuse him of being scatological, diffuse, and violent. It was the European critics and a few stalwart Americans who gave him his true value, and who led to his receiving the Nobel Prize in literature early this year.

His twentieth book, *Requiem for a Nun*, is a novel, almost half of which is written as a play set in the midst of three explanatory historical interludes, "The Courthouse" and "The Jail" in Jefferson, center of his fictional county, and "The Golden Dome," the state capitol in Jackson. These passages represent Faulkner at his best, his native humor, imaginative sense of history, his eloquence; and they provide a background and meaning to his play as the judges and the condemned in courtrooms over the land are symbolically enclosed in walls of stone and towering pillars.

The play is the story of the Temple

Drake of *Sanctuary*, the wretched college girl who was kidnapped by a pervert on her way to a football game with alcoholic young Gowan Stevens, then raped, and held for weeks in a sporting house in Memphis. In the play she is five years older, married to Gowan, with her shocking past shielded, but still isolated, by the family's wealth and distinction. The "Nun" of the title is the colored maid and nurse for her two children, who has murdered her baby, and in the first brief scene is condemned to death. The sordid events that lead to this crime and the desperate attempts of Temple and Gavin Stevens, her lawyer uncle, to free the murderess, including a midnight appeal to the Governor, make up the body of this extraordinary drama. Temple had not been able to escape her past in the Stevens mansion; the loathsome creature who had seduced her, if it can be called that, had been killed, but Popeye's brother was blackmailing her. She was about to run away with him when Nancy, the nurse, once a prostitute and "dope fiend" and now her only intimate companion, strangled her baby, in an apparently mad and yet successful attempt to prevent the ruin of her mistress and the total destruction of the family.

Temple and her husband fled to California but were driven back by their conscience to Jefferson in an effort to prevent somehow Nancy's execution. To the reader their motive may seem to be as unbalanced as that of the murderess. The story that Temple would have to tell in court of her passion for a blackmailing scoundrel and thief could not conceivably release Nancy; as a reason for mercy no judge would give it a second thought. The midnight scene in the Governor's mansion takes the form and the meaning of a confessional which can purge but cannot cure. Faulkner has bestowed on Nancy the dignity of a sacrificial heroine in a Greek drama. She is endowed with one gift that no one else in the cast possesses, religious faith. When Gowan Stevens asks her a few hours before her execution if she believes in salvation she answers, "You don't need it. All you need, all you have to do is just believe." She believes that "when folks suffer they are too busy to get into devilment, won't have time to worry and meddle one another." In killing the baby she brought suffering to Temple, prevented her from doing more evil, and as the baby went straight and untarnished to Heaven her act was merciful, and therefore she herself would go to Heaven. Gowan asks, "Can a murderess go to Heaven?"; her response is in three words, "I can work."

If Faulkner had written his play as a novel, his talent would have illuminated this strange woman. For the success of the play it is also necessary to comprehend how Temple, her husband, and her uncle can understand the dignity and purity of the murderess's conception; can believe that she is in a way a saint, or a nun as Faulkner names her, and that her act has brought to Temple forgiveness of her own past sins and her own part in the tragedy. Whether Faulkner has accomplished this in his play remains in doubt to the readers. On the stage where it will be presented with the devices of light and shadow which he has invented it might become one of the most remarkable dramas of our times.

Malcolm Cowley.
"In Which Mr. Faulkner
Translates Past into
Present."
*New York Herald Tribune
Books*, September 30,
1951, pp. 1, 14.

Requiem for a Nun is among the most successful of Faulkner's many experiments in narrative form. It is a three-act play, written in a genuinely tragic spirit, with each act preceded by a historical account of the scene on which the curtain is about the rise. The first history is that of the courthouse in Jefferson, Miss., where Nancy Mannigoe, a Negro maid who used to be a prostitute, is standing trial for the murder of her mistress's baby. The second is that of Jackson, capital of the state, where the mistress pleads vainly with the Governor to pardon Nancy. The third and last is that of the old jail in Jefferson where Nancy is waiting to be hanged.

Besides being good in themselves, the historical narratives serve a double purpose in Faulkner's scheme for the book. First, they emphasize his feeling that the past survives in the present. "The past is never dead," says our old friend Gavin Stevens, who reappears from *Intruder in the Dust* and *Knight's Gambit* to serve as Nancy's lawyer and the author's spokesman. "It's not even past," he says in the next breath. By writing the three narratives, Faulkner translates the past into present and gives his action a sense of historical depth, like a fourth dimension. A book that might otherwise be merely a printed play, without actors or setting, now reads like a thoughtful novel.

But the narratives have a second pur-

pose, too, and one that is connected with the Yoknapatawpha series as a whole. For the last quarter of a century Faulkner has been writing the story of an invented county in northern Mississippi; it now extends through a dozen novels and thirty-odd shorter stories. It is an imaginative creation on a larger scale than any other in serious American fiction; but there have been gaps in the story and Faulkner is beginning to fill them. In the present histories he gives us information about Yoknapatawpha County families—the Sartorises, the Compsons, the Sutpens, the Ratliffs—that we missed in the novels in which they first appeared. Most of the novels had been written subjectively, that is, the events with which they dealt had been presented through the rather murky consciousness of the characters, so that we seemed to be moving in perpetual twilight. Now some of the same events are presented objectively, as if in the light of day.

Sometimes we have the impression that the events are being retold by a second author and that Faulkner himself has become a different man. Once, there was an unregenerate Faulkner, careless of his readers but not unwilling to shock them; the author of novels about incest, rape, arson, and miscegenation. Now there is a reformed Faulkner, conscious of his public duties, who has become the spokesman for the human spirit in its painful aspirations toward "love and honor and pity and pride and compassion and sacrifice," to quote from his Nobel Prize address. Soon his readers on the five continents will have to decide which of the two authors they prefer.

Requiem for a Nun, like the earlier *Intruder in the Dust*, is a book by the regenerated Faulkner. As if to mark the separation from his earlier self, the three acts of the play—as distinguished from the historical narratives—deal with the further adventures of the heroine of the most notorious novel written by the other Faulkner, who seemed to regard himself as a rebel and a scamp. The young woman is Temple Drake, of *Sanctuary*, and her reappearance makes it necessary to compare the two books.

Sanctuary—so Faulkner told us in an introduction written for the Modern Library edition of the novel—was "a cheap idea, because it was deliberately conceived to make money." It was written in 1929, when he was a penniless writer whose stories were being rejected by magazine editors. "I took a little time out," he said, "and speculated what a person in Mississippi would believe to be current trends, chose what I thought was the right answer and invented the most horrific tale I could imagine and wrote it in about three weeks and sent it to Smith, who had done *The Sound and the Fury* and who wrote me immediately, 'Good God, I can't publish this. We'd both be in jail.'" Two years later Harrison Smith changed his mind and had the novel set in type. When Faulkner saw the galley proofs, he tore them to pieces and rewrote the book from the beginning, "trying," so he said, "to make out of it something which would not shame *The Sound and the Fury* and *As I Lay Dying* too much."

In spite of the revision *Sanctuary* has never been one of the author's favorites, but it is a better novel than Faulkner and most of his critics have been willing to admit. His imagination was working at full speed when he wrote it, and was working on different levels at the same time. He was trying to tell a horrific story about bootleggers, rape, murder and lynching, but he was also brooding about the moral situation of the South, and the two problems became interfused. Popeye the gangster, who was always described in mechanical terms, came to stand for the industrial civilization of the North that was making a second invasion of Mississippi. His victim, Temple Drake, stood for the violated South that finally became as corrupt as the invader.

Although Temple was symbolic, she was also a real and convincing person. Nobody could read the book without wondering what happened after her father rescued her and after we last saw her sitting in the Luxembourg Gardens, not repentant, but merely "sullen and discontented and sad." Faulkner himself wondered, and he gives us the rest of her story in *Requiem for a Nun*.

Eight years have passed (or six or five; Faulkner is always careless about chronology). Temple has married Gowan Stevens, wise old Gavin's nephew, the alcoholic Southern gentleman who took her to Popeye's hideout and deserted her there. Gowan has stopped drinking. Temple and he belong to the country club set and have two children, one a little boy, the other a baby six months old. Suddenly Temple meets the younger brother of "Red," the night-club bouncer who had been her paramour in a Memphis sporting house. The old temptations revive in her and, even though she is being blackmailed by the brother, she falls in love with him and prepares to desert her husband. That is one reason why Gavin tells her, "The past is never dead."

But although the past lives in her, Temple has changed since we first met her in *Sanctuary*. There she never once exercised the faculty of conscious choice; instead she followed her instincts blindly as if living in a dream. She didn't even try to escape from the sporting house where Popeye was keeping her a prisoner. In her helplessness and willessness she was like the other principal characters in Faulkner's early novels, including Popeye himself; all of them seemed to be haunted and compelled by some blind necessity that made all their actions foreordained. The new Temple is different. Shocked into life by

342

the example of Nancy Mannigoe, the murderess and former prostitute who is also something of a saint, Temple makes a difficult choice between good and evil. For the rest of her years she will live in torment—that was a condition of the choice she made—but she will also live as a morally responsible human being.

Requiem for a Nun—the nun is Nancy, of course—is a drama conceived on a level of moral consciousness that made me describe it as being genuinely tragic. In that respect it is vastly superior to *Sanctuary*, where the only morality was in the dim background of the author's mind. Yet the comparison between the old book and the new isn't as simple as this would make it seem. *Sanctuary* had the compelling power of nightmare images and there were meanings hidden beneath the surface of a headlong and violent story. *Requiem for a Nun* propounds the sort of traditional wisdom that we must respect, because we feel that it has been learned at the cost of suffering. It has a much richer surface than *Sanctuary*, but I would guess that it has less beneath the surface. Faulkner is writing now with more attention to logic and with somewhat less help from his subconscious mind.

Moreover, there are flaws in his logic that are likely to disturb his readers. Nancy Mannigoe, the saint, kills Temple's baby. She does it to save Temple and her older child, but we can't help feeling that she might have saved them without sacrificing a baby that had a right to its own salvation. The painfully wise Gavin Stevens is Nancy's lawyer and might have kept her from the scaffold—we are told—if he had entered a plea of insanity. Instead he lets her be sentenced to death, then forces Temple to visit the Governor and confess her own sins—and he does this even though he knows that Temple's utter humiliation will be useless, since the Governor has already decided not to pardon Nancy.

After meeting Uncle Gavin in three of Faulkner's novels, I still don't know whether he is wisdom incarnate or a monster of cruelty; I only know that he talks too much. As for my choice between the two Faulkners, I still haven't made up my mind. The new one I vastly respect for his defense of human dignity, but I'm not sure the old unregenerate and scampish Faulkner wasn't the greater novelist.

Robert Penn Warren. "The Redemption of Temple Drake." *New York Times Book Review*, September 30, 1951, pp. 1, 31.

William Faulkner has often dealt with bold, shocking, or implausible materials. His triumph has been to make such materials acceptable by developing their symbolic significance, striking down to some unsuspected, mysterious level of motive, or creating by the hypnotic power of his narrative voice the atmosphere of his special world.

Some time ago in the Mississippi of Faulkner's special world a 17-year-old girl named Temple Drake slipped off the rear platform of a train bound for a college baseball game and got into the car of a young man named Gowan who had learned his drinking at a good school, the University of Virginia. Her subsequent career was checkered and included violation by a pervert, being witness to a murder, doing a rather privileged hitch in a Memphis sporting house, falling in love with a young tough named Red who was bouncer in a gambling establishment, perjuring herself in court to save the gangster Popeye, who had been the agent of her degradation, and getting shipped off to Paris to let the dust settle.

Temple's adventures made some stir twenty years ago and continue, in the paper cover, to titillate the drug store trade. Now Temple reappears, but her current adventures, even with the benefit of the jacket decorator when the paper-cover edition is issued, will scarcely make *Requiem for a Nun* a serious contender for the favor long enjoyed by *Sanctuary*. For one thing, Temple is now engaged in saving her soul, and that is never quite as exciting a subject as losing one.

Not that Temple has set out to save her soul. She is trapped into salvation by tragedy, trapped by tragedy and prodded by her husband's kinsman, the lawyer-philosopher Gavin, who earlier has been best known for his hand in the fortunes of Lucas Beauchamp of *Intruder in the Dust*. Temple is trapped into salvation long after everything had seemed to be happily settled and forgotten.

It is now eight years (Jefferson, Miss., time) since the great scandal. Gowan, full of remorse and chivalry, has gone to Paris to marry her, and a wedding at the embassy with a reception at the Crillon have done their work as a disinfectant. Now the young couple live in Jefferson, in an attractive modern apartment made over in one of the old houses, go to the country club on Saturday night, and are buttressed by a host of loyal friends of their own age and privileged set and the presence of two children, a boy of 5 or so and a baby girl.

However, the marriage is false. It is poisoned by Gowan's forgiveness, by his grim determination to do the "right thing," by his swearing off drink after the scandal, by his groundless suspicions regarding the paternity of the first child. And it is poisoned by Temple's official gratitude, by her resentment, and by her recollections of Red. She secretly gratifies her nostalgia for the mud of her past by long kitchen conversations with Nancy Mannigoe the colored woman, a reformed dope-fiend whore, whom she and Gowan have, in their informed modernity, brought in to raise their children.

This is the situation when a young brother of Red appears, a hard, ruthless, handsome, not immoral but simply unmoral young man who has in his pocket a batch of letters written by Temple to Red in the old sporting-house days. He is, of course, bent on blackmail, but he nearly gets more than he had bargained for. Temple is prepared to give him not only the cash looted from her husband's strong-box and her jewelry, but herself as well, and the baby thrown in for good measure.

When Nancy Mannigoe, Temple's confidante, learns of Temple's decision to elope with the hoodlum, she takes the money and jewelry to prevent it. She wants to save the children, whom she has grown to love. Yet she can't keep the money and jewelry, and when a direct appeal to Temple fails, she plays her last card and smothers the baby. She is tried and convicted, despite the defense by Gavin, and is to be executed. During the trial she has had nothing to offer for herself and when the sentence is pronounced exclaims, "Yes, Lord!"

This is a summary of the action, but as a summary it gives no notion of the peculiar form the action in fact takes. The story of Temple's redemption is given as a play, a fully developed and rounded play in three acts, opening with the scene in court when Nancy hears her sentence and ending in the jail with the interview between Nancy and Temple. In between, by dramatized cutback and Temple's narrative to the Governor, we find the body of the story.

It has long been clear that Faulkner has a powerful dramatic sense. He can catch the strong inner voice of a character, the

344

one phrase that will sum up being and situation. And he constantly probes for the conflict that will be basic for his view of the world. But ordinarily this dramatic sense is somewhat obscured. It is obscured by Faulkner's narrative "voice," which tends to override and absorb the other voices. It is obscured by his fundamental concern with the massive coilings of human motive and with the interpenetration of past and present.

The voice and the fundamental concern are still here, but somewhat differently managed. It is true that though the hands are the hands of Temple Drake the voice is sometimes the voice of William Faulkner; but at other times in the play Temple has a voice all her own. The massive concern with human motive remains: Temple must try to disentangle her motives and say them. Yet the difference between the situation here and that in most of Faulkner's other work is that the issue now is the saying and not the exploration of the thing to be said. And as for the concern with past, that is the very essence of Temple's problem: the past is not even past.

This new treatment of the voice and the fundamental concerns makes for sharpness and dramatic concentration; and the general development of theme and the manipulation of suspense are enormously effective, except, perhaps, in the scene with the Governor where the mass of material to be narrated clogs the dramatic outline, even if the work is taken as a closet drama. Yet despite the general dramatic effect, a certain price has been paid for transferring Faulkner's characteristic materials and concerns into the present form. The price is the credibility of Nancy Mannigoe.

The act of Nancy Mannigoe is shocking and implausible, and as a dramatic fact stands bare and alone without the benefit of Faulkner's voice to delineate motive and bemuse us into acceptance. And even the symbolic meaning seems somewhat dry and schematic. To be clearer, I may remark that we might understand Dilsey of *The Sound and the Fury* in such a role as Nancy's, for we know Dilsey and Dilsey's world massively and hypnotically. Dilsey's act would be a projection of Dilsey. Yet Nancy's act is all; we have no context for it. If anything, the act must project Nancy. It is true, of course, that in the last scene when Nancy and Temple meet and Nancy begins to talk, the mere veracity of her idiom almost persuades us and her voice almost bemuses us. However, the mischief, if it is a mischief, has already been done.

Let us come back to the larger context of Yoknapatawpha history in which the play is set. There is nothing in all Faulkner's work finer than most of these sections for their cranky humor, profound and grotesque poetry, simple pathos, precise visualization, and driving eloquence. But aside from their own merits, what is the relation of these sections to Temple Drake's play?

First, I may observe that the difference between the play and the context gives a shock. It is not merely a difference in method; or rather, the difference in method seems to indicate a more drastic difference. Under the bemusing power of the voice we enter into the world of old Yoknapatawpha, not to identify ourselves with it, for there is always a sense of history, or irremediable pastness, but to yearn toward and believe in its fullness and significance.

The world of Temple Drake is, however, staged, and, in a quite deliberate sense, stagey. It is as though we could say of the sections dealing with Yoknapatawpha County, "This is the way it really was, and the way we must feel about it." And of the play, "This is the kind of play one would have to make about a girl like Temple Drake." The kind of illusion set by the play is very different—more arbitrary, more abstracted, more stylized—

than that set by the account of Yokna-patawpha. The illusion is by consent. The illusion of the other sections is illusion by compulsion.

I am not certain but that the contrast between the sections dealing with the past and the play itself is not a way of saying that the arbitrary, the abstracted, the schematic, the stagey is the only kind of story possible for the world of Temple Drake. Just as salvation through the black Nancy Mannigoe is salvation through one of the despised and rejected derelicts of the old order. We accept her, if we accept her, because we know the world she came from, the world of old Yoknapatawpha.

Checklist of Additional Reviews

"*Requiem for a Nun.*" *Kirkus*, July 15, 1951, p. 356.
"*Requiem for a Nun.*" Buffalo *Evening News*, September 22, 1951, p. 7.
"Faulkner's Latest 'Soul' Work Poetry and Pathos." New Orleans *Times-Picayune*, September 23, 1951, Section 11, p. 8.
"A Time for Tears." Wichita *Beacon*, September 23, 1951, p. 2.
"No Sanctuary." *Newsweek*, September 24, 1951, pp. 90–92.
"Sanctuary Revisited." *Time*, September 24, 1951, p. 114.
Syracuse *Post*, September 29, 1951.
Columbus *Citizen*, September 30, 1951.
"Faulkner Writes a New Tragedy." Miami *Herald* September 30, 1951, p. 4-F.
Charm, October, 1951.
"*Requiem for a Nun.*" *Booklist*, October 1, 1951, p. 49.
"*Requiem for a Nun.*" San Francisco *Call Bulletin*, October 3, 1951, p. 12.

Hartford *Courant*, October 7, 1951.
Buffalo *Courier Express*, October 10, 1951.
Kalamazoo *Gazette*, October 19, 1951.
"*Requiem for a Nun.*" Vancouver *Sun,* October 20, 1951, Magazine Supplement, p. 11.
"Herald Book Reviews." Calgary (Alberta) *Herald,* October 20, 1951, p. 4.
Fort Worth *Star-Telegram*, October 21, 1951.
"Author of the Week." *Sunday Olympian* (Olympia, Wash.), October 28, 1951, p. 22.
"*Requiem for a Nun.*" *College English,* 8 (November 1951), 128.
"*Requiem for a Nun.*" *U.S. Quarterly Book Review*, 7 (December 1951), 357.
Esquire, December, 1951.
Yale Review, Winter, 1952.
"*Requiem for a Nun.*" *Extension,* January 1952, p. 32.
The Free Press (Burlington, Vt.), February 28, 1952.
"The Library Corner." Kalama (Wash.) *Bulletin,* March 7, 1952.
"*Requiem for a Nun.*" *Philippine Education Company Sunday Chronicle,* April 6, 1952.
"*Requiem for a Nun.*" *Stephens College Literary Magazine Standard*, Spring 1952.
Abernathy, Cecil. "The Many Becomes One and All, and Time Becomes a Moment." Birmingham *News,* September 23, 1951, p. 6-E.
Abernathy, Harry. "Sequel to Faulkner's *Sanctuary* Is Told in Drama Form." Clarksdale (Miss.) *Press-Register,* October 6, 1951, p. 6.
Allison, Elizabeth. "The Old and a New Faulkner." *Arkansas Gazette* (Little Rock), September 30, 1951, p. 6-F.
Ashford, Gerald. "Faulkner's New Novel Shows Typical Faults and

Virtues." San Antonio *Express,*
September 16, 1951, p. 5-D.

Aswell James. "Faulkner Revives His
Sanctuary People." Houston *Post,*
September 30, 1951, Section IV, p. 14.

Ault, Phil. "Faulkner Experiments." Los
Angeles *Mirror,* September 28, 1951,
p. 32.

Barkham, John. Hartford *Times,*
September 22, 1951. (*Saturday
Review* Syndicate.)

Beck, Warren. "Mr. Faulkner's New
Surprise." Milwaukee *Journal,*
September 23, 1951, Section V, p. 4.

Bradley, Van Allen. Chicago *Daily
News,* September 26, 1951.

Brantley, R. H. "Faulkner Is the Man to
Say lt." Durham *Morning Herald,*
September 30, 1951, Section IV, p. 7.

Breit, Harvey. "William Faulkner."
Atlantic Monthly, October 1951,
pp. 53–56.

Bruni, T. G. "Books in Brief." *Daily
News Digest* (Allentown Pa.), October
25, 1951, p. 8.

Byam, Milton S. "*Requiem for a Nun.*"
Library Journal, 76 (August 1951),
1220.

B., K.L. *Standard Times.*

C., J.F. "Faulkner Novel Has Message
of Expiation." Arizona *Republic*
(Phoenix), September 23, 1951,
Section 111, p. 7.

C., J.L. "Temple Drake's Redemption."
Columbia *Missourian,* December 19,
1951, p. 4.

Canfield, Francis X. "Honor and
Dishonor: Black and White." *Books
on Trial,* November 1951, pp. 115–
16.

Cantwell, Robert. "Sequel to
Sanctuary." *The Freeman,* February
11, 1952 , pp. 317–18.

Chapman, John. "Novel by Nobel Prize
Winner Faulkner." Dallas *Morning
News,* September 23, 1951, Part VII,
p. 4.

Chism, Cecil. "Faulkner at His Best."
Chattanooga *Times,* October 7, 1951,
p. 17.

Clipper, Patrick M. St. Paul *Sunday
Pioneer Press,* September 30, 1951.

Coe, Callie Mae. "*Requiem for a Nun.*"
Sunday Enterprise (unidentified city),
September 30, 1951, p. 8-C.

Collins, Carvel. "Mississippi's Nobel
Prize Winner Experiments with Play
Form in Middle of His Newest
Novel." *Delta Democrat-Times*
(Greenville, Miss.), September 30,
1951, p. 15.

D., P. "Faulkner Probes Further into
Story of Temple Drake." Corpus
Christi *Caller-Times,* October 21,
1951, p. 16-C.

D[ouglas], C[laude] L. "*Requiem for a
Nun.*" Fort Worth *Press,* September
29, 1951, p. 6.

Dwight, Ogden. "Faulkner, Recalling
Temple's Sins, Ponders Now Their
Atonement." Des Moines *Sunday
Register,* September 30, 1951,
p. 17-G.

Elconin, Victor A. "Faulkner Reaffirms
Man's Ability to Triumph over Evil."
Daily Oklahoman (Oklahoma City),
September 23, 1951, Magazine
Section, p. 14.

Elliott, J. K. "Faulkner's Play-Novel
Sultry Epic." London (Ontario)
Evening Freepress, October 6, 1951,
p. 11.

Emerson, O. B. "Faulkner Continues
Characterizations of People of South."
Jackson (Tenn.) *Sun,* May 18, 1952,
Section III, p. 3.

Engle, Paul. "*Requiem for a Nun.*"
Chicago *Sunday Tribune,* October 7,
1951, Magazine of Books, p. 6.

English, H. M., Jr. "Reviews." *Furioso,*
7 (Winter 1952), 60–63.

Fadiman, Clifton. "Party of One."
Holiday, November 1951, pp. 8–11.

Ferguson, Milton James. "*Requiem for* a

Nun." Brooklyn *Eagle,* October 7, 1951, p. 25.

Flowers, Paul. "Nobility Out of Depravity." Memphis *Commercial Appeal,* October 14, 1951, p. 7-E.

Flynn, Peggy. "*Requiem for a Nun.*" Radio broadcast on WTAL (Tallahassee), November 8, 1951 (copy in Random House files).

Ford, Jesse Hill, Jr. "Intricate Faulkner Work Symbolizes Destruction." Nashville *Tennessean,* September 30, 1951, p. 18-C.

Fowler, R. "Experiment Effective." Greensboro *Daily News,* November 4, 1951, Feature Section, p. 3.

Fratoni, Alba. "*Requiem for a Nun.*" Red Hook (N.Y.) *Advertiser,* October 11, 1951.

Gannett, Lewis. "*Requiem for a Nun.*" (N.Y.) *Herald Tribune,* September 27, 1951, p. 21.

Gardiner, Harold C. "Two Southern Tales." *America,* October 6, 1951, p. 18.

Gardiner, John. "Requiem in Mississippi." Windsor (Ontario) *Daily Star,* October 6, 1951, p. 10.

Gellert, Leon. "The Book of the Year?" Sydney (Australia) *Morning Herald,* January 5, 1952, p. 7.

Gingras, A. de T. "Key Books." Key West *Citizen,* December 18, 1951, p. 2.

G[lackin], W[illiam] C. "Faulkner Writes a Play Like a Novel." Sacramento *Bee,* December 22, 1951, p. 23.

Glenn, Taylor. "Books and Authors." Bridgeport *Sunday Post,* September 23, 1951, p. 4-B.

Groseclose, Frank. "*Requiem for a Nun.*" *Carolina Quarterly,* 4, No. 1 (December 1951), 59–62.

Grove, Lee. "Faulkner Writes of Redemption." Washington *Post,* September 23, 1951, p. 6-B.

Guerard, Albert. "*Requiem for a Nun*: An Examination." *Harvard Advocate,*

November 1951, pp. 41–42; also reviewed in *Perspective U.S.A.,* 1 (Fall 1952), 171–72.

Hass, Victor P. "Mr. Faulkner—as Before." Omaha *World Herald,* October 21, 1951, Magazine Section, p. 29.

Heilman, Robert B. "Schools for Girls." *Sewanee Review,* 60 (Spring 1952), 304–9.

Hicks, Granville. "Faulkner's Sequel to *Sanctuary.*" *New Leader,* October 22, 1951, pp. 21–23.

Hoch, Henry George. "Evil World of Faulkner." Detroit *News,* February 10, 1952, Women's Section, p. 18.

Horowitz, Irwin M. "*Requiem for a Nun.*" Elizabeth (N.J.) *Daily Journal,* September 26, 1951, p. 20.

Howes, Larry. "Happy Ending—Practically." Portland (Oregon) *Sunday Journal,* October 21, 1951, p. 12-M.

Hoyt, Elizabeth North. "Southland Corruption." Cedar Rapids *Gazette,* September 23, 1951, Section III, p. 2.

Hughes, Riley. "New Novels." *Catholic World,* 174 (December 1951), 232.

Hunter, Anna C. "Books in Review." Savannah *Morning News,* September 23, 1951, p. 29.

Jackson, Margot. "*Requiem for a Nun.*" Akron *Beacon Journal,* September 30, 1951, p. 4-B.

Jessup, Lee Cheney. "Faulkner's Most Complex Work." Nashville *Banner,* November 2, 1951, p. 30.

Johnson, Stanley. "Further Adventures of Temple Drake Who Is Back in Yoknapatawpha County." Salt Lake City *Tribune,* November 11, 1951, p. 4-M.

Jones, Carter Brooke. "Sequel to *Sanctuary* New Faulkner Novel One of His Most Persuasive Stories." Washington *Sunday Star,* September 23, 1951, p. 3-C.

Kass, Bob. "Artists and Actors." Radio broadcast on WFUV, November 3, 1951 (copy in Random House files).

Keeling, John Mason. "A Panegyric at a Requiem." Wilmington (N.C.) *Sunday Star,* October 28, 1951, Magazine Section, p. 9.

K[lein], F[rancis] A. "Books—What's New." St. Louis *Globe Democrat,* October 21, 1951, p. 3-G.

Kohler, Dayton. "Faulkner's Latest Brooding Concern for Man's Fate." Louisville *Courier Journal,* October 7, 1951, Section III, p. 10.

Laycock, Edward A. "Faulkner Still Baffles." Boston *Sunday Globe,* September 23, 1951, p. 29-A.

Littlefield, J. Wesley. "The Story of Temple Drake Joins Yoknapatawpha Fable." Toledo *Blade,* September 30, 1951, p. 5.

Looby, James F. *"Requiem for a Nun."* Hartford *Courant,* October 7, 195l, Magazine Section, p. 19.

Loveman, Amy. *"Requiem for a Nun."* *Book-of-the-Month Club News,* September 1951.

M., W. J., Jr. "New Distinguished Faulkner Novel." Montgomery *Advertiser,* September 23, 1951, p. 4-D.

Mason, Jack. "Faulkner Novel Is Three-Act Play." Oakland *Tribune,* October 21, 1951, p. 2-C.

Match, Richard. "The 'New' Faulkner." *New Republic,* November 5, 1951, pp. 19–20.

McClipper, Patrick M. "William Faulkner Writes Play." St. Paul *Sunday Pioneer Press,* September 30, 1951, Women's Section, p. 18.

McGann, George. "Faulkner's New Novel Has Religious Savorings." Dallas *Times Herald,* September 23, 1951, Section V, p. l0.

McGovern, Hugh. "Prowler in the Backstalls." Denver *Monitor* (East Side Edition), October 12, 1951, p. 1.

McHugh, Miriam. "Today's Books." *The Trentorian* (N.J.), October 6, 1951.

McLaughlin, Richard. "Requiem for Temple Drake." *Theatre Arts,* October 1951, pp. 50, 77.

Merlin, Milton. Los Angeles *Times,* October 7, 1951.

Minot, George E. "New Faulkner Novel Sharp, Provocative, Exasperating." Boston *Sunday Herald,* September 30, 1951, Section III, p. 4.

Morgan, Frederick. *"Requiem for a Nun."* *Hudson Review* 5 (Spring 1952), 154.

Moritsugu, Frank. "Yoknapatawpha Revisited." *The Varsity* (Univ. of Toronto), October 16, 1951.

Morrissy, W. B. "Return Ticket to *Sanctuary.*" Montreal *Gazette,* September 29, 1951, p. 29.

Murphree, Alex. "New Faulkner Novel Neither Detracts, Adds to Stature." Denver *Post,* September 23, 1951, p. 6-E.

Nichols, Luther. *"Requiem for a Nun."* San Francisco *Chronicle,* October 14, 1951, p. 19.

O'Neill, Frank. "New Faulkner Novel Is Story-Drama Headed for Broadway This Fall." Cleveland *News,* September 25, 1951, p. 9.

Parsons, Eugene O. "Faulkner Finds Good in the 'Mud and Scum of Things.'" Worcester (Mass.) *Sunday Telegram,* September 23, 1951, p. 7-B.

Patrick, Corbin. "Faulkner's Latest Work Is Play-Novel." Indianapolis *Star,* September 23, 1951, Section VI, p. 8.

Perkin, Robert L. "Faulkner Better than Ever." *Rocky Mountain News* (Denver), September 23, 1951, p. 6-A.

Pfaff, William. "The Future that Is Already Here." *Commonweal,* September 28, 1951, p. 601.

Philbrik, Charles H. Providence *Sun Journal*, September 30, 1951.

Pooley, E. M. "*Requiem for a Nun.*" El Paso *Herald Post*, September 29, 1951, p. 4.

Poore, Charles. "New Books." *Harper's Magazine*, October 1951, p. 102.

Posner, Arthur. "Faulkner's Latest Sure to Please." Rochester *Democrat and Chronicle*, October 7, 1951, p. 4-C.

Poster, Herbert. *American Mercury*, December, 1951, pp. 106–12.

Powers, Clare. "*Requiem for a Nun.*" *The Sign*, November 1951, pp. 73–74.

Prescott, Orville. "Books of the Times." New York *Times*, September 27, 1951, p. 29.

Price, Emerson. "Tragic Faulkner Novel Has Spiritual Message." Cleveland *Press*, September 25, 1951, p. 10.

Richards, Robert. "The Value of Faith Comes to Us Again in Faulkner Book." Memphis *Press-Scimitar*, October 13, 1951, p. 6.

Ridgely, Joseph V. "A Moral Play." *Hopkins Review*, 5, No. 3 (Spring 1952), pp. 81–83.

Rogers, W. G. "New Faulkner Book Combines Novel, Drama." Atlanta *Journal-Constitution*, September 23, 1951, p. 12-B.

Sain, Bob. "The Same Temple as of Old." Charlotte *News*, October 6, 1951, p. 8-A.

Schott, Webster. "Faulkner's Experiment a Play in a Novel." Kansas City *Star*, October 13, 1951, p. 16.

Schuyler, J[osephine]. "Faulkner's Remarkable New Novel." Pittsburgh *Courier*, December 15, 1951, Magazine Section, p. 15.

Scott, James. "Nobel Prize-Winner Experiments Again." Toronto *Telegram*, September 29, 1951, p. 15.

Shaw, John Bennett. "Faulkner Both Good, Bad in *Requiem for a Nun.*"

Tulsa *Daily World*, November 4, 1951, Section V, p. 9.

Sherman, John K. "Incredible Plot Trips Old Faulkner Heroine." Minneapolis *Sunday Tribune*, October 7, 1951, p. 6-F.

Sherman, Thomas B. "Faulkner's New Novel a Departure in Form." St. Louis *Post-Dispatch*, September 30, 1951, p. 4-C.

Simcoe, Selma. "*Requiem for a Nun.*" *Daily Bruin* (U.C.L.A.), December l, 1951.

S[mith], B[lanche] H[ixson]. "*Requiem for a Nun.*" Meriden (Conn.) *Record*, November 9, 1951, p. 6.

Spearman, Walter. "Literary Lantern." Greensboro *Daily News*, September 23, 1951, Feature Section, p. 3.

Stanley, Robert. *The Stormy Petrel* (Oglethorpe University, Georgia), 3 (April 16, 1952), 4, 6.

Stobie, Margaret. "New Faulkner Novel." Winnipeg (Manitoba) *Free Press*, October 20, 1951, p. l0.

Swanson, Jean. "Faulkner Fulfils What He Considers to Be the Duty of a Writer." Saskatoon (Saskatchewan) *Star Phoenix*, November 3, 1951, p. 12.

Truax, Charles. "Newest Faulkner 'Novel' Sequel to Earlier Book." Dayton *Daily News*, October 7, 1951, Section II, p. 8.

Tunstall, Caroline Heath. "Faulkner Reaches into *Sanctuary* to Weave a Play among 3 Stories." Norfolk *Virginian-Pilot*, September 23, 1951, Part V, p. 4.

Van Dewerker, John. "Latest Faulkner Yarn Is Bizarre." Spokane *Daily Chronicle* (Final Fireside edition), October 18, 1951, p. 34

W., H. "*Requiem for a Nun.*" Auburn (N.Y.) *Citizen Advertiser*, September 27, 1951.

Weigel, John A. "Faulkner's Novel Pictures Dramatic Scene in Court." Dayton *Journal Herald,* November 3, 1951, p. 22.

W[eissblatt], H[arry] A. "William Faulkner." Trenton *Sunday Times-Advertiser,* December 30, 1951, Part IV, p. 8.

West, Ray B., Jr. "William Faulkner: Artist and Moralist." *Western Review,* 6 (Winter 1952), 162–67.

White, Charles E. "About Faulkner's New Requiem and How Time Heals." Houston *Chronicle,* September 23, 1951, p. 7-E.

Whitson, Robley Edward. "*Requiem for a Nun.*" *Fordham Monthly Bulletin,* 68, No. 1 (1951).

Wicker, Tom. "William Faulkner's Domain." Winston-Salem *Journal and Sentinel,* September 23, 1951, p. 4-C.

Wiener, Max. "Faulkner and His Work." (N.J.) *News,* October 27, 1951, Section III, p. 52.

Williams, Ernest E. "New Novel Viewed as Epitaph to an Earlier Faulkner Work." Fort Wayne *News-Sentinel,* September 29, 1951, p. 4.

Wilson, W. Emerson. "*Requiem for a Nun.*" Wilmington (N.C.) *Morning News,* October 8, 1951, p. 11.

Wilson, William E. "A Faulkner Novel in a 'New' Form." Baltimore *Evening Sun,* September 24, 1951, p. 18.

W[ood], D[aniel]. "Faulkner's Latest Odd Jumble of Novel and Play." Pasadena *Star-News,* October 14, 1951, p. 23.

Yeiser, Frederick. "More about Temple Drake." Cincinnati *Enquirer,* September 23, 1951, p. 48.

MIRRORS OF CHARTRES STREET

Mirrors
of
Chartres Street

by

William Faulkner

Introduction by
WILLIAM VAN O'CONNOR

Illustrated by
MARY DEMOPOULOS

Carvel Collins.
"As Faulkner Saw New
Orleans."
*New York Times Book
Review*, February 7,
1954, p. 4.

In 1925 the Sunday Magazine section of *The New Orleans Times-Picayune* printed a series of sketches by William Faulkner. This was his first extended prose publication, his earlier published work having been chiefly poetry. The staff of the journal of *Faulkner Studies*, after searching through the Picayune files and finding eleven sketches, has reprinted them here in a limited edition.

At the end of 1924, when he was 27, Faulkner went to live in New Orleans and stayed there until he sailed for Europe the next June. These months were important in his development. For the first time he was in association with writers and artists and their shop talk; partly under their influence he put poetry somewhat to the side and began to concentrate on fiction. Among his associates in New Orleans were Sherwood Anderson, Roark Bradford, and the artist William Spratling, with whom Faulkner prepared a picture book about these men and others of their group.

Faulkner wrote the pot-boiling sketches for *The Picayune* under the general heading "Mirrors of Chartres Street." A famous book of that time was Begbie's *Mirrors of Downing Street*, with its accounts of such personages as Lloyd George, Winston Churchill and Lord Kitchener. Faulkner's series set out to describe vagabonds, aspiring hoodlums, racing touts and workmen whom he saw in New Orleans' French Quarter, of which Chartres Street is a major thoroughfare.

William Van O'Connor points out in his helpful introduction that at the back of Faulkner's observation of this hard-pressed street life was "a desire to see the world as high romance." For example, Faulkner admires the crippled panhandler of the opening sketch for his "untrampled spirit," his "heaven-sent attribute for finding life good... which gave King Arthur to a dull world, and sent baron and knight... to flap pennons in Syria, seeking a dream."

Some of these apprentice sketches seem forced and awkward, but several give indications of the genius their author was to display in such masterpieces as *The Sound and the Fury* and *Light in August*. The disappointing ones have the air of being either too skillfully aimed at the newspaper fiction reader or too hurriedly produced for small but needed fees—probably in time stolen from *Soldiers' Pay*, the first novel Faulkner was tapping out in his ground-floor corner room halfway down the little street now known, for the tourist trade, as Pirate's Alley.

The most interesting sketches show Faulkner working with methods and themes he was to develop in his finest fiction. "Sunset" tells of a Negro's confusion and destruction in a way which suggests later stories such as "Pantaloon in Black." Here awkwardness of style and conception disappears and Faulkner's revelatory method is itself revealed. "The Kingdom of God," a sketch inferior to "Sunset" but superior to several, is of interest because it centers on a character who anticipates the idiot of *The Sound and the Fury*. Paragraphs of another sketch, "Out of Nazareth," also anticipate parts of *The Sound and the Fury* and *Light in August*. And "The Kid Learns" introduces the motif of meeting "little sister Death" which Faulkner was to use later in more than one work.

In making these eleven early pieces available, the compilers have done a service for the reader interested in William Faulkner, and they are to be commended. It is unfortunate, however, that in examining the 1925 files of *The Picayune* they did not come upon the March first issue, which contains "Jealousy," the fourth sketch in the "Mirrors" series, a skillful treatment of the dilemma of a restaurant owner in the Quarter, the aging husband of a young wife. And the issue of Aug. 16, published after Faulkner's departure for Europe, contains his "Episode," another sketch of the "Mirrors" type which should have been included here. Because Faulkner's contributions to *The Picayune* seem to be unknown to most of his bibliographers, biographers and critics, the reprinting of all thirteen sketches would have increased the value of this already interesting and useful book.

Checklist of Additional Reviews

"*Mirrors of Chartres Street.*" *New Yorker*, January 30, 1954, pp. 103–4.
Halsband, Robert. "Early Faulkner." *Saturday Review*, July 24, 1954, p. 34.

THE FAULKNER READER

THE
FAULKNER
READER

Selections from the works of

WILLIAM
FAULKNER

 RANDOM
HOUSE
NEW YORK

Charles Poore. "Books of the Times." New York *Times*, April 1, 1954, p. 29.

Who reads Faulkner, the Nobel laureate of Yoknapatawpha County? Is he, as we have occasionally been told, a terrifically difficult writer whose stories are veiled in unutterable lore? Well, that's the legend. And legends die hard.

The truth, however, seems to be spectacularly otherwise. It shows, in fact, that he is hardly least among the popular writers of America. A survey made for this morning's column reveals that his publishers have sold more than 600,000 copies of his books in the Random House and Modern Library editions. And the New American Library reports that the total sales of nine Faulkner titles in paperback editions are nearing 5,000,000 copies. A roundish sum. Furthermore, the fact that three of the stories in his new anthology, *The Faulkner Reader*, appeared first in *The Saturday Evening Post* in 1932, 1942, and 1943, calls for a certain amount of revision in the cultists' theory of his abounding obscurity.

Would it not be fair to say, then, that—among book readers—those who find this distinguished Mississippi hunter, fisherman, farmer, and author hard to understand are in the minority? Those who think he is hard to read underestimate the intelligence of Americans. Anyone who can follow the punctuationless cadence of a telephone conversation can follow Faulkner. As Eudora Welty has pointed out: "His stories seem to race with time, race with the world"—and "the reason Faulkner's unwieldy looking sentences can

race is of course their high organization, a musical organization."

Also, I think he likes to leave out periods to bedevil the critics. The thing to do is to plunge into the stream of Faulkner's writing and enjoy it, along with several million other Americans.

You get the full sweep of Faulkner in *The Faulkner Reader*. Here is a great romantic storyteller at his best, represented by the Nobel Prize address, *The Sound and the Fury*, "The Bear," *Old Man*, "Spotted Horses," "A Rose for Emily," and a number of other pieces—including "An Odor of Verbena" from *The Unvanquished* and "The Courthouse," from *Requiem for a Nun*. Personally, I wish that *Sartoris* had been included, for that novel is the best introduction to Faulkner's astounding world of plumes and turnip greens.

However, he has provided a superb introduction to this anthology that touches many matters in the Faulknerian Ring. In it he politely ignores the moss and mistletoe that solemn, pavement-bound Northern critics have tried to graft on the great tree of his stories—as well as the poison ivy some have planted around the trunk. He tells us here what we confirm in his own books, his own style, that he read Scott and Dumas as a child, and that in a preface by Sienkiewicz he found his most satisfying answer to the why of writing: "To uplift men's hearts."

Reading Faulkner's article on Mississippi in the current issue of *Holiday* magazine while crossing that state from the Gulf of Mexico to Memphis a couple of weeks ago, I found themes that run through all his works. Here are the key Faulkner words: Invincible, inviolable, indomitable, sailing down the page like a class of British warships.

He writes in *Holiday* about the times when Old Man River rises so high that the boats can cross the cotton fields, and you see what follows in this anthology's story, *Old Man*. You read a new text of Faulkner's boyhood drive to be a beribboned aviator, and news of the ups and downs of the Walter-Scott-proud Sartoris clan, the terrible flounderings of the sad, seedy Compsons, the devouring rise of the Snopeses. He is never blind to the desperate inequities that strew the way of the world, any more than he is blind to the squalor or the splendor.

The world of Faulkner is not always decaying. It is growing. You can dramatize that, I think, in the fact that on the streets of his Mississippi towns this spring you see many men in uniform, particularly the gray-blue of the Air Force. It's not the corps he joined as a boy eager to fight in the skies of France, and the color is not a true blend of the contending forces in the Civil War that lives again so often in his books. Yet it suggests all three, somehow.

The last paragraph in his salute to Mississippi might stand for Faulkner's works: "Loving all of it even while he had to hate some of it because he knows now that you don't love because: you love despite, not for the virtues, but despite the faults."

Charles H. Nichols.
"The Achievement of
William Faulkner."
Phylon, 15 (2nd Quarter
1954), 209–10.

The career of William Faulkner is one of the most extraordinary in our literary history. For here is the writer who in twenty novels, from *Soldiers' Pay* to *Requiem for a Nun*, has violated virtually all the rules of good fiction. Yet he is widely regarded as the foremost literary man in America. Perhaps no contemporary author is better known abroad, and it was not surprising that he was chosen for the Nobel Prize in 1950. The publication of *The Faulkner Reader*, which contains much of his best work, forces upon us the same insistent question: what has Faulkner actually achieved?

This fine volume makes possible a rapid review of the author's work during the last quarter of a century, for it takes the reader deep into Yoknapatawpha County, Mississippi, and impresses us with the power of the author's imagination, the intensity of his feeling, and the strangeness of his tortured, high-flown rhetoric. This book contains the novel, *Sound and Fury*, first published in 1929, three long stories—"The Bear," *Old Man*, and "Spotted Horses" as well as nine short stories and the Nobel Prize Address. Faulkner is at his best in the stories where he does not get lost in fantastic rhetorical flourishes, where there is some singleness of purpose and clarity of idea. And the original aspects of his talent—the emotional intensity, the virtuosity and inventiveness, the capacity to re-create the terror and guilt of the South—can be seen in "The Bear," "That Evening Sun," "Dry September," "Wash," and "A Rose for Emily." There is no space here for an analysis of *Sound and Fury*, but one is tempted to say that it signifies nothing. The first part cannot be understood until one has read the other two parts. It is so confused in plot, so full of false starts, delays, repetition and rhetorical absurdities, it operates on so many levels of consciousness simultaneously that as an "experiment" it is a monstrous failure. Nevertheless, this account of the tragic decline of the Compson family, of Quentin's brooding over his sister's nymphomania and his eventual suicide has an immediacy which is striking.

But what is Faulkner getting at anyway?

In his Nobel Prize Address he said: "I decline to accept the end of man . . . I believe that man will not merely endure; he will prevail . . . It is the writer's privilege to help man endure by lifting his heart, by reminding him of the courage, and honor and hope and pride and compassion and pity and sacrifice which have been the glory of his past." This is a fine statement, but where in Faulkner is it justified? How can we reconcile with this his pervasive sense of doom, decay and damnation? Is there courage, honor or pity in his Snopeses, Compsons or Popeyes? Is the heart lifted by his picture of the constant triumph of rape, madness, suicide, incest and every form of violence and depravity? I do not quarrel here with Faulkner's subject matter, but with his denigration of man. Apart from guilt and terror and romantic dreams of an *ante bellum* myth of "honor," what do his characters feel? They wrestle with their guilt, but they have no sense of purpose, no visions of greatness. They react to their surroundings in much the same way as "Lion" or "Old Ben." But men are not dogs and bears. Only a few Negroes, children and old women in Faulkner "endure." And it is a question whether his portrait of the psychopathic South is ever held up against a standard of normality. His own attitudes are curiously ambivalent. He sees the injustice toward the Negro, yet clings to the views of his Mississippi neighbors in race relations. He sees the barbarism of the South, yet glories in the Cavalier myth which holds the region in thrall. He is like Quentin Compson shouting, "I don't hate the South!"—tortured, guilty, sick, lacking the courage to destroy the causes of the South's sickness.

One has the feeling that all the grandeur of Faulkner's style—his Mississippi baroque—all his grotesqueries and posturing, all his high-flown bombast are attempts to wrest from his material a pro-

found meaning which has persistently eluded him. It is high time that someone pointed out that the emperor has no clothes.

Webster Schott. "Unstinted Praise Reward of Faulkner, Once Rated 'Obscure and Degenerate.'" Kansas City *Star*, July 24, 1954, p. 14.

In 1945, it was impossible to obtain any of the then sixteen books of William Faulkner except *Sanctuary, The Sound and the Fury* and *As I Lay Dying.*

Four years after the Nobel prize at least a dozen of these books are back in print between either hard or paper covers; four new books by Faulkner are very much available; three volumes of commendable Faulkner criticism have been published. And now we have a new collection of Faulkner's writings, dating back to his early career, as well as another critical investigation of William Faulkner's "tangled fire" by a University of Minnesota English professor, William Van O'Connor.

In ten years Faulkner's standing in American letters has obviously undergone a considerable change. When some of us read Faulkner in college, it was fashionable to dismiss his fiction as obscure and degenerate. Presently it's equally fashionable to praise everything Faulkner writes, without selecting the good from the bad. But whatever stature the writings of William Faulkner may have in the future, we have at least not refused him recognition commensurate with his gifts, as past generations withheld it from Henry James or Theodore Dreiser, for example.

This new regard for William Faulkner's fiction largely accounts for the publication of *The Faulkner Reader*. And indeed, it's an excellent introduction to Faulkner, superior in a number of ways to *The Portable Faulkner* in which Malcolm Cowley tried to relate excerpts of Faulkner's fiction into an 1820-to-1945 saga of the mythical Yoknapatawpha County, Mississippi, where much of Faulkner's writings are laid. *The Faulkner Reader*, enclosing within one set of covers a broad selection of Faulkner's works largely intact, may well persuade more of us to dig into the early writings which are once more in print.

Faulkner's most recent novels, *Intruder in the Dust*, *Requiem for a Nun*, are by no means his most distinguished, as Professor O'Connor reminds us. And *Sanctuary*, Faulkner's best known early novel, is a melodramatic "potboiler," as Faulkner called it, written in three weeks, early in the mornings while Faulkner tended a factory furnace, with only one purpose—to sell 10,000 copies.

The selections in *The Faulkner Reader* present Faulkner at his best; the entire novel *The Sound and the Fury* (1929), his twisting, pathetic story of the destruction of the Compson family; the novelette, "The Bear" (1942), a grim kind of idyl suggesting our return to nature to find fellowship in the human race; the novelette, *Old Man* (1939), which depicts man as a moral creature even within the unnatural confines of prison or the natural walls of a great Mississippi flood; the short stories, "Barn Burning" (1938) and "A Rose for Emily" (1931), which illustrate the decay of the South that lies outside the main stream of traditional morality; ten other stories, including "Spotted Horses" and "Dry September," Faulkner's Nobel prize address, and an introduction

in which Faulkner states for the first time in a book his hope as a writer.

It is a formidable array of reading, not the kind of fiction that can be handled casually in a few evenings. Faulkner is not an easy writer. But after following *The Faulkner Reader* to the last passage of "The Courthouse" and hearing the clock strike and shatter "the virgin pristine air with the first long dingdong of time and doom," one has a clearer understanding of why Faulkner's works won the Nobel Prize.

Faulkner writes in his introduction that the writer's duty is to "uplift the hearts" of men as if he were "saying 'no' to death." It's not unreasonable to ask, is it possible that the heart can be uplifted by the violence, perversion, corruption, and malicious humor which Faulkner's characters, the Snopeses, Compsons, and Sartorises portray?

But it seems equally reasonable to answer yes. For how else, but through knowledge of himself and the forces which propel human nature, can man's heart be uplifted? Faulkner's turgid style is his own. But the tragedy he writes of belongs to the ages. The harshness and evil Faulkner explores are no more harsh or evil than that of classic Greek or English tragedy. The telling is different but *Hamlet* and *Macbeth* are in Faulkner's genre.

In Stockholm, William Faulkner said, "I believe that man will not merely endure; he will prevail. He is immortal, not because he alone among creatures has an inexhaustible voice, but because he has a soul, a spirit capable of compassion and sacrifice and endurance." William Faulkner's novels and stories provide the catharsis which makes us sense this kind of immortality.

In *The Tangled Fire of William Faulkner*, William Van O'Connor suggests that these values are drawn "without question from the Christian doctrines . . ." that "men cannot live as automatons, without traditional values. Though the world at large no longer affirms the fact, man is a spiritual creature. If man does not live with dignity, self-respect, responsibility, and love, he will go the way of the Compsons. . . . He lives in a harsh world, and he should recognize it as such. But he has his compensations. He can know a sense of his own significance and being by violating his aloneness, by accepting what he has to accept to be decently human."

As he covers Faulkner's works book by book, Professor O'Connor not only reconstructs plots, which makes the book generally more useful and less abstract than most literary criticism, he observes things which haven't been apparent along the way.

He shows for example how much a romantic Faulkner was when he first began writing (poetry) in his late twenties. He was a "clever young writer" who could not quite overcome the pose, the "will to rhetoric." Soon Faulkner's smooth, wan verse gave way to a prose rhetoric that was alternately subconscious and a fire for paragraph after paragraph. But Faulkner, unlike his expatriate contemporaries, learned to write untutored. He acquired a copy of *Ulysses*, James Joyce's classic stream-of-consciousness novel, only after he had written *The Sound and the Fury* and was unaware that his experiment closely paralleled Joyce's.

Professor O'Connor observes, too, that Faulkner's critical successes have dealt consistently with the "spirit left over from the heroic past." Ironically, these finest of Faulkner's novels and stories were written at midpoint in his career, when he was drawing the heaviest on Mississippi's history. His progress recently has been almost "crabwise."

However, his new novel, *A Fable*, which Random House will publish early in August is supposed to be his magnum opus. Ten years in the writing, it is said to be the story of the unknown soldier, dealing with "war and peace, the world, humanity."

The biography that reveals the extraordinary personality of the taciturn, withdrawn William Faulkner is still to be written. In the meantime, the chapter notes at the end of *The Tangled Fire of William Faulkner* make fascinating reading. We learn that Faulkner rates himself second among America's four leading twentieth century novelists, behind Thomas Wolfe, but ahead of Ernest Hemingway and John Steinbeck.

He writes his first draft, in longhand at a neat, orderly study desk. Then he transcribes just once with his typewriter. He reads practically no novels. He has granted more interviews than one might have thought. But the rule is still seclusion. Faulkner's typical answer to a request for an interview might go like the one I received in 1950: "Sorry but no. Am violently opposed to interviews and publicity. What I write is in public domain of course and the writer has no right to dictate. But I hold that his private life is his own, to be—the privacy—defended. Sorry, and thank you for the courtesy of your letter."

(Signed) Faulkner.

Checklist of Additional Reviews

"*The Faulkner Reader.*" *Kirkus*,
    February 1, 1954, p. 79.
Sunday *Olympian*, February 22, 1954.
St. Louis *Globe Democrat*, April 4, 1954.
"'To Uplift Man's Heart.'" San Jose
    (Calif.) *Mercury-News*, April 11,
    1954, Section III, p. 16.

"*The Faulkner Reader.*" *New Yorker*, April 17, 1954, p. 139.

"Faulkner's Stories in Shortened Form." Detroit *News*, April 18, 1954, p. 12-F.

Delta Democrat-Times (Greenville, Miss.), April 18, 1954.

"Faulkner Writings Collected." Dayton *Daily News*, April 25, 1954. Section II, p. 9.

"The Best of Faulkner." San Francisco *Argonaut*, April 30, 1954, p. 18.

Think, May 1954.

The Freeman, May 17, 1954.

The Writer, June 1954.

Arizona Days and Ways, June 6, 1954.

Pasadena *Independent*, August 1, 1954.

Perspectives U.S.A., Winter 1955.

Abernathy, Harry. "*Faulkner Reader Has Best Work.*" Clarksdale (Miss.) *Press Register*, April 3, 1954, p. 2.

B[arkham], J[ohn]. "Whole Bookful of Faulkner." Youngstown *Vindicator*, May 16, 1954, p. 21-C.

Beck, Warren. "Faulkner Guide and Samples." Milwaukee *Journal*, April 11, 1954, Part V, p. 4.

Beshera, John. "Farmer Who Tells Stories." *Daily Tar Heel* (Univ. of North Carolina), April 8, 1954, p. 2.

Chapman, John. "Faulkner's Uplifting Fiction." Dallas *Morning News*, April 18, 1954, Section VI, p. 13.

Collier, Bryan. "A Writer's Creed." Charleston (S.C.) *News and Courier*, April 4, 1954, p. 10-C.

Comans, Grace P. "A Cross Section." Hartford *Courant*, April 11, 1954, Magazine Section, p. 18.

Davis, Evangeline. "William Faulkner Reader." Greensboro *Daily Times*, April 25, 1954.

Engle, Paul. "Life around Faulkner." Chicago *Sunday Tribune*, April 18, 1954, Magazine of Books, p. 4.

Flynn, Stephen. "Faulkner Works Are a Treasure." Miami *Herald*, April 25, 1954, p. 4-F.

Govan, Gilbert E. "Of Books and Writers." Chattanooga *Times*, May 16, 1954, p. 24.

Gribben, J. C. "The Faulkner Reader." Cincinnati *Enquirer*.

H., E. "The Basic Philosophy." Durham *Morning Herald*, April 18, 1954, Section IV, p. 7.

Haselmayer, Louis. "*The Faulkner Reader.*" Burlington (Iowa) *Hawkeye-Gazette*, August 2, 1954, p. 4.

Hermel, Olive Dean. "Nobel Prize Novelists." *Christian Science Monitor*, August 5, 1954, p. 11.

Herzberg, Max. "Selections from Books of William Faulkner." Newark (N.J.) *Sunday News*, April 18, 1954, p. 2-E.

Hogan, William. "The Non-Faulknerian's Guide to the Master." San Francisco *Chronicle*, February 13, 1959, p. 29. (Review of reissue. Also February 12, 1954.)

Horowitz, Irvin M. "*The Faulkner Reader.*" Elizabeth (N.J.) *Daily Journal*, April 1, 1954, p. 28.

Howe, Irving. "William Faulkner's Enduring Power." *New York Times Book Review*, April 4, 1954, p. 1.

J., C.W. "*Faulkner Reader Real Treasure.*" Springfield (Mo.) *News and Leader*, April 4, 1954, p. 5-B.

J., R.C. "The Faulkner Reader." Flint (Mich.) *Journal*.

Jensen, Arthur E. "Here's an Excellent Selection of Novels." Boston *Sunday Herald*, April 11, 1954, Section I, p. 4.

K., F.T. "*The Faulkner Reader.*" Long Beach *Independent Press Telegram*, April 25, 1954, Southland Magazine, p. 28.

Kelton, Lorena. "A Sampling of Faulkner: Stark and Unforgettable." Beaumont (Tex.) *Enterprise*, May 2, 1954, p. 6-C.

Kinnaird, Clark. "*The Faulkner Reader.*" New York *Journal American*, April 11, 1954, p. 21-C.

(King Feature release April 10, 1954.)

Knezevich, Nick. "*Faulkner Reader Typical*." Pittsburgh *Press*, April 18, 1954, Section II, p. 6.

Kubasek, John R. "*The Faulkner Reader*." *Night Owl Reporter* (N.J.), February 24, 1959, p. 2. (Review of reissue.)

Miller, Lillian Beresnoch. "*The Faulkner Reader*." *Jewish Advocate*, January 27, 1955, Section II, p. 16.

Morrissey, Ralph. "Domain of William Faulkner." Nashville *Tennessean*, March 28, 1954, p. 21-C.

North, Sterling. "The Hounds of Spring." New York *World-Telegram and the Sun*, April 8, 1954, p. 30.

O'Neill, Frank. "Faulkner Saga in Fat Reader." Cleveland *News*, April 2, 1954, p. 11.

Richards, Robert. "William Faulkner Always Stands Up for Man in His Struggle to Live." Memphis *Press-Scimitar*, April 10, 1954, p. 4.

Rubin, Harold. "*Faulkner Reader* Good Sample of Old and New." New Orleans *Times-Picayune*, April 11, 1954, Section II, p. 4.

Santillan-Castrence, Pura. "*The Faulkner Reader*." Manila *Bulletin*, September 20, 1954, p. 24.

Shapiro, Charles. "A New Collection of Faulkner Work." Louisville *Courier Journal*, May 16, 1954, Section III, p. 11.

Shapiro, Norman. "Books." *Education Sun*, March 31, 1954.

Sherman, Thomas B. "William Faulkner's 'Sound and Fury.'" St. Louis *Post-Dispatch*, April 11, 1954, p. 4-B.

Tunstall, Caroline H. "16 Selections by Faulkner." Norfolk *Virginian-Pilot*, May 16, 1954, Part V, p. 10.

Waterfall, W. K. "New Faulkner Collection Offers Best Works from Yoknapatawpha County." Fort Wayne *News-Sentinel*, April 10, 1954, p. 4.

W[eissblatt], H[arry] A. "Faulkner." Trenton *Sunday Times-Advertiser*, April 10, 1954, Part IV, p. 12.

Winterich, John T. "Faulkner in Perspective." *New York Herald Tribune Book Review*, July 11, 1954, p. 11.

Wolff, Anthony. "Views and Previews." Publication unknown. (Chapel Hill, N.C.), March 24, 1959.

A FABLE

A
FABLE

WILLIAM FAULKNER

Random House

Warren Beck.
"A Gigantic Faulkner
Fable."
Milwaukee *Journal*,
August 1, 1954, p. 4.

A Fable, on which William Faulkner worked from 1944 to 1953, is a magnificent novel, in concept and in drama, characterization and style. Though not easy reading, or immediately transparent, it is resonant with meanings and its gamut of tones is immense. A tremendous venture in symbolic composition, it requires attention like that demanded by fugue or symphony, and should be viewed both closely and in perspective, like great architecture.

Besides its complexity of design and symbolic subtleties, there are the difficulties inherent in Faulkner's characteristic methods. The cryptic narrative unfolds slowly, like experience itself, and details are sometimes multiplied and magnified in a dreamlike vision which intensifies mood but must be closely noted, like concentrated poetry.

Thus *A Fable* will disconcert and perhaps irritate those uninclined to such attentiveness. However, serious readers of fiction will give this novel a high place, though conflicting interpretations will abound.

The scene, except for one episode in the United States, is France in World War I. The story shifts among many characters, in a counterpoint of contrasted attitudes and actions. A central event is a French regiment's refusal to attack, and the consequent lull on the front, both sides sensing that men might will peace. This spirit of nonviolence and conciliation has been promulgated by a mysterious corporal, about whom are many implied parallels to Jesus, culminating in his execution after he has been taken to a high place and offered worldly power and after his betrayal by one of 12 followers.

Faulkner has interpolated a previously published narrative, "Notes on a Horse Thief." It tells how an English groom, assisted by a negro Preacher-hostler, stole an injured racehorse from a train wreck, healed it and raced it in remote American communities, eluding arrest. Concerned at first with winning bets, the groom, like the old Negro, then wants simply to see the extraordinary horse run rather than have it penned on a stud farm.

Later the Negro, as preacher, seeks the groom, now a soldier, intent on saving him, having seen a spark of idealism in this corrupt, bitter man. Thus the American episode, though only tenuously connected with the war scenes, is relevantly symbolic, since a main theme is spiritual conversion. While plainly satirical of war and the military mind, *A Fable* also deprecates by implication all hardness of heart, and affirms men's recurrent idealism and susceptibility to grace.

The English groom's conversion proceeds slowly; first he only appreciates the horse but finally among fellow soldiers he can say "we" instead of "I." Conversion touches the deputy sheriff who pursues the horse thief and then resigns, his sympathies having gone over to those who cherish the wonderful animal. Another convert is a British soldier, who gives up a commission and returns to the ranks, repudiating military stratification. Still another searcher for truth is the French quartermaster general, lifelong friend of the commander in chief, deterred from resigning only when told that the corporal's execution is part of a pattern, since martyrdom will enhance his teaching.

Among the inflexibly unreconstructible is the mutinous soldier's commander, so insistent on executing the whole regiment that he himself must be assassinated. A British flier and a French priest, unable to question their loyalties, commit suicide. The commander in chief, an enigmatic figure, has a foot in both worlds, seeming omniscient and compassionate but insisting on a full rendering to Caesar.

His role is complicated in that the corporal is his unacknowledged son. Their interview dramatizes undeniable relation and irreconcilable conflict between the expedient world of affairs and the realm of absolute spirit. The novel has two symbolic climaxes, first when the corporal's body, blown out of its grave by resumed barrages, is buried as the unknown soldier, and second, when six years later the war crippled groom flings the corporal's medal at the commander in chief's coffin during the state funeral.

Women related to the corporal suggest Biblical parallels supporting the novel's religious implications. Episodes concerning minor characters range from grotesque or starkly realistic to eloquently poetic. The varied style is complex but controlled; Faulkner has refined ... his unique, dynamic mode. That some passages are fantasies is not a lapse but a studied use, enlarging ... fiction's scope.

This book makes Faulkner more than ever our greatest novelist.

Malcolm Cowley. "Faulkner's Powerful New Novel." *New York Herald Tribune Books*, August 1, 1954, pp. 1, 8.

William Faulkner's new book is simultaneously a novel, a golden legend, and a passion play. Forsaking Yoknapatawpha county, Mississippi, and the whole South, which has been the scene of all his other novels, he takes us to the Western battlefront in the spring of 1918. Forsaking the novelist's world of probable actions and plausible characters, he imagines that the Passion of Christ is re-enacted by a corporal in the French army determined to redeem the world from evil. War is evil, and the corporal tries to stop the war.

With the twelve men in his squad, who are his disciples, he persuades a regiment to stay in the trenches on a Monday morning when it has been ordered to make an attack. News of the mutiny spreads up and down the line and across No Man's Land, and by three o'clock of Tuesday afternoon fighting has ceased from Switzerland to the North Sea. The rest of the long novel tells how the corporal is betrayed by one of his men, imprisoned on Wednesday, and executed on Friday between two thieves; then it tells how fighting was resumed on the seventh day. *A Fable* is a fable indeed.

Faulkner spent nine years on the book, beginning in December, 1944. Three years later, when he interrupted work on the longer novel to write *Intruder in the Dust*, he had already accumulated five hundred manuscript pages, which had carried him a little more than halfway through the story. "Notes on a Horsethief," which would be an episode in the finished novel, was privately printed in 1950. *Requiem for a Nun* (1951) was strictly an interruption, but after that he worked on the big book steadily, at home in Oxford, Mississippi, and in New York, until it was finished in November, 1953. He had done much more planning and rewriting than on any of his earlier novels. Except for the Yoknapatawpha cycle as a whole—now consisting of a dozen books—*A Fable* is Faulkner's most ambitious work.

It contains some of the most powerful

scenes he has ever conceived. There is, for example, the symbolic and dramatic scene in which an English battalion puts down its weapons and walks out through the wire toward the German lines. A German battalion also puts down its arms and comes out to meet the Englishmen. Just as they are beginning to mingle peaceably, an artillery barrage is opened by both sides, on orders from both the Supreme Commands, and the two battalions are wiped out.

There is the ghostly scene in which a German general is flown across the lines in a two-seater plane, to consult with Allied generals about how to restore military discipline. Three English aviators try to shoot him down. They watch their tracers march along the fuselage and up the German's back, but he doesn't slump in his seat, and the plane flies on through harmlessly bursting anti-aircraft shells. What the Englishmen don't know is that their bullets and those of the AA batteries have been removed, by secret order, and replaced with soft pellets covered with phosphorus.

The New Testament parallels are worked out ingeniously and with a feeling of reverence. Among them are miracles reduced to homely terms; healing the sick, the loaves and fishes, the marriage at Cana. Among the characters are Peter (who denies the corporal thrice), Judas (who tries to give back thirty pieces of silver), Mary and Martha, and Mary Magdalene (who is rescued from a house of prostitution in Marseille). Among the events are the temptation by Satan in a high place, the Last Supper, and even a sort of resurrection, though not of the flesh.

The temptation is another of Faulkner's great scenes, one that might be compared with Dostoevski's fable of the Grand Inquisitor. In order to destroy the corporal's influence among the soldiers, which might persist after his death, the supreme

commander of the Allied forces wants him to accept a pardon. He drives the corporal up to the old Roman citadel overlooking the city and shows him the world beneath; then he offers him in succession (and in Faulknerian rhetoric) liberty, dominion over peoples, and life itself. Each time the corporal refuses thinking of the disciples who trusted him and saying: "There are still ten," without Judas and Peter. Then he is taken back to the prison and finds that Peter, who had won his release by denying the corporal, has refused to accept freedom and has been returned to their common cell. "There are eleven now," he says to the old marshal.

The scene has something huge about it, and at the same time something old-fashioned or even ancient. Among the rather timid and academic novelists of the new generation, Faulkner is like a hairy mastodon in the midst of sleek tan dairy cattle. He is more impressive when he stumbles along than the tan Jerseys are when they gather in a herd and amble off to the barn to be milked.

In this new novel he stumbles more than once, because the footing is unsure. I mean to say—forgetting the mastodons now—that *A Fable* is based on a contradiction between feeling and logic. The feeling of the novel is deeply pacifist. It says that war is wrong and that men who refuse to have any part in it are saints or even incarnations of the Christ. Faulkner's logic, on the other hand, says that some wars are right, or at least necessary, and that men who refuse to have any part in them are fools. If the corporal is a fool, he cannot be truly Christlike.

This fundamental contradiction appears even in great scenes like that of the temptation. Here as elsewhere in the book, the corporal says little; Faulkner seems to feel that the best way to suggest an attitude of reverence toward him is to have him be silent and suffer rather than act. The result is to make him a shadowy figure, where the old marshal is vivid, speaks a great deal, and achieves something like grandeur.

But we don't know what to think of the marshal either. He plays a double and even a triple role. He is the judge, or Pontius Pilate, and he is also the tempter, or Anti-Christ, but he is something more than either of these. In this great scene he speaks with such foreknowledge of the future, and with so much loving pity for the sinful and foolish but enduring race of man, that he seems to embody something of the divine. When he leaves the corporal at the gate of the prison, the corporal says to him, "Good-bye, Father." Does that mean that Pilate or Satan is really the father of the Redeemer?

There is something murky in Faulkner's theology, as at times in his style, and there is something confused in the lesson of the book. One result of Christ's mission was to change, in some measure, the hearts of men. The result of the corporal's mission is to stop the fighting on the Western front for the six days of a new Holy Week, and that is an enormous achievement, but afterward everything returns to what it was before.

The disciples vanish, except for Judas, who hangs himself; we aren't told whether the others were executed. Mary Magdalene goes back to the house of prostitution in Marseille. The marshal dies peacefully, rich in honors. There is only a horribly crippled Englishman—he had survived the barrage in which the two unarmed battalions were wiped out—who tries to carry on the corporal's work. At the marshal's state funeral, he bursts through the guards to fling a military medal—it had been the corporal's—at the draped coffin. He shouts at the corpse:

"You too helped to carry the torch of man into that twilight where he shall be no more."

It is another of Faulkner's magnificent scenes, but, as a French general said of a brave but useless charge, it isn't war and it isn't the change to which we had hoped the corporal's mission and passion would lead. There is, however, one more statement in the book, and perhaps—though we can't be certain—Faulkner intends it as the moral of his fable. The crippled Englishman has been beaten by the spectators at the marshal's funeral. Now he lies bleeding in an alleyway, while he looks up at the faces bending over him. After spitting out blood and teeth he says, as if speaking for the effort of mankind to redeem itself:

"That's right. Tremble. I'm not going to die. Never."

I have set down my reservations, thinking of Faulkner's talent, his daring, and his great aims in this book. Perhaps I expected too much of it, though it offers a great deal. Its many readers will wonder and argue about it for a long time to come. It is likely to stand above other novels of the year like a cathedral, if an imperfect and unfinished one, above a group of well built cottages.

Paul Engle. "Faulkner's Vast Vision, Clouded with Rhetoric." Chicago *Sunday Tribune*, August 1, 1954, Magazine of Books, p. 3.

In *A Fable* Faulkner says of a small town courtroom in the United States that it is "the postulation of an invincible way of life: the loud strong voice of America itself out of the westward roar of the tremendous and battered yet indomitably virgin continent, where nothing save the vast unmoral sky limited what a man could try to do, nor even the sky limit his success and the adulation of his fellow man." In a way, here is the heart of the book: a strong affirmation of hope, expressed in language more complex than is necessary.

William Faulkner's new novel is a world of powerful imagination clouded, at times, with tedious rhetoric: a legend of man's fate in the 20th century. Far more than his other novels, it is a story of human pride and dedication.

Its theme is exactly what Faulkner stated in his speech accepting the Nobel prize. An old general says, "I don't fear man. I do better: I respect and admire him." He goes on to say, as Faulkner said in Stockholm, that man will not only endure, he will prevail for, "he has that in him which will enable him to outlast even his wars." Even when the final "ding-dong of doom" has sounded this earth's destruction, there will be one more sound, the voice of surviving man "planning still to build."

The whole novel is one vast vision, centered on a corporal in the French army of 1918, who himself had seen a vision and had tried to get all armies on the western front to make a cease-fire on their own. He almost succeeds, but is shot, although his action was not entirely vain, for he had lifted the old dignity of man one additional ten-thousandth of an inch above his equally old barbarity.

In a Christlike episode, women take the dead body and bury it. In a further religious parallel, the body is taken from its grave and consecrated, being removed to Paris, through the drunken corruption of some soldiers, as the Unknown Soldier.

There are times when one wishes that Faulkner would give up stretching the English language so hard and make a simple, clear statement. But the book's weakness, as compared with the best of his earlier novels, is that we are offered abstractions instead of men and women leading their dusty, harsh, proud, and life crammed existence.

The book is properly called fabulous by its author, yet there is enough of military and peasant Europe to give it the daylight of reality, and to give a living foundation to the spiritual structure Faulkner has built out of the noble and appalling times in which we live.

Maxwell Geismar. "Faulkner Pens Parable on 1918 False Armistice." Philadelphia *Evening Bulletin*, August 1, 1954.

William Faulkner's new novel, entitled, simply, *A Fable*, is in part a religious allegory based on the events of the false French armistice near the end of the First World War. It is by far the best novel Faulkner has published in the past decade. His last two, *Intruder in the Dust* and *Requiem for a Nun*, had to my mind the mark of Hollywood and of Broadway on them; only, as if to atone for his earlier use of shock and sensationalism, Faulkner imposed a high-flown morality upon very dubious narratives. In *A Fable* he has, to a certain degree, reconciled his rhetoric and his instincts.

The false armistice of 1918, in Faulkner's version of it, was based upon the mutiny of a French regiment, which simply failed to move when it was ordered to attack. A form of passive resistance to any further fighting, the mutiny spreads to other French regiments along the battleline and to their German counterparts. The first memorable portrait in *A Fable* is that of General Gragnon, the division commander, who orders an artillery barrage to be thrown down on his rebellious troops, and then requests authority to shoot the entire regiment.

Some of these episodes of war are excellent. Faulkner's gift has always been that of narrative power. Even when his stories are difficult to follow, they are interesting to read, and the new novel uses his familiar techniques. There is the long cut-back (sometimes within a long cutback) where we follow the adventures of "the runner," a mysterious soldier who has apparently been clubbed to death at the beginning of the story—we are never quite sure. There is the silence of the "aghast and suspended city"—in these typical Faulknerian phrases—when the Parisian crowds learn that their husbands, brothers and lovers are to be executed for the mutiny. The narrative itself moves by a series of brilliant, if sometimes momentarily inscrutable detours to the inmost center of the Allied high command. Only here do we begin to realize that the novel in turn has been shifting from the level of realism to that of religious symbolism and mysticism—that it is, in effect, a modern version of the Christ story.

It is on this last level that the novel fails. Its failure, it seems to me, throws a significant light not only on Faulkner's earlier career but on that whole famous "lost generation" of American writers to which his youth and apprenticeship belonged. In the foreword to *The Faulkner Reader*, a collection of representative selections from the whole body of his work, recently published, this gifted and eloquent novelist stresses again, as he did in his Nobel Prize speech, and as he does once more in *A Fable*, that the function of literature is "to uplift men's hearts." Nobody can quarrel with this; all great writers have done it; the only question is how. I think that Faulkner's great error during the last decade of his writing has been to substitute an empty moralism, however sincere, for the true uses of his own genius.

In *A Fable*, too, one notices the vestigial suspicion of city life and city people—the symbols of the 20th century—on the part of this deep-country novelist. There is the "open reliant incorrigibly bucolic face" of the Iowa farm boy in uniform, who is compared with the killer Buschwald, grandson of a Polish rabbi and on the way to becoming an American gangster. Another of these soldiers, Polchek, with a "knowing, almost handsome metropolitan face," is the modern Judas among the 12 military disciples who have conspired with a French corporal to instigate and direct the mutiny.

In the novel's climax, when we discover that this "corporal" is the illegitimate son of the French Marshal who sentences him to death, with God and with love, we realize that Faulkner has intended these two poles of man's mundane power and his eternal spiritual aspirations. But these "aspirations" are never really embodied in the novel itself; they are still sermons. They represent Faulkner's own "need to believe," in the maturity of his art, but they also represent a kind of abstract belief which has never been rooted in the life around him, the life of his own country, and of his own time. This remains his central problem as a writer, just as it remains the problem which so far has not been grappled with successfully by other gifted literary figures of his generation.

Granville Hicks. "Faulkner's *Fable* Is Powerful, Heroic." New York *Post*, August 1, 1954, p. 12.

In indiscreet moments Ernest Hemingway has talked as if the writing of novels were a kind of athletic competition—a prize fight or an endurance test—in which the author matches himself not only with his contemporaries but also with the great of all ages.

William Faulkner has never made such boastful claims, and I do not believe that he thinks of himself as competing with other novelists, living or dead. It is the task itself that challenges him. He approaches the writing of a major novel in a mood of furious determination, a mood akin to that in which Thomas Sutpen, in *Absalom, Absalom!* undertook the building of his mansion.

For him the writing of a novel is as ineluctable a mission as that performed by the tall convict in *The Wild Palms*, and no more than the convict can he say why it has to be done. It is a kind of ritual, like the pursuit of the bear in the most famous and finest episode of *Go Down, Moses*.

If Faulkner's most ambitious novels— *The Sound and the Fury, Light in August*, and *Absalom, Absalom!*—have proved to be his best work, this is not because he is a master of sustained narrative. On the contrary, as Malcolm Cowley has said in his introduction to *The Portable Faulkner*, his imagination deals most easily with the shorter units of fiction.

But it is the "big" books that have challenged him most and called into action most fully his diverse and magnificent talents. To say that *A Fable* is a novel of that order—with that kind of achievement—is to give it the highest possible praise, which is what it deserves.

Unlike the other major novels, *A Fable* is not part of the Yoknapatawpha Saga, that extended and wonderful re-creation of Faulkner's region, northern Mississippi. The scene is France in the first World War, and there is only one faint echo of Yoknapatawpha—the appearance of a minor character named Philip Manigault Beauchamp, who must be related to the

Lucas Beauchamp of *Go Down, Moses* and *Intruder in the Dust*, and to the Nancy Mannigoe of "That Evening Sun" and *Requiem for a Nun*.

Indeed, Faulkner has indulged his old habit of introducing familiar characters only in references to an aviator named Monaghan, who figures in an early short story, "Ad Astra," and appears briefly in *Sartoris*.

The central person of the novel is a corporal in the French army, name uncertain, whose life parallels that of Jesus of Nazareth. The corporal was born in a stable on Christmas Day because, or perhaps because, there was no room at the inn. Early in the war he appeared out of nowhere with twelve disciples, and he is believed to have performed miracles.

The parallel is not exact: Mary and Martha, called here Marya and Marthe, are the corporal's half-sisters, and he is married, or perhaps is to be married, to an unnamed prostitute who may be identified with Mary Magdalene. On the other hand, the events of the week with which the novel deals, the Passion week, correspond closely with the events of the gospel story.

As readers of *The Sound and the Fury* and *Light in August* know, Faulkner has long been preoccupied with the Christ legend, and it is not surprising that he has at last directly confronted the figure of Jesus.

What does seem surprising, at least at first, is that the corporal is deliberately kept in the background. He appears only briefly, says almost nothing. We are told that he has had a great influence on the men in the trenches, but we do not know what he has taught nor much of what he has done. All we really know is that, as a result of what he says or does or is, a French regiment, one Monday in May 1918, refuses to obey an order to attack, and the war stops for some 48 hours.

The novel is less concerned with how

the corporal does what he does than it is with the effect of his accomplishment on other people. In telling what happens when the war stops and how it is started again, Faulkner presents a series of extraordinary characters.

We begin with General Gragnon, commander of the division to which the revolting regiment belongs. Then there is Levine, a young British aviator who is assigned a part in the plot of the generals by which the war is resumed, and who, with that passionate inquisitiveness so often found in Faulkner's characters, discovers for himself what the plot is.

Next we come to a nameless character, a man who has renounced his commission out of hatred of war and is now a private soldier, a runner, in the British army. He introduces us to the fabulous tale of the English groom, the old Negro preacher, the young Negro jockey, and the three-legged race horse—a magnificent example of Faulkner's compelling narrative power. (Part of this appeared in a limited edition in 1950 as "Notes on a Horsethief.")

And finally there is the old marshal, center of the resistance to the 20th century Jesus—and related to him not merely as antagonist but actually, it turns out, as father.

The climax comes when the runner persuades the groom, who has achieved a wide influence among the soldiery, to accept the corporal's challenges and to fraternize with the enemy. But the generals have done their work, and the runner's labors are in vain.

Now the novel moves strongly through the death, the burial, and the ironic resurrection of the corporal, its emotional impact growing steadily greater until it ends with laughter and tears, on the twin notes of defiance and compassion.

It will be many years, I think, before we begin to exhaust the meanings of A Fable.

On one level, obviously, it is an anti-war novel, full of passion for peace and a searing contempt for the military mind. Faulkner's sympathy lies with the peace-lovers—with the corporal himself, with the runner, and with that strange, pathetic figure, the quartermaster general of the French army.

Yet in the interview between the old marshal and the corporal, a passage that reminds one of Dostoevsky's famous parable of the Grand Inquisitor, the marshal makes a case for himself. And Faulkner chooses to put his own words in the marshal's mouth, for it is he who says, anticipating Faulkner's Nobel Prize speech, that man not only will endure but will prevail.

Rather than being a book about the evils of war, A Fable is about the qualities in man that make for survival and victory. And, as one looks back, one can see that this has always been Faulkner's theme. He is constantly amazed at what human beings are capable of.

Think how many arduous pilgrimages there are in his books, from Lena Grove's in Light in August to the tall convict's in The Wild Palms, how many Herculean labors, from Sutpen's in Absalom, Absalom! to Chick's and Aleck's and Miss Habersham's in Intruder in the Dust.

Even the characters Faulkner dislikes have their own kind of greatness: the Snopeses in The Hamlet, for instance, are no ordinary rednecks; Flem Snopes is so mean that he literally beats the devil.

This is the key of A Fable. The wonderful story of the race horse, which has only a tenuous connection with the plot of the novel, has the closest thematic relationship, for here is a perfect example of that heroic devotion to a mad cause that has always fascinated Faulkner. There is a wild extravagance in this tale, as there is in the account of the German general's flight to confer with the Allied officers and in many other episodes of the book. Extravagance is an inherent part of Faulkner's vision of life, of the thing he has been trying to express since he began writing 30 years ago.

His whole career, indeed, is a kind of extravagance, and he himself is, as a writer, just such an amazing and bizarre person as he has chosen to write about. His style, about which there has been so much controversy, becomes, at times that seem appropriate to him, a wild and frightening outburst. (It is interesting to note that the racehorse story is now told in sentences of ordinary length—and is the better for it.)

He has brought to *A Fable* all of his prodigious resources in an effort to render his vision of the grandeur and strangeness of human life. The meanings of the book, as I have said, will be argued about for a long time, but we shall make no mistake if we regard it as a great novel and an act of Faulknerian heroism.

Dayton Kohler.
"William Faulkner's New Work Is a Novel of Faith in a World of Doubt."
Louisville *Courier Journal*, August 1, 1954, Section III, p. 12.

While the materials and techniques of fiction seem capable of almost endless variation, novelists themselves fall roughly into one or the other of two divisions: those who from a social point of view reflect the world about them and those with the rare ability to project in their books a wholly personal vision of life. To writers of the first group—Jane Austen, Flaubert, Trollope—we give ungrudging recognition. This, we say, is the way life is. But among writers of the second group—Dickens,

Melville, Dostoevsky, for example—there is always an air of the imaginative and fabulous which transforms everyday reality into something rich and strange. Theirs is the way of exaggeration, fantasy, symbol and myth, and acceptance of their art waits until we can accustom our own point of view to a picture of life as they see it.

William Faulkner shares with these older writers the power to impose his tragic vision on the nature and condition of man. In his Yoknapatawpha novels he has taken furious, imaginative possession of the social and historical details of his Southern region. Because he has made a single Mississippi county his measure of the larger world and his Jefferson the center of a moral universe, his version of the regional experience is one which mirrors also the social confusion and moral sterility of our time. Now, in *A Fable*, he has taken a single event, the mutiny of a French regiment on the Western front in 1918, and against that wartime background written a deeply symbolic and moving novel which parallels on more than one level the story of the Passion and the Crucifixion.

Nine years went into the writing of *A Fable*. When Faulkner in his Nobel speech at Stockholm, spoke of his books as work produced "in the agony and sweat of the human spirit," he may have had this novel particularly in mind. Certainly, it still shows evidence of difficulties encountered in his attempt to re-create within a framework of contemporary conflict and disaster a parable of the source of man's faith and its abiding nature. For much the same reason this is not an easy book to read, so closely knit are the planes of action and thought as well as the secondary and multiple symbols which reflect crises of belief and action in our century.

Thematic treatment of religious experience is not new, of course, so far as Faulkner's fiction is concerned. Symbols and motifs of sacrifice, redemption, atonement and the Crucifixion appear in several of his novels and some of his best short stories. But there are a number of approaches to Faulkner and we are just beginning to see the religious half-light suffusing his world and penetrating even into its murkiest corners.

Although *A Fable* makes explicit and meaningful this aspect of his work, readers will be disappointed if they expect to find in his new novel a point-by-point correspondence with the Gospel story. Faulkner's method is still one of symbolism and the fabulous, not history. The time of the story is late May of 1918, shortly after the disastrous breakthrough on the Western front. At dawn, when a scheduled attack is to begin, a French regiment refuses to leave the trenches. Under arrest, the regiment is returned to headquarters at Chaulnesmont, where the three Allied commanders meet to deal with this emergency. Since the regiment has been recruited in the district, relatives and friends of the mutineers flock into the town. Their peasant bewilderment and grief change to rage against a squad of 12 men and their corporal, who had instigated the mutiny by preaching behind the lines a creed of peace and good will. Meanwhile the war grinds slowly to a false armistice between French, British and Americans on one side and Germans on the other.

All that happens between the mutiny at dawn on Monday and the execution of the corporal on Friday—two thieves and murderers are shot at the same time—must be interpreted in terms of the Passion and the Crucifixion, but on a symbolic rather than a literal level. A few of the events and characters are more recognizable than others. Martha, Marya and Magda we know by their names, also Pierre Bouc who was born Piotr. Others we identify by their actions, as when the old French commander-in-chief is forced

into the role of Pilate and compelled to ask the nature of truth and justice. Still others we know according to the way in which they are affected by the consequences of the mutiny—the old Quartermaster General who speaks for man's conscience, the priest who commits suicide, Polchek, the betrayer, and his burden of guilt, the German general who, arriving for a secret conference at Chaulnesmont, shoots with Prussian thoroughness the pilot who has landed him on an English airfield, and the English runner dedicated to human suffering.

Ironic as well as symbolic are the circumstances by which the dead corporal is buried at last in the Unknown Soldier's tomb. Equally ironic is the burial of the old French marshal, whose funeral procession is disturbed by the crippled runner when he hurls upon the dead man's coffin the corporal's Medaille Militaire. Present also at the scene is the ex-Quartermaster General, whose depth of compassion brings this latter-day parable sharply into focus.

In addition, *A Fable* illustrates the integrated quality of Faulkner's world. Several years ago he published a long short story, "Notes on a Horsethief," which caused some perplexity among readers when it appeared. This story of an English groom, a stolen racehorse and an old colored preacher has now become one of the sections of *A Fable*, with the groom and the minister figuring significantly in the development of the theme. Faulkner has also put into a speech by the French commander-in-chief a paraphrase of his Stockholm address and relates it to the basic pattern of the meaning.

A novel of faith in a world filled with forces that would deny the meaning or even the nature of that faith, *A Fable* is likely to become a subject of controversy which will have little to do with literary merit. Faulkner himself is said to regard this as his major work. As a novel, it is a profound story of man's capacity for love, duty, suffering, honor, compassion, sacrifice and faith. The most unusual novel out of World War I, it may become the great novel of that war as well, a work of enduring power because Faulkner's vision of the age and man's predicament joins the 20th Century condition of crisis to the Christian tradition of the living past.

Randall Stewart. "Faulkner Tells a Wartime Fable." Providence *Sunday Journal*, August 1, 1954, Section VI, p. 8.

The fame of Faulkner is one of the extraordinary phenomena of the present time. Hemingway and Faulkner have steadily emerged in recent years as the chief of our contemporary prose fictionists, and while Hemingway is undoubtedly the more popular of the two, and is still much more widely read, Faulkner would appear now to be receiving the lion's share of the critical acclaim.

This acclaim is solidly based upon such remarkable fictions as *The Sound and the Fury, As I Lay Dying, Absalom, Absalom!, Light in August,* "The Bear," and perhaps a dozen others—some long and some short. These fictions, as everyone knows, all have to do with Yoknapatawpha County, Mississippi, whose county-seat is Jefferson, whose area is 2,400 square miles, whose population consists of 6,298 whites and 9,313 Negroes, and whose sole owner and proprietor is William Faulkner: it is already one of the most famous of all mythical realms. Yoknapatawpha is Faulkner's proper milieu; in it he lives and moves and has his being; he understands its traditions and social arrangements; he is master of its vernacular; he probes profoundly its comedies and tragedies; concerning it, he speaks with unimpeachable authority, and with passion and insight.

A writer's choice of subject is one of his indefeasible rights, and it is foolish for a mere reviewer to cavil at any choice which he may make. But even the casual reviewer may express preferences, and the present reviewer may be forgiven for saying that he likes Faulkner much better when he operates within the metes and bounds of Yoknapatawpha, and that he greatly prefers any of the works mentioned above to the one whose publication tomorrow furnishes the excuse for this piece.

Faulkner, of course, is under no obligation to stay on in Yoknapatawpha (any more than Melville was obligated to stick to his whaler or merchantman or frigate, or Hawthorne to Salem and Boston, or Mark Twain to the River). He is now 57, and his literary output may eventually contain works on other subjects—though this seems to me very unlikely—as good as those dealing with Jefferson and its environs. But it seems to say that this is not true at the present moment, and that the claim of the Random House editors that *A Fable* is Faulkner's greatest achievement to date is absurd. For Faulkner does not speak in *A Fable* with the same authority.

The action of *A Fable* is laid in France during World War I. The actors are drawn from France, England, America, and the Near East. The key event is the failure on a certain day in May, 1918, of a certain French regiment on the Western Front to attack as ordered: when the French general commanding the division watched from his observation post, expecting to see the start of a preconcerted action, nothing happened— the men did not leave their trenches. The "mutiny" spread to other regiments, and to the enemy also. Our attention is drawn in many directions, but it is centered chiefly upon the division commander (a military formalist who insisted eventually upon being shot, from behind), the French Marshal (a benignant and casuistical presiding deity), the thirteen leaders of the mutiny, and their ringleader the mysterious corporal from Asia Minor (with "the high calm composed, not wary but merely watchful, mountain face"), and the three women associated with the ringleader— his sisters Marthe and Marya, and his "wife" Magda.

We have obviously here the framework of a fable patterned after the Christ story. The author, in fact, introduces many parallels; the corporal's birth 33 years before, in a stable, because there was no room at the inn; his "ministry" of three years, during which he had spread the gospel of mutiny among the soldiers of the Western Front; the element of the miraculous in his ubiquity; the temptation, offering him the world, and its rejection; his execution with two culprits, one on either side; the attendance of the women at his burial; and so on. The height of the irony is reached when, by a tragi-comical deception, the corporal's body is made to do service, with pomp and circumstance, as the Unknown Soldier, reputedly a defender of Verdun. By a similar fraud, perhaps the author means to imply, Christ through the centuries has been made the symbol of fratricidal war.

A re-reading would doubtless reveal a wealth of carefully contrived symbolical meanings. But one misses the passion and the mirth of Yoknapatawpha. The characters of A Fable seem scarcely realized; they move across the stage somewhat cloudily, like figures in an allegory; one's sympathies are not deeply engaged. Occasionally, the pristine Faulkner breaks through: the description of the crowd gathered in the Place de Ville to witness the execution of the "traitors" was obviously written by the same pen which has described with awesome effect many a crowd awaiting some tragical denouement at the courthouse or jail in Jefferson; the story of the drunken soldiers sent to obtain a cadaver from Verdun is clearly the work of the master-raconteur who is the chief living heir of the old Southwestern yarnspinners; and the tale of the Negro preacher and the horse that won races running on three legs is a long interlude, or episode, which boldly transplants author and reader to the author's home base. But the book as a whole, I venture to say, lacks drama; it is polemical rather than dramatic; it derives more from the author's recent speeches—several passages, in fact, directly echo the Stockholm speech—than from felt experience.

The Stockholm speech was a good speech. But Faulkner's true affirmation is to be found, not in direct statement, but indirectly in the powerful revelation of the cataclysmic personal tragedies of the great fictions. It is one thing for the old Marshal to deliver a longwinded speech about man's "enduring" and "prevailing," but it is something very different when Dilsey in *The Sound and the Fury* delivers herself of the pronouncement, "I seed de first en de last." What is lacking in the one instance, whose presence in the other makes all the difference, is a moving dramatic context.

Let us take the tentative view, then, that what we have in *A Fable* is probably an experiment, or a digression, or a mere sequel to the Stockholm speech, and that it is a work which is likely to interest many readers less than it interested its author.

A great author, though, is entitled to his diversions, his indulgences, and even his indiscretions. He is none the less great because of them, for the great work is there, still. It is more lasting than bronze. It is indestructible.

Sterling North.
"Mr. Faulkner's Strange Fable."
New York *World-Telegram and the Sun*, August 2, 1954, Feature Magazine, p. 12.

This is William Faulkner's best book in many years and the most ambitious of his whole career. It is the only one from which I have derived much profit or pleasure since *Light in August*, some 13 miasmic volumes ago.

The core of his disturbing and compassionate tale is the central story of Christendom itself, complete with a Messiah, 12 disciples, Mary, Martha, Magdalene and all other characters essential to the drama.

This re-enactment of the Passion Week, however, occurs in the spring of 1918, when, as you may remember, there was wholesale mutiny, principally among the French. Mr. Faulkner has extended the passive revolt to virtually all troops on both sides of the barbed wire, which may stretch history a bit, but is an effective use of poetic license.

After swimming through many chapters of remarkably moving but often highly confusing prose, the reader begins to get his head above water. A very high-ranking French officer hopes, before he dies, to earn his marshal's baton. For some reason never quite clarified, he feels this will become a certainty if he sacrifices a regiment in what he knows will be a futile and suicidal attack. The regiment mutinies and refuses to make the assault. As though by telepathy or prearranged signal, passive resistance sweeps like a tidal wave from the English Channel to the Alps. Blessed silence reigns along hundreds of miles of trenches where for four long years men by the millions have been mangled.

The question now arises at the highest level of command as to who is guilty and who shall be punished. Shall the whole regiment be shot as a lesson? Can other scapegoats be found? Who is the strange Christlike figure who with 12 disciples seems to have been able to wander almost at will through all the armies in France? Who are the women among his followers? How deeply has his gospel of peace penetrated the fiber of all the fighting men? And shall this man die for the "sins" of all these others?

In tracing all the possible ramifications of this allegory, Mr. Faulkner takes us into almost every rank of the French, British and American armies. He even brings over a haughty Prussian officer complete with monocle. One feels the terror of the families of the regiment who know their men may be executed.

In short, this is a novel which largely fulfills the stirring demand Mr. Faulkner himself made in accepting the Nobel Prize, when he said that the writer must rediscover ". . . the old verities and truths of the heart, the old universal truths lacking which any story is ephemeral and doomed—love and honor and pity and pride and compassion and sacrifice."

There is no evidence in this book of the sloppy, first draft writing which Mr. Faulkner so frequently has before us. This prose is the result of blood, sweat and tears. Even so, long years of intentional obfuscation and complete lack of discipline have left their exasperating idiosyncrasies. Mr. Faulkner will not (or perhaps cannot) tell a story simply. He will not identify his speakers nor reveal the antecedents of his pronouns. Those verities which he extols never extend to compassion for the reader, or even acknowledgment of his existence.

If Mr. Faulkner really wishes to put across his universal message he should have some of the modesty of the central character in this fable. There is no reason for attempting to give American readers the Sermon on the Mount in Sanskrit. May I also add that the story of the Cockney jockey and Negro groom who steal the great race horse, interesting as it is in itself, seems to me almost completely extraneous to this story.

Nevertheless, and despite Mr. Faulkner's stubborn resistance to clarifying his medium, this is a very important and powerful novel, dealing with a theme which concerns our continued survival on this planet. Perhaps Mr. Faulkner did not previously deserve the Nobel Prize in Literature. But after this novel he at least deserves the Nobel Prize for Peace.

Orville Prescott. "Books of The Times." New York *Times*, August 2, 1954, p. 15.

First and foremost was the absurdity— the ludicrousness,—the impossibility of it: he, there by the counter where rings for fifty cents and one dollar were sold (he, the book reviewer, hounded and harried by consciousness of lost time, taking shelter from the storm which bounced raindrops like squashed persimmons on the pavement of Times Square and all the time the music from the juke box roaring in his ears and the suspicious trying to sell him glass rings and the fat woman staring with her cheap cotton dress sticking to her with wet—moisture—rainwater) and trying to read a book while he waited for the storm to stop, laughing at himself, knowing that

it couldn't be done, that in all the interminable indomitable tragic heroic and repulsive history of man no book reviewer had ever been able to read William Faulkner and understand what he was reading without rereading many paragraphs twice and some a dozen times, least of all standing up in a crowded Woolworth's on Times Square, New York City.

It may be easy to write a paragraph that sounds vaguely like Faulkner. It's harder to reach a fair judgment on the most extravagantly admired, the most ignorantly denounced and the most controversial of modern American writers. It is particularly hard to be judicious about Mr. Faulkner's new novel, A Fable, for this is the most ambitious work Mr. Faulkner has yet written, a book on which he worked intermittently for nine years.

There are three facts about A Fable which cut it off sharply from the main body of his work. It is not about Yoknapatawpha County. It is not concerned with vice or degeneracy. It is a desperately earnest parable with an elaborately worked-out Christian message. But if Mr. Faulkner's subject is new his manner is unchanged. A Fable is as clogged and clotted with the familiar Faulknerian assaults on the English language as any of his books. And, unlike most of his books, it lacks the demonic power, the darkly eloquent poetry and the gaunt and gruesome characters driven by private furies that have cast a spell on so many of Mr. Faulkner's readers.

The interest of A Fable lies solely in its symbolical message. And the symbolism is so complex (not in its simple major figures but in its intricate pattern of minor points) that it would be obscure even if Mr. Faulkner's prose were coherent and lucid. Consequently, it seems to me, A Fable must be regarded as an experiment noble in purpose which, as a novel, is inferior to most of its predecessors. Dull, tortuous and marvelously soporific, its nearly impenetrable prose and its weirdly Faulknerian dialogue yield only to persistent assaults.

Like Humphrey Cobb's *Paths of Glory*, which was published nineteen years ago, *A Fable* is inspired by the execution of several French soldiers for mutiny in World War I. Mr. Faulkner begins with an attack that failed to take place because a whole regiment refused to leave its trenches. The instigators of this demonstration in favor of peace were the members of one squad, a corporal and twelve men. Circling through many points of view, trailing backward in time and telling several long and almost irrelevant stories, Mr. Faulkner slowly edges up to his central situation, never trying to individualize his characters, leaving them ponderously symbolical and usually nameless.

The principal figures in his large cast are: the divisional commander, who wanted to execute the entire regiment, all 3,000 men; the "old general," a mysterious representative of military eminence and the father of the corporal; a British private, a former groom, loved by his men, who conducted an intricate business betting on his chances of survival; a British officer who refused to remain one and became a private; three women symbolically associated with Mary, Martha and Mary Magdalene; and the corporal, who preached peace, who was betrayed by one of his disciples, who participated in a grisly last supper, and was put to death between two thieves.

The general thesis of *A Fable* is clear enough and familiar: a bitter lament over the nature of mankind which would doom Christ (or any Christlike figure) to be crucified again if He should return and a particularly bitter protest against war and military organization, military tradition and military might. But if the broad outlines of *A Fable* are clear, the details are not. Much of the activity of several characters seems almost meaningless. Mr. Faulkner is always oblique, cryptic and obscure. Sometimes he withholds essential information. Often he digresses and then digresses within a digression. He allows his characters to make prolonged speeches of stupefying dullness and artificiality.

Since Mr. Faulkner's private style is world famous, there is no need to list the various verbal traps he lays for unwary readers. They are all familiar, including the sentences 100 lines long. But in *A Fable* the dramatic emotion which suffuses other Faulkner books with a fiery glare is missing. Instead there are admirable but essentially undramatic emotions— Mr. Faulkner's pity for suffering mankind and his reverent feeling for the Christian message of peace among men. These command respect. But they cannot make this stiff and lifeless novel an interesting reading experience.

Carlos Baker.
"Cry Enough!"
Nation, August 7, 1954, pp. 115–18.

This remarkable story centers on the origin, development, and aftermath of the mutiny of a French regiment in the trenches one Monday night in May, 1918. Its intellectual and to some extent its emotional force arises from the fact that Faulkner has chosen to project his story through a modern and ironic version of the ministry, the betrayal, the passion, the death, and the resurrection of Jesus Christ. As the false, mutiny-induced armistice comes to an end and the novel moves toward its Easter Sunday denouement, images and events flower into recognizable parallelisms: the Last Supper, the triple denial, the Judas figure, the execution between thieves, Mary-Martha-Magdalene, the crown of thorns, the burial, the disappearance of the body, and even an ironic suggestion of resurrection.

Neither his theme nor his method should occasion great surprise among regular readers of Faulkner. Both are extensions rather than essential innovations. All his best work—*The Sound and the Fury, As I Lay Dying, Light in August, Absalom, Absalom!*, and *The Hamlet*—has employed themes and images derived from the Bible. Several short stories, as well as novels like *The Wild Palms* and *Pylon*, have left the environs of Yoknapatawpha County, Mississippi. He has dealt with war before in *Sartoris* and *The Unvanquished*. The freshness here is in the recombination of familiar elements, and the fascination is to watch them being inexorably fitted into that complex, interlocking, cross-indexed mosaic work which comprises Faulkner's narrative method.

Nine years in the making, the novel is datelined, after the manner of Joyce's *Ulysses*, "Oxford–New York–Princeton, December, 1944—November, 1953." The comparison with Joyce in instructive. Both books are modern fables, moral by intent, ironic by execution. Where Joyce used a Homeric mythus, Faulkner's ground-pattern is the most celebrated story in the Hebraic-Christian tradition. For unity and intensity Joyce concentrates his action into a single passionate day. For the same and other reasons Faulkner confines his own within the limits of Passion Week. Both novels are over-long, too heavily populated with rather shadowy minor figures. Vast stretches in both books strain the reader's patience by what seems like unnecessary complication or obscurantism. Sometimes both writers appear to revel unduly in the manipulation of rhe-

torical language, though both, when they choose, can handle straight narrative like old masters. In brief, different as the two novels are, Faulkner's work ascends into virtues and succumbs to temptations not unlike those which distinguished, but also diminished, Joyce's huge opus of thirty-odd years ago.

The memorable opening, deliberate, impersonal, and massive as a passage from Hardy's *Dynasts*, comes in Paris on a Wednesday morning. An enormous crowd has converged to see the arrival of a fleet of Army trucks bearing the three thousand mutineers. One vehicle contains the illiterate thirty-three-year-old corporal and his twelve squad members. To these thirteen can be traced the central event of Monday morning—the zero-hour refusal of an entire regiment to attack. The French command pulled out the regiment, thrust in replacements, and laid down a heavy barrage to keep the Germans out of the gap. Yet the Germans did not move either: the conspiratorial message had reached them from the same source, spreading like light among the common soldiers. By noon all guns were silent along the French sector; by mid-afternoon the undeclared armistice had extended across the whole front from the Alps to the sea. For this long, anyhow, no one had been killed in anger in what Faulkner calls the "ancient familiar abattoir" of France. Now the mutineers have come to judgement. And Gragnon, commander of their division, is urging the higher echelons to shoot them all.

As always in Faulkner, the reader is not so much told or given this information: the oblique narrative method compels him to glean it through the eyes, minds, chance remarks, or incidental observations of a variety of participant characters. The corporal, one slowly learns, was born in a stable somewhere in the Middle East at Christmas, 1885. He was brought first to

Beirut, then to Europe. His relatives live on a small farm near the village of Vienne-la-Pucelle, north of St. Mihiel. He has rescued and rehabilitated a Marseilles prostitute whom he intends to marry. Since the beginning of the war he has been quietly at work in France. He wears a blue uniform; his papers are in perfect shape; his squad has gathered round him. Like him they seem to move at will among the soldiery of the embattled nations. At intervals they disappear and return, A.W.O.L.'s who are never reported. The corporal is said by a British colonel to have been killed in a cavalry charge in 1914; he is said by an American captain to have died of influenza and been buried at sea from an American transport in 1917. Yet for over a year now he has been known "among all combat troops below the grade of sergeant" in the allied armies.

"You don't need to understand," says an aged British private to a message-runner. "Just go and look at him." "Him?" says the runner. "So it's just one now?" "Wasn't it just one before?" says the old private. "Wasn't one then enough to tell us the same thing all them two thousand years ago: that all we ever needed to do was just to say, Enough of this—us, not even the sergeants and corporals, but just us, all of us, Germans and Colonials and Frenchmen and all the other foreigners in the mud here, saying together: Enough. Let them that's already dead and maimed and missing be enough of this—a thing so easy and simple that even human man, as full of evil and sin and folly as he is, can understand and believe it this time. Go and look at him."

The runner as it happens, never meets the corporal face to face, though converted to the cause, like St. Paul, and spreading the gospel wherever he can persuade or harass listeners into attention, not only while the corporal lives but long after the execution and the war are over. Even when we are brought into the corporal's presence in the Paris prison, or watch a priest of God commit bayonet suicide for not having recognized and followed him before, we see him as through a glass darkly. He remains, no doubt by the author's intent, an enigmatic figure. Yet supremely dangerous, too; not to be tolerated in a world organized to continue what the French Maréchal calls man's "most expensive and fatal vice . . . so long ingrained in man as to have become an honorable tenet of his behavior and the national altar for his love of bloodshed and glorious sacrifice . . . a pillar of his national survival." War is now, says the Maréchal, the last recourse of politics, and it will soon become the last refuge from bankruptcy. "A nation insolvent from overpopulation will declare war on whatever richest and most sentimental opponent it can persuade to defeat it quickest, in order to feed its people out of the conqueror's quartermaster stores." Against this contingency stands the equally terrible simplicity of the corporal's message: cry Enough, and back it up with action for peace. Whoever understands it has seen the corporal face to face, whether in the flesh or not, and called by whatever name.

Most of the other available attitudes toward war are summed up through subordinate characters. To the division commander Gragnon it is a profession; to the caricatured and stagy German lieutenant general who flies over the front lines for a conference it is a religion; to the American Buchwald, a prelude to gangsterism; to the Maréchal, a challenge in the statesmanship of survival. For Levine, the naive young aviator, a Sartoris-like figure, it is a romance followed swiftly by an overpowering disillusion. For the Quartermaster General it is a sick disgust from which he cannot resign. To the bandy legged British groom (Harry, 'Arry, Mister 'Arry, Mistairy, Mystery), whose story is a revised version of Faulkner's previously published "Notes on a Horsethief," war is a business, a money-lending private insurance business among the common soldiers, over whom his influence is almost godlike. Even though the story of his abduction and exploitation of the wonderful three-legged horse is intrinsically a great yarn, it seems intrusive in this new context. Still, his allegorical right to be present is clear enough. He is the type of the eternal gambler. When the Pauline message-runner would persuade the groom to use his great influence in the corporal's cause, old Harry, old anti-Christ, kicks him in the face and tries to bash in his head with a rifle butt.

By thirty years of memorable work Faulkner has earned the right to his own method of exposition, and one does not, therefore, attempt to revise him. Yet he has never been one to whom the matter of pace was of any special importance, and the pace, for a fact, of the whole middle part of the book is snail-like. Speeches are often prolonged past reason or requirement; seemingly extraneous detail is agonizingly built in; and biographical data on the representative men is occasionally excessive, as if Faulkner enjoyed inventing too much to stop. Rhetoric, a notable pace-slacker elsewhere in Faulkner, crops out like lava from time to time. The sunset gun at Paris does not merely thud: its sound is "a postulation of vacuum, as though back into its blast-vacated womb the regurgitated martial day had poured in one reverberant clap." The funeral train does not merely whistle; it makes a "sound of protest and insensate anguish and indictment of the hard dark earth it rushes over, the vast weight of sky it burrows frantically beneath, the constant and inviolable horizon it steadily clove." Through something more than half the novel the roadblocks are insistent.

About the 333d page, however, the pace quickens, the blocks fall away, and the novel rises with rapidity and into its climactic phase, as good a hundred-page sequence as Faulkner has ever done. In this part of the book he exploits to the full—and perhaps a little beyond the full—the cosmic irony of man's periodic rejection of that power which, if ever accepted, would be the means to redemption. On the afternoon of Thursday, for example, great bands of common soldiers come out of the trenches again. Friendly and without arms, they move together, Allies and Germans, into no man's land. After the false armistice of Monday, of course, such fraternization is not to be countenanced. The batteries on both sides simultaneously open up on the soldiers in the foreground. The ministry is over, and the rulers of man begin, through persuasion, subterfuge, violence, and betrayal, the task of getting back to what men call normal. How the corporal's body is brought home for burial, how a barrage and a battle exhume and lose the body, how a squad of soldiers, having secured from Valaumont Fortress an anonymous cadaver for the Tomb of the Unknown Soldier, trade it for brandy to a demented war widow, how they find a substitute in a ravaged field north of St. Mihiel, and how years after the war's end the crippled message-runner appears at the Maréchal's funeral with the corporal's medal and (still) the corporal's message—these stories provide the denouement of the book. It is a good series of interwoven stories, and it is a good message that the message-runner brings. As for his experience at the funeral, it is about what one would have expected. He gets his teeth kicked in again.

James Aswell.
"Faulkner's Fable Massive
Hoax, Seen as 'Monstrous
Absurdity.'"
Houston *Chronicle*,
August 8, 1954, Feature
Magazine, p. 24.

That William Faulkner is actually loony could not be established with certainty by this book alone. Loonier books have been written (but not often) by sane people; and more lucid books have come from lunatics.

The question might be irrelevant if it were not for the issue of Faulkner's guilt: If he deliberately and cynically concocted this monstrously unintelligible and pretentious hoax, he ought to be hanged.

Imitations of this stuff will taint a generation of young writers—solely because a committee of Swedish professors knowing schoolbook English or none, handed Faulkner a hunk of dynamite money and a scroll—and thereby made him a Great Writer.

Unlike poor Pearl Buck, the chow mein lady who got the same accolade but not the paranoia and kept on writing pleasant, thin books of horrible, naked clarity, Faulkner, always shaky on sense, soared off into the empyreal blue after telling the committee: "I refuse to accept the end of man."

Translated this means: "I, Willie Faulkner of Oxford, Miss., refuse to accept the end of man and if Destiny has any such projects under her hat, I'd better be told."

After that the real fable of Faulkner was off to the races, helped along by one of the best publicity squads in the book business, helped along by the old-maid school teachers of all sexes and callings who make up the cheering section of beautiful letters.

That no one could decipher what the man was driving at was an immense advantage, as generations of metaphysical philosophers, avant-garde literary marvels and "social scientists" have found out.

Pretty soon the taboo closed down on heretics tempted to point out the king's lack of clothing. Sense was adjourned, skeptics intimidated by talk of ravishing and subtle meanings to which only the intellectual elite were hep, and another face was cut on the mountain, perhaps forever.

I predict that at least 100,000 copies of *A Fable* will be sold, of which maybe 201 will be sweated through in a daze by martyrs like this reviewer. Professors of English will assign it sadistically to advanced classes, and the gassier and emptier the resulting gobbledygook of the themes, the higher the marks.

"He was a Norman, son of a Caen doctor whose grandfather while an art student in Paris, had become the friend and then the fanatic disciple of Camille Desmoulins until Robespierre executed them both, the great-grandson come to Paris to be a painter too but relinquished his dream to the Military Academy for the sake of France as the great-grandfather had done his to the guillotine for the sake of Man: who for all his vast peasant bones had looked at twenty-two even more impermanent and brittly-keyed than ever had his obsession at seventeen—a man with a vast sick flaccid moon of a face and hungry and passionate eyes, who had looked once at the one which to all the world else had been that of any seventeen-year-old youth and relinquished completely to it like a sixty-year-old longtime widower to that of pubic unconscious girl, who picked up the three figures—uncle, nephew and godfather—like so many paper dolls and turned them around and set them down again in the same position and attitudes but obversed."

That, gentle scholars, is one of the sharper and more coherent character vignettes with which the book abounds. I could find you far more idiotic passages, but it's best to start with something relatively simple.

That is the sort of goo you must wade through to discover that this "fable" is laid in World War I and concerns an old supergeneral and his illegitimate son who seems to be wandering around at the head of a squad of 12 men (Christ and the Apostles, naturally) in French uniforms who stop the war by making the men on both sides mutiny.

There is a great deal of other heavy symbolism; there are jumbled characters which appear suddenly and disappear, events unresolved, the beginnings and tag-ends of episodes, clouds of strangulated syntax which must be inhaled in agony like a dentist's gas.

It is a dead cinch that if this book had been printed backwards, chapter by chapter, perhaps even paragraph by paragraph, the critical reaction to it would be precisely the same as what it is going to get.

Most reviewers, in either case, would smirk and pant and mutter about the book's transcendental symbolism and social significance, perhaps with a guarded admission here and there that the going may be a bit "hard" for tyros and Philistines and "definitely not for casual readers." But the glorious rewards for real esthetic hep-cats willing to work? Boy! Pied Sanskrit—from Faulkner—would have got the identical tune.

What can Mrs. Vanderbilt's guests do, given place settings of twigs and a fare of gelatin slabs, but roll their eyes in ecstasy over the handsome silver and the prime beef? Dolts attending such a function would even begin to believe their cant. That's the power of self-hypnosis in the grip of snobbery. That's the power of it in the book racket today.

But the sorrow implicit in this massive absurdity is the thing that has happened to Faulkner. He's no lifelong literary quack to be brushed off like Gertrude Stein.

Faulkner has written prose of superlative poignancy and power. He has even written memorable novels like *Light in August, Soldier's Pay* and *Pylon*. He wrote a story called "Turn About," using some of the World War I materials he scrambles in *A Fable*, which had the keen, clear kick of a flagon of white mule. It appeared—this is recalled only to drive the eggheads crazy—in the *Saturday Evening Post*.

Even in *A Fable*, despite the fact that the sum of its parts is chaos and gibberish is its warp, Faulkner produces phrases, sentences—rarely ever paragraphs—of astoundingly sharp loveliness and fire. The fact that he can do this raises an appalling (and subversively stimulating) possibility.

He admits that he concocted *Sanctuary* as a cheap horrifier to make money. He made it. Has he now contrived this thing flaunting pretensions and hollow nonsensicality because it is precisely the sort of bundle today's crop of critics would be certain to swallow with banshee shrieks of acclaim? Can solid fame be brought to heel, like notoriety, by a shrewd pitchman? Is the book world so full of easily conned fools?

It is a shocking and probably far-fetched alternative to his having let some of his marbles roll out at Stockholm. His guilt is great if he be guilty, and only the hangman can ever give him atonement. Somehow, though, the idea pleases me far more than contemplation of the old fellow gone off his rocker. And there are only two possibilities.

Leslie A. Fiedler. "Stone Grotesques." *New Republic*, August 23, 1954, pp. 18–19.

A Fable finds William Faulkner at the critical point in his career when his ideas and themes, striving desperately to open out come into conflict with his style which has been for several years closing in, rigidifying. There is something terrifying about the present furious immobility of his writing—so much rage and so little motion! One is reminded of the children's game in which at a given signal the players who have been mugging and writhing freeze into whatever contortions they have attained; a moment before there has been violent action, a moment later there will be laughter, but for one instant they are grotesques of stone. "Statues," the game is called; and just so Faulkner's rhetoric seems to me now a statue of what it once was, its passion turned to stone. There are no new flaws: the pronouns without reference set straight by an impatient parenthesis; the constant straining of meaning as if the dictionary were a conspiracy in restraint of trade; the syntax abandoned like a world well lost; the compulsive words, "aghast" "endure"—returning like the rimes of a sestina—all these have been a part of his style since *Absalom, Absalom!*; and if they seem now devices, or even tics, it is because they are *stranded* in all their absurdity like the trash carried by a flood and deposited in the mud when the waters have gone down.

It is not merely a matter of time, of the natural tendency of any rhetoric to turn into its own parody, but of Faulkner's having surrendered on *principle* the two main motions of his earlier books: the accumulation of horror to the point of nausea, sustained by the sense that nausea is amoral attitude; and the circular, tortured progress toward the Secret, the revelation of hidden guilt. Either of these motivations has sufficed in the past to save Faulkner from the static tendencies of his style and his confirmed inability to move plot forward in any ordinary way—the former alone in *Sanctuary*, for instance, the latter in the popularizing detective stories involving Gavin Stevens; but the two have usually worked in concert, as in *As I Lay Dying* and "A Rose for Emily," where the final nausea and the final disclosure are simultaneous and indistinguishable.

But Faulkner apparently wants now to disclose not the secret of guilt but that of innocence, not the ultimate revulsion before the world's horror, but the acceptance which transcends it. Driven on the one hand by a desire to live up to his status as our greatest living writer, and on the other, by a growing religiosity, he insists upon making explicit the sentimental, Protestant ethos that has always informed his writing. There is something especially appealing in Faulkner's willingness to accept (against his own temperamental reluctance) the public role his tortured talent has forced upon him, and to translate that role back into his work itself. In *A Fable*, which is a political book as well as a religious one, he takes it upon himself to be "our" plenipotentiary, to deliver for America, for the people and for the democratic principle which gives meaning and weight to the people, a manifesto which is also a poem on war and peace.

On the face of it, it is hard to imagine anyone ideologically less qualified for the job; for politically Faulkner is, I suppose, our most naïve, certainly our least informed novelist. And yet—precisely the

"GI" nature of his political notions, the fact that no one of them is different from the paranoid fantasies of the man in the street—a southern street, of course (not the newspaper-learned patriotic phrases the citizen parrots, but the disingenuous cynicisms he confides to his buddies once in the barracks), gives to them a special pathos; and once dressed in the most un-GI of rhetorics, a special irony.

A Fable deals with the temporary stopping of an entire war when a single regiment refuses to make an attack to which it is ordered; and of the maneuverings of the generals on both sides to get the slaughter going again, before the men in the ranks realize finally their power to stop this war, all wars, war itself whenever they choose. There is even a scene where the enemy generals (each the ultimate stereotype of his nationality, transported from the darkest mass mind to printed page without the loss of an eyelash) sit about a single table in nefarious conclave. It is all out of the Poor Man's Dictionary of Received Ideas (which is to say, out of the letter column in the *Daily News*): War as the product of the Munitions Makers, the Politicians, the Brass—some postulated Other, whose absolute guilt makes the People absolutely innocent, always the Victims of a Conspiracy.

And it fits into a total conspectus of civilization out of Science Fiction: this war seen as a part of the long process of our enslavement by vast, semi-intelligent machines for combat which must drive toward the holocaust that will destroy the entire earth; though meanwhile, man will have ensured his continuance by rocketing through space to the stars. This is "fable" enough, the truest (because quite unconscious) myth which underlies the book; but it is not the legend to which the title points, being understood rather as "history," and "this war" itself identified with the First World War.

As a history of the War of 1914–19, *A Fable* is strangely expurgated; Russia for example does not exist, its very name unrecorded, and the Revolution never referred to, though it was long accomplished by the time of the novel's action, and, indeed, motivated the actual mutinies which perhaps suggested the story. No, Faulkner's war is that of pure legendary war between Germany and the Allies, "The War" of the sentimental-pacifist literature of the twenties, "The War," of course, of some of Faulkner's own early stories, his other mythical theme beside the South. Indeed, there is in 1954 something almost absurdly old-fashioned about *A Fable*, with its concluding warning that the epitaphs of man are: "They shall not pass. My country right or wrong . . ." Surely, one thinks, this must have been written sometime between *The Enormous Room* and *All Quiet on the Western Front*—before a second World War had betrayed the stereotypes we thought eternal; and the emergence of Hitler and Stalin made the comforting fantasies of a conspiracy in the Brass viable only to the backwoods mind.

But a book can triumph over its politics; it is by its imposition of reality, by the conviction of its symbols that it finally stands or falls. And the fate of his fiction Faulkner confides to the archetype his title declares: a reliving of Christ's passion inside of this pseudo-history, through the seven days which give to the book whatever pattern it finally has. The initial mutiny is led by a group of thirteen men, who follow a corporal born in a stable on Christmas Day, etc., etc. The gospel parallels are made with somewhat annoying pointedness, but the Corporal-Christus they are intended to illuminate never quite makes it into the spotlight they focus for him. Through most of the book, Faulkner, shifting point of view in his accustomed style, lets us see all around the Leader of the Twelve, without ever directly introducing him onto the scene; but when he can resist no longer, he is able to show us only a somewhat surly and illiterate peasant, suspicious of ritual and without rhetoric, who we are loath to believe could have led the mutiny much less be the representative of Christ.

This churl who is intended to be the center of the book's affirmation of faith in man Faulkner can give no positive lines, making him finally Christ as the spirit who denies and thus endures, the most negative of all literary Christs—as he is also the most naturalistic: the Son of Man but not the Son of God. Faulkner's faith is, like his politics, a case of Hamlet without the Prince, as his First World War exists without the Russian Revolution, his Religion survives without God.

And insofar as his story is not merely a reliving of the Christ Pattern but a reinterpretation of the Bible story, it is disconcertingly without mystery or miracle; saved only by the figure of the Old Marshal, who is Commander of the Allied Armies, chief enemy of the peace, condemner of the Christ to death, but also (and here is the one real ingenuity of the re-telling) Christ's actual father.

In Faulkner's condensed fable, the Marshal plays finally the combined roles of the Devil as Tempter, Pilate as Judge, and Caesar as the Prince of this World; and if there is a God, the book mockingly (unintentionally?) suggests, he can only be this father image: Satan—Caesar—Pilate—the Enemy of all as the father of what alone can destroy him.

The generalissimo is fundamentally, of course, a stereotype among stereotypes, the very essence of that imagined Insider, whom the GI dreams as the controller of his destiny; but he is a stereotype raised to the level of the demonic and hence of poetry.

Christ the Corporal, however, does not exist even in this sense; indeed, though the title of the book declares him at its center, he seems finally a supernumerary, an intruder in the story Faulkner must always write, whatever he intends to set down. For there is a rival savior in the book, a more adequate mouthpiece for Faulkner's back-country, sentimental, unchurched Faith: The Reverend Tobe Sutterfield, an old Negro who has wandered into battle-ridden France, or rather has been insolently introjected into it by Faulkner out of his old books and his compulsive concerns, a self-appointed savior of men, who has helped steal a race horse, and is called by the French "Toolyman," which is to say *tout le monde*. Here is a real rather than a literary Christ, a Christ adequate to Faulkner's obsessions rather than his ambitions; and where the Negro touches the book it comes most alive; for it is the Negro who must save Faulkner, whoever else is to be the savior of the rest of us.

Elsewhere the book remains static, unmoving and unmoved, except where flashes of the old violence and disgust break through the planned affirmation (a scene for instance, which begins with a platoon scrabbling among the decaying dead for the Unknown Soldier, and ends with their trading his corpse to a halfmad old woman for some bottles of brandy; or another, where three Americans, yokel, gangster and Negro queer, attempt to shoot a reluctant French general in the face); for finally, nausea is to Faulkner the supreme moral attitude, and where he does not betray it in the name of "affirmation" or "faith in man," he is most himself— and still the greatest writer among us.

Norman Podhoretz.
"William Faulkner and
the Problem of War."
Commentary, 18
(September 1954),
227–32.

A Fable may not be William Faulkner's worst book; one would have to re-read *Pylon* to make a definitive judgment, and I personally could not face the ordeal. But whether or not it is his worst, this new novel is for the most part so dull, so tortured, above all so pretentious, that it forced me back to "Red Leaves" and "Spotted Horses", *Light in August* and *The Sound and the Fury*, for reassurance. Perhaps Faulkner was always as bad as this; perhaps some obsolete piety prevented us from seeing him truly. But the reassurance was there: those earlier works are wonderful, they are masterpieces. Nevertheless they struck me as the consummation of a minor, not, as I once thought, a major talent. I found them narrower than I remembered, and what was more surprising, not in the least complex. Faulkner's prose style, perhaps, fooled us into attributing complexity to his mind. It now seems obvious, however, that he really is what he always claims to be: a simple man. His warmest admirers have usually refused to take him at his word, insisting that the pettish autobiographical remarks he has made to interviewers were a pose, the great artist's secret revenge on the impertinent intruders who came south to pester him. Yet how much more impressive, after all, and how fitting, that it should be this way!

The narrowness I am speaking of is a narrowness of range. I am not suggesting that Faulkner's work exhibits just one mode of feeling or a single quality (it is often forgotten how funny this most solemn of writers can be), but rather that he deals best with only one kind of person acting in one kind of situation. Think of his greatest achievements: the transcription of how Issetibbeha's condemned Negro slave ran from his pursuers, never resting and finally eating a nest of ants to keep himself alive; or Lena Grove walking across two states with the patience of the stupid and the saintly, expecting to find the father of her unborn child; or the picture of Quentin Compson, crazed with a sense of honor so powerful that it drives him to suicide, buying a dirty little girl soggy cakes, only to be arrested for molesting her, and laughing when he is arrested; or the description of Lion, the great yellow hunting dog hurling himself time after time after time against a door he can never crash through. These marvelous images share one overriding conception: a sense of all living things as possessed, fated, doomed—and the possessed are the simplest of creatures. They do and feel only as they must, and if they do what they must with dignity, beauty, and submission, Faulkner finds glory in their lives. "Come," his captors tell Issetibbeha's slave, "you ran well. Do not be ashamed." But the glory Faulkner attributed to the man is no different from the glory he sees in the dog—which tells us something about his view of reality.

Think also what is missing from his books. Perhaps it can be summed up by saying that as far as Yoknapatawpha is concerned, the Enlightenment might just as well have never been. The qualities of reasonableness, moderation, compromise, tolerance, sober choice—in short, the antiapocalyptic style of life brought into the modern world by the middle class—no more exists for Faulkner than plain ordinary folks do (everyone is at least a demigod to him). To a whimsical observer, his work might almost seem a gigantic fantasy fulfilling the wish that the middle class had never been brought forth onto this earth. He doesn't even hate it accurately, as those great haters Flaubert and D. H. Lawrence did. In the very act of damning industrial, urban, middle-class man, he reveals nothing more than an abstract conception of what the type is like. Jason Compson, for example, is one of Faulkner's supreme triumphs, but he hardly represents the corrosive effects of the business ethos on a man's soul. For Jason is really another variety of the possessed creature Faulkner always writes about. There is nothing mean or diminutive—or middling, for that matter—in him, except perhaps his objectives. He has the same overwhelming compulsiveness, the same superhuman drive exhibited by his characteristic adversary, Quentin Compson—whereas the truth is that the middle class, if it stands for anything at all, supports the immediate exorcising of all known demons. Its great cultural triumph is precisely that it brought obsession into disrepute.

The view that takes Faulkner as a chronicler of war between pre-industrial civilization and the new world of the middle class seems to me unfounded. I cannot discover a genuine sense of history in the Yoknapatawpha series; unlike Stendhal, say, who saw a new kind of personality emerging from major historical changes and understood the drama and significance in its clash with a moribund type, Faulkner has always taken refuge from historical change in a vague sense of doom. We can speak without exaggeration of Julien Sorel's struggle with the de la Moles as the 19th century versus the 18th—two different worlds quite literally meet in *The Red and the Black*, two different temperaments, two different attitudes toward the self. Jason Compson, on the other hand, is merely Quentin Compson

gone wrong. And who can blame him?

Faulkner's narrowness, then, has always stemmed partly from an unwillingness or an inability either to love or to hate the world of the 20th century enough to understand it. But it isn't contemporary reality alone that Faulkner has shied away from. The very effort to explain, to understand any living thing, seems to him sheer blasphemy. Moreover, he is utterly indifferent to subtlety and qualification. When he qualifies—and often he will do so at tiresome length—it is not with the Jamesian intent of suggesting how much the naked eye never sees. Nor does he wish to refine the gross perception and focus it on a delicate point. The fine points are a swarm of motes irritating to Faulkner's eyes; occasionally he can descend to a crude, surly tone in dismissing them as irrelevant:

"But tell me why—No, I know why. I know the reason. I know it's true: I just want to hear you say it, hear both of us say it so I'll know it's real"—already—or still—speaking, even through the other's single vicious obscene contemptuous epithet: "You could have surrendered the horse at any time and it could have stayed alive, but that was not it: not just to keep it alive, any more than for the few thousands or the few hundred thousands that people will always be convinced you won on it"—stopping then and even waiting, or anyway watching, exultant and calm while the prisoner cursed, nor toward him nor even just at him, but him, the ex-deputy, steadily and for perhaps a full minute, with harsh and obscene unimagination, then the ex-deputy speaking again, rapid and peaceful and soothing: "All right, all right. The reason was so that it could run, keep on losing races at least, finish races at least even if it did have to run them on three legs because it was a giant and didn't need even three legs to run them on but only one with a hoof at the end to qualify as a horse."

Is it fanciful to suggest that Faulkner's sympathies are with the obscene prisoner who thinks that the young man in quest of reasons is a fool and a monster? Faulkner frequently takes a kind of mischievous delight in tantalizing us with long passages which pretend to be explanations, but whose point is that no explanations are possible. These passages almost always consist of crude metaphysical assertions written with an ineptitude even translations of Hegel rarely match. He hurls his convoluted rhetoric and clumsy thought into the air like an educated version of his own prisoner cursing those of us who ask for a reason or two now and then. In any case, the notion that nothing can be explained is a half-truth which, in my opinion, has limited Faulkner's creative range. For let us be bold and admit it: a lack of ideas is no virtue in a novelist. I do not believe that Faulkner ever had ideas. Convictions, yes, and a terrifying energy behind them, but not ideas, not the wish to understand the world, only the wish to feel deeply and to transcribe what he felt and saw. (Compare him to Dostoyevsky and the difference between a demonic writer with ideas and one who has none becomes clear.) Heaven knows that what Faulkner did have was enough to make him one of the two or three first-rate writers in modern American literature. But it was not enough to make him a truly great writer.

It was also not enough to sustain his creative energy. For the paradox is that after awhile the imagination of a novelist who has maintained merely an equivocal flirtation with ideas begins to flounder. At the very point when he needs more than his original enthusiasm about a subject to keep him going, he finds himself without resources. He may feel his subjects as intensely as ever, but the convictions which once were enough to make him certain that it was a *significant* subject no longer appear self-evident. Eventually this loss of confidence will also affect his capacity to distinguish between emotion which refers to something outside and feeling which is created by the will to feel. (The rhetorical mode of *A Fable* seems to me evidence of Faulkner's present inability to recognize a self-generated paroxysm when he works his nerves into one.) And finally, it will betray the novelist into choosing subjects that he has no business dealing with.

The more explicitly Faulkner declares his "values"—as he has been doing lately —the more we suspect that he is terribly unsure of himself these days, unsure of the relevance of his way of looking at things. For what has the Glory celebrated in Yoknapatawpha got to do with the Korean War, that tiresome, drab, plodding, inconclusive war, from which not a single national hero emerged, a war uninspiring, nay meaningless, to the Yoknapatawpha mind, and thrilling only to children of the Enlightenment who understand its moral sublimity? What has become of Faulkner—when a speech like his Nobel Prize address affirming the nobility of man and his power to endure and to prevail despite atom bombs, falls on our ears with a sound dangerously like irrelevant cant? We do have our own kind of glory and our own kind of miraculousness, but Faulkner's vocabulary is somehow inadequate to describe them. And I think *A Fable* proves that he knows it and is trying to do something about it.

As everyone must have heard by now, the book is Faulkner's version of the Passion of Jesus Christ. It is difficult not to

394

see in it also his attempt to bring Yokna-patawpha up to date. The allegory is superimposed upon the story of a false armistice which takes place toward the end of World War I. Faulkner portrays the war as an endless, frustrating affair which seems meaningless to those caught in it, a war so devastating to the spirit that it doesn't even provide ambitious young men with their chance for glory: a war, in fact, rather like the one we have all been living through since 1948. Into this atmosphere, Faulkner introduces his extremely shadowy Christ figure, an illiterate corporal serving in the French army who inspires a whole regiment to mutiny. The mutiny frightens all the top brass of both sides so thoroughly that they suspend hostilities long enough to hold a conference for the purpose of forming a united front against this revolutionary move. People must never learn that they can end a war as simply as all that. But at least one man does learn. He is a former officer who has intentionally had himself degraded to the ranks and become a runner. When he hears of the mutiny, he experiences what can only be called a conversion, and though he has never met the corporal, he dedicates himself to spreading (among the "Gentiles") the new gospel, the secret that can transform the whole world:

> "Don't you see? If all of us, the whole battalion, at least one battalion, one unit out of the whole line to start it, to lead the way—leave the rifles and grenades and all behind us in the trench: simply climb barehanded out over the parapet and through the wire and then just walk on barehanded, not with our hands up for surrender but just open to show that we had nothing to hurt, harm anyone; not running, stumbling: just walking forward like free

men—just one of us, one man; suppose just one man, then multiply him by a battalion; suppose a whole battalion of us, who want nothing except just to go home and get themselves into clean clothes and work and drink a little beer in the evening and talk and then lie down and sleep and not be afraid. And maybe, just maybe that many Germans who don't want anything more too, to put his or their rifles and grenades down and climb out too with their hands empty too not for surrender but just so every man could see there is nothing in them to hurt or harm either—"

That William Faulkner should be able to take such stuff not seriously but reverently, that he should see the trench mutiny as anything but a touchingly pathetic gesture of desperation! What are we to make of it?

Well, it is all done for the sake of an affirmation. Two years ago, in his Nobel Prize address, Faulkner "declined to accept the end of man." The passage in which he insisted most intensely on his faith is in *A Fable* also, spoken by the corporal's father, the Commander-in-Chief of Allied Forces in France, who acknowledges his (illegitimate) son in the act of condemning him to death:

> "I don't fear man. I do better: I respect and admire him. And pride: I am ten times prouder of that immortality which he does possess than ever he of that heavenly one of his delusion. Because man and his folly will endure. They will do more. They will prevail."

Heavenly immortality, then, is a "delusion"; man's true immortality lies in his glorious career on earth. There may or may not be a God (if the corporal is Christ, are we to take the Marshal of France as God the Father?), and he may or may not have actually given his son to save the world. For all we can tell from *A Fable*, it does not matter to Faulkner. Though Faulkner is a very religious writer, his work surely constitutes a paean to Man, not to God. He has turned to the Gospels as the source of his affirmation, not because he has suddenly discovered traditional Christianity but because he rightly sees in the Gospels the greatest tribute to Man ever conceived: they tell how God became man and man became God for a brief moment, and it therefore presumably lies in man's power to become "God" again. Even today.

Yet, as far as this novel is concerned, the affirmation is empty. *A Fable* is just another one of those proofs that an artist must either accept the religious view of the universe as a literal truth or leave its myths alone. The Gospel According to Matthew is a literary masterpiece because the author saw no contradiction in the idea of a man-God. He was not disturbed by qualities in the Messiah which many modern Christians would consider a blasphemy to attribute to the Son of God. The character of Jesus, as it appears in Matthew, Mark, and Luke, is not in the least monolithic: his Godliness is conveyed mostly through his ideas, thus never deteriorating into insipid virtue, while the plentiful evidences of his humanity are unabashedly displayed: we get glimpses of his arrogance, his impatience, his playfulness, his capacity to suffer. As for Faulkner's corporal, the trouble with him is not just that he is monolithic; he simply doesn't exist. Nor does the Olympian marshal. Nor do any of the characters who take part in the religious allegory. How could they exist when Faulkner doesn't seem to believe that they ever did? Under these conditions not all the

Biblical parallels in all the testaments ever compiled could give them life.

And there are parallels aplenty in *A Fable*. The corporal brings a complete biblical retinue along with him. Of the twelve men in his squad, one betrays him; he is "engaged" to a whore from Marseilles who he has said was really "a good girl"; he even has a virgin mother of sorts (his real mother had died in childbirth after having been cast off by her husband for committing adultery, so the corporal was raised by his sister who, being nine years old at his birth, could only be called his mother in a spiritual sense, I suppose). Many other analogies come to mind, including the traditional chronology of the Passion. The corporal is captured on a Wednesday, executed on a Friday, and "resurrected" on a Sunday. He is killed (at the age of 33) together with two other criminals, and though he is executed by means of a firing squad, Faulkner still contrives to have him die with a crown of "thorns" around his head:

> The corporal's post may have been flawed or even rotten because . . . the plunge of the post had jammed it and its burden too into a tangled mass of old barbed wire, a strand of which has looped up and around the top of the post and the man's head as though to assail them both in one unbroken continuation of the fall, into the anonymity of the earth.

Before he dies, however, he performs miracles. The miracle at Cana is given a particularly "modern" naturalistic interpretation, where either Faulkner's sense of humor or his lack of reverence has got the better of his judgment. It seems that the corporal met a young American soldier who wanted to marry an orphan girl. Neither of them had any money and consequently could not prepare a wedding feast. To help them out of their predicament, the corporal walks into a crap game and calmly picks up the money lying on the floor, explaining to the soldiers (who are on the point of dealing with him as we might expect) that he needs it for one of their buddies. Miraculously, the soldiers experience a burst of sentimental enthusiasm and "adopt" the wedding, buying up all the wine in town, thus, I assume, turning water into wine. This sort of thing, embarrassingly silly as it is, can almost be compared to some of the details in D. H. Lawrence's version of Jesus' resurrection (*The Man Who Died*) which, in the monstrous reaches of its bad taste, strikes even an unbeliever as a blasphemy.

It would be dishonest to pretend that the occasional spurts of life in *A Fable* redeem the book. The story which Faulkner worked into the allegory about the wretched Cockney groom and the Negro preacher who steal a crippled racehorse was written nine years ago, and though it is a good story, it certainly falls short of his best work on animals and men (for example, "The Bear"). As for the character of General Gragnon, the commander of the mutinied regiment who wants to execute all three thousand men, and would be prepared to execute a whole army for the sake of his reputation, he is Yoknapatawpha itself dressed in a French uniform. But Gragnon is buried in the allegoric mess; Faulkner never gives him the chance he deserves.

A Fable, then, is one of those disembodied, religiose affirmations that we have learned to regard as the typical literary symptom of a failure of nerve in difficult times. It can be read as a fantasy in quest of some optimistic statement on our present predicament. Faulkner offers us a "pure," primitivistic Christianity that we are meant to feel is nobler, more beautiful, somehow more effective than our worldly politics. For he can see nothing but silliness in the machinations of the political mind; his satiric chapter on the conference of the generals seems to me astonishingly simple-minded, a worthy foil to his conception of the Christian lesson for our time. We are confronted here with Faulkner's impulse to escape the complexity of a world he has no patience with, a world he cannot understand. He is saying to us: "I am tired and bored and bewildered by the way you go about things; I am sick of your conferences and your bickerings. They don't matter, they are little childish games. What matters is Love and Faith and Hope." Love of what? Faith in what? Faulkner never tells us. How could he, when he cannot realize that today as perhaps never before the question of man-and-his-destiny is inseparable from the hard, dull, wearisome details of EDC's and NATO's and Austrian Peace Treaties? Indeed, it is even possible that the committees and conferences and legalistic bickerings *are* the very question itself. The fact that this possibility is inconceivable to Faulkner may indicate that *A Fable* is something more than the usual product of social unrest.

I think this book marks conclusively, and as it were officially, the end of an era. The "modern" world of which Faulkner, Hemingway, and Dos Passos were the most penetrating interpreters, the world of the 20's and 30's whose articulate consciousness they were, froze to death in 1948. As I have suggested Faulkner's point of view—and the same might be said of both Hemingway and Dos Passos—already has taken on that so slightly stilted, archaic look; the tint of brown begins to stain the photograph, the poses seem a little awkward and artificial. Even the best works of these writers, reread today, induce nostalgia rather than the exhilaration of discovery. We are living now in a limbo that is neither war nor peace, yet it has given rise to a generation not "lost" but patient, acquiescent, careful rather than reckless, submissive rather than rebellious. We will recognize fully what a new world this is only when it finds a voice of its own. Meanwhile, however, the extent to which Faulkner has lost touch with contemporary experience—the way he has been bamboozled by irrelevant religiosity, while blinding himself to the real drama of salvation being played out before his very eyes—is enough to bring home the gap between his reality and ours. In the end, *A Fable* leaves us wondering whether the time will ever come again when a writer will be able to dismiss politics in favor of the Large Considerations without sounding like a chill echo from a dead world.

V. S. Pritchett.
"Time Frozen."
Partisan Review, 21 (September–October 1954), 557–61.

Mr. William Faulkner has been working on this novel—if that is what it is—for the last nine years and it is, appropriately, a work of ambitious theme and dimension. It has the diffused moral gloss of affirmation that writers of talent seem bound to hanker after sooner or later. In nearly all his novels he has been the regionalist and one of those who lay down the foundations of a culture. He has been called, in this respect, bardic, a worker in legend and saga and although he has been a good deal compared with Hawthorne in American literature, he will suggest to an English critic an even greater resemblance to Scott. But there has always been alien irritant in his talent: the contact with Eu-

rope through the Europeanized Eliot and through Joyce in literature, and through the First World War in life. The last has occasionally been explicit, as in *Soldiers' Pay* or in one or two short stories—"Turn About" is one of the best stories he has ever written. Europe is explicit also in *A Fable*.

Mr. Faulkner has always turned his subjects into history: that is to say the story has stopped, Fate has had its say, the thing is settled before it begins; we go back over it as it rots down in the compost of time. Mr. Faulkner has no sense of what things may become, instead he has the mythmaker's sense of the different ways in which experience is repetitive and over. In *A Fable* he moves from the native past of Yoknapatawpha to history on a larger scale. He goes to the Europe of 1916 which, as we know, so profoundly affected the writers of his generation. Old Kaspar sits in the sun and tells us he does not know what the war was about except that, in the end, people began to feel it must be the last war of all. Mr. Faulkner has always loved the land; he has always hated mechanical civilization and the castrated man it is thought to produce; but like Crane and Hemingway before him he is romantically curious about military *virtu* and ritual. The clash of rifle butts as the guard changes, the sounding of the *Last Post*, the pulling down of the flag, the self-mutilations of hierarchy and command, the privileged speeding of cars to headquarters, and so on, have an almost religious connotation for him and are certainly marked by rhetoric and nostalgia. Mr. Faulkner is far from the same sort of thing in Vigny's *Servitude et Grandeur Militaire*; he is close to the romanticism of Crane and strikes the European as very American of its period. He describes an initiation. And there is another point to note when we consider where Mr. Faulkner's historical compulsion has taken him in this book. It is this. The tragedy of the First World War lay in the conjunction of mass slaughter with the feeling of meaninglessness. The war was felt to be an outrage committed inexplicably against each human person. This could not be said or felt of the Second World War and it cannot be said of the warlike state of the world today, for our wars are revolutionary and revolutions have meaning. They are also fought by technicians and technicians are notoriously absorbed in their work and are morally segregated and sustained by it. They may become traitors; they will never mutiny—and mutiny is Mr. Faulkner's subject. The truly symbolical figure of our time is the traitor or divided man, not the mutineer; it is Judas not Christ. *A Fable* is a fantasy natural to a past dispensation. The novel ends, with unconscious literary "placing" in the now barren ceremony at the Arc de Triomphe before the tomb of the unknown soldier. One might say that the 1914 war was the final gift of European culture to America.

It is rarely easy to disentangle the narrative of Mr. Faulkner's novels. We can simplify it however. When the book opens we are in the penultimate phase of the 1914 war. Hardly any Americans have arrived. There is a mutiny in the French army. It is a protest on the part of the ordinary human being against the terror and misery of the trenches. Why not make a simple act of will and just refuse to go on? The mutiny is seen as a rumor, a mystery which has, as it turns out, been fomented by a corporal from the Middle East who has acquired French nationality and who has twelve secretive assistants, one of whom eventually betrays him. The story opens wonderfully with the arrival of the arrested men at Headquarters. Presently the disgraced general in command hands over his sword and the disaffected regiment is unloaded into a prison camp. They will be shot. The population is di-

vided between its own desire for peace and its anger at the rebellion. In the meantime there is a false armistice and the Germans have been contacted. Another regiment (I believe I am right in saying: one can never be sure of one's facts after reading Mr. Faulkner), setting out to emulate the doctrine of non-resistance, is shot up by its own guns. Mr. Faulkner's business is to take the situation at all levels, though not in the rule of thumb manner of realism, and to explore the conflict between the moral claims of war as an exorable but pitying institution and the anguish of man, to put man's need of hierarchy against the heart, to set Saint Paul against Christ. The crisis of the allegory lies in the interviews of the Supreme Commander with some of the prisoners, but above all with the leader. The analogy with Christian myth is covertly insinuated: the leader is in fact the bastard son of the once dissolute and immensely wise Supreme Commander, who is admirably drawn; he tempts the son with freedom, with the arguments of Saint Paul, but finding him obdurate, leaves him to be shot. By an odd chance he falls dead, with two others, still tied to the post of the execution yard and with a crown of barbed wire on his head. It is a crucifixion. By accident or design he is identified with the unknown soldier, a symbol of the will of man in his solitude to prevail.

Such a simplification of the theme is necessary but intolerable. Mr. Faulkner may be playing rhetorical poker with the marked cards of myth and symbol, but he is not a purveyor of melodrama. He is enriched by his vices and his idiosyncrasies as a novelist. There is the characteristic digression into the garrulous story of the stolen racehorse which can win races on three legs. There is the tale of the horse's foul-mouthed and crooked English groom, who is later seen getting the soldiers to gamble with him on their expectation of death, at a shilling a day. There is the absurd figure of the exalted negro preacher. There are the women. These are entangled in the allegory and, with Mr. Faulkner, that means their declamatory unconscious is entangled with their physical presence. The prose is written as incantation, in swelling and diminishing monologue; it is filled with purple patches, conceits, epigrams, and lapidary phrases, and those images that paralyze movement, but intensify the moment. For Mr. Faulkner's aim, as an historian, is to isolate and freeze each moment of the past:

> And that was all. Then it was sunset. As they stood in the turning flood of night, the ebb of day rang abruptly with an orderly discordant diapason of bugles, orderly because they all sounded at once, discordant because they sounded not one call, but three; the *Battre aux Champs* of the French, the *Last Post* of the English, the *Retreat* of the Americans, beginning inside the city and spreading from cantonment and depot, rising and falling within its own measured bruit as the bronze throat of orderly and regulated war proclaimed and affirmed to the end of day, clarion and sombre above the parade rite of *Mount and Stand Down* as the old guards, custodians of today, relinquished to tomorrow's, the six sergeants themselves appearing this time, each with his old guard or his new, the six files in ordered tramp and wheel facing each its rigid counterpart juxtaposed, the barked commands in the three different tongues ringing in the same discordant unison as the bugles, in staccato *poste* and *riposte* as the guards exchanged and the three sentries of the new ones as-

sumed the posts. Then the sunset gun went from the old citadel, deliberate and profound, as if a single muffled drumstick had been dropped once against the inverted bowl of hollow and resonant air, the sound fading slowly and deliberately until at last, with no suture to mark its close, it was lost in the murmur of bunting with which the flags, bright blooms of glory myriad across the embattled continent, sank, windless again, down.

or to give each moment of time or experience its final own fatal judgment or epithet. The only criticism we make is the old one: that all Mr. Faulkner's moments have the same intensity.

The whole conception is poetic. We shall read of "day dream's idle un-expectation." Or

> One more day I would have missed him which should have told me, warned me that what faced us was doom, not destiny, since only destiny is clumsy, inefficient, procrastinative, while doom never is.

But behind the rhetorician and the dizzy dialectician who is metaphysically wonderstruck at the way one idea, or even one word, turns into its opposite there is another Faulkner. This is the sardonic, the "judgmatic," the garrulous old writer, as incurably repetitive and his life story of the blasphemous English groom; he drawls out the night talk in the trenches, the professional talk of the aerodrome; the nasty talk of the assassins or the burial squad and what they will do for one, or preferably, two bottles of brandy. The native Faulkner is the old pungent Faulkner and, in trying to pick his way through this consciousness and that, the reader is grateful for this survival. For what one notices is that there is no equivalent to Popeye in this book. The precise, brutal, bleeding savage pity we recall in *Soldiers' Pay* is missing—except in the murder or execution of the French Commander in the end—and this from a theme which would seem to demand all Mr. Faulkner's capacity for horror. Instead, evil is generalized by words like "anguish" and so on. The war is an atmosphere that pervades like the smell of refuse and rules by some implicit yet mysterious moral and physical force of its own. There is no doubt that Mr. Faulkner's supreme gift is the creation of atmospheres of one kind or another; but we are now dealing with a writer who has moved from destructive despair, in his own work, to conscious affirmation: to that extent his world becomes more recognizable than the earlier one of idiots, sadists and derelicts, because it is more comprehensive and humane; but it is recognizable solely on the sympathetic, engaging and immensely ingenious level of allegory. The moral Faulkner of *A Fable* represents the sort of accomplished retreat one notices, say, in Tolstoy's *Resurrection*.

In the novels of his generation, like *Ulysses* or *Finnegans Wake*, which have influenced Faulkner (novels which had worked back through the chaos of the mind's associations toward archetypal myth), the human representative figures like Mr. and Mrs. Bloom for example, have been more powerful than their myth. Mr. Faulkner's are weaker. But his richness of texture is still there and, above all, there is that capacity for passion which—combining, as it does, with literary artificialities—gives him his intensity, his thwarted power and his integrity as an artist. I am not one to defend a novelist for being exasperating to read, or for being difficult; no amount of intellectual sophistry can make the unreadable read-

able and, after all, we have learned to do our best by the "difficult" writers of the last thirty years. Some private worlds are nuts that cannot be cracked except by one university on behalf of another and not on behalf of readers. But if the difficulty of Faulkner is partly the result of too much reading in an isolated society, it springs from a genuine judgement on our time. He has been a writer divided between idiosyncrasies of regional genius and a nostalgia for a contemporary means of dealing with a universal subject. The division is still apparent in the rather laden majesty of his allegory where a universal subject has been treated as the compendium of a word-drunk mind.

Delmore Schwartz. "William Faulkner's *A Fable.*" *Perspectives U.S.A.*, No. 10 (Winter 1955), pp. 126–36.

Faulkner toiled over *A Fable* for more than nine years, a long time for most novelists, and particularly long for a writer of Faulkner's kind of inspiration which Malcolm Cowley has rightly compared to a state of demonic possession. The novelist's long labor suggests that the difficulty was one of conception, not of composition, and this should be enough in itself to indicate that the book must be read several times. This is true of much of Faulkner's fiction, but hitherto the reason has been the novelist's style and narrative method. In *A Fable* the same effort must be directed to style and method, but there is a greater difficulty in the theme itself. Within the literal story of a mutiny on the

401

Western Front during the First World War, the Gospel account of Christ's passion emerges in a peculiar and unique way. The illiterate French corporal who leads the mutiny is the modern representative of Christ; his twelve followers are like the twelve apostles; one of them betrays him, another denies him thrice; he is tempted by the Supreme Commander of the Allied armies as Christ is tempted by Satan; and when, rejecting all temptation, he refuses to repudiate the mutiny, he is tied to a post and shot by a firing squad, his head, as he falls, caught in barbed wire to make a modern crown of thorns. And there are a good many other genuine and powerful realizations of the Gospel pattern—a delightful modern version of the marriage in Cana of Galilee (which begins in a French village with American soldiers in a crap game), and a touching version of the Last Supper (in which the corporal who represents Christ simply urges his followers to eat more and talk less or afterward they will be hungry and sorry).

The peculiar way in which the Gospel pattern functions can perhaps best be suggested by metaphor: it is as if, during a play, the actors were seen at recurrent, important moments, varying in length and meaning, in a lighting which like an X-ray machine showed their bone structure, brain, and heart in black, beneath and together with their ordinary visual appearance. This use of the Gospel story is quite unlike the prevailing mythical techniques of modern literature because it has only one purpose and meaning, the representation of supreme nobility, instead of the manifold meanings of contrast, simultaneity, irony, analogy, and the like, which other modern authors seek through mythical reference. Faulkner's sole purpose is to unite the theme of modern war with the theme of the appearance of Christ in the modern world (an aim which could be surpassed in daring and ambition only by

the like one of the second coming of Christ as a Negro in the South) in order to give adequate actuality to the real subject of *A Fable*. The real subject is: are human beings worthy of supreme nobility? The wholesale impersonal brutality of modern war, intensified by the crisis of a mutiny, might by itself reduce this question to that of whether human beings are worth anything at all. By making the Gospel pattern emerge within the mutiny through the corporal who is its leader, the question is made to include the noble sacrifice which the corporal embodies, and at the same time it is strengthened by the most famous of precedents, the most vivid and tragic of all stories.

Hence this complexity of intention and meaning in *A Fable* (a complexity which is also, in part, a remarkable simplicity) makes two kinds of misunderstanding possible and even likely. The reader who is a devout Christian may misinterpret the novel as a hideous parody, pacifist and sacrilegious in intention. The reader without religious belief may mistake the book for a religious affirmation; so powerfully does the Gospel pattern assert itself, and with so much of a magical radiance, that one overlooks, at first, the numerous points at which the Gospel pattern is ignored, avoided, contradicted, or modified. And the possibility of misunderstanding is increased by the style which, at first, seems bombastic and overwritten when it is not hysterical or frenetic. Once the book is mastered, this first and false impression vanishes: Faulkner has converted various extreme traits of his style into a systematic elevation and intensity, comparable to the mannerisms of opera, and perfect as a preparation and context for simple directness of the illiterate corporal. Hence, although the complexity of conception in *A Fable* makes it the most difficult of all his books, the rewards, if one persists, are astonishing: *A Fable* is a masterpiece, a unique fulfillment of Faulkner's genius which gives a luminous new meaning to his work as a whole.

The extent to which *A Fable* is governed by a radically new attitude and point of view cannot be overemphasized. Throughout his career Faulkner has been concerned with the First World War; and he was directly concerned with the disillusioned or mutilated veteran of modern war in his first novel, *Soldiers' Pay* (the same title might also serve for his latest book twenty-eight years after), in his third novel, *Sartoris* (which is, as Robert Cantwell has remarked, his first characteristic book and contains all his later work in embryo), and in many of his best stories, such as "Ad Astra" and "Victory." But in all this fiction the governing attitude which motivates the author, although it is that of the most intense disillusion, is the disillusion of one recently and severely deprived of important illusions. To use the stock phrase, it is the antiwar attitude of the lost generation to which Hemingway and Dos Passos also belonged. The point of view of *A Fable* is far beyond illusion and disillusion; there is no effort to show at the start that the mutiny has been provoked by the meaningless horror which common soldiers suffer; and from the beginning, it is taken for granted that the war is wrong so that antiwar sentiment is the starting point, and not the conclusion.

This is but one of the important and radical differences which distinguish *A Fable* from other fiction which deals with modern war: the degree of difference is so important that it must be characterized at length by comparing an episode in *A Fable* with an anecdote about the Civil War in *Sartoris*. The Civil War anecdote, set in deliberate contrast to the emotional paralysis of the modern Bayard Sartoris as a veteran of modern war, deals with his remarkable ancestor, the Bayard Sartoris

of the Civil War. He is an officer of the famous Southern cavalry leader Jeb Stuart and with Stuart he raids a Union encampment for the sole purpose of securing coffee, capturing, along with the coffee, a Northern officer, but not his horse. Stuart out of chivalry and courtesy determines to secure a mount by making another unnecessary raid, and when the Northern officer protests that this is heedless and foolish behavior, particularly for a mere prisoner's comfort, Stuart's haughty reply is that he is acting not for the prisoner but "for an officer suffering the fortunes of war. No gentleman would do less." The Union officer answers that "No gentleman has any business in this war . . . he is an anachronism, like anchovies. At least General Stuart did not capture our anchovies . . . Perhaps he will send General Lee for them in person." Bayard Sartoris, hearing the interchange, dashes off for the anchovies, and Stuart turns to follow him, as one of his own officers protests. But the captured Northern major, converted, cries out to Stuart: "Forward, sir . . . What is one man to a renewed belief in mankind?"

A good many episodes in *A Fable* concern the English battalion runner, who is not only one of the most important and moving characters in the new novel, but is as gallant a hero as Bayard Sartoris. When five months as an officer have made him hate himself and all other human beings, he feels that his loss of belief in mankind makes it necessary that he go to his company commander, resign his commission, and return to the ranks. The company commander advises him to shoot himself in the foot; in the same way, with the same useless advice, the battalion commander and finally the brigadier refuse his resignation. After three months, however, a simple method occurs to him, that of copulating with a girl in public. Since this jeopardizes the honor of the regiment, he is now permitted to resign and return to the ranks as a private: the request he has made with dignity as a human being is granted only after the performance of an obscene pantomime. When the girl hired to help him discovers that his true motive is not cowardice, as she supposed, but the extraordinary courage of an extraordinary protest, she then experiences the same immense renewal of belief in mankind as the captured Union major in *Sartoris*. The explicit meaning which Faulkner gives to the Civil War episode is so close to that of the episode in *A Fable* that the latter might almost be characterized as the former is, apart from the irrelevant details:

"... what had been a hare-brained prank of two heedless and reckless boys became a gallant and finely tragical point to which the [human] race had been raised from spiritual sloth ... by two angels ... purging the souls of men ..."

Yet although the meaning of both episodes is the same, in this sense of a renewed belief in man, the extreme difference in point of view is defined by comparing public copulation to a heedless prank, as the difference in attitude shows itself when an officer's greatest heroism becomes his effort to resign his commission as an officer.

The runner has convinced the girl that at least one human being is not worthless, but he cannot convince himself until he hears of the mutiny. Before it occurs, he visits an old Negro preacher, who, unlike himself and most other human beings of the book, is in serene possession of belief in God and Man. Perceiving the runner's spiritual desperation, the old preacher tells him the story of a marvelous horse,[1] and although this episode has been dismissed by some critics as interpolation, its function is quite clear and very important. Two years before the war, in the American South, this marvelous horse has broken a leg in a train wreck, and the old preacher and the horse's English groom have stolen him, knowing that otherwise, because of the accident, the horse's millionaire owner will use him only for breeding purposes instead of racing him. After stealing the marvelous horse, and patching up his leg, the preacher and the groom race him in small towns all over the countryside, and though he now must run three-legged, the horse continues to be a marvel of speed and wins most of the time. When the millionaire owner sets all the forces of the law in motion to regain the horse and arrest the thieves, the succession of officers who come in pursuit suppose like everyone else that the motive of the abduction is money, and that the horse must be winning enormous sums. But as each officer comes to recognize that the preacher and the groom are dedicated purely to the horse as a marvel of speed, they too experience a renewed belief in mankind: convinced that they have come upon a love and nobility which transcends the enforcement of the law, they are transformed into fanatical protectors of the horse's cause and his keeper's safety.

Hearing this story, the runner perceives that what he needs is the ability to believe in belief: "... Maybe what I need is ... To believe. Not in anything: just to believe." The horse is thus a stupendous narrative metaphor, since he is the cause of belief and nobility in other human beings just as the illiterate corporal is, an identification which does not become explicit until, after much mystery, the corporal's true nature is made clear.[2]

Several other characters in *A Fable* are comparable in interest and meaning to the runner, but perhaps most significant of all is the French general Gragnon, who commands the division in which the mutiny originates. Gragnon has lived by a belief in the Army to the exclusion and scorn of all else; he has been the perfect soldier, making his way up the military hierarchy solely by virtue of a brilliant record of personal merit. But just before the mutiny he is ordered to launch an offensive the sole purpose of which, as he immediately perceives, is failure, a failure which will enable a superior officer to gain his marshal's baton but which will at the same time ruin Gragnon's career. The mutiny occurs at the moment the offensive is scheduled to begin, and when both Gragnon's troops and the enemy's fail to attack, Gragnon demands successively of his immediate superior, the group commander for whose promotion he is being sacrificed, and finally of the supreme commander that, in accordance with military law, the mutinous regiment be shot. This request is refused as is his demand for a court-martial and lastly his resignation. "But to me? What will happen to me?" Gragnon asks when all his illusions have been exposed. "I don't know," a superior general answers, "but it will be glorious." What does happen to Gragnon is exactly what he has demanded for the mutinous regiment: instead of shooting the regiment, the high command decides that Gragnon had better be shot so that it can be maintained that he was killed in action, leading his troops against the enemy. The episode of his execution, which is written with a spectacular narrative power Faulkner has never surpassed, is one of the consummations of A Fable's extraordinary originality and insight. Most novelists of war are committed to the platitude that generals die in bed, which remains a literary platitude, no matter what the actual statistics may be. For Gragnon's agony of shocked disappointment would hardly be diminished if he had died in bed: the infamous manner of his death is the final dramatization of the fact that in modern war anything may happen to anyone, that a general may be just as expendable as a common soldier, and that most generals' hopes and ambitions are likely to be disappointed or rendered essentially meaningless by the very character of modern war, whether or not they die in bed. Since it is by hope that everyone, including generals, must live and die, Gragnon has suffered a death of the heart long before he is shot. He is, in fact, a martyr, like the illiterate corporal, for in an ironic symmetry which may not be immediately clear, he is crucified by three soldiers because of his dedicated belief in the Army. The novelist's attitude toward him, combining compassion and contempt, is worthy of Dante who also felt compassion for the most arrogant and despicable of the damned.

Like Gragnon, other significant characters are overtaken by the mutiny in ways as various and meaningful. Within the limits of a review, one cannot be adequate to Gragnon, and certainly not to the complexity of characterization of the entire book. But it probably must be said, in view of some of the first reviews of A Fable, that until the reader is capable of a detailed synopsis of the novel, he has really not read it at all. This is also true as long as the reader suffers from the impression that some characters are melodramatic stereotypes: one review's instance is a German general's monocle! For once the characters are seen in full relation, not in isolation or out of focus, the reader will know that the melodrama is in his own mind or in the characters'. It can be regarded as a great novelist's triteness only if, with a great literary critic, the reader supposes that the cruel actions of cruel characters suffice to make a book cruel and prove that the author is a sadist.

The extreme complication of meaning throughout A Fable is typified in the climactic interview between the corporal and the supreme commander. The complication is justified and necessary; and its nature is such that the least diminution of attention or oversimplification of interpretation results not in perplexity but in what is worse, a false impression of understanding which occurs because part of the total meaning has been taken as the whole meaning of an episode. For example, the supreme commander's avowed purpose in the climactic interview is to persuade the corporal to repudiate the mutiny; and this, certainly, is one of his purposes; but he has a purpose more serious and important to himself, which is to reveal to the corporal that he is his father and that he has devoted his career to enigmatic and strange courses in order to gain a son worthy of his inheritance; the interview is thus also a trial of the success or failure of his own life. These and other motives are involved in the interview, and if any one is overstressed or entirely unnoticed, a systematic kind of misunderstanding is bound to occur.

There is a further and somewhat different difficulty in the fact that the interview also corresponds, up to a point, to Christ's temptation by Satan; after that point there are serious and remarkable developments which are missed unless the Gospel analogy is disregarded. If Satan's temptation of Christ were the primary basis of the interview, and not merely one dimension of it, Satan, Caesar, Pontius Pilate, and God would have to be one and the same being. The chief reason that these oversimplifications lead to radical misunderstanding, instead of partial understanding, is that the supreme commander is often misrepresenting his own point of view and the real issues. He affirms repeatedly at great rhetorical length that he believes in mankind and admires human beings, a claim which is quite false. Thus, offering the corporal the temptation of freedom, the general points out that one

follower, the modern Peter, has denied him; and that all can soon be persuaded to the betrayal of the corporal. The corporal's simple answer is that for each human being who betrays him many more will spring up to follow him. Clearly the general's accusation is a denial of the admiration and belief which he claims that he has for humanity, as well as the "base underestimation" of the corporal which he also disclaims, since he asks the corporal to be a traitor too. It is thus the way in which the general articulates each of the temptations that demonstrates his essential contempt for all human beings, including the corporal and himself. This fact is most marked in the offer of the temptation of recognition as the general's son which will mean, he says, the chance to be the first emperor of the world, a throne which would give the corporal the opportunity of providing human beings with "sweeter bread" and "bloodier circuses"; but the corporal, who has shown no interest in making circuses bloodier or bread sweeter, is in the position Gandhi would have occupied, had a British Prime Minister offered him the chance to be Viceroy of India and to provide his fellow countrymen with superior teahouses and cricket matches. Though the general is not a foolish man, he becomes foolish as the interview continues and he must contend with the corporal's simple desire to be faithful to his followers and to himself. The last, most subtle and damning of the general's temptations is another and still more ignorant appeal to the corporal to be treacherous: "I will be dead in a few years," the general says, "and you can use your inheritance to win the trick tomorrow which today my ace finessed."

Each of the corporal's answers is hardly a direct refusal, so little is he tempted, so strong and clear is his belief in human beings. Sometimes he says, "there are still ten [men]," and when he is offered the temptation of the kingship of the world, he says only: "Are you that afraid of me?" His final refusal is just as brief and bare, yet declares his own attitude toward existence and humanity.

"Don't be afraid," the corporal said. "There's nothing to be afraid of. Nothing's worth it." This is the summit of the interview as of the book. Its negative phrasing may not reveal sufficiently that it is a supreme affirmation of what it is to be a human being, of how much depends upon courage if one is human. But in addition the corporal has said to the general that the general's entire view of existence is rooted in fear, an accusation all the more awful for being spoken with kindness, sympathy, and unemphatic directness. The immense sum of the corporal's moral triumph is thus that the supreme commander, seeking to tempt an illiterate corporal, has succeeded only in making himself pitiful!

Silenced for a time by the unbearable humiliation of the corporal's compassion, the general, when he regains self-possession, utters the most torrential and passionate of his perorations, denying that he suffers from fear and predicting man's catastrophic future to affirm once again that he really admires human beings. The future, he says, will be made inconceivably catastrophic by new instruments of warfare, but nevertheless man will survive and prevail over them even if he has to migrate to another planet as a result of war, the most perverse vice of man's deathless folly! His esteem for man is nothing more or less than the admiration reserved for successful criminals and homicidal maniacs. All that he has said to the corporal is based on the view that human beings are worthless, and this is illustrated perfectly when he calls himself "the champion of the mundane earth" and the corporal "the champion of man's baseless hopes": the one word, baseless, is sufficient to show

his inexhaustible contempt of everything truly human.

The corporal for his part possesses hardly more than a belief that human beings are not worthless, and human hope and aspiration not baseless. He himself is the living proof that man has a unique worth; and all the complexity of the book moves toward the establishment and acceptance of the reality of the corporal as a simple illiterate noble human being: *Ecce Homo!* Behold the Corporal! The two phrases contain the simple ultimate meaning of *A Fable*, as if they were the plain nails or hooks from which the large and intricate tapestry depended.

The minimal character of the corporal's belief is the measure of Faulkner's ambition and daring: the corporal's belief in mankind can be neither helped nor hindered by coffee, anchovies, chivalry or cowardice, betrayal or loyalty. It is a belief which justifies itself and is independent of all else, including supernatural sources or sanctions. And it is a simple belief because it supposes that hope is necessary, fear is foolish, and life is only worth living if human beings are worth dying for.

It should be entirely clear that in the course of the interview the book has moved outside the Gospel pattern, outside religious belief or disbelief, beyond the question of war or pacifism. There is no discussion of religion, apart from one scornful reference to immortality of the soul which the corporal ignores and to which the general does not return; there is almost as complete an absence of any argument about the mutiny as such.

It is in the light of this interview that everything else must be understood; and this fact makes it important to deny the comparison (which has been made twice in reviews and will doubtless be made often) of the climactic scene of *A Fable* to the legend of the Grand Inquisitor in Dostoevski's *The Brothers Karamazov*, which is itself one of the most misinter-preted passages in the history of litera-ture. The two scenes have a surface re-semblance which makes the comparison worse than misleading: for Dostoevski's scene is an imaginary poem composed by a leading character, Ivan Karamazov; its primary purpose is religious, as the whole of Dostoevski's novel is also; its substance shows Ivan's character as an intellectual, as a human being in torment because he cannot believe in God's existence, nor dis-believe and ignore the question of God; and among Ivan's chief reasons for being unable to believe is his difficulty in believ-ing in man because of that side of man revealed in the crimes which newspapers report. Faulkner's intention—and his tri-umph—is utterly unlike Dostoevski's be-cause he attempts to cut below the ques-tion of God's existence to a question which, for many modern human beings, is prior, the root conception of Man. The contrast is extreme and complete because Dostoevski is intent upon asserting par-ticular religious, doctrinal, and national meanings which Faulkner is equally de-termined to avoid. Dostoevski's purpose is to show the true church of Christ as opposed by the church of the Grand In-quisitor, who is a cardinal and hence a symbol of Roman Catholicism. The true church belonged to the Russian people and to the Czar, and gave men freedom to be good or evil, while the false church deprived man of freedom to prevent him from being evil. Faulkner's very different intention is to establish man as worthy of devotion, belief, and love, whatever his misdeeds and failings, and whether or not he is God's creature. Thus Dostoevski sought to prove that without belief in God man is capable of every crime; but Faulkner seeks to show that man is capa-ble of goodness purely because he is hu-man. Dostoevski's curious and wholly bi-ased views linked the church with Czarism;

Faulkner is concerned with no particular church's claims, but writes from a point of view which is radically modern pre-cisely because it seeks to avoid the ques-tion of God's existence so that a vision of humanity can be grasped which will be valid to readers of any and every shade of religious belief and disbelief. His attempt, it must be said again, depends only on the corporal's reality as a human being, then it is possible for all human beings to be noble.

Another important reason for distin-guishing between Dostoevski's religious intention and Faulkner's intention as nei-ther religious nor antireligious is illustrated by the scene, subsequent to the interview with the supreme commander and similar to it, in which a military chaplain, also seeking to persuade the corporal to repu-diate the mutiny, claims that it is contrary to the doctrines of the Church, and, through his arguments so perverts Chris-tian doctrine and the character of Christ that, when he fails, he commits suicide. If *A Fable*'s intention were religious, the priest's effort would be wholly false and without meaning; if the intention were essentially antireligious, then the priest's suicide, demonstrating his knowledge and guilt that he has betrayed the priesthood, would not have occurred, a point which seems worth making only because the epi-sode has been thus interpreted as an at-tack on institutional Christianity and on all organized religion.

It is true, however, and it is important to note that throughout the book the ques-tion of whether or not the corporal has a supernatural status presents itself sharply. The most representative instance, typical in its systematic ambiguity, is the meeting summoned by the supreme commander at which the corporal is present (but silent except when he says that he knows only one language, French). Three officers, all stubborn in their certainty, testify that they have separately known the corporal at three different places and that he has died in 1914 and in 1917. The supreme commander queries the three officers scornfully, but each refuses to surrender his own certainty or to deny the conviction of the other two. The English officer, taunted by the supreme commander as to whether he has not also seen the ghosts of Agincourt above the trenches, replies: "I'm sorry, sir, I've got to believe in something," a new version of the runner's need to believe in something or anything. The supreme commander summarizes his own attitude and contempt thus: ". . . one of our allies' officers . . . saw him slain . . . another buried him . . . so all that remains for us is to witness his resurrection." His irony is an assertion that he himself believes in nothing whatever, but that he expects others to assert foolish supernatural conviction with absolute certainty, now and henceforward. Here, as throughout, he speaks as one involved in a tragic masquerade of which he has foreknowledge, and in which, like an actor in a play he detests, he must play an assigned part conceived by another. In contrast to this nihilism, the officers' certainty that the corporal has died and returned among the living three times is their unwitting, intuitive expression of the necessity of such a being as Christ or the corporal every day, every week, every year. His perpetual death and return is a perpetual necessity.

But this need on the part of other human beings does not give the corporal a literal supernatural status, a point which Faulkner makes with the utmost emphasis in the last chapter, a year after the corporal's execution. The battalion runner has come to visit the corporal's sisters on their farm, and when the sister called Martha offers to show him the corporal's grave, the runner, refusing, says: "What for? He's finished." Martha is offended but Mary reassures her sister, telling her:

"He didn't mean it that way. He just means that brother did the best he could and now he doesn't need to worry any more." This is a kind of credo which neither denies nor affirms a belief in Christianity. So too, in the penultimate episode, when the corporal's body by mischance becomes that of the Unknown Soldier, the apotheosis is the corporal's ironic failure and yet, in a sense, his triumph. And then there is the brutality of the final scene, at the supreme commander's funeral, where the runner, kicked into unconsciousness by a French mob, recovers and laughs and says that he will never die: never. This affirmation is indomitable but desperate because he now has only one arm, leg, eye, and ear, and it inspires only tears in the one sympathetic character who is present.

The only true affirmation in the book is the corporal's "Don't be afraid." The only belief asserted without ambiguity is the belief that such a being as the corporal exists. But the reality of the corporal has endless implications. One important implication is that the test of any religious belief is such a person as the corporal, and no justifiable social or political movement can succeed without the help of such a person. Thus the chief reason for the Gospel parallel and one of the reasons that it is so successful is that the Gospel story represents the kind of a being who must exist if any aspiration is to be worthy of realization.

The question of the worth of man has profoundly troubled such peers of Faulkner as Malraux and T.S. Eliot. After the Second World War, Malraux observed that the chief question of the nineteenth century, Is God dead? had now become, in the twentieth century: Is Man dead? In a poem written after the First World War, T. S. Eliot wrote, "After such knowledge, what forgiveness?" a comment on human history which, in its context, was compelled by the same fundamental anxiety as Malraux expressed. But Malraux sought salvation in political action and Eliot in religious belief; Faulkner, however, believes that it must be found in man first of all.

It may be that this view is caused by a new desperation far more than by a new hope and belief in man. Throughout *A Fable* and above all at the climax of the book, the supreme commander uses the same words as Faulkner himself in his Stockholm speech in 1950 to an extent which verges upon self-quotation and with an intention which admits of a variety of interpretations, including self-mockery, self-criticism, and the assumption that if the devil can quote Scripture, a modern Satan can quote Faulkner. But whatever the intention, the speech itself rehearses the themes which have obsessed the novelist and inspired *A Fable*. The speech declares the novelist's belief that man will endure and prevail very much as the runner declares that he will never die, in a tone at once desperate and indomitable. In the same way, the novelist's speech asserts that other writers have been distracted from the themes of nobility, courage, pride, sacrifice, compassion and love by the terrifying question: "When will I be blown up?" Yet it is likely enough that the novelist's obsessed consciousness of this question (which is clearly an awareness of the atomic age) inspired the tormented hope and tragic recognition which make *A Fable* a masterpiece.

Notes

1 This story appeared in *Perspectives 9* under the title "Notes on a Horsethief."
2 Faulkner underscores the underlying meaning of the episode when the preacher and the groom share their religious beliefs during the period which must be called the passion of the horse: the groom makes the old Negro a

Mason, and the old preacher baptizes the groom into his own religious sect. There are further meaningful connections: the horse runs, though crippled; the runner "runs" toward belief; though crippled too, he is equally indomitable. One of the thieves who is shot with the corporal is named Horse and wants only to go to Paris, as the horse wants only to race. The groom, capable of complete self-sacrifice for the sake of the horse, is ruthless toward all human beings. And the preacher declares that he is a witness not to God, who needs none, but to man. Finally the horse is a natural symbol of the way in which the games and sports of American life provide objects of pure devotion and admiration: the chief reason is that in a country committed to a democratic ethos, the intrinsic skill of the individual attracts the greatest and most disinterested esteem and prestige.

Nathan A. Scott, Jr. "A Fable." *The Intercollegian*, February 1955, pp. 20–21.

The public was given a new book by Mr. William Faulkner a few months ago, and for our generation that is an event of considerable importance, for, since Henry James, his has been the most impressive talent at work in American fiction. He has, with the great European masters of fiction in our time—with Joyce, Proust, Kafka, and Lawrence—staked out as his own a part of the world inhabited by the modern imagination, and he has *added* something undisposable and permanent to the apparatus of our sensibilities, as only genius can.

When we think of it, this appears to be rather a remarkable achievement, for there is no major writer of our period who has remained more bound to place and to a body of purely local experience than Faulkner; and at a time when we have become an international people, and when our more important literature has therefore become, in a way, an international literature, it may at first strike us as a little curious that a writer who in the past has remained as stubbornly parochial as Faulkner should have become the source of so pervasive an influence. His story has been a story of the mythical kingdom that forms the landscape of his books and that he calls Yoknapatawpha County, Mississippi. He has offered this story as a legend not only of the patch of land in Mississippi in which he has his own familial roots but of all the Deep South; his myth has been the Southern myth which has as its subject the fate of a ravaged land. But his relation to this myth has, of course, been highly complicated, and it can by no means be responsibly construed as having yielded, on his part, any simple program of Southern apologetics. Indeed, the critical tactic that takes as its starting-point the notation of the Southern elements in Faulkner's writing itself involves considerable peril, since it may well betray us into an over-emphasis upon these aspects of his work—when, of course, actually, we must never forget that in *The Sound and the Fury*, in *As I Lay Dying*, in *Light in August*, and in *Absalom, Absalom!*, though his materials derive from the American South, Faulkner's essential comment is upon issues of human existence that are common to the modern world. The doomed and accursed place which is the scene of the dramatic action in these books is a scene through whose nocturnal glow we are expected to behold the scene of our own tragic time.

In recent years, however, Faulkner has shown signs of wanting to move beyond the confines of Yoknapatawpha County and into a more direct and immediate traffic with the contemporary world. He has

recently chosen, not alone on the occasion of his Nobel Prize Award speech, to deliver lay sermons about the nature of man and "the old verities and truths of the heart"—"love and honor and pity and pride and compassion and sacrifice," apart from an understanding of which we are, indeed, doomed. And the present book represents, I suppose, the latest culmination of this new tendency. The setting here is no longer the state of Mississippi but France, a few months before the end of the First World War, and the subject is the destiny of modern man, as seen under the aspect of Passion Week and the Crucifixion.

At the center of the story is an illiterate corporal in the French army (born in a stable on Christmas Day) who, together with his twelve men, persuades his entire regiment to disregard an order to attack. The overt act of mutiny is itself the culminating result of the long endeavors of this platoon to spread a gospel of peace not only amongst the Allied forces but also amongst the German enemy—though, curiously, the officers have been completely unaware of these developments. And once the regiment lays down its arms, the mutiny spreads contagiously, even to the Germans in the opposite trenches—so that, in a relatively short time, the entire front is quiet, the common soldiers on both sides of the conflict having themselves contrived their own uneasy peace.

The top brass in both the German and the Allied headquarters are deeply shaken by the whole affair, and after the corporal and his twelve followers have been thrown into jail, they hold a conference for the purpose of undertaking a collaborative effort against the uprising, for the soldiers in the ranks must not be allowed to suppose that war can be ended so simply. An attempt is made to strike a bargain with the corporal, his freedom being offered him on the condition that he repudiate

411

the whole revolt, thus placing his influence among his comrades in the service of military authority. The French marshal who is at the head of the Allied forces and who makes this offer does not really expect the corporal to accept it, nor does he want him to accept it, and both realize that the cause to which the corporal has borne witness can be effectively asserted only by his martyrdom.

So there is a last supper—this time held in a prison cell—and the re-enactment of the earlier drama moves inexorably through its final stages. There is a Judas, and there is one Piotr who denies the corporal. Two women, Marthe and Marya, wait silently for the end—which does finally come, when the corporal is thrown one Friday into a cell with two thieves and later is shot between them.

Here, then, is Mr. Faulkner's fable whose structure clearly indicates his intention to rehabilitate the drama of Christ as an archetypal drama disclosing the ultimate stratagem by which the human adventure is to be redeemed from futility and frustration. And, in the list of so serious and noble a purpose, one wishes that it might be possible to say that it has been successfully achieved, but the book is, I fear, the worst book that Faulkner has ever written—though, like such books as Melville's *Pierre* or Tolstoy's *Resurrection*, it never allows us to forget that it is the failure of a truly great writer.

The book is, of course, on the first level a political novel, and so it must be judged; and it is on this level that we are perhaps most embarrassed by its naiveté and ineptitude. His view of the War is incredibly simplistic: it is completely without meaning for its participants and is regarded as a vast and awful holocaust brought into being by means of a sinister conspiracy between the makers of armaments and the politicians and the top brass: the People are thus divested of all responsibility for the happenings of history which, when they take tragic turns, are, it appears, to be understood in the light of the nefarious machinations of the Conspirators.

Nor is the book any more impressive on the level of religious affirmation. This churlish, illiterate peasant who is Faulkner's Christic figure is hardly a believably charismatic personality and certainly doesn't begin to approach, in vividness and attractiveness, in spiritual grace and intellectual vigor (which is surely a necessary requirement for a Christic figure in literature) Ignazio Silone's Pietro Spina, who is perhaps the most impressive instance of the type in recent literature. All he can dumbly offer is the idea of resistance and the presentation of himself as a particular example of what Faulkner believes to be man's greatest capacity—the capacity to endure. The most radical imperative he is capable of voicing is only this: "Don't be afraid. There's nothing to be afraid of. Nothing is worth it."

Even this, of course—the ethic of resistance—might have been given an impressive incarnation in fiction had Faulkner hewn close to the line of his central narrative, telling it with the restraint and simplicity, say, with which M. Albert Camus treated a similar theme in *The Plague*. But he is so bent upon beating his story into life with the mechanical fury of his rhetoric that this theme is completely ravaged by the verbal pyrotechnics and the grating convolutions of syntax which seem in this book to function as a kind of tic, now quite beyond the author's control.

So let us not be intimidated by the impulse to be pious about the latest work of a distinguished writer—intimidated into accepting the publisher's claim in the jacket-blurb that here is a book that we shall soon have to acknowledge as "a classic" of modern literature. It is not that at all: let us rather, without making any cheap and easy predictions about what it portends about Faulkner's future as a writer, simply regard it as a great failure of our greatest novelist today.

Checklist of Additional Reviews

"*A Fable.*" *Kirkus*, July 1, 1954, p. 402.

"Faulkner Passion Play." *Time.* August 2, 1954, p. 76.

"Faulkner's Faults Evident in *Fable.*" Knoxville *News Sentinel*, August 8, 1954, p. 2-C.

"*A Fable* Best Faulkner Novel in a Decade." Erie *Times*, August 15, 1954, p. 10-E.

"Books New and Noticeable." Cleveland *Plain Dealer*, August 22, 1954, p. 53-D.

"William Faulkner's *A Fable* Slated to Be Recognized as One of Classics." Vallejo (Calif.) *Times-Herald*, August 29, 1954, p. 35.

"*A Fable.*" *Southern Observer* (Nashville), 2 (September 1954), 201.

"*A Fable.*" *Booklist*, September 1, 1954, pp. 14–15.

"*A Fable.*" *Wisconsin Library Bulletin*, 50 (October 1954), 506.

"A Fable." *U.S. Ouarterly Book Review*, 10 (December 1954), 506.

"Something New in the Book World." *The Tablet* (Catholic Press, Brooklyn).

Abernathy, Harry. "*A Fable* a Masterpiece? Faulkner, Critics Disagree." Clarksdale (Miss.) *Press-Register*, August 7, 1954, p. 2.

Allen, John F. "A New Faulkner." Carmel (Calif.) *Spectator*, August 6, 1954, pp. 3-D, 4-E.

B., R.H. "Jesus Transplanted." Durham *Morning Herald*, August 15, 1954, Section IV, p. 7.

Babcock, Frederick. "Among the Authors." Chicago *Sunday Tribune*, July 4, 1954, Magazine of Books, p. 4.

Baily, Angus. "Book of the Week." Fall River (Mass.) *Herald News*, August 3, 1954, p. 24.

Barley, Rex. "Faulkner Novel Disappointment." Los Angeles *Mirror*, July 30, 1954, Part II, p. 3.

Barry, Leslie. "*A Fable.*" Burlington (Vt.) *Sunday News*, August 15, 1954, p. 6.

Barth, J. Robert. "A Rereading of Faulkner's Fable." *America*, October 9, 1954, pp. 44–46.

Bedell, W. D. "Split Decision on Faulkner's *A Fable.*" Houston *Post*, August 1, 1954, Section V, p. 4.

Betts, Doris. "Today's Book Review." Chapel Hill *News Leader*, October 11, 1954.

Bivins, Dan. "Faulknerian Fable on Universals." *Daily Reveille* (Louisiana State Univ.), August 2, 1954.

Blackburn, F. M. "Faulkner's Fable Difficult, Great." Wichita *Daily Times* (Wichita Falls, Texas), August 29, 1954, p. 7-D.

Bond, Alice Dixon. "The Case for Books." Boston Sunday *Herald*, August 15, 1954, Section I, p. 7.

Bradley, Dwight J. "*A Fable.*" *Advance*, January 26, 1955, p. 15.

Bradley, John L. "*A Fable.*" Boston *Post*, August 8, 1954, p. 8-A.

Bradley, Van Allen. "Faulkner's *Fable* His Greatest Effort." Chicago *Daily News*, August 4, 1954, p. 16.

Brady, Charles A. "'*A Fable*' by Faulkner Has Surging Prose, but Fails on Theme." Buffalo *Evening News*, July 31, 1954, Section II, p. 7.

Breit, Harvey. "The Gospel according to Faulkner." *New Leader*, September 13, 1954, pp. 18–19.

Broaddus, Marion Howe. "*A Fable.*" El Paso *Times*, August 29, 1954, p. 8-C.

Burgess, Jackson. "Faulkner's *Fable.*"

413

Greensboro *Daily News*, August 8, 1954, Feature Section, p. 3.

Butler, G. Paul. "Faulkner Fable." New York *Sunday Mirror*, August 1, 1954, p. 32.

Cahoon, Herbert. *A Fable.*" *Library Journal*, 79 (August 1954), 1400.

Chamberlain, Dud, Jr. "*A Fable* Shows Vagaries of War." Columbus *Citizen*, September 19, 1954, Magazine Section, p. 15.

Chametzky, Jules. "Some Remarks on *A Fable.*" *Faulkner Studies*, 3 (Summer–Autumn 1954), 39–40.

Cheney, Frances Neel. "Faulkner's Fable." *Virginia Quarterly Review*, 30 (Autumn 1954), 623–26.

Coleman, Arthur L. "Faulkner's *Fable.*" San Antonio *Express and News*, August 8, 1954, p. 5-G.

Collier, Bert. "Faulkner's Fable Full of Debate." Miami *Herald*, August 1, 1954, p. 4-F.

Collins, Carvell. "War and Peace and Mr. Faulkner." *New York Times Book Review*, August 1, 1954, pp. 1, 13.

Coughlan, Robert. "Is *A Fable* William Faulkner's Masterpiece?" Chicago *Sun-Times*, August 1, 1954, Section II, p. 1.

Cross, Austin F. "*A Fable.*" Ottawa (Ontario) *Evening Citizen*, September 4, 1954, p. 17.

Dammarell, William J. "*A Fable.*" *National Catholic Monthly* (Chicago), October 1954.

Derleth, August. Faulkner Novel. Madison (Wis.) *Capital Times*, August 5, 1954, p. 14.

Donnelly, Tom. "Oh, What a Tangled Web Will Weaves." Washington *Daily News*, August 2, 1954, p. 29.

Durham, Frank. "Faulkner's *Fable* Is Noble as an Experiment, but Dull." Charleston (S.C.) *News and Courier*, September 19, 1954, p. 9-C.

Dwight, Ogden G. "Faulkner the Master Affirms Faith in His Great *Fable.*" Des Moines *Register*, August 1, 1954, p. 5-M.

Dwyer, Daniel N., S.J. "Faulkner's Latest Novel Parallels Incidents of Passion of Our Lord." *The Pilot* (Boston), August 21, 1954, p. 2.

Elconin, Victor A. "Faulkner Is Still Brooding." *Daily Oklahoman* (Oklahoma City), August 22, 1954, p. 20.

Emerson, William. "William Faulkner— after Ten Years, *A Fable.*" *Newsweek*, August 2, 1954, pp. 48–52.

Fairfax, Montgomery. "Faulkner Novel Has a Big Theme." *Army Times*, August 28, 1954, p. 5-M.

Flint, R. W. "What Price Glory?" *Hudson Review*, 7 (Winter 1955), 602–6.

Flowers, Paul. "Faulkner Addicts May Hail *Fable* but Casual Readers May Be Bored." Memphis *Commercial Appeal*, August 1, 1954, Section V, p. 12.

Fretz, Gene. "Confusion and Faulkner: *A Fable* Is a Baffling Book." *Arkansas Gazette* (Little Rock), August 1, 1954, p. 6-F.

G., M. Wichita *Beacon*, August 1, 1954.

Gannett, Lewis. "*A Fable.*" New York *Herald Tribune*, August 2, 1954, p. 13.

Gardiner, Harold C. "William Faulkner's *A Fable.*" *America*, August 21, 1954, p. 502.

Geismar, Maxwell. "Latter-Day Christ Story." *Saturday Review*, July 31, 1954, pp. 11–12.

Gill, Brendan. "Fifth Gospel." *New Yorker*, August 28, 1954, pp. 78–80.

Glackin, William C. "The New Faulkner Novel Hits Home with Plea for Peace, Good Will in Men." Sacramento *Bee*, September 4, 1954, p. 18.

Glenn, Taylor. "*A Fable.*" Bridgeport *Sunday Post*, August 1, 1954, p. 4-B.

Govan, Gilbert E. "Faulkner's Ambitious Bid Falls Short of Its Mark." Chattanooga *Times*, August 22, 1954, p. 16.

Grady, R. F., S.J. "*A Fable.*" *Best Sellers* (Scranton), September 1, 1954, pp. 1–2.

Harding, Walter. "Faulkner's *Fable* Is His Finest Work." Richmond *News Leader*, August 4, 1954, p. 11.

Hart, Robert A. "Faulkner's Involved Style Well Suited to War Prose." Indianapolis *Star*, August 8, 1954, Section II, p. 3.

Hass, Victor P. "From a Bookman's Notebook." Omaha *World Herald*, July 4, 1954, Magazine Section, p. 20.

Hayes, E. Nelson. "Recent Novels." *Progressive*, November 1954, pp. 40–41.

Herzberg, Max. "Faulkner's *Fable* May Stir Warm Discussion." Newark (N.J.) *Sunday News*, August 1, 1954, Section III, p. 2.

Highet, Gilbert. "Sound and Fury." *Harper's Magazine*, September 1954, pp. 98–104.

Hillestad, Paul C. "The Month in Books." *Athletic Club Events* (St. Paul), September 1954.

Howe, Irving. "Thirteen Who Mutinied: Faulkner's First World War." *Reporter*, September 14, 1954, pp. 43–45.

Hughes, Riley. "*A Fable.*" *Catholic World*, 180 (November 1954), 150.

Hunter, Anna C. "Events of Passion Week Are Symbols for Faulkner Novel." Savannah *Morning News*, August 1, 1954, p. 46.

Hurley, Doran. "*A Fable.*" *The Sign*, August 1954, p. 61.

Hutter, Trent. "A Revolutionary Novel." *Fourth International*, 16 (Summer 1955), 105.

Hyde, Frederic G. "Faulkner Pens an Indictment of War in a Modern Parable." Philadelphia *Inquirer*, August 1, 1954, p. 10-C.

Imes, Cristel Hurst. "All the Flaws, Virtues Found in 'Masterwork.'" Columbus *Dispatch*, August 8, 1954, p. 14.

Jessup, Lee Cheney. "Man's Inevitable Triumph." Nashville *Banner*, August 6, 1954, p. 26.

Jones, Carter Brooke. "New Faulkner Novel Is Parable Against Futile Waste of War." Washington *Sunday Star*, August 1, 1954, p. 11-C.

Justice, Blair. "Man's Survival Theme of Faulkner's 'Fable.'" Fort Worth *Star-Telegram*, August 1, 1954, Section II, p. 7.

K., W. J. "Faulkner Ponders Man, Good and Evil." Rochester *Democrat and Chronicle*, September 19, 1954, p. 7-F.

Kass, Bob. "Best Sellers." Radio broadcast on WFW-FM, August 9, 1954 (copy in Random House files).

Kelley, William P. "Man-Battleground and Mediator of the Cosmos." *Brown Daily Herald Book Review* (Brown Univ.), January 14, 1955, p. 1.

Kennedy, Gerald. "Browsing through the Fiction." *The Pastor*, April 1955, p. 36.

Kenner, Hugh. "Book Reviews." *Shenandoah*, 6 (Spring 1955), 44–53.

Kervin, Roy. "Shadow of a Cross." Montreal *Gazette*, August 14, 1954, p. 20.

Kincheloe, H. G. "Reviewer Dislikes Faulkner's *Fable.*" Raleigh *News and Observer*, August 22, 1954, Section IV, p. 5.

Kippax, H. G. "A Modern Version of Christ's Passion." Sydney (Australia) *Morning Herald*, September 11, 1954, p. 10.

Klein, Francis A. "*A Fable.*" St. Louis *Globe-Democrat*, August 1, 1954, p. 8-F.

Laggard, Gerald. "Fable Born of

Travail." Long Beach *Independent-Press-Telegram*, August 15, 1954, Southland Magazine, p. 24.

Laycock, Edward A. "He's Sound and Fury." Boston *Sunday Globe*, August 1, 1954, p. 5-A.

Leaming, Delmar. "Midwestern Book Shelf." Newton (Iowa) *Daily News*, December 4, 1954, p. 4.

Leigh, Micheal. "Books and Authors." Pensacola (Fla.) *News Journal*, August 8, 1954, Section II, p. 4.

Lucchese, Sam F. "A Bore, a 'Chore to Read.'" Atlanta *Journal-Constitution*, August 1, 1954, p. 6-F.

M., A. "The Corporal Had Twelve Disciples." Winnipeg (Manitoba) *Free Press*, September 18, 1954, p. 28.

M., C.J. "Faulkner's Folly." Chicago *Sunday Tribune*, August 8, 1954, Magazine of Books, p. 1.

Maner, William L. "Faulkner Has Traveled Far since *Sanctuary*." Richmond *Times-Dispatch*, August 15, 1954, p. 5-F.

Mankel, Siegfried. "William Faulkner on Man's 'Love of Bloodshed.'" *Newsday*, July 31, 1954, p. 3.

Mason, Jack. "*Fable* Labor of Love for Author and for Most of Its Readers." Oakland *Tribune*, September 5, 1954, p. 44-A.

McCarthy, David. "Faulkner's Novel Reaffirms Faith." Charleston (S.C.) *Evening Post*, July 30, 1954, p. 7–B.

McCarthy, John Russell. "Faulkner's *Fable*." Pasadena *Star-News*, August 15, 1954, p. 27.

McCaslin, Walt. "Faulknerian Fable Probes Idea of Man's Redemption." Dayton *Daily News*, August 1, 1954, Section II, p. 7.

McGill, Ralph. "Faulkner's Cry for Compassion." Atlanta *Constitution*, August 10, 1954, p. 1.

McLaughlin, Richard. "Faulkner Forsakes South for French Locale of 1918." Springfield (Mass.) *Sunday Republican*, August 22, 1954, p. 5-C.

McManis, John. "Faulkner Lets Fame Trip Him." Detroit *News*, August 1, 1954, p. 6-B.

Mercier, Vivian. "A Search for Universality that Led Too Far from Home." Commonweal, August 6, 1954, pp. 443–44.

Merlin, Milton. "Striking Biblical Parable Seen in Faulkner's *Fable*." Los Angeles *Times*, August 15, 1954, Section IV, p. 6.

Mims, Puryear. "Faulknerian Version of Christ Story." Nashville *Tennessean*, August 1, 1954, p. 22-C.

Murray, Don. "Faulkner Novel Heroic Attempt." Boston *Herald*, August 23, 1954, p. 6.

Muste, A. J. "War the Enemy." *Fellowship*, December 1954, pp. 23–24.

Naeseth, Henriette C. K. "Passion Story Rephrased by Faulkner." Davenport (Iowa) *Times-Democrat*, August 1, 1954, Section II, p. 19.

Norris, Hoke. "Flesh, Blood, and Bones: *A Fable* from Faulkner." Winston-Salem *Journal and Sentinel*, August 1, 1954, p. 5-C.

O'Bryant, Arch. "Faulkner's *Fable* Is Seen as Modern Biblical Parallel." Wichita *Eagle*, August 8, 1954, Feature Magazine, p. 12.

O'Dell, Scott. "Fables by Faulkner." Los Angeles *Daily News*, August 9, 1954, p. 16.

O'Leary, Theodore M. "Faulkner's Anti-War Novel." Kansas City *Star*, August 7, 1954, p. 16.

O'Neill, Frank. "Faulkner 'Vote' Is Mostly Nay." Cleveland *News*, September 7, 1954, p. 7.

P., C.L. "*A Fable*." *Florida Times-Union* (Jacksonville), October 3, 1954, p. 51.

P., E.L. "*A Fable*." *Arizona Republic* (Phoenix), September 12, 1954,

Arizona Days and Ways, p. 21.

Parsons, Eugene O. "He Struggled to Write It: We Struggle to Read It." Worcester (Mass.) *Sunday Telegram*, August 1, 1954, p. 7-D.

Past, Ray. "*A Fable.*" El Paso *Herald Post*, August 28, 1954, Section II, p. 10.

Paulding, Gouverneur. "A Note in Rejoinder." *Reporter*, September 14, 1954, pp. 45–46.

Peckham, Stanton. "Is It Ever Hard to Read!" Denver *Post*, August 8, 1954, Roundup Section, p. 19.

Perkin, Robert L. "Faulkner's Greatest?" *Rocky Mountain News* (Denver), August 8, 1954, p. 52.

Pettigrew, Richard. "Faulkner's Latest Is Amazingly Different from Those of Past." Birmingham *News*, August 1, 1954, p. 6-E.

Pickrel, Paul. "Outstanding Novels." *Yale Review*, 44 (Autumn 1954), viii-xii.

Portuondo, José Antonio. "The Brush of Faulkner." *Américas*, January 1955, pp. 40–41.

Price, Emerson. "*A Fable.*" Cleveland *Press*, August 3, 1954; May 10, 1955, p. 24.

Rascoe, Burton. "The Truth about Faulkner's *Fable*" *Literary Journal*, August 8, 1954.

Raymund, Bernard. "*A Fable.*" *Arizona Quarterly*, 10 (Winter 1954), 361–63.

Ready, W. B. "A Work of Genius—Perhaps Even a Classic." *Books on Trial* (Chicago), October 1954, p. 9.

Reed, Doris T. "Great Power, True Beauty in This Novel." Dayton *Journal-Herald*, August 7, 1954, p. 22.

Reynolds, Horace. "Dramatizing a Misconception." *Christian Science Monitor*, August 5, 1954, p. 11.

Rice, Philip Blair. "Faulkner's Crucifixion." *Kenyon Review*, 16 (Autumn 1954), 661–70.

Richards, Robert. "Faulkner's Faith in Fellow Man Shows in His *Fable.*" Memphis *Press-Scimitar*, August 14, 1954, p. 4.

Ritchie, Elisavietta. "Faulkner Masterpiece." San Francisco *Aragonaut*, August 13, 1954, p. 18.

Rogers, W. G. "Nobel Prize Not in This." Omaha *World Herald*, August 8, 1954, Magazine Section, p. 25.

Rolo, Charles J. "Reader's Choice." *Atlantic Monthly,* September 1954, pp. 79–80.

Rubin, Harold. "Faulkner at Brilliant Best in Novel of World War I." New Orleans *Times-Picayune*, August 1, 1954, Section II, p. 4.

Rubin, Louis D., Jr. "Faulkner's *Fable.*" Baltimore *Evening Sun*, August 5, 1954, p. 28.

Russell, H. K. "Faulkner Novel is 'Important.'" Charlotte *Observer*, August 8, 1954, p. 12-C.

Russell, Robert. "Faulkner's 'Good Friday' Fable." *Jubilee*, October 1954, pp. 52, 54.

S., D.T. "That Man Will Prevail Is Faulkner's New Theme." Columbia *Missourian*, October 11, 1954, p. 4.

Sampson, Paul. "Faulkner's *Fable* Packs Power." Washington *Post and Times-Herald*, August 1, 1954, p. 6-B.

Shedd, Margaret. "Passion Week Paralleled in New Faulknerian Fable." *Mexico News Weekly*, August 15, 1954, p. 2-B.

Sherman, John K. "Faulkner Echoes Christ's Passion in War Novel." Minneapolis *Star-Tribune*, August 8, 1954, Feature Section, p. 6.

Sherman, Thomas B. "A Novel of Tremendous Magnitude." St. Louis *Post-Dispatch*, August 1, 1954, p. 4-E.

S[mith], B[lanche] H[ixson]. "*A Fable.*" Meriden (Conn.) *Record*, August 17, 1954, p. 6.

Smith, Norman. "Basic Conflicts in

417

Faulkner's *Fable*." *Bharat Jyoti* (Bombay), Independence Day, 1954.

Spearman, Walter. "New for Faulkner." Rocky Mount (N.C.) *Sunday Telegram*, August 8, 1954, p. 2-B.

Spicehandler, Miriam. "*A Fable*." *Justice*.

Tawes, Roy Lawson. "Religion in Books." Wilmington (N.C.) *Morning News*, September 4, 1954, p. 26.

Theall, D. Bernard. "Faulkner Allegory Falls Flat." *Catholic Standard and Times*, August 13, 1954, p. 13.

Thomas, Walt. "Faulkner Worked Nine Years to Turn Out Latest Book." *Oregon Sunday Journal* (Portland), September 5, 1954, p. 11-M.

Tinkle, Lon. "Faulkner's Vision of Moral World." Dallas *Morning News*, August 1, 1954, Part V, p. 8; and "Faulkner's 'Emotional Incident': Or, a Rose IS; a Rose Is a Rose," August 8, 1954, Part V, p. 8.

Tunstall, Caroline. "Faulkner's New Novel a Diatribe Against War." Norfolk *Virginian-Pilot*, August 1, 1954, Part III, p. 10.

Turner, Decherd. "A 'Work on the Agony and Sweat of the Human Spirit.'" Dallas *Times Herald*, August 1, 1954, Section VIII, p. 2.

Vogler, Lewis. "*A Fable* by William Faulkner Is Called His Greatest Work." San Francisco *Chronicle*, August 8, 1954, This World Section, p. 18.

W., E. "*A Fable*." Auburn (N.Y.) *Citizen Advertiser*, July 31, 1954, p. 4.

W., H. "*A Fable*." *American Scholar*, 24 (Winter 1955), 125.

Wagner, Charles A. "Books." New York *Sunday Mirror*, August 22, 1954, Home Edition, p. 8.

Watkins, Walter. "*A Fable*." *Guide to Current Reading* (Laurel, Miss.), 1 (August 1954), 1–4.

Watts, Richard, Jr. "Random Notes on This and That." New York *Post*, August 17, 1954, p. 21.

W[eissblatt], H[arry] A. "Faulkner." Trenton *Sunday Times-Advertiser*, August 8, 1954, p. 10.

Wetterberg, David. "*A Fable*." *Quarterly—University of Massachusetts*, Spring 1955, pp. 37–38.

Williams, Ernest E. "Faulkner's *Fable* of World War I Is Allegory of Christ's Crucifixion." Fort Wayne *News-Sentinel*, July 31, 1954, p. 4.

Wilson, W. Emerson. "*A Fable*." Wilmington (N.C.) *Morning News*, August 2, 1954, p. 11.

Wobbe, James A. "The Fury 'Lay Dying.'" New Orleans *Item*, August 8, 1954, p. 27.

Wyrick, Green D. "*A Fable*." Topeka *Daily Capital*, January 9, 1955, p. 5-C.

Yeiser, Frederick. "Some of the Recent Fiction." Cincinnati *Enquirer*, August 1, 1954, Section IV, p. 9.

Zailian, Marian. "William Faulkner's *Fable* Complex Novel of Humanity." San Rafael (Calif.) *Independent-Journal*, October 30, 1954, p. 2-M.

Zaiman, Jack. "The Twelve and One." Hartford *Courant*, August 8, 1954, Magazine Section, p. 18.

Zink, Karl E. "Faulkner, Tortuous yet Exciting Reading." Gary *Post-Tribune*, January 22, 1955, p. 2.

BIG WOODS

BIG WOODS

BY WILLIAM FAULKNER

DECORATIONS BY Edward Shenton

RANDOM HOUSE · NEW YORK

Lewis Gannett.
"Big Woods."
New York *Herald Tribune,*
October 14, 1955, p. 27.

This is Mr. Faulkner's hymn to the Mississippi he has lived and loved. The dust-jacket calls the book "The Hunting Stories of William Faulkner." Indeed, it consists of two of Mr. Faulkner's finest stories, "The Bear" and "The Old People," somewhat rewritten, which appeared in *"Go Down, Moses"* in 1942 and have been often reprinted since; of "A Bear Hunt," which appeared in *Dr. Martino* in 1934, and of a new story, "Race at Morning," which carries on into old age the saga of Ike McCaslin, hunter. But, put together with new connective tissue—story, legend, poetry and memory—it is something new. It is Mr. Faulkner's fabulous Old Testament.

"It was his native land," the old man meditates who was young in the first of the stories. "He had been born in it, and his bones would sleep in it . . . the hills along whose edge the plantation lay where he had been born and where old Sam Fathers, son of a Negro slave and a Chickasaw king, had trained and taught him how to use a gun with care and respect, in order to be worthy to enter the Big Woods when the time came."

The Big Woods had been the wilderness where nameless Indian tribes built mounds and buried their dead; home for tribe after tribe which gave way to the white men who first came in a Chippewa canoe; "owned" for a time by Frenchman, Spaniard and Anglo-Saxon, "the tall man, roaring with Protestant scripture and boiled whisky"; also home to "the strong, irritable, loud-reeking bear, the gallant high-headed stags looking longer than comets and pale as smoke, the music-ed and untiring dogs and the splattered horses and the men who rode them"; and to small boys proud in the knowledge that old men had faith in them.

The Big Woods were, are, being pushed back by the lumber mills and the cotton seed and the paved roads. And beyond the inviolable hills and the violable woods was "the great invincible almost inattentive river . . . piling up the water while white man and Negro worked side by side in shifts in the mud and the rain, with automobile headlights and gasoline flares and kegs of whisky and coffee boiling in fifty-gallon batches in scoured and scalded oil drums; lapping, tentative, almost innocently, merely inexorable (no hurry, his) among and beneath and between and finally over the frantic sandbays," while in the flotsam on the levees "the young continued to be born and the old to die . . . as if man and his destiny were in the end stronger even than the river."

But *Big Woods* is, after all, a series of stories, not primarily a statement of a philosophy. It may be significant that Mr. Faulkner has here chosen to omit the much-discussed moralistic section of the original version of "The Bear," which has so often been called his finest story; that he has omitted various other hunting stories from this collection, and retold, in his prologue, interludes and epilogues, fragments of others. It may well be argued that Mr. Faulkner, beginning with an old man, half Indian, half slave, communicating his woods lore to the boy who in his last story is himself old and a legend to the young, is saying something about the continuity of tradition in the midst of superficial change. Does it matter?

To attempt to analyze and define the philosophy behind Mr. Faulkner's stories has always been as thankless a task as to attempt to distill the pure colors of the rainbow. It has been tried many times and produced various answers. The whole remains greater than the sum of any analyzable parts. The important fact is that Mr. Faulkner has here assembled and retold some of his finest stories, with the emotional intensity that is his special gift and a simplicity which he has not always chosen to exhibit. "Big Woods" is Faulkner at his best.

Peter Grevas.
"Faulkner—Forever Faulkner."
Davenport (Iowa) *Democrat Times*, October 15, 1955, Features Section, p. 25.

Out comes a new book by an author of importance, and out come the "hatchet men" ready to do bloody battle. But contrary to popular opinion, critics would much rather lay their weapons to the ground and praise a good piece of work. They are seldom wrong in their collective evaluation.

When Ernest Hemingway's not-so-good *Across the River and into the Trees* hit the book stalls, the reviewers carried hatchets in both hands and managed to do a little kicking on the side. Only one notable, Malcolm Cowley, was brave enough to stand up for "Papa." He not only laid his tools to the ground, he buried them while uttering "Papa" was the greatest writer since Shakespeare.

But then, periodically, along comes the

writer William Faulkner with a new epic which invariably throws the whole critical world into paradoxical dither. He is stalked by the most diverse group of critics since James Joyce's *Ulysses* hit Judge Woolsey's U.S. District Court in the early '30's.

To be sure, some come after Faulkner brandishing two hatchets, but often as not, their feet drag a bit. Others come with a hatchet in one hand and a divining rod in the other; and still others with open arms and naked as the day is long. And often there's quite a bit of perceptible bickering amongst the group.

Meanwhile, back at the plantation in Oxford, Miss., Faulkner sits in his own literary holy see, upheld by the Nobel Prize for Literature, the Pulitzer honor and the National Book Award and his own indomitable feeling that he's a pretty darn good writer.

It is our purpose here not to praise Faulkner, nor to bury him. That chore is much better left to those whose business is scholarship in literature.

This week, an anthology of Faulkner's hunting stories called *Big Woods* appears. The stories are entitled "The Bear," "The Old People," "A Bear Hunt," and "Race At Morning." All of them have been published before in one form or another. Each of them is introduced by long poetic preludes, and the final story is followed by an epilogue.

Those hoping to find a departure from the Faulkneresque characters, the unbelievably glued together syntax, the extensive genealogy of the characters, enough to make one's head swim, or a county and state other than Jefferson, Miss., won't find it here.

But that is not to say there is not much worth reading because, as always, the stories are laden with good things. Save for the lapses in which Mr. Faulkner might decide to beat to death the genealogy of his main characters, or present in astounding brevity (it doesn't seem brief) what leads up to the "kill" of a buck or bear, and this entails history from back to the days of slavery and the Old South, a story definitely emerges that is not only memorable it is compelling. And it is graphic beyond any fiction written today.

The *Big Woods* stories concern the "youth" and the "kill," the first shot, the warm blood of the animal; the aura of the Old South today—proud, but quiet.

Faulkner demands perhaps more from the reader than any writer has a right to ask. The reader gleans what he can. And what he gleans is what is the finest in our literature.

Coleman Rosenberger. "Four Faulkner Hunting Stories, Rich in Narrative and Symbol." New York *Herald Tribune*, October 16, 1955, pp. 1, 16.

In the world of William Faulkner, in life and in fiction, the camp in the big woods has a cherished if subordinate place. When the announcement came in 1950 that Faulkner had been awarded the Nobel Prize for literature, an enterprising reporter found him taking his turn as the camp dishwasher at the annual deer hunt near Anguilla, Mississippi. In Faulkner's mythical Yoknapatawpha County, the "Hunting and fishing camp where Wash Jones killed Sutpen: Later owned by Major de Spain," as he designated the camp on a map which he once drew, lies on a bend in the Tallahatchie River which forms one of the boundaries of his land of the imagination.

Big Woods brings together four of Faulkner's hunting stories from this corner of Yoknapatawpha, "The Bear," "The Old People," "A Bear Hunt" and "Race at Morning," and joins them with evocative passages. The first three of the stories are well known; "Race at Morning" has not previously been published.

When "The Bear" (which Robert Penn Warren has called a "profoundly symbolic story," and whose symbolism has had much critical exegesis) was included a decade ago in Malcolm Cowley's *The Portable Faulkner*, Cowley wrote of it: "It is divided into five parts. If you want to read simply a hunting story, and one of the greatest in the language, you should confine yourself to the first three parts and the last. . . ." It would appear to be something unique in the way of an author's tribute to a critic's perception that the story as Faulkner now publishes it consists only of the first three parts and the last.

In "The Bear," when the hunt's "yearly pageant-rite of the old bear's furious immortality" finally comes to an end under Boon Hogganbeck's knife, and young Isaac McCaslin is sixteen, the frontier is already passing.

It is Isaac McCaslin's fortune to come of age before it wholly passed. "The Old People" is the moving story of the boy's first deer, under the tutelage of Sam Fathers, son of a Negro slave and a Chickasaw chief. In initiation Sam stood over the boy's kill and "dipped his hands in the hot smoking blood and wiped them back and forth across the boy's face," and later led him to see the great phantom buck which the elder McCaslin, too, had once seen after he had killed his first deer.

"A Bear Hunt" is the slightest of the stories here, hardly more than an extended anecdote, told by the sewing-machine agent, Ratliff. If concerns one of the sons of the hunter Boon Hogganbeck and how, with fright, he was cured of the hiccups, and the mild, twenty-year delayed revenge of the Negro Ash was accomplished. It must be noted, for those who would keep straight the dramatis personae of Yoknapatawpha, that when "A Bear Hunt" was published in the *Collected Stories of William Faulkner*, the principal character was Lucius Provine of the Provine gang. Lucius Provine has here been metamorphosed into Lucius Hogganbeck, a transmutation not unique in the Faulkner legend.

Faulkner's new "Race at Morning" is a delightful story of a new generation of the hunter and the fresh wonder of the recurring world of youth. It is narrated by a new character, the nameless ("I don't need to write my name down," I said. "I can remember in my mind who I am.") twelve-year-old ward of Mister Ernest. Isaac McCaslin is now Uncle Ike, past eighty, the oldest man in camp. The world has changed. But to the boy, in his two November weeks in camp, the race is still at morning, the "pageant-rite" has its old power.

The virtues of Faulkner's hunters prevail and endure.

But only in part and perhaps only in the very young and very old. The last word of *Big Woods* is a monologue by the old hunter, who was Isaac McCaslin and is now Uncle Ike. He sees the rifle put aside for the slaughter of the shotgun's blind handful of pellets, the deer brought in on a tarpaulin, and he broods on the ravaged woods and the devastated game: "This land, said the old hunter. No wonder the ruined woods I used to know don't cry for retribution. The very people who destroyed them will accomplish their revenge."

Lee Cheney Jessup. "Power, Poignancy Mark Hunting Tales." Nashville *Banner*, October 28, 1955, p. 28.

This is the twenty-sixth book to go to press under the name of William Faulkner and, in my judgment, if it was his only contribution it would entitle him to his present high place in American literature. Under the sub-title "Hunting Stories," this is a collection of three long short-stories published before and one new one, with a long prelude before each one and the final one followed by an epilogue. Evocations of the scene and mood of the individual tales are profoundly moving and memorable tributes to both the hunters and the hunted. Bound together through such a medium, these fine tales take on a new continuity, presenting a pattern of life to be forever cherished and preserved, indelibly imprinted upon the minds and hearts of the reader through the exquisite beauty of word and concept.

In this slender volume is all the power of description, the richness of life, the poignancy of expression that Faulkner at his best produces. The quality of his imagination and the sensitive regard with which he writes can come only from a complete understanding and deep love of his subject; and that subject is—for Faulkner—first and always, the South. In the words of old Ike McCaslin, "this land, this South, for which God has done so much, with woods for game and streams for fish and deep rich soil for seed and lush springs to sprout it and long summers to mature it and serene falls to harvest it and short mild winters for men and animals," Faulkner speaks his own feelings; and in these tales of great simplicity and merit he proves his thesis.

The four stories are "The Bear"—a magnificent saga of the killing of "Old Ben," "The Old People"—the momentous event in a boy's life when he kills his first deer, "The Bear Hunt," a hunting episode of frontier humor, and "Race at Morning," a traditional chase of an old man and a boy for a buck who outwits them, leaving another hunting season in the future. In all four tales there is interrelation of characters and scenes, and each contributes its part toward the unity of the thesis as a whole. Each, however, is a separate and highly individual story in itself and can be enjoyed as such. And to any who loves a good hunt, woods in the morning, nature in all its beauty, the South—past or present—I recommend this book!

Mr. Faulkner needs no identification from this reviewer. He is the most distinguished and controversial American writer of today. Born and bred in the South, he has written indefatigably about her life and her problems. Some twenty or more novels and many short stories have come from his pen which have achieved for him world-wide recognition. The highest literary honor—the Nobel Prize—has been awarded him but he has not rested on his laurels as the superb quality of his latest production proves.

Carlos Baker. "Happy Hunting Grounds." *Nation*, October 29, 1955, pp. 365–66.

Faulkner and Hemingway, America's two Nobel-prize winners in the field of fiction, would both rather hunt than eat, provided they can eat after hunting, and write about it a little later on. Their work is never so idyllic, so nostalgic, so full of a sense of the good earth's teeming poison, her unremitting plenitude, as when they speak of the pursuit of game among the mountains, the streams, and the big woods from Africa to Michigan, to the far west, or down in the rich delta of the state of Mississippi.

The idyllic quality arises from their evident belief in the nobility, bravery, and mystery of the wild creatures who serve as quarry, or on another plane, as totems; and from their love of the mode of life which the pursuit of game engenders and fosters—excitement, endurance, humility, humor, rough comradeship or rivalry among men who share the vacation spirit, the sense of pastoral renewal in the primitive conditions of tent camp or hunting lodge. The nostalgia comes from the shared convictions of both writers that the happy hunting-grounds are fast vanishing, swallowed up or cut down by the onslaughts of materialist civilization, so that this last of the frontiers grows steadily farther and farther away. In sundry ways, but chiefly through the machinations of the lumbermen and the land grabbers, the idol of Mammon is inexorably banishing the idyll of the Big Woods. All things are a flowing, all good things are going, runs the rhyme. Among these are the wilderness where game still abounds, where nature still natures, where men may go for annual rest and for refreshment, including Bourbon.

This double sense of the value of the hunting-grounds and their imminent final destruction is what gives Faulkner's hunting stories, now assembled in a single handsome volume, their considerable emotional impact. But this is only one side, the upper side, of the total effect. Under the surface opposition stretches the vaster ground of Faulkner's moral and metaphysical belief: that the destroyer, whether hunter or waster, ultimately defeats himself, and that his destruction has been implicit in the scheme of things since the Creation. Faulkner's hunter-philosopher Ike McCaslin recognizes the double aspect of the ethical and metaphysical problem. His argument almost seems to combine Plato's myth of the creation with the thoughts of the Pentateuch on man's freedom of choice and his accursed capacity to choose wrongly. God made the Eden-like wilderness for man's use and enjoyment. Owing to the basic recalcitrance of things, God did not wholly succeed in creating man in the ideal image, but He granted man both power and free will. "I reckon," says Ike McCaslin, that God said, "I will give him a chance. I will give him warning and foreknowledge too, along with the desire to follow and the power to slay. The woods and the fields he ravages and the game he devastates will be the consequence and signature of his crime and guilt, and his punishment." So McCaslin on man's choice. And on man's fate: "No wonder the ruined woods I used to know don't cry for retribution. The very people who destroyed them will accomplish their revenge." For the destroyers are already accomplishing, by and upon themselves, the vengeance the woods might seek if it were possible or necessary. Implicit in the very act of destruction are the seeds which, growing up, will destroy the destroyer.

The four tales and five interludes which make up the present volume have all appeared before in one form or another. The tales are "The Bear," "The Old People," "Bear Hunt," and "Race at Morning." The last of these is a new story, first published last March in the *Saturday Evening Post*. Three of the interludes are extracts, considerably revised, from the short stories "Red Leaves," "A Justice,"

and "Delta Autumn." The other two, on the state of Mississippi and its great river, are made over from the *Holiday* magazine article of April, 1954. Out of this apparent diversity, Faulkner and his editor have achieved a real unity, both of theme and development. By dint of rearrangement, rewriting, and the new emphases produced by the modifications and interactions which each of the tales and interludes exerts upon the others, the book emerges as a fresh entity, a piece of huge acreage of Faulkner's heart never fully visible, because never surveyed and ridden over in quite this way before.

The book has both range and concentration. The range is in time, the slow swing of the seasons from November round to November, the deliberate spiral down the years from reconstruction to modern times. When General Compson and Major De Spain vanish from the scene, a new generation is prepared to make, as eagerly as ever, the annual autumnal pilgrimage to the big woods. And over their shoulders other generations still to come, as over De Spain's shoulder the old ghosts of the Chickasaws move through the flickering woods. Boon Hogganbeck and his dog Lion may kill the legendary bear. But other creatures as noble and as elusive will arise, like the huge stag in "Race at Morning" with a set of antlers like a rocking chair. If they survive this November, all the better. "Which would you rather have?" cries the hunter to the tyro. "His bloody head and hide on the kitchen floor yonder and half his meat in a pick-up truck on the way to Yoknapatawpha County, or him with his head and hide and meat still together over yonder in that brake, waiting for next November for us to run him again?" The bear and the buck are the concentrators, unkillable, though killed; the spirits of this solitude, the unvanquishable geniuses of this place. That is why Ike McCaslin, who begins hunting

426

on the under side of twenty, is still going back, as to a class reunion, when he has reached the upper side of eighty. For the forest is a timeless place arrested in the flux of time.

It is a grace note in a fine book that Edward Shenton has done the handsome decorations, as he did twenty years ago for Hemingway's *Green Hills of Africa*. For those who remain, even in the face of these delights, epithet to the genre of the hunting-story, the words of Boon Hogganbeck may be pertinent: "Them that's going, get in the goddamn wagon. Them that ain't, get out of the goddamn way."

Harrison Smith. "Lament for the Forest." *Saturday Review*, October 29, 1955, p. 16.

There can be few men, whether or not they have ever hunted with rifle and dogs, who would not be stirred by the four epic tales of William Faulkner in Random House's collection of his hunting stories, "The Bear," "The Old People," "A Bear Hunt," and his latest, "Race at Morning." All of these four stories are based on two major themes: the tenacious need of men to destroy at the risk of their own lives the bear or the stag at bay, and a bitter lament for the wilderness which once sheltered them but which has now been ravaged in only two generations—"this land where white men rent farms and live like niggers and Negroes crop on shares and live like animals."

André Gide said of Faulkner long ago that there is not one of his characters who has a soul. But it should be obvious that many of his characters certainly have a soul as well as a sense of responsibility. Certainly this is true of the hunters in this collection, who year after year track down the giant bear, then let him live, scarred though he is with the teeth of dogs he had killed and with lead slugs from old battles under his hide, until they know his time has come for his last battle. Is it not better, Faulkner seems to ask, for the bear and the stag to die fighting against their enemies than to perish of hunger or senescence in the diminishing forest?

"I decline to accept the end of man—man will not only endure but prevail," Mr. Faulkner said in his memorable Stockholm speech; but in the prefaces to each of these stories and in the epilogue to "Race at Morning" he infers that while man is doubtless endurable he can also look forward to an existence that may not be worth living. At least in Faulknerian terms it may not be worth living in a world without a wilderness, with its rivers tamed, with its wild animals gone, and with the only dangers left being the diseases and wars to which man is heir.

Big Woods is, in a sense, a memorial to the courage of the hunters which Mr. Faulkner brings back to memory. It is a collection of tales which have been told to him or which his genius has created. "The old," he writes, "had innocent tumultuous eupeptic tomorrowless days, now obsolete, when men were without bowels for avarice or compassion or forethought either, changing the face of the earth, felling a tree which took two hundred years to grow, in order to extract from it a bear or a capful of wild honey."

The boy of these stories, in which Faulkner's readers will find familiar names, is sixteen, and there is a mongrel puppy, Lion, who in the end brings death to Old Ben, the monstrous bear. The boy had listened during the yearly expeditions to the forest to tales of the big woods and of the vanished Indians and of the Civil War and of the disappearance of old steamboats from the Mississippi. There is Major de Spain, General Compson, old Thomas Sutpen, the boy's cousin McCaslin, and old Sam the Negro. They talk endlessly of the hunts of other days and of life itself, and of the death of what was worth living for. Old Ben, the savage bear, is never forgotten, and the tale of his death when it comes his time to die, is without question one of the great hunting tales in our literature. The training of the huge savage mongrel, Lion, for the sole purpose of killing Old Ben is a vital part of the narrative. The last story in this enthralling collection, "Race at Morning," illustrates Faulkner's attitude toward hunting. It is told by a lonely boy whose parents have deserted him and who has been taken into the house of a kind and lonely planter. As in the earlier stories the heroic stag, Old Eagle, has won the affection of all the hunters in the neighborhood. His time, they think, has come, but the story ends not in his death but in the gift of perhaps another year or so of life to Old Eagle when Mr. Ernest, after a wild ride with the boy clinging to his back and his gun ready, aims at his old foe while the boy realizes that Mr. Ernest knows that there are no shells in the rifle. "Don't worry," the boy says, "I won't tell them you forgot to load your gun. For that matter they don't need to know we ever seed him."

John C. Weston, Jr. "Faulkner as Anthologist." *Carolina Quarterly*, 8 (Fall 1955), 69–70.

Faulkner's new collection, *Big Woods*, is composed of four hunting stories, all but one already printed in previous books; four preludes to the stories, three of them

stories themselves and all excerpted and considerably altered from previously published works; and a postlude adapted from a story in *Go Down, Moses*, the principal source for the entire collection. One's first reaction after glancing over its pages is to reject the whole of it. But after the careful reading required of all new books by America's greatest living writer of fiction, one's reaction is a seriously qualified but considerable admiration.

There are many indications that the book was designed to make money: Faulkner has removed the fourth part of one of his best stories, "The Bear," and with it his most difficult prose and a disturbing theme; he has altered the source of the postlude to remove the same theme; he directs the whole to people who hunt or like to read about hunting; the publishers have had the book neatly but not thoughtfully illustrated; and they have published it in time for the Christmas trade. But Faulkner, notwithstanding his money-making trips to Hollywood and his magazine publications, has never prostituted his awesome art in a novel or collection of stories between covers. Anyone who doubts this should consider the few concessions in style and diction he makes to his readers and should read his seemingly tough and cynical Preface to the Modern Library edition of *Sanctuary*. There he tells how he selected the most sensational subject he could think of and wrote it into *Sanctuary* to make money; but he goes on to say that after he saw how "terrible" it was in the galley proofs, he tore them down at his own expense and rewrote it so that it would not "shame" *As I Lay Dying* and *The Sound and the Fury*. And it does not.

Faulkner assembles and adapts his stories with an artistry one would expect from the author who shaped the delicate complexities of *Absalom, Absalom!*. The collection achieves a fine unity. It has the single topic of hunting; it deals with a single theme, the passing of the wilderness; and it involves the same characters—Ike McCaslin, his kinsmen, his friends, and the Indians or the "People" as Faulkner calls them. The collection has an effective time-progression, beginning with Chickasaw Indians viewing French explorers on the Mississippi in the first prelude and then "The Bear" in which Ike McCaslin is baptised fully into manhood at the age of fourteen in 1881, and ending with an account of the same character made for this printing to be over eighty in the late 1940's. Finally, each prelude admirably sets the tone for the following story: the prelude for "The Old People" is appropriately wild and tense, and that for the humorous "A Bear Hunt" is wryly funny.

If, as is probable, a lot of hunters and readers of male adventure magazine fiction discover Faulkner for the first time this Christmas through this book, its publication is justified without further question. They will experience him with a serious and characteristic theme, with his remarkable story-telling ability, with his flexible and effective and difficult style, with a wealth of recurring and blood-related characters, with his inventive and experimental structures and viewpoints, and with two qualities we associate with Twain: a skill with local speech patterns and an ability to communicate the dry and ironic humor of the folk tale. "A Bear Hunt" is one of a half-dozen funniest stories in American literature. It is conceivable that this book may help to persuade that distressingly large group of people who think Faulkner is a cynical and despairing realist of the now-outmoded school, people who have this opinion through a reading of *Sanctuary* alone—and necessarily a careless reading—that Faulkner is a deep and warm romantic idealist.

But while feeling happy for those who

will experience Faulkner for the first time, or nearly the first time, through this book, those old lovers of this man's works must lament (painfully and humbly it must be said) his lack of judgment in separating the two great themes, both resulting from man's cupidity and misuse of property: the passing of the wilderness and the sin against the Negro. In removing the latter from this book, a theme bound to the other in its principal source with profound and moving art, Faulkner has made this work less complex and disturbing for hunters, but also less significant for serious students of American literature. "The Bear" is incomplete without the fourth section. What McCaslin did there is a direct result of what he learned by hunting the bear in the first parts, and the killing of the bear lacks a deep meaning without one's experiencing the consequences of it. And the postlude, without the theme of the white man's sin against the Negro with its continuing, terrible consequences, carries the same message, with some overtones certainly, as would a government circular on forest conservation. We can hope that Faulkner's audience may grow. But we can also hope that "The Bear" and "Delta Autumn" do not go down to posterity in these forms.

Checklist of Additional Reviews

"*Big Woods*." *Kirkus*, September 1955, p. 668.
The Pastor, October 1955.
"New Faulkner Collection Is Hunting Stories." *Delta Democrat-Times* (Greenville, Miss.), October 16, 1955, p. 19.
"*Big Woods*." Auburn (N.Y.) *Citizen-Advertiser*, October 22, 1955, p. 4.
Omaha *World-Herald*, October 22, 1955.

Syracuse *Post Standard*, October 30, 1955.

"Four Short Stories of William Faulkner." San Francisco *Argonaut*, November 4, 1955, p. 18.

New Yorker, November 19, 1955, p. 236.

St. Louis *Post Dispatch*, November 27, 1955.

Literary Cavalcade, December 1955.

"*Big Woods*." *Booklist*, December 1, 1955, p. 146.

Cleveland *Plain Dealer*, December 11, 1955.

The Journal (Franklin Park, Illinois), January 25, 1956.

The Record (Sigma Alpha Epsilon), February 1956.

Daily Texan, February 19, 1956.

"*Big Woods*." *U.S. Quarterly Book Review*, 12 (March 1956), 43–44.

English Journal, April 1956.

Bulletin of the National Association of Secondary School Principals, May 1956.

Asplundh Tree (Jenkintown, Pa.), Summer 1956.

"*Big Woods*." Los Angeles *Free Press*.

New Haven Register.

Abernathy, Harry. "Short Stories, Long Sentences." Clarksdale (Miss.) *Press Register*, November 19, 1955, p. 2.

Aby, Hulette F. "Men, Boys and Hounds." Tulsa *Sunday World*, November 27, 1955, Magazine Section, p. 22.

Arnold, Stanleigh. "For Hunter and Fisherman—The Pageant of the Out-of-Doors." San Francisco *Chronicle*, November 27, 1955, Book Section, p. 25.

Beck, Warren. "Faulkner and His Haunted Woods." Milwaukee *Journal*, October 16, 1955, Part V, p. 4.

Brady, Charles A. "Faulkner Catches Magic of the American Woods." Buffalo *Evening News*, October 22, 1955, Magazine Section, p. 10.

Brown, James. "Faulkner's Stories Are Profound, Engrossing." Wichita *Daily Times* (Wichita Falls, Texas), January 15, 1956, p. 5-D.

Cahoon, Herbert. "*Big Woods*." *Library Journal*, November 1, 1955, p. 2521.

Cowley, Malcolm. "Life of the Hunter." *New York Times Book Review*, October 16, 1955, pp. 4, 44.

Crume, Paul. "In Wilderness with Faulkner." Dallas *Morning News*, October 16, 1955, Part VII, p. 6.

Dawson, Hal. "New Faulkner Volume Now at Post Library." *Fort Bliss News*, May 19, 1956.

Farrow, Robert. "Book of Hunting Stories States Faulknerian Themes." Pasadena *Enterprise*, November 23, 1955.

Frank, Armin. Unidentified clipping.

Glass, Mrs. W. D. "*Big Woods*." Radio broadcast on WAVE (Louisville, Kentucky) (copy in Random House files).

Glenn, Taylor. "A Report on William Faulkner's *Big Woods*." Bridgeport *Sunday Post*, October 16, 1955, p. 4-B.

Govan, Gilbert E. "*Big Woods*." Chattanooga *Times*, January 1, 1956, p. 16.

Gruel, George E. "*Big Woods*." *Best Sellers*, November 15, 1955, pp. 225–26.

Hains, Frank. "Paging." *Jackson* (Miss.) *Clarion-Ledger–Daily News*, October 16, 1955, Section IV, p. 6.

Hathorn, Isabel. "Faulkner 'Romances' with Woods in Latest Collection of Tales." Shreveport *Times*, November 13, 1955, p. 2-F.

Hayes, E. Nelson. "Fiction Assorted." *Progressive*, February 1956, p. 38.

H[oey], R[eid] A. "Faulkner Hunting Stories." Baltimore *Sun*, October 30, 1955, p. 11-A.

Hunt, Trudie. "*Big Woods*." Pasadena

Independent, October 30, 1955, Scene Section, p. 23.

Hyde, Frederic G. "Faulkner's Magic." Philadelphia *Inquirer*, October 30, 1955, Society Section, p. 13.

Imes, Cristel. "Faulkner Takes to the Woods." Columbus *Dispatch*, November 6, 1955, Tab Section, p. 14.

Jacks, L. V. "*Big Woods*." *Books on Trial*, December 1955, p. 184.

Jakes, Paul R. Unpublished review from Baptist Sunday School Board, October 28, 1955.

Kirsch, Robert R. "The Book Report." Los Angeles *Times*, October 26, 1955, Section II, p. 5.

Kohler, Dayton. "Hunting Tales by Faulkner." Louisville *Courier Journal*, October 23, 1955, Section III, p. 11.

May, Hoke Smith. "Power in Faulkner's Stories of the Hunt." Charlotte *Observer*, October 16, 1955, p. 16-E.

McDavid, O. C. "Safari in Woods with W. Faulkner." Jackson (Miss.) *State Times*, December 18, 1955, p. 2-E.

M[inot] , G[eorge] E. "For the Hunter." Boston *Sunday Herald*, October 16, 1955, Section IV, p. 4.

Moore, William. "*Big Woods*." Columbus *Citizen*, October 23, 1955, Magazine Section, p. 20.

N., E.A. "Prey or Pursuer?" Columbia *Missourian*, July 6, 1956, p. 4.

Nichols, Luther. "Faulkner in the Woods." San Francisco *Examiner*, October 17, 1955, Section III, p. 3.

O'Neill, Frank. "*Big Woods*." Cleveland *News*, October 17, 1955, p. 21.

Poore, Charles. "Books of the Times." New York *Times*, October 19, 1955, p. 31.

Ray, William I., Jr. "All Faulkner's Hunt Stories." Atlanta *Journal and Constitution*, October 30, 1955, p. 8-E.

Rogers, W. G. "Reviewer Parodies Faulkner." Gary *Post-Tribune*, October 30, 1955, Panorama Magazine, p. 14.

Rothermel, J. F. "Faulkner at His Best as Hunter." Birmingham *News*, November 6, 1955, p. 27-A.

S., H.L. "Faulkner Hunting Stories." Richmond *Times-Dispatch*, December 4, 1955, p. 16-E.

Sandeen, Ernest. "*Big Woods*." *America*, November 12, 1955, p. 190.

Speake, Farroll. "Four of Faulkner's Hunting Stories Combined in Volume." Indianapolis *Star*, November 13, 1955, Section VIII, p. 4.

Sullivan, Shirley K. "*Big Woods*." Radio broadcast on KTIB (Thibodaux, Louisiana), October 13, 1955 (copy in Random House files).

Tunstall, Caroline. "Man's Relation to Wilds." Norfolk *Virginian-Pilot* and Portsmouth *Star*, October 16, 1955, p. 6-C.

Washburn, Beatrice. "Faulkner and Long Sentences." Miami *Herald*, October 23, 1955, p. 4-G.

Williams, Ernest E. "Faulkner Hunting Stories Sparkle." Fort Wayne *News-Sentinel*, February 11, 1956, p. 4.

THE TOWN

The
TOWN
William Faulkner

RANDOM HOUSE · NEW YORK

Louis Dollarhide.
"Rich Detail, Energy,
Humor; One of His
Strongest Books."
Clarion-Ledger–Jackson
(Miss.) *Daily News*,
April 28, 1957, p. 11-C.

They came up the trails from the swamps, down paths from the hills, along roads from God-knows-where, to Jefferson; and they worked and cheated and stole, but they won for nothing could stop them. Their victory was as assured as their rapacity, their vast empty hunger to be fed and filled, was always present.

Readers of Faulkner will recognize "they" as the Snopeses, the pale-eyed, shrewd, omnivorous white trash who move into and up in the world of Jefferson, using and taking the old settlers for their possessions and positions. As Gavin Stevens comments early in *The Town* "They none of them seemed to bear any specific kinship to one another; they were just Snopeses, like colonies of rats or termites were just rats and termites."

In *The Town* Faulkner is returning after seventeen years to a theme first begun in *The Hamlet*, the chronicling of the Snopes family. Again the central figure, the indifferent patriarch of his immense tribe, is Flem. In the first book of the projected trilogy, Flem, a young man, moved into Frenchman's Bend, the hamlet, and married Eula, the daughter of landowner Will Varner. This was his start.

In the present book, Flem moves like an irresistible force into Jefferson, the town. This arrival Gavin Stevens calls "the first summer of the Snopeses." And seen alternately from the point of view of three authorities on the Snopeses, Charles Mallison, who looks and listens, and Lawyer Gavin Stevens, and V. K. Ratliff, who are drawn actively into Snopes affairs, the rise of the family is explored to the final emergence of Flem as president of the bank, deacon, and respectable, if not respected, citizen.

The two people most aware of the danger which the Snopeses present to the old order and the two who dedicate themselves to stemming the tide are Gavin Stevens and V. K. Ratliff. But powerless to halt the relentless march of Flem, even they are reduced to fascinated, often horrified, onlookers of the show. Trying to outguess Flem becomes a game, a sort of driving compulsion with them; and the reader joins them in their fascination.

The Snopes family is a numberless breed, and there is much to observe, much to outguess. Besides the name Flem bears, they wear such unlikely tags as Byron and Eck, Bilbo and Vardaman, Mink, Wallstreet Panic, and Montgomery Ward; and they present characters to outweigh, even to justify, their names. Two remarkable women shine among them, Flem's wife Eula and her daughter Linda, the daughter Flem gave his name to only by marriage. Eula Snopes, loved and desired by all men, emerges almost a figure of tragedy.

The Town illustrates one aspect of Faulkner's writing which has not been sufficiently emphasized by his commentators, the fact that he is a supremely great humorist. A reader would have to go all the way back to Chaucer to find writing comparable in richness of humor and tone to at least episodes in the book—the episode of the stolen brass, the Rouncewell panic, and the episode involving Miss Mamie Hait, old Het, and I. O. Snopes's mule, which has appeared earlier as a short story called "Mule in the Yard."

In many ways, *The Town* is one of Faulkner's strongest novels. *The Hamlet* is more directly told and is less complex. But what *The Town* may lose in directness of narrative it gains immeasurably in richness of detail, energy and variety of character.

It has the strength of the great English Renaissance writing, which, like Faulkner's, was a deeply traditional art. It may well prove to be one of the most acceptable of Faulkner's novels with readers at large, not because it is more removed from life as the writer sees it (which is often what readers require of artists), but because in moving from hamlet to town he presents, with the exception of the Snopeses, characters of a social order with which most people who read novels can identify. The Snopeses, whoever they are, do not read novels.

As an interesting postscript, it should be noted that Faulkner pays Lawyer Phil Stone of Oxford an age-old tribute of friendship, first, by dedicating the book to him, and secondly, in the story itself by having Linda Snopes seek out Mr. Stone of Oxford, who "was a competent lawyer or at least he had a license saying so," when she makes her will.

Arthur MacGillivray, S.J. "*The Town*." *Best Sellers*, May 1, 1957, pp. 52–53.

Everywhere you look about Yoknapatawpha County, there is a moon shining over shacks and post offices and banks and district courts—and you (I mean you) wonder why the Snopes are Snopes and South is South, where mules turn loose and dash away, widows fret while houses burn, and Flem (catarrh trouble)—he's just one of the Snopes (and who doesn't know the Snopes—or is it Snopeses?) seems to get his way into the real Jefferson way of life (Mississippi, that is), which is a manner of speaking about what you haven't much time for, if you have no veneration for Nobel prizes and what Flem his-self says might—and you never can tell, that is, if you are a person not knowing what you are coming up against, especially when a cotillion ball is in swing and the florist shop is out of flowers—how did this sentence begin?—no matter, the board of aldermen will come up with dark rooms, post cards, and did I mention a mule on the loose? Drugs, too. Jefferson is mah town, and Jefferson's mah destination, end of the line, no baby doll.

Yes, suh, is you a Southerner or is you ain't? Is you a Europeener or a Sweed? Noble or not, I said to Flem (call me Gavin, I'm a Stevens; Flem is a Snope), whose tribe increases daily, whether in tents or out, but there are flaps where messages come into directors whose purpose it is to detect what the words mean in language, unlike this chap Beckett whose world is a bucket, or ash cans, I forget which, how can the characters (Sam, meet Bill) get together except in Yoknapatawpha County? To be at home. "Because he missed it. He missed it completely"—that's chapter nine complete.

You see? This is Faulkner's problem, to revivify the saga of the Snopes whose chronicle he introduced in *Sartoris* (1929) and continued in *The Hamlet* (1940). So, *The Hamlet* and *The Town* and *The Mansion* (forthcoming) will be a trilogy about the Snopeses, who not only exploit the community but each other as well, who contrive to undermine the South with bad manners along with guile; and, in a way, they take over America.

There is no plot, but what is in the book is a series of picaresque chapters which don't necessarily tie together. Will Flem Snopes send Linda away from Jefferson to school? Did you hear about

436

the Riddell boys having polio? Don't miss chapter nineteen. Sweet Linda, are you a Snopes? Try to marry Flem. Try! V. K. Ratliff, Uncle Gavin, Montgomery Ward, Mayor de Spain, and many others plod their tiresome way through this tiring chronicle. All that they do is of the utmost importance to the narrator who thrives on the slimmest morsel of gossip that Jefferson hears. Faulkner should have titled his book *Snopeslore*, a term he uses once in the course of the narrative. Too many demands are made on the reader who too often is allowed to remain in the dark. Presuming that the reader knows what he is talking about, the narrator goes off on too many tangents, as smalltown people who are gabbers often do, so that clarity is lost and interest dwindles.

Amid the chaff, there are some golden grains; "the lean umbilicus of bare livelihood"; "born a generation too soon, he would have been by acclamation ordained a high priest in that new national religious cult of Cheesecake as it translated still alive the Harlows and Grables and Monroes into the hierarchy of American cherubim"; "a monument only says *At least I got this far* while a footprint says *This is where I was when I moved again*"; "there's always somebody handy afterward to prove their foresight by your hindsight." In general, however, Faulkner has mastered the art of writing much without saying anything worthwhile, and for that reason this book will appeal only to dyed-in-the-buckram Faulkner fans.

Harrison Smith. "Story of Greedy, Indomitable Men Told in Humorous Not Grim Fashion." Hartford *Times,* May 4, 1957; St. Petersburg (Fla.) *Times,* May 5, 1957; Toledo *Blade,* May 12, 1957, p. 4.

It is not necessary for the reader of William Faulkner's 23rd novel to have read *The Hamlet,* published in 1940, the first volume of the trilogy which will be completed when he writes *The Mansion. The Town* stands on its own solid base, an integral part of the small world he has created which he has named Yoknapatawpha County, and of Jefferson, its county seat, which has many of the aspects of Faulkner's own home town of Oxford, Mississippi.

It is not a mythical domain created by the author's imagination, but a revelation of the slow emergence of the Deep South from the chaos and destitution that followed the Civil War.

It was not due to the carpetbaggers from the victorious North, who with sound money swarmed into the Southern States, but to a new breed of greedy and indomitable men, who, starting with nothing, slowly took over the townships and villages and the ruined industry of Mississippi.

Faulkner has given them a family name, the "Snopeses." They followed the once-powerful and wealthy Sartorises who were stained with the guilt of slavery and who had to explain their sin in a penance which still continues.

The Town is an account of the early conflict between the Sartoris clan (a generic name for the aristocracy—the Compsons and Mallisons, the de Spains, the Varners, the Stevenses) and the Snopeses, whose wiles and industry they were incapable of resisting and whom they considered poor white trash.

It is a humorous and even hilarious, rather than grim novel. The Snopeses were never hostile: they acted like poor folk, and their wives and daughters were occasionally available for amorous aristocrats who were slowly loosening their hold on reality. Apparently humble, Flem Snopes conquered the town, slowly penetrating the power plant, the bank, the ramshackle boarding house which turned into Snopes's Hotel. Mayor de Spain fell under his spell.

When young Gowan at the age of 13 got the job of night watchman at the plant, his Uncle Gavin, now the city attorney, said, "It's time for him to begin to stay out all night." And what better place than down there at the plant where Mr. Harker and the fireman could keep him awake, for Harker talked endlessly about Mr. Snopes "with the kind of amoral amazement with which you would recount having witnessed the collision of a planet."

In a sense, though Snopes and his kin had brought new life to a stagnant town, as well as new ideas, he was despised and admired. Lawyer Gavin Stevens argued that they were "like a herd of tigers." Wouldn't it be better to have them shut up in a mule-pen where you could at least watch them, even if you did lose an arm or a leg every time you got within 10 feet of the wire, than to have them strolling loose over everywhere in the country? It was up to them to cope, to resist, to endure and (if they could) survive.

The villain of the novel is Flem Snopes; but Faulkner has not presented him as wholly evil. He had been cheated in Frenchman's Bend, and in Jefferson was willing to have Mayor de Spain sleep with his wife; his revenge when he decided to put an end to it was simply to ruin the man and destroy Eula as a woman no one would want.

The Town must be rated as one of Faulkner's greatest books. His central theme, "Snopesism," goes to the core of the matter, the gradual erosion of the Deep South at the hands of remorseless and avid men; but the novel is enriched with living characters, good or evil, and by the author's knowledge of the human mind and heart.

Paul Engle. "New Faulkner Is Richly Rewarding." Chicago *Sunday Tribune*, May 5, 1957, Part IV, p. 4.

With this novel by Nobel Prize Winner Faulkner, we can see more exactly why he received that honor for this country. For it is now fully apparent that these tangled stories Faulkner has been writing for so many years are not just anecdotes of Mississippi hunting, and Civil War veterans, and violent young men.

These novels are the image of an entire society, a human scene wide in range and deep in psychological insight.

This is to say that you will not find Faulkner easy reading. He has attempted a most difficult job, and the reader must meet him halfway. In Faulkner's case, halfway is a long, hard journey, but it is worth it.

Here is the mortal landscape of these people: the fine old Sartoris family, trying to keep alive the values of quiet decency in the post–Civil War world where corruption hung in the still air; the Snopes family, pushing, ruthless, the absolute example of the dollar-dedicated people, not consciously thrusting the old values aside, but actually unaware that they existed, and Ratliff, the man of humor and good will, the sad viewer of that scene.

This novel follows the earlier *The Hamlet*, and is the middle of a trilogy. Where the first novel brought the Snopes tribe to Mississippi, *The Town* shows the manner in which the Snopes legion established itself in a community too relaxed and unaware to realize the poison that was penetrating it.

The third volume, *The Mansion*, will presumably prove the final triumph of the new type of predatory man in our times, the man who does not shoot you but simply takes over your house and land and occupation.

The reward for staying with Faulkner is a rich one. Here is the old humor, when Faulkner speaks of a lady as "fat old Eve long since free of the danger of inciting a snake or anything else to tempt her." Here is a deeply realized chronicle of one American region, deserving more than one quick look. Read it over, and over.

Murray Kempton.
"Another Day in the
Creation of a World."
New York *Post*, May 5,
1957, p. 11-M.

Saxe Commins, who is William Faulkner's editor, as he was O'Neill's, Anderson's, and Dreiser's, once said that it is a great mistake to confuse writers with thinkers. He meant, I think, that they were something more, or, as Richard Blackmur has it, that in the best of them, the thought begins in the senses.

So Faulkner's genius occasionally runs ahead of his mere critical intelligence, as it runs ahead of his mere critics, and it is necessary, before attempting to engage him, to say the simple things publishers hope for.

The Town, except for those first readers who were thrown off by *A Fable*, is likely to sell in greater quantities than anything of his in its first hardcover edition; we could even, for once, have a novel of truly extraordinary proportions at the top of the best-seller list.

I think this is a first thing which has to be said early, because *A Fable* was, as early Faulkner goes, a great popular success, and it is said to be his favorite among his own works, although it has always seemed one of the few failures of a great man of great talent which was not even an interesting failure.

The Town is in that range of Faulkner's work where he is to be compared not with any contemporary novelist but only with himself.

It does not reach quite so deep in me as *The Sound and the Fury* or *Absalom, Absalom!* or *Go Down, Moses*; but if it lacks the dark interior magnificence of these works, it is simpler and less rigorous with its audience, and it has none of those stretches which occasionally seem almost willful in their failure to communicate.

Or could it be that Faulkner looks back to the 19th Century as a period of private, and at the 20th, along with its other faults, as one of public, or common speech?

Now, having rested with *A Fable*, Faulkner has finished another day in the creation of his world. In sum, *The Town* seems to me a fair and shining regimen of his first work. As Mr. Blackmur says, about one of his own comments in this vein, "This is to say nothing," but it ought to be said, before anything is said.

I have never met many persons with

any direct experience of Mississippi who thought much of that quality of myth about which we hear so often in Faulkner. I know an honest man who swears he has been introduced to Temple Drake and in Oxford too.

Faulkner, even on the basis of my own slender experience with his country, seems to me anchored to his ankles in reality. I rather think of him as writing from the clips.

It was impossible to look at the Till trial without seeing a Sartoris in the judge, a Snopes in one of the defense attorneys, a Lucas Beauchamp in Moses Wright, the Till boy's uncle, although none were entirely recognizable as Faulkner's since they had not been transformed by his heightened sensibility, any more than a piece of stone is recognizable as a final work of Phidias to anyone but Phidias.

I think the sensibility, heightened even beyond Faulkner's equipment, is part of that lack of proportion which has disturbed the most creative critics about him.

"Why has he left the harmony out of the level of notation, at the level where the reader is instructed to read?" Mr. Blackmur asks.

"It is precisely what the reader cannot be trusted to put in. In his books, the words, if not the people, fall out of relation ... Why is so much of *The Sound and the Fury* told deliberately through the putative mind of the idiot Benjy?"

The gravamen of Mr. Blackmur's complaint is largely absent from *The Town*; there is in it nothing quite so wrenching to the ordinary intelligence as Faulkner's insertion of a long wedding hymn into the head of the idiot Snopes during his passion with the cow in *The Hamlet*.

There is, however, some of the same lack of proportion in Eula Varner Snopes— we unite with Faulkner in thinking of her as Eula Varner, never having been a Snopes or having known one. Her first spoken words in *The Hamlet* were: "Stop pawing me, you old headless horseman, Ichabod Crane." Her last words in *The Town*, 24 years later, nearly her last words in life for that matter, run like this:

"If you are a man, you can lie unconscious in the gutter bleeding and with most of your teeth knocked out and somebody can take your pocketbook and you can wake up and wash the blood off and it's all right; you can always get some more teeth and even another pocketbook sooner or later. But you can't stand meekly with your head bowed and no blood and all your teeth too while somebody takes your pocketbook because even though you might face the friends who love you afterward you can never face the strangers that never heard of you before."

Everything has happened to Eula Varner in the generation between except the capacity to talk like that, and she is here near the end much more William Faulkner than Molly Bloom was ever James Joyce. We bear that distortion of probability, because Faulkner's characters are Romans at moments and they would be less than themselves if they did not speak then in the high Roman fashion.

The Town's style is in the frontier tradition, almost that described under that horrid word "folk," and we are due to hear again a little too much about Faulkner's humor. There are persons—a majority, I suppose—who think the spotted horse sequence in *The Hamlet* is funny, and they will find it duplicated in wonderful grotesqueries here.

But Faulkner's contribution to frontier tradition is more than refinement and happy echo. Told any other way, these scenes would break the heart; they come close enough to doing so anyway; and, in them, Faulkner is doing something with the tradition that not even Mark Twain, except in moments of absolute self-command, was ever able to do.

Now Flem Snopes has his bank, and in Faulkner's final chapter he has his mansion, and he has done all these things not with country trickeries which served him to Frenchman's Bend's cost but by converting himself to a pillar of Oxford propriety.

He is no longer outside society and at war with it. Faulkner has written him into the center of Oxford's life, as though our century were so empty that it can worship only Snopes and raise such of its children who remain behind to be themselves Snopeses.

We are all of us in this fight Snopeses. It is a terrible thought, and I'm afraid the next and final volume will be unbearable.

Dayton Kohler. "Faulkner's Second Novel in the Snopes Trilogy." Louisville *Courier Journal*, May 5, 1957, Section IV, p. 6.

Members of the rapacious Snopes clan came into William Faulkner's fiction as early as *Sartoris*, but he did not give them a chronicle of their own until *The Hamlet* appeared in 1940. That novel, rich in folk comedy, grotesque in horrors, sharp in social criticism, defined the characteristic role of the Snopeses in Faulkner's legend of the South and confirmed what his earlier novels and short stories had already suggested: that these landless exploiters were to become the locust-like destroyers of the economic, social and moral integrity of the Yoknapatawpha world.

Faulkner's rendering of regional myth is now recognized if not always accepted. In its broadest outlines it shows that the earliest settlers in the deep South were aristocrats like the Sartorises, Compsons and McCaslins, or ambitious men of no family background like Thomas Sutpen. They took the land, built their homes, planted their crops, all in the determination to found a lasting social order for their sons. But because they accepted the institution of chattel slavery, there was an element of guilt in their design, a curse on their way of life and even on the land itself.

After conquest from without—the Civil War—had destroyed the old order, a new exploiting class, the bushwhacking Snopeses of Civil War days, appeared and with the carpetbaggers climbed to power by economic control and demagoguery. This myth is the story of the dissolution of a traditional order and the growth of a new society with an accumulated heritage of enmity, hatred, greed and guilt.

The Town, second novel of the Snopes trilogy, traces Flem's activities through his next 18 years in Jefferson. We see him operating a cheap café, becoming a superintendent of the power plant (a job that gives him the opportunity to steal brass fittings and junked metal), turning private usurer and property grabber until, shrewdly turning to his advantage the fact that Manfred de Spain, the new president of the Sartoris bank, is also his wife's lover, he manipulates a stock deal to have himself named vice-president of the bank.

But Flem is not satisfied to be a mere vice-president. At the end, having played the willing cuckold for years, he uses Linda, his nominal daughter, to force a threat of scandal, outmaneuver his father-in-law, ruin de Spain, and drive his wife to suicide in order to become the president and owner of one of the finest houses in Jefferson.

Flem Snopes is one of Faulkner's notable villains. Some critics have tried, quite mistakenly, to equate him with Popeye, the gangster in *Sanctuary*. But the quality of evil and the lack of ethical will found in Snopesism is of a different order. To

441

call Flem amoral is to define his characteristic but not to explain his motivation. Ratliff, the wry-humored, compassionate, observing sewing machine salesman who has spoken for Faulkner on other occasions, does this in *The Town*. Flem's goal is respectability, says Ratliff, that quality for which, when a man "finds out he wants and has got to have, there aint nothing he wont do to get it and then keep it . . . there aint nothing he will stop at, aint nobody or nothing within his scope and reach that may not anguish and grieve and suffer."

These comments may suggest that *The Town* is a grim book. Actually, it is not. In addition to its social theme, a skein of folk humor running back through Mark Twain to the frontier tale-tellers helps to hold its episodes together. Faulkner has never hesitated to rewrite his short stories in order to fit them into the larger pattern of his Yoknapatawpha novels. *The Town* contains several examples of his tall tales. Among them readers familiar with the canon will recognize "Centaur In Brass" and "Mule In the Yard," now revised and given their proper place in the Snopes saga.

Faulkner's characters also have a habit of shifting from book to book. The writer's method of shifting from one narrator to another may seem awkward at first reading, but this device of technique, as Faulkner has demonstrated several times in the past, also has the advantage of presenting the story from several different angles of vision—in this case that of Gavin Stevens; Ratliff, the man of reason and a shrewd commentator on the human condition, and Charles Mallison, initiate from childhood into a social situation and a moral problem of conduct which allows him at the end to understand the way in which the predatory Snopeses rose through mule-trading and storekeeping to become the bankers and suspender-snapping politicians of the new South.

The second part of a trilogy still to be completed, *The Town* may nevertheless be read as a self-contained novel adding to our understanding of the Sartorises and Compsons doomed to defeat in their contacts with the codeless tribe of Snopes.

Milton Rugoff. "Faulkner's Old Spell in a New Novel of Yoknapatawpha." *New York Herald Tribune Books*, May 5, 1957, p. 1.

The publisher describes this as the second volume in a trilogy on the Snopes family, the first, published seventeen years ago, being *The Hamlet*.

Now, the Snopeses are an authentic Faulkner subject, yielding the kind of warped and stunted men (but no women, curiously enough) on which his imagination thrives and his reputation rests. In part our interest in the Snopeses is doubtless morbid, for many of them are degenerate or mad. But they also fascinate us because they are sometimes grotesquely funny, and because of what they portend, for they are apparently becoming, in the Yoknapatawphas of America, the master class, and finally because they afford us the spectacle of a magician pulling trick after trick out of the same old bag without diminution of power.

But in *The Town* the Snopeses (or at least Flem, their chieftain) have achieved success and move in wider and wider— that is, non-Snopesian—circles, so that they are in danger, so to speak, of being lost in the crowd. In a backwater hamlet they are monstrous; in a university town merely queer. *The Hamlet* described how they spread, feral and supremely predatory, across a mythical Mississippi county, outcheating or outworking the old elite (which had become too complacent, effete or possibly decent to cope with them), so that its pages are filled with a fierce primitivity and a sensational mingling of horror and humor. In particular, it traced Flem Snopes' climb out of the primordial ooze, his worming himself into the Varner enterprises and his capture of Eula Varner, that supercharged vessel of female sexuality, when her first lover abandoned her with child. In his wake came others of the breed, such as Montgomery Ward Snopes, who sells obscene pictures, but they are only sucker fish to the shark.

In *The Town*, however, Flem, having won money and power, seeks respectability. After scraping off the sucker fish, he grapples with his wife, who still has a lover; then with her illegitimate daughter Linda, who is growing up to be equally desirable, if not so fabulous; and finally with Gavin Stevens, County Attorney, Heidelberg Ph.D., something of a Quixote (Sherwood Anderson might have created him), who once unsettled Eula with his love because it was so high-minded, and now would teach Linda the way to escape from the Snopesian condition. How Flem gains his end, or nearly; how Linda escapes, but not unscathed; how Gavin wins, but loses; and how Eula, somewhat melodramatically, pays the high penalty constitute the climax of what in the old popular ballads would be called a domestic tragedy.

Thus, where *The Hamlet* moves on the edge of a backwoods underworld in which rapine is an art, *The Town* introduces the almost bourgeois background of a respectable community. Snopes is still Snopes, still repulsive, a character still worlds away from the genteel tradition, but Gavin is a highly civilized and subtly drawn figure, Linda an intellectually curious young woman, and even Eula has subsided into staying with one lover for eighteen years. Moreover, we learn about the Snopeses through such men as the ubiquitous sewing-machine salesman Ratliff, an ironist of parts, Gavin, an unreconstructed idealist, and Charles, a fresh-eyed youngster, so that we seem to be watching, with an acute sense of helplessness, some fearful invasion from outer space, the spreading of a plague of rats or termites or other non-human things.

The Snopeses still being Snopeses, the macabre humor is still here, and in a few sections, such as that in which Byron Snopes sends back to Flem his four halfbreed, wholly wild offspring, it casts its spell once again. But the account of Flem's machinations requires so much space that little is left for those episodes that, like slow-motion nightmares, or things seen at the bottom of a murky sea, make Faulkner's novels a unique experience. Although there is less of outrageous incident and the hypnotic, somnambulistic style of some of the earlier novels, there is in *The Town* (especially in the fate of Gavin and Eula and even in the development of Flem) more of such gentler and subtler emotions as pity and pathos. The style is still a series of unoriented episodes that gives us an extraordinary lifelike sensation of groping our own way through such experience, but the world here is much closer to the outside one, and by so much the more accessible to our sympathies. If *The Town* is a tamer book than *The Hamlet*, it is because the time and the people are tamer. Tameness is of course relative, and a tamer Faulkner is still wilder than a whole bookshelf of other novelists.

Granville Hicks.
"The Question of William Faulkner: His New Novel, *The Town*, as Test."
New Leader, May 6, 1957, pp. 6–8.

A couple of years ago, William Faulkner published in *Harper's* a bitter article about the decline of privacy in American life. In a general way, his indictment was accurate, but, so far as his own experience was concerned, his indignation and surprise seemed naive. For a century and a half, famous writers have been public figures, and many of them, including some of the good ones, have welcomed the invasion of their privacy. Faulkner sincerely dislikes public attention, but it would seem that he might have reckoned with it as an occupational hazard.

As a matter of fact, Faulkner has been luckier than most writers of his stature, for he had twenty working years in which he was pretty well able to preserve his privacy because he was scarcely known to the larger public. About ten years ago, the situation began to change. Malcolm Cowley's *Portable Faulkner*, published in 1946, pointed the way for a multitude of critical and biographical studies. The success of *Intruder in the Dust* in 1948 and the success of the movie made of it gave his name popular currency. And, of course, the bestowal of the Nobel Prize in 1950 doomed forever his dream of privacy.

As a consequence of all this, Faulkner became the object of vulgar curiosity, and he also—and this is more important—became acutely self-conscious. He was now a man whose opinions on any subject whatsoever were news, and this was a role for which he was not well adapted.

Unlike Hemingway, he refused to lapse into irresponsibility; on the contrary, when he gave an opinion he gave it seriously. But on this level his mind functioned badly, as one can easily see by looking at his agonized but inconsistent and often almost incoherent statements on desegregation.

At the same time, he became increasingly self-conscious about his work. For many years, all that mattered deeply to Faulkner was the act of writing; what happened to his books after they were finished scarcely concerned him. (He thought of *Go Down, Moses* as a novel, but he didn't bother to tell his publishers and didn't protest when they brought it out as a book of short stories.) One of his activities in recent years has been the gathering together and tidying up of previous efforts. The *Collected Stories* was needed and was a magnificent volume, but one cannot feel so much enthusiasm for either *Knight's Gambit* or *Big Woods*, and even *Requiem for a Nun* is tail to a kite that was flown a long time ago.

There was one major creative effort in this decade, *A Fable*. Faulkner worked on the novel for seven years, and he made no bones about saying that he believed it to be his greatest work. Few critics, I am afraid, will give it that rank, though some of us find much that is magnificent in it. The trouble is that, taken as a whole, it is an act of will, not, like his last novels, an organic growth. One recognizes the tremendous mastery the man has achieved in his craft, but too much of the time the skill is being used to conceal absence of insight. It is as if this wonderful rhetoric, which he had so boldly fashioned to serve his purposes, had taken over and was plunging ahead like a runaway locomotive.

Now we have *The Town*, in which Faulkner has returned to Yoknapatawpha County and to one of his finest themes, the Snopes family. This is neither a reworking of old material—although it does include, as Faulkner's novels so often do, episodes that have already been used in short stories—nor is it an excursion into foreign territory. In conception *The Town* is an integral and important part of the great Yoknapatawpha saga, and we can and must compare it with its illustrious predecessors—especially with *The Hamlet*, to which it is a direct sequel.

The Snopeses were introduced in the first novel Faulkner wrote about Yoknapatawpha, *Sartoris*, published in 1929. Here, presenting a member of the tribe, he wrote:

"This Snopes was a young man, member of a seemingly inexhaustible family which for the last ten years had been moving into town in driblets from a small settlement known as Frenchman's Bend. Flem, the first Snopes, had appeared unheralded one day behind the counter of a small restaurant on a side street, patronized by country folk. With this foothold and like Abraham of old, he brought his blood and legal kin household by household, individual by individual, into town, and established them where they could gain money. Flem himself was presently manager of the city light and water plant, and for the following few years he was a sort of handy man to the municipal government: and three years ago, to old Bayard's profane astonishment and unconcealed annoyance, he became vice-president of the Sartoris bank, where already a relation of his was bookkeeper."

The Hamlet, as everyone knows, tells how the Snopeses overran Frenchman's Bend. *The Town* describes the conquest of Jefferson. The general theme of *The Mansion*, which is to complete the trilogy, can be surmised.

Many of the events in *The Hamlet* are seen through the eyes of a sewing-machine agent, V. K. Ratliff—introduced in *Sartoris* as V. K. Suratt—who is fascinated by the Snopeses and who is eventually outwitted by Flem Snopes. In *The Town*, Ratliff is one of three narrators, the others being Chick Mallison and Gavin Stevens. Chick is the boy who played so important a part in *Intruder in the Dust* and the character from whose point of view the story is told. Stevens in recent years has become one of Faulkner's favorite characters, often serving as his spokesman. As we know from his earlier works in which they have appeared, each of these individuals is intensely curious about what people do and why they do it.

Faulkner has written from the point of view of a speculative bystander who observes what goes on or, as in *Absalom, Absalom!*, reconstructs what has gone on in the past. *A priori* three such observers would seem to be excessive, but the method proves not to be cumbersome. Chick much of the time is describing events that took place before he was born or while he was too young to understand them, but this imaginative reconstruction serves, as it served in *Absalom*, to give the incidents a legendary quality. Ratliff, the shrewdest of the observers, functions as he did in *The Hamlet*, except that he now speaks in the first person. Stevens is more involved in certain of the events than the other two, but he retains his detachment. By playing one interpretation against another, Faulkner achieves a kind of counterpoint and sometimes a good deal of humor, as in Chapter 9, a Ratliff chapter following a Stevens chapter, which is made up of just two sentences: "Because he missed it. He missed it completely."

As a novel about the Snopeses, *The Town* raises questions concerning the role of the family in the Yoknapatawpha saga. George Marion O'Donnell, one of the first critics to look for a pattern in Faulkner's work, emphasized the contrast between the decaying aristocrats and the aggressively upsurging poor whites, and suggested that Faulkner saw the struggle as one in which evil was triumphing over good. This seems a simplification. In many of his works—for instance, *As I Lay Dying*—Faulkner portrays poor whites with great sympathy. Furthermore, not all Snopeses are bad; think of Eck Snopes and Wallstreet Panic Snopes. Snopesism is a disease of individuals, not the characteristic of a class.

Even in *The Hamlet* there appeared to be two varieties of Snopesism, and we see this clearly in *The Town*. There are the uncivilized Snopeses: the barn-burning Ab, patriarch of the tribe; Mink the murdered, "the only out-and-out mean Snopes we ever experienced," as Ratliff says; the uncouth and meanly dishonest Montgomery Ward Snopes; the stupidly dishonest and brutal Byron Snopes, and a host of others. Then there is Flem Snopes, coolly rapacious, boundlessly ambitious, without principle, honor or pride, the man who, in *The Hamlet*, literally beats the devil. Just as was forecast in *Sartoris*, *The Town* shows how the Snopeses moved in on Jefferson, but it turns out, with amusing and unexpected irony, that much of the book is devoted to telling how Flem succeeded in ridding the town of his uncivilized kinsfolk. The last episode, and one of the best, tells how "Byron Snopes's children out of a Jicarilla Squaw in Old Mexico" descended on Jefferson, terrorized its citizens, and were disposed of by Flem. Ratliff describes their departure as "the last and final end of Snopes out-and-out unvarnished behavior in Jefferson." Flem's kind of Snopesism now has a free hand, which indicates the direction *The Mansion* is likely to take.

Snopesism is one theme of *The Town*; the other is love. Readers of *The Hamlet* are unlikely to have forgotten Eula Varner, who becomes Flem's wife. In describing her, Faulkner says that "her entire appearance suggested some symbology out of the old Dionysiac times—honey in sunlight and bursting grapes, the writhen bleeding of the crushed fecundated vine beneath the hard rapacious trampling goat-hoof." As Robert Penn Warren has said, she is a kind of fertility or earth goddess. Her effect on the males of Jefferson is as great as the effect she has had in Frenchman's Bend, and Gavin Stevens is only one of the men that fall in love with her. Nor is he the successful suitor, for Major Manfred de Spain, soon to be mayor of the town, becomes and for many years remains her lover. (There is irony in the fact that a barn belonging to Manfred de Spain's father was burned by Flem's father.)

Gavin Stevens loses Eula, but some years later he falls in love, in a somewhat different sense of that term, with her daughter Linda. Linda seems to be another Eula but is not, for, as Gavin reflects, "you realized that she must not, must not duplicate: very Nature herself would not permit that to occur, permit two of them in a place no larger than Jefferson, Mississippi, in one century, let alone in overlapping succession, within the anguished scope of a single generation." From the start, Gavin's feeling for Linda is partly paternal, and in the end it is predominantly so, as it becomes his great concern to protect her from disillusionment with regard to her mother. Flem, who is nominally her father, has practical reasons for worrying about Linda because of the way her maternal grandfather, Will Varner, has drawn his will. Thus, Flem's intrigues to capture the old Sartoris bank, of which he is vice president and Manfred de Spain president, become involved with the whole romantic theme, the complex relationship between de Spain and Eula, between Eula and Gavin Stevens, between Gavin and Linda. Flem triumphs, for, being single-minded, he gets what he wants and loses nothing that matters to him. The others lose much, but each gains something, too.

Although *The Town* has many details

that cannot be reconciled with other details in other volumes in the Yoknapatawpha saga, it is in itself more consistent than most of Faulkner's novels. In the old days, one surmises, he never worried about consistency, but now he does. This self-consciousness has its drawbacks, but it also has advantages. In the three narrative and descriptive passages that accompanied the three acts of *Requiem for a Nun*, he displayed a wonderful awareness of the past and present, the length and breadth of Yoknapatawpha County. The same awareness is in many sections of this book and especially in the account of Gavin Stevens's thoughts as, in a moment of crisis, he stands upon one of the county's high points at twilight: "They are all here, supine before you, stratified and superposed, osseous and durable with the frail dust and the phantoms—the rich alluvial river-bottom land of old Issetibbeha, the wild Chickasaw king, with his Negro slaves and his sister's son called Doom who murdered his way to the throne and, legend said, . . . stole an entire steamboat and had it dragged intact eleven miles overland to convert into a palace proper to aggrandize his state; the same fat black rich plantation earth still synonymous of the proud fading white plantation names whether we—I mean of course they—ever actually owned a plantation or not: Sutpen and Sartoris and Compson and Edmonds and McCaslin and Beauchamp and Grenier and Habersham and Holston and Stevens and de Spain, generals and governors and judges, soldiers . . . and statesmen failed or not, and simple failures, who snatched and grabbed and passed and varnished, name and face and all. Then the roadless, almost perpendicular hill-country of McCallum and Gowrie and Frazier and Muir translated intact with their pot stills and speaking only the old Gaelic and not much of that, from Culloden to Carolina, then from Carolina to Yoknapatawpha

still intact and not speaking much of anything except that now they called the pots 'kettles' though the drink (even I can remember this) usquebaugh: then and last on to where Frenchman's Bend lay beyond the southeastern horizon, cradle of Varners and ant-heap for the northeast crawl of Snopes." This is very fine, and there are many fine things in the book. Indeed, when one has said the worst about it—I shall be saying what is bad enough— it remains both an exciting and an impressive novel, one that only William Faulkner could have written. But we have only to compare it to *The Hamlet* to see what it is not: It is not a richly inventive novel, the expression of a tremendously original and fertile imagination. There is nothing in it to compare with the humor of the spotted-horse episode, the bizarre romanticism of Ike's love affair with the cow, the intensity of the feud between Houston and Mink Snopes. The Eula of *The Town*, whom we see chiefly as she carries on long conversations in the office of Gavin Stevens, conversations in which she is as wordy as he, is only a pale reflection of the Eula who was courted by Labove and won by McCarron, and even Flem seems endowed with a human greediness rather than demonic rapacity. Two of the best episodes, one cannot help noticing, are derived from stories—"Centaur in Brass" and "Mule in the Yard"—written 25 years ago. Only in the concluding chapter, another but a new story about the wild Snopeses, do we find the same inventiveness. And in between there is a great deal of Gavin Stevens's loquacity— along with much else, to be sure.

It is only when we compare it with Faulkner's earlier work that the novel disappoints us, but, alas, that is the comparison that has to be made. I read it with great though not continuous pleasure, relishing the shrewdness and the humor, liking Ratliff as well as ever, liking Gavin

Stevens some of the time. The rise of Flem Snopes is described with great precision and skill, though the plot, like the plot of *Intruder in the Dust*, has a complexity that seems over-ingenious. And there is a real tenderness in Gavin's feeling for Linda, though here, too, Faulkner's ingenuity—which is very different from inventiveness—gets out of hand. Yes, there are many fine things, but except for a few sections, some of which, as I have said, were written many years ago, *The Town* is on a lower literary level than *The Hamlet*.

This is something that I do not enjoy saying. At no time in the past decade have I been willing to conclude that Faulkner's creative powers were waning: You cannot expect even a very great writer to produce nothing but masterpieces, and in any case the work he was doing was in one way or another different in intention from the work he had done in earlier decades. For *The Town*, however, there are no excuses. It would be preposterous to announce that Faulkner is "finished," but he has produced a book that is obviously less than it was intended to be. Whether its shortcomings are a consequence of his new position as a recognized man of letters and a public figure is hard to determine, but I would argue that this is at least a possibility. The distractions that he avoided for so long, going his own way with an unmatched tenacity, caught up with him at last, and it may be that they have been too much for him.

Walter Sullivan. "Faulkner Writes New Unit of His Trilogy." Nashville *Tennessean*, May 12, 1957, p. 5-H.

Viewed as an individual novel, *The Town* is a love story which concerns Eula Varner Snopes, who is attractive beyond imagination of any man's powers to resist; and Manfred de Spain and Gavin Stevens, who love her; and Flem Snopes, who owns her but is impotent. Read simply as a love story, *The Town* is a fine and beautiful book, and it is filled with the heartbreak which attends man's innocence and man's idealism, his sense of honor and his search for perfection in the world.

But if we intend to do ourselves and Mr. Faulkner justice, we do not take his novels singly. We read each into the pattern of those that have come before, and this book is the second volume of what is to be a trilogy about the Snopeses. It begins with the arrival of Flem Snopes in Jefferson; it ends with the elevation of Flem to the president of Colonel Sartoris' bank, and with the death of Eula—whom we remember as the earth goddess in *The Hamlet*—and with the tears of Gavin Stevens, who is doomed by his own soul's lofty ambition and the tawdriness of the Snopes-ridden town.

We can see now, that just as *Absalom, Absalom!* is a microcosmic representation of Southern history from frontier days to the Civil War, so the Snopes trilogy will, when it is completed, bring Southern history up to date. Or, to fit this book into the scheme of Faulkner's work another way, if *Absalom, Absalom!* and *The Sound and the Fury* are Faulkner's *Macbeth* and his *Hamlet*, then *The Hamlet* and *The*

Town are his *Winter's Tale* and his *Tempest*. There is a richness in these later novels that we did not find in Faulkner's earlier work.

All good novelists are aware of the essentially tragic nature of the human situation. The very good novelists are able to show within this tragic framework a fundamental human grandeur and to predict the ultimate victory of man. Many great novelists are sufficiently sure of man's nobility to make hilarious comedy out of his very misery and frustration without denying one stern syllable of life's tragic circumstances or reducing their concept of man's dignity by the breadth of a hair. Fielding was such a novelist. So was Dickens. And so in our time, as the publication of *The Town* proves, is William Faulkner.

It may or may not be Faulkner's most significant book, but it must be counted among his finest. Without doubt it is his best novel to appear since *The Hamlet*, his best work since *Go Down, Moses*, which included "The Bear."

Victor P. Hass.
"From a Bookman's Notebook."
Omaha *World Herald*, May 19, 1957, Magazine Section, p. 30-G.

Most of the reviews are in now and critics all over the nation have been trumpeting that William Faulkner has written another "masterpiece" in a novel called *The Town*.

This is embarrassing and humiliating for me personally for I have made three attempts in the past five weeks to get enough out of the book to make up a review. I count it as a feather in my hat that I managed to finish the novel for, as with its predecessor, *The Hamlet*, it is an exhausting journey from Page 1 to Page 371.

But finish the journey I did and a more boring, tiresome and rewarding literary trip I have never taken.

I did get a spot of salve for my ragged feelings from the review of the novel Alfred Kazin, one of the finest of our literary critics, wrote for the *New York Times Book Review*.

Mr. Kazin weighed most of Mr. Faulkner's work and even he could not tear himself away from the notion that what he had read was the work of a genius even though he found *The Town* was "tired, drummed-up, boring and often merely frivolous" and a "bad novel by a great writer."

At the risk of losing my professional standing, I'd like to go on record as suggesting that Mr. Faulkner has been grotesquely over-rated by the long hairs and that they, rather than his work, keep his reputation afloat.

I did not understand at the time, nor do I understand now why Mr. Faulkner was awarded the Nobel Prize in Literature. It seems to me that even Ernest Hemingway, shoddy and empty and unwholesome as much of his work is, comes closer to being a major writer than does Mr. Faulkner.

This, of course, is critical heresy because Mr. Faulkner now has become a cult, the darling of the intellectuals, the idol of the "New Critics," a really monumental figure as literary figures go these days.

Yet I find it impossible to pay even lip service at the Faulknerian shrine. His brooding grief over the collapse of the Old Order in the Old South to the rapacious, mean and feral Snopeses of his Yoknapatawpha novels leaves me cold.

And his deliberate obscurantism, his refusal to communicate so that a person with normal intelligence can get his meaning without knocking himself out, his tired jokes and corny anecdotes, his outrageous exaggerations of character until his people are something less than subhuman, his Joycean glee at silly syntax and his endless repetition of meaningless mumbo-jumbo seem to me a waste of his time and the reader's.

It wouldn't surprise me, years from now, to learn that it has all been a vast joke and that Mr. Faulkner has sat in his decaying Mississippi mansion and howled with laughter over the solemn wrestling of critics trying to make sense of his novels.

For myself, I have always held that good fiction interprets human life in a manner understandable to human beings. If it fails to do that I cannot see how it can be good fiction.

Walter J. Slatoff.
Epoch, 6 (Spring 1957), 130–32.

It would be foolish and dishonest for me to pretend that I can report on Faulkner's latest novel, *The Town*, with any sort of real objectivity. I came to it with firmly preconceived notions about Faulkner's writing and with such an argument to pursue. I expected the book to reinforce those notions and to strengthen the argument. And, of course, it did.

My chief notion is that while one can be moved or troubled or excited or delighted or even hypnotized by Faulkner's novels one cannot really understand them, that they may be brilliantly vivid, highly evocative, infinitely suggestive, but that they do not finally make sense, are not rationally coherent entities, anymore than are many of his blatantly incoherent sentences and paragraphs. What is more, I do not believe that Faulkner intends them

to be comprehensible. His works are designed not for the understanding but for the emotions. They are designed not for critical exegesis, but largely to prevent it, to prevent us from using the "mind's reason[s]," which Ike McCaslin explains (in *Go Down, Moses*) we have to give ourselves "because the heart don't always have time to bother thinking up words to fit together." As McCaslin claims was true for God, Faulkner "didn't have His Book written to be read by what must elect and choose, but by the heart." Faulkner does not respect the mind. That is why he is so infatuated with oxymorons, pseudo-logic, and non-sequiturs, and why he makes his intellectuals like Rosa Coldfield and Gavin Stevens so incoherent, and uses incoherence as his chief structural device. It is no accident that every one of Faulkner's experiments with form and style—his rapidly shifting points of view, his use of more or less incoherent narrators, his distorted time sequences, his juxtapositions of largely independent incidents and stories, his unsyntactical marathon sentences, his whole method, as Conrad Aiken puts it, "of deliberately withheld meaning, of progressive and partial and delayed disclosure"—is a movement away from order and coherence. And it is no accident that every one of his novels involves one or more of these experiments and that in most of the novels we find all of them.

My argument is with those critics who insist upon giving to Faulkner's work the coherence and meanings which he has refused to give them. It is not that most of the interpretations are entirely wrong. The patterns the critics find in the works are usually in them to some degree. The trouble is that in every work there are many such patterns suggested, and that Faulkner does not worry about how they fit together. The evil in this sort of criticism is that it blurs the vital distinctions between sense and non-sense, meaningful complexity and sheer suggestiveness, profundity and confusion. My quarrel with Faulkner is that he does not believe in these distinctions. That is why he is so fond of describing events as being "at once futile and tragic," "empty and profound," and why the endings of every one of his novels not only fails to resolve but further complicates the questions of what the novel was about and the meanings it suggested.

Conceived and announced as Volume II of a trilogy devoted to the Snopes family, *The Town* depicts the impact of the Snopeses on the town of Jefferson much as Volume I, *The Hamlet*, treated their effect on the rural community of Frenchman's Bend. As in *The Hamlet*, the dispassionately ambitious Flem Snopes is at the center, and we watch with mixed amusement, horror, admiration and bewilderment as he manipulates his way toward social and financial success, a success which seems less a conscious goal than an instinctive need. And we conclude, I think, that like his wife, Eula, he too, is an amoral rather than an immoral being. But he is amoral not only because he apparently has no consciousness of wrongdoing but because he seems, finally, to lack any human interior at all. I say "seems" because we have no way of knowing whether or not Flem does have human emotions, because Faulkner has been careful to portray him only from the outside. And we cannot deduce his interior from the exterior because Flem's chief characteristic is his inscrutability and opaqueness. We can understand why Faulkner does this. If we were to look within Flem or to understand him, he might cease to serve as a comic character (as Eula says, "You've got to be careful or you'll have to pity him") and he would be less effective as a symbol of Snopesdom, which is by definition non-human and non-humane.

At the same time, this means that we are reading a trilogy in which the central character is an enigma. Faulkner obviously delights in this and much of the book is devoted to Ratliff's and Gavin Stevens's clearly inadequate attempts to understand Flem's motives. But the reader who desires to understand as well as to be amused or flabbergasted feels dissatisfied or even cheated, especially when the book develops serious or even tragic overtones and compels him to ponder the moral implications of Flem's conduct and the causes of the suicide of his wife, Eula. The suicide, too, is an enigma. The Faulkner "interpreters" will find many explanations for it. It will be argued that Stevens and/or the town made her into a guilt-knowing creature at last, or that natural and healthy sex and love cannot survive in a world that we and Flem Snopes have made, or as Gavin and Ratliff suggest at one point, that she was "bored" because there was no one big enough to fulfill her need to give and accept love. But for the reader who has tried to understand or feel Eula as a human being and not merely as a symbolic or thematic one, her suicide is incomprehensible. The Eulas of this world do not commit suicide. If one does, it is a very important matter, worth some thought. Is it possible that by living with Flem, she had, like Kurtz in Conrad's *Heart of Darkness*, finally seen "the horror"? Is it simply that she can neither run away with de Spain or stay in Jefferson? Or is it to save her daughter? We have no way of knowing; Faulkner will not explore the matter. It is possible that he may do so in the final volume of the trilogy, *The Mansion*. If he does, I predict he will offer a variety of conjectures, but little clarification or illumination.

The final problem for the reader, which is, I have suggested, the case in all Faulkner's novels, is to know what meaning to attach to the events he has witnessed, or more precisely, to know which of the many meanings Faulkner has suggested or hinted at, he is to accept. At the end of the book all of the main characters except Flem have suffered terrible misery and defeat. Why? Is it that Eula and de Spain have committed mortal sin by violating valid and real moral law or that they have violated merely the bigoted tyranny established by "incorrigible and unreconstructible Baptists and Methodists"? Charles Mallison suggests both on page 307. Are we to feel that Eula's death is a necessary and justified retribution for the terrible waste of something brave and pure and clean? In a word, are we to take a pagan or a Christian view? Both are strongly urged. Is the outcome of events primarily a matter of doom and fate or are human will and choice important? Both are strongly suggested.

In his introduction to the French edition of *Sanctuary*, one of the best and most thoroughly ignored pieces of Faulkner criticism, André Malraux wrote that Faulkner has no psychology and no philosophy. Or to be more precise, we may say that he has many and will not commit himself to any, which is, in effect, the same as having none. Many admirers of Faulkner will find such a statement infuriating. I think that Faulkner, himself, would accept it. For I think he sees even our best efforts to explain and understand our world as both pathetic and absurd. He may be right, but I cannot forgive him for not trying, and for doing everything he can to further confuse us. We are confused enough already.

For those who do not share my view or who are not troubled by the kind of intellectual failing I have outlined, I fear that *The Town* may still be something of a disappointment. There are moments of brilliance in the work and there is a chapter of wild grotesquerie which will stand with the "Spotted Horses" episode of *The Hamlet*, but essentially the work seems that of a tired or too busy man, one who

is writing out of habit rather than fresh inspiration and perception, relying heavily on the momentum of his systolic mannerisms and his previous creations. There is more repetition than in his earlier books, more recapitulation of events he has presented elsewhere, less effort to distinguish between the voices of his various characters, less sheer rhetorical magnificence, fewer unforgettably vivid scenes.

There is still, of course, much that is very good, considerable evidence that Faulkner is still one of the most talented voices of our time. (If this were not the case there would be little point in being angry with him for lacking the intellectual discipline which would place him in the very first rank.) There are a number of wonderfully comic episodes, one involving two old ladies, two Snopeses, a cow, seven mules, a rooster and eight white hens. The comic-pathetic portrait of Gavin Stevens that emerges from the book is a memorable achievement, and so, of course, is the continued conception and development of the Snopes family. And here again, as in all the Yoknapatawpha novels, Faulkner has brilliantly conveyed the sense that the events he depicts are part of a community history and that his characters are inescapably involved in that community, something which few contemporary writers are able to do persuasively.

Arthur Mizener. "Spring Fiction." *Kenyon Review*, 19 (Summer 1957), 484–88.

Far and away the most important book in this selection of novels from the publishers' spring lists is certainly Faulkner's *The Town*, the middle novel of the Snopes trilogy, which began with *The Hamlet* and will be completed by *The Mansion*. We know the reason for the title of the last volume already; by the end of *The Town* Flem Snopes owns the de Spain house and is refurbishing it in the style he has painstakingly learned to think is the right one for the home of the town's leading banker, a position which he has seized by an extremely complicated manoeuvre which—incidentally for him—involves his wife's suicide. V. K. Ratliff—V.K. for Vladimir Kyrilytch, we now know, since everyone who is wise and human in Faulkner must have a romantic ancestry to take pride in—Ratliff describes what Flem is doing to the de Spain house by saying "it was going to have colyums across the front now, I mean the extry big ones so even a feller that never seen colyums before wouldn't have no doubt a-tall what they was, like in the photographs where the Confederit sweetheart in a hoop skirt and a magnolia is saying good-bye to her Confederit beau jest before he rides off to finish tending to general Grant." For Flem is creating the appurtenances of past, mostly with the help of advertisements and the advice of second-rate Memphis department stores.

There is something almost pitiful about it, for Flem has only desire for these things and no traditional objects to fix his desire on, or, as Eula puts it, "He knew exactly what he wanted. No, that's wrong. He didn't know yet. He only knew he wanted, had to have." However primitive this impulse, however sham its satisfaction, however horrible Flem's method of achieving it, it is the beginning of humanity, just as are Flem's desire for a proper wife (he is impotent) and a proper child (Linda is the daughter of Hoak McCarron, who disappears for good after one meeting with Eula). So Flem has the tasteless, loveless, lying appearance of what counts as respectability: he even persuades Linda to love him as a father, and Gavin Stevens, who has never lied to her before, is forced to lie to her to support that necessary and terrible illusion. (Ratliff says Gavin's relation to the Snopeses is "like that one between a feller out in a big open field and a storm of rain," and certainly he and his world have "given them all.") Faulkner's vision of Jefferson in the period covered by this novel (from 1909 to 1929) is implicit in Flem Snopes's commitment to respectability and in the substitution of the advertiser's parasitic culture for the created culture of the Southern tradition.

Like most of Faulkner's novels, *The Town* has not had a very good press, and judged by the criteria of the well-made novel it has, like all Faulkner's books, its faults—not that these criteria have much to do with Faulkner's kind of novel. It is not, however, easy to see how this novel is inferior in its kind to the earlier works in the Yoknapatawpha saga. Faulkner makes a few slips that might indicate a relaxed imagination (for example, when he casually calls Virginia Du Pre "Old" Bayard's sister instead of his aunt). It is not, however, a mistake, but a calculated change, that the whole Mallison family history, including the history of Gavin Stevens, Mrs. Mallison's twin brother, has been set back ten years: it has to be if Flem Snopes's usurpation of power is to take place at the right time in Jefferson history, for what Faulkner is doing here is to re-imagine his whole set of values in new time in Jefferson's history and in Gavin's life and they must be made to fit one another.

In any event, *The Town* is not, as some reviewers have said it is, a mere string of anecdotes, even though it is episodic (we ought not to forget Faulkner's passion for Cervantes, whom he is reported to have said he rereads every year). Some of the episodes are, taken simply as anecdotes, marvelous enough; perhaps the best one is the pursuit of the mules around Mrs.

Hait's yard, with old Het firmly in command ("'They tightening on the curves!' she hollered at Mrs. Hait. 'They already in the back again'"). But this episode, like all the rest, has its purpose; it is the occasion when I. O. Snopes (who has driven the mules into Mrs. Hait's yard) finally becomes unendurable to Flem in his new respectability and this forces Flem to spend a considerable sum of money to get him out of town for good. "Gentlemen, hush," says old Het. "Ain't we had a day." Indeed we have.

In episodes like this we watch Flem painstakingly cleaning up his family, getting rid of I. O. and—by a characteristic trick—Montgomery Ward Snopes, who comes back from France after World War I wearing "a black thing on his head kind of drooping over on one side like an empty cow's bladder made out of black velvet, and a long limp-ended bow tie" and opens something called "Atelier Monty," where he exhibits dirty postal cards in the back room. After Flem got rid of those relations he furnished himself with a house and the right kind of wife and daughter for the vice-president of a bank.

In another group of episodes we see the contemporary generation of the old Jefferson families. Manfred de Spain, Major de Spain's son, still has some of the old panache, but is, as Chick Mallison says, essentially Café Society, born too early to lead "That new national cult of Cheesecake as it translated still alive the Harlows and Grables and Monroes into the hierarchy of American cherubim." Even Bayard Sartoris is slightly downgraded: "The Jefferson ladies said [Bayard drove too fast] because he was grieving so over the death in battle of his twin brother that he too was seeking death," Gavin thinks, "though in my opinion Bayard liked war and now that there was no more war to go to, he was faced with the horrid prospect of having to go to work." What

the Jefferson ladies said is very close to what William Faulkner said twenty-eight years ago.

There is a third set of episodes in the novel from which the slightly absurd and wholly heroic attitudes of Gavin Stevens emerges. One may resent Faulkner's romantic attitude, not toward the society of the South or even its history, though they are sometimes involved, but, essentially, toward a certain view of man. Perhaps it is easier to accept this view of man when it is applied to the Bayard Sartoris of "An Odor of Verbena" than when it is applied to the young Gavin Stevens, a citizen of the age of the internal combustion engine. But if Faulkner cannot show that it does apply in that age, he will have to surrender man to the horrible respectability of Flem Snopes or to the soiled gallantry of Manfred de Spain. In an eloquent review of *The Town* in the New York *Times*, Alfred Kazin remarked that "Gavin Stevens . . . here becomes a completely silly character." Maybe so. Faulkner certainly sees Gavin's absurdity; it is the absurdity of elevated passion, of naive knightliness, of the awful daring of a moment's surrender, as when Charles Mallison, suddenly discovering that Gavin wants his sister to call on Eula, says:

> "No, by Jupiter. My wife call on that———"
>
> "That what?" Uncle Gavin said, hard and quick. And still Mother hadn't moved: just sitting there between them while they stood over her.
>
> "'Sir,'" she said.
>
> "What?" Uncle Gavin said.
>
> "'That what, sir?'" she said. "Or maybe just 'sir' with an inflection."

Absurd, but never silly, for Gavin is Faulkner's hope. It is he who can conceive of himself and of Eula in terms that make them wholly human, can truly love her, as neither Flem nor Manfred can. "Maybe," Eula says in Gavin's office, where she offers herself to him and he refuses—"Maybe it's because you are a gentleman and I never knew one before." Near the novel's beginning, after Gavin has fought de Spain because of de Spain's attitude to Eula, Mrs. Mallison brings him a rose which she says Eula has taken from her corsage and sent him.

> "You lie," Uncle Gavin said. "You did it."
> "Lie yourself!" Mother said. "She sent it."
> "No," Uncle Gavin said.
> "Then she should have!" Mother said.

In the end, she does. The night she dies "in order to leave her child a mere suicide for a mother instead of a whore," she comes to Gavin's office for the second time, to make him promise to take care of her daughter. The request is not necessary. Gavin has always thought of Linda as the child of his passions for Eula and he has already tried to take care of her, often making himself look absurd in the process, just as he had looked absurd in his love for Eula. The request is Eula's way of telling Gavin she now understands his kind of love, as she had not when she came to his office that other time. Because she does, she dies so that Linda may have Gavin's kind of life—"Not her mother's fierce awkward surrender in a roadside thicket . . .; but love."

You may find it impossible to accept this vision of experience, may find Flem's respectability less horrible than Faulkner does, may find Manfred de Spain less trivial, may find Gavin hopelessly silly because he is willing to risk "acting like a high-school sophomore." But I think it is impossible to deny that the action of The Town, however episodic, is controlled by this vision with a grandeur and complexity which testify to the imaginative pressure under which the book was made.

M. J. Bruccoli. "Faulkner Continues the Snopes' Story." Richmond *News Leader*, July 2, 1957, p. 13.

The Town, the second volume of William Harrison [*sic*] Faulkner's saga of the rise of Flem Snopes appears to have reached a small peak of popular success and is now fading from the current literary scene. In the six weeks it has been on the *N. Y. Times*' best seller list, *The Town* climbed to number six and then dropped to number eight. If the book is only a slight success with the reading public, it was even less appealing to the reviewers. In general those critics grunted in relief that Mr. Faulkner had not brought forth another *A Fable*, but instead they went on to note that *The Town* falls far short of *The Hamlet*.

In *The Hamlet*, the book which brought about the emergence of Flem Snopes, the facts of the narrative were not always perfectly clear; but there was plenty of the peculiar Faulknerian drive and brooding energy and lush eloquence. The characters, too, exercised a special claim on the reader's attention. Although they were rather bigger than life, they were also full of life. Flem's unmitigated cupidity had real fascination, and Eula was little short of a primal goddess of fleshy delights. Now, seventeen years after the publication of *The Hamlet*, a mellower and duller Flem and Eula appear in *The Town*. The trip from Frenchman's Bend to Jefferson seems to have been too much for them.

Flem is hell-bent on respectability, and he wiggles his way to bank president before the novel is over. He even undertakes the chore of ridding the town of undesirable Snopeses. Eula, or Mrs. Snopes, has managed to add 50 or so points to her intelligence quotient.

She still yields to the call of the libido, but manages to end her life with a lady-like noble suicide for the sake of her daughter—who is not really a Snopes. Mr. Faulkner also debases another character, Gavin Stevens, the brilliant scholar-lawyer of *Knight's Gambit*, who is here depicted as a romantic clown. Stevens and V. K. Ratliff—no dope himself—seemingly squander all their energy in trying to anticipate Flem's next coup; but Flem outfoxes them every time. However, the biggest problem with *The Town* is that it is dully repetitious. Mr. Faulkner wastes a lot of time in *The Town* just retelling whole chunks of *The Hamlet*. Even worse, he employs a wearying narrative structure. Ratliff, Stevens, and Charles Mallison (Stevens' nephew) take turns telling the Snopes saga to the reader and to each other; then they retell what they have told and what have been retold. All this seems like a great deal of sweat over a thin story. No wonder that Alfred Kazin in his fine review for the New York *Times* called *The Town* "Tired, drummed-up, boring, often merely frivolous." Perhaps the best measure of the tiresomeness of the novel is the fact that Mr. Kazin got Flem confused with his kinsman, I. O. Snopes. The anonymous critic on *Time* committed an even bigger bungle by confusing the hophead Jefferson druggist with Montgomery Ward Snopes, who is in the porny-picture peep show business.

During his recent stint as a writer-in-residence at the University of Virginia, William Faulkner remarked that he rarely knows what his books will be like when he finishes them. Mr. Faulkner claimed that he lets the characters take over and that his job is to run alongside of them writing down what they do.

Gouverneur Paulding. "Many Souths." *Reporter*, September 19, 1957, pp. 47–48.

Even in France they get a little tired of their literary South, even in Italy, just as we do here. When first discovered, any country's literary South is a great excitement, but that discovery necessarily grows less and less exciting when it is made again and again, generation after generation. It grows so much less exciting that it is replaced by a deep suspicion of any and every book written about any South whatever.

Thus the French no longer rush to read one novel simply because its action takes place in Marseilles and therefore can be presumed to be comic, or another simply because the narrative concerns the love of a goatherd for a shepherdess in the hills back of the Riviera and therefore can be presumed to be poetic. (It is true that the French are discovering a South that is still virginal, Algeria, which Camus writes about.)

The Italians, with the Southern resources of Sicily long since exhausted by Giovanni Verga (*I Malavoglia*) and Pirandello (*Novelle per un Anno*) as well as by Mascagni and Leoncavallo in their enthusiastic little operas, recently fell back upon their neglected Southern mainland. Ignazio Silone, Carlo Levi, and a host of younger explorers of dialect, folklore, and misery have overrun Lucania, Apulia, the Basilicata, and Calabria. To the northern Italian, everything south of Rome is Africa, but by now that Africa must have been thoroughly surveyed and mapped, and the charm of the familiar is somewhat less captivating.

Mistrust of the picturesque—any South is always picturesque to any North—follows the rapture of discovery. This suspicion, this reluctance to read books with Southern trappings, has the excellent effect of compelling Southern writers, along with tourists, salvationists, and literary profiteers exploiting the South, to write better and better if they want to be read.

In our own country, pillared mansions, Negro jokes—in pre–Civil War novels Negro slaves and horsewhipping—aristocratic ladies dancing with gentleman gamblers in the mansion hall, all these once sufficed almost in themselves to make a story. The slightest connective brought them into juxtaposition, and this could be, and usually was, of the simplest kind. These books were coasting down the hill where once stood *Uncle Tom's Cabin*. They have come to the bottom. Their failure is not commercial, for year after year there will be young people who have still to make their discovery of the South and can make it pleasurably through bad books as well as good ones. Yet as a matter of literary history, easy times for Southern writers are past.

The reason the traditional Southern figures and landscapes no longer suffice in themselves is not that social and economic progress has rendered them obsolete or effaced them. They may seem to have gone, but no traditional figure ever disappears—unless the whole civilization, the Greek, the Aztec, in which he is a part disappears carrying him with it. And certainly in the United States many traditional Southern concepts, no matter how archaic their embodiment, have not disappeared and need only to be treated with some seriousness in order to become recognizable as enduring.

This is exactly what William Faulkner has done. He has breathed new life into the traditional Southern figures. Anyone who parades them lifeless and trite henceforth will be recognized for what he is. Faulkner's new discovery of the South has brought back all the excitement of the first.

He plays with the conventional cards—the knave, Queen, Joker—dealt him at birth, not asking permission to procure new ones—Freudian, or Rorschach blobs—with which to play a new game. He rejects none of the traditional Southern figures with whom he has lived. In *The Town*, his latest novel, all of them are there, none of them un-Southern, none of them imported from alien literatures or created of nothing to project hysteria (Tennessee Williams) or brutality (Erskine Caldwell). They are there in this novel just as they have always been in the Southern legend all through the period when that legend found no true voice to narrate it comprehensibly. They are there, the Southern clichés and puppets, just as in that other South, in Sicily, the puppet knights and ladies, Saladino, Angelica, and Armida of Tasso's poem, hang in the closet awaiting the puppeteer to set them moving and speaking before the children crowding the hard wooden benches. Tom Tom the jealous Negro with the butcher knife, Major de Spain with the first speedster in town, Gavin Stevens the gentle lawyer, Eula the proud and passionate, or Snopes the intruder against whom the Southern code finds no defense—no sooner has one recognized them as traditional figures than they are made corporeal; the obvious is made subtle; the puppets live.

How does William Faulkner do it? If one could answer, that would be knowing why a man is a great writer. Gavin Stevens, the lawyer, is standing on a hill overlooking Yoknapatawpha County: "... yourself detached as God Himself for this moment above the cradle of your nativity

457

and of the men and women who made you, the record and chronicle of your native land proffered for your perusal in ring by concentric ring like the ripples on living water above the dreamless slumber of your past; you to preside unanguished and immune above this miniature of man's passions and hopes and disasters—ambition and fear and lust and courage and abnegation and pity and honor and sin and pride—all bound, precarious and ramshackle, held together by the web, the iron-thin warp and woof of his rapacity but withal yet dedicated to his dreams." The knowledge of how great writing is achieved, supposing it could ever be reached, is surely less useful than one sentence—or even part of a sentence—by a great writer.

John L. Longley, Jr. "Galahad Gavin and a Garland of Snopeses." *Virginia Quarterly Review*, 33 (Autumn 1957), 623–28.

Now that *The Town* has been out for a few months, there is little in the reviews of it that was not entirely predictable. Those reviewers who in 1936 and 1942 decided never to forgive Mr. Faulkner have not done so. Most of the journalistic comments in the weeklies and dailies have, as usual, taken Mr. Faulkner to task for not writing the sort of books that a dedicated "I Love Lucy" fan would enjoy. Most of the reviews could have been written without a reading of the novel, and some of them sound as if they had been. They show the usual indifference to what the novel is trying to do, in favor of showing how Faulkner's view of reality is inferior

to the reviewer's own. In short, they have missed the forest by looking at the trees.

Not that some of the trees aren't worth looking at. *The Town* is the second volume in the Snopes saga, and a Snopes, when he is not simply disgusting or nasty or vicious, can be very funny indeed. Sooner or later, as the predatory battalions move into Jefferson, all the Snopeses encountered in *The Hamlet* turn up again; not only Flem, but I. O., Mink, Lump, and even old Ab. As if this were not more than enough, there is the whole new rising generation to contend with. There is, for instance, Montgomery Ward Snopes, who volunteers to go to France with the Red Cross in World War I, but only to escape the draft, and who manages to run a canteen and a bawdy house under the same roof. After the war he returns to Jefferson wearing "... a black suit and a black overcoat without any sleeves and a black thing on his head kind of drooping over one side like an empty cow's bladder made out of black velvet ..." and opens an establishment he calls Atelier Monty. Eventually it is discovered he is running a dirty-postcard show in the darkroom.

Or, there is Byron Snopes, who runs off to Mexico with all the cash in the bank, and so can never return to Jefferson. But he does send back his half-Apache offspring to terrify the town. There are Vardaman Snopes and Bilbo Snopes (what's in a name?), and Clarence, whom Faulkner readers will remember as the unwashed state senator in *Sanctuary*.

Since *The Town* is a novel about Snopesism, a good deal of previously-published Snopes-lore, including "Centaur in Brass" and "Mule in the Yard," are found in it. In one sense, all this is window-dressing, however legitimate and however amusing. But in another sense, it details part of the essential process of the novel. To change the figure a bit, a novel is properly concerned with the man, the moment, the milieu. In this case, the man is Flem and the milieu is Jefferson. The significant moment is not precisely in time, but at least the narrators are able to tell us what it contained. It was the moment when Flem Snopes discovered respectability.

This is both the central point of the novel and a startling word to use in connection with Flem. To realize how startling, especially when he begins to run his relatives out of town, it is helpful to recall what he was like in *The Hamlet*, before the Jefferson period. In those days his pure and undivided attention was held by the process of getting money. No human feeling or sympathetic impulse was allowed to interfere. It would be entirely inaccurate to speak of him as calloused or hardened, since this implies he once had human emotions which he had successfully overcome. Flem is an inhuman monster, and up to now there has been absolutely no check upon his rapacity: not the law, since he merely ignores it; not his own lusts and weaknesses, since he is incapable of pleasure; and God knows, not the opinion of his neighbors, since such trivia never came to his notice. But now a new factor has come in.

It will be recalled that on Flem's first day of work in the Varner store he appeared wearing a white shirt and tiny black bow tie. It is chilling to think what twisted yearnings these may have symbolized. Perhaps no one else knew, but Flem evidently knew what he wanted. Now it appears that what he most wants is most tangibly represented by the presidency of the bank. But that in itself is not enough. It has to be right: complete, whole, unflawed. With the same unflagging single-mindedness that has made him rich, Flem sets out to complete his personal image of the respectable banker. This means getting rid of his less respectable relatives, painful as this may be in wasted money and effort. Having used the affair between his wife, Eula

Varner, and Manfred de Spain, mayor of Jefferson and president of the bank, to parlay his way into a vice-presidency of the same bank, he now sees that one cannot in respectability continue with a wife who is mistress to one's employer. So with the same efficiency and dislike of waste that characterize him, he manages to bring about his wife's suicide and Manfred's removal from the town; in one operation getting control of the bank and rid of the scandal, and acquiring Manfred's home in the bargain. There is only one item left over; Eula's child, Linda, now eighteen.

Flem is only putatively her father, but it is necessary to the image of himself in the town's eyes that she be what a banker's daughter should be; a dutiful and obedient child who loves her father. He controls his wife by threatening to tell Linda she is illegitimate. Hence Eula kills herself, to leave her daughter "... a mere suicide for a mother, instead of a whore." When her grandfather and Gavin Stevens see to it that Flem will never get her money, Flem still will not let her get away until her mother's tombstone is set up for the town to see. Flem insists that she ride to the cemetery with him in his new car:

> ... and him sitting there and chewing, faint and steady, and her still and straight as a post by him, not looking at nothing and them two white balls of her fists on her lap. Then he moves. He leant a little and then spit out the window and then set back in the seat.
> "Now you can go," he says.

There are three major narrators in the novel: Ratliff, who began fighting Snopesism long ago, Gavin Stevens, the new champion, and young Charles Mallison, who is being groomed for the position of Chief Snopes—Warden of Yoknapatawpha County. He explains the

459

strategy of Snopes-watching in this way: "... Snopeses had to be watched constantly like an invasion of snakes or wildcats and Uncle Gavin and Ratliff were doing it or trying to because nobody else in Jefferson seemed to recognize the danger."

There is another story in the novel as well: Gavin's hopeless and hopelessly romantic love for Eula Varner Snopes, that "bucolic Venus" first described in *The Hamlet*, and now seen as a mature and still more beautiful woman in *The Town*. In the earlier novel, she was discovered to be with child out of wedlock, and so, dishonored by Yoknapatawpha standards, she was given in a loveless and barren marriage to Flem, who is impotent and did not care. In the later novel she has given her love, illicitly, to Manfred de Spain, who too is unworthy of her. To Gavin, the waste of all Eula's potential magnificence is horrible, and he alone perhaps has the gentleness to love her for what she is, and for herself. She can realize this, but simply does not happen to love him in return. The essence of his struggle against Flem is to protect her and her daughter from Snopesism.

The relationship is seen from a variety of angles, and the treatment is now tragic, now outrageously funny. One of the most richly comic sections of the novel is Gavin's symbolic duel with Manfred for Eula's affections, involving a Stutz Bearcat (c. 1912), a sharpened garden rake, fist fights, and a corsage with unmentionable components. One of the most moving passages is Gavin's attempt to protect Linda. He is successful to this extent, as Ratliff puts it: "... the relationship between him and anybody named Snopes ... was like that one between a feller out in a big open field and a storm of rain: there aint no being given nor accepting it: he's already got it." It does not matter, of course, that Eula does not seek Gavin's help at first, and is not particularly interested in him.

Nor does it matter that the town misinterprets his love for Linda. What does matter is that Gavin, in the name of humanity, decency, kindness, and human love, is willing to make the effort, doomed to failure as it is.

In some reviews of ... *The Town* it has been rather testily asserted that Gavin's attitude is "excessive," "foolish," "old-fashioned," "romantic," or, most horrible of all, "unrealistic." This is all quite true; no one wishes to deny it. Mr. Faulkner (he wrote the book) is deliciously, ironically aware of the foolishness of Gavin, and no one is more keenly aware of it than Gavin himself. But he chooses to persist, and it is very difficult to understand how anyone could fail to sympathize with his motives. Of course Gavin is impractical, ineffectual, and romantic, but this reviewer, at least, is happy to remember the voice of mundane practicality in another context:

> "Ah, master," cried Sancho through his tears, "don't die, your Grace, but take my advice and go on living for many years to come; for the greatest madness that a man can be guilty of in this life is to die without good reason.... Look you, don't be lazy but get up from this bed and let us go out into the fields clad as shepherds as we agreed to do. Who knows but behind some bush we may come upon the lady Dulcinea, as disenchanted as you could wish...."

Gavin is defeated because he is human, committed to fighting humanely against inhumanity. The significance of his defeat is that he prefers to be defeated by Snopesism, rather than become a Snopes in order to win. What Flem stands for is terribly clear, but has not yet run its complete course. Perhaps the worst is yet to come. In *The Hamlet* we saw Flem merciless, inhuman, and rapacious. But there was at least one despicable quality he did not have: hypocrisy. He did not need to deceive his neighbors nor lie to himself. At the end of *The Town*, he has acquired a black hat, a car, a house, a bank and is a deacon in the Baptist church. He is still moving fast; he has learned dissimulation, hypocrisy, the theory that appearances are more valuable than facts, and that reality is subjective. He is making up a picture of himself, and he has begun to believe in the picture. We are promised a third volume in the trilogy, to be called *The Mansion*. Who knows, perhaps in this one Flem will emerge some bright morning in a grey flannel suit, a sincere tie, and an office on Madison Avenue. God help us all.

Louis D. Rubin Jr. "Snopeslore; or, Faulkner Clears the Deck." *Western Review*, 22 (Autumn 1957), 73–76.

In Yoknapatawpha County, Mississippi, the Age of the Heroes ended sometime back. Mostly its demise occurred in the nineteenth century, after the Civil War, when Thomas Sutpen and his grand design fell before the scythe, and Colonel Sartoris died of an assailant's bullet, and the Great Bear who symbolized not The Kill but The Hunt was finally slain. It may have lingered on into the present century, but when Quentin Compson realized he could not defend a concept of honor which no longer existed, and so drowned himself, the titans had surely all gone from Mississippi. Now it is the age of the common man, and Flem Snopes, who in many ways seems to personify

it, is about as common as they come.

The common man does not make a very satisfactory tragic hero. *The Town*, William Faulkner's newest Yoknapatawpha novel, is not a tragedy. Nor was its thematic predecessor, *The Hamlet*, a tragedy, and it is not likely that the third and last volume of the Snopeslore trilogy that Mr. Faulkner promises to write will be a tragedy, either. Contemporaries seldom make good tragic heroes, and Mr. Faulkner knows better than to connect a Snopes with tragedy, anyway. There can be pathos in the doings of the Snopeses, and there is plenty of that in *The Town*. But there must also be comedy, and there is an abundance of that, too. In fact, *The Town* is one of Mr. Faulkner's funniest books. There are some hilarious Snopes misadventures, the ubiquitous V. K. Ratliff is in fine form (along wit additional etymological information about his name), and Gavin Stevens shows to good advantage when young. The sequence with which *The Town* closes, involving some half-Snopeses, half-Jicarilla Apache children consigned to Flem Snopes' care, is one of Mr. Faulkner's finest comic episodes.

The Town centers about the rise of Flem Snopes, the Full Man of that tribe of weaselly ridge-runners of which Ab was patriarch. They descended from that progenitor Snopes who stole horses during the Civil War, and was hanged by his fellow confederates because of his inability to distinguish between Union and Confederate purchasers. In *The Hamlet* we learned how the Snopeses infiltrated the County. They burned barns, cheated, connived. They were amoral, unscrupulous, untouched by any motivations save avarice. They were sterile, loveless, yet they swarmed like locusts. Now, in *The Town*, they move from their rural hitches in the county into Jefferson, the county seat, "covering Jefferson like an influx of snakes

461

or varmints from the woods," as V. K. Ratliff describes it.

Gavin Stevens reveals the true nature of a Snopes. "It was rather," he says, "as if *Snopes* were some profound and incontrovertible hermaphroditic principle for the furtherance of a race, a species, the principle vested always physically in the male, any anonymous conceptive or gestative organ drawn into that radius to conceive and spawn, repeating that male principle and then vanishing; the Snopes female incapable of producing a Snopes and hence harmless like the malaria-bearing mosquito of whom only the female is armed and potent, turned upside down and backward. Or even more than a mere natural principle: a divine one: the unsleeping hand of God Himself, unflagging and constant, let alone just Jefferson, Mississippi."

In Jefferson, Flem Snopes does battle with the Old Order, personified by Mayor Manfred de Spain, in whom past family glories have become rodomontade and tinsel. So insidious is Flem's infiltration that his victims seldom know they are endangered, and sometimes even aid Flem in his endeavors. Mr. Faulkner begins by recounting Flem Snopes' previously chronicled attempt to steal the brass safety valves of the town waterworks. It was a defeat for Flem, but only a momentary one. A mere tune-up for the campaign that lay ahead, it taught Flem that his operations must be less petty and more subtle. The water tower where the brass was hid, as Gavin Stevens agrees, was not Flem's monument, but a gigantic footprint, marking his passage.

Flem, who is himself impotent, is married to Eula Varner. His espousal, as related in a previous story, was the result of a bargain whereby he agreed to marry Eula and give her unborn child his name, in return for some property in the county. Once in Jefferson, Eula, who is the female principle personified, immediately becomes mistress of Manfred De Spain. And for the succeeding eighteen years, the period covered in *The Town*, Flem uses his own cuckoldry to build his fortune, for many years by his seeming ignorance of it, ultimately by pretending to discover the infidelity at last.

At the close, Eula is dead, De Spain has departed, and Flem is president of the bank that old Colonel Sartoris had founded and De Spain had headed, and he resides in the old De Spain mansion, having remodeled it to the proper neo-Confederate specifications. In thus achieving status and respectability, Flem also cleans out various petty Snopeses who might inconvenience him, such as Montgomery Ward Snopes with his pandering tendencies, Byron Snopes, a smalltime embezzler, and I. O. Snopes, a cheap horse-trader. For these Snopeses are puny crooks, whose activities are so blatantly obvious that they would make respectability impossible for the name Snopes. And what Flem Snopes desires, must attain, places above all other considerations, is respectability, community status. In V. K. Ratliff's words, "there aint nothing he wont do to get it and then keep it. And when it's almost too late when he finds out that's what he's got to have, and that even after he gets it he cant jest lock it up and set—sit down on top of it and quit, but instead he has got to keep on working with ever—every breath to keep it, there aint nothing he will stop at, aint nobody or nothing within his scope and reach that may not anguish and grieve and suffer."

When *The Town* concludes, Flem is secure, powerful, ostensibly ready for any new challenges. Yet if the novel is the saga of his rise to power and respectability, it is also the story of Gavin Stevens's bitter education in the ways of Snopesism, and how to combat it. Gavin is at his most attractive in *The Town*, being neither ponderously windy as in *Intruder in*

462

the *Dust* nor merely clever as in *Knight's Gambit*. Though chronologically those adventures occur after the battle with the Snopes tribe in *The Town*, it is in this book that Gavin acquires the depth and stature to become a full-fledged Faulknerian protagonist, and to defend the community against Snopesism in the future. That Snopesism must be fought, Gavin and his friend Ratliff agree. But not until late in *The Town* does Gavin discover the true goals of the enemy. He wastes his energies in taking on De Spain—a lengthy, hilarious bout—because of the Mayor's too brazen liaison with Eula Varner Snopes, a foolish business, for De Spain's flouting of decency is unimportant compared to Flem's greater and more hidden scheming. Then Gavin attempts to save Linda, Eula's daughter born of the affair which caused her mother to be married to Flem, from the Snopes heritage, thinking he can do it merely by teaching taste and respect and sensibility to Linda. But such things are not enough; when Flem eventually strikes, he uses the knowledge of Eula's ties with her lover De Spain to get control of the bank. To save her daughter from finding out of her illegitimacy, Eula takes her own life. Only her suicide can protect Linda from Flem Snopes.

But Linda is saved, thanks to Gavin and to her mother's sacrifice, and as the second book of Snopeslore closes, Linda goes away to seek a decent, Snopes-free life, possibly even to achieve happiness.

And the question that remains is, where does Flem Snopes go from here? He cannot stand still; he must expand his domain or perish. Wherever he goes, whatever he next tries to do, this much is now sure: he must defeat Gavin Stevens to get there, and Gavin is no mean antagonist. He is forewarned, he is intelligent, and he understands the menace fully now.

Such is Flem's problem, and such is Gavin Stevens'. And such, too, is William Faulkner's. For he cannot avoid the issue now. He has built his Yoknapatawpha saga through two dozen books covering in scope a century and a half of time, until now the hour is almost Now and the problem our own. The Manichean duality of good and evil confronts Yoknapatawpha. In the Old South of the Heroes, the ending was tragedy—heroic virtues and tragic vices, until at last the imperfect social order tumbled. Now the twentieth century is half done, and though the protagonists have shifted, the issue remains. On the one side is Flem Snopes and Snopesism—pure acquisitive force, compounded of greed, the low cunning of amoral desire, loveless, pitiless. On the other side is, shall we say, Gavin Stevensism, with its idealism, intelligence, kindness. But is it strong enough, ruthless enough, to win out?

Three times Mr. Faulkner has attempted a sort of answer, but each time it has been unsatisfactory, because each time the real issue has been circumvented. In *Intruder in the Dust*, Lucas Beauchamp was saved from a lynch mob, but ethically and dramatically it was not a convincing solution to the tragic plight of Joe Christmas as delineated in *Light in August*. In *Requiem For a Nun*, Mr. Faulkner's proposed answer to the nihilistic dilemma of Temple Drake in *Sanctuary* was a tenuous and unsatisfactory mysticism. In *A Fable* the issue was projected into cosmic terms, and Faulkner the Southern myth-maker became Faulkner the murky and rhetorically-drunk symbolist, but the problems of Yoknapatawpha remained unsolved. Diversions, abstractions, short cuts, these have failed to give Mr. Faulkner his answer; he must fight it out with the persons and places of that particular universe he has created in Mississippi. It is in the town of Jefferson, county of Yoknapatawpha, William Faulkner sole proprietor, that our greatest contemporary novelist must join the issue. This he seems ready to do at last. The third and final volume of the Snopes triptych is now in order.

Dorothy Parker. "Best Fiction of 1957." *Esquire*, December 1957.

. . . Now about those books we all want to give. For myself, to open the holiday exercises, I should dearly wish to send those I most love and respect William Faulkner's *The Town*. The only drawback to this otherwise smooth-flowing plan is that the beloved and venerated go buy and read every Faulkner book as soon as it comes out—which is among the reasons for my feelings toward them, and *The Town* must long have been on their bed tables. It is presumptuous to offer such small awards as these to the greatest writer we have (oh, all right, all right; to the man I believe to be the greatest writer we have, then), even if there were any room left on Mr. Faulkner on which to hang them. Nor can I say that this is William Faulkner's finest work, for his books are so variegated that comparisons among them are not possible. *The Town* comes after *The Hamlet* in his triptych of the horrible, evil, greedy irresistible Snopes family, on their way to taking over full power in Yoknapatawpha County. I hope you will permit me to crawl back to those words I once said about this being no banner year for American novels. This is the year in which *The Town* appeared; I was a fool and a liar.

Checklist of Additional Reviews

Virginia Kirkus Review, March 15, 1957.
Monroe (Ala.) *Morning World*, April 28, 1957, p. 1-D.
Script of WNNT (Warsaw, Va.) broadcast, May 1, 1957 (copy in Random House files).
"Novel Tells of Deep South Erosion." Wichita *Beacon*, May 5, 1957, p. 4-D.
"The Superb Storyteller." *Newsweek*, May 6, 1957, p. 116.
"The Snopeses." *Time*, May 6, 1957, p. 110.
"Snopeses' Progress." Charlotte *News*, May 11, 1957, p. 9-A.
Dayton *Daily News*, May 12, 1957.
"Faulkner's Snopeses Revisited." Denver *Post*, May 12, 1957, Roundup Section, p. 8.
"*The Town*." Pasadena *Independent-Star News*, May 12, 1957, Scene Section, p. 7.
"In Faulkner's World." Erie *Times-News*, May 26, 1957.
"Faulkner's *The Town* Rewarding." New York *Mirror*, May 26, 1957, Home Edition, p. 7.
Bangor (Maine) *News*, June 1, 1957.
"*The Town*." Auburn (N.Y.) *Citizen-Advertiser*, June 1, 1957, p. 4.
"*The Town*." The Baronette (Steubenville, Ohio), June 4, 1957.
Town Crier (Cal.), June 6, 1957.
Denver *Register*, June 9, 1957.
"Characters Continued." Fayetteville *Observer*, June 23, 1957, p. 3-C.
"*The Town*." *U.S. Lady*, Midsummer, 1957.
Inn Dixie (Hotel Ansley, Atlanta), July 1957.
"*The Town*." *Booklist*, July 1, 1957, p. 500.
"*The Town*." *The Record*, August 1957.

"*The Town*." *The Cresset* (Valparaiso Univ.), September 1957.

"*The Town*." South Bend (Ind.) *Tribune*, February 2, 1958, p. 10.

"Faulkner Falters." Jacksonville *Journal*.

Abernathy, Harry. "Episodes of *The Town* Make Delightful Tall Tales." Clarksdale (Miss.) *Register*, August 9, 1957, p. 2.

Adams, Francis R., Jr. "Faulkner at His Best." Richmond *Times-Dispatch*, April 28, 1957, p. 10-L.

Alexander, Charles. "Faulkner's Snopeses Dig in Old Graves." Albany (Oregon) *Democrat-Herald*, May 11, 1957, p. 7.

Allen, John F. "Recent and More or Less Readable." Los Gatos *Times–Saratoga Observer*, June 4, 1957, p. 3.

Andre, Carl F. "Faulkner Tale One of Series." Jackson (Miss.) *State Times*, June 9, 1957, p. 10-B.

Babcock, Frederick. *Chicago Sunday Tribune: Magazine of Books*, June 9, 1957, p. 8.

Banister, John R. "Latest Faulkner Tells New Snopes Adventures." Columbus (Ga.) *Sunday Ledger-Enquirer*, May 5, 1957, p. 8-D.

Banta, Ruth Fark. "Faulkner Continues Theme of Snopesism." Indianapolis *Star*, May 12, 1957, Section VII, p. 12.

Barret, Paul. "Faulkner's *Town* Is Second Book In Mississippi Author's Trilogy." Greenville (S.C.) *Piedmont*, May 9, 1957, p. 48.

Barrington, Kay. "Books and Authors." *International News Service Features*, May 1, 1957, p. 1.

Battendfeld, David H. "*The Town*." *Ave Maria*, May 11, 1957, p. 24.

Bellman, Samuel. "Faulkner Returns to Predatory Snopes Family in New Novel." Fresno *Bee*, May 5, 1957, p. 34-D.

Blagden, Ralph M. "Faulkner Writes Story of 'White Trash' Attack on South's Traditions." Sacramento *Bee*, August 10, 1957, p. 5-A.

Bradley, Van Allen. "His Finest Hour." Chicago *Daily News*, May 1, 1957, p. 16.

Brady, Charles A. "Faulkner Writes Again about the Snopeses." Buffalo *Evening News*, April 27, 1957, Magazine Section, p. 8.

Branam, George. "Faulkner's *The Town* Is Sequal [*sic*] to His *The Hamlet*." Baton Rouge *Morning Advocate*, May 12, 1957, p. 2-E.

B[rock], C[harles]. "Rapacious Termites Nibble Away at South's Old Order." *Florida Union Times* (Jacksonville), June 16, 1957, p. 66.

Burlingame, Robert. "*The Town*." El Paso *Herald Post*, May 4, 1957, p. 4.

Burton, Hal. "The South, Eviscerated." *Newsday*, April 27, 1957, p. 23.

Butler, G. Paul. "Faulkner's Novel Tops." New York *Mirror*, May 5, 1957, p. 32.

Cheney, Frances Neel. "Depth of Vision Marks Saga of a Town." Nashville *Banner*, May 3, 1957, p. 28.

Coleman, Arthur L. "Snopes Clan Rise Related." San Antonio *Express*, May 5, 1957, p. 14-G.

Copeland, Edith. "Bitter Smile Is Provoked." *Daily Oklahoman* (Oklahoma City), May 12, 1957, Magazine Section, p. 30.

Coulbourn, Keith. "Faulkner, Saroyan, Marquand and Steinbeck Are Criticized." Shreveport *Times*, May 19, 1957, p. 4-F.

Daly, Jim. "Latest Novel by Faulkner Hard Reading." Fort Lauderdale *Sunday News*, May 26, 1957, p. 13-E.

Dame, Lawrence. "Looking at Books." Sarasota *Herald-Tribune*, luly 7, 1957, Section I, p. 9.

Derleth, August. "Faulkner's *Town*: Snopes Family Saga Continued." Madison (Wis.) *Capital Times*, May 2, 1957, p. 24.

Dolbier, Maurice. "*The Town*." New York *Herald Tribune*, May 1, 1957, p. 21.

Duncan, Bruce. "New Faulkner Novel, *The Town*, Praised." *Colorado Daily*, May 7, 1957.

Durston, J. H. "Come, Come, William Faulkner." *House and Garden*, June 1957, pp. 16–17.

Dwight, Ogden, G. "Snopeses Inch Forward in New Faulkner Panel." Des Moines *Sunday Register*, May 12, 1957, p. 21-G.

Dwyer, Daniel N., S.J. "Progress of an Artist." *The Pilot* (Boston), May 25, 1957, p. 12.

Elliot, George P. "Fiction Chronicle." *Hudson Review*, 10 (Summer 1957), 292–93.

Ellmann, Richard. "Faulkner Genius Shines in New Novel." Chicago *Sun-Times*, May 5, 1957, Section III, p. 1.

Fecher, Charles A. "*The Town*." *Books on Trial*, June–July 1957, p. 448.

Ferch, Ellsworth A. "*The Town*." *Yale Literary Magazine*, May 1957, p. 23.

French, Marion Flood. "*The Town*." Bangor *Daily News*, June 1–2, 1957, p. 3.

Fretz, Gene. "Snopeses Take Over Yoknapatawpha as Faulkner Resumes Story-telling." *Arkansas Gazette* (Little Rock), April 28, 1957, p. 6-F.

Frost, Derland. "Yoknapatawphians in New Faulkner Novel." Houston *Post*, May 5, 1957, Now Section, p. 37.

Galphin, Bruce. "Faulkner's Poetic *The Town*, Second in Snopes Trilogy." Atlanta *Journal*, May 5, 1957, p. 16-E.

Gauvreau, Winifred R. "Of Books, Publishers and Writers." Suffolk *News Herald*, May 19, 1957, p. 7.

Gildea, Michael M. "Characters Live on Heroic Scale in Second Volume, Snopes Trilogy." Charleston (S.C.) *Evening Post*, April 27, 1957, p. 8-B.

Gill, William. "Faulkner Paints Town." Pittsburgh *Press*, May 19, 1957, Section VI, p. 4.

Glenn, Taylor. "Faulkner: A New Masterpiece." Bridgeport *Sunday Post*, May 5, 1957, p. 4-B.

Gorman, Thomas R. "Faulkner Novel Found a Fizzle for Dreariness." *Catholic Standard*, May 3, 1957.

Govan, Gilbert E. "New Faulkner Novel Again Traces Rise of Man without Standards." Chattanooga *Times*, May 19, 1957, p. 20.

Greene, A. C. "Biting Humor Gives Tang to Latest Novel on South." Abilene *Reporter News*, May 19, 1957, p. 5-B.

Gunter, James. "Memphian Complains of Obscurantism in Trilogy's Second." Memphis *Commercial Appeal*, May 12, 1957, Section V, p. 10.

Gutekunst, E. H. "Snopes Family Tiresome to Reader: To Author Too?" Buffalo *Courier-Express*, May 30, 1957, p. 43.

H., J. "Faulkner's Latest a Disappointment." Jackson (Tenn.) *Sun*, September 15, 1957, Section III, p. 3.

Hall, Barbara H. "*The Town*." Anniston (Ala.) *Star*, September 19, 1957, p. 4-A.

Hanscom, Leslie. "Faulkner's Latest Snopesish Humor." New York *World Telegram*, May 1, 1957, p. 31.

Harrington, Michael. "Uneven Addition to a Magnificent Whole." *Commonweal*, June 21, 1957, p. 306.

Haselmayer, Louis. "*The Town*." Burlington (Iowa) *Hawkeye-Gazette*, July 15, 1957, p. 2.

Hoffman, Frederick J. "The Snopes Balance: 1940 and 1957."

Progressive, September 1957, pp. 33–35.

Hofstra, J. W. "William Faulkner's Epos." *De Tijd*, April 26, 1958.

Holland, E. L., Jr. "Faulkner Returns Snopeses." Birmingham *News*, May 5, 1957, p. 7-E.

Hood, John. "175–Word Sentences Slow Faulkner Work." Houston *Chronicle*, May 5, 1957, Feature Section, p. 35.

Horowitz, Bob. "Wallstreet Panic Snopes Stays in Yoknapatawpha." *Navy Times*, May 18, 1957.

Howard, Edwin. "Snopeses Flow like Lava over Yoknapatawpha in *The Town*." Memphis *Press-Scimitar*, April 27, 1957, p. 4.

Hunter, Anna C. "Snopes Again Corrupt Morals of Small Southern Community." Savannah *Morning News*, April 28, 1957, p. 22.

Hyde, Frederick G. "Faulkner Again Visits the Snopes." Philadelphia *Inquirer*, May 5, 1957, p. 37-B.

Imes, Cristel. "Less Obscurantism in His Latest Novel." Columbus *Dispatch*, May 12, 1957, p. 10.

Irby, James E. "Faulkner Power Shows Slow, Steady Decline." *Michigan Daily*, May 12, 1957.

Jackson, Margot. "Family Seeks Power and a Town Changes." Akron *Beacon Journal*, May 5, 1957, p. 4-D.

Jacobs, Jack. "*The Town*." Birmingham (Mich.) *Eccentric*, June 27, 1957, p. 6-B.

Johnson, Robert J. R. "Faulkner's Revolting Snopeses in New Novel." St. Paul *Sunday Pioneer Press*, April 28, 1957, TV Tab Section, p. 14.

Jones, Carter Brooke. "New Faulkner Novel May Be His Best." Washington *Sunday Star*, May 5, 1957, p. 6-E.

K., A. "Faulkner Back in Literary Spotlight with *The Town*." Galesburg (Ill.) *Register-Mail*, June 5, 1957, p. 13.

Kazin, Alfred. "Mr. Faulkner's Friends, the Snopeses." *New York Times Book Review*, May 5, 1957, pp. 1, 24. Also see letters by Joseph V. Wilcox, Orlan L. Sawyer, and S.P.C. Duvall, and Kazin's reply, June 9, 1957, p. 30.

Keister, Don A. "Faulkner's Evil Hero Top Dog in a New Tale." Cleveland *Plain Dealer*, May 5, 1957, p. 16-G.

Kelleher, Elise. "*The Town*." *Argus*, August 9, 1957.

Kennedy, Gerald. "*The Town*." *Together*, November 1957, p. 52.

Kincheloe, H. G. "Novel of Power and Enduring Value." Raleigh *News and Observer*, May 5, 1957, Section III, p. 5.

Kirk, Irene. "*The Town*." Honolulu *Saturday Star Bulletin*, September 7, 1957, p. 8.

Kirsch, Robert R. "The Book Report." Los Angeles *Times*, April 26, 1957, Section III, p. 5.

Klein, Francis A. "*The Town*." St. Louis *Globe-Democrat*, May 12, 1957, p. 4-F.

Knickmeyer, W. L. "Just Snopeses." Ada (Okla.) *Evening News*, July 7, 1957, p. 7.

Korg, Jacob. "Buckboard to Model T." *Nation*, June 8, 1957, pp. 503–4.

Lawton, Georgeann. "Faulkner's Snopes in New Rise by Osmosis." Riverside (Calif.) *Press-Enterprise*, August 11, 1957, p. 7-C.

Laycock, Edward A. "Back Fence Gossip." Boston *Sunday Globe*, May 5, 1957, p. 28-A.

Leaming, Delmar. "Two Bitter Thumbs." Newton (Iowa) *Daily News*, August 3, 1957, p. 3.

Leigh, Michael. "Books and Authors." Pensacola *News-Journal*, May 5, 1957, p. 7-B.

Lindau, Betsy. "*The Town* on Snopes." Asheville *Citizen-Times*, August 4, 1957, p. 3-D.

Long, Ulman E. "Faulkner's South Is Study in Contrast." Wichita *Daily Times* (Wichita Falls, Texas), May 12, 1957, p. 3-D.

Longstreet, Stephen. "Off the Bookshelf." Los Angeles *Free Press*, May 2, 1957, p. 2.

Lytle, Andrew. *Sewanee Review*, 65 (Summer 1957), 475–84.

Magill, Lewis M. Radio broadcast on network of twelve stations in Washington, Oregon, and Idaho (copy in Random House files).

Malcolm, Donald. "Faulkner Returns to Yoknapatawpha." *New Republic*, May 27, 1957, pp. 20–21.

Marcus, Stephen. *Partisan Review*, 24 (Summer 1957), 432–41.

Maslin, Marsh. "Flem Snopes Wins Again." San Francisco *Call-Bulletin*, May 2, 1957, p. 11.

Mason, Jack. "Lost in Deep, Dark Forest of Faulkner's Trackless Prose." Oakland *Tribune*, May 19, 1957, p. 12-C.

May, William. "Faulkner Novel." Newark (N.J.) *Sunday News*, May 5, 1957, Section IV, p. 10.

McCaslin, Walt. "The Snopes Clan Move into Town." Dayton *Daily News*, May 12, 1957, Section III, p. 23.

McGloin, Joseph T., S.J. *"The Town." Extension*, August 1957, p. 32.

McManis, John. "Faulkner Fogs Family Record." Detroit *News*, April 28, 1957, p. 9-E.

Meriwether, James B. "Snopes Revisited." *Saturday Review*, April 27, 1957, pp. 12–13.

Merlin, Milton. "Faulkner Scores Success with *The Town*." Los Angeles *Times*, May 19, 1957, Part V, p. 7.

Moore, William G. "Faulkner at His Best." Columbus *Citizen*, April 21, 1957, Magazine Section, p. 20.

Morse, Samuel F. "The Second Panel."

Hartford *Courant*, May 26, 1957, Magazine Section, p. 14.

Nelson, Stan. "Second in Faulkner's Trilogy Holds Interest." Fort Worth *Star-Telegram*, May 12, 1957, Section II, p. 8.

Nichols, Luther. "Faulkner: A New Novel by the Architect of Southern Gothic." San Francisco *Examiner*, April 28, 1957, Modern Living Section, p. 11.

O., T. "Snopes Family Ran *The Town*." Columbia *Missourian*, June 6, 1957, p. 4.

O'Leary, Theodore M. "Faulkner at His Best in His Latest Novel." Kansas City *Star*, May 11, 1957, p. 6.

O'Neill, Frank. "Faulkner at Peak." Cleveland *News*, May 1, 1957, p. 17; and "Up from Snopery?" May 3, 1957, p. 9.

Owen, T. C. Library Review in Emporia, Kansas (copy in Random House files).

P., A. *News and Courier*, July 14, 1957.

Parsons, Eugene O. "Town Swamped by Outsider." Worcester (Mass.) *Sunday Telegram*, May 5, 1957, p. 11-D.

Payne, Henry. "Book No. 2 in Trilogy." Tulsa *Sunday World*, May 19, 1957, Magazine Section, p. 24.

Perkin, Robert L. "The Snopes Swarm Again." *Rocky Mountain News* (Denver), May 5, 1957, p. 55.

Perry, Martin. "Sinister, Evil Family Moves Through Faulkner Novel." Wichita *Eagle*, May 26, 1957, Feature Magazine. p. 12.

Phelps, Robert. "Faulkner Recovered." *National Review*, July 6, 1957, p. 43.

Pickrel, Paul. "The New Books." *Harper's Magazine*, June 1957, pp. 85–86.

Podhoretz, Norman. "Snopesishness and Faulknerishness." *New Yorker*, June 1, 1957, pp. 110, 113–16.

Popkin, George. "Faulkner's Paradoxical

New Novel." Providence *Sunday Journal*, May 5, 1957, Section VI, p. 6.

Porterfield, Waldon. "A Townful of Snopeses." Milwaukee *Journal*, May 5, 1957, Part V, p. 4.

Prescott, Orville. "Books of the Times." New York *Times*, May 1, 1957, p. 35.

Price, Emerson. "Faulkner's Snopes Clan Depicts South's Decay." Cleveland *Press*, May 14, 1957, p. 18; Knoxville *News Sentinel*, June 2, 1957.

Reynolds, Horace. "The Snopes Story Continues." *Christian Science Monitor*, May 2, 1957, p. 7.

Richards, Robert. "Let's Talk about Books." Duarte (Colo.) *Dispatch*, June 13, 1957, p. 5.

Richman, Charles. "About Books." Brooklyn *Daily*, May 6, 1957, p. 4.

Rogers, Thomas H. "Farce and Anecdote." *Chicago Review*, 6 (Autumn 1957), 110–14.

Rogers, W. G. "Faulkner Teases His Followers as Usual." Indianapolis *News*, May 4, 1957, p. 2.

Rolo, Charles J. "Reader's Choice." *Atlantic Monthly*, May 1957, pp. 80, 82.

Rose, Ruth G. "Literary Guidepost." *The Scrantonian*, May 26, 1957, p. 19.

Rubinstein, Annette. "Close to Parody." *Mainstream*, September 1957, pp. 60–61.

S., W. J. *Epoch*, Spring 1957, pp. 130–32.

Scott, Glenn. "New Faulkner Novel Adds Chapter to the Snopes Saga." Norfolk *Virginian-Pilot* and Portsmouth *Star*, May 5, 1957, p. 6-C.

Scott, Nathan A., Jr. "The Vision of William Faulkner." *Christian Century*, September 18, 1957, pp. 1104–6.

Seward, William W. "William Faulkner: Folk Legends of Frenchman's Bend." Radio broadcast over WMTI-FM (Norfolk), May 16, 1957; reprinted in *Contrasts in Modern Writers*. New York: Frederick Fell, Inc., 1962, pp. 59–61.

Shedd, Margaret. "Faulkner So Good One Wants to See Better." *Mexico News Weekly*, May 26, 1957, p. 2–B.

Sherman, John K. "Faulkner Drops Symbolism for Humor in *The Town*." Minneapolis *Sunday Tribune*, May 5, 1957, p. 6-E.

Sherman, Thomas B. "Faulkner Continues Saga of Yoknapatawpha County." St. Louis *Post-Dispatch*, May 5, 1957, p. 4-C.

Simmons, Mabel C. "Back Home in Jefferson: Coming of the Snopeses." New Orleans *Times-Picayune*, April 28, 1957, Section III, p. 8.

S[izer], A[lvin] V. "Faulkner Returns Home, Recovers His Old Touch." New Haven *Register*, May 12, 1957, Magazine Section, p. 8.

S[mith], B[lanche] H[ixson]. "*The Town*." Meriden (Conn.) *Record*, September 19, 1957, p. 6.

Spearman, Walter. "William Faulkner's *The Town*." Rocky Mount (N.C.) *Sunday Telegram*, May 12, 1957, p. 2-B.

Stanback, Betty Anne. "William Faulkner's Second Volume of Snopes Trilogy." Greensboro *Daily News*, May 12, 1957, Feature Section, p. 3.

Sullivan, Shirley K. Radio broadcast on KTIB (Thibodaux, La.), May 3, 1957 (copy in Random House files).

Taylor, Robert. "Faulkner and His New Snopes Novel." Boston *Herald*, April 29, 1957, p. 20.

Thompson, Ralph. "*The Town*." *Book-of-the-Month Club News*, May 1957.

Tinkle, Lon. "Of Snopes and Sin in Faulkner Country." Dallas *Morning News*, May 5, 1957, Part VII, p. 5.

Tribble, Hal. "Faulkner Has Big Message." Charlotte *Observer*, May 12, 1957, p. 5-B.

Trotter, Margaret G. "*The Town.*" *Georgia Review*, 12 (Summer 1958), 226–28.

Turner, Decherd. Dallas *Times Herald: Roundup*, May 5, 1957, p. 22.

Ujcic, Albert. *Mexico News Weekly*, May 26, 1957, p. 2-B.

Upton, Bob. "Faulkner Probes Deep to Inscribe the Town." Winston-Salem *Journal and Sentinel*, May 5, 1957, p. 5-C.

Vogler, Lewis. "Faulkner's Rapacious Snopeses Are Back Again." San Francisco *Chronicle*, May 5, 1957, This World Section, p. 32.

Wandell, Walt. "A Book to Convince Critics of Faulkner." Colorado Springs *Free Press*, May 19, 1957, p. 4.

W[arren], M[ark]. "*The Town* Tells More of Snopeses." Columbus (Ga.) *Enquirer*, September 2, 1957, p. 5.

Washburn, Beatrice. "Town Probed by Faulkner." Miami *Herald*, May 5, 1957, p. 4-G.

Wasson, Ben. "New Faulkner Book Shows Snopes' Progress into Control of Town." *Delta Democrat-Times* (Greenville, Miss.), May 5, 1957, p. 20.

Watts, Richard. "Random Notes on This and That." New York *Post*, May 7, 1957, p. 44.

Weigel, John A. "Maneuvering Snopeses Take Over Jefferson."

Dayton *Journal Herald*, June 29, 1957, p. 29.

W[eissblatt], H[arry] A. "Faulkner." Trenton *Sunday Times-Advertiser*, May 5, 1957, Part IV, p. 16.

Wilder, Charles. "Faulkner Clan Arrives." Washington *Post and Times-Herald*, May 5, 1957, p. 6-E.

Williams, Ernest E. "Yoknapatawpha Doings Involves Civic Virtues." Fort Wayne *News-Sentinel,* May 4, 1957, p. 9.

Willingham, John R. "*The Town.*" *Library Journal*, May 15, 1957, pp. 1319–20.

W[ilson], W. E[merson]. "*The Town.*" Wilmington (N.C.) Morning *News*, May 6, 1957, p. 13.

Winn, Marie. "Faulkner's New Novel Has Imagination, Style." San Francisco *News*, May 4, 1957, Magazine Section, p. 16.

Wobbe, James A. "More Story Telling in Faulkner's Novel." New Orleans *Item*.

Worley, Eleanor. "The Old 'Pro.'" San Francisco *Argonaut*, May 17, 1957, p. 22.

Yates, Donald A. "*The Town.*" Detroit *Sunday Times*, May 1, 1957, Section III, p. 3.

Yeiser, Frederick. "Some of the Recent Fiction." Cincinnati *Enquirer*, May 5, 1957, Section IV, p. 13.

NEW ORLEANS SKETCHES

WILLIAM FAULKNER

New Orleans Sketches

INTRODUCTION BY CARVEL COLLINS

Rutgers University Press, NEW BRUNSWICK, N. J.

1958

Alfred Kazin.
"Faulkner Forecast."
*New York Times Book
Review*, March 2, 1958,
pp. 4–5.

Once upon a time—1925—there was an unknown American writer whose name was William Faulkner. In that far-off day there was no Faulkner Studies Associations; no academic conclaves were held to hunt down symbol and image in his work, and he gave no comfort to the ghost of Jefferson Davis. He was not merely a heavily neo-Swinburnian poet; but he lived in bohemian quarters in New Orleans writing compassionate sketches for the Sunday features section of the *Times-Picayune* about crippled beggars, jockeys, bootleggers, idiots, Italian shoemakers, desperate Negroes. He had a passion for low company and an enormous admiration for Sherwood Anderson, who also lived in New Orleans at the time, and whose tender little story, "I'm a Fool," Faulkner ranked with Conrad's *Heart of Darkness* as the two finest stories he had ever read.

Under the influence of Anderson—and of artists and literary friends in New Orleans who were trying to escape the heavy scent of magnolia—the poet from the wastes of north Mississippi, who had tried everything and who was regarded back home as a failure and wastrel, now became, through the traditional opening step for American writers of newspaper sketches, a writer of prose and soon of fiction.

These sketches—most of them are from the *Times-Picayune* but some were first published in a famous New Orleans literary magazine of the Twenties, *The Double-Dealer*—are apprentice work, and the first ones are pretty bad. Although eleven of these sketches were reprinted a few years ago in a volume titled *Mirrors of Chartres Street* and two in *Jealousy and Episode*, Mr. Collins found in them many misreadings and omissions, and with the addition of three stories he presents here a more accurate text.

Faulkner began as a "prose-poet" in the arch, Beardsleyan manner of the esthetic Nineties, and the opening pages remind one in their dribbling despair of the tone once favored in high school literary magazines. But the book as a whole is curious and valuable. Some of the last sketches and tales show that Faulkner, although inexperienced in fiction, already commanded certain themes and devices that were to become central in his later work. The book is interesting not only for the biographical account of Faulkner at this period by Carvel Collins, but because of Faulkner's own concern with isolated and rejected figures in New Orleans.

One of the most depressing aspects of the canonization of Faulkner today is the attempt by excessively comfortable people to turn his accounts of Southern life into arguments for "orthodoxy" and "tradition." The fact is that Faulkner has more in common with writers of the Mississippi Valley like Mark Twain than he has with literary agrarians. Many of the principal figures in Faulkner's work are the marginal, wretched and even outcast types of Southern society. The great writer's combination of strength and compassion that one sees in his portraits of Benjy in *The Sound and the Fury* and Joe Christmas in *Light in August* is suggested here in the tenderness of a bootlegger toward an idiot brother who was calm only when he held a narcissus in his hand, in a French veteran adrift on the streets of New Orleans, in a young tramp of supernatural gentleness, in a desperate Negro stevedore, trying to make his way back to Africa and used by everyone he meets.

"'When I holp loadin' yestiddy, Ah thought us was all goin' on dis boat.'

"The white man bore down on him with tides of profanity 'Don't you know where this boat is going? It's going to Natchez.'

"'Dat suit me all right, jes' so she pass Af'ica. You jes' tell me when we gits dar and if she don't stop I kin jump off and swim to de bank.'"

Hard-luck stories used to be a traditional subject of Sunday feature stories. But Faulkner's identification of himself with these marginal characters in American society is emphasized by his enormous admiration for Anderson's story of the boy who made a lasting mistake in "I'm a Fool." If Faulkner thought of Anderson as "a giant" surrounded by pygmies, Anderson knew Faulkner to be "gentle." "Life may be at times infinitely vulgar. Bill never is." There seems to be something in every great writer's make-up that is not "integrated," as most people now want to be, but that brings into simultaneous play an unforgivingness toward the world and an immense sympathy for human beings. Faulkner's early sketches are often spoiled by a quality of loose religious emotion, which in his later work is concentrated and objectified into dramatic power.

The interesting thing for us now, who can see in this book the outline of the writer Faulkner was to become, is that before he had published his first novel he had already determined certain main themes in his work, he had already worked out his imaginative place in American society. Even when he puffed words like soap bubbles, it was because he really loved words for themselves, for what they are, as only a writer can.

Horace Reynolds.
"Faulkner Before He Was Famous."
Christian Science Monitor, April 24, 1958, p. 11.

In 1925 when William Faulkner was 27, he lived for six months in New Orleans, joining the group of writers and artists who there clustered around Sherwood Anderson in this Louisiana Bohemia. Those were the years when John McClure was editing the book pages of the New Orleans *Times-Picayune* and *The Double Dealer* magazine of which McClure had been one of the founders, was printing not only early Faulkner and Hemingway but also Sherwood Anderson, Hart Crane, Robert Penn Warren, Ezra Pound, Edmund Wilson, and many others whose names have since become well known in American letters.

The early work of a distinguished writer is always interesting for its forecast of what is to come, and the sixteen sketches here reprinted from the *Picayune*, are no exception. Thirteen of these have been reprinted in book form before but, according to Mr. Collins, with such "misreadings, omissions, and additions" as to justify their second reprinting here. In addition, this collection reprints from *The Double Dealer* a group of thumbnail sketches of New Orleans types, and three long stories never before reprinted from the *Picayune*.

All are the work of a man so young he can write, "The moon is a silver sickle about to mow the rose of evening from the western sky." But they are also the work of a young man who can write that the sunlight flashed "through the window, crashing in my head like last night's piano."

474

Most obvious of the foreshadowings are the use of the pattern of fable, in this case that of "The Country Maid and Her Milk Pail," here in the story "Chance." There are also two characters, one in "The Kingdom of God," another in "Yo Ho and Two Bottles of Rum," both of which come in for much more extensive treatment in *The Sound and the Fury*, and *As I Lay Dying*, respectively.

The horse which here runs through old Miss Harnion's house, in "The Liar," later runs through houses in both *The Hamlet* and *The Town*. A horse in a house is a favorite Faulkner image of incongruity.

The story in which the horse appears is perhaps the best in the collection and certainly the most indicative of what is to come. Its background is not New Orleans but the Deep South back country: the platform of its action is the porch of a country store. It also holds Faulkner's fondness for violent, highly seasoned actions, the expanded episode (here in miniature), and the cadential joke, often ironic or grim.

Mr. Collins, who teaches English at MIT, has provided an introductory essay which well sets these stories in the stream of Faulkner's life and work. We are grateful to him for reminding us that in the 1920's New Orleans once again played host to American letters as it had in the century before to Walt Whitman and Lafcadio Hearn, among others. We are grateful also for his letting us see how early the love of soliloquy dominated the writing of the man who is widely considered America's foremost living novelist.

Checklist of Additional Reviews

"Early Faulkner." *Newsweek,* December 30, 1957.

"*New Orleans Sketches.*" *Booklist,* April 15, 1958, p. 476.

Burns, John A. "*New Orleans Sketches.*" *Library Journal,* May 1, 1958, p. 1436.

Engle, Paul. "Early Faulkner Tales." Chicago *Sunday Tribune,* February 16, 1958, Magazine of Books, p. 3.

Garrett, George P. "The Earliest Faulkner." *Prairie Schooner,* 32 (Fall 1958), 159–60; also reviewed in *Georgia Review,* 14 (Summer 1960), 215–16.

Kane, Harnette T. "Faulkner's Early Work Gave Hints." Washington *Post,* August 10, 1958, p. 7-E.

Poore, Charles. "Books of the Times." New York *Times,* April 1, 1958, p. 29.

Ridgely, Joseph V. "William Faulkner." *Modern Language Notes,* 74 (February 1959), 175–76.

Rumley, Larry. "Faulkner's 'Sketches' Show Seeds of His Later Imagery." Baton Rouge *Morning Advocate,* May 10, 1959, p. 2-E.

Simmons, George E. "*New Orleans Sketches.*" New Orleans *Times-Picayune.*

THREE FAMOUS SHORT NOVELS

Three Famous Short Novels

by

WILLIAM FAULKNER

SPOTTED HORSES

OLD MAN

THE BEAR

VINTAGE BOOKS

A DIVISION OF RANDOM HOUSE

New York

Philip Y. Coleman. "Debt Repaid to Faulkner." *Daily Illini* (Champaign, Ill.), May 13, 1958.

The publishing of *Three Famous Short Novels* by William Faulkner is both an act of publishing inequity and a payment of retribution for previous inequity which well serves to point out what is wrong with the American publishing industry and why what's wrong cannot be corrected.

William Faulkner wrote for years, a novelist unnoticed, hardly known outside his home town—known there as a bum. His attempts to get recognition as a novelist met with dismal failure as book after book went unnoticed and unbought. He wrote ably—if not consistently, flashily. But it was not until he wrote *Sanctuary*, a novel he professes to have written only because he knew it would attract attention, that he had a publishing success.

Now things are different. William Faulkner is a Nobel Prize winner. All his works have made money, including the earlier failures. He is universally acclaimed.

So now the publishing people are repaying William Faulkner for all those hard years. They have not only published everything he has written, but they have used all the tricks available to republish the same works time after time.

Three Famous Short Novels is one of those tricks. It contains in order "Spotted Horses," "Old Man," and "The Bear."

"Spotted Horses" is a seventy page excerpt from a full length novel, *The Hamlet*. It is funny and entertaining, much lighter than the usual Faulkner writing. But it is not a novel.

"The Bear" is a novel. It is built around a central character who goes through a profound change. Not only that, it is also typically Faulkner: the subject matter is straight from Yoknapatawpha County and the style, especially in the fourth chapter, is involuted, periodic, involved and impressive. "The Bear" is a good novel, but not so good as to merit being reanthologized ad infinitum.

"Old Man" on the other hand is a worthwhile novel, underrated and too seldom read. If this volume has any merit, that merit lies in the republication of this novel.

The Old Man of the story is old man river—the Mississippi at flood time. The protagonist is a convict who is pulled off a Mississippi penal farm to fight the flood and who is sent on an errand which takes him seven weeks to fulfill.

He is told to take a skiff out on the river to rescue a woman in a tree and a man on the roof of a cottonhouse. In the process of retrieving the woman, who turns out to be nine months pregnant, he bumbles the skiff into the current and is washed way down stream.

For the next several days he is washed by the flood, finding only temporary haven on an Indian mound (there the woman's baby is born) and afterwards at an alligator hunter's cabin and a Red Cross rescue center. He leaves the last of these because the flood has begun to subside, and he begins the laborious journey back upstream, working along the way to earn money for food, always dragging the skiff and mother and child with him.

Finally arriving back at the penal farm, he walks up to the deputy warden and pronounces the perfect mock heroic: "All right, yonder's your boat, and here's the woman. But I never did find that bastard on the cottonhouse."

479

In spite of the punch line, this is a serious novel, one worth reading. That it is sandwiched between two other pieces is to be regretted, but a publishing company must make money first and then make sense.

The inclusion of "Spotted Horses" and "The Bear" guarantees the volume a certain success—a profit which will pay for other failures. If it weren't for bread and butter publications such as this, a company could never afford to publish the early novels of other young novelists who don't yet have an audience.

THE MANSION

The
MANSION
William Faulkner

RANDOM HOUSE · NEW YORK

R. E. L. Masters. "Faulkner Concluding Novel of Snopes Family Is Unwieldy, Irritating and Dull." Shreveport *Times*, November 1, 1959, p. 4-G.

William Faulkner's chronicle of the Snopes family, which began with *The Hamlet* (1940) and was extended in *"The Town"* (1957), is concluded with this third volume, *The Mansion*. How Mr. Faulkner may feel about having at last wound up this complex, unwieldy narrative is anyone's guess, but this reviewer's most overpowering response to having finally reached the end is a heartfelt "thank goodness!"—couched in somewhat stronger terms for private consumption.

The three Snopeses who dominate this last book are Mink Snopes—the small, almost invisible, and infinitely patient killer, whose monomania makes him, despite his waifish appearance, about as sympathetic as a water moccasin; Flem Snopes—equally monomaniacal, but in the direction of acquiring everything within his reach; and Linda Snopes—no real Snopes at all, but going through life as Flem's daughter—whose hearing is lost fighting for the Communists in Spain, and who returns to the town of Jefferson to agitate among the Negroes, be investigated by the FBI, and eventually to bring about the novel's bloody and mildly surprising climax.

A large number of other characters—of greater or lesser importance—also skip, hop, meander, slither or skulk across those 436 pages. Only a few of them come to life—notably, Old Meadowfill, whose warfare against a neighbor's hog provides several hilarious scenes. The character who most lamentably fails to be brought to life is Eula Varner, Flem's wife and Linda's mother, who, as a kind of incarnate Venus, moves briefly across the Jefferson scene before taking her own life. Most of the other characters are shadowy figures, whose utterances are almost indistinguishable, and who serve largely to add bulk to a story that might have been better told in a third the space.

Such suspense—and, for the most part, such interest—as the novel possesses, revolves around Mink Snopes who, sent to prison for killing a man, patiently waiting 38 years, never wavering from his plan to kill his cousin, Flem. What does happen when Mink is finally released—and the circumstances under which he is released—is all supposed, no doubt, to be tragically inevitable. Instead, it is perhaps at this point that one is most of all conscious of Faulkner as the manipulator of events.

All in all, *The Mansion* is a tedious tale, made more irritating in places by the here false-ringing language of rural Mississippi, crammed with superfluous material, and unduly complicated by the presence of characters who add nothing and detract considerably.

Mr. Faulkner, as it has become painfully evident in recent years, is not the writer he once was. Despite occasional flashes of brilliance, something has gone out of his work—or he is trying to do too much. One waits in vain for another novel as lean and taut and true as *Sanctuary*, or some of the other, earlier works.

"Saga's End."
Time, November 2, 1959, p. 90.

U.S. literature registers a milestone this week: Flem Snopes in dead. His death in *The Mansion* closes a William Faulkner trilogy that stands alone in U.S. writing for its wild, weird comedy, its savage indictment of rapacity and greed, its haughty indifference to the reader's bewilderment as he tries to follow some of the most obscurely motivated characters in any literature. *The Hamlet* and *The Town* proved that the Snopeses were never far from Faulkner's mind even as he was writing other books that in sum won him the Nobel Prize.

Like a singular breed of evil locusts, Flem Snopes and his clan showed up in Mississippi's Yoknapatawpha County at precisely the moment when the old Southern aristocracy had become a pushover for vulgar, illiterate climbers. Flem's god was money, because money was power, and in the end it even led to respectability. To get money, he trampled over the less cunning, blandly jobbed the unsuspecting; he married the casually pregnant daughter of the big man in Frenchman's Bend, and with equal blandness allowed himself to be cuckolded by a banker because it helped Flem become the bank's president. Behind him he left a trail of foreclosed mortgages, underhanded legal victories, cold-blooded assaults on human decency. In him Faulkner raised a monument not only to the worst kind of Southerner, but to the worst in man everywhere. When, in the present book, Flem is murdered by a pathetically ignorant relative for the best of Snopes reasons, the killing seems not only justifiable but long overdue.

Even more than most windups of multiple novels, *The Mansion* ties up so many loose ends that the string can sometimes hardly be seen for the knots. For a good deal of the way, *The Mansion* recapitulates the first two books. Flem's dirty deals. Wife Eula's electric sexiness. Daughter Linda's womanly inheritance from her mother, nice Lawyer Stevens' frustrated hankering for them both—none of these can easily be appreciated without some help from *The Hamlet* and *The Town*.

In this volume, Faulkner carries the story well beyond World War II, and it is precisely the new material that seems least convincing. Characters get in and out of wars in a way that seems merely to pass time. Linda marries a New York sculptor who is also a Jew and a Communist, but by the time he gets himself killed fighting the Spanish Civil War, the whole episode has the look of merely trying to keep up with the times. Jefferson, Miss. (really Faulkner's home town of Oxford) sees dramatic changes after World War II, but the comments on housing developments, new cars and the Negro problem sound tacked on, like dutiful after-dinner small talk.

The best things in *The Mansion* are the old things: Flem pulling a dirty stratagem to latch on to more property, the heartbreaking description of the raw deal that led ignorant Mink Snopes to murder a rich landholder, the devastating characterization of Huey Long–like politician Clarence Snopes, who rises from rural bully to candidate for Congress. If the Snopes family is unforgettable, it is because author Faulkner understands them as deeply as he hates them. And like so many hates, it seems like a first cousin to love. As always, the Faulkner writing has its quota of awkwardness, irritation, downright sloppiness. And just as surely, much of it seems in the end like some kind of smoldering, personal poetry that stands out defiantly imperfect and unassailable.

484

Time magazine has broken the Nov. 13 release date in William Faulkner's new book, *The Mansion*. A note to me from Random House, the publishers, says the early appearance of the review, "surprised us, too . . . and we are trying to find out what happened."

Time's action lifts the release date insofar as I'm concerned. Actually, I've only completed about 150 pages of *The Mansion*—but I hadn't intended to read any more. The style is too involved, and I spent about 15 hours digesting the first third of the book. It wasn't worth it, to me.

Faulkner is a Nobel Prize winner and a gray-haired veteran, so I can't criticize him without opening myself to the accusation of finding fault with an elder and better.

Just the same, I think he is a silly poseur. Talented. Certainly. But so affected that he refuses to—or at any rate does not—write prose that can be readily understood.

I find passage after passage after passage that I have to re-read in order to understand what he's driving at. Sometimes I never do get what he means. On those occasions when the meaning finally comes through, the message is seldom worth the time or effort.

Is it too much to expect an author to write so that he can be understood?

I wonder why Faulkner does it? What is the literary merit in deliberate confusion and obliqueness? Mind you, there are no ringing words, alliteration, symbolism allegory. There is no question of setting a mood. Just confusion.

Here's an excerpt picked pretty much at random:

"It ain't never too late and won't never be, providing, no matter how old you are, you still are that 'ere 19-year-old boy that said that to that 16-year-old gal at that one particular moment outen all the moments you might ever call yourn. Because how can it ever be too late to that 19-year-old boy, because how can that 16-year-old gal you had to say that to ever be violated, it don't matter how many husbands she might a had in the meantime, provided she actively was the one that had to say 'Of course' right back at you?"

That is not the most oblique or even one of the more oblique passages of Mr. Faulkner. Actually, in context, I can figure out the meaning of that particular quote. But only after going back and re-reading it. And why should anyone bother to do that, when there is so much nice, direct, easy reading on the market, like *Finnegans Wake, Studs Lonigan, Four Saints in Three Acts* and *Titus Andronicus*.

Some Southerners don't like Faulkner because he pictures Southern people as depraved. But, Lord, that don't hardly bother me none a-tall, after reading (well, hearing about, anyway) *Peyton Place*. And, really, Faulkner pictures ALL people—not just Southerners—as depraved, so there's no need for sectional affront.

You do meet some pretty earthy individuals in *The Mansion*, though. In the part I plowed through, the main characters are Mink (don't you LOVE it!) Snopes, who bushwacks and kills in cold blood a hateful neighbor after an argument over a $10 cow; Flem Snopes, an impotent and grasping Cracker who marries a promiscuous and pregnant rich babe so he can shake down his new father-in-law; Montgomery Ward, a noisome ferret who is in the business of selling feelthy peectures; State Sen. Clarence Eggleston Snopes who spends most of his time (on per diem pay) in Memphis brothels and is the "apostolic venereal ambassador" from Gayoso Avenue, Memphis, to the entire north Mississippi; and . . . But what's the use!

In those 150 pages, these must be 20 or 25 characters, and not a single one of them is anything but stupid, depraved, despicable or a combination of all three.

In Faulkner's world, men occasionally do such things as go to church, all right; but their motive invariably is to meet some gal out in the bushes. In fact, he seems to be a bit obsessed with the extra-curricular aspect of church-going, Mississippi-style, for he mentions it a couple of times, with considerable relish, and I think it comes up in his other books.

I do not object to any of that. In fact, I plead guilty to the vice of finding a titillation in salty and salacious *Tobacco Road* characters. I am perfectly willing to admit, too, that Faulkner often writes with humor (although seldom with compassion). The "apostolic venereal ambassador" is a good example. What I object to is simply that he isn't worth the effort. That's why I stopped in annoyance, after spending 15 hours lip-reading 150 pages. I wish someone would tell me, in phrases I can understand, how the story came out. Did jailbird Mink finally kill rich old Flem, the cuckold?

Walter Sullivan.
"New Faulkner Novel Completes a Trilogy."
Nashville *Tennessean*,
November 8, 1959,
p. 20-D.

The Mansion is the third volume of Faulkner's trilogy about the Snopes fam-

ily. It is not, I think, so good a book as *The Town* and certainly not so fine as *The Hamlet*, which many critics judge to be Faulkner's best work. Indeed, a case could be made that *The Mansion* is superfluous, that the story of Flem Snopes and Eula Varner and V. K. Ratliff and Gavin Stevens had its proper ending in the death of Eula at the end of *The Town*. On the other hand, the three books taken together have an obvious formal relationship; *The Mansion* is a proper rounding off.

To speak first of the faults of *The Mansion*, it is repetitive. To anyone at all familiar with the earlier volumes, half of *The Mansion* had already been told in better style. There are places in this book where the humor falls flat, where the drama becomes melodrama. There are times when Faulkner tends to sermonize. These are faults that might be disastrous to a lesser writer. But to make much of them in the presence of Faulkner's genius is a little like saying the staging facilities in the Globe theater were rather poor. There are virtues enough to make up for the deficiency.

The story, which takes place mostly just before, during and after the Second World War, has two major plot lines. Mink Snopes, the murderer of Jack Houston in *The Hamlet*, will get out of prison soon and seek vengeance against Flem, who abandoned Mink to justice during his trial. Linda Snopes, who went to New York at the end of *The Town*, marries a Communist sculptor named Barton Kohl and goes to Spain with him to fight against Franco. Kohl is killed. Linda is rendered deaf by an explosion and returns to Jefferson to move in with Flem and to resume the glorious, heartbreaking love affair that her mother began with Gavin. Like Mink, Linda and Gavin have reasons to hate Flem, for it was Flem, after all, who drove Eula to suicide.

For Gavin, the end is triumphant

486

unfulfillment. Other men marry the beautiful women, other men make love to them. Gavin serves them and worships them from afar. But to judge from the many references to it throughout his work, Faulkner's favorite poem must be Keats' "Grecian Urn." The medallion on Eula's grave in *The Town* must certainly call to mind the marble figures on the vase, and in the present volume, the deaf Linda is referred to as the "unravished bride of quietness." Unravished, at any rate by Gavin, as Eula was unravished by him. Yet it is he, and not Flem or Eula's lover, De Spain, who can say at the end, "I have everything. We have had everything." Gavin and Eula and Linda are images of the terrible paradox of love and beauty.

Finally, Gavin's victory balances the triumph of Flem in *The Hamlet* and *The Town*.

Tom Donnelly.
"Wild Bill's Yonder in the Cornfield."
Washington *Daily News*, November 13, 1959, p. 41.

William Faulkner winds up the saga of the Snopes family with *The Mansion*, and I am pleased to report that black-hearted, larcenous, sadistic Flem Snopes gets his in the end. I won't tell you how, because I don't want to give away any of Faulkner's surprises.

Actually, there are lots of things I can't tell you about this novel, because Wild Bill is up to his usual tricks. He doesn't write what you could call real plain, and he is very coy about letting you know who's doing the talking. Sometimes, even when I'm sure about who's doing the talk-ing, or thinking, I'm not sure what's being said, or thought, or meant. You know how Wild Bill operates. He feels that every reader should be a do-it-yourself man. He offers you three verbs in a clump, and you can select the one you think helps most. Helps, illuminates, elucidates. Also, there are plenty of sentences for you to put a subject in, if you feel so inclined. It will probably help, or aid, or assist you with *The Mansion* if you've read the first two installments of The Snopes Saga: *The Hamlet* (1940) and *The Town* (1957). But not a hell of a lot. The best part of *The Mansion* deals with Mink Snopes. Mink is a small, child-like moron, who goes to prison when he is 25 for murdering a big cattleman. Mink had the notion of hiding his solitary scraggly cow in the cattleman's herd and getting it, the cow, fed for nothing. But he, Mink, winds up killing him, the cattleman, and he, Mink, doesn't get out of prison until he, Mink, is 63. Mink blames Flem Snopes for a lot of his troubles, and he, Mink has reasons. (I always tell myself, when I'm sitting down to spread the word about a new Faulkner, that this time I won't feebly ape his, Faulkner's tricks, but I do it every time, because his, Faulkner's, bad habits are bigger than both of us.)

Actually the story of squalid, long-suffering, confused, betrayed, violent and peaceful Mink Snopes, and how he got his revenge on Flem, is quality stuff: a funny and pathetic cornpone version of David and Goliath. In other sections of the book, which is not beautifully orchestrated, Mr. Faulkner rambles on about Linda Snopes, who got shot up on the Communist side in the Spanish Civil War, and Lawyer Gavin Stevens, who is still mooning over Linda's late mother, the Yoknapatawpha County Helen of Troy. Flem Snopes is mostly an off-stage presence, his diabolism conveyed by what the other characters think, or remember, about him.

The non–Mink Snopes passages don't amount to much, either dramatically or thematically, and if Mr. Faulkner had presented them in a simple, straightforward, grammatical manner, even die-hard Faulknerites might be forced to reflect that there is a mighty pulpy foundation here. To be sure, you can't separate an artist from his style, and one must concede that Faulkner's annoying mannerisms add up to a splendid, or at any rate, crafty camouflage.

Lee Cheney Jessup. "Chronicle of Snopes Clan Comes to Close." Nashville *Banner*, November 13, 1959, p. 32.

The Mansion is the third and last volume in William Faulkner's trilogy of the rise of the Snopes clan in Jefferson, Mississippi. The chronicle was conceived and begun in 1925, producing *The Hamlet* in 1940, and *The Town* in 1957 and is concluded with this latest novel. Faulkner, in a forenote, explains what he refers to as "discrepancies and contradictions in the thirty-four year progress of the chronicle as due to the fact that the author has learned, he believes, more about the human heart and its dilemma than he knew thirty-four years ago; and is sure that, having lived with them that long time, he knows the characters in the chronicle better than he did then." This he proves by his infinitely detailed and poignant interpretation of even the least of his characters, often to the point of confusion and exhaustion to the reader. It is not necessary to have read the two preceding novels to become familiar with and hypnotized by the machinations of the abominable Snopeses!

Mr. Faulkner is a superb story-teller and no matter how disagreeable his theme or how obnoxious his characters, he holds the reader spell-bound by the richness of his imagination and his compelling power with words. He plumbs the depth of human degradation and tears hypocritical respectability to shreds but never loses his compassion for man as a human being. He even establishes a somewhat repugnant and reluctant rapport between the best and the worse, leveling the barriers between with the blindly-driven instincts of mercy and courage. His understanding of human emotions is both awesome and terrifying.

Three Snopeses dominate the story of *The Mansion*—Mink, Linda and Flem. Mink, serving a life sentence for the murder of Jack Houston, passes the long years in planning vengeance against Flem, who according to Mink's view, betrayed him by deliberately withholding help. Flem, who knows a Snopes' feeling about blood ties, has used his ill-gotten money and power to double Mink's sentence, in order to prevent his own murder. Linda, who had earlier gone to New York, married a Communist sculptor and gone with him to Spain to fight Franco, is home, widowed and completely deaf from an explosion. She lives with Flem, her stepfather, who drove her mother to suicide, and has taken control of all the family's possessions—home, bank, money. Gavin Stevens, a brilliant lawyer and a gentleman of honor, loves Linda devotedly and hopelessly, as he had loved her mother before her, and is her confidante, protector and slave. Linda loves Gavin but refuses to marry him for many and obscure reasons. However, because of her love for him, she lets him make the supreme sacrifice, of aiding and abetting her in her revenge, and her triumph. As he says to her, "I have had everything. We have had everything."

Mr. Faulkner, who is a Nobel Prize winner, has already attained sufficient fame to be indifferent to further accolades. However, with this last volume of his trilogy he has completed a powerful and moving chronicle which maintains his literary reputation with fitting honor. No one who has read the first two volumes or who has missed the first two, will want to lose the satisfaction of sharing the triumph of Linda and Gavin Stevens over the most abominable of all the Snopeses!

Orville Prescott. "Books of the Times." New York *Times*, November 13, 1959, p. 27.

Well, it had to happen sometime. Flem Snopes, the spider, weasel and all-around curse of Jefferson City, Yoknapatawpha County, Miss., was bound to get his some day. Whether that means we have heard the last of the Snopes family no one knows, probably least of all William Faulkner, who has been writing, off and on, about the loathsome Snopeses since 1940.

He first wrote about them in one of his most characteristic and most extravagantly ill-written novels, *The Hamlet*. He next wrote about them in a much simpler and much better novel, *The Town*. Now he has completed the third volume of his Snopes trilogy, *The Mansion*, which is published today.

By this time every literate American citizen who reads contemporary fiction at all has made up his mind about William Faulkner and reached one of two possible verdicts: He thinks that the demon-ridden chronicler of a score of fantastic novels about a nightmare South is a master novelist who eminently deserved the Nobel Prize. Or he thinks that Mr. Faulkner is one of the most naturally gifted, but most disastrously undisciplined and sadly self-indulgent of American writers.

Critical restatements of either view will never convert holders of contrary opinions. All they can do is provide each critic with the opportunity to take his stand on previously prepared positions.

I will now report that in the opinion of one reader, who has always held that William Faulkner is the most overrated of Modern American writers, *The Mansion* is an intolerable bore. It isn't even as good as *The Town*, which was enlivened by far more flashes of lusty humor and which contained far more amusing bits. Both novels are written in a much simpler style than the convoluted and labyrinthine prose that did so much to make Mr. Faulkner famous. There is no real trouble in either one about knowing what is going on. The trouble is to care.

It is difficult to care because in *The Mansion* Mr. Faulkner repeats himself frequently and repeats also material from *The Town*. He makes use of the conventional third person and of four different narrators: V. K. Ratliff, a garrulous sewing-machine salesman and corn-pone-fed philosopher; Montgomery Ward Snopes, a seller of filthy pictures (stupid when Mr. Faulkner writes about him, surprisingly bright when he speaks up for himself); Charles Mallison, an idealistic young war veteran, and Gavin Stevens, a lawyer and romantically self-sacrificing lover of Eula Varner Snopes (the Helen of Troy of Yoknapatawpha County) and of her daughter Linda, rebellious do-gooder and high-minded patricide.

One main thread of plot in *The Mansion* might have made an excellent short story, but, stretched on the rack of Mr.

Faulkner's rambling and discursive narrative method, it loses much of the interest it might have had. This is the story of Mink Snopes, who went to the state penitentiary in 1908 for life because in a moment of exasperation he had murdered an arrogant neighbor.

Mink was "small, and frail and harmless as a dirty child," and as ignorant. When his wily cousin, Flem, who could fix anything, failed to come to Mink's aid, Mink found a mission in life. He would kill Flem. He did, too, but only after thirty-eight years in prison and a re-emergence at the age of 63 as a sort of innocently murderous Rip van Winkle.

Mink is a pathetic, comic and sinister character, and, in his own way, likable, which makes him unique among his atrocious kinfolk. He is believably real, too, which makes him almost as exceptional. Most of his relatives—Flem, or Wall Street Panick Snopes or Byron Snopes or Clarence the politician Snopes—are monstrous caricatures.

But in *The Mansion* Mr. Faulkner is diverted from Mink's story for a hundred pages at a time. Sometimes he just lets Ratliff talk at stupefying length. Sometimes he tells all over again the story of Gavin Stevens's chaste and chivalrous love life that was told better in *The Town*, although its last lap as told in *The Mansion* is new. Sometimes he just rambles, mentioning familiar characters out of earlier novels for the sheer pleasure of recalling them and briefly introducing new characters who may well turn up again in future books. Of these the most promising is a Marine sergeant who believed that, while he lay wounded and thought himself dead, Jesus, disguised as a Marine officer, ordered him to return to life. Home from the wars, the sergeant became a preacher, a tough one who mixed his sermons with a lot of authentic Marine lingo.

As in all Faulkner novels, there are flashes of brilliance, of insight and of compassion in *The Mansion* and as in many Faulkner novels there are episodes in which the motivation of major characters seems absolutely unbelievable.

Granville Hicks. "The Last of the Snopeses." *Saturday Review,* November 14, 1959, pp. 20–21.

In a brief introductory note William Faulkner describes *The Mansion* as "the final chapter of, and the summation of, a work conceived and begun in 1925." The Snopeses, then, have been on his mind and in his imagination for a long time. He introduced them to the public in the first of his Yoknapatawpha novels, *Sartoris*, published in 1929, as "A seemingly inexhaustible family which for the last ten years had been moving into towns in driblets from a small settlement known as Frenchman's Bend." There were allusions to members of the family in the novels that followed—*The Sound and the Fury, As I Lay Dying*, and *Sanctuary*—and in the next few years he wrote several short stories about this Snopes or that. In 1940, he published a Snopes novel, *The Hamlet*, some parts of which were based on earlier stories.

Faulkner told Malcolm Cowley, when the latter was editing *The Portable Faulkner*, that he intended to write a Snopes trilogy, but the second volume waited until 1957. *The Town*, as expected, described Flem Snopes's rise to wealth and eminence in Jefferson, but it turned out to have other themes as well. Flem's wife, Eula, who figured in *The Hamlet* as a kind of fertility or earth goddess (Robert Penn Warren's description) was the novel's dominant character. And Gavin Stevens, who had once played the role of amateur detective in a series of stories and had been prominent in *Intruder in the Dust* and *Requiem for a Nun*, turned up as one of Eula's worshipers.

The Mansion, as the title suggests, portrays Flem at the pinnacle of prestige and respectability, but he is given even less attention than he was in *The Town*. A cousin, Mink Snopes, is the central character, and only slightly less important is Linda, Eula's daughter and, legally, but not otherwise, Flem's. There are also, as in *The Town*, episodes that stand by themselves, that belong to the Snopes legend but are not essential to the two major themes.

The novel begins with Mink Snopes's murder of Jack Houston in 1908. Faulkner described this murder first in a story, "The Hound," published in 1931, which, considerably changed, became part of *The Hamlet*. Now he presents in more detail and from Mink's point of view the events leading up to the shooting. He goes on to tell of Mink's determination to avenge himself on Flem, who he feels has betrayed him, a determination that does not abate during Mink's thirty-eight years in prison. Released at last, he does what he has resolved to do.

Meanwhile we have the story of Linda Snopes. As in *The Town*, there are three voices telling the story: there is V. K. Ratliff, who from the outset (though at first he was named Suratt) has been a fascinated observer and now and then a victim of Snopesism; there is Gavin Stevens, who is also an observer, but, because of his involvement with both Eula and Linda, more than that; and there is Gavin's nephew, Charles Mallison, the courageous youngster of *Intruder in the Dust*, who has acquired his uncle's manner

of speaking as well as his curiosity. The story tells of Linda's marriage, of her husband's death in the Spanish Civil War, of her return to Jefferson, of her prolonged and complicated relationship with Gavin and of her life with Flem.

Like the story of Eula and Gavin in *The Town*, the story of Linda and Gavin is enigmatic and less than satisfactory. On the other hand, Mink's story is magnificent. He is one of Faulkner's driven men—like Thomas Sutpen in *Absalom, Absalom!*, like the horse thief in *A Fable*, like many another Faulkner character. He labors fantastically to outwit Jack Houston, and when Houston gets the better of him, he is ineluctably committed to murder. Again there are vast labors to be performed, and again he performs them. Fate, indeed, always imposes upon him a greater burden than he had reason to expect, though what he has expected is more than most men can bear. Thus his stay in prison is lengthened, by a trick of Flem's devising, to thirty-eight years, but his resolution is equal even to this ordeal. It is also equal to all the frustrations and bafflements that beset his search for the instrument of his vengeance against Flem. An ugly little man, bestial in appearance and manner, he is heroic in his pursuit of his evil ends.

The incidental episodes enriched the novel. In one of them, which was published as a short story a few years ago, Ratliff manages to end the political career of one member of the Snopes clan, Senator Clarence Snopes. In another, Faulkner juxtaposes the two meanest men he has created: Flem Snopes and Jason Compson, whom we last encountered in *The Sound and the Fury* three decades ago. Although both men are inspired by "their mutual master, the Devil," Flem is the better disciple or at any rate the easy victor. Faulkner still relishes a contest of wits as much as he did when he wrote *The*

Hamlet, and both of these episodes have the vitality of the traditional tall tale of the early nineteenth century.

Flem's triumph over Jason Compson is but one of a long series of successes that makes up his career as it is portrayed in the trilogy, but that career ends in defeat and despair. For Flem acquiesces in his murder by Mink; Stevens and Ratliff have no doubt about that, although they can only speculate concerning his motives. Mink, indeed, for all his resolution, turns out to be merely an instrument—Linda's but also Flem's. Flem, who in *The Hamlet* quite literally beat up the devil, no longer has anything to live for.

That the trilogy ends on this particular note invites us to re-examine Faulkner's conception of the Snopeses. In an article he wrote for the *Kenyon Review* in 1939, George Marion O'Donnell, one of the first critics to look for a pattern in Faulkner's work, emphasized the contrast between the decaying aristocrats and the aggressively upsurging poor whites, and suggested that Faulkner saw the struggle as one in which evil was triumphing over good. Even at the time when it was put forth, this thesis seemed a simplification, for in some of his works—for instance, *As I Lay Dying*—Faulkner had treated poor whites with great sympathy. Then in *The Hamlet* he indicated that there were good Snopeses as well as bad, and this was made even more obvious in *The Town*. Now, in *The Mansion* he invites us to look with tolerance on two of the worst of the Snopeses: Mink is as dangerous as a rattlesnake, but his powers of endurance demand our admiration; Flem to the end is as innocent of scruples as a hyena, but ultimately we see that he is pitiful.

It has to be said clearly that *The Mansion* is not one of Faulkner's great novels. Faulkner's literary life divides sharply into two parts. Between 1929, when he published *The Sound and the Fury* as well as *Sartoris*, and 1942, when he published *Go Down, Moses*, he wrote at least six books for which greatness can be claimed. His second period began in 1948 with *Intruder in the Dust*, and it includes *A Fable* in addition to *The Town* and *The Mansion*. Because the novels of this period do not measure up to the standard Faulkner himself had set, it is hard not to underestimate them. We have to remind ourselves that they contain, all of them, passages that are absolutely first-rate: some of the Mink episodes in *The Mansion*, for example, are as good as anything Faulkner has ever done. Moreover, there is not a page in any of them that lacks the characteristic Faulknerian touch. They are very good indeed. But one feels in them strength of will and mastery of technique rather than the irresistible creative power that surged forth so miraculously in the earlier work.

Faulkner has become more self-conscious in this second period, and he is now troubled about consistency as he wasn't in the old days. "There will be found discrepancies and contradictions in the thirty-four-year progress of this particular chronicle," he says in his introduction; "the purpose of this note is simply to notify the reader that the author has already found more discrepancies and inconsistencies than he hopes the reader will." *The Mansion* itself, like *The Town*, is free from inconsistencies: the chronology and the relationships of the characters have carefully been worked out. But there are many details that cannot be squared with those in other books. (Gavin Stevens must have half a dozen birth dates.)

Consistency is a good thing, but it happens in this instance to be further evidence of the decline of spontaneity. At the beginning Faulkner spun the Yoknapatawpha saga out of his imagination, and it had a marvelous wholeness that was unspoiled by the discrepancies, even though these were more numerous than the critics have recognized. Now he is consciously fabricating and reshaping it, and much of the magic has gone out of the process.

Faulkner had what (giving up the attempt to define it more closely) we call genius. It is what Herman Melville had when he wrote *Moby Dick* and rarely manifested thereafter. We know that genius seldom lasts, but we are always saddened when it goes.

On the other hand, if something has been lost, something has been gained. In his note, Faulkner says that "the author has learned, he believes, more about the human heart and its dilemma, than he knew thirty-four years ago." Indeed he has. He has learned, for one thing, to respect deeply the human capacity for sheer endurance. He has also acquired compassion. "People just do the best they can," says Gavin at the end of the book. "The pore sons of bitches," Ratliff replies. And Gavin echoes him: "The poor sons of bitches." It is what we say too. The Snopeses, it turns out, are not personifications of greed or anything of the sort; they are poor sons of bitches like the rest of us.

V[ictor] P. H[ass]. "Tiresome Faulkner Ends Tiresome Trilogy." Omaha *Sunday World Herald*, November 15, 1959, Magazine Section, p. 29.

With this wild, obscure, sloppy and punishingly dull novel, William Faulkner concludes his trilogy about the mean, dirty, ignorant Snopeses of Yoknapatawpha County in Mississippi.

The trilogy began with *The Hamlet* in 1940, continued with *The Town* in 1957 and now—Allah be praised!—has been ended with *The Mansion*.

As I understand it, the aristocratic Mr. Faulkner has been trying to say all these years that vulgar and illiterate climbers have just about taken over the Dear Old South and that it is a shame. If the real takers-over are even remotely like the Flem Snopeses then I think it is a shame, too.

But, unlike Mr. Faulkner, I cannot mourn the event. The Snopeses were what was left when feudalism decayed. There might have been no Snopeses, no "poor white trash," if the aristocrats had not kept them trashy. Since the Old South deliberately sowed this whirlwind it is difficult for me to appreciate Mr. Faulkner's sorrow at what has been reaped.

All that aside, I do not think that Snopeses were worth writing about any more than I think the degenerate sub-humans of Erskine Caldwell's novels were worth writing about. Mr. Faulkner, brooding in his Oxford, Miss., mansion, leaves me cold just as his novels leave me cold.

Perhaps it is the measure of my limitations as a critic but I have never been able to understand why the body of Mr. Faulkner's work was considered worthy of the Nobel accolade. I have, I believe, read nearly every line that Mr. Faulkner has published but I cannot honestly say that I have enjoyed more than a few hundred lines of it, not even the finest of the lot, *The Sound and the Fury*.

A writer's mission, if he has any pretensions to being "major," is to mirror and interpret the "human comedy." This, certainly, Mr. Faulkner attempts but over his mirror he drapes a sort of grey, pulpy mass of words that obscure his meaning and bewilder the reader. This tiresome obscurantism, this irritating obfuscation, to me, is maddening and not worth the struggle.

Plato, Shakespeare and a host of other giants managed to be clear. I have often wondered why Mr. Faulkner considers he need not make the effort.

But to get back to *The Mansion*. This is the mixture as before only this time Flem Snopes gets murdered at last as payment for his mean foreclosures, his assaults on human decency. Mink Snopes got him— Mink who had spent 30 years in prison for murdering a man who tried to do him out of a cow. It is characteristic of Mr. Faulkner that he should use so pathetically ignorant a tool as Mink to rub out the ghastly Flem who stands in here for the worst in every man.

It takes the entire book for Mink to get Flem but Mr. Faulkner runs in snippets of other stories, along with some ill-digested history of the past 40 years. The publishers insist you need not have read *The Hamlet* and *The Town* but I insist *The Mansion* would be meaningless if you have not read its predecessors— which I do not recommend any more than I recommend *The Mansion*.

The Nobel committee says Mr. Faulkner is good, the French say he is wonderful, various American critics of substance call him our greatest living novelist but, as far as I can see, Mr. Faulkner has taken care never to prove it.

James B. Meriwether. "Flem Snopes' Come-Uppance." Houston *Post*, November 15, 1959, Now Section, pp. 36, 38.

With *The Mansion*, William Faulkner has brought to a close his great Snopes trilogy, which began in 1940 with *The Hamlet* and continued in 1957 with *The Town*. In the two other volumes of the trilogy, Faulkner told of the rise of Flem Snopes, first in the little crossroads hamlet of Frenchman's Bend, then in the town of Jefferson, during the first quarter of this century.

The Mansion is the story of the fate that finally caught up with Flem, and its setting, like that of its predecessors, is Faulkner's imaginary Mississippi county, Yoknapatawpha.

This is a long and very moving novel, typical of Faulkner in that we have learned to expect of him a blend of beauty and humor that is unique in our time. The two dozen books he has produced in his long and distinguished career (he is now 62) have already proved Faulkner's position as America's greatest's 20th century literary pioneer, and have accustomed his readers to expect each of his books to differ, sometimes radically, from his previous work.

The Mansion has its share of surprises, but it does not present the structural or stylistic innovations which mark a good deal of his work, and which have unfor-

494

tunately obscured for many readers the more conventional aspects of his genius: his profound sense of drama, with its Shakespearean vitality and combination of the humorous and the tragic; his perfect ear for dialogue; his abundant range of characters; and the sheer beauty of much of his writing. These are all present in *The Mansion*, and obvious here, too, is another attribute of his genius, the deeply moral quality which has often been overlooked, not so much because of the difficulties of his technique, but because of the violence that is often a part of his subject matter. Faulkner has never been a purveyor of horrors, but the intensity of his indictment of the human baseness he loathes has occasionally been expressed with a directness, as in *Sanctuary*, that some readers have been unable to accept.

The Flem Snopes who dominated the first two books of this trilogy was a ruthless, ambitious, wholly amoral creature who worked his way up from the desperate poverty of his tenant-farm background to the presidency of a bank. Flem was more a symbol than a character, an almost unbelievable monster who was made acceptable to the reader only because he was treated in a prevailingly comic mode. *The Hamlet* is one of the funniest books ever written by an American, a 20th-century development of the once-crude tall-tale tradition that in the 19th century had produced *Huckleberry Finn*. *The Mansion* has some fine comic episodes, but its mode is not prevailingly that of comedy. Nor is its central figure Flem Snopes. It is Flem's kinsman Mink Snopes who dominates the novel, and it is the strength of the compassion Faulkner shows for this warped and violent figure that produces in *The Mansion* its greatest surprise and its deepest meaning.

From its beginning in *The Hamlet*, an important part of Flem's success came from the use he made of his innumerable Snopes relations, whose clan loyalty he relied upon. In turn, it is clan loyalty which finally destroys him. Flem had refused to help Mink when Mink needed it, and he had sacrificed Eula, his wife, to gain control of the bank. The agent of Flem's destruction becomes Mink, the man he betrayed, and Mink is aided by Linda, Eula's daughter, when she discovers what really happened to her mother.

Like any Faulkner novel, there is a complexity of meanings beyond the simple surface action of its plot. In the lives of old characters and new ones Faulkner chronicles the progress of the 20th century, which he sees here in terms of a continuing struggle to preserve older standards of decency in the face of an increasingly dominant, and perhaps essentially valueless, urban and commercial culture. No sentimentalist, Faulkner makes grimly plain, in the lives and characters of Flem and Mink Snopes, what was done to them by the grinding poverty of their tenant-farmer background. But it is typical of Faulkner that he has been careful to give us another character who comes from the same background that produced Mink and Flem, and to make him one of the most sympathetic and admirable characters. This is V. K. Ratliff, the itinerant sewing-machine salesman and shrewd backwoods philosopher and humorist, who escaped from the poverty of tenant farming, like Flem, by the avenue of commerce, but who carries with him all the qualities of decency and honor and humanity that Flem lacked. Ratliff and Flem Snopes are two characters who are important in all three books of the Snopes trilogy: in them Faulkner shows the positive good and positive evil that any environment can engender.

But in *The Mansion* it is not Ratliff, nor his talkative but honorable friend, lawyer Gavin Stevens, nor Linda Snopes whom Stevens loves but doesn't marry, to whom Faulkner gives the burden of overcoming Flem Snopes and all he stands for. This is Mink's book, and it is to Mink's quarrel with Flem, and to his relationship to the land that bore him and finally claimed him, that Faulkner brings his finest qualities as a writer. To make of this fierce little figure of vengeance a sympathetic character is one of Faulkner's greatest triumphs, and if *The Mansion* is not one of Faulkner's greatest books, it is filled with his genius. It deserves to be read, and it can be read, by itself, though its greatest impact and deepest meaning come from the unexpected, yet satisfying way it brings to a conclusion the Snopes trilogy, which is surely one of the finest achievements of our century in our language.

William Van O'Connor. "Best in Faulkner Comes Out Again." Minneapolis *Sunday Tribune*, November 15, 1959, Home and Hobby Section, p. 12.

When little Bill Faulkner was newly born, a good fairy and a bad fairy stood at either end of his crib, and the good fairy said, "You, William, are destined to be the greatest novelist of your age," and the bad fairy said, "But you are also destined to be garrulous and careless."

Having been told of these auguries, William Faulkner tried to be a scrupulously conscientious novelist and spent as much as four years on a novel, trying to perfect it to the best of his abilities. Eventually, he won the Nobel prize.

Believing the good fairy had routed the bad fairy, Faulkner relaxes. He then wrote three garrulous and careless books, *Requiem for a Nun, The Fable* and *The Town*. And some of the critics (including this one) said, "Ah, Faulkner is through. His important work is all behind him."

But the critics were wrong, because the good fairy and the bad fairy had obviously been wrestling all night through many nights, and the good fairy may be said, on an average, to have won two out of every three falls. With *The Mansion*, the final Snopes novel, Faulkner is back in something near his old form, and that is very good indeed.

The Mansion is divided into three sections, "Mink," "Linda" and "Flem." "Mink" and "Flem" are a unit and would have made a fine short novel. The Linda section is garrulous, careless and unnecessary.

About 12 years ago Faulkner began to use lawyer Gavin Stevens, a compulsive talker, as a narrator. He dominates the middle section, leading the action into unrewarding back alleys and dead-end streets. In *The Mansion*, Faulkner kills off Flem Snopes. He should have saved the bullet for lawyer Stevens.

In *The Hamlet*, published in 1940, Mink killed a man named Houston. In *The Mansion*, Mink's story is picked up at that point. He is sentenced to the state penitentiary at Parchman, Miss. For 38 years he devotes his attention to hating Flem Snopes, his cousin, because Flem had made no attempt to help him. His anger is crystalline, distilled. No other emotion contaminates the purity of his hatred.

Ironically he is a slight, wraith-like little man— Faulkner describes his hands as "child-sized," like "the hands of a pet coon"—but his anger is enormous. Mink is a miserable, even mad creature, yet one comes to admire him, to have a kind a perverse affection for him. He feels the earth pulling at him, asking him to lie down, to die—but he refuses, and his anger is the sustaining force in his life. It transcends ordinary human anger.

Twenty and more years ago, Faulkner was creating characters like Joe Christmas and Addie Bundren. Their anger and determination were uncontainable. They moved with some strange, irresistible force, and even in death there seemed to be something inexorable about them; their spirits had won a paradoxical victory over matter. Mink Snopes is such a character.

The Mansion also picks up the careers of many figures from other Faulkner novels. There is a short section devoted to Miss Reba Rivers from *Sanctuary*, and one learns some of the subsequent events in the lives of certain of the Compsons, from *The Sound and the Fury*.

But Mink alone is worth the price of admission.

Paul H. Stacy.
"End of the Snopeses."
Washington *Post*,
November 15, 1959,
p. 7-E.

The latest novel of William Faulkner completes a trilogy on the rise and fall of the Snopes family. The trilogy of *The Hamlet*, *The Town* and now *The Mansion* is one of the extraordinary achievements of American literature.

For equal brilliance of style one must look all the way back to Melville and Hawthorne. *The Mansion* is particularly uneven and complex; it demands close attention. Still, it is a lucid and tense and marvelous book.

In *The Hamlet*, the vicious tribe of Snopes invades Jefferson City; in *The Town*, they rise to ugly eminence. Their degradation and destruction begins in *The Mansion* when Mink Snopes' cow goes onto Jack Houston's land. Houston demands payment for the cow's return—37 $\frac{1}{2}$ days of work. An obscure and unfair law demands that Mink also pay one dollar.

Mink murders Houston. Given a "life" sentence, and then an additional 20 years for an attempted escape, Mink, nonetheless, after 38 years, is released. He heads for home, intent upon killing his cousin, Flem Snopes, the banker who might have helped him earlier but didn't.

The next section skips to Linda, Flem's daughter. She returns from the University after her mother's suicide, goes to Greenwich Village and becomes a sort of wife to Kohl, a Communist sculptor.

They go to Spain, to war; Kohl is killed, Linda loses her hearing. Back in Jefferson, Linda falls in love with Gavin, the lawyer. The love scenes between Gavin, who writes his declarations on a tablet, and deaf Linda, who shrieks when she thinks she is whispering, are profoundly touching, though sometimes on the very edge of sick humor.

Faulkner interrupts the flow of plot with fascinating observations about New York City, modern art, war, politics, class structure and jail life. His descriptions are as magnificent and simple as his dialogue.

The whole novel, as uneven as *Moby Dick*, moves forward in splendid fits of intensity. Faulkner is most intense in his penetrations into human nature, even of minor characters, penetrations as telling as Dostoievsky's.

The final section of the novel concludes the story of Mink on a doubly controversial note. Mink succeeds and very dramatically—in murdering Flem. It is a cosmic death, a deed of mythic grandeur.

"Equal to any, good as any," Mink seems to rise gloriously to a place among "the beautiful, the splendid, the proud and the brave, right on up to the very top itself among the shining phantoms and dreams which are the milestones of the long human recording—Helen and the bishops, the kings and the un-homed angels, the scornful and graceless seraphim."

The paradox of this celestial reward for Mink, the criminal with the animal name, indicated that whoever is on the earth—of grass, of worms, of elemental love—he will ultimately prevail. The Flems, parasites who deny their capacity for love, they rightly perish.

Technically there are puzzles. *The Mansion* is a large cubist painting put together in enormous chunks.

Points of view change, minor themes and characters push to the foreground, transitions are startling, repetitions and variations confuse, and digressions and broken continuity often halt the pace completely. This means that the book (particularly the last third) is often tough going.

But one hesitates before assuming that toughness is a defect, for clearly *The Mansion* is not merely a suitable climax to a trilogy that is monumental in scope and technique; it is, even by itself, as impressive as very few books are—very few indeed.

Louis D. Rubin Jr. "The Trilogy of the Snopes Family Complete." Baltimore *Evening Sun*, November 27, 1959, p. 26.

William Faulkner's *The Mansion* is the third and culminating novel of the trilogy about the Snopes family begun in 1940 with *The Hamlet* and continued in 1957 with *The Town*. It has been long and eagerly awaited.

In *The Hamlet* Flem Snopes, most formidable of that greedy and unscrupulous tribe of ridge-runners who took over Yoknapatawpha county after the Civil War, won control of the village of Frenchman's Bend and prepared to make his descent upon the town of Jefferson, the County Seat.

In *The Town* he did so, and finally attained the presidency of one of the two local banks, withholding his master stroke until the last when he drove his wife to suicide in order to oust the bank president.

Now we see what he does with his power. He is clever, scheming, hungry for respectability, and to reach the top he had permitted his kinsman Mink Snopes, to go to prison undefended. Mink spends 38 years in prison, plotting revenge. Finally he is discharged, and sets out for Jefferson.

So long as Mr. Faulkner writes of Mink Snopes and Flem Snopes, he is at his best, which is close to unsurpassable. The description of *Mink* in prison, and of his attempts to cope with a world that has changed in a bewildering fashion while he has been away, is among the finest writing that Mr. Faulkner has ever done.

Unfortunately, that is not all that happens in *The Mansion*. There is Gavin Stevens, the Heidelberg-educated lawyer, and Linda Snopes, Flem's "daughter" by another man. Linda left for New York at the close of *The Town*, a beautiful and high-minded young girl. She comes back to Jefferson in *The Mansion*. She has married a New York sculptor, who was killed during the Spanish Civil War. She herself has turned stone deaf, the result of an explosion during that war. Now she is a crusader for Negro rights, and a card-carrying Communist (Flem steals the card to use for blackmail).

Gavin, whom Mr. Faulkner had unfortunately married off in one of the stories of an earlier work, *Knight's Gambit*, idolizes Linda, and wants to marry her. But theirs is a love which, Mr. Faulkner tells us, is so noble and pure that it can dispense with sex; as Linda puts it, "How did we say it? the only two people in the world that love each other, and don't have to? I love you Gavin."

So Linda goes to work in a war plant, then comes home and finally Mink shows up—Linda has helped him get out of the state penitentiary—and despite all of the guards—he gets into Flem's sitting room and the deed is done. Pure evil has succumbed to its own deviltry. Snopesism is dead, a victim of Snopesism.

Well, it is pretty bad, much of it. It is amazing that Mr. Faulkner could create so absurd a character as the adult Linda Snopes, could develop Gavin Stevens into what he becomes in this book, could have the two of them do and say and think the things they do. And because Mr. Faulkner is so accomplished a stylist, when what he is writing is preposterous it becomes incredibly, embarrassingly preposterous. Some of the most absurd fiction of our time is contained in *The Mansion*.

On the other hand, some of it is very good. Who, having read this novel, will ever forget the picture of Mink Snopes come back to the world after decades in prison? The scene in Memphis when Mink purchases a pistol and waits about is hauntingly beautiful work. And at the close, Mr. Faulkner's rhetoric comes close to saving the situation, doing as much as rhetoric ever can to bring something off when dramatic technique has failed.

But of course it cannot succeed, and *The Mansion* is a failure as a novel, an unbelievably awkward failure.

All of which goes to prove something about Mr. Faulkner. So long as this great Mississippi novelist deals with rural Southern life, so long as his milieu is primitive and pre-modern, he is matchless. From the earliest Yoknapatawpha tales right down through Mink Snopes in the present

novel, Mr. Faulkner is the greatest novelist of his generation.

But when he attempts to deal with a sophisticated, modern milieu, with characters living in the present and requiring the subtle, intellectual characterizations of moderns, his technique fails, his rhetorical gifts emphasize the failure, and our greatest American writer falls flat on his face. It is not his world; as a writer, his universe is bounded by Nineteenth and early Twentieth Century Yoknapatawpha county. Within those boundaries he has no peers. But let him attempt to step outside the time or the place and he is lost.

So now all the small voices can come out and carp, and this time they will be right. But it is well to remember before joining the chorus, that the author of *The Mansion* is also the author of *The Sound and the Fury* and *Absalom, Absalom!* and may not be done yet.

Durant DaPonte. "William Faulkner's New Novel." *Southern Observer* (Nashville), December 1959, pp. 121–22.

More than just an object of a cult, William Faulkner has become an institution, like Congress or the Church, and it is only with an attitude of reverence or at least awe that one nowadays presumes to approach his work. His fame, like that of the Church, is well-nigh universal, and his every utterance, like those of Congress, are recorded and preserved. And all this, I think, is a pity, for it tends to elevate him beyond the reach of the common reader, who feels intimidated by the Olympian distance which separates him from the creator of the world of Yoknapatawpha County, Mississippi.

For some thirty-five years Mr. Faulkner has been painstakingly detailing the lives and times of as original and fantastic a gallery of characters as can be found in contemporary fiction. Viewed in total perspective, the dozen novels and countless short stories which make up the Yoknapatawpha chronicle take on the epic proportions of a *Comédie Humaine* or a *Remembrance of Things Past*. A fictional analysis of the decline and fall of an American way of life, these works provide a picture of the modern South which is as graphic and compelling as anything produced in this century. The most recent installment to come from the seemingly inexhaustible pen of the Mississippi novelist and Nobel prize winner is *The Mansion*, the final chapter of a trilogy of which *The Hamlet* (1940) and *The Town* (1957) are the other two parts. This trilogy is merely one connected segment of the total picture, but it is in many respects the most impressive part. For sheer gusto and fecundity of imagination it is unrivalled. Whereas certain of the earlier works seem unnecessarily sensational (degenerate, even) and others are so experimental in their technique as to present almost insuperable barriers, the trilogy (especially *The Mansion*) brings us Mr. Faulkner at the peak of his narrative skill, at the height of his mature analytical powers.

Although an acquaintance with *The Hamlet* and *The Town* is desirable for a full understanding of *The Mansion* (as indeed some knowledge of the various other Yoknapatawpha novels will help in untangling the complex narrative threads), the new work may be read as a complete and self-sufficient entity. Viewed as such, it becomes simultaneously a number of different things: a "suspense-thriller," telling an absorbing story of revenge and murder; a sociological study of the corrupting forces in modern life, symbolized by the Snopes blight which creeps relentlessly across the once-fair land of the deep-Delta South; a parable of good and evil and of what the author on a notable occasion called "the human heart in conflict with itself"; a psychological study of moral decline and degeneration; an ironic drama of fate and destiny in almost the classic Greek sense, involving crime and guilt, retribution, doom, and catastrophe.

Three things seem to fascinate Mr. Faulkner (obsess may not be too strong a word): the characters he has created, the technique he has developed for detailing their actions, and the theme of disintegration which is the persistent motif of the entire series.

The characters of *The Mansion* are by now well known to most Faulkner readers: Flem Snopes, who loved only money, finally rich and respectable, sitting in splendid isolation in the mansion he had fraudulently obtained from the rightful owners, staring vacantly and chewing the cud of impotence and nothingness which is his life; a banker now, but morally, spiritually, intellectually bankrupt; Eula, his wife, a combination of Eve, Semiramis, Lilith, and Helen of Troy, the epitome of fatal femininity, "a natural phenomenon like a cyclone or a tide-wave," who escapes her doom by taking the easy way out; Linda, her daughter, no Snopes though she called Flem father, herself a replica of her mother but destined to live a life of isolation through deafness caused by an injury sustained in the Spanish Civil War, and ultimately doomed to be the instrument of vengeance (however indirectly) upon Flem; Mink Snopes, "a little kinless tieless frail alien that never really belonged to the human race to start with," mean, illiterate, comic and pathetic, whose single-minded obsession survives a sentence of thirty-eight years in the state penitentiary to become the focal point around which the action of the novel revolves; V. K. Ratliff, "rural bucolic grass-roots philosopher" and sewing-machine salesman, who knows more about what goes on in Jefferson and Frenchman's Bend than probably anyone else and who is one of Mr. Faulkner's chief narrators; Gavin Stevens, one of the "nice" people in Yoknapatawpha County, worldly, literate, compassionate, morally responsible, sensitive, a lawyer, who comes under the spell of the two women in the novel and whose apparent meddling in the lives about him is merely his way of being, however modest, one of the instruments of fate and destiny; Charles Mallison, Gavin's nephew, older now than when he figured as hero of *Intruder in the Dust,* like his uncle a basically decent person whose life is touched by the fate of the doomed figures about him. These are the main characters, but there are assorted Snopeses—Clarence, the corrupt senator; Montgomery Ward, who made filthy postcards; Wallstreet Panic; I.O.; Orestes; and others almost apparently without number, so that Gavin Stevens, adept as he is at "Snopes-dodging," can remark with stoic resignation: "Even when you get rid of one Snopes, there's already another one behind you even before you can turn around."

As for Mr. Faulkner's now famous (or perhaps even infamous) technique, it remains a controversial aspect of his literary art. One might suggest that it is largely responsible for whatever alienation exists between him and his readers (although there are those who question the validity of the Faulkner world view). The fact is, however, that Mr. Faulkner seems almost willfully to have cultivated a determinedly opaque style. Its defenders may find in it a kind of fierce and highly personal poetry, but the average reader is apt to be somewhat dismayed by the manner in which the Mississippi author explores the dark regions over which he holds undisputed sway. The efforts to forge a no doubt unique style, compounded of a dithyrambic, highly elliptical, convoluted, somewhat ornate and labyrinthine prose, are largely wasted on readers conditioned to expect succinctness, clarity, and facility from those who would communicate with them. It is certainly to Mr. Faulkner's credit that, despite a certain arbitrary obtuseness, an apparent tendency to enjoy obfuscation for its own sake, he manages (in *The Mansion,* at least) to be so eminently engrossing.

As for the theme of this latest opus, it may be stated merely that it is familiar. As Gavin Stevens puts it: "Just to hate evil is not enough. You—somebody—has got to do something about it." If the conclusion tends to be somewhat pessimistic ("There aren't any morals," Stevens said. "People just do the best they can.") the reader may take whatever small comfort he will from the knowledge that here in the concluding volume of a marvelously graphic and profound commentary upon modern life one of our country's most distinguished men of letters has done the best he could. And the result is something of a triumph.

501

Irving Howe. "Faulkner: End of a Road." *New Republic*, December 7, 1959, pp. 17–18, 20–21.

The Snopeses have always been there. No sooner did Faulkner come upon his central subject—how the corruption of the homeland, staining its best sons, left them without standards or defense—than Snopesism followed inexorably. Almost anyone can detect the Snopeses, but describing them is very hard. The usual reference to "amorality," while accurate, is not sufficiently distinctive and by itself does not allow us to place them, as they should be placed, in a historical moment. Perhaps the most important things about the Snopeses is that they are what comes afterward: the creatures that emerge from the devastation, with the slime still upon their lips.

Let a world collapse, in the South or Russia, and there appear figures of coarse ambition driving their way up from beneath the social bottom, men to whom moral claims are not so much absurd as incomprehensible, sons of bushwhackers or *muzhiks* drifting in from nowhere and taking over through the sheer outrageousness of their monolithic force. They become presidents of local banks and chairmen of party regional committees, and later, a trifle slicked up, they muscle their way into Congress or the Politburo. Scavengers without inhibition, they need not believe in the crumbling official code of their society; they need only learn to mimic its sounds.

In a prefatory note to *The Mansion*, the new novel which completes the Snopes trilogy, Faulkner says that he has been working on this clan since 1925. We can well believe it. The Snopeses have appeared in earlier books, *Sartoris* and *Sanctuary*, which contain snatches of portraiture or anecdote later to be worked up in *The Hamlet, The Town* and *The Mansion*. One would speculate that by the mid-twenties, after Faulkner had returned to Mississippi from World War I, the originals of Snopesism, red-neck rascals and demagogues, had come back to the social forefront. Perhaps it was some shock of perception, some encounter with an adulterated (because real-life) model of Flem or I.O. or Ike Snopes, which first prompted him to look back into the fate of the homeland, mulling over the collapse of the Sartorises and Compsons which left the field open for Flem Snopes and his plague of relatives.

In Faulkner's version—it is amply grounded in historical reality—the South by the turn of the century had come to resemble a social vacuum. The homeland drifted in poverty and xenophobia, without social direction or moral authority. Traditional relationships had decayed but there were no workable new ones. Into this vacuum, with a shattering energy, came the Snopeses. And insofar as they are both its sign and product, Faulkner's description of them in *The Hamlet* as "sourceless" is extremely brilliant.

Most of *The Hamlet,* published in 1940, was written during the previous ten or twelve years, and together with *Go Down, Moses*, brings to a close Faulkner's great creative period. It is a comic extravaganza, half family chronicle and half tall tale, strung together in loosely-related episodes that portray the swarming of the Snopeses upon Frenchman's Bend, a hamlet in a rich river-bottom, "hill-cradled and remote," at the Southern rim of Yoknapatawpha county. By the end of the book Flem Snopes, who had begun as a clerk in the village store, is ready to leave for Jefferson, the town where he will become a bank president and then owner of a splendid mansion.

Flem towers over the book, a figure with a marvelous energy for deceit, an almost Jonsonian monomania in pursuit of money. In Flem, Faulkner has embodied the commercial ethos with a grotesque purity, both as it represents the power of an undeviating will and as it appears in its ultimate flimsiness. This *tour de force* depends on Faulkner's refusal to make Flem "human," his steadiness in holding Flem to an extreme conception which, violating verisimilitude, reaches truth. Though Flem stands for everything Faulkner despises and fears, he is treated in *The Hamlet* with a comic zest, a sheer amazement that such a monster could exist or even be imagined. The danger is real, but the battlefield still confined, and opposed to Flem there stands as a mature antagonist, if in the end a defeated one, the humane sewing-machine agent V. K. Ratliff. One of the few positive characters in Faulkner's novels who is utterly convincing and neither hysterical nor a canting windbag, Ratliff provides an aura of security for the book. His very presence makes possible a sustained comic perspective upon the Snopes invasion, and in its own right speaks for the possibilities of civilized existence.

Seventeen years intervened between *The Hamlet* and *The Town*, years not merely of honors, prizes, public declamations and communiqués, but of a slowly mounting crisis in Faulkner's career. The more he kept assuring us that man would "endure," the less assurance his own work showed. Though the novels he wrote in the forties and fifties contain many fine and even brilliant parts, they are on the whole forced, anxious and high-pitched, the work of a man, no longer driven, who drives himself. *Intruder in the Dust* launches

marvelous Negro curmudgeon Lucas Beauchamp, but goes utterly dead with pages of barren Southern oratory. *Requiem for a Nun* contains some exquisite rhapsodic interludes, but in the central sections, so clearly meant to be dramatic, it falls into inert statement. *The Fable*, which may come to hold a place in Faulkner's work somewhat analogous to *Pierre* in Melville's, is a book noble in conception but incoherent and hollow in execution.

What went wrong? It would be idle to try to say in a brief article, but let me at least note a few symptoms of the trouble. In all these works there is a reliance upon a high-powered rhetoric which bears the outer marks of the earlier Faulkner style, but is really a kind of self-imitation, a whipped-up fury pouring out in wanton excess. There is a tendency to fall back upon hi-jinks of plot, a flaunting arbitrariness and whimsicality of invention— as if Faulkner, wearied of telling stories and establishing characters, were now deliberately breaking his own spell and betraying an impatience with his own skill. Consciously or not, he seems to be underscoring the incongruity between the overwrought, perhaps incommunicable seriousness of his intentions—his having reached a point where language seems no longer to suffice—and the triviality of the devices to which he turns.

There is, further, an apparent disengagement, perhaps even a disenchantment with the Yoknapatawpha locale which had so fruitfully obsessed him in the past. Faulkner has now entered the familiar workaday world in which you and I live, at least one part of him has, the man you see in the photographs dressed in a natty grey topcoat; and no longer is it possible to imagine him, like Balzac, calling for his doctor—"get old Doc Peabody!"— from his own novels. His creative journey, begun with the nihilism of the twenties in

Soldiers' Pay, has led him, not as his conservative critics have maintained, to the strength of a traditionalist morality, but to the more perilous edge of the nihilism of the fifties.

Faulkner has become our contemporary. He can no longer work within his established means; one senses a bewilderment and disorientation spreading through his pages, by which the subject of his earlier novels now becomes the force constraining his later ones. How else can one explain the frantic verbal outpourings of Gavin Stevens, the character so disastrously his *alter ego*? Anyone with a touch of feeling, to say nothing of respect, must respond to this new Faulkner who so evidently shares our hesitations and doubt. But in truth this is no longer the man who wrote *The Sound and the Fury*, not even the one who wrote *The Hamlet*.

By the time he turned back to the Snopeses, completing the trilogy in the last few years, Faulkner could sustain neither his old fury nor his old humor. Both, to be sure, break out repeatedly in *The Town* and *The Mansion*; there are sections which, if torn out of context, read nearly as well as anything he has done in the past. But they have to be torn out of context.

Nor is the difficulty to be found in the over-all design of the trilogy. That, on the contrary, is superb. Faulkner sees how Flem Snopes must assume the appearance of respectability, which in turn will rob him of a portion of his demonic powers and pinch him into ordinary helplessness. Faulkner also sees how Flem, though safe from attack by the "traditionalist" moral leaders of the county, must meet his destruction at the hands of a Nemesis from within his tribe: Mink Snopes, a pitiful terrier of a man who spends 38 years in jail because, as he believes, Flem has failed him, and who knows that the meaning of his life is now to kill Flem.

Indeed, one can anticipate scores of critical essays which will trace the ways in which each incident in the trilogy contributes to the total scheme, and which thereby will create the false impression that a satisfying congruence exists between the conceptual design and the novels as they are. (This, I think, is the single greatest weakness of American criticism today: that, in its infatuation with the ideas of literary structure as a system of thematic strands, it fails to consider performance, execution as the decisive measure.) Yet, as regards *The Town* and *The Mansion*, such a congruence is not to be found, for only fitfully do these novels fulfill the needs and possibilities of Faulkner's over-all design.

Let me cite an example. One of the Snopeses, Cla'ence, goes in for politics and in 1945, running for Congress, suddenly declares himself an opponent of the KKK. This shrewd maneuver, apparently made in response to the changing atmosphere of the South, greatly upsets Ratliff and Gavin Stevens, who fear that the minority of "liberal" Yoknapatawpha citizens will now be taken in. Ratliff then arranges that, at a picnic in Frenchman's Bend, a gang of dogs should mistake Cla'ence for a familiar thicket which they visit regularly each day—and this dampening of the candidate makes him so ridiculous that he must withdraw from the race. For as Uncle Billy Varner, the Croesus of Frenchman's Bend, says: "I ain't going to have Beat Two and Frenchman's Bend represented nowhere by nobody that ere a son-a-bitching dog that happens by cant tell from a fence post."

Simply as an anecdote, this comes off beautifully. It has a plausibility of its own. Faulkner can tease this sort of joke along better that anyone else, just as he knows the mind of a grasping little demagogue like Cla'ence Snopes better than anyone else. But in the context of the trilogy the incident is damaging, since it suggests that the threat of Snopesism can easily be defeated by the country shrewdness of a Ratliff—an assumption which all the preceding matter has led us gravely to doubt and which, if we do credit it, must now persuade us that the danger embodied by the Snopeses need not be taken as seriously as the whole weight of the trilogy has seemed to argue. The incident is fine, and so is the over-all pattern; but their relationship is destructive.

There are other, more important difficulties. Through both *The Town* and *The Mansion* Flem Snopes moves steadily toward the center of Yoknapatawpha economic power. The meaning of this is fully registered, but Flem himself, as a represented figure, is not nearly so vivid in these novels as in *The Hamlet*. Partly this seems due to a flagging of creative gifts, so that, for the first time, one feels Faulkner is dutifully completing a cycle of novels rather than writing for the sheer pleasure and immediate need of writing. Partly it is due to his propensity for avoiding the direct and dramatic, for straining the action through the blurred—and blurring—consciousness of the insufferable Stevens and the mediocre young Charles Mallison. Partly it is the result of a genuine literary problem: that Faulkner, having set up Flem with such a preference of malevolence in *The Hamlet,* now faced the difficult task of finding ways to dispose of him, as a character, in the two later books. Apparently aware of this problem, Faulkner tries to outflank it in *The Mansion* by keeping Flem in the background as a figure whom we barely see, though his impact upon the other characters is always felt. That Flem Snopes, of all the marvellous monsters in American literature, would end up seeming shadowy and vague—who could have anticipated this?

Faulkner has made the mistake of softening Flem; he verges at times on sociological and psychological explanations of Flem's behavior; and he even shows a few traces of sympathy for Flem, which is as unfortunate as if Ben Jonson broke into tears over Volpone. When the Flem we see—or, alas, more often hear about—is "the old fishblooded son of a bitch who had a vocabulary of two words, one being No and the other Foreclose," all is for the best in the best of Faulknerian worlds; but when it is a Flem who becomes still another item in the omnivorous musings of Gavin Stevens, then he suffers a fate worse than even he deserves.

The greatest trouble, finally, with *The Mansion*, as with *The Town*, is that Faulkner feels obliged to give a large portion of his space to material that does not directly involve the Snopeses. Again, there is a conflict between the design of the trilogy and what Faulkner can bring off at the moment of composition. The trilogy requires that a new force of opposition to the Snopeses be found, since they have moved to the town where, presumably, Ratliff can no longer operate with his accustomed assurance. In both *The Town* and *The Mansion* Ratliff suffers a sad constriction, all too often playing straightman to Gavin Stevens. For the new force of opposition to the Snopeses, as the Faulkner *aficionado* can sadly predict, now comes largely from Stevens, the District Attorney with a degree from Heidelberg and a passion for rant. Stevens not only speaks the underbaked wisdom that has become Faulkner's specialty since his Nobel Prize speech in Stockholm; he also betrays how deluded Faulkner is in his notion of what an intellectual can or should be.

The middle section of *The Mansion* deals with Stevens' relation to Linda Snopes, stepdaughter of Flem and daughter of Eula Varner Snopes, whom Gavin had worshipped in vain throughout *The*

Town. Linda has left Jefferson; married a Jewish sculptor in New York; gone off to the Spanish Civil War, where she suffered a puncture of her eardrums; returned to Jefferson as a member of the Communist Party; and now loves Gavin (also in vain), "meddles" with the Negroes, and shares a home with Flem in cold silence, until her schemes lead to Mink being freed from jail, destroying Flem and thereby avenging the suicide of her mother. Gavin loves Linda too, but once more in vain. For reasons that two readings of the novel do not yield to me, they fail to marry or do anything else that might reasonably be expected from a man and a woman in love, except to purr sympathetically at each other. Very likely some exegetes will discover or infer a reason for this curious situation, but that will not be at all the same as justifying it in the context of the novel.

In any case, this whole section is poorly managed and frequently tedious. The New York locale, Linda's venture into Communism, the snooping of an FBI man— these are not matters that Faulkner can handle with authority. The relationship between Gavin and Linda, never allowed to settle into quiet clarity, elicits at most a mild pity, since Faulkner seems unable to face up to whatever remnants of Southern "chivalry," romantic ideology or plain ordinary repression drive him to think of love as a grandiloquent "doom." The truth, I suspect, is that Faulkner cannot treat adult sexual experience with a forthright steadiness, despite the frequency with which sex appears in his earlier books as a symptom of disorder and violation. Only at the end of the novel, as Stevens and Linda kiss goodnight and he slides his hand down her back, "simply touching her . . . supporting her buttocks as you cup the innocent hipless bottom of a child," does Faulkner break into that candor for which this whole section cries out.

If the Snopes trilogy, bringing together nearly the best and nearly the worst in Faulkner's career, is both imposing and seriously marred, *The Mansion* taken more modestly, as a novel in its own right, has some superb sections. Perhaps the reader who is not so steeped in Faulkner's work and cares nothing about its relation to his previous books is in the best position to accept it with pleasure. For whenever Mink Snopes appears, the prose becomes hard, grave, vibrant, and Faulkner's capacity, as Malcolm Cowley has well put it, for "telling stories about men or beasts who fulfilled their destiny," comes into full play. Like the convict in *The Wild Palms*, Mink drives steadily toward his end, without fear or hope, unblinking and serene.

Faulkner begins *The Mansion* by retelling a story told in *The Hamlet*, but with far greater depth of feeling. Mink Snopes, galled by the arrogance of his wealthy neighbor Houston and himself full of a bitter meanness as well as a bottom-dog dignity which draws the line beyond which humiliation is not to be borne, finally kills Houston and stands trial for murder. He expects Flem to rescue him, since for him, as for all the other Snopes, Flem is the agent, the connection between their clan and the outer world. Flem, however, coldly abandons Mink, and Mink, sentenced to prison, lives only for the day he can destroy Flem. A stratagem of Flem's lures Mink into attempting an escape; his sentence is doubled; but he waits patiently, sweating out his blood over the state's cotton. At the age of 63, his body as puny as a child's, he comes out a free man.

The portrait of Mink is beyond praise: a simple ignorant soul who sees existence as an unending manichean struggle between Old Moster (God) and Them (the world), with Them forever and even rightly triumphant, always in control of events as they move along, yet with Old Moster

506

standing in reserve, not to intervene or to help but to draw a line, like Mink himself, and say that beyond this line no creature, not even a wretched little Mink, dare be tried. Mink's is the heroism of the will, a man living out his need: what we might call his destiny.

In the opening part of the novel, as well as in its brilliant final pages—where Mink goes to Memphis to buy a gun, gets caught up in a superbly-rendered revivalist sect led by Marine Sergeant Goodyhay, mooches a quarter from a cop and supposes that this is one of those dispensations he had dimly heard described as the "WP and A" and finally, as if in a pageant of fatality, returns to Jefferson to kill his cousin—Faulkner is writing at very close to the top of his bent. The pages quiver with evocation, the language becomes taut, and Faulkner's sense of the power of life as it floods a man beyond his reason or knowledge, becomes overwhelming. Here is Mink reflecting:

"In 1948 he and Flem would both be old men and he even said aloud: What a shame we cant both of us jest come out two old men setting peaceful in the sun or the shade, waiting to die together, not even thinking no more of hurt or harm or getting even, not even remembering no more about hurt or harm or anguish or revenge—two old men not only incapable of further harm to anybody but even incapable of remembering hurt or harm. . . . *But I reckon not*, he thought. *Cant neither of us help nothing now. Cant neither of us take nothing back.*"

And here is Mink approaching Jefferson after 38 years, as he rests on a truck:

"He was quite comfortable. But mainly he was off the ground. That was the danger, what a man had to watch against: once you laid flat on the ground, right away the earth started in to draw you back down into it. The very moment you were born out of your mother's body, the power and drag of the earth was already at work on you . . . And you knew it too."

Reading such passages in the fullness of their context, is like returning to a marvelous world that has gone a little dim, the world Faulkner made; and then all seems well.

David L. Stevenson. "Faulkner's Subliminal World." *New Leader*, February 1, 1960, pp. 26–27.

Faulkner is the one living, functioning American novelist who, during the past quarter century, has produced a sustained body of work of a very high order, with an identifiable tone and style that is itself a special creation. And yet, we are apparently too close to him to feel wholly comfortable in exploring in public our sense of his very great stature as a writer. Indeed, it has recently seemed much more tempting to critics to indulge their carping faculties at his expense and to let themselves go in chiding his failure to be 100 per cent genius.

It is easy enough, to be sure, to react with irritation to the lack of a firm, "novelistic" structure in Faulkner, whether the work be the early *Light in August* or the more recent *Requiem for a Nun*. It is pure pleasure to resist his sometimes insistent moralizing (as in "The Bear," or *A Fable*) and his occasional glides into mere rhetoric.

But with his new novel, *The Mansion*, I feel that we have little right to quibble over such matters. It may be that Faulkner will, finally, be judged as the great American novelist "Manqué," as Maxwell Geismar thinks. I wish to assert quite bluntly, however, that in reading *The Mansion* I have been in the presence of the best in Faulkner—that is to say, in the presence of magnificent writing.

The Mansion, as a novel, is the third and last of the trilogy of connected episodes in the lives of the Snopeses, begun in *The Hamlet* (1940) and continued in *The Town* (1957). Its main narrative focus is on Mink Snopes, a wretched, half-literate share-cropper member of Faulkner's tribe of Cain, who first murders the wealthy plantation owner, Jack Houston—ostensibly in a protracted quarrel over the pasturing of a cow, actually in retaliation against Houston's ineradicable contempt. Then, because his cousin Flem Snopes, a bank president and the leading member of this avaricious family of emotional idiots, had refused to help him beat the jail sentence, Mink served 38 years at hard labor in the state penitentiary to earn the pardon which will free him long enough to kill Flem. This study in hate is told largely from the point of view of the omniscient author, with two shorter views described both by V. K. Ratliff, the detached, philosophic character of earlier novels, and then by Mink's distant relation, Montgomery Ward Snopes, a dealer in pornographic pictures.

A secondary narrative focus of *The Mansion* is concerned with Linda McCarron Snopes, the illegitimate daughter of Flem Snopes's wife Eula (the Helen of Troy or the Venus symbol to the novel's town of Jefferson, Mississippi). This portion of the novel is concerned with

Linda's marriage to a Greenwich Village sculptor, his death in the Spanish Civil War, her return to Jefferson to engage in social work among Negroes, and, finally, her arranging Mink's pardon so that he might avenge her mother's suicide on Flem. This section of the novel deals with Linda's search for love and for personal identity. It is presented by Ratliff, by Gavin Stevens (Jefferson's lawyer, in love first with Eula and then with her daughter Linda), and by Charles Mallison, Stevens's nephew, a Harvard-educated, World War II veteran, self-intoxicated by the lustful thoughts Linda generates in him.

This is the surface, nameable content of *The Mansion*. It is concerned with Freud's intertwined polarities of love and hate and Catullus' *Odi et amo,* as they have thrived among the Snopeses and their more sensitive townsfolk in Faulkner's Jefferson. But it is below this surface that the novel truly functions. Its importance, it seems to me, has to do with the kind of knowledge or understanding of its characters which Faulkner gives us, and with the unimpeded flow of his stylized, suggestive prose which makes this knowledge to us. It is the kind of knowledge of a Mink Snopes and, to a lesser extent, of a Linda McCarron Snopes, which involves the reader with these characters at the level of the deep, tentacular roots of his being.

Mink Snopes is somehow recognizable as Lear's "unaccommodated man," the "poor, bare, forked animal" in all of us, existing in this hatred. This is communicated to us below the level of our conditioned lives, where each of us has heart, secular business identities and definable moral identities. Linda McCarron and her mother, Eula Snopes, likewise function in the novel (though a shade less successfully, I think) to make us aware of our personal liability to the fascinations and the terrors of love and lust which float beneath our everyday surface identifications

508

of love as institutionalized romance, courtship and marriage.

In *The Mansion*, we commune with Faulkner over the emotional stuff lying deeply within us. We are made aware, through his characters and his art, of the subterranean, unconditioned sources of our own capacity for love and hate. As Richard Rovere has put it, in his introduction to the Modern Library edition of Faulkner's *Light in August*: "When we respond to [Faulkner] at all, we do not so much observe experience as undergo it. We do not recognize a mood; we are overcome by it."

In *The Mansion*, then, through Faulkner's very great skill, we are "overcome" by our sense of a subliminal world of feeling. We are gratified as we read what John Crowe Ransom has called "a perceptual impulse [which] exhibits the minimum of reason." But it is difficult to isolate passages from this novel which, torn from context, would exemplify its submerged content. It is faintly suggested, perhaps, in Gavin Stevens' comment on the Snopeses and on humanity in general: "There aren't any morals. . . . People just do the best they can" and in Ratliff's reply, "The pore sons of bitches."

This subliminal world is better caught, in isolation, in the long passage on Mink, lying out in the open farm country at night, after he has killed Flem: "It seemed to him he could feel the Mink Snopes that had had to spend so much of his life just having unnecessary bother and trouble, beginning to creep, seep, flow easy as sleeping: he could almost watch it, following all the little grass blades and tiny roots, the little holes the worms made, down and down into the ground already full of the folks that had the trouble but were free now, so that it was just the ground and the dirt that had to bother and worry and anguish with the passions and hopes and skeers, the justice and the injustice and the griefs, leaving the folks themselves easy now, all mixed and jumbled up comfortable and easy so wouldn't nobody even know or even care who was which any more, himself among them, equal to any, good as any, brave as any, being inextricable from, anonymous with all of them."

No American writer of fiction other than Faulkner has so consistently made available to us (sometimes with incredible skill, sometimes with a turgidity that makes us wince) a perception of the deep, tidal currents of unclassifiable love and hate, the great hidden links of common human nature. It is also no doubt true that we cannot and would not wish to escape for long, even with the best of Faulkner, from our plain, everyday, conditioned feelings and perceptions, set easily in motion by the phrases and the dogmas of our culture. We may have an occasional Tillich-like existential intimation of something deeper. But our comfortable, homey identities as individuals reside in the fact that we fall in love and make love, that we hate and make hate, at the conventional surface of our 20th century existence.

Hence my final praise of *The Mansion* is that in it Faulkner reasserts those elements of perception which have always been his greatest strength. This new novel, once again, gives us the uncommon, exhausting and deeply rewarding pleasure of letting go our surface identity. For the length of time it takes to read the novel, we are plunged, if only momentarily, into the almost inscrutable pool of feeling that lurks below all our superficial and incessant questing for satisfaction and happiness.

Geoffrey Moore.
"Mink Agonistes."
Kenyon Review, 22 (Summer 1960), 519–22.

The Mansion is divided into three parts: "Mink," "Linda," and "Flem." It begins *in media res,* with Mink's thoughts as the jury says "Guilty" and the Judge says "Life." Unlike Gavin Stevens, V. K. Ratliff and Charles Mallison, who between them tell the rest of the story, Mink is not allowed to speak for himself—Faulkner presumably having learnt his lesson from the Benjy experiment in *The Sound and the Fury.* At any rate, by reporting Mink's thoughts and actions Faulkner retains the privilege of using his own words instead of limiting himself to those of an illiterate dirt farmer. The result is strangely compelling except for certain lapses in that Faulkner rhetorical style (which had its high point in *Absalom, Absalom!*). In these places it simply looks like a good style gone to seed.

The incident in "The Long Summer" section of *The Hamlet* in which Mink kills Jack Houston for impounding his cow is re-told with considerable embroidery. Mink is endowed with a presence and a power of sarcasm at least equal to Houston's and emerges from the encounter with some justice on his side. The pasturage fee has become eighteen dollars and seventy-five cents, not three, which sum Houston makes Mink take out in work at a time when Mink needs to plant his crop for his livelihood. The last straw is Houston's demand for a one dollar pound fee. For this Mink kills him, not, we may feel, without considerable provocation. He has become more than just another of the faceless tribe. He is a Snopes understood, a Snopes allowed feelings. Seldom has Faulkner presented the grinding day-laboring plight of the poor white farmer with such force and conviction. Technically, too, the opening chapters of Mink's section are extremely well-managed. His fanatical resolve, which is also the main theme of the book and the subject of its closing pages, is released like a bombshell in the last sentence *(It looks like I done had to come all the way to Parchman jest to turn around and go back home and kill Flem.).*

At this point, however, Faulkner turns the story over to V. K. Ratliff, the sewing machine salesman for whom he has an especial fondness, and Ratliff goes rattling on in an idiom which is a mixture of country Mississippi and sophisticated reference, as if he were one of O. Henry's Western characters gifted with Faulknerian imagination. Ratliff has to tell about Montgomery Ward Snopes, who had been showing pornographic lantern slides. (The year, we gather, is 1923; Mink's trial had been in 1908.) Knowing that Mink will probably be out for good behavior in five years, Flem decides to have Montgomery Ward sent to Parchman, where Mink is, rather than to Atlanta, Georgia. This is ensured by planting Moonshine whiskey in what Ratliff calls Montgomery Ward's "a-teelyer" and having him convicted for illicit distilling rather than illicit exhibiting. Montgomery Ward is to suggest to Mink that he escape in a Mother Hubbard and bonnet (shades of *Huckleberry Finn*) thoughtfully supplied by Flem. Mink allows himself to be persuaded, is grotesquely caught, and sentenced to twenty more years. By this time the reader should be really sorry for Mink, although slightly ashamed that he should be caught with such charitable feelings for a man who, Faulkner makes abundantly clear, is as lovable as a water-moccasin. In the last chapter of Mink's section he is being interviewed by the Warden as we leave him on the road to Jefferson to kill Flem.

Linda's story is told by Ratliff, Charles Mallison and Gavin Stevens. She is the daughter of Eula Varner by Hoake McCarron. Linda Snopes becomes Linda Kohl, wife— after living with him for seven years—of a Jewish sculptor in Greenwich Village. Together they go off to the Spanish War where Kohl is killed and Linda is made permanently deaf.

Linda loves Gavin, and needs him, but will not marry him, which would be, of course, the only way that Gavin, the honorable man, could have her. In the end she persuades him to marry Melisandre Backus (that was), she who is the widow of the New Orleans gangster and owns a Southern mansion with electrically-lighted stables.

And so back to Mink, whose encounters with a civilization that has grown up outside the walls of Parchman during the thirty-eight years of his imprisonment are vividly and convincingly imagined. After various frustrating encounters, he buys a rusty old gun in a Memphis pawn shop and makes for Jefferson. The denouement is held up by a comic relief story, but when Mink finally reaches Flem, Flem sits still like some ancient hero resigned to his fate, not even attempting to overpower his assassin when the latter fumbles a second time with the impossible gun.

After the murder Mink digs himself into the ruins of his former shack and at the end, an old man with his task accomplished, feels his life ebbing out into the earth to which he has given so much. He passes (there is no other word) in such a manner as to make one feel that it is his apotheosis which is being described, thinking that he is "equal to any, good as any, brave as any, being inextricable from, anonymous with all of them: the beautiful, the splendid, the proud and the brave, right on up to the very top itself among the shining phantoms and dreams which are the milestones of the long human recording—Helen and the bishops, the kings and the unhomed angels, the scornful and graceless seraphim."

What are we to make of all this? Photographs of William Faulkner most commonly in circulation show the Squire of Yoknapatawpha County. The one on the dust jacket of *The Mansion* is no exception. Faulkner looks "Country." He is wearing a thick, voluminous check raglan overcoat with huge sleeves and leather buttons over a tweed suit. The striped tie looks very much like that of the Royal Air Force Reserve. His hair is a distinguished and springy white and he sports a Marshal Foch mustache. Holding a smoked-out briar pipe in his right hand, he contemplates the middle distance with a look which might be interpreted as Augustan reserve but which is probably the result of being photographed. The classic pillars of an ante-bellum mansion show faintly in the background, across an expanse of immaculate greensward. Here is the compleat Southern gentleman. Hollywood could not do better.

Turn however (secretly, of course, since no reader of *The Kenyon Review* could afford to be caught with an anthology) to page 1187 of the 1957 edition of Norman Foerster's *American Poetry and Prose* and you will find a different Faulkner. This is the Bill Faulkner who never completed high school and who worked as a subpostmaster in Oxford until he refused to be "at the beck and call of every son-of-a-bitch with two cents in his pocket." This is the Faulkner who claims to be "just a farmer" and who quietly goes hunting each year with the citizenry of Oxford, washing the dishes with the rest, and listening, no doubt, with an ear like a gramophone horn, to the conversation that flows around him. The face has the look of an old snapper-turtle, with a little of craft in it, too. The neck is stringy, the hair grizzled, the face lined and weathered. It is the face of a country man.

Then there is that other Faulkner who left Mississippi in the twenties to go to New Orleans, William Faulkner the Bohemian friend of Sherwood Anderson "and other Creoles," contributor to the *Double Dealer* and the *Times-Picayune,* author of *Mosquitoes* and *Soldiers' Pay,* aspirant to international literary fame. This is the Faulkner who returned to Oxford and, on the advice of Phil Stone, settled down to hoe his own literary patch, the first result being *The Sound and the Fury.* This is the Faulkner who (and why not?) was determined to be the Marcel Proust, James Joyce and Virginia Woolf of Yoknapatawpha County, heir of symbolism and the nuance. And he did in fact carry the experiments of the twenties to a transatlantic extreme. Under his hand, the mysterious and panoplied myth of the South (Faulkner's style is catching) became, to modify Gide's prescription for a truly modern novel, not *légèrment,* but *violemment déformé.* And all three Faulkners being co-present in this one writin' man from Mississippi, the results have been sometimes puzzling, sometimes frightening, sometimes amusing, and sometimes breathtaking in their imaginative power and heady rhetoric.

Which Faulkner wrote *The Mansion?* If we could have taken a spirit photograph of the author at the time of writing it would probably have been Persona Two, the country man, which we should have seen most clearly, the Faulkner whose literary lineage is that of the tall-tale tellers, of Calaveras County, *Huckleberry Finn* and the Sut Lovingood stories. Most of the incidents in *The Mansion* are superbly told, with just that edge to the style which holds an audience. But every now and then the cracker-barrel philosopher appears, the Faulkner to whom we were introduced in *Intruder in the Dust.* Like

Robert Frost in his old age, he has undertaken to accept the role of popular sage, a function which America apparently demands of all her authors once they have reached a certain age and a certain elevation in that pantheon whose membership may be suggested by the Nobel Prize Committee but which must be ratified by *Time* and *Life.* And yet that is not quite it. There is as much of chastisement, admonition, in his remarks as there is of worldly wisdom.

If there has seemed to be a hint of the pejorative in these comments it was not wholly unintended. And yet when I come to ask myself why, I cannot for all the life of me find a satisfactory answer. If *Tom Jones, David Copperfield* or *Vanity Fair* are good novels then *The Mansion* is also. The comparison is not wholly apt since Faulkner is highly conscious of the twentieth century's experiments, and in his tale-telling role he uses flashbacks, different facets of narration and a mild form of "stream of consciousness." Yet in its gusto, its characterization and the vividness of its tale-telling *The Mansion* seems to capture something of the spirit of the traditional novel, if not its form. We can say that it is Faulkner writing with his left hand, spinning out a tale told of Flem and Eula, Mink and Jack Houston in *The Hamlet* and continued in *The Town.* But it is more than that. A much better novel than *The Town, The Mansion* is also quite different in tone than *The Hamlet.* If there is less art, there is more humanity in it. At first it is a shock to have the allegorical (almost) or historical characters of the Snopes saga brought up to date. But one grows fond of the new Faulkner. One could not exactly believe in the Eula of *The Hamlet,* but one can in the Linda of *The Mansion.* Mink's conversation with Jack Houston at the fence, Captain Strutterbuck's ejection from the Memphis storehouse, Ratliff buying an Allanova tie,

Tug Nightingale knocking down Skeets McGowan, Senator Clarence being wetted on by the dogs, Gavin and Linda at Pascagoula—these are some of the things that one immediately remembers. Hardly, the carping critic will answer, the stuff of great literature. Perhaps not, but it is encouraging to see Faulkner writing like this, rather than plodding with ill-humor towards the high impossible peaks of the "art novel." Not that *The Mansion* is wholly free from fine writing, but the rhetoric is here carried along on the storytelling rather than existing in static patches. At any rate, if I had to choose between *A Fable* and *The Mansion* I know what my choice would be.

Checklist of Additional Reviews

Virginia Kirkus, November 13, 1959.

The Mansion. Long Beach *Independent Press Telegram*, November 15, 1959, Southland Magazine, p. 23.

"Enthralling to the End." *Newsweek*, November 16, 1959, pp. 119–20.

Pensacola (Fla.) *News Journal*, November 29, 1959.

U.S. Lady, December 1959.

"Another from Mr. Faulkner, 40-Year Project Concluded." Durham *Morning Herald*, December 27, 1959, p. 5-D.

"*The Mansion*." *Booklist*, January 1, 1960, p. 266.

"*The Mansion*." Fort Wayne *Journal Gazette*, January 3, 1960, p. 11-E.

Bulletin of the National Association of Secondary School Principals, March 1960.

Fresno Guide, March 24, 1960.

"*The Mansion*." *Victorian*, May 1960.

Abernathy, Harry. "Critical Consensus Favorable to 'Farewell to the Snopses' [*sic*]." Clarksdale (Miss.) *Press Register*, December 5, 1959, p. 2.

Addison, Eleanor B. "Winding Up the Saga of the Sordid Snopes." Columbus *Dispatch*, November 22, 1959, p. 10.

Anderson, Charles. "The End of the Snopes Saga." Baltimore *Sun*, November 15, 1959, p. 12-A.

Baisler, Albert W. "*The Mansion* Deals with Unsuccessful Attempt of Individual to Gain Selfhood." Jamestown (N.Y.) *Post-Journal*, May 28, 1960, p. 60-M.

Barley, Rex. "Between These Covers." Los Angeles *Mirror News*, November 16, 1959, p. 14.

Barth, J. Robert. "Faulkner and the Snopes Trilogy." *America*, February 27, 1960, pp. 638–40.

Beck, Warren. *Virginia Quarterly Review*, 36 (Spring 1960), 272–92.

Bellman, Samuel. "Riding the Literary Circuit." San Jose (Calif.) *Resident*, February 4, 1960.

Blum, Ann. "*The Mansion* Is Good but Not William Faulkner at His Best." Baton Rouge *Morning Advocate*, February 7, 1960, p. 2-E.

Boswell, George. "Faulkner at His Best—Murder Dominates Book." Atlanta *Journal and Constitution*, November 15, 1959, p. 7-E.

Bradley, Van Allen. "Faulkner Completes a Great Trilogy." Chicago *Daily News*, November 11, 1959, p. 8.

Brady, Charles A. "A Mellower Faulkner Winds Up Chronicle of Snopes Family." Buffalo *Evening News*, November 7, 1959, p. 6-B.

Burton, Hal. "Faulkner Ends a Family Saga." *Newsday*, October 31, 1959, p. 23.

Butcher, Fanny. "Faulkner's 'Final' Snopes Novel by Far the Best in the Trilogy." Chicago *Sunday Tribune*, November 15, 1959, Magazine of Books, p. 3.

Casper, Leonard. "Reviews of Books." *Southwest Review,* 45 (Spring 1960), viii-x, 186.

Cevasco, George A. "*The Mansion.*" *The Sign,* February 1960, pp. 77–78.

Chase, Richard. "The Snopeses at an End." *Commentary,* 29 (February 1960), 179–81.

Cohan, Barney. "*The Mansion* Completes Trilogy." Los Angeles *Herald Express,* December 7, 1959, p. 9-C.

Coleman, Arthur L. "Faulkner's Snopeses Just Keep on Coming." San Antonio *Express and News,* November 15, 1959, Magazine Section, p. 10.

Coleman, Irwin W., Jr. "Faulkner 'Eradicates' Flem Snopes in Last of 'Jefferson' Trilogy." Unidentified newspaper, April 6, 1960.

Copeland, Edith. "Books in Orbit." *Daily Oklahoman* (Oklahoma City), November 29, 1959, Magazine Section, p. 26.

Cowley, Malcolm. "Flem Snopes Gets His Come-Uppance." *New York Times Book Review,* November 15, 1959, pp. 1, 18.

D[atisman], D[on] F. "Snopes Family Returns." Gary *Post-Tribune,* November 15, 1959, Sunday Panorama, p. 10-D.

Daw, Richard. "Faulkner Brings to an End His Snopes Family Story." Pensacola (Fla.) *News-Journal,* November 29, 1959, p. 8-D.

DeMott, Benjamin. "Monge and Other Destinations." *Hudson Review,* 12 (Winter 1960), 618–20.

Derleth, August. "*The Mansion.*" Madison (Wis.) *Capital Times,* January 28, 1960, p. 18.

Dolbier, Maurice. "*The Mansion.*" New York *Herald Tribune,* November 14, 1959, p. 6.

Dwight, Ogden G. "A Devious Ell Is Added in Faulkner's Grand Design." Des Moines *Sunday Register,* November 15, 1959, p. 15-G.

Ellison, Virginia P. "Trilogy Ends—but Not the Snopeses!" New Orleans *Times-Picayune,* November 8, 1959, Section II, p. 19.

Emch, Tom. "Faulkner Tries Reader in Completing Trilogy." Houston *Chronicle,* November 15, 1959, Feature Magazine, p. 39.

Fadiman, Clifton. "Reading I've Liked." *Holiday,* January 1960, p. 23.

Feinstein, George. "Snopeses Not Nice but Gamey Reading." Pasadena *Independent-Star-News,* November 29, 1959, Scene Section, p. 30.

Field, Roscoe C., Jr. "*Mansion* Typical Faulkner, Long Excursions Leave Gaps." Memphis *Commercial Appeal,* November 8, 1959, Section IV, p. 10.

Freeman, Gordon N. "Newest Opus by Faulkner Is Boring, Offers Little." Pine Bluff (Ark.) *Commercial,* November 22, 1959, p. 24.

Fry, Hal. "Snopeses Are Done." Akron *Beacon Journal,* November 15, 1959, p. 4-D.

Gardiner, Harold C. *America,* May 14, 1960.

Garske, Allan. "Faulkner's Latest Book Cannot Stand by Itself." *Minnesota Daily.*

Gay, Alva A. "Flem Snopes Rides Again." Detroit *Sunday Times,* November 15, 1959, p. 5-E.

Glikes, Erwin. "'A Man Speaks to Men.'" *Columbia* (College) *Spectator,* November 20, 1959, Supplement, pp. 1–2.

Govan, Gilbert E. "Flem Snopes Comes to the End of Faulkner Road in Mississippi." Chattanooga *Times,* December 6, 1959, p. 24.

Hall, Barbara Hodge. "Faulkner Completes Snopes Family History."

Anniston (Ala.) *Star*, November 15, 1959, p. 8-B.

Hanrahan, Virginia. "Here's Another of Those Works by William Faulkner." Napa (Calif.) *Register*, November 28, 1959, p. 3-A.

Harrington, Joe. "Last of the Snopes." Boston *Sunday Globe*, November 22, 1959, p. 71-A.

Hart, Jack. "Faulkner Finally Kills Off His Intriguing Snopes Clan." Lincoln *Sunday Journal and Star*, November 15, 1959, p. 9-B.

Hoffman, Frederick J. "This Is the End of Flem Snopes." *Progressive*, March 1960, pp. 55–57.

Hopper, Lynn. "Final Touch Given Snopes by Faulkner." Indianapolis *Star*, November 15, 1959, Section VI, p. 20.

Howard, Edwin. "Faulkner Writes Last on the Snopeses—Is It Farewell to Yoknapatawpha, Too?" Memphis *Press-Scimitar*, November 28, 1959, p. 4.

Hunter, Anna C. "Curtain Falls on Snopes Family of Famous Yoknapatawpha County." Savannah *Morning News*, November 15, 1959, Magazine Section, p. 12.

Jones, Carter Brooke. "William Faulkner's New Novel One of His Finest and Strongest." Washington *Sunday Star*, November 15, 1959, p. 5-B.

Kaftal, Isa. "A 'Final Chapter' by Faulkner." *Cornell Daily Sun*.

Keister, Don A. "Faulkner Saga Ends on Note of Optimism." Cleveland *Plain Dealer*, November 15, 1959, p. 10-F.

Kempton, Murray. "Here Lies Snopes." New York *Post,* November 15, 1959, p. 10-M.

Kennedy, Gerald. *"The Mansion." Together*, April 1960, p. 56.

Kincheloe, H. G. "To the Climax in Obfuscation." Raleigh *News and Observer*, November 15, 1959, Section III, p. 5.

King, Paul. "Faulkner Winds Up Trilogy in *Mansion." Sunday Olympian* (Olympia, Wash.), December 13, 1959, p. 18.

Klein, Francis A. "Faulkner Winds Up Trilogy." St. Louis *Globe-Democrat,* November 15, 1959, p. 4-F.

Kohler, Dayton. "Flem Snopes Gets His Just Desserts." Richmond *News Leader*, November 18, 1959, p. 15.

Lemay, Harding. "Faulkner and His Snopes Family Reach the End of Their Trilogy." *New York Herald Tribune Books*, November 15, 1959, pp. 1, 14.

Lindau, Betsy. "Books." Asheville *Citizen-Times*, December 20, 1959, p. 3-D.

Lowenstein, Ralph. *"The Mansion."* El Paso *Times,* December 6, 1959, p. 10-C.

Lowry, D. M. "Faulkner Reaffirms Optimism." Rochester *Democrat and Chronicle*, November 22, 1959, p. 7-H.

Maner, William. "The Saga of the Snopes Family." Richmond *Times-Dispatch*, December 6, 1959, p. 6-L.

Maslin, Marsh. "A Genius like Faulkner Gets under Your Skin." San Francisco *News-Call Bulletin*, November 7, 1959, p. 15-TV.

Masterman, John. "Faulkner Concludes Era of Flem Snopes." Amarillo *Daily News*, November 15, 1959, Section I, p. 16.

Masters, Ann V. "Flem Snopes Saga Closes in Best Faulknerian Style." Bridgeport *Sunday Post*, November 15, 1959, p. 4-B.

May, William. "New Faulkner Novel." Newark (N.J) *News*, November 15, 1959, Section III, p. 7-E.

McCabe, Adeline. "Requiem for the Snopes." *Wyoming State Tribune*

(Cheyenne), December 20, 1959, p. 12.

McKinley, Kent S. "Faulkner's *Mansion* Excellent." Sarasota *News*, November 15, 1959.

McLarn, Jack. "Snopes Trilogy Is Completed with *Mansion*." Charlotte *Observer*, November 15, 1959, p. 2-C.

McManis, John. "Farewell to Snopes Tribe Is Faulkner at His Best." Detroit *News*, November 15, 1959, p. 3-G.

McPherson, Hugo. "The Last of the Snopeses." *Tamarack Review*, Spring 1960, pp. 87–89.

Meriwether, James B. "The Snopes Trilogy Completed." *Carolina Quarterly*, 12 (Fall–Winter 1959), 30–34.

Mertena. "Swan Song of the Snopeses." Lake Charles (La.) *American Press*, November 29, 1959, p. 17.

Miller, Milton. "Faulkner Continues Story of Mississippi." Riverside (Calif.) *Press-Enterprise*, January 10, 1960, p. 11-C.

Moore, Harry T. "Faulkner Pens Final Volume of Trilogy." Boston *Sunday Herald*, November 22, 1959, Section I, p. 17.

Moreland, John. "Critic on the Hearth." Oakland *Tribune*, November 17, 1959, p. 19.

Nelson, Stan. "Mansion Wraps Up Snopes Saga." Fort Worth *Star-Telegram*, November 15, 1959, Section II, p. 11.

Nichols, Luther. "Faulkner and the Last of the Snopeses." San Francisco *Examiner*, November 8, 1959, Highlights Section, p. 10.

Nordell, Rod. "Faulkner Trilogy Complete." *Christian Science Monitor*, November 12, 1959, p. 15.

Norman, Jerry. "Faulkner Writes End to Snopeses." San Angelo (Tex.) *Standard Times*, November 15, 1959, p. 10-B.

Norris, Hoke. "Faulkner Kills, Destroys, Demolishes Snopes." Chicago *Sunday Tribune*, November 15, 1959, Section III, p. 1.

O'Connor, William Van. *Virginia Quarterly Review*, 36 (Winter 1960), 147–51.

O'Neill, Frank. "Faulkner Finds Snopes Chronicle." Cleveland *News*, November 13, 1959, p. 19.

Owens, Patrick J. "*Mansion* Is Final Faulkner Snopes Story." *Arkansas Gazette* (Little Rock), November 8, 1959, p. 6-E.

Ownbey, E. S. "Finale to Story of Snopeses." Birmingham *News*, January 17, 1960, p. 7-E.

Parsons, Eugene O. "Decline of Morals in Our Time Is Trilogy's Theme." Worcester (Mass.) *Sunday Telegram*, November 15, 1959, p. 9-D.

Patrenella, Luke L., Jr. "*The Mansion* Might Be Faulkner's Best Seller." Tyler (Tex.) *Courier-Times-Telegraph*, November 22, 1959, Section I, p. 9.

Patterson, William D. "Saga of Snopes Clan Ends in Faulkner's *The Mansion*." Youngstown *Vindicator*, January 31, 1960, p. 12-B.

Paulding Gouverneur. "Right Wind, Right Rain." *Reporter*, November 26, 1959, pp. 41–42, 44.

Peckham, Stanton. "William Faulkner Completes a Great Trilogy." *Sunday Denver Post*, November 8, 1959, p. 9.

Perkin, Robert L. "Trilogy Finale." *Rocky Mountain News* (Denver), November 15, 1959, p. 20-A.

Pickrel, Paul. "The New Books." *Harper's Magazine*, November 1959, pp. 102, 104.

Popkin, George. "No Justice for Mink." Providence *Sunday Journal*, November 15, 1959, p. 20-W.

Porterfield, Waldon. "Bell Tolls for a Snopes in a Faulknerian Knell."

Milwaukee *Journal*, November 8, 1959, Part V, p. 4.

Price, Emerson. "William Faulkner." Cleveland *Press*, November 17, 1959, p. 22.

Price, Martin. "Dreams and Doubts: Some Recent Fiction." *Yale Review*, 49 (December 1959), 278–80.

Prince, J. Roy. "More Snopes." *The Rebel* (East Carolina College), Fall 1960.

R., W. "Snopeses Turn Up in Faulkner Novel." Santa Barbara *News Press*, November 15, 1959, p. 11-D.

R., W.H. "Long-Range Faulkner Trilogy Completed." Springfield (Mass.) *Daily News*, January 8, 1960, p. 12.

Ready, William. "*The Mansion*." *The Critic*, February 3, 1960, p. 26.

Redman, Ben Ray. "Faulkner Country Revisited, Revised." New York *World-Telegram and the Sun*, November 17, 1959, p. 27; Saturday Review Syndicate, November 14, 1959.

Robb, Mary C. "Endurance Rewarded in Faulkner's Latest." Pittsburgh *Press*, November 15, 1959, Section IV, p. 10.

Rogers, W. G. "The Snopes Gang." Trenton *Sunday Times*, November 22, 1959, p. 14; AP Release: Indianapolis *News*, January 2, 1960; Allentown *Call Chronicle*, December 26, 1959.

Rolo, Charles. "Reader's Choice." *Atlantic Monthly*, November 1959, pp. 170–71.

Rowland, Stanley J., Jr. "End of a House." *Christian Century*, December 23, 1959, p. 1503.

Rubin, Louis D., Jr. Roanoke *Times*, December 27, 1959.

Rubinstein, Annette T. "Poorly Furnished." *Mainstream*, January 1960, pp. 60–61.

Ryan, Stephen P. "*The Mansion*." *Ave Maria*, March 19, 1960, pp. 27–29;

Best Sellers (University of Scranton), 19 (November 15, 1959), p. 278.

S., D. "Snopes Epic Concluded with *The Mansion*." Salt Lake City *Tribune*, January 3, 1960, p. 13-W.

Schott, Webster. "The Snopes Era Is Now Brought to Conclusion." Kansas City *Star*, November 21, 1959, p. 7.

Scott, Virgil. "*The Mansion*." Lansing *State Journal*, February 28, 1960, p. 42.

Serebnick, Judith. "*The Mansion*." *Library Journal*, November 15, 1959, p. 3586.

Shedd, Margaret. "William Faulkner Brings Snopes Trilogy to Balanced Conclusion in Latest Novel." *Mexico News Weekly*, November 15, 1959.

Sherman, Thomas B. "Continued Chronicle of the Snopes Family." St. Louis *Post-Dispatch*, November 8, 1959, p. 4-B.

Slatoff, Walter J. "*The Mansion*." *Epoch*, 10 (Winter 1960), 124–25.

Smeltzer, Robert. "William Faulkner Finally Ends History of Snopes Family." Greenville (S.C.) *Piedmont*, November 19, 1959, p. 12.

S[mith], B[lanche] H[ixon]. "*The Mansion*." Meriden (Conn.) *Record*, November 27, 1959, p. 6.

Spearman, Walter. "Is This the Kind of Person Who Will Inherit the South?" Rocky Mount (N.C.) *Telegram*, November 22, 1959, p. 6-A.

Swift, Pat. "Last of Trilogy Is Published." Niagara Falls *Gazette*, November 15, 1959, p. 10-B.

Swiggart, Peter. *Sewanee Review*, 68 (Spring 1960), 319–25.

Taillefer, Anne. "*The Mansion*." *Catholic Worker*, April 1960, p. 4.

Taylor, Robert W. "World of Books." *The Diplomat*, February 1960, p. 52.

Tinkle, Lon. "In Faulkner Country with Sinful Snopes." Dallas *Morning News*, November 15, 1959, Section V, p. 8.

Tucker, William. "Snopes Trilogy Comes to End." Unidentified newspaper, November 22, 1959.

Tunstall, Caroline H. "Snopeses Inherit the Earth." Norfolk *Virginian-Pilot* and Portsmouth *Star*, November 15, 1959, p. 6-F.

Turner, Decherd. "Rise and Victory of Flem Snopes." Dallas *Times Herald*, November 15, 1959, Roundup Section, p. 13.

Vogler, Lewis. "Snopesism Returns— Full of Surprises." San Francisco *Chronicle*, November 15, 1959, This World Section, p. 26.

W., J. "*The Mansion*." Auburn (N.Y.) *Citizen-Advertiser*, December 12, 1959, p. 4.

Walker, Gerald. "William Faulkner Settles Flem Snopes' Fate." *Cosmopolitan*, December 1959, pp. 24–25.

Washburn, Beatrice. "Faulkner Writes Movingly of South." Miami *Herald*, November 15, 1959, p. 23-E.

Wasson, Ben. "Snopes Invade Everywhere as Faulkner Pens Last of Trilogy." *Delta Democrat-Times* (Greenville, Miss.), November 22, 1959, p. 18.

Watts, Richard. "Random Notes on This and That." New York *Post*, November 18, 1959, p. 77.

West, Anthony. "A Dying Fall." *New Yorker*, December 5, 1959, pp. 236–43.

Williams, Ernest E. "Faulkner Ends His Saga." Fort Wayne *News-Sentinel*, November 14, 1959, p. 4.

Williams, George. "*The Mansion*." NEA *Journal*, February 1960, p. 71.

Williams, Wirt. "A Genuine Novel by Faulkner." Los Angeles *Times*, December 29, 1959, Section III, p. 5.

Wills, Garry. "The Thin World of the Snopeses." *National Review*, November 21, 1959, pp. 498–99.

W[ilson], W. E[merson]. "*The Mansion*." Wilmington (N.C.) *Morning News*, November 16, 1959, p. 13.

Wilson, Walter. "What Knighthood Is This?" *Berkshire Eagle* (Pittsfield, Mass.), December 26, 1959, p. 14.

Yeiser, Frederick. "The Last of the Snopes." Cincinnati *Enquirer*, November 15, 1959, p. 8-D.

Young, Thomas Daniel. "Book Reviews." *Journal of Mississippi History*, 22 (July 1960), 208–11.

THE REIVERS

THE
REIVERS

A Reminiscence

WILLIAM
FAULKNER

RANDOM HOUSE
New York

George Plimpton.
"The Reivers."
New York Herald Tribune Books, May 27, 1962, p. 3.

The first two words of William Faulkner's new novel are GRANDFATHER SAID, in bold caps, followed by a colon, and then three-hundred-odd pages of what Grandfather (Lucius Priest) does say—an uninterrupted turn-of-the-century reminiscence of such length that one marvels at the staying power of his listener, presumably his grandson. Reckoning two minutes to read a page of Faulkner aloud, a bit more if the print collapses into such inevitable avalanches as "secure behind that inviolable and inescapable rectitude concomitant with the name I bore," etc., one arrives at a total of 10 straight hours of Grandfather Priest's storytelling without any interruption indicated—not the slightest complaint from the attentive grandson (one wonders at his deep silence), no time out for a meal, or a call to the telephone, or an unruly hound to be set outside the screen door, or even, for that matter, a moment for refreshment. One remembers that Joseph Conrad's Marlow pounds the table and calls for the bottle to get through his recounting of the sea disaster of *Youth*. But not Lucius Priest. He pegs along with his story, much of it very funny indeed and worth any number of cramps to sit and listen to, until he has at hand what must be one of the longest spoken monologues in literature.

A few weeks ago, Mr. Faulkner tried out a section of *The Reivers* on the cadets at West Point, who surely in carriage, at least, are listeners of the finest order. He prefaced his reading by remarking that they were going to hear from the "funniest" novel he (Faulkner) had ever read, much less written. One imagines the sudden anticipatory half-moon smiles illumine the faces of the corps—the squad leader checking to make sure ("Plebes! Dress up those smiles!")—before settling back to compose themselves accordingly. Faulkner has a thin slow voice, as faint as the sound of sand rustled around in a fruit jar— hardly an instrument of delivery—and so one imagines that with those first dry sounds the cadets, respectful, as one man in the vast hall, leaned forward from their chairs ... towards the podium, every manjack of them smiling. [Ellipsis dots throughout are in the original review.]

What they heard, and what Lucius Priest's grandson heard, and what you'll read when you buy *The Reivers* is a boy's adventure story, almost a classic example, utilizing to the extent of parody all the time-honored devices that distinguish boy's fiction—an impressionable 11-year-old youngster away from home for the first time (*Treasure Island*), the odyssey through the complexities of the outside adult world (*Huckleberry Finn*) accompanied by boon companions (*The Rover Boys, Stalky & Co.*), then the adventures in the thick of the night (*Tom Sawyer*), the 100–1 shot temperamental racehorse (*National Velvet*), and, of course, the big race itself (our hero, Lucius Priest in saddle) on which everything rides, not quite the old homestead (Faulkner knows how far he can go), but climax certainly in the spirit of every film with Kentucky in the title. There is a somewhat strained and abrupt happy ending, hardly Mr. Faulkner's long suit, in which everything is gathered up swiftly, brushed together in a heap, one might say, as if Lucius Priest in getting into the 11th hour of his tale was either wearying and in need of a shot of bourbon, or perhaps noting his grandson nodding a bit.

Should one then rush out and buy *The Reivers* to supplement the birthday-gift baseball mitt? Does this book belong up there on the shelf under the college pennant with *The Tennessee Shad*, *Stover at Yale*, *PT–109*, the Mark Twain books, and the *Black Arrow*? Well, not exactly. Mr. Faulkner has seen to that. He has made a few concessions to the boy's adventure genre—in plot, theme, and the untypical general warmth of the book—but neither style, weight, nor intensity is sacrificed. He is as prolix as ever—"thinking it out interminably" as Alfred Kazin has described it. As usual, the text abounds with the names of people one hasn't met (unless one reads the works thoroughly) and isn't going to meet, what's more. To put it mildly, the locales are somewhat out of the ordinary for a boy's adventure story. No caves, or moonlit graveyards. Much of the action of *The Reivers* takes place in a Memphis maison de joie—the same house, in fact, in which a generation later Popeye incarcerates Temple Drake. The villainy in the book is not healthy or straightforward—Injun Joe's or Long John Silver's—but often twisted or grotesquely funny . . . the sadism of the deputy, Butch, or the voyeurism of Otis, a 15-year-old peep-show czar who roams the "rooming house" with an auger. It is unlikely Faulkner could have turned out 300 pages without dark fancies of this sort cropping up, and in fact, their appearances against the wholesomeness of a boy's adventure story is one of the curious delights of the book.

In applying himself to the form of his adventure-story, Mr. Faulkner is forced into a mellow turn of the theme. The theme of his past works is familiar: the disintegration of the southern traditional life, or, in a broader sense, the slow collapse of the antique and traditional virtues on which society is formed. His world is grim—peopled either with the obsessed, the obsessors themselves, or the guilt-ridden. All of this would have been stiff and heady fare for a grandson to listen to. If Isaac McCaslin, who more often is Faulkner's philosopher and conscience, had told the story he would have inflicted on the grandson a grim saga that would have left him pop-eyed and shaken in his rocker, perfectly willing to give the country back to the Chickasaws. But Lucius Priest is a story teller first, a moralist second. He has set about to tell his grandson about the circumstances and the temptations which in his eleventh year brought about his fall from the grace of childhood into a pragmatic world—a move from the state of what Faulkner calls virtue to that of nonvirtue. It is not so much a "fall" as a calculated step. Priest tells his grandson: "When grown people speak of the innocence of children they don't really know what they mean. Pressed, they will go a step further and say, well ignorance then. The child is neither. There is no crime which a boy of eleven has not envisaged. His only innocence is, he may not yet be old enough to desire the fruits of it, which is not innocence but appetite; his ignorance is, he does not know how to commit it, which is not ignorance but size."

Often Lucius Priest regrets his appetite. Much of what he sees of human action and nature is distasteful to him. But though often longingly expressing the state of virtue, he continues to absorb and adjust, horrified by what he learns and sees, but continuing to stare.

His first tempter is Boon Hogganbeck—one remembers him from *The Bear* ("four inches over six feet, he had the mind of a child, the heart of a horse, and little hard shoe-button eyes without depth"). Boon wants to "borrow" Lucius' grandfather's 1904 Winton Flyer, one of Jefferson's first automobiles. The Priest Family with the exception of Lucius is off in Bay St. Louis at a funeral. It is Boon's idea that if he can persuade young Priest to accompany him in the Flyer to Memphis (he has a girl in a "rooming house" there) his "borrowing" action is somehow sanctioned. Young Priest must make the decision, it is forced on him—the temptation such that virtue is no longer a shield; he cannot resist; so the act is thus sanctioned by him and the odyssey underway.

The "borrowing" is reflected in the title *The Reivers*, which means "thieves" or "plunderers." But it is typical of the tone of the book that the crimes committed— the "borrowing" of the Winton Flyer, the theft of the race-horse, and so forth—are somehow within the family. There are no truly injured parties, each act no more harmful or severe than Huck and Tom's pilfering of Aunt Sally's pie-plates and sheets. Which is all in the spirit of wholesomeness. But then of course, there is Otis, the youthful voyeur. He commits one of the great light-fingered crimes of all time— extricating with consummate skill a big front gold tooth (it unscrews apparently) from the mouth of one of the wearied and sleeping "rooming-house" girls, or "aunts" as the younger generation of *The Reivers* refers to them. Somehow it is reassuring. No matter what the genre, Mr. Faulkner is irrepressible.

Granville Hicks. "Building Blocks of a Gentleman." *Saturday Review*, June 2, 1962, p. 27.

Once one accepts the fact that *The Reivers* isn't a major Faulkner novel, nor, I should say, was meant to be, one can settle down to enjoy it, for minor Faulkner may be very good, and this is. It is not comparable, of course, to *Light in August* or *Absalom, Absalom!* but I liked it better than I did either *The Town* or *The Mansion*, the considerably more pretentious novels that preceded it. The novel that it most closely resembles is *Intruder in the Dust*; it is less topical and less grim, but it has the same kind of excitement.

The subtitle, *A Reminiscence*, alludes to the fact that the narrator, Lucius Priest, is telling, as if to his grandchildren, about an adventure that happened to him in 1935, when he was eleven years old. Faulkner makes good use of the device, for he gives us the young innocent, excited, frightened Lucius, put to a test that is almost beyond his strength, at the same time that he gives us the aging Lucius, who comments on events, not quite so loquaciously as Gavin Stevens but in somewhat the same vein, and talks amusingly about mules, autos, the population problem and other matters.

Lucius's adventure is spectacular enough. He and Boon Hogganbeck, with an unsolicited assist from Ned William McCaslin, steal Lucius's grandfather's automobile in Jefferson, and drive to Memphis, where they put up at Miss Reba's whorehouse, celebrated in *Sanctuary* and other portions of the Yoknapatawpha saga. As if that were not enough, Ned involves them with a stolen horse, and, after a series of races with young Lucius as jockey, the climax is reached by way of a dizzying series of twists and turns.

Each of the three principal characters is given his appropriate place in the saga. Lucius is a newcomer, but he is descended from the McCaslins and thus is related to a dozen characters we have met before. Ned is the son of a slave who was the natural daughter of Lucius Quintus Carothers, and hence he is a cousin, I guess, of Lucas Beauchamp in *Intruder in the Dust*. Boon Hogganbeck appears in "The Bear," and there as here is a notoriously bad shot. Indeed, the episode with which the novel begins is based on a sentence or two in the earlier work. (This involves Faulkner in some chronological difficulties, which he tries with little success to straighten out. The time was when he made nothing of such discrepancies, but he has grown more self-conscious about the saga.)

Once the story gets under way, it moves at a splendid pace. Faulkner's characters are always setting out on perilous pilgrimages or undertaking almost or quite impossible tasks: the funereal mission of the Bundren family in *As I Lay Dying*; Lena Grove's long pursuit of Lucas Burch in *Light in August*; Thomas Sutpen's grand design in *Absalom, Absalom!*; the convict's quest in *The Old Man*. In *The Reivers*, as in *Intruder in the Dust*, a boy finds himself confronted with a task that has to be done over and over again, but Lucius Priest is even younger than Chick Mallison, and perhaps that makes his gallantry all the more admirable.

In his Nobel Prize speech Faulkner said, "I believe that man will not merely endure: he will prevail." What this means in terms of his novels is perfectly clear: his characters do endure; they endure endlessly; and in one way or another they prevail. So poor little Lucius, brought to tears more times than he likes to admit, endures and prevails. Ned McCaslin prevails, too, but his triumph comes by way of intelligence whereas Lucius's is achieved by character.

Ned, a middle-aged Negro, is a major character in the book. Faulkner has made him quite different from Lucas Beauchamp in *Intruder in the Dust*, the statuesque figure of impervious dignity. Ned plays Uncle Remus when it serves his purpose, and he knows how to turn away the white man's wrath, which he often provokes, with a "Hee, hee, hee!" He lives by his wits, and his wits have a fine edge. Faulkner loves a wily strategist, and Ned, whom one would bet on even in a contest with Flem Snopes, is one of his best. He is so sure of himself that he can play the buffoon without losing his self-respect.

It is Ned who precipitates the wild adventure and guides its course, but Lucius is the hero. He knows that he is doing wrong when he connives in Boon's borrowing of the car, and his conscience troubles him constantly, but he accepts the consequences of what he has done, even when they seem certain to overwhelm him. He has weak moments, when he thinks he can simply walk out from under, but he refuses to give in: "Because I couldn't now. It was too late. Maybe yesterday, while I was still a child, but not now. I knew too much, had seen too much. I was a child no longer now; innocence and childhood were forever lost, forever gone from me." Thus he accepts the maturity that has been thrust upon him. He has been disciplined by his father and especially his grandfather in the code of a gentleman; he is truthful, responsible, considerate, brave; and these virtues enable him to endure and even to prevail.

The style is basically that which Faulkner has cultivated since *Intruder in the Dust*: a voice that starts out, qualifies, interrupts itself, lunges ahead, and sometimes never gets anywhere at all—which is the way voices do behave, as anyone can tell who keeps an ear open at a party. It is a style that is really a good deal like Henry James's, except that James tucked away the qualifications and digressions in neatly grammatical phrases and clauses, as most people don't do in ordinary speech. Faulkner has used the style here with somewhat more restraint than he has sometimes shown—there are fewer breathless, nonstop sentences—and on the whole it is well suited to the kind of story he is telling.

There is in the book none of the demonic power and little of the dazzling originality of the half dozen great books that appeared from 1929 to 1943, but there is excitement, and there is humor, and there is a strong moral sense. When Lucius has his final reckoning with his grandfather, he wants to be punished, so that, as he puts it, he can get rid of all he has done. But his grandfather knows better, telling him that he must and he can live with it: "A gentleman can live through anything. He faces anything. A gentleman accepts the responsibility of his actions and bears the burden of their consequences, even when he did not himself instigate them but only acquiesced to them, didn't say No though he knew he should." Lucius, only eleven after all, begins to bawl. After a while his grandfather tells him to wash his face. "A gentleman cries too," he says, "but he always washes his face."

M. E. Bradford.
"Faulkner Novel Described as Comedy of Manners."
Nashville *Tennessean*, June 3, 1962, p. 12-F.

The Reivers is the best we have had from Mr. Faulkner in many years. It is not a pretentious novel, not a raw exploration of social problems, creeping Snopesism, or the meaning of the Christian story in our times. It is instead, a comedy—in part a study in manners, in part roaring farce and highjinks in the tradition of Longstreet, Baldwin, Hooper and the rest of the humorist raconteurs of the Old Southwest.

The last two novels of the Snopes trilogy, *The Mansion* and *The Town*, are also comic or serio-comic but they were written to fulfill an obligation, to finish an old story.

This novel, I suspect, Mr. Faulkner wrote to please himself. It is another of his superb stories of turning points, formative experiences in the lives of young men of good family.

A product of memory, *The Reivers* (thieves) is a story told by an old man to his grandson. The narrator is Lucius Priest, at the time of the story the 11-year-old grandson of a Jefferson banker—and one of the McCaslin connection.

He recalls and comments on the events of one week in his life, a week in early May of 1905, when he, Boon Hogganbeck, and Ned William McCaslin (a very real, multi-dimensional Negro—and, on top of that, a McCaslin Negro) steal his grandfather's car and "light out" for Memphis.

The youthful odyssey that follows is, as seen through the eyes of age and wisdom, unspeakably funny—innocent saturnalia in Miss Reba's bawdy house, a box car, a rural resort hotel, and a race track.

Young Lucius Priest reminds us of Chick Mallison in *Intruder in the Dust* (minus Chick's self-righteousness). His struggle with what he calls "non-virtue," his final surrender to it with the theft of his grandfather's car, and his acceptance of the consequences of that surrender make for just the sort of story a grandfather would want to tell his grandson.

His is not a merely funny story. Young Lucius in a short week has an intensive course in human frailty, cunning, dignity, and deceit. He acquires from his experience something of that manliness which he hopes to commend to his grandson with this account of it.

His intention explains much of the novel's tone and the perspective from which it is written.

But the presence of this "story-teller" narrator, this speaking voice so often heard in or behind Faulkner's novels and tales does more than give the novel its unity.

It also gives Faulkner a chance to indulge in his love for the tall tale, the potentially independent yarn done in the manner of the oral tradition of the Southern frontier.

The like of Boon's shooting spree early in the novel we have had before in "The Bear." Ned's adventure on Beale Street, in Miss Reba's kitchen, and with a rural Tennessee deputy offer further proof of Faulkner's understanding of Negro humor and character.

The account of the second-rate race horse who will do anything for sardines runs throughout the book and provides it with a climax.

But the longest of these extractable episodes is best; Boon's contest with the mudhole farmer of Hell's Creek bottom (a man who gave up farming his land and farmed instead the highway into a quagmire which cannot be crossed without the expensive assistance of his mules), is in the best folk tale tradition, hyperbolic, extravagant, uproarious.

However, none of these vignettes fail to move forward the narrative, none are extraneous in function, or thematically digressive.

This novel is complete and certainly no collection like Go Down, Moses or The Unvanquished—though resonant at times (like all of the Yoknapatawpha books) with overtones, echoes from the great unified corpus of legendry from which it is drawn.

And it is on the social and moral norms (even on the idiom itself) native to the world that produced and is sustained by that legendry that this novel largely depends for its effect.

By definition true comedy exists in and is a comment on a social matrix, a set of manners. And the fabric of manners, the characters' sense of "place" and of propriety, of "what's fittin" in an established scheme of relations make this novel comic.

Lucius Priest dramatizes and affirms the importance of such a sense of place and manners to civilized life; and only to those who share with Old Lucius and his creator such a sense will the full comic wisdom of this novel be available.

To those who expect in a novel from or about the South only annals of protest, abuse and violence, only thinly disguised preachment (of which we have had God's plenty in supposedly Southern novels of late), The Reivers will be a disappointment. To those who know better, it is a welcome relief.

R. A. Jelliffe. "Fabulous Tale Has Humor, Wisdom, and Rare Artistry." Chicago Sunday Tribune, June 3, 1962, Magazine of Books, pp. 1–2.

Nothing in Faulkner's previous work, nothing in Sanctuary, for instance, or in A Fable, to mention only two of his former novels, quite prepares the reader for this latest production. The Reivers is in an entirely different vein from its predecessors.

The range of the author's work, that is to say, the variation in theme and tone, is astonishing. He shifts at will, it would seem, from dire sensationalism, from the macabre representation of warped and thwarted human nature, to the symbolic portrayal of religious mysticism, the reproduction, in terms of World War II, of the central legend of our Christian faith. And now, with an equally amazing change of key, he captures our fascinated attention with an absorbing situation, a story steeped in a solution of the plausibly preposterous.

All these variations in mood and spirit, he would seem to say, are but changes in the primary colors in the total spectrum of the truth of life. His concern is with a number of those hues, not with any one of them alone. He expressed this idea much better, himself, one day in Japan at a seminar meeting of Japanese professors of American literature, over which I presided.

One of the Japanese scholars asked him this question: "They say you are not so interested in what is called 'literary classification.' You have been called a lot of things, such as naturalist, traditionalist, symbolist, etc. I wonder what school you belong to." Faulkner replied: "I would say, and I hope, the only school I belong to, is the humanist school." By this time, assuredly, he has matriculated.

Fundamentally different as these stories are from one another in nature, they nevertheless have in common his unmistakable and inimitable stamp. There is in all of them the same sense of throbbing mentality, of breathless suspense, of multiple levels of meaning, of an intricate, involuted style of expression. *The Reivers*, like its predecessors, belongs in the Faulkner canon.

"Grandfather said:"

So begins this fabulous tale, this "reminiscence," narrated with vivid exactitude of detail and with affectionate total recall by a virtuoso storyteller. It recounts the sequence of amazing adventures brought upon themselves by a trio of "reivers" [borrowers], who, in the year of grace 1905, appropriated for their own use a brand new Winton Flyer and set forth in it on the 80 mile jaunt from Jefferson, Miss., to Memphis, Tenn.

One of the trio, Lucius Priest by name, the "grandfather" who now tells the tale, was then a boy of 11. His companions, attached by ties of service of loyalty to the Priest household, were Boon Hogganbeck, a giant of a man, physically, who had lost his heart to the car at first sight, and a Negro youth, a stable boy, Ned McCaslin. Into the limited space of four days they managed to cram a whole odyssey of riotous and marvelous experience.

The story would be engrossing as a story alone, if that were all. Singly and cumulatively, the incidents that comprise the plot hold us in their spell. The fording of Hell Creek Bottom, for instance, constitutes a thrilling episode, an epic exploit of itself. The horse race, in its climactic series of heats, between Acheron and Lightning, those noble steeds—the trio had bartered the automobile for a horse—stirs the reader's pulse to a pitch of feverish anxiety, so much is at stake. At the moment of supreme climax, the sudden apparition of "the Boss" (Lucius' grandfather) startles us (even as it did the culprits) almost as if a *deus ex machina* had descended from on high.

But the story itself is far from all. There is more to it, much more. It is told by one who is no longer a boy; it is told by a man well along in years, by one old enough, wise enough in the experience of life, to enrich the telling with all his accumulated wealth of reflection and understanding. In retrospect, he becomes aware of the essentially fantastic in the nature of this escapade that, when he was a boy, engulfed him with its immediate stress and impact. So told, the story takes on much greater depth and dimension. It is interspersed, in the telling, with bits of wisdom, of insight, of perspective. His innate sense of humor, mellowed with the years, colors all he says. "A Republican," he finds himself saying on one occasion, "is a man who made his money; a Liberal is a man who inherited his; a Democrat is a barefooted Liberal in a cross-country race; a Conservative is a Republican who has learned to read and write."

"Grandfather" and William Faulkner would seem to have much in common; such dry comments as these come natural to him. They have in common, also, the undertone of the authority of a social and moral code that governs the personal behavior and the human relationships of both whites and Negroes of that time and place. The code is a law unto itself, not to be violated.

Most significantly of all, Faulkner and "grandfather" have in common the magic gift of communication, the power of expression that frequently sums up in a single utterance the character of the speaker, the particular time and place, the very key of language, "A banker, president of the older Bank of Jefferson, the first bank of Yoknapatawpha County, he believed then and right on to his death many years afterward, by which time everybody else even in Yoknapatawpha County had realized the automobile had come to stay, that the motor vehicle was an insolvent phenomenon like last night's toadstool and, like the fungus, would vanish with tomorrow's sun."

If the author, as he has testified on occasion, liked best of all his novels, *The Sound and the Fury*, because it "caused him the most trouble," he might well, by the same reasoning, it might seem, like this one least; for *The Reivers* sounds as if it had been written effortlessly, as if it were a piece of unpremeditated art.

The reminiscence as a whole gives the initial impression of being the spontaneous, impromptu recollection of events as dictated by memory and recorded verbatim. The style has the irregularity, the scrambled syntax, the colloquial idiom, of improvisation. In truth, however, as we know to our cost, such an effect is achieved only by consummate artistry. It is a great accomplishment in itself.

Winfield Townley Scott. "Faulkner." Santa Fe *New Mexican*, June 3, 1962, pp. 3, 8.

Let's say to begin with that—perhaps barring some Faulknerian stylistic tricks—this is a complete delight. Among his many gifts, we may incline to forget that for one thing William Faulkner is a first-rate storyteller, and in *The Reivers* all stops are out for a really fantastic and often hilarious yarn about an 11-year-old boy, his two more or less adult and weird companions, and their adventures with a stolen car which they swap for a dubiously gifted race horse. Or, like Huck Finn's watermelons, a "borrowed" car—Faulkner's title derives from a variant of the word "reave."

The novel is subtitled "a reminiscence," and it begins: "Grandfather said." The rest is 300 pages of monologue in which Lucius Priest recalls the few days' saga of childhood that so wildly altered his life. (I think I can improve on a good-natured appellation already applied to this novel—it incongruously involved Tom Swift of the once-famous boys' series—and say we can consider this "Penrod in the Whorehouse.")

We are once again in Faulkner's kingdom, Yoknapatawpha County. The time when Lucius is 11 is the year 1905. Automobiles are a rarity and Lucius' banker grandfather purchased one principally to defy Colonel Sartoris who aimed to bar autos from the town of Jefferson, Miss. Driver, caretaker and general custodian of the car is Boon Hogganbeck, a huge childlike man. When a death in the family summons all Lucius' immediate adult kin out of town for several days, it is Boon who conspires with the boy to improve their time by a—in those days—Herculean drive to Memphis. Ned McCaslin, an aging but amorous and imaginative Negro employee of Grandfather's, goes along, at first as a stowaway.

Without ever being quaint or nostalgic or sentimental—indeed it is all simply alive—Faulkner gets an amazing amount of juice out of the time and the situation. The crank-up; the kerosene headlights; the "dusters" and goggles alarmed passengers wore; the mild "speed"; the block and tackle carried aboard in case of emergencies; the alarmed horses, too, that had to be passed with such care; the bad and sometimes nonexistent roads; extrication of the car by leverage or mule team or both from disastrous mudholes—this sort of thing Faulkner brings back as historic comedy on the journey to Memphis.

Well, Lucius and Boon and Ned make it and they repair boy and all to a nest well known to Boon, Miss Reba's bawdy house on Catalpa Street. (Years later *Sanctuary* happened there.) Again Faulkner gets every ounce of color, somehow without any golden-hearted distortion. Miss Reba and her girls, particularly big Corrie, are matter-of-fact, profane, delightful. And it is almost as soon as they arrive that the dumfounding Ned swaps the car for the unpromising horse. All the crazy rest of it—Lucius' riding Lightning in horse-races—depends on what may be termed Ned's talented know-how.

The stylistic tricks I mentioned lie chiefly in Faulkner's basing his style on garrulity. Particularly in the first part of *The Reivers* we have those sag-bellied sentences complicated by interpolation and parentheses. Yet, take the book altogether, I can only however awkwardly, record my curious sensation that I was reading a book which had long been classic American literature. I daresay that's what's going to happen to it.

John Chamberlain. "A Car, a Horse and Virtue." *Wall Street Journal*, June 4, 1962, p. 12.

If you're looking for a tradition to hitch William Faulkner's *The Reivers* (misspelled for "reavers," meaning "those who take away by stealth") on to, you can go back, scrambled syntax and all, to the tradition that produced Mark Twain's "Jumping Frog," or Gus Longstreet's "Georgia Scenes," stories in which the rubes turn out to be more sophisticated than the city slickers, or at least so unreconstructed as rubes that they are going to have their way, anyway, even if it takes them just about as long to get it as to finish a William Faulkner sentence (like this one is supposed, in a probably, no a certainly, parody way to be).

To dispense, for the moment, with the Faulknerese (and, by the way, how was it ever translated into Swedish for the Nobel Prize Judges?), this is a comic tale of growing up in Yoknapatawpha County, Mississippi, in the early days of the automobile age. Literally speaking, our accounts of primitive automobiling have been largely limited to Edith Wharton's reminiscences of touring the back country all dressed up in linen duster and veil and to the accounts of Glidden Tours that may be found in the social histories. (There are also the Ford joke books.)

But Faulkner, whose memory has the tenacious quality of old-fashioned tanglefoot glue, knows that in scores of American hamlets in 1905 A.D. there were monomaniacs like Boon Hogganbeck (good native stock, even to the part that was Chickasaw Indian) who would give their eyeteeth to get their hands on a car (a budding railroad mechanic named Walter Chrysler once borrowed every cent he could just to buy one to take apart).

The car that Boon Hogganbeck found in Jefferson, Mississippi, was a Winton Flyer, and it was owned by Banker Priest, who had bought it to flout Banker-Colonel Sartoris, who without consulting anybody had put an "ordinance" into the Jefferson archives prohibiting the operation of any mechanically propelled vehicle within the town's limits.

Banker Priest didn't care to drive the car himself, which was the cue for Boon Hogganbeck to take over. Possession being nine points of the law, it merely needed Banker Priest's temporary absence from town to tempt Boon Hogganbeck to a pioneering expedition. With Banker Priest's 11-year-old grandson, Lucius, and a horse-loving Negro named Ned McCaslin, Boon set off for Memphis, Tennessee.

There were, of course, no good roads across the southern creek bottoms (for that matter, there was not a single mile of concrete road anywhere in rural America in 1905). But, by virtue of a few lifts from crow-bars and rented mules, Boon got the Winton to Memphis.

Up to this point the story has been merely hilarious. Once Boon and the 11-year-old Lucius are ensconced in Miss Reba's house, which-is-not-a-home, however, Faulkner turns on the insight. The boy Lucius has already chosen "Non-Virtue" by electing to make the trip with Boon; now he will learn that Non-Virtue brings mental anguish in Memphis even as in the Garden of Eden. Lucius is still much too young to be seduced physically—but merely to know that there is shame in the world is enough to make him wish he were back at home in Jefferson, with "Boss" (his grandfather and his mother).

He could, of course, have called the whole thing off by telling Boon to get the car and take him back to Jefferson. But along with the knowledge of evil, Lucius has learned something else: That if you set out to do something with comrades, you go through with it for loyalty's sake. You go though with it even when a comrade—in this case, the Negro horse-lover, Ned— crosses you up by succumbing to a temptation that hadn't been allowed for in the original compact. Ned had seen a horse he liked—and he had traded the "borried" Winton Flyer for the animal.

The rest of the story revolves around the attempt to win enough money by racing the horse (who turns out to be a stolen animal) to buy the Winton Flyer back again. The horse, Lightning, is Mr. Faulkner's own Jumping Frog.

The wildly improbable race track seems to involve all sorts of moral issues, in which one of Miss Reba's Non-Virtuous ladies discovers the sinfulness of her ways and reforms, only to backslide just once in order to keep a self-appointed sheriff from impounding the horse. (This bit of step-by-step progression toward Virtue is forgiven by Boon, who marries the lady.) The 11-year-old Lucius learns that redemption is just as much a worldly part of the world as the practice of Non-Virtue—and Grandpa forgives all, telling the boy that a "gentleman accepts the responsibility of his actions" and learns to "live with it."

If the book ends with a hearts-and-flowers throb, that, too, is Faulkner, who can be conventional or non-conventional with equal aplomb or disdain.

530

John K. Hutchens. "The Reivers." New York Herald Tribune, June 4, 1962, p. 21.

All the way from Yoknapatawpha County to Memphis, the only Nobel Prize winner in literature known to have come from Oxford, Miss., kicks up his heels in *The Reivers*, and the spectacle turns out to be as engaging as it is surprising. For some years now William Faulkner has been a quite solemn gentleman, as if not only Yoknapatawpha County but the world weighed upon his pen, as indeed they may have done. If this surmise happens to be correct, then *The Reivers* may be called a happy holiday from tragedy's tenebrous glades, somewhat like Eugene O'Neill's comic *Ah, Wilderness!* when that playwright took a day off from Euripides and Strindberg.

To be sure, Mr. Faulkner does not surrender to this impulse at once or easily. *The Reivers* opens with a slow-motion, largely irrelevant incident, set in the familiar surroundings of Jefferson, Miss., and phrased in Mr. Faulkner's most strangling prose, as if to dare the reader to go on reading. But then—that barrier hurdled—things picked up at a fine pace. The story tightens, the style lightens, and here we all are in Jefferson in 1905, about to have a good time.

If it doesn't belong with the work that took its author to Stockholm in 1950 to join the immortals, it reminds us that in his deadpan fashion Mr. Faulkner has always been a considerable humorist, even a farceur. Here, for instance, he presents old Grandfather Lucius Priest looking back on one exciting week of his childhood as he reminisces to his grandson in terms variously literary and lusty, and sustained over a solid 300-page stretch, unless at one point or another the old gentleman paused to say:

"Now that you have heard about my enlightening stay in a Memphis brothel at the age of 11, good night and pleasant dreams, and we'll go on with this saga in the morning."

Anyhow, as Grandpa Priest recalls it, it's 1905 and *his* Grandpa is the reluctant owner of one of Jefferson's two motor cars, a Winton Flyer in which the then pre-adolescent Lucius Priest and the gigantic, child-like Boon Hogganbeck (you have met him before, in "The Bear"), take off on a highly unauthorized trip to Memphis while their elders are away from Jefferson attending a funeral. With them in the Winton, as they discover rather suddenly, is Uncle McCaslin, the Priest family's wayward old family retainer.

Having made off with Grandpa's car, they are "reivers" (from "reave," to take away by stealth), but that's only the beginning. On the way to Memphis, their journey could be no more innocent if it were Clarence Young's deathless *The Motor Boys Overland*. However, if memory isn't loafing unduly, Mr. Young never let his motorists wind up in a place like Miss Reba's—the same Miss Reba well remembered as a hostess in Mr. Faulkner's *Sanctuary*.

One seems to sense Mr. Faulkner grinning, if invisibly, as he goes on from there to spin a tale which on its own terms is impeccably moralistic. Well, yet, old Ned does secretly trade off the car for a stolen horse and Miss Reba's language is not all that it might be, and we are obliged to hope that a doped horse will win a race. But does not an innocent lad persuade a soiled dove to quit her life of shame while

531

a lecherous sheriff gets his comeuppance and a monstrous little voyeur will be sent packing?

Apparently hopeless complications, sharp suspense, neatly rounded-off conclusion, a good many laughs along the way, a narrative whose events plausibly suggest that one small resident of Yoknapatawpha County has received an insight into humanity that will serve him all his life—what more, Mr. Faulkner might ask, could his public ask of him in this vein. And the answer is: nothing more at all.

Brooks Atkinson. "New Picaresque Novel by Faulkner Gives Academic Theory of Comedy." New York *Times*, June 5, 1962, p. 38.

If William Faulkner had intended his new novel *The Reivers*, to illustrate the academic theory of comedy, he could hardly have done better.

All the characters in this picaresque yarn are funny, but none of them regards himself as funny. They are comic because they are desperately trying to ride a whirlwind they have raised out of their own foolishness. Inadvertently, they represent the philosophy of comedy, which is the topic of today's discussion.

To write in general terms, it is not true that a comic character does not laugh at himself. Falstaff is a great laugher; he exudes merriment over his own buffoonery. But in the strictest sense, a comic character, like Pickwick, is not aware of the ludicrous relationship he bears to the rest of the world. He does not know that the image other people have of him is a comic distortion of the image he has of himself. Puck's "Lord, what fools these mortals be" puts the human world into perspective. Living just outside that world, Puck, a sprite, has enough detachment to regard people as witless, bumptious, irrational and vain.

If Puck were a god and not a sprite, he would regard mortals not as fools, but the pawns of an inhuman universe. In the deepest sense, life is tragic.

"As flies to wanton boys are we to the
    gods,
They kill us for their sport"

says Gloucester in *Lear*, revealing Shakespeare in his bleakest mood. But comedy is the defense that humans erect against the inexorability of fate. It is less a spiritual than a mental form of energy. Instead of submitting, it resists by laughing at human folly. When Hazlitt was on his deathbed he declared: "Well, I've had a happy life"—a purely human benediction.

The jokes that are told in comedy are only surface decor. Fundamentally, comedy consists in a sense of proportion. The true comedian knows that life cannot be made to conform to the idealist's aspirations, that the millennium is impossible because human beings are not organized on the heroic scale.

We are full of grandiose plans. We found the United Nations to ensure the peace of the world; we write a noble charter in an exalted frame of mind. But human beings with human passions bring noble conceptions down to human size. The prophets become the saboteurs of the temple they have helped to erect, and the United Nations becomes, not an organ of peace, but a clearinghouse for suspicion and hatred. From the long point of view, this would be tragic. From the short point of view, it neither disillusions nor discourages the realist because, in the grand tradition of civilization, men will keep trying.

Or, take the Presidential campaigns, which are part of the folklore of an excitable nation. During the campaign the candidates solve national and international problems with easy logic and on high principle; and the party blueprints for justice, prosperity and happiness. But as soon as he has won the campaign, the new President is confronted by problems that no one can solve without creating new problems raised by the perversity of human beings. Nothing can ever be quite finished. When Taft was asked during his second campaign how a certain problem can be solved, he replied: "God knows!" As comedy, the statement was sound. But the nation does not vote comedians into the White House—knowingly.

To come back to Mr. Faulkner's novel, it does not concern people in high stations, and no great people are at stake. If Mr. Faulkner were in a melancholy mood, he could indict the human race on the evidence of the knaveries of Boon Hogganbeck, the loose morals of Miss Carrie and the skulduggery of Ned. Laws are broken and the code of civilized behavior is repeatedly smashed.

But Mr. Faulkner never loses the common touch, whatever the mood. Human beings in all their pride and frailty are always in the foreground of his novels. In *The Reivers*, he is in his happiest mood; and his story of townsfolk on the loose, soberly trying to control a mad situation they have created, is pure comedy. The characters are bizarre figures on a bright screen. Exploding with friskiness, they outlaw common sense. No one enjoys their escapades except the author and the readers.

Note that no serious harm comes to any of them. For the most winning aspect of comedy is that human beings must be forgiven—all mortals being fools, as Puck has said.

"Prospero in Yoknapatawpha." *Time*, June 8, 1962, p. 92.

On the mythical island of Shakespeare's *Tempest*, the forces of human bestiality, which raged so freely in his earlier tragedies, are held peacefully in check by the benign white magic of Prospero. Now in Yoknapatawpha County, an equally mythical but heretofore relentless dark and bloody portion of Mississippi, a similarly pacific sea change has taken place. Evil still exists there, but it makes no serious headway. No one is raped. No one is lynched. No one is murdered.

In *The Reivers*, William Faulkner plays a mellowed Prospero and proves an engaging fellow. Like an old man gossiping on the back stoop, he delights in sentimental recollection, revels in his roles as a teller of tall tales, at which only Mark Twain is his equal. Above all, Faulkner carries on the flagrant, 30-year love affair he has had with Yoknapatawpha County and its ornery, enduring and, until now, doom-ridden people.

The time is 1905, and the principal character in the story is a Winton Flyer, one of the first automobiles ever seen in Yoknapatawpha County. Its owner is old Lucius ("Boss") Priest, a member of the cadet branch of the country's first families (the Edmondses and McCaslins), but its proud chauffeur is Boon Hogganbeck, the childlike, "tough, faithful, brave and completely unreliable" part Indian who became famous in "The Bear" for not being able to hit anything with a shotgun, rifle or weapon of any kind.

Boon yearns after the car with the innocent lust of man for machine. Somehow enlisting the help of Boss Priest's grandson, young Lucius, Boon "borrows" the car. Twenty-three and a half hours later—a record for the 80 miles of swamp road they heroically cover—Boon and Lucius reach Memphis. Just four days after that, they are back home in Jefferson again. In a series of outlandishly comic episodes, they have somehow lost the car and won it back, found a stolen horse and raced it, spent an innocent night in a Memphis bordello run by young Miss Reba, the madam who, some 25 years later (Yoknapatawpha time), was to figure in the downfall of Temple Drake in *Sanctuary*.

"There is no such thing as *was*," Faulkner once said, and in his country—partly because it cannot let go of the nostalgic, bittersweet memory of the Civil War, partly because Faulkner had arranged it—everything that has happened for nearly a hundred years exists in an instantaneous, perpetual, heroic present. Faulkner does not so much invent as he does recollect his action and anecdote from an existing, constantly growing body of lore. *The Reivers* is no exception. The outrageous doings of Boon and Lucius in 1905 are told, in 1962, by Lucius to his grandson. Mostly, Lucius remembers things as the eleven-year-old boy he was when they happened. But on occasion, usually to compare the present unfavorably to the past, he speaks with the knowledge of what has been going on in the U.S. and the county up till today. In almost the same breath, he refers to the rush of automobiles that have all but swamped modern-day Yoknapatawpha, and to the Gayoso Hotel in Memphis where he always stayed because, in 1864, an ancestor rode into the lobby trying to lay hands on a Yankee general.

"Nothing is ever forgotten," Lucius' own grandfather tells him at the end of the story. "Nothing is ever lost. It's too valuable."

"Then what can I do?" asks the boy, who has been shaken by his escapade. "Live with it," Grandfather says.

Readers may not want to live with quite so much of it as Faulkner does. But the continual digression and anecdote that embroider the story are more than decoration. They are part of a way of life, and a way of seeing life, and a system of values that Faulkner has celebrated for years. Mules are among the most intelligent animals, he explains, because intelligence "is the ability to cope with environment: which means to accept environment yet still retain at least something of personal liberty."

The Tempest is not *King Lear*. *The Reivers* is not *The Sound and the Fury*. Critics hot for pessimistic reality may find this autumnal story a retreat into anecdotal escapism. More important, readers who know the body of Faulkner's work will miss, as they have in much of his recent writings, the matchless (even when flawed by excess), surging power of his earlier and darker creations. Occasionally the book falls into something close to pure sentimentality. But what the heart holds, Faulkner once wrote, becomes the truth. Faulkner's heart has held Yoknapatawpha County, its gentleness and comedy as well as its terror, for more than a generation. Whatever else it may be, *The Reivers* is a work of love.

Clifton Fadiman. *"The Reivers." Book-of-the-Month Club News*, July 1962, pp. 1–5.

REIVER, says the dictionary, is *arch.* or *poet.* for robber or plunderer. In *reft* we still retain the past participle of the original verb *reave* or *reive*. Perhaps down in Jefferson, Mississippi, the word was in common use in 1905, the year in which is set this story about the oddest band of thieves the reader is likely to have encountered in the pages of a novel.

Novel isn't quite the right word to describe *The Reivers*, even though the book is designed to fill its niche in the vast structure of the Yoknapatawpha saga, and mentions characters we have met before. Somehow it doesn't have the feel of fiction. Mr. Faulkner's subtitle "A Reminiscence" has the proper sound, suggesting a long, complicated, true anecdote. Like *Huckleberry Finn*, about a boy very different from the young hero of *The Reivers,* the story may have been drawn from the author's own early experience. But, whether or not autobiographical, here is a tale pervaded by reality. One overhears it being told.

A highly sophisticated folk comedy, with touches of broad humor, *The Reivers* has, playing through it like light, a quality rather rare in Faulkner, a curious tenderness. I intend no left-handed compliment in saying that to enjoy it there is no need to be a Faulkner devotee. I am not one, yet *The Reivers* caught, held and delighted me, despite the impediments of the famous style, the crisscross structure, the acrobatic play with time sequences. Not as ambitious as Mr. Faulkner's major efforts, it is more successful than some of them. Faulkner fans will revel in it; those who have tried to be Faulkner fans but haven't been able to make the grade should give themselves another chance with *The Reivers*; and those who have never read Faulkner now have the opportunity to enjoy a fresh experience.

The story retraces an episode that occurred during the 11th year of Lucius Priest, at a time when the world, if not more innocent, was simpler than it is today. For reasons too obscure to summarize here, Lucius' grandfather buys a motorcar, a Winton Flyer, one of the first to be seen in the quiet streets of Jefferson.

Young Lucius and a moronic motor-mad family retainer named Boon Hogganbeck "steal" the car and set off on a junket. They haven't traveled far before the Negro family coachman, Ned, discloses himself from under a tarpaulin on the back seat. The strangely assorted trio reach Memphis, where they stay, in Boon's words, at "a kind of boarding house." This turns out to be a brothel, the same one we are to meet twenty-one years later in *Sanctuary*. But, to forestall raised eyebrows, let me state that there is not even a faint suggestion of the scabrous in Mr. Faulkner's handling of the bordello background. He manages to be both comic and moral.

It now develops that the coachman, Ned, by far the most admirable and brainy character in the book (and so viewed by the author), has not come along just for the ride. He swaps the car for a racehorse, whose peculiar habits he happens to be well acquainted with, and then sets up a three-heat race, with whose presumed winnings he expects to buy the car back. The story now gets extremely complicated. In it are involved, among others, Miss Reba, who runs the bordello; Corrie, one of the girls, with whom Boon is in love; Corrie's nephew, a sprig of Satan, on a visit to Corrie's place of business because she claims "he don't get enough refinement on that Arkansas tenant farm"; young Lucius, who runs the race on Lightning; Lightning himself, a horse as real as any human character in the book, "strong and willing [with] every quality you could want in fact except eagerness"; and preeminently the sagacious, farsighted Ned, who alone knows the secret of inducing eagerness in Lightning.

The word delightful is not one ordinarily applied to Mr. Faulkner, whose genius is a dark one. But it applies here. The car-and-horse intrigue on which the plot rests is delightful in its absurdity; the sweetness and decency, is charming; his family, and particularly his grandfather, obeying codes of behavior of extraordinary graciousness and refinement, are no less charming.

Here is a book in which figure ladies of pleasure, a near-maniac, a degenerate adolescent and similar ingredients. Yet the net effect is one of wholesomeness, of moral soundness quite unalloyed by conventional piety or optimism. It is a book about the meaning of virtue, cast in terms of comedy and indeed at times in terms of farce. There is no Faulknerian brooding in it (or very little) and, while one senses a tragic temperament behind the high jinks, the temperament is not allowed to dominate.

Particularly attractive is the implied tribute to the Negro contained in the figure of Ned, who is not only a connoisseur of mules and horses, but a first-rate businessman, a sly comedian, and something of a philosopher. He is the particular triumph of a book rich in triumphs of characterization.

The Reivers was the immediate and unanimous choice of your judges. They believe that it will please a large audience, consisting both of those familiar with the work of the Nobel Prize winning novelist and those who have still to make his acquaintance.

The sole proprietor of Yoknapatawpha County, Mississippi, will be 65 years old next September. He has been writing about its inhabitants old and new, its masters and slaves and dispossessed Chickasaws, its upstarts and gentry, its grotesques and primitives, its livestock and landscape, for most of these 65 years—or ever since 1929, when a novel called *Sartoris* appeared, followed shortly by another called *The Sound and the Fury.*

It is hardly a secret any longer that Mr. Faulkner's county does not figure on Mississippi roadmaps. Nor do Hardy's Wessex and Trollope's Barsetshire on matter-of-fact maps of England. Yoknapatawpha

resembles the actual county of Lafayette, up in the rural north central part of Mississippi (the nearest metropolis, Memphis, lies to the northwest, across the Tennessee line), for here Mr. Faulkner was born, here he lives today and here his ancestors lived before him. But it is primarily the county of his extraordinary and often anguished human insights and of his rich, relaxed comic imagination.

To the conception and quality of Mr. Faulkner's work a long series of public honors bears witness, from the Nobel Prize awarded in December, 1950, to the gold medal of the National Institute of Arts and Letters announced in February, 1962. Still too rarely appreciated, nevertheless, are the several strains of American folk humor which crop out in almost everything he writes—sometimes abrasive and harshly sardonic (as in the notorious episode of Ike Snopes and the cow in *The Hamlet*), more often backwoodsy-laconic, genial and dry, salted with Southern crossroads comedy about mules and such and with the traditional wit and lingo of the Southern Negro.

The Reivers is much the best example to date among all Mr. Faulkner's books, now about thirty in number, of his comic invention—indeed, the first book he has ever written that may be called comedy virtually unalloyed. Its literary ancestry runs back, via Yoknapatawpha County, to Mark Twain, Joel Chandler Harris and George W. Harris of "Sut Lovingood" fame, and probably ultimately to Aesop.

536

James B. Meriwether. "Faulkner's Gentle Comedy of Rustic Rustlers." Houston *Post*, July 1, 1962, Now Section, p. 30.

The Reivers begins ominously: Boon Hogganbeck, who is part Indian but mostly white, grabs a revolver and at the range of 20 feet blasts away at Ludus, a Negro who Boon thinks has insulted him. It might be the beginning of another strong and tragic account of the race problem like *Light in August,* or perhaps another *Go Down, Moses.*

But the bullets, all five of them, miss Ludus a mile—the only damage is to a plate glass window (broken, but easily paid for), to a passing Negro wench (creased across the buttocks, but she gets a bag of candy and a new dress and her father gets $10), and perhaps to Boon's ego (but he never did think he was much of a marksman, and besides he can restore his spirits by stealing a car and going to Memphis).

So *The Reivers* is a comedy. It's a book where the bullets not only miss but they miss a mile; where any damage done is easily amended. And it comes as a shock, to this reader at any rate, to realize that it is Faulkner's first full-length comedy, his first book which is neither a tragedy or, to adopt a word from the terminology of Elizabethan drama, a tragicomedy. As Katherine Anne Porter once put it, much of Faulkner's fiction walks a knife-edge, a fine line between comedy and tragedy that keeps the reader in suspense at every point during the progress of a story.

But *The Reivers* shows evil routed all along the line, and innocence firmly in command. Like some of Faulkner's short stories, this novel is easy, genial, anecdotal. It is told by a grandfather to his grandchildren, and since the narrator was born at about the same time Faulkner was, in the late 1890's and like Faulkner spent his boyhood around a livery stable owned by his father, we might guess that the five names he gives in the dedication are those of his grandchildren.

The Reivers lacks tragedy but not drama. The date is 1905, and the dramatic conflict is between the automobile and the horse. Boon Hogganbeck works in Maury Priest's livery stable, but when the first automobile appears in Jefferson, Mississippi, Boon falls in love with it. And he promptly takes advantage of the absence of his employer to steal the car and set off in it to see his other love, Corrie (for Corinthia Everbe), who works in an establishment in Memphis to which Faulkner's readers were introduced in *Sanctuary.* (That Boon's two loves are an automobile and a whore, and quite ignores that noble animal the horse, may be one of Faulkner's comments on 20th century progress.) To take an automobile from Jefferson 80 miles to Memphis in 1905 takes either courage or stupidity or both. Boon has both but he tries to take out insurance by carrying with him his employer's 10 [*sic*] year old son, Lucius Priest. On the way they pick up Ned William McCaslin, an aging Negro ostler from the stable.

In Memphis Ned swaps the stolen automobile for a stolen race horse, Coppermine. A little while later the whole party—by this time including Corrie, Corrie's madam Miss Reba Rivers, and Corrie's poisonous little nephew from Arkansas, Otis—has moved from the little whistle-stop town of Parsham for a match race between Coppermine (now renamed Lightning) and the pride of Parsham (which they call Possum), a black gelding named Acheron (which they call Akron). The action is swift and maybe a little confusing;

537

it involves gambling, fixed races, goatish small-town constables, and a reformed prostitute (Corrie); Lucius rides Lightning and wins once and loses once before his grandfather appears, and everything turns out all right in the end with Corrie married to Boon and naming their first baby Lucius Priest Hogganbeck.

The publishers have been calling *The Reivers* another *Adventures of Huckleberry Finn*, and of course Faulkner has many things in common with Twain, whom he has called his literary grandfather. (He has also put Sherwood Anderson and Theodore Dreiser in there somewhere as literary relations.) One is the device of the innocent narrator—like Huck, Lucius is humorless, and there is a sort of double-barreled effect to the comedy of the book, which the reader is apt to get once when he sees the humor of the situation, and again when he sees that Lucius doesn't see it. But there is more to Faulkner's way of telling his story than just the boy's point of view. From time to time we are reminded that the boy has grown to be a grandfather himself. In one of the final scenes Lucius confronts his own grandfather after the theft and the fight and the discovery.

"I lied," the little boy tells his grandfather, and begs to be whipped, punished, anything that will bring him back to the way things were before. But the old man tells him that this can't be done.

"There ain't anything to do? Not anything?" the boy asks, pleading to be told how he can forget what he has done.

Yes, his grandfather replies—Lucius himself can do something, though not forget it. "Nothing is ever forgotten," he tells him. "Nothing is ever lost. It's too valuable."

"Then what can I do?" asks Lucius.

"Live with it," his grandfather replies. To the boy's protest that he can't bear to live with his failure forever, he replies:

"Yes you can. You will. A gentleman always does. A gentleman can live through anything. He faces anything. A gentleman accepts the responsibility of his actions and bears the burden of their consequences. . . . There. That should have emptied the cistern. Now go wash your face. A gentleman cries, too, but he always washes his face."

In the 40 years Faulkner has been writing books he has created a body of American work which is not only unmatched for its sheer bulk (25 books of fiction) and seriousness, but for variety too. At the age of 65 he has given us a different kind of book from any he has written previously. Faulkner is a strong individual writer, in most of his fiction, and some readers have been repelled by his stylistic and structural innovations. But I should guess that *The Reivers* will prove to be the best introduction to Faulkner's world for anyone not immediately sympathetic with his technical experiments.

The Reivers is, comparatively speaking, low-voltage Faulkner, but the reader who is rewarded by it may be ready for the greater strains of his work, which established Faulkner as the greatest novelist in English in his time—a position which *The Reivers* confirms if not strengthens.

Stanley Edgar Hyman. "Taking a Flyer with Faulkner."
New Leader, July 9, 1962, pp. 18–19.

To start with a platitude, American success is often hollow. Here is William Faulkner, accepted by all the world, at least since the death of Hemingway, as our greatest writer. He has received the Nobel Prize and every other critical accolade, his books sell in the millions, and at 65 he stands at the pinnacle of success. Yet I do not think that he has published anything first-rate since *Go Down, Moses* in 1942, when he was a relatively obscure *avant-garde* novelist. Now we have *The Reivers*, a Book-of-the-Month Club selection. It is listed facing the title page as Faulkner's 25th book, and the list is far from complete. Unfortunately, *The Reivers* is a boy's book, and not even a superior specimen of that genre.

Faulkner has always occupied an anomalous position in our literature. If we use "writer" to refer to imaginative power, moral earnestness, and ability to create an effective imitation of life in Aristotle's sense, Faulkner is a great writer. If we use "writer" to mean prose stylist, Faulkner is one of the worst writers who ever lived, worse even than that other ornament of American letters, Theodore Dreiser. In such novels as *Sartoris*, *The Sound and the Fury*, *As I Lay Dying*, and *Light in August*, and in such stories as "The Bear," Faulkner has produced masterpieces on some of the major themes of the American experience: the blood guilt on the land, Indian blood and Negro blood; the difficulties of attaining manhood in our world of overgrown boys; the crippling burden of history on personal relations; the loss of conviction by the best, while the worst continue full of passionate intensity.

Yet even in those works, the reader is maddened by impenetrable thickets of time-switching, broken-backed sentences that squirm along for pages, figures of speech from some high school magazine, and horrid little editorials on topics of the day. Then there are other works that are no more than pretentious nonsense—*Requiem for a Nun*, *A Fable*—and still others that are carefree hacking—the *Post* stories published as *Knight's Gambit*, the movie script published as *Intruder in the Dust*.

The Reivers is written in Faulkner's habitual prose. The long awful sentences are too long to quote, but a short example or two should suffice. When Faulkner wants to say that Miss Reba's whorehouse was quiet because the girls were still afraid of the absent pimp, he writes: "But decorously: no uproar either musical or convivial; Mr. Binford's ghost still reigned, still adumbrated his callipygian grottoes." Arguing that frightened horses are not graceful, Faulkner explains: "Fright demands fluidity and grace and bizarreness and the capacity to enchant and enthrall and even appall and aghast, like an impala or a giraffe...."

The figures of speech aghast like an impala indeed. Eyes are "like two bluebird feathers moulted onto a small lump of coal," teeth are "like small richly alabaster matched and evenly serrated headstones," events stop one cold "like a basilisk," someone vanishes "like a mouse into a lump of stillsoft ambergris." With them are little interpolated essays: on the afterlife of old soldiers; on the vulnerability of virtue; on the comedy of party politics in 1961; on the hierarchy of animals from the rat down; on the mule as a gentleman.

Worst of all are the spots where comic essay and simile combine. Thus a horse avoids the bit "as if the bit were a pork rind and he a Mohammedan (or a fish spine and he a Mississippi candidate for constable whose Baptist opposition had accused him of seeking the Catholic vote, or one of Mrs. Roosevelt's autographed letters and a secretary of the Citizens Council, or Senator Goldwater's cigar butt and the youngest pledge of the A.D.A.)."

The Reivers tells of the initiation into adult life of the 11-year-old Lucius Priest in 1905. He, the simple strong man Boon Hogganbeck, and Lucius' grandfather's Negro coachman (and kinsman), Ned McCaslin, steal the grandfather's 1904 Winton Flyer and drive it from Jefferson to Memphis. (Thus the title, an archaic word meaning "robber.") In Memphis, they make Miss Reba's whorehouse their headquarters, and after Ned trades (or appears to trade) the car for a horse, they spend their time in a complicated series of private horse races until Lucius' grandfather appears to straighten things out. Lucius narrated the story to *his* grandson in 1961.

As a boy's initiation with the help of Boon, the book is a redoing of "The Bear" as farce: as a vision of golden hearts and redemption by love at Miss Reba's, it is *Sanctuary* turned into musical comedy; as a paean to the virtue of and wisdom of elderly Negroes, it is a more inspirational *Intruder in the Dust.*

The car-and-racehorse plot is melodrama of the most preposterous sort; for example, Ned's magic for making the reluctant horse run and win turns out to be feeding it a sardine. It is the hardly-meant-to-convince plot of a boy's book, and there are two melodramatic villains to fit it. One is Otis, the wicked nephew of Everbe the Virtuous Prostitute, who tells Lucius the facts of life, says bad words to his elders, pulls a knife in a fight with Lucius, and is eventually exposed as a rotter and a coward and properly punished. The other is a deputy sheriff named Butch Lovemaiden (yes, Lovemaiden), "with a red face and a badge and a holstered pistol," stinking of sweat and whisky, who uses the power of his badge to topple Everbe from her new pedestal of virtue. He eventually gets his comeuppance too, and has his badge ripped off by the sheriff.

Balancing these two vile critters are the book's two noble heroes: the sheriff, little old Mr. Poleymus, a brave and just man; and Lucius' grandfather, Boss, a figure of Olympian wisdom and understanding. Actually, they are just the book's two noble *white* heroes. Looming above them are two noble Negro heroes: Ned, and a

saintly old figure called "Uncle Parsham" Hood. Ned pretends to be Uncle Remus, but like Lucas Beauchamp of *Intruder in the Dust* he is prematurely dignified, brilliant, and wise, his understanding of human psychology rivals that of Sigmund Freud, and his powers of ratiocination rival those of Sherlock Holmes. At the end Ned's motive for the whole operation turns out to have been to save another Negro family retainer and kinsman of the Priests, Bobo Beauchamp, who was being blackmailed (or whitemailed) by a "white blackguard."

As for Uncle Parsham, he is "the patrician, the aristocrat of us all and judge of us all"; "regal prince and martinet in the dignity of solvent and workless age." He says grace "briefly, courteously but with dignity, without abasement or cringing: one man of decency and intelligence to another." Lucius recognizes that Uncle Parsham is just like Boss, even to the same gold toothpick. Lucius and Uncle Parsham go fishing together, then in a final rite of kinship, they go innocently to bed together. (How about that, Fiedler?)

The book's ultimate absurdity, perhaps even too much for a juvenile audience to stomach, is its subplot, The Magdalen's Redemption. Touched by Lucius' fighting Otis in defense of her reputation, the whore Everbe promises that she will give up prostitution, and does. She demonstrates her new domesticity by washing Lucius' clothes, then takes a job helping Sheriff Poleymus care for his invalid wife. "If you can go bare-handed against a knife defending her," Boon says to Lucius, "why the hell cant I marry her?" He can and does, and on the book's last page they have a baby, named, of course, Lucius Priest Hogganbeck.

True, Miss Reba is not redeemed, but she is not the ignorant blowsy madam of *Sanctuary*, rather, a young woman "with a kind hard handsome face" and heart of gold, who is compelled by circumstance "to make a living in this hard and doomed and self-destroying way." Perhaps *her* conversion is being saved for the next novel.

A few things in *The Reivers* transcend its absurdity and juvenility, and remind us of Faulkner's earlier accomplishments. There is a valid and moving nostalgia, almost obsessive, for the wilderness of Mississippi, full of bear and deer before our century's civilization destroyed it. There is a real sense of the hard and painful initiation from the child's world into the adult's, with its loss of one kind of innocence at least. A single scene in the book, an encounter with a pirate who digs the road by his place into bog in order to charge for pulling out automobiles, is the colorful comedy of Faulkner at his best.

Some of the book's speech carries the same conviction, and brings the characters momentarily to life. "If you got any business still hanging," Butch says to Boon, with a leer toward Everbe, "better get it unhung before I get back or something might get tore." Asked why she takes out her gold tooth to eat, Minnie, the whorehouse servant, says: "I aint going to have it all messed up with no spit-mixed something to eat." Sometimes, when a character uses strong hard verbs like "tomcat" and "ramshack," or when Faulkner uses an effective figure of speech ("He ate like you put meat into a grinder") one comes temporarily to believe that he really could write decent English prose if he chose.

At one point, when Lucius fears for Uncle Parsham, because if Butch is frustrated in his pursuit of Everbe he will take it out on Uncle Parsham, who stands watching "white people behaving as white people bragged that only Negroes behaved," the book suddenly comes out of Roverland and shows us the real South in which Faulkner lives. In 1956 he told an interviewer on the subject of segregation that, forced to a choice, he would "fight for Mississippi against the United States even if it meant going out into the streets and shooting Negroes." The statement is absurd, and malign. The pastoral glorification of Negro wisdom and nobility in *The Reivers* may be equally absurd, but at least its absurdity is benign. We can be grateful for that.

Robert Drake. "Yoknapatawpha Innocence Lost." *National Review*, July 31, 1962, pp. 70, 72.

In *The Reivers* (from the now archaic or "poetic" verb *reive* or *reave*: to take away by stealth or force; to plunder) William Faulkner is primarily concerned with the initiation into knowledge—almost, one might say, into manhood—of eleven-year-old Lucius Priest (naturally of Jefferson, Yoknapatawpha County, Mississippi—or as it is usually spelled in the book's dialogue, "Missippi"). Lucius is related to the McCaslin and Edmonds families who figure so prominently in "The Bear" and "Delta Autumn," with their dark history of miscegenation and incest; so it is entirely proper that his initiation be in some measure prompted, if not always guided, by Boon Hogganbeck, the part-Indian white who finally killed Old Ben in "The Bear."

Boon, as Lucius recounts the story to his grandson in 1961 (the subtitle of the novel is "A Reminiscence"), really "belongs" to three Yoknapatawpha "proprietors": the McCaslin-Edmonds-Priest connection, Major de Spain, and General Compson. He is a sort of "corporation, a holding company in which the three [proprietors] had mutually equal but completely undefined shares of responsibility" to keep him out of trouble and leap into "whatever breach Boon had this time created or committed or simply fallen heir to" because he is "tough, faithful, brave, and completely unreliable." Furthermore, Boon is six-feet-four, weighs 240 pounds, has the mentality of a child, and couldn't hit the broad side of a barn with a gun.

The action involved in Lucius' initiation is complicated in the extreme. One May day in 1905 young Lucius' parents are hurriedly summoned to Bay St. Louis by the death of his maternal grandfather and accompanied there by his Grandfather ("Boss") and Grandmother Priest, thus leaving the field open to Boon (who works at Lucius' father's livery stable when he isn't being the "dean of Jefferson motor-car drivers") and Lucius to light out for that Earthly Paradise, Memphis (where else *can* you go from Yoknapatawpha?) on a wild stolen holiday in Boss' adored (by Boon) Winton Flyer automobile. And Lucius doesn't have to be strongly tempted by what he calls "non-virtue"; he, even as a child, is as much "fallen" as Boon, if not more so. (Lucius seems already to know the tune that "non-virtue" plays; he just hasn't had the occasion—or need— to learn all the words yet.) Matters are further complicated when Boss' Negro coachman-valet, "Ned William McCaslin Jefferson Missippi," as he calls himself, stows away on the journey because he wants a trip, too. And where else should Boon take the young boy in Memphis but Miss Reba's brothel on Catalpa Street (of storied memory from *Sanctuary*), where he has arranged an assignation with "Miss Corrie" (really a Kiblett, Arkansas, girl whose given names are Everbe Corinthia)?

Faulkner is operating here in the Pelion-on-Ossa Division of Old Southwestern tall-tale–telling, but he's only just gotten started. Suddenly Ned appears with a horse which he has "acquired" in a swap for the Winton Flyer (the "business" transactions here are as complicated as some of Flem Snopes' finest efforts in *The Hamlet*) and proposes that they all leave for "Possum" (Parsham), Tennessee (probably a pseudonym for an actual town called Grand Junction), where he proposes to race the horse, Lightning, against "Akron" (Acheron), who has already beaten him twice before. But this time Lightning will *win* because Ned *knows* secretly how to make him run. (He'd had a mule once which he "worked" the same way: with "sour deans"—sardines—which the mule couldn't resist running for!)

Before it's all over, Boon, Miss Reba, and Miss Corrie have all been jailed, Boon for complicity in acquiring a stolen horse and for defending Miss Corrie from the overtures of a red-hot deputy sheriff called "Butch," the ladies for "fragrancy," as Ned so well puts it; Miss Corrie has decided to "go straight" (because Lucius has fought Miss Corrie's fifteen-year-old nephew, Otis, for degrading her honor to him); Boon finally decides he'd better marry Miss Corrie; *and* Lightning (really a horse named Coppermine belonging to Mr. van Tosch, a Yankee "foreigner") does beat Acheron, in a hair-raising race with Lucius as Lightning's jockey. Boss, apprised somehow of the reivers' whereabouts and suddenly arriving on the scene, then proceeds to settle matters with Mr. van Tosch and Col. Limbscomb, Acheron's owners, and escorts the sadder and wiser trio back home to Jefferson in the recovered Winton Flyer.

The Reivers certainly ought, as the dust jacket so enthusiastically blurbs, to be "one of the funniest books in our literature"; but it most certainly is not. This may be partially because Faulkner was trying to make this potentially marvelous (and I use this word in its original sense) narrative carry more weight than it will bear. It is essentially funny, but he wanted to make it *mean* too seriously. Lucius is supposed to experience all sorts of revelations and acquire all sorts of insights into the human condition—or predicament (and some of them are valid indeed). He is supposed to learn just how difficult—and tedious—lying and all forms of "non-virtue" really are; to learn moreover, that one *is* always free to say "no" to them (that's what Miss Corrie decides to do); and to learn at the end, from Boss, that one can't "forget" or cancel out his errors because, as Boss puts it: "Nothing is ever forgotten, Nothing is ever lost. It's too valuable." One simply has to "live with it" because "a gentleman can live through anything."

But these "serious" insights, however valid, are wrong for the type of narrative Faulkner conceived here. What we want—and expect—is that Old Southwestern tradition of humorous story-telling which Faulkner knew so well how to handle—one where the events themselves (as perceived and recounted by the master raconteur) carry their own "moral" weight. Still, Faulkner remains our greatest contemporary novelist, and in his "failures" there is always much to admire. In *The Reivers*, despite some stock Faulknerian figures, there are descriptive passages—particularly those concerning the countryside and the elements—as fine as any he ever wrote. There are also, despite some mawkishness, exalted tributes to those who "endure" and "prevail"—especially women and Negroes— as moving as those in his greatest novels. In our day, when the novel is all too often liable to be more *craft* than *art*, it is invigorating to see a real artist like Faulkner, who failed, as he succeeded, with nobility and grandeur.

William Van O'Connor. "Young Boy Discovers the World." Minneapolis *Sunday Tribune*, August 19, 1962, Home and Hobby Section, p. 10.

The Reivers is a comedy, with a good many sententious asides. In his later years, Faulkner rather frequently indulged himself in high-sounding moralistic preachments, usually at the expense of the story. There is some preaching in *The Reivers*, but it is usually overcome by Faulkner's humor and self-irony.

Probably this is the "happiest" book in the Faulkner canon. It is full of nostalgia, as the elderly narrator recalls a slower-paced world, when the town of Jefferson boasted two automobiles, and the country roads were a foot deep. The narration is leisurely, relaxed, humorous and anecdotal.

Faulkner felt at home in writing about the early years of the 20th century. The setting of *The Reivers* is Jefferson and Parham, Miss., and Memphis, Tenn. The year is 1905. Once again we meet Boon Hogganbeck, from *Go Down, Moses* and Miss Reba, from *Sanctuary*.

The narrator is someone very like William Faulkner, Nobel Prize winner, remembering incidents that happened when he was 11 years old. The boy is named Lucius Priest. His grandfather, like Faulkner's, was a banker. There is also Aunt Callie, very like the servant who lived out her 100 years in the Faulkner family. Faulkner labeled this novel "a reminiscence."

The subject is a boy's discovery of the world—his recognition of his own capacity for duplicity and trickery, his discovery of the degradation experienced by one of the prostitutes in Miss Reba's Memphis house of ill fame, and the concomitant discovery of honesty, honor, courage and selflessness.

In watching the workings of Lucius' 11-year-old mind one seems to be watching the growing up of the boy William Faulkner.

The Reivers is superior to a number of Faulkner's most recent books, but it is not up to *Light In August, The Sound and the Fury* or *The Hamlet*. One can spot weaknesses, even carelessness, that the younger Faulkner would have eliminated. The old intensities and violence are missing. Yet *The Reivers* is more than nostalgic comedy. It is a reassurance of the ancient virtues, seen newly and clearly by a sensitive boy who knows he is incapable of lying to himself.

Warren Beck.
"Told with Gusto."
Virginia Quarterly Review, 38 (Autumn 1962), 681–85.

The Reivers is an intricately plotted, pell-mell story, figuring the theft of an automobile and a horse and the fixing of a horse race, and displaying, besides its principals, such gamey items as a corrupt deputy sheriff, Memphis prostitutes, and an utterly delinquent juvenile from Arkansas; it is also, in the Faulknerian mode, a highly moral tale. Told retrospectively in first person with unabated natural human gusto for the outrageous, it expresses as well an awareness of consciousness and conscience in many sorts of persons, variously situated. In typical Faulknerian vein it adumbrates, behind elaborations of

behavior, even more extreme complexities of motive and fluidity of mood. The novel abounds in sin and—being the work of a complete realist—in sentiment. Some, no doubt, will read one side of the coin and neglect or else condemn the other. But that has always been Faulkner's fate, which plainly he has survived.

What this book may encounter is a supercilious latter-day depreciation as the benign foolery of an elder citizen—whether Grandfather Priest, the reminiscent narrator, or Faulkner himself, grandfather and chief of American fiction. *The Reivers* merits recognition for a true virtuosity that combines exuberance, implicativeness, and commitment, as a narrative wherein humor and wit spring from judicious insight, in a nice fusion of value judgements and hearty tolerant interest. The funniest stories are always the most pointed ones, and they most require a conceptually oriented perspective for their appreciation. Read with such acknowledgment, *The Reivers* may be found a substantial work, significant in the Faulkner canon.

Connections are not lacking. Some scenes are in Miss Reba's Memphis bordello, with a glimpse of the Mr. Binford lamented in *Sanctuary*. The anecdotal opening, which primarily introduces thematic elements in burlesque guise, shows Boon Hogganbeck of "The Bear," here too a main character, still an incredibly bad marksman. He is also an intensely passionate man, as enamored of his employer's automobile ("this was 1905") as he was devoted to the great dog Lion. More important than connections are parallels, especially with *Intruder in the Dust* as well as "The Bear," for *The Reivers* too tells of a boy's maturation, accelerated by acquaintance with a sagacious, self-possessed Negro.

Parallels with *Huckleberry Finn* are conspicuous, in a picaresque progress through eye-opening encounters with idiosyncratic folk. A basic difference is more significant; Huck is a well-scarred waif, of disreputable parentage, whereas well-fostered eleven-year-old Lucius Priest lapses from social status and family regimen, and while Huck lives by solitary empirical assertions, whether against his father or Mississippi valley society or Tom Sawyer, Lucius—after conniving in what Huck would have called borrowing his grandfather's automobile—faces up to the whorehouse and racetrack worlds by the code of a gentleman.

Indeed, the word recurs pointedly, though with no sense of caste or taint of snobbish pretense. It suggests the essence of the social, a mutual reckoning and regard, as in the tacit assumption between Lucius' father and the Negro hostler John Powell that John's prized pistol would be kept out of sight, mention, or use at the stable; and in such matters of conduct agreed and depended upon, John (as Grandfather recollects it) "was a gentleman." The rough, childish Boon recognizes a rule of reciprocal assent, letting the boy drive the automobile to "seduce" him into conspiracy, and thereby beating him "in fair battle, using, as a gentleman should and would, gloves." When the incorrigible Otis calls Ned nigger, Lucius remembers his grandfather's teaching that "no gentleman ever referred to anyone by his race and religion." Finally Lucius' grandfather, bringing the boy to judgement for his escapade, says, "A gentleman accepts the responsibility of his actions and bears the burden of their consequences," and adds more specifically that "A gentleman cries too, but he always washes his face."

Lucius' tears are not just the ready penance of a caught culprit but an overflow from the four-day adventure become ordeal, his "having to learn too much too fast, unassisted," especially of "non-virtue's" awful potency while the devotees of Virtue must depend besides on "luck." Yet the boy had acted, and not just in providing strategy for Boon's making away with the automobile, not in winning the horse race under Ned's direction; enraged at Otis' vileness concerning the beset prostitute Corrie, he attacks the older boy, and his defense of her revives Corrie's self-esteem. Her reformation and marriage to Boon may be disparaged as facile sentimentality, but that implies denial of the way common vital people break through adverse circumstance into idealistic assertion, and thus "endure." It is to this basic human quality quite as much as to the concept of gentleman that the ethos of Faulkner's new novel is keyed.

This is most subtly shown (and strikingly too in denouement) through Ned, the Priests' middle-aged coachman, a never-daunted, wily, wry-spoken Negro, stowaway in the back seat on the Memphis expedition. When he trades automobile for horse, it seems irresponsible caprice until a gentlemen's court of inquiry finds that Ned in his mysterious ways has performed wonders to extricate a young Jefferson-born Negro from a white blackmailer. Like his creator, Ned is a fantastic improviser with an unshakable sense of fact; a principled opportunist, determinedly aligned on the side of the angels, he gets there by the long way around, yet with full effect.

As Grandfather Lucius Priest's deliberate "reminiscence" concerning a too-crowded and crucial period in his twelfth year, *The Reivers* has qualities typical of recollection in old age, a sharpness of detail but under an abstracting light. Sometimes the tone is like Huck's in its boyish immediacy:

> Then there was all the spring darkness: the big bass-talking frogs from the sloughs, the sound that the woods makes, the big woods, the

wilderness with the wild things: coons and rabbits and mink and mushrats and the big owls and the big snakes—moccasins and rattlers —and maybe even the trees breathing and the river itself breathing, not to mention the ghosts—the old Chickasaws who named the land before white men ever saw it, and the white men afterward. . . .

Sometimes though not so often the old man, envisaging no less clearly but more impressionistically, voices the Old Master, as on pulling the automobile out of a mud-hole by the mule team:

There was something dreamlike about it. Not nightmarish: just dreamlike—the peaceful, quiet, remote, sylvan, almost primeval setting of ooze and slime and jungle growth and heat in which the very mules themselves, peacefully swishing and stamping at the teeming infinitesimal invisible myriad life which was the actual air we moved and breathed in, were not only unalien but in fact curiously appropriate, being themselves biological dead ends and hence already obsolete before they were born; the automobile; the expensive useless mechanical toy rated in power and strength by the dozens of horsepower, yet held helpless and impotent in the almost infantile clutch of a few inches of the temporary confederation of two mild and pacific elements—earth and water. . . .

and so on. Yet it all enters fluently into composition. There is real antiphony between the recalled rush of action, with all the drive and quick elliptical talk of the unforgettable characters, and the prolonged musings, in the perspectives of a lifetime, over the essence of events once so keenly sensed and now so deeply reassessed. What the boy felt the old man now defines, chorus to his own drama. It is not an uncommon fictional procedure, but Faulkner has used it uncommonly well. The alternations are not interruptive but responsive and complementary, the two periods and levels of experience are made real, each in its kind, and the modulations between them are part of a spontaneous continuum of remembering as act revived.

It is thus that the grotesqueries of this tall tale can comprise raucousness, kindliness, vulgarity, gentility, brutality, manly honor, passion and poise, the impulsive and the meditative, comic exuberance and *lacrimae rerum*, while embracing it all is the felt sense of life, dynamic in all the characters who whatever else they may be are never indifferent, never enervated, never wholly lost or beat—not even an eleven-year-old boy in a crude and tricky world he was unprepared for, not even an old man, recollecting the irrevocable and relishing its evocation even as he judges it and himself in it.

Mary Jo Hatfield. "*The Reivers*—Waste of Talent." Peoria (Ill.) *Catholic Register*, January 21, 1963.

A rose by any other name still smells the same. It's not how you say it, but what you say that counts. It's a crying shame that a man of such great literary talent as Faulkner possessed, shouldn't write about things of value.

Rather, in this, his last novel, published just before his death on July 6, he freely and frequently has his characters "god damn" everybody, or loosely use the term s.o.b. until it becomes "old hat."

He even innocently weaves into his story of The Reivers (or plunderers) the taking of an 11-year-old boy into a bawdy house. Of course, the boy does nothing immoral, but he receives a pretty complete education . . . of sorts. [Ellipsis dots throughout appear in the original review.]

Faulkner's vocabulary is fabulous . . . and he is often referred to as "the intellectual's Mickey Spillane."

His rambling way of telling his story through a talkative, windy, and wordy great-grandfather is excellently done . . . to the point that I could even feel the presence of my Grandfather DeBold who tried to corner us, and often did for many hours, to tell us of things he had done as a boy or a much younger man . . . or of items of historic interest that had happened to . . . or because of particular family members.

Faulkner's writing totaled 17 novels and 91 stories. He stressed, he said, "the dignity and worth of the individual, his right and duty to be responsible for his own actions and to direct his own faith." In his writings, he asserted the inherent wickedness of the world, the winning out of desire over conscience.

In this novel, however, conscience overpowers . . . and the book has a relatively wholesome ending.

Many books about immoral places and people become best sellers. They are funny to some . . . just as dirty jokes or sadistic stories keep lots of people laughing.

So this book might depict the way of life of some of the people in this mythical Yoknapatawpha County . . . actually Oxford, Miss., where the author lived . . . and died! So I may be learning something about a few characters who could have lived there in 1905 . . . or finding a few laughs in the so called "steady stream of rustic humor and comedy," . . . or keeping tab on the last work of the noted author who wrote well and at length of life in the South, and who in 1949 received The Nobel prize for literature for "his forceful and independent artistic contribution to the new American novelistic literature." So what!

Why waste good God-given moments on literature of this type. Recognized or not, it's still basically trashy.

Checklist of Additional Reviews

Anaheim (Calif.) Bulletin, May 26, 1962.

Hayward (Calif.) Review, May 27, 1962.

"The Reivers." Booklist, June 1, 1962, p. 682.

"The Reivers." Philadelphia Evening Bulletin, June 1, 1962.

Hobbs (N.Mex.) News-Sun, June 3, 1962.

San Jose (Calif.) Mercury, June 3, 1962.

Virginia Kirkus, June 4, 1962.

"Picaresque and Puzzling." Newsweek, June 4, 1962, p. 100.

Life, June 8, 1962.

"Are Writers Smarter than Politicians?" Miami News, June 10, 1962, p. 6-B.

(Ontario) St. Catherine Standard, June 16, 1962.

Middleton (Ohio) Journal, June 17, 1962.

"The Reivers Mirrors Faulkner in a Distinctive, Penetrating Way." National Observer, July 9, 1962.

"The Reivers." Dixie Guide, August 1962.

"Books." Glamour, August 1962, p. 66.

"Books." McCalls's, August 1962, pp. 12, 14.

"The Reivers." Playboy, August 1962, p. 24.

"The Reivers." Negro Digest, October 1962, p. 96.

Monsieur, February 1963, p. 6.

Adams, Robert M. "Fiction Chronicle." *Hudson Review*, 15 (Autumn 1962), 423–25.

Alexander, Holmes. "What's Minor for Faulkner Remains Major for Most." Tampa *Tribune*, June 10, 1962, p. 13-D.

Alexander, James E. "Book Choices of the Week." Pittsburgh *Post Gazette*, June 2, 1962, p. 19.

Allen, Morse. "A Memphis Memoir." Hartford *Courant*, June 24, 1962, Magazine Section, p. 14.

Anderson, Charles R. "Faulkner in a Lighter Vein." Baltimore *Sun*, June 10, 1962, p. 5-A.

Attaway, Roy. "Faulkner's Novel Called Classic of Comic Literature." Charleston (S.C.) *News and Courier*, June 3, 1962, p. 13-C.

Badger, Edward. "Funny Faulkner Tops Earlier Solemn Writer." Birmingham *News*, June 10, 1962, p. 23–D.

Banks, Ade. "Rich Faulkner Legacy." *Valley Times Today*, August 10, 1962, p. 20.

Barkham, John. "Faulkner's Last Book Rated Work of a Mellowed Author." Newport News *Daily Press*, July 22, 1962, p. 4-D. *Saturday Review* release, June 2, 1962; *Telegraph*, June 4, 1962; New York *World*, June 4, 1962; St. Petersburg (Fla.) *Times*, June 3, 1962; Hartford *Times*, June 9, 1962.

Barley, Rex. "Faulkner's Latest Lacks Early Skill." *Arizona Republic* (Phoenix), June 10, 1962, p. 1-C.

Barret, William. "Reader's Choice." *Atlantic Monthly*, July 1962, pp. 109–10.

Bartlett, Lynne. "The Lighter Faulkner." Palm Beach *Times*, July 28, 1962, p. 2-A.

Bauer, Malcolm. "New Faulkner Novel Compares Well." *Oregonian*, July 10, 1962.

Bonner, Ruth Hard. "Books in Town." Brattleboro (Vt.) *Daily Reformer*, August 22, 1962, p. 4.

Boswell, Margaret. "Slapstick—Can This Be Faulkner?" Springfield (Ill.) *State Journal-Register*, June 3, 1962, p. 8-C.

Botts, Jack C. "Promise of Comic Classic Lost in Faulkner Tangle." Lincoln *Sunday Journal and Star*, June 3, 1962, p. 8-C.

Bouise, Oscar. "Fiction." *Best Sellers*, June 15, 1962, pp. 126–27. Reprinted *Catholic Telegraph*, March 8, 1963; *Catholic Standard*, July 6, 1962, p. 7.

Bradley, Jack. "Fast-Paced *The Reivers* Faulkner at His Best." Fort Worth *Star-Telegram*, June 3, 1962, Section II, p. 15.

Bradley, Van Allen. "Ribald Humor in a Faulkner Tale." Chicago *Daily News*, June 3, 1962, p. 20. Reprinted Rochester *Times-Union*, June 9, 1962.

Branche, Bill. "New Faulkner Novel Is 'Richly Alive.'" Niagara Falls *Gazette*, June 3, 1962, Magazine Section.

Brown, David. "Faulkner in a Humorous Vein Is in Top Form with New Novel." *Delta Democrat-Times* (Greenville, Miss.), June 10, 1962, p. 16. Reprinted from *Chronicle Star*, June 7, 1962.

Brown, Irby B. "Wit Marks Faulkner's New Book." Richmond *Times-Dispatch*, July 1, 1962, p. 8-L.

Burger, Otis Kidwell. "Laughs on a Lark to Memphis." *Village Voice*, August 2, 1962, p. 9.

Campbell, Mary. "Faulkner Characters Return in New Novel." Cleveland *Plain Dealer*, June 3, 1962, p. 7-H. Associated Press, June 3, 1962. Reprinted Jackson (Tenn.) *Sun*, June 10, 1962; Bridgeport *Post*, June 3, 1962; Tulsa *World*, June 10, 1962; Allentown *Chronicle*, June 3, 1962; San Jose (Calif.) *News*, June 3, 1962; Durham *Herald*, June 10, 1962.

548

Carberry, Edward. Cincinnati *Post and Times Star*, June 9, 1962.

Cargill, Oscar. "American Literature." *Collier's Encyclopedia 1963 Yearbook*. Eds. Louis Shores *et al.* New York: Crowell-Collier 1963, p. 68.

Cevasco, George A. "*The Reivers.*" *The Sign*, August 1962, pp. 66–67.

Chametzky, Jules. "How Much More Might Have Come?" Holyoke *Transcript-Telegram*, August 4, 1962, p. 9.

Cheney, Frances Neel. "His Last Book the Human Comedy." Nashville *Banner*, July 13, 1962, p. 22.

Collier, Bert. "Faulkner's Novel Truly Fine, Funny." Miami *Herald*, June 3, 1962, p. 8-J.

Conant, Mike. "World Is Humorous in Faulkner's Last." *Sunday Olympian* (Olympia, Wash.), July 8, 1962, p. 18.

Cook, Don L. "Faulkner's Latest Tall Tale Charming and Full of Surprises." Louisville *Courier Journal*, June 3, 1962, Section IV, p. 7.

Copeland, Edith. "Faulkner Comedy Simply Told." *Daily Oklahoman* (Oklahoma City), June 10, 1962, p. 9-D.

Corke, Hilary. "Faulkner across the Water." *New Republic*, July 16, 1962, pp. 20–22.

Cox, Bud. "What a Lot of Fun." Charlotte *News*, June 9, 1962, p. 19-C.

Crawford, William. "*The Reivers.*" El Paso *Times*, June 17, 1962, p. 8-C.

Culligan, Glendy. "Faulkner Still Tracks the Grail in Southern Accent." Washington *Post*, June 3, 1962, p. 6-E.

Curley, Thomas F. "Faulkner Smiles." *Commonweal*, June 22, 1962, pp. 331–32.

D., E.J. "Faulkner's Last Bow." New Bedford Mass. *Standard*, August 12, 1962, Section III, p. 29.

Daniel, Frank. "Faulkner's *The Reivers* Small, Fresh Masterpiece." Atlanta *Journal*, June 3, 1962, p. 8-D.

D[atisman], D[on] F. "Faulkner Finally Fathomed." Gary *Post-Tribune*, June 10, 1962, Sunday Panorama, p. 8.

Delmont, James. "*The Reivers.*" *Minnesota Daily.*

Demerest, Donald. "Latest Book Reviewed." *Central California Register* (Fresno), July 27, 1962.

Derleth, August. "Faulkner's Comic Note." Madison (Wis.) *Capital-Times,* July 12, 1962, p. 6.

Diebold, Michael. "Philosophical Huckleberry." Pittsburgh *Press*, June 3, 1962, Section IV, p. 13.

Donnelly, Tom. "Everything's Simple but the Syntax." Washington *Daily News*, June 1, 1962, p. 23.

Downey, Matthew T. "Faulkner's *Reivers* Is Good Reading but Is Not New Life." Baton Rouge *Sunday Advocate*, June 10, 1962, p. 2–E.

Dwight, Ogden G. "Faulkner Spins a Spree." Des Moines *Register*, June 3, 1962, p. 21-G.

Emch, Tom. "Faulkner in Surprise Comic Vein." Houston *Chronicle*, June 10, 1962, Zest Magazine, p. 13.

Epstein, Aaron. "Final Faulkner Is Comic Escapism." Sacramento *Bee*, September 9, 1962, p. 18-L.

Feinstein, George W. "William Faulkner Revisits the South." Pasadena *Independent-Star-News*, June 10, 1962, Scene Section, p. 10.

Finestone, Harry. "A Pleasant Faulknerian Tale, but Not His Best." Greensboro *Daily News*, June 10, 1962, p. 3-D.

First, Helen G. "Curl Up and Read." *Seventeen*, October 1962, p. 18.

Forsyth, Malcolm. "Faulkner Succeeds in Humorous Novel." New Orleans *Times-Picayune*, June 10, 1962, Section III, p. 5.

549

Frankel. Chuck. "Faulkner Novel Humorous, Racy." Honolulu *Star-Bulletin*, June 3, 1962, Hawaiian Life Section, p. 16.

Freedley, George. "Faulkner's *Reivers* Hilarious." *Morning Telegraph* (unidentified city), June 8, 1962.

G., D. "*The Reivers*." Kitchener-Waterloo (Ontario) *Record*, July 7, 1962, Section III, p. 21.

Gardiner, Harold C. "*The Reivers*." *America*, June 16, 1962, pp. 405–6.

Gilomre, Jane L. "Faulkner's New Novel Robust, Earthy, Comic." Omaha *Sunday World Herald*, June 10, 1962, Magazine Section, p. 28.

Gingras, Angelo de T. "*The Reivers*." *U.S. Lady*, September 1962.

Goolrick, Esten. "Faulkner's Last Book Wondrously Hilarious." Roanoke *Times*, August 19, 1962, p. 14-C.

Govan, Gilbert E. "Intriguing and Delightful." *Chattanooga Times*, June 24, 1962.

Graham, Philip. "Concentrated Maturing." *American Statesman*, June 18, 1962.

Greene, A. C. "Back to Yoknapatawpha." Dallas *Times Herald*, June 3, 1962, p. 5-E.

Greenwood, Walter B. "Faulkner Switches Style, Turns Out Light, Funny Tale." Buffalo *Evening News*, June 2, 1962, p. 8-B.

Griffin, Lloyd. "*The Reivers*." *Library Journal*, June 1, 1962, p. 2156.

G[utekunst], E. H. "Faulkner Light Touch Shows a Heavy Hand." Buffalo *Courier-Express*, July 22, 1962, p. 16-D.

Hayes, Ben. "*The Reivers*." Columbus *Citizen-Journal*, June 2, 1962, p. 13.

Hening, Wayne. "*The Reivers*." *The Peddie News* (unidentified city).

Hobby, Diana Poteat. Houston *Post*, July 22, 1962.

Hogan, William. "It's Yoknapatawpha County, with Fun." San Francisco *Sunday Chronicle*, June 3, 1962, This World Section, p. 30.

Holmesly, Sterling. "A Reiver Is a Plunderer: Faulkner Tells a New Tale with Fewer Semicolons." San Antonio *Express and News*, June 3, 1962, p. 6-G.

Hopper, Lynn. "Faulkner Finally Chuckles." Indianapolis *Star*, June 10, 1962, Section VIII, p. 5.

Howard, Edwin. "Lots of Horse Sense, Cumulative Horse Laughs in Picaresque Faulkner Tale." Memphis *Press Scimitar*, May 25, 1962, p. 6.

Howe, Irving. "Time Out for Fun in Mississippi." *New York Times Book Review*, June 3, 1962, pp. 1, 24–25.

Hoyt, Elizabeth N. "William Faulkner Turns to Humor." Cedar Rapids *Gazette*, June 10, 1962, pp. 2-C, 10-C.

Hunter, Anna C. "Lonesome Road to Maturity." Savannah *Morning News*, June 3, 1962, Magazine Section, p. 8.

Isbell, John. "Faulkner's Last Story Tells of Boy, Automobile and Trip." Anniston (Ala.) *Star*, July 15, 1962, p. 6-B.

Jackman, F. J. "Barefoot Boy with Shoes on Yoknapatawpha Scene." Worcester (Mass.) *Sunday Telegram*, June 3, 1962, p. 12-E.

Jacobson, G. I. "Eggs Sometimes Wear Covers." Dayton *Daily News*, June 24, 1962, Section II, p. 15.

Jay, Leah. "A New '*Huck*' by Faulkner." Detroit *Free Press*, June 10, 1962, Amusement Section, p. 5.

Jeffries, Phil. "*The Reivers*." Indiana *Sunday Courier and Press* (Evansville).

Jones, Nard. "New Novel: High Comedy in Low Society." Seattle *Post-Intelligencer*, June 9, 1962, p. 8.

Kazan, Chris. "William Faulkner on His Usual Theme." *Arkansas Gazette* (Little Rock), June 10, 1962, p. 8-E.

Keown, Don. Indianapolis *Journal*, June 1962.

Kervin, Roy. "Strange and Wonderful Story." Montreal *Gazette*, June 30, 1962, p. 19.

Kincheloe, H. G. "Faulkner Leavens His Touch with Laughter." Raleigh *News and Observer*, June 3, 1962, Section III, p. 5.

Knickerbocker, Conrad. "The Blessings of Yoknapatawpha." Kansas City *Star*, June 3, 1962, p. 5-E.

Kohler, Dayton. "Faulkner Writes of Comical Journey." Richmond *News Leader*, June 6, 1962, p. 15.

Kyle, Clason. "Faulkner's *Reivers* Termed Blessed with Humor and Lacking in Violence." Columbus (Ga.) *Enquirer*, July 30, 1962, pp. 8–9.

Lacy, Bernard. "Felicitous Finale." *Christian Century*, September 19, 1962, pp. 1136–37.

Laycock, Edward A. "Faulkner's Kind of Fun." Boston *Sunday Globe*, June 10, 1962, p. 67.

Leclair, Edward E., Jr. "*The Reivers*—by Faulkner." Albany *Times-Union*, June 10, 1962, p. 6-H.

Lewisohn, Thelma Spear. "Interfaith in Art, Music and Literature." *Interfaith Observer*, August 1962.

Lockerby, Frank M. "Author of the Week." Tacoma *News Tribune*, June 12, 1962, Magazine Section, p. 2.

Lovell, James H., Jr. "The Reivers Provide a Spectator Sport." Charlotte *Observer*, June 3, 1962, p. 7-D.

MacLure, Millar. "A Grandfather's Tale." *Saturday Night*, November 10, 1962, pp. 29–30.

Mahoney, Ruth. "Faulkner's *Reivers*." *National Guardian*, October 15, 1962, p. 9.

Malin, Irving. "*The Reivers*." *Wisconsin Studies in Contemporary Literature*, 3 (Autumn 1962), 250–55.

Maslin, Marsh. "The Browser." San Francisco *News-Call Bulletin*, June 2, 1962, p. 6.

McIntosh, Joan. "Bitter-Sweet Faulkner." South Bend (Ind.) *Tribune*, June 3, 1962, p. 12.

McLellan, Joseph. "*The Reivers*." *Ava Maria*, November 10, 1962, pp. 27–28.

Meeker, Joseph W. "Faulkner's New Adventure Leans toward the Comic." Los Angeles *Times*, June 10, 1962, Magazine Section, p. 13.

Miller, Mabel. "Time Out for Printed Page Fun." Sioux City (Iowa) *Journal*, July 6, 1962, p. 4-C.

Miller, Milton. "An 80 Mile Comedy on the Horse Paths of the South, by Faulkner." Riverside (Calif.) *Press-Enterprise*, August 5, 1962, p. 10-C.

Moody, Minnie Hite. "Faulkner Proves He Can Still Spin a Yarn." Columbus *Dispatch*, June 10, 1962, Tab Section, p. 24.

Moore, Harry T. "Faulkner Humor Is Superb." Boston *Sunday Herald*, June 3, 1962, Section I, p. 14.

Morton, Robert. "Fiction." *Show*, July 1962, p. 93.

Murray, James G. "Faulkner and the Comic Tradition." *The Delphinian* (Adelphi College), October 11, 1962, pp. 7, 10.

Newquist, Roy. "New Volume Proves Prejudice Unjustified." Chicago Heights *Star*, June 3, 1962, Section I, p. 6.

Nordell, Roderick. "A Wild Ride with Faulkner in 1905." *Christian Science Monitor*, June 7, 1962, p. 7; and "Book Report," June 27, 1962, p. 9.

Norris, Hoke. "A Comic Movement Moves Faulkner." Chicago *Sunday Sun-Times*, June 3, 1962, Section III, p. 1.

Northrup, Guy. "Finales—Horselaugh and Moral." Memphis *Commercial Appeal*, June 3, 1962, Section IV, p. 10.

Norton, Gayle. "Faulkner Turns to Humor, Scores." Pensacola (Fla.) *News-Journal*, May 20, 1962, p. 2-D.

Partain, Floydene. "*The Reivers*." Unidentified journal, syndicate release.

Pasley, Virginia. "Critic's Corner." *Newsday*, June 2, 1962, p. 27.

Paul, Charlotte. "*The Reivers*." *Argus*, June 8, 1962.

Paulding, Gouverneur. "Running Away." *Reporter*, July 5, 1962, p. 38.

Peckham, Stanton. "Faulkner's Tall Tale Tops Mark Twain's." Denver *Post*, May 27, 1962, Roundup Section, p. 11.

Perkin, Robert L. "A Comic Faulkner." *Rocky Mountain News* (Denver), June 3, 1962, p. 22-A.

Petran, Eleanore. "*The Reivers* Reveals Faulkner as Humorist." Columbus (Ga.) *Sunday Ledger-Enquirer*, June 17, 1962, p. 5-B.

Porterfield, Waldon. "Mr. Faulkner Has Fun in a World of Boyhood." Milwaukee *Journal*, June 3, 1962, Part V, p. 4.

Powers, Dennis. "Faulkner's Comic Novel Is a Rare Delight." Oakland *Tribune*, June 3, 1962, p. 2-EL.

Prescott, Orville. "Books of the Times." New York *Times*, June 4, 1962, p. 27.

Reid, Margaret W. "Comic Novel Has Moral Undertones." Wichita *Daily Times* (Wichita Falls, Texas), June 3, 1962, Magazine Section, p. 4.

Richards, Keith. "William Faulkner Tells a Tale and Points a Moral." St. Louis *Globe-Democrat*, June 9–10, 1962, p. 4-F.

Riley, Kathryn. "*The Reivers*—a Tale of Two Plunderers." Delray Beach (Fla.) *Daily-News Journal*, June 22, 1962, p. 2.

Ryckebush, Jules. "*The Reivers*: William Faulkner's Book Is Compared with Mark Twain's Huckleberry Finn."

Springfield (Mass.) *Sunday Republican*, June 24, 1962, p. 12-D.

Rzepecki, Arnold. "*Reivers* Reveals Faulkner's Humor." Detroit *Catholic*.

S., R.H. "*The Reivers*." *Publisher's Weekly*, April 16, 1962, p. 93.

Sales, Jack. "Faulkner Acquires Twain-Like Humor." Indianapolis *News*, June 9, 1962, p. 2.

Sandeed, Ernest. "*The Reivers*." *The Critic*, June–July 1962, pp. 62–63.

Schneider, Michael. "The Silly-Sad Creature, Man." Newark (N.J.) *Sunday News*, June 17, 1962, p. 8-E.

Shedd, Margaret. "William Faulkner's Latest Odyssey of Old Car Is Not Sentimental." *Mexico News Weekly*, July 25, 1962.

Sherman, Thomas B. "Faulkner's New Novel a Pastoral Comedy." St. Louis *Post-Dispatch*, June 3, 1962, p. 4-B.

S[izer], A[lvin] V. "The Old Master Isn't Dead Yet: Faulkner Novel Is Riotously Funny." New Haven *Register*, June 10, 1962, p. 5.

Smith, F. A. "*The Reivers*." AAUP-ATPI-NACS (Cottey College, Missouri), February 21, 1963, p. 3.

Smith, Lois. "Faulkner Lets the Humor Shine Through." Charleston (W.Va.) *Sunday Gazette-Mail*, July 15, 1962, p. 6-C.

Smith, Ruth. "Gift of a Genius." Orlando *Sentinel*, July 22, 1962, p. 30-E.

Southern, Terry. "Tom Sawyer in the Brothel." *Nation*, June 9, 1962, pp. 519–21.

Stanley, Donald. "A New Trip to the Land of Faulkner." San Francisco *Examiner*, June 3, 1962, p. 2-H.

Stephens, Steve. "Reminiscent *Reivers* Reflects Best Humor." *Emory* (University) *Wheel*.

Thomas, Phil. "The Making of a Southern Gentleman: Faulkner Turns to Reminiscent Humor." Detroit *News*, June 10, 1963, p. 3-G.

Thorpe, Day. "Faulkner's Newest: A Jovial Amalgam." Washington *Sunday Star*, June 3, 1962, p. 5-C.

Tift, Judy. "Kathryn T. Garten Gives Book Review." Kalamazoo *Gazette*, October 31, 1962, p. 18.

Tinkle, Lon. "New Faulkner Novel Gentle to Old South." Dallas *Morning News*, June 3, 1962, Section V, p. 9.

Tredway, Martha. *"The Reivers."* St. Louis *Review*, September 7, 1962, Book Section, p. 3.

Troy, George. "Bill Faulkner's Lively Comedy." Providence *Sunday Journal*, June 10, 1962, p. 24-W.

Tunstall, Caroline. "Faulkner Writes a Cheerful Odyssey." Norfolk *Virginian-Pilot*, June 3, 1962, p. 6-F.

Turner, Lucille. *"The Reivers."* *Club Dial*, October 1962, p. 14.

Wade, Gerald. "Gentleman Accepts Consequences of His Actions, Faulkner Contends." Beaumont (Tex.) *Journal*, June 1, 1962, p. 17.

Walker, Gerald. "Faulkner Writes a Comedy." New York *Post*, June 3, 1962, p. 11-M.

W[eissblatt], H[arry] A. "Mellow Faulkner." Trenton *Times*, July 2, 1962, p. 14.

Wellejus, Ed. "Bookshelf." Erie *Times*, June 17, 1962, p. 11-E.

White, Ellington. "Throw Out the Paddle and Get a Reactor." *Kenyon Review*, 24 (Autumn 1962), 753–54.

Williams, Ernest E. *"The Reivers* Delights." Fort Wayne *News-Sentinel*, June 2, 1962, p. 4.

Williams, Henry. "Of a Car, a Racehorse and Some People." Peoria (Ill.) *Journal Star*, June 9, 1962, p. 11-C.

Williams, Paul. "Faulkner Rich Wit Filled His Last Book." Norfolk Ledger–Portsmouth *Star*, July 11, 1962, p. 17.

Wilson, W. Emerson. "Faulkner Writes Very Funny Tale." Wilmington (N.C.) *Morning News*, June 4, 1962, p. 11.

Woolsey, Bill. "A Faulknerian Sally into the Past." Louisville *Times*, June 8, 1962.

Yeiser, Frederick. "Novels from Late Spring Crop." Cincinnati *Enquirer*, June 9, 1962, p. 14.

Young, Scott. "William Faulkner Unconvoluted." *Globe and Mail* (unidentified city), August 11, 1962, Magazine Section, p. 2.

Index

557

566

Waterfall, W. K., 365
Watertown (N.Y.) *Times*, 184, 205
Watkins, Walter, 418
Watts, Richard, 470, 518
Watts, Richard, Jr., 418
WAVE (radio station), 430
WDNC (radio station), 296
Weeks, Edward, 73, 95, 137
Weigel, John A., 350, 470
Weigle, Edith, 205, 244
Weissblatt, Harry A., 231, 279, 350, 365, 418, 470, 553
Wellejus, Ed, 553
Wellington, Gertrude, 244
Welty, Eudora, 269, 279
Wemer, Willis, 137
West, Anthony, 329, 518
West, Ray B., 351
Westchester Life, 319
Western Review, 351
Weston, John C., Jr., 428
Weston, Sam, 244
Westporter Herald, 319
Wetterberg, David, 418
Weymouth (Mass.) *Gazette*, 276
WFM (radio station), 415
WFUV (radio station), 349
WFW-FM (radio station), 415
Wheeling *News-Register*, 271
Wheelright, Philip E., 60
White, Charles E., 351
White, Ellington, 553
White, Kenneth, 50
White, Mary Ann, 279
White, William Allen, 165
Whitson, Robley Edward, 351
Wichita *Beacon*, 346, 414, 464
Wichita *Daily Times*, 413, 430, 468, 552
Wichita *Eagle*, 276, 297, 365, 416, 468
Wicker, Tom, 351
Wiener, Max, 279, 351
Wilder, Charles, 470
Wile, Florence, 165
Williams, Ernest E., 251, 418, 470, 518, 553
Williams, George, 518
Williams, Henry, 553
Williams, Paul, 553
Williams, Sidney, 95, 137, 165, 184, 206
Williams, Wirt, 518
Willingham, John R., 320, 470
Wills, Garry, 518
Wilmington (N.C.) *Morning News*, 276, 351, 418, 470, 518, 553
Wilmington (N.C.) *Morning Star*, 244
Wilmington (N.C.) *Star*, 49, 64

Wilmington (N.C.) *Sunday Star*, 349
Wilson, Edmund, 251, 279, 298, 320, 325
Wilson, Emma, 184
Wilson, Gloria, 320
Wilson, Robert H., 95
Wilson, W. Emerson, 251, 418, 470, 518, 553
Wilson, Walter, 518
Wilson, William E., 251
Windsor (Ontario) *Daily Star*, 348
Wings, 163
Winn, Marie, 470
Winnipeg (Manitoba) *Free Press*, 350, 416
Winston-Salem *Journal and Sentinel*, 49, 351, 416, 470
Winterich, John T., 365
Wisconsin Library Bulletin, 29, 318, 413
Wisconsin State Journal, 73, 115
Wisconsin Studies in Contemporary Literature, 551
WMTI-FM (radio station), 469
WNNT (radio station), 464
Wobbe, James A., 418, 470
Wolff, Anthony, 365
Wolin, Don, 320
Wood, Daniel, 279, 351
Woolsey, Bill, 553
Worcester (Mass.) *Sunday Telegram*, 278, 320, 349, 417, 468, 516, 550
Worcester *Telegram*, 226, 244, 297
Worley, Eleanor, 470
Wright, John A., 279
Writer, 364
WSAY (radio station), 319
WSTC (radio station), 318
WTAL (radio station), 348
Wylie, Elinor Hoyt, 220
Wyoming *State Tribune*, 516
Wyrick, Green D., 418

Yale Literary Magazine, 466
Yale Review, 205, 225, 244, 279, 297, 346, 417, 517
Yates, Donald A., 470
Yeiser, Frederick, 280, 298, 320, 351, 418, 470, 518, 553
Young, Scott, 553
Young, Thomas Daniel, 518
Youngstown *Vindicator*, 72, 182, 204, 244, 364, 516
Yust, Walter, 35

Zailian, Marian, 418
Zaiman, Jack, 418
Zink, Karl E., 418
Zwart, Elisabeth Clarkson, 244